Learn Latin from the Romans

Learn Latin from the Romans is the only introductory Latin textbook to feature texts written by ancient Romans for Latin learners. These texts, the 'Colloquia', consist of dialogues and narratives about daily life similar to those found in modern-language textbooks today, introducing learners to Roman culture as well as to Latin in an engaging, accessible, and enjoyable way. Students and instructors will find everything they need in one complete volume, including clear explanations of grammatical concepts and how Latin works, both British and American orders for all noun and adjective paradigms, 5,000 easy practice sentences, and over 150 longer passages (from the Colloquia and a diverse range of other sources including inscriptions, graffiti, and Christian texts as well as Catullus, Cicero, and Virgil). Written by a leading Latin linguist with decades of language teaching experience, this textbook is suitable for introductory Latin courses worldwide.

ELEANOR DICKEY was educated at Bryn Mawr College and the University of Oxford, has taught in Canada and the United States, and is currently Professor of Classics at the University of Reading in England. She is a Fellow of the British Academy and of the Academia Europaea and has published widely on the Latin and Greek languages and how they were studied in antiquity, including *Greek Forms of Address* (1996), *Latin Forms of Address* (2002), *Ancient Greek Scholarship* (2007), *The Colloquia of the Hermeneumata Pseudodositheana* (2012–15), *Learning Latin the Ancient Way* (2016), and *An Introduction to the Composition and Analysis of Greek Prose* (2016). She is a dedicated and passionate language teacher with extensive experience of teaching both Latin and Greek at all levels and has brought this experience to bear on her adaptations of ancient Latin-learning materials for modern students.

Learn Latin from the Romans

A Complete Introductory Course Using Textbooks from the Roman Empire

ELEANOR DICKEY

CAMBRIDGE
UNIVERSITY PRESS

CAMBRIDGE
UNIVERSITY PRESS

University Printing House, Cambridge CB2 8BS, United Kingdom

One Liberty Plaza, 20th Floor, New York, NY 10006, USA

477 Williamstown Road, Port Melbourne, VIC 3207, Australia

314–321, 3rd Floor, Plot 3, Splendor Forum, Jasola District Centre, New Delhi – 110025, India

79 Anson Road, #06–04/06, Singapore 079906

Cambridge University Press is part of the University of Cambridge.

It furthers the University's mission by disseminating knowledge in the pursuit of education, learning and research at the highest international levels of excellence.

www.cambridge.org
Information on this title: www.cambridge.org/9781107140844
DOI: 10.1017/9781316493182

First published 2018

Printed in the United States of America by Sheridan Books, Inc.

A catalogue record for this publication is available from the British Library

Library of Congress Cataloging-in-Publication data
NAMES: Dickey, Eleanor, author.
TITLE: Learn Latin from the Romans : a complete introductory course using textbooks from the Roman Empire / Eleanor Dickey.
DESCRIPTION: Cambridge, United Kingdom : Cambridge University Press, 2018. | Includes bibliographical references and index.
IDENTIFIERS: LCCN 2018012018 | ISBN 9781107140844 (alk. paper)
SUBJECTS: LCSH: Latin language – Textbooks.
CLASSIFICATION: LCC PA2087.5 .D53 2018 | DDC 478.2421–dc23
LC record available at https://lccn.loc.gov/2018012018

ISBN 978-1-107-14084-4 Hardback
ISBN 978-1-316-50619-6 Paperback

*Dedicated to Latin students and Latin teachers
who put their hearts and souls into the subject*

Contents

Preface: What This Textbook Is

During the Roman empire many speakers of Greek and other ancient languages learned Latin. To do so they used materials known as 'colloquia', short dialogues and narratives for reading and speaking practice. First created in the first century AD or earlier and greatly expanded in later centuries, the colloquia were heavily used throughout antiquity and still employed in the middle ages and early Renaissance, but they largely disappeared from Classicists' awareness after that point.[1]

As language-learning materials the colloquia have great advantages, for they were composed by native speakers of Latin specifically for learners. English-speaking Latin learners normally have to choose between reading 'fake' Latin composed by modern teachers, which is easy but inauthentic, and 'real' Latin composed by Romans for other Romans, which is too difficult for beginners. But the colloquia offer an ideal compromise: having been written for beginners by native speakers, they are both authentic and easy. Their language is idiomatic, their grammar simple, and their sentences short. Moreover, their subject matter is daily life in the Roman empire (shopping, bathing, banking, dining, going to school, engaging in litigation, visiting friends, etc.); such material is highly interesting to modern students and far more accessible than much Latin literature.

In their original form, however, the colloquia do not completely meet the needs of a modern student. They consist only of reading material, without any grammatical explanation; of course grammars of Latin were also composed for the ancient learners, and some of these survive today, but those grammars are not suitable for most English speakers since they presume knowledge of ancient Greek. Moreover the colloquia are not long enough to form a complete Latin course; ancient students used them only at the beginning of their Latin study and then moved on to reading literary texts accompanied by full running vocabulary lists. And some portions of the colloquia are unreadable today, either owing to textual corruption or because enthusiastic users expanded them into gigantic vocabulary lists, hopelessly obscuring the original narrative. Lastly, many passages use post-Classical Latin grammar and syntax, including forms that could cause serious confusion for beginners.

In this book, therefore, the colloquia are presented in a format suitable for modern students. The most readable passages have been selected, vocabulary is glossed as

---

[1] For more information on the colloquia and other texts used for learning Latin in antiquity see E. Dickey, *The Colloquia of the Hermeneumata Pseudodositheana* (Cambridge 2012–15) and *Learning Latin the Ancient Way* (Cambridge 2016).

necessary, and any non-standard grammar and syntax that might make it harder for a beginner to learn Latin has been standardized. The texts have then been embedded in the framework of a modern textbook.

In fact the purpose of this textbook is twofold: to enable today's students to learn Latin using the ancient materials, and to meet the need that I and some other Latin teachers have felt for a particular type of book. There are many different ways to learn Latin, of course, and none of them is best for everyone; the choice of method needs to depend at least in part on the age, background, and goals of the student. But it seemed to me that many Latin students fell into a group not ideally served by any of the available books: students who have a certain intellectual maturity and want to understand fully everything they learn, but who do not necessarily have any background knowledge of grammar or of the ancient world; who want to master the essentials rapidly in order to move on to reading real texts as soon as possible, but who nevertheless need to have a firm grasp of those essentials to avoid fear and confusion; who want lots of practice exercises but do not want to buy or carry around extra workbooks; who want interesting reading material but disagree completely with one another about what counts as interesting; and who would like the people designing their Latin course to pre-select the most important concepts for learning rather than pouring out a deluge of details.

This is the group whose needs I have tried to meet. Therefore a thorough grounding in grammar is provided, so that those who like to understand things can feel confident rather than confused, and care has been taken to explain major concepts clearly, sometimes at the cost of omitting, or relegating to footnotes, details whose inclusion might make a concept too hard to understand. When it comes to grammatical terminology, a middle course has been taken between avoiding any terminology that might intimidate the reader and using all the terminology employed by a full-scale Latin grammar: I have used grammatical terminology only when it is strictly necessary (i.e. when it will make the learners' task easier rather than harder). Thus readers will not find in this book names for different uses of the dative (one can understand *auxiliō eī sum* without deciding whether to call it a predicative dative or a double dative), but they will find the parts of speech, the cases, the moods, etc. All terminology used is explained clearly and explicitly, in small increments suitable for a beginner, and the explanations in the main text are supplemented by a complete glossary of grammatical terminology (chapter 65) as well as exercises on the more challenging grammatical concepts (chapter 63, with answer key in chapter 64). A student who comes to this book knowing no grammatical terminology whatsoever can use it without the assistance of any other English reference work and will emerge with an ability to understand English as well as Latin grammar. Such an understanding is widely held to be an important reason for learning Latin, as it is generally thought to improve one's ability to write good English.

One drawback to grammatical terminology is that it is not uniform across the English-speaking world; indeed even the analysis underlying that terminology is sometimes different in different countries. In the twenty-first century such local customs are no longer really local: some Americans learn from British books, and some British students from American ones, so in the production of a new book the choice of either terminological framework would be arbitrary. Having taught Latin in both these countries as well as Canada, I find that on most points where terminologies or analyses diverge they are both equally good, and that it is often helpful to teachers and students to have both; therefore I provide both whenever I consider both to work well. (The point on which this is most noticeable is the order of the cases, but it is a principle that runs throughout the book.) The inclusion of a range of terminology also makes it easier for students to move from this book to consulting major reference works such as grammars, which do not all use the same terminology. On a few points, however, I find one way of putting things distinctly more helpful than the other, and on those points I have preferred the more helpful version irrespective of its place of origin.

Many students learn Latin as their first foreign language, and therefore many users of this book will be thinking for the first time about those aspects of English that are unproblematic until English is compared with another language, such as the fact that English tenses shift in indirect speech. Some students will also be thinking for the first time about aspects of English that ideally ought to have been understood earlier, such as the difference between *girl's* and *girls'*. For this reason certain features of English are explained in some detail, and Latin and English grammatical principles are explicitly compared and contrasted. (Incidentally, the ancient Latin teachers made extensive use of such teaching methods, though the other language involved was Greek rather than English.)

The book also provides more than 5,000 modern sentences and exercises for grammatical practice, for although the colloquia make learning Latin from ancient texts easier, it still is simply not feasible for elementary students to get enough practice on every individual point purely from reading ancient texts. It is not expected that every student will translate all these sentences; most students will find that they grasp most concepts after doing fewer than half the exercises provided. The other exercises are there for those times when an individual student needs more practice in order to master a particular concept – they should be seen as an opportunity and a resource in times of need, not as an obligation. The sentences and exercises in the main chapters of the book have no answers provided, so that they can easily be set for homework. But more than 700 are revision sentences and exercises on points of grammar that students often find particularly difficult, and these are separated into an appendix for which a key is provided, to allow students to use them as and when they are needed.

A principle behind the construction of the sentences is that they should not only illustrate whatever construction is under discussion while being otherwise as easy to translate as possible, but also help students develop the right thought processes for reading real Latin. For example, when producing sentences for beginners it is tempting to put the words in an order close enough to that of English that an English speaker can naturally make the right words into subjects and objects even if he or she does not pay attention to the Latin case endings: such word order allows students to read more easily and gain confidence quickly. But that confidence is produced at the cost of a belief that one does not need to pay attention to the case endings, something that will prove a major handicap to the student's later Latin studies. This book, therefore, starts off with sentences that cannot be correctly translated except by paying attention to the endings and thus helps students develop the skills that in the long run will be most helpful in reading real Latin texts. For the same reason macrons are not used on translation exercises: given the usual conventions for the printing of Latin texts, ability to read Latin means ability to read Latin without macrons, and many people read by word shape. Therefore people who learn to read Latin seeing words in precisely the shape that those words will have when encountered in a real Latin text have an easier time later than those whose initial learning occurs on sentences with macrons. But the absence of macrons on the sentences should not be taken as a disincentive to learning the quantities, for which much opportunity is given elsewhere: long vowels are marked on all vocabulary, on grammatical exercises, and on all Latin quoted in the main text.

The core of the reading material is not the sentences but 159 passages from Latin texts, 43 from the colloquia and 116 from other sources. These have all been carefully chosen for comprehensibility as well as illustration of relevant concepts and have been glossed with the information needed to understand them at the point where they are inserted. The passages come from a wide range of Latin genres, authors, and periods, for students differ greatly from one another in their interests and only a broad selection has a chance of appealing to a substantial percentage of the people in any given Latin class. Therefore literature is represented by Virgil (ten passages comprising the first ninety-one lines of the *Aeneid*, a text that ancient Latin students often used early in their studies), Martial (twenty-seven passages), Cicero (sixteen passages), Catullus (six passages), Terence (five passages), Livy (four passages), the Vulgate Bible (four passages), Apicius' cookbook (four passages), St Augustine (three passages), Plautus (one passage), Vitruvius (one passage), and Caesar (one passage);[2] documentary texts are represented by fourteen inscriptions, ten graffiti, four Vindolanda tablets, one papyrus letter, and one mosaic. Four medieval Latin songs are also included.[3] Non-standard spelling and grammar in late and documentary texts have been standardized, and some passages have been further adapted, but poetry is almost always presented in its original form.

---

[2] The inclusion of more Caesar has been deliberately avoided in order to prevent annoying repetition for people who read Caesar immediately after elementary Latin.

[3] See the index of Latin passages for precise details.

The passages begin at chapter 11, and at least one is found in each chapter from that point onwards, with more in the later chapters. Ten chapters consist entirely of such reading practice and introduce no new grammar. The idea of these chapters is to give students the opportunity to tackle longer passages than those provided at the ends of the other chapters: reading longer texts is an important skill, and students often find it more enjoyable than reading little extracts. These chapters also offer the teacher a certain safety valve in scheduling: if a class is under time pressure they can be postponed or even skipped without impairing students' ability to understand subsequent chapters.

The amount of vocabulary learning required has been kept as small as possible, in the belief that since an intermediate-level student reading a Latin literary text can always look up unfamiliar words in a dictionary but will have much more difficulty finding out about unfamiliar forms and constructions, elementary students need to learn grammar more than they need vocabulary. But the vocabulary that does get included in the 'vocabulary to learn' sections should be taken seriously and memorized: those words are used constantly in the sentences. As a result of the prioritization of grammar, by the end of this book most users will have a command of all the major forms and constructions and a good understanding of how to use them, but only a limited vocabulary. Therefore it is recommended that at the next level they read texts with a comprehensive glossary or word list.

The work involved in learning elementary Latin consists of two very different types of mental activity: memorization of forms and vocabulary, and practice at reading and translating. In many existing textbooks all the forms (i.e. the memorization work) are presented early in the course, with the constructions (i.e. the work that can be done only via reading practice) largely reserved for the second half. This arrangement has the disadvantage that the rate of progress in the first half of the course is restricted by the speed at which the students can accomplish the memorization. Latin has a very large number of different forms to learn, and when vocabulary is added to this (for it is undoubtedly necessary for the beginner to learn *some* vocabulary) the burden of memorization becomes so great that many students never reach the stage at which they would learn the constructions; for this reason they can never read any 'real' Latin, even after spending considerable time and effort on memorization. If one is learning Latin because one enjoys grammar, or to improve one's English, Latin-learning that never leads to independent reading is not necessarily wasted, but most people prefer the sense of accomplishment and independent enjoyment that comes from being able to read real ancient texts. In this book, therefore, forms and constructions are systematically interspersed with one another, so that the work of memorization is spread out over the entire book and constructions are introduced early; this arrangement reduces the burden of the memorization and allows the introduction of more interesting reading material earlier in the course.

Throughout this course students are encouraged to use Latin actively as well as passively, by translating into Latin as well as out of it. The reason for this practice is not a belief on my part that all students should learn to write good Latin; I do want to give students the opportunity to learn to write good Latin if they so desire, but many quite reasonably want to learn the language in order to read what the ancients wrote, rather than in order to add to our store of Latin literature. The point of translating into Latin is that good reading knowledge can never be attained without some active capacity in a language. Language learners forget material almost as fast as they learn it; individual students often see this as some peculiar shortcoming in themselves, but it is actually a feature of the way human memory works, and one has to accept it and work with it rather than being ashamed of it. The best way to deal with the problem of forgetting things, of course, is to re-learn them, and every student has to do a lot of re-learning throughout an elementary language course (though each time around is easier than the time before – this is a more fortunate feature of the way human memory works). But even with extensive re-learning, most people are unable to retain simultaneously all the material that they learn; sometimes each word that enters the brain seems to push another one out.[4] And yet it is not possible to read a page of Latin literature without retaining nearly all the material in this book.

A solution to this problem is to learn on each point somewhat more than you will actually need for reading a text; that way when you forget part of it you still have enough knowledge to read the text. Thus if you learn vocabulary from Latin to English, so that you can recognize the meaning of a word when you see it but nothing more, in a few days you will lose that recognition ability and have nothing. But if you learn vocabulary from English to Latin, so that you can produce the Latin word along with its gender or principal parts, in a few days you may lose the ability to produce the Latin, but you will retain the ability to recognize it for a much longer period. And if before losing active command of the Latin word you learn to use it in Latin constructions, you can end up with a passive knowledge of both words and constructions that is as close to permanent as anything in our memories can be. Therefore in this book the main purpose of the English to Latin translation is to enable users to acquire a basic reading knowledge that can survive the natural and inevitable process of forgetting that occurs during language learning. For this reason users are advised that if they skip the active exercises and do only the passive ones, this apparent shortcut will in the long run make learning passive reading skills harder rather than easier.

This book is designed to be used in a Latin course meeting three times a week for at least twenty-two weeks; each chapter can be completed in forty-five minutes of class

---

[4] This phenomenon has in fact been documented by scientists and is known as 'retroactive interference'. An understanding of memory and how it works can be very useful to language students; one good work on this topic is A. Baddeley, *Your Memory: A User's Guide* (London 1996).

time. It works best if students memorize the forms and vocabulary of each chapter before moving on to the next one, and if cumulative tests on paradigms, vocabulary, and translation skills are given at intervals. The division of the book into five parts suits a system in which five such tests are given during the year, one at the end of each part; in the course in which this book was created, one test was given four weeks into the first semester, a second four weeks later, a third at the start of the second semester (chapter 31 was designed to be done independently during the intervening vacation), a fourth halfway through the second semester, and the last at the end of the second semester. Many other schedules would, however, work equally well.

The author of this book did not have an easy time learning Latin. I struggled repeatedly with concepts that ought to have been easy, took years to reach the stage where I could read any original literature at all, and was the only member of my (originally large) Latin class who made it to that stage. I only got there thanks to dedicated teachers at the more advanced levels, who insisted that I re-learn all the grammar from scratch and helped me to do so. Throughout my time as a student and my decades of teaching since then, I have thought about what could have made my task as an elementary Latin student easier and more enjoyable: this book is the result. Probably it will not work for everyone, for different people have different strengths and there is no one best method of learning anything. But I hope that for a significant number of students this course will offer the chance to obtain more knowledge of Latin more enjoyably and with less confusion than most other available Latin courses.

Credit for whatever is good in this book – but certainly not blame for any mistakes – must be shared with, and gratitude offered to, everyone who taught me Latin, especially Mr Barako, Miss Bloch, Julia Gaisser, Jasper Griffin, David Raeburn, and Donald Russell. Particular thanks go to Philomen Probert and Stephen Colvin, who read the work before publication and made many useful corrections, and to Martin West, Harm Pinkster, Christoph Pieper, David Langslow, Jim Adams, Wolfgang de Melo, and Michael Weiss, who provided help with particular points. Any mistakes remaining in this book are definitely my own fault, not theirs. I am also grateful to my students at the University of Exeter, for their patience and good humour in testing trial versions of this book; Marion Osieyo and Priscilla Del Cima made particularly valuable contributions with their interpretive insight and sharp eyes spotting mistakes. Generous funding from the Leverhulme Trust and from a period as Spinoza Visiting Scholar at the University of Leiden provided time to prepare the work for publication. Last but not least, I am deeply grateful to Michael Sharp, Malcolm Todd, and Henry Maas for their invaluable contributions to the book's production process.

I hope very much that no mistakes remain in the published version of this book, but if any do appear, I hope even more that readers will bring them to my attention so that they can be eradicated from subsequent versions. All corrections will be very gratefully received at E.Dickey@reading.ac.uk.

Introduction: What Latin Is

Latin is an ancient Indo-European language; that is, it is one of the oldest known members of a large family of languages. It is related, with varying degrees of closeness, to all the other members of that family, including ancient languages such as Greek, Sanskrit, Gothic, Old Irish, and Hittite, as well as modern languages including English, German, Welsh, Russian, Hindi, Persian, and Armenian. The languages to which it is most closely related are the 'Romance' (i.e. Roman) languages that descend directly from Latin; these include Italian, French, Spanish, Portuguese, and Romanian. English is a 'Germanic' language and not descended from Latin, but rather related to it as a niece to an aunt; the structure of English is very different from that of Latin. English vocabulary, however, has been heavily influenced by Latin (often via French), so that many Latin words have English derivatives.

Latin was originally the language of a small area of Italy called Latium, in which the city of Rome (traditionally believed to have been founded in 753 BC) was located. But as

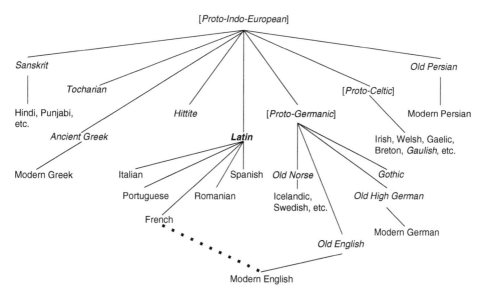

FIGURE 1 Latin and a few of the other Indo-European languages (ancient languages are in italics; brackets indicate ancient languages that do not survive in written form but can be reconstructed from surviving languages)

Rome's power grew the range of the language expanded, not only because Romans travelled all over the Mediterranean but also because many of the peoples conquered by the Romans gradually abandoned their own languages and went over to using Latin. Thus for example in most of what is now France and Spain the pre-Roman people were Celts who spoke languages related to Welsh and Irish, but they gave up those languages for Latin. In other parts of the empire, however, the pre-Roman languages survived the Roman conquest and sometimes even persist to this day; one obvious example of such survival is Greek, but there are numerous others including Welsh.

When the Roman empire collapsed in the fifth century AD, Latin rapidly disappeared from those parts of the world where it had not become people's native language; it also largely disappeared from places like England where the end of the empire was accompanied by a major influx of invaders speaking a different language. (Modern English does, however, still contain a few words that entered the language due to the Roman occupation of Britain, such as 'wall' from Latin *vallum*.) In other regions Latin survived, but it was transformed into a variety of forms sufficiently different from the original that they are now considered distinct languages: Italian, French, Spanish, etc. The original Latin language, or at least something closer to the original language, was also maintained after the fall of the empire, as a medium for international communication and for literature, by the more educated members of society (a group which for much of the middle ages was largely synonymous with priests, monks, and nuns). During this period much ancient Latin literature disappeared; virtually the only works to survive were those copied by hand in monasteries.

During the Renaissance and for several centuries afterwards Latin continued to be widely used as an international scholarly and scientific language; important thinkers who published their ideas in Latin included not only scholars like Erasmus but also scientists such as Isaac Newton. But the rise of first French and later English as international languages made Latin less useful for this purpose, and nowadays most people who learn Latin expect to use it for reading, not for expressing their own ideas. Nevertheless there are some neo-Latin enthusiasts who publish books and periodicals in Latin, converse in Latin, and even produce radio broadcasts in Latin; some but by no means all these people are connected with the Vatican, which still translates all its official documents into Latin. Because of this continuous usage the vocabulary of Latin has been constantly updated to include modern inventions, so that just as a medieval priest could use Latin to discuss points of feudal law that had not existed in ancient times, today's neo-Latin enthusiasts can easily discuss computers and aeroplanes in Latin.[1]

---

[1] Those who would like to learn to speak Latin may want to look at the resources available via e.g. www.maierphil.de/SeptLat/, www.fundatiomelissa.org/, mcl.as.uky.edu/conventiculum-latinum/, www.latin.org/, and yle.fi/radio/yleradio1/ohjelmat/nuntiilatini/.

But not all forms of Latin have acquired the same status. Already during the Roman empire the Latin prose of the end of the Republic (especially that of Cicero) and the poetry of the beginning of the Empire (especially that of Virgil) had assumed a special position, because the works of these writers seemed to native speakers of Latin better than anything else produced in their language. For prose in particular Cicero has usually set the standard that subsequent users of Latin aimed at. Extensive criticism of this practice (Erasmus, for example, ridiculed it on the grounds that using only words known to Cicero made it impossible to use any of the updated vocabulary that rendered Latin useful as a medium of communication in his own day) has by and large failed to change it, because when dealing with a language as internally diverse as Latin, and in the complete absence of native speakers whose judgements of comprehensibility would be reliable, it is generally felt that *some* objective standard must be used to decide what is and is not right. To most people, therefore, 'Latin' means ancient Latin, and to most of those who distinguish among different types of ancient Latin it means Ciceronian Latin.

The Pronunciation of Latin

1 Background

There are many different pronunciations of Latin. Currently the most common in English-speaking countries is the restored ancient pronunciation described below, which is a fairly close approximation of the way educated Romans of the late Republic pronounced Latin.[1] Even in antiquity, however, there was some variation in pronunciation, and this variation greatly increased in the middle ages, when Latin was commonly pronounced like the pronouncer's native language. Remnants of the diverse pronunciations produced by this system can be found in what is now known as ecclesiastical or church Latin (which is effectively pronounced like Italian) and in Latin names that have become part of the English language (which are effectively pronounced like English). For example the name *Cicerō* is pronounced *Kikero* in the restored pronunciation, *Cheechero* in the ecclesiastical pronunciation, and *Sisero* in the English pronunciation. This diversity can lead to serious misunderstanding, because the various pronunciations are not easily mutually comprehensible, so when learning Latin it is important to master the pronunciation used by those who will be teaching you (normally the one described below), so that what you say will be understood correctly.

2 Consonants

In the restored pronunciation most consonants are pronounced in Latin like one of their pronunciations in English, but Latin consonants normally have only one sound regardless of what other letters appear nearby, whereas in English the same letter may have very different sounds in different words. The differences, therefore, can be considerable in practice. The most important of them are:

c **is pronounced hard, like the** *c* **in 'cold'**, never soft like the *c* in 'city' (i.e. always like *k*, never like *s*).

g **is pronounced hard, like the** *g* **in 'get'**, never soft like the *g* in 'gem' (i.e. never like *j*).

i **is pronounced like the** *y* **in 'yet' when it is a consonant** (*i* is usually a consonant when a word begins with *i* + vowel, and when *i* appears between two vowels).

---

[1] For more information on how the Romans pronounced their language and how we know, see W. S. Allen, *Vox Latina* (2nd edition, Cambridge 1978).

qu is pronounced like the *qu* in 'quick', never like the *qu* in 'unique' (i.e. always like *kw*, never like *k*).

r is always fully pronounced, regardless of where it occurs in a word. The Romans pronounced their *r* more like a modern Italian *r* than like a modern British or American *r*, but many English speakers use their own type of *r* when pronouncing Latin.

s is pronounced voiceless like the *s* in 'sink', never voiced like the *s* in 'ease' (i.e. never like *z*).

t is pronounced like the *t* in 'type', never like the *t* in 'ration' (i.e. never like *sh*).

v is pronounced like *w*, never like *v*.

double consonants are pronounced double: *nn* lasts longer than *n*, and the *dd* in *reddō* is pronounced as in 'red dough'.

3 Vowels

Latin has no silent vowels: every letter is pronounced, even the final *e* in a word like *sine* (pronounced *si-ne*). English vowel letters usually have two very different pronunciations according to what other letters follow them: compare the vowels in 'rat' and 'rate', 'bit' and 'bite', and 'not' and 'note'. But in Latin the spelling of the rest of the word makes no difference to the pronunciation of vowels: every vowel has its own sound. That sound can be long or short, a difference that is always important in a few specific forms and more generally important in poetry, but that is not normally indicated in writing; in order to know which vowels are long and which short, one has to learn that information individually for each word and form. In the forms where vowel quantity (i.e. which vowels are long and which short) is an important distinguishing marker, it is vital to learn it, but in other forms teachers often leave it up to students whether to master the quantities. As a result not all Latin students learn the quantities, and some of those who do not later regret that decision. Once you have learned all your Latin vocabulary without quantities it is considerably more difficult to re-learn it so as to know the quantities, with the result that for the rest of your life you face certain handicaps.

In this book, all long vowels are marked with macrons (a macron is a line over the vowel, e.g. *ā*) in paradigms, vocabulary lists, discussions, and grammatical exercises (i.e. everywhere except in translation exercises); in sections where long vowels are marked, any vowel not marked is short.[2] The purpose of marking the long vowels is to give readers who wish to learn the quantities a chance to know what they are; the reason that no such marking is provided in translation exercises is that because Latin texts are

---

[2] A complication is that some vowels can be either long or short. Generally speaking these are not marked as long, but readers may want to be aware of them. The most important words involved are *mihi, tibi, sibi, ego, ibi, ubi, nisi,* and *modo,* all of which sometimes have a long vowel in the final syllable. In endings, the third person plural perfect indicative active ending *-ērunt* can also be found as *-erunt* with short *e*.

normally printed without macrons, it is better to learn to read Latin without them from the beginning.

The pronunciations of the vowels are as follows:

Short:	Long:
a as in 'h<u>a</u>t'	*ā* as in 'f<u>a</u>ther' (never as in 'd<u>a</u>te')
e as in 'g<u>e</u>t'	*ē* as in '<u>ai</u>r' (never as in 'tr<u>ee</u>')
i as in 'b<u>i</u>n'	*ī* as in 'tr<u>ee</u>' (never as in 'tr<u>y</u>')
o as in '<u>o</u>ff'	*ō* as in 'l<u>aw</u>n'
u as in 'p<u>u</u>t'	*ū* as in 'sch<u>oo</u>l'

In many books, including this one, the letter *i* can stand for either a vowel or a consonant; it is usually a consonant when it occurs at the beginning of a word followed by a vowel or between two vowels, and in other positions it is usually a vowel. (In some older texts consonantal *i* is written *j* – but it is still pronounced like English *y*, not like *j*.) In many texts there is a similar situation with *u*, which can be either a consonant (in this book written *v*) or a vowel according to position. Latin writers make occasional use of the letter *y* to represent a Greek upsilon; originally this sound was like a French *u*, but later it came to be pronounced like Latin *i*, and English speakers often prefer to use this later pronunciation.

When two vowels come together they are usually pronounced separately as two distinct vowels, for example *ia* in *glōria* (pronounced as in English) and in *grātia* (pronounced 'grat-ee-a', not 'gray-sha'), *iu* in *Lūcius* (pronounced 'Luke-ee-us', not 'Loo-shus'), *iō* in *capiō* and in *faciō* (pronounced 'cap-ee-o' and 'fak-ee-o'). But some particular vowel combinations form diphthongs, that is, a single vowel sound made up of several parts. Diphthongs are always long. The most common Latin diphthongs are:

ae pronounced like the *i* in 'bike'
au pronounced like the *ou* in 'cloud'
oe pronounced like the *oi* in 'oil'

4 Accent

In Latin, as in English, one syllable of each word is stressed. In Latin the placement of the stress is predictable, as follows.

1) If the word has only two syllables, the first syllable is stressed.
2) If the word has more than two syllables, and the second syllable from the end contains a long vowel, or a short vowel followed by two or more consonants, the second syllable from the end is stressed.
3) Otherwise the third syllable from the end is stressed.

Thus *docēre* is stressed on its second syllable, but *dūcere* is stressed on its first syllable. Regardless of whether one learns the quantities, it is important to stress Latin words correctly, as doing otherwise leads to miscommunication.

Practice

For each word in passages 1–5 below, work out which syllable should be stressed and mark it with an accent. Then read the passages aloud with correct pronunciation. Passages 6 and 7 are poetry and somewhat more complicated to pronounce (see chapter 66); you should listen to someone who has learned to read Latin poetry aloud and try to imitate his or her pronunciation of these passages.[3]

1   Quoniam videō multōs velle Latīnē loquī et Graecē, neque facile posse

propter difficultātem et multitūdinem verbōrum, meō labōrī et industriae

nōn pepercī, ut in tribus librīs interpretāmentōrum omnia verba scrīberem.

multōs enim videō cōnātōs esse, nōn prō dignitāte sīcut ipsa rēs postulat,

sed suae cupiditātis et exercitātiōnis causā. propter quam causam nōn audeō

plūra verba facere, sed volō omnibus palam facere, nēminem melius neque

exquīsītius interpretātum esse quam mē in tribus librīs quōs scrīpsī; quōrum

hic liber prīmus erit. quoniam parvīs puerīs incipientibus docērī

necessāriam vīdī esse audītiōnem interpretāmentōrum sermōnis

cottīdiānī, ut facillimē Latīnē et Graecē loquī discant: idcircō paucīs verbīs

dē sermōne cottīdiānō scrīpsī haec quae subiecta sunt.

    (*Colloquia Monacensia-Einsidlensia* 1b–q, an ancient language teacher's preface to his textbook; you will read this passage in chapter 30)

2   Gallia est omnis dīvīsa in partēs trēs, quārum ūnam incolunt Belgae, aliam

Aquītānī, tertiam quī ipsōrum linguā Celtae, nostrā Gallī appellantur. hī

---

[3]   Recordings of these passages can be found for example at www.rhapsodes.fll.vt.edu/aeneid1.htm (Robert Sonkowsky), www.fas.harvard.edu/~classics/poetry_and_prose/Aeneid.1.intro.html (Wendell Clausen), www.youtube.com/watch?v=orzrnEzKbaE (Evan der Millner). These three differ considerably from one another in certain respects: it is the features they have in common that are useful to master.

omnēs linguā, īnstitūtīs, lēgibus inter sē differunt. Gallōs ab Aquītānīs Garumna flūmen, ā Belgīs Mātrona et Sēquana dīvidit. hōrum omnium fortissimī sunt Belgae.

(Caesar, *De bello Gallico* 1.1.1–2, the conqueror's explanation of the geography of Gaul; you will read this passage in chapter 32)

3 Cum vocātus essem, ad praeceptōrem accessī et tabulam, in quā erat lēctiō mea, eī dedī. et coepī reddere memoriā quae accēperam ut discerem: versūs ad numerum et distīnctum et clausulam, cum aspīrātiōne ubi oportēbat, et versuum metaphrasin dedī. dum reddō ēmendātus sum ā praeceptōre, ut vōcem praeparem bonam.

(*Colloquium Stephani* 13a–15, the tale of a boy who can pronounce Latin well; you will read this passage in chapter 47)

4 Cicerō Pūbliō Caesiō salūtem dīcit. Pūblium Messiēnum, equitem Rōmānum, omnibus rēbus ōrnātum meumque perfamiliārem, tibi commendō eā commendātiōne, quae potest esse dīligentissima. petō ā tē et prō nostrā et prō paternā amīcitiā, ut eum in tuam fidem recipiās eiusque rem fāmamque tueāris.

(Cicero, *Epistulae ad familiares* 13.51; you will read this passage in chapter 44)

5 Cicerō Atticō salūtem dīcit. cum quod scrīberem plānē nihil habērem, haec autem reliqua essent quae scīre cuperem: num Caesar profectus esset, quō in statū urbem relīquisset, in ipsā Italiā quem cuique regiōnī aut negōtiō praefēcisset, ecquī essent ad Pompeium et ad cōnsulēs ex senātūs cōnsultō dē pāce lēgātī – cum igitur haec scīre cuperem dēditā operā hās ad tē litterās mīsī.

(Cicero, *Epistulae ad Atticum* 10.3; you will read this passage in chapter 56)

6   Arma virumque canō, Troiae quī prīmus ab ōrīs

Ītaliam fātō profugus Lāvīniaque vēnit

lītora, multum ille et terrīs iactātus et altō

vī superum, saevae memorem Iūnōnis ob īram,

multa quoque et bellō passus, dum conderet urbem

īnferretque deōs Latiō; genus unde Latīnum

Albānīque patrēs atque altae moenia Rōmae.

mūsa, mihī causās memorā, quō nūmine laesō

quidve dolēns rēgīna deum tot volvere cāsūs

īnsignem pietāte virum, tot adīre labōrēs

impulerit. tantaene animīs caelestibus īrae?

(Virgil, *Aeneid* 1.1–11; you will read this passage in chapter 31)

7   urbs antīqua fuit (Tyriī tenuēre colōnī)

Carthāgō, Ītaliam contrā Tiberīnaque longē

ōstia, dīves opum studiīsque asperrima bellī,

quam Iūnō fertur terrīs magis omnibus ūnam

posthabitā coluisse Samō. hīc illius arma,

hīc currus fuit; hoc rēgnum dea gentibus esse,

sī quā fāta sinant, iam tum tenditque fovetque.

prōgeniem sed enim Troiānō ā sanguine dūcī

audierat Tyriās ōlim quae verteret arcēs;

hinc populum lātē rēgem bellōque superbum

ventūrum excidiō Libyae; sīc volvere Parcās.

(Virgil, *Aeneid* 1.12–22; you will read this passage in chapter 31)

PART I

1 | Verbs: Inflection and Word Order

1.1 Inflection

The key element of every sentence, both in English and in Latin, is a verb: a word indicating the action described by the sentence (e.g. 'go', 'is', 'learn', 'eat'). English verbs can be identified by the way they inflect (change shape): a word to which '-ed' and '-ing' can be added is a verb. Thus 'learn' can be identified as a verb because of the forms 'learned' and 'learning'. Likewise, if you put a verb after 'they' and then replace the 'they' by 'he', you will usually find that the verb then gets an '-s' at the end. Thus 'they eat' → 'he eats', 'they learn' → 'he learns', etc. Some common verbs inflect in other ways, but they still indicate that they are verbs by the fact that they have different forms for past and present and for use after 'they' and after 'he': 'run' and 'sit' become 'ran' and 'sat' in the past, and 'they are' becomes 'he is'. A problem, however, is that some English verbs are periphrastic (formed of two or more separate words): 'is running', 'had run', 'did run', 'will be running', and 'will have been running' are all periphrastic verb forms and each express one single idea – and each would be expressed with just one word in Latin. It is important to be able to spot English verbs, and to be able to identify periphrastic verb forms as units, in order to deal successfully with Latin. Those who are uncertain of their abilities in this area would benefit from doing the exercises on these points in chapter 63.1–2.

Verbs normally have subjects, that is, a word for the person or thing that does the action expressed by the verb (in the examples above, 'he' and 'they' are the subjects). In English every sentence must have a subject and a verb, so the shortest possible sentence is 'I am', where 'I' is the subject and 'am' is the verb. But in Latin sentences do not all have an expressed subject, because the verbs have endings that often make it unnecessary. The Latin for 'I am' is simply *sum*, and the Latin for 'he rules' is *regit*, but the Latin for 'Julia runs' is *Iūlia currit*, because the Latin endings can only supply pronouns such as 'I', 'you', 'he', 'she', 'it', 'we', or 'they' as subjects, not a name like 'Julia'. When translating Latin one needs to think carefully about whether the verb has an expressed subject, and if not, which pronoun to add in English.

Like English verbs, Latin verbs have different forms with different meanings, for example present versus future ('rule' versus 'will rule'), active versus passive ('rule' versus 'be ruled'), and indicative versus infinitive ('rule' versus 'to rule'). All these will be encountered in due course; we begin with the present active indicative. In the present active indicative English verbs normally have two forms ('rule' and 'rules', as in 'he rules'), but Latin verbs have six forms. A Latin verb can appear in the first person (indicating a subject 'I' or 'we'), second person (subject 'you'), or third person (subject 'he', 'she', 'it', 'they' or almost any other word); and it can be singular (indicating just one subject) or plural (more than one subject, or a subject composed of multiple individuals). For example:

Regō 'rule' (present active indicative)		*Dūcō* 'lead' (present active indicative)	
regō	'I rule'	dūcō	'I lead'
regis	'you (singular) rule'	dūcis	'you (singular) lead'
regit	'he rules', 'she rules', 'it rules', 'rules'	dūcit	'he leads', 'she leads', 'it leads', 'leads'
regimus	'we rule'	dūcimus	'we lead'
regitis	'you (plural) rule'	dūcitis	'you (plural) lead'
regunt	'they rule', 'rule'	dūcunt	'they lead', 'lead'

These two verbs, and many others like them, have the same endings as each other (*-ō, -is, -it, -imus, -itis, -unt*): once you know how one of them conjugates (takes different endings), you can also conjugate (put the endings on) the other. A sample verb written out this way is known as a 'paradigm', and once you know a paradigm you can use it to produce the equivalent forms for all other verbs that take the same endings. For example, if you know that *currō* 'run' is conjugated like *regō*, you also know that *curris* means 'you run' and *currunt* means 'they run' or 'run'.

When there is more than one possible translation of a Latin verb, it is necessary to pick the one that fits the context. Thus *Mārcus regit* would be translated 'Marcus rules', but *regit* by itself would be translated 'he rules' or 'she rules'.

Practice

A Conjugate in the present active indicative:

1 regō 'rule'   3 currō 'run'
2 dūcō 'lead'   4 petō 'seek'

B Translate, adding subjects in English as necessary (note *et* 'and'):[1]

1 regitis.   5 regit.
2 regunt.   6 rego.
3 currimus.   7 petitis.
4 petis.   8 currunt.

---

[1] Remember that in this book translation exercises do not have macrons on the long vowels, so the words in these sentences will not look exactly as they do in the paradigms or the grammatical exercises.

9   Iulia regit.

10   curro.

11   Quintus currit.

12   duco.

13   Marcus et Quintus regunt.

14   regis.

15   Iulia et Maria ducunt.

16   regimus.

17   Maria ducit.

18   ducis.

19   petunt.

20   peto.

21   Iulia et Marcus currunt.

22   Marcus et Iulia ducunt.

23   ducitis.

24   petimus.

C Translate into Latin:

1 We run.

2 Maria runs.

3 She runs.

4 You (singular) run.

5 Marcus leads.

6 He leads.

7 Marcus and Quintus lead.

8 I lead.

9   Maria rules.

10 Julia and Maria rule.

11 You (plural) rule.

12 They rule.

13 He seeks.

14 Marcus seeks.

15 I seek.

16 We seek.

1.2 Multiple Translations

English has a number of different verb forms that are all equivalent to the present tense in Latin. *Regō* could be translated not only 'I rule', but also with the periphrastic form 'I am ruling'; in the negative *nōn regō* could be either 'I do not rule' or 'I am not ruling'. To form a yes/no question English can use a present tense made with 'do' ('Do you rule?'), while Latin adds *-ne* to the end of the first word of the sentence: *regisne?*. Therefore a more complete list of the English translations of the *regō* paradigm for the present active indicative would be as follows:

regō	'I rule', 'I am ruling', 'I do rule'
regis	'you (singular) rule', 'you (singular) are ruling', 'you (singular) do rule'
regit	'he/she/it rules', 'he/she/it is ruling', 'he/she/it does rule', 'rules', 'is ruling', 'does rule'
regimus	'we rule', 'we are ruling', 'we do rule'
regitis	'you (plural) rule', 'you (plural) are ruling', 'you (plural) do rule'
regunt	'they rule', 'they are ruling', 'they do rule', 'rule', 'are ruling', 'do rule'

Practice

D Give all the possible translations of:

1 ducimus	7 duco	13 ducunt
2 curritis	8 currit	14 currunt
3 petit	9 petis	15 petimus
4 ducis	10 ducitis	16 ducit
5 curro	11 curris	
6 petunt	12 peto	

E Translate, picking the one of the possible translations that makes the best English (n.b. *-ne* indicating questions, *nōn* 'not'):

1 regitisne?	13 Marcus et Quintus regunt.	
2 non regunt.	14 regisne?	
3 currimus.	15 Iulia et Maria non ducunt.	
4 petisne?	16 regimusne?	
5 non regit.	17 Mariane ducit?	
6 non rego.	18 non ducis.	
7 petitisne?	19 petuntne?	
8 curruntne?	20 peto.	
9 Iulia non regit.	21 Iulia et Maria non currunt.	
10 non curro.	22 Marcus et Iulia ducunt.	
11 Quintusne currit?	23 ducitisne?	
12 non duco.	24 non petimus.	

F Translate into Latin:

1 I am running.	9 Julia is leading.
2 I am not running.	10 Julia is not leading.
3 Are you (plural) running?	11 Is she leading?
4 Maria is running.	12 She is not leading.
5 Is Maria running?	13 Are they leading?
6 Does she run?	14 They are not leading.
7 Maria does not run.	15 Are you (singular) leading?
8 Do you (singular) run?	16 We are leading.

1.3 Word Order

Latin word order is not usually the same as English word order. In Latin a verb normally goes at the end of a sentence, but if there is a question with *-ne*, the verb normally comes first: *Mārcus et Quīntus dūcunt* 'Marcus and Quintus are leading' but *dūcuntne Mārcus et Quīntus?* 'Are Marcus and Quintus leading?'. (If another word comes first in a question, as in *Mariāne dūcit?*, that word is emphatic: 'Is *Maria* leading?'.)

Practice

G Translate, changing the word order as necessary:

1 reguntne Maria et Iulia?

2 curritne Marcus?

3 ducuntne Maria et Iulia?

4 regitne Maria?

5 curruntne Quintus et Iulia?

6 petuntne Maria et Quintus?

7 ducitne Marcus?

8 petitne Iulia?

H Translate into Latin with normal word order:

1 Are Marcus and Quintus running?

2 Does Marcus run?

3 Are Marcus and Julia leading?

4 Is Julia leading?

5 Does Maria run?

6 Is Julia running?

7 Are Marcus and Quintus ruling?

8 Does Marcus rule?

9 Is Marcus leading?

10 Is Julia ruling?

1.4 Additional Exercises

The exercises below offer further practice on all the material covered in this chapter.

Practice

I Conjugate all the verbs in the vocabulary (section 1.5) in the present active indicative.

J Translate:

1 Maria scribit.

2 scribitne Maria?

3 Marcus et Quintus legunt.

4 Marcus et Quintus non legunt.

5 legitne Iulia?

6 Iulia non legit.

7 scribuntne Marcus et Iulia?

8 Marcus et Iulia non scribunt.

9 Marcus non scribit.

10 leguntne Maria et Iulia?

K Translate into Latin with normal word order:

1 Is Quintus reading?

2 Quintus is not reading.

3 Are Marcus and Quintus writing?

4 Marcus and Quintus are not writing.
5 Do Julia and Maria write?
6 Julia and Maria do not write.
7 Does Julia read?
8 Julia does not read.
9 Julia is buying.
10 Is Julia buying?

11 Are Marcus and Quintus buying?
12 Marcus and Quintus are buying.
13 Is Quintus conquering?
14 Quintus is not conquering.
15 Are Maria and Julia conquering?
16 Maria and Julia are conquering.
17 Do Maria and Marcus run?
18 Maria and Marcus do not run.

1.5 Vocabulary to Learn

Verbs

currō	'run'
dūcō	'lead'
emō	'buy'
legō	'read'
mittō	'send'
petō	'seek'
pōnō	'put'
regō	'rule'
scrībō	'write'
vincō	'conquer', 'defeat'

Other words

et	'and'
-ne	*introduces questions*
nōn	'not'

2 | Nouns: Nominative, Vocative, and Accusative of First and Second Declensions

2.1 Cases

Nouns are words for people, places, or things. In English, word order tells us how the nouns and verbs in a sentence are related: 'Maria leads Julia' has a very different meaning from 'Julia leads Maria.' The noun (or pronoun) that comes before the verb is usually the subject, the doer of the action of the verb. Likewise, in English, if there is a noun (or pronoun) after the verb, that is normally the object, the recipient of the action of the verb. In Latin, however, the information as to which noun is the subject and which is the object is conveyed not by word order, but by the endings of the words (inflection). The subject has an ending that identifies it as belonging to the nominative case, and the object has an ending that identifies it as belonging to the accusative case. Therefore any word order can be used in Latin without altering the basic meaning of the sentence, and when translating a Latin sentence into English one normally has to change the order of the words.

Names like *Marīa* and *Iūlia* belong to the first declension, a group of nouns that end in *-a* in the nominative singular (when they are subjects) and in *-am* in the accusative singular (when they are objects). Thus 'Maria leads Julia' could be written in Latin *Marīa Iūliam dūcit*; this would be the normal order with the verb at the end. But 'Maria leads Julia' could also be *Iūliam Marīa dūcit, dūcit Iūliam Marīa, dūcit Marīa Iūliam, Marīa dūcit Iūliam,* or *Iūliam dūcit Marīa*. These six sentences are not identical in meaning; there are differences of emphasis depending on how they vary from the normal order. But all six could be translated into English as 'Maria leads Julia'. Similarly 'Julia leads Maria' could be written in Latin *Iūlia Mariam dūcit, Mariam Iūlia dūcit, dūcit Mariam Iūlia, dūcit Iūlia Mariam, Iūlia dūcit Mariam,* or *Mariam dūcit Iūlia*.

Names like *Mārcus* and *Quīntus* belong to the second declension: these words end in *-us* in the nominative and *-um* in the accusative. So 'Marcus leads Quintus' could be *Mārcus Quīntum dūcit, Quīntum Mārcus dūcit*, etc. In sum:

	First declension	Second declension
Nominative singular	*-a*	*-us*
Accusative singular	*-am*	*-um*

Practice

A Translate:

1 Maria Iuliam petit.
2 Mariam duco.
3 Mariam Iulia mittit.
4 petisne Marcum?
5 Iuliam non petit Maria.
6 Mariam non peto.
7 ducitne Maria Iuliam?

8 Mariam ducit.
9 petitne Mariam Iulia?
10 Marcum et Quintum petimus.
11 regitne Marcus Quintum?
12 petitne Quintum?
13 Marcum Quintus petit.
14 Iuliam peto.

B Translate into Latin with normal word order:

1 Maria is sending Julia.
2 I am seeking Maria.
3 Is Marcus seeking Quintus?
4 We are leading Marcus.
5 Marcus does not rule Quintus.

6 Are you (singular) seeking Julia?
7 Is Maria seeking Julia?
8 He does not rule Quintus.
9 Julia is not leading Maria.
10 Are they leading Julia?

2.2 Vocative

When calling to someone or addressing him/her directly, the Romans used another case, the vocative. In the first declension the vocative has the same endings as the nominative, but in the second declension it is different.

	First declension	Second declension
Nominative singular	*-a*	*-us*
Vocative singular	*-a*	*-e*
Accusative singular	*-am*	*-um*

Thus when calling to Marcus, one says *Mārce*, but when calling to Julia, one says *Iūlia*. A vocative can appear anywhere in the sentence, even in front of the word that has *-ne* in a question: 'Marcus, are you reading?' could be *Mārce, legisne?* or *legisne, Mārce?*. (The *-ne* cannot be attached to the vocative itself.)

Practice

C Translate:

1 Marce, currisne?
2 scribisne, Quinte?
3 Quinte, petisne Mariam?
4 scribitne Quintus?

5 ducisne Quintum, Maria?
6 curritne Maria?
7 Marce, petitne Iulia Mariam?
8 currisne, Maria?

9   Quinte, Iulia Mariam ducit.
10 legisne, Iulia?
11 Maria, legitne Marcus?
12 legitne Iulia?

13 Iulia, Mariam peto.
14 regisne, Maria?
15 Marce, Iulia Mariam petit.
16 regitne Maria?

D Translate into Latin:

1 Marcus, are you writing?
2 Quintus, is Iulia writing?
3 Julia, do you run?
4 Maria, I am seeking Marcus.
5 Marcus, are you sending
   Quintus?

6   Quintus, are you leading Maria?
7   Julia, I am not seeking Quintus.
8   Maria, we are reading.
9   Marcus, are you seeking Julia?
10 Quintus, you are not writing.

2.3 Declensions

Like the verbs in chapter 1.1, these names illustrate paradigms, large groups of words that all take the same endings. Many nouns end in -*a* and belong to the first declension, and many others end in -*us* and belong to the second declension. These nouns take the endings we have just seen; in addition, they can be plural (refer to more than one person/thing), and when they are plural they take different endings: nominative and vocative in -*ae* (first declension) or -*ī* (second declension), accusative in -*ās* (first declension) or -*ōs* (second declension). One example of a first-declension noun is *puella* 'girl', and one example of a second-declension noun is *servus* 'slave'. We can now decline (i.e. put the endings on) these two nouns as follows:

	First declension		**Second declension**	
	Singular	**Plural**	**Singular**	**Plural**
Nominative	puella	puellae	servus	servī
Vocative	puella	puellae	serve	servī
Accusative	puellam	puellās	servum	servōs

Practice

E Determine which declension each of these nouns belongs to:

1 agricola 'farmer'
2 dea 'goddess'
3 equus 'horse'
4 amīcus 'friend'

5 poēta 'poet'
6 deus 'god' (has no vocative
   singular)

F Decline the nouns in exercise E in these three cases, singular and plural.

2.4 Multiple Translations

Like the verb forms in chapter 1.2, these nouns can be translated into English in more than one way. Latin has no articles (i.e. no equivalent of English 'the' or 'a'). So *puella* can be translated 'girl', 'a girl', or 'the girl', and *puellae* can be translated 'girls' or 'the girls'. A sentence containing two nouns and a present-tense verb therefore has a wide variety of translations: *puella servum dūcit* could be rendered 'The girl leads the slave', 'The girl is leading the slave', 'A girl leads the slave', 'A girl is leading the slave', 'The girl leads a slave', 'The girl is leading a slave', 'A girl leads a slave', or 'A girl is leading a slave'. When the sentence is presented in isolation any one of these can be used, but when the sentence has a context (as is almost always the case in real Latin literature) the context normally determines which translation is appropriate. Therefore *puella servum dūcit* might mean 'A girl leads a slave' in one place and 'The girl is leading the slave' in another place.

Practice

G Translate, adding articles as necessary in English and remembering the following meanings: *agricola* 'farmer', *amīcus* 'friend', *dea* 'goddess', *deus* 'god', *equus* 'horse', *poēta* 'poet', *puella* 'girl', *servus* 'slave'.

1	agricolae equos ducunt.	21	puellas equi non petunt.
2	agricolas deae ducunt.	22	deae petunt puellam.
3	servos agricolae ducunt.	23	servi, ducitisne equos?
4	deae agricolas non ducunt.	24	servum poeta petit.
5	ducuntne deae agricolam?	25	poetae agricolas petunt.
6	amice, petisne puellam?	26	petuntne poetam agricolae?
7	puellas deae ducunt.	27	agricola equum emit.
8	deae ducunt puellam.	28	poeta, scribisne?
9	poetae, scribitisne?	29	servum agricola non emit.
10	servum poetae non ducunt.	30	puellae servum emunt.
11	poetae agricolam ducunt.	31	emitne poeta servos?
12	ducuntne poetas agricolae?	32	emuntne servos poetae?
13	poetas agricola non ducit.	33	puellae, petitisne servos?
14	puella, petisne servos?	34	agricolae equos non emunt.
15	agricolam servi petunt.	35	puellas non petimus.
16	agricolas servus non petit.	36	emisne servum?
17	servum agricolae petunt.	37	puellae equum ducunt.
18	servi agricolas petunt.	38	equos ducit puella.
19	petitne servus agricolas?	39	agricolas poetae ducunt.
20	agricolae, emitisne servos?	40	serve, ducisne equos?

41 puellae equos petunt.

42 agricola, emisne servos?

43 amicos petunt puellae.

44 equum puella non emit.

45 equos agricolae emunt.

46 amici, petitisne puellas?

47 reguntne dei poetas?

48 servum non emo.

49 amice, mittisne servum?

50 poetae scribunt.

51 agricolae non legunt.

52 serve, currisne?

H Translate into Latin:

1   The farmers lead the poets.

2   The poets lead the farmers.

3   Girls are seeking the farmers.

4   Farmers are seeking the girls.

5   Goddesses lead girls.

6   A girl leads the goddesses.

7   Friend, are you buying a horse?

8   Friends, are you sending slaves?

9   The poets seek a girl.

10 The girls seek a poet.

11 A farmer leads the poets.

12 A poet leads the farmers.

13 The girls are sending the farmer.

14 A farmer is sending the girls.

15 A goddess leads the girls.

16 The girls lead the horses.

17 Slave, I seek the farmer.

18 Girls, are you writing?

19 Poets seek girls.

20 The girls seek poets.

21 We are sending slaves.

22 Farmer, are you buying slaves?

2.5 Vocabulary to Learn

Nouns

agricola	'farmer'
amīcus	'friend'
dea	'goddess'
deus	'god'
equus	'horse'
poēta	'poet'
puella	'girl'
servus	'slave'

3 | Adjectives: Gender, Agreement, Neuters, and Vocabulary Format

3.1 Gender

In Latin, all nouns have a gender; that is, every noun is inherently masculine, feminine, or neuter. Words for male humans are normally masculine and words for female humans are normally feminine, but words for things can belong to any of the three genders. Gender is important because adjectives in Latin assume the same gender as the nouns they modify; often you cannot tell which noun an adjective goes with unless you know the genders of the nouns in the sentence. The genders of the nouns we have seen so far are:

Masculine	Feminine
agricola 'farmer'	dea 'goddess'
amīcus 'friend'	puella 'girl'
deus 'god'	
equus 'horse'	
poēta 'poet'	
servus 'slave'	

All the second-declension nouns in this list are masculine; in fact most nouns of the second declension ending in *-us* are masculine – but not all, so it is important to learn their genders. Likewise most nouns of the first declension are feminine – but not all, as you can see from *agricola* and *poēta*.

3.2 Neuters

So far we have not seen any neuter nouns. Neuters decline similarly to masculines, but they always have one form for the nominative, vocative, and accusative; in the second declension this form is *-um* for the singular and *-a* for the plural. For example, the noun *bellum* 'war' declines as follows:

	Singular	Plural
Nominative	bellum	bella
Vocative	bellum	bella
Accusative	bellum	bella

This paradigm requires alertness on the part of the reader. It can be difficult to tell whether a neuter noun is nominative or accusative, and if you encounter an unfamiliar word ending in *-a*, it may be difficult to tell whether it is a neuter plural or a first-declension nominative singular.

Practice

A Decline the following neuter nouns:

1 verbum 'word'   2 oppidum 'town'

B Translate and explain how you know what the subject is:

1 puella verba legit.   7   agricolae oppida petunt.
2 poeta verba scribit.   8   oppida poetae petunt.
3 puellae verba legunt.   9   verba scribimus.
4 verba poetae scribunt.   10 petitisne oppida?
5 dea oppida vincit.   11 verbane legis?
6 deae oppida vincunt.

C Translate into Latin:

1 I seek the town.   6 Are you (plural) seeking the
2 Are you (singular) writing words?   towns?
3 The goddess rules the town.   7 I am writing words.
4 Poets rule the towns.   8 Gods send wars.
5 We are reading words.

3.3 Adjectives

Adjectives agree with nouns in gender, number, and case; therefore they can be masculine, feminine, or neuter; singular or plural; and nominative, vocative, or accusative. They take different endings to reflect these different possibilities, as you can see from the declension of *bonus* 'good'.

	Singular			Plural		
	Masculine	**Feminine**	**Neuter**	**Masculine**	**Feminine**	**Neuter**
Nominative	bonus	bona	bonum	bonī	bonae	bona
Vocative	bone	bona	bonum	bonī	bonae	bona
Accusative	bonum	bonam	bonum	bonōs	bonās	bona

You will observe that adjectives take second-declension endings in the masculine and neuter, and first-declension endings in the feminine. But this does not mean that an adjective necessarily has the same ending as the noun it agrees with, since a first-declension noun may be masculine (and a second-declension noun may be feminine, though we have not yet seen any such). 'A good friend' is *amīcus bonus* or *bonus amīcus*, and 'a good girl' is *puella bona* or *bona puella*, but 'a good farmer' is *agricola bonus* or *bonus agricola*, and 'a good poet' is *poēta bonus* or *bonus poēta*.

Practice

D Give the form of *bonus* 'good' that would be used to agree with the following nouns (i.e. *bonus* in the same gender, number, and case):

1 amicum	8 equos	15 poetas
2 bellum	9 agricolas	16 deos
3 puellam	10 puellae	17 agricola
4 agricolae	11 poeta	18 amice
5 dei	12 serve	19 poetae
6 deae	13 agricolam	20 equum
7 poetam	14 equus	

E Decline the following adjectives in the genders and numbers indicated:

1 *magnus* 'big', masculine singular
2 *novus* 'new', masculine plural
3 *tuus* 'your' (singular 'you'), feminine singular
4 *meus* 'my', feminine plural
5 *magnus* 'big', neuter singular
6 *tuus* 'your', neuter plural

F Translate:

1 agricolae equos magnos ducunt.
2 agricolas bonos deae ducunt.
3 servos novos agricolae emunt.
4 deae bonae agricolas non ducunt.
5 ducuntne deae bonae agricolam?
6 amice, petisne tuum oppidum?
7 servus tuus verba mea non legit.
8 dei bella nova mittunt.
9 oppidum meum peto.
10 servum meum poetae non ducunt.
11 poetae boni agricolam ducunt.
12 ducuntne poetas bonos agricolae?
13 verba bona agricola non scribit.
14 puella, petisne servos tuos?
15 poeta bona verba scribit.
16 dei oppidum bonum regunt.
17 servum tuum agricolae petunt.
18 servi novi agricolas petunt.
19 petitne servus tuus agricolas?
20 agricolae, emitisne servos bonos?
21 servine vincunt oppidum tuum?

22 oppidum novum petimus.

23 servi, ducitisne equos meos?

24 servum novum poeta petit.

25 poetae bonos agricolas petunt.

26 petuntne poetam boni agricolae?

27 agricola bonum equum emit.

28 poeta nova verba scribit.

29 servum novum agricola non emit.

30 puellae meum servum emunt.

31 emitne poeta bonos servos?

32 emuntne servos boni poetae?

33 puella, petisne servos tuos?

34 agricolae equos meos non emunt.

35 puellas bonas non petimus.

36 emisne servum bonum?

37 puellae magnae equum magnum ducunt.

38 equos tuos ducit puella.

39 poetae oppidum tuum petunt.

40 serve, ducisne equos meos?

41 puellae equos tuos petunt.

42 agricola, emisne servos novos?

43 amice, scribisne nova verba?

44 equum magnum puella non emit.

45 equos novos agricolae emunt.

46 amici, petitisne puellas bonas?

47 amice, petisne nova bella?

48 servum tuum non emo.

49 amice, mittisne tuum servum?

50 poetae boni verba non scribunt.

51 agricolae verba mea non legunt.

52 bone serve, currisne?

G Translate into Latin:

1 Your slaves are seeking your horse.

2 I am writing your words.

3 They seek a new town.

4 The gods send good words.

5 Farmers rule my town.

6 He is reading your words.

7 A good poet does not write.

8 Good farmers buy good horses.

9 Do the gods rule your town?

10 Friend, are you seeking a new horse?

11 Friends, you are leading my horse.

12 Slave, you do not rule the town.

13 We are seeking good poets.

14 He is seeking new slaves.

15 You (plural) do not rule the towns.

16 The new slave is running.

3.4 Vocabulary Format

When nouns are listed in Latin dictionaries or vocabulary lists, they are accompanied by two pieces of information in addition to their meanings. One of these is the gender, usually abbreviated to 'm.', 'f.', or 'n.' The other is information on what declension a noun belongs to, since there are more than two declensions and it is not normally possible to tell how a noun declines simply by seeing the nominative singular. Declensions are given by adding a case form we have not yet seen, the genitive singular: first-declension genitives singular end in -*ae*, and second-declension genitives singular (both masculine and neuter) end in *-ī*. Thus a proper dictionary or vocabulary entry for *puella* would be '*puella, puellae* (f.) "girl"' (sometimes abbreviated to '*puella, -ae* (f.) "girl"'), and one for *bellum* would be '*bellum, bellī* (n.) "war"' (sometimes abbreviated to '*bellum, -ī* (n.) "war"'). Such entries tell the reader that *puella* is a feminine noun of the first declension and *bellum* is a neuter noun of the second declension. It is necessary to memorize this information along with the word itself in order to understand a Latin text, for without knowing that *bellum* is a second-declension neuter one does not know that the form *bella* may be accusative plural.

Adjectives are accompanied by different information: they show the endings that they take in the nominatives singular of all three genders. Thus a proper dictionary or vocabulary entry for *bonus* would be '*bonus, bona, bonum* "good"' (sometimes abbreviated to '*bonus, -a, -um* "good"'). Again it is necessary to memorize this information along with the words themselves. The vocabulary from the previous chapter is therefore repeated here, for re-learning with this additional information.

3.5 Vocabulary to Learn

Nouns

agricola, agricolae (m.)	'farmer'
amīcus, amīcī (m.)	'friend'
bellum, bellī (n.)	'war'
dea, deae (f.)	'goddess'
deus, deī (m.)	'god'
equus, equī (m.)	'horse'
oppidum, oppidī (n.)	'town'
poēta, poētae (m.)	'poet'
puella, puellae (f.)	'girl'
servus, servī (m.)	'slave'
verbum, verbī (n.)	'word'

Adjectives

bonus, bona, bonum	'good'
magnus, magna, magnum	'big'
meus, mea, meum	'my'
novus, nova, novum	'new'
tuus, tua, tuum	'your' (singular 'you')

4 | Tenses: Future, Perfect, and Principal Parts

4.1 Future Tense

So far all the verbs we have seen have been in the present tense, but Latin has a future as well. Third-conjugation verbs (the only type we have seen so far) form their futures by changing the vowel in the ending to *e*, except in the first person singular.

Present active indicative	Future active indicative	
regō	regam	'I will rule', 'I shall rule'
regis	regēs	'you (singular) will rule', 'you (singular) shall rule'
regit	reget	'he/she/it will rule', 'he/she/it shall rule', 'will rule', 'shall rule'
regimus	regēmus	'we will rule', 'we shall rule'
regitis	regētis	'you (plural) will rule', 'you (plural) shall rule'
regunt	regent	'they will rule', 'they shall rule', 'will rule', 'shall rule'

Practice

A Conjugate in the future active indicative:

1 currō
2 dūcō
3 emō
4 legō

5 mittō
6 petō
7 pōnō
8 scrībō

B Translate:

1 curres
2 ducent
3 emetis
4 legemus
5 mittam
6 petet
7 ponent
8 scribet

9 vincam
10 curretis
11 ducemus
12 emes
13 leget
14 mittent
15 petam
16 ponemus

C Translate into Latin:

1 they will write	7 we shall send
2 we shall conquer	8 they will seek
3 he will run	9 he will put
4 I shall lead	10 you (plural) will write
5 you (singular) will buy	11 you (singular) will conquer
6 you (plural) will read	12 I shall run

4.2 Principal Parts

Most Latin verbs have more than one stem (basic form of the word to which endings are added); one stem is used for the present and future and a different one for (most) past tenses. Many English verbs also have this arrangement: consider 'sing, sang, sung' or 'go, went, gone'. In most cases it is not possible to predict from the present stem what the others will be, so one has to learn a set of stems for each verb. These are known as 'principal parts' and consist of four elements (though not every verb has all four): the first person singular of the present active indicative (this is the standard reference form that you have already been using), the present active infinitive (this tells you which conjugation the verb belongs to and therefore how to conjugate it in the present; since all the verbs we have seen so far belong to the third conjugation, they all have infinitives in -*ere*), the first person singular of the perfect active indicative (the tense you are about to learn now) and the supine or perfect passive participle.[1] Thus the principal parts of *regō* are: *regō* ('I rule'), *regere* ('to rule'), *rēxī* ('I ruled'), *rēctum* ('ruled'). The principal parts of all the verbs we have seen so far are:

> currō, currere, cucurrī, cursum
> dūcō, dūcere, dūxī, ductum
> emō, emere, ēmī, ēmptum
> legō, legere, lēgī, lēctum
> mittō, mittere, mīsī, missum
> petō, petere, petīvī, petītum
> pōnō, pōnere, posuī, positum
> regō, regere, rēxī, rēctum
> scrībō, scrībere, scrīpsī, scrīptum
> vincō, vincere, vīcī, victum

In some verbs (*emō, legō*) the only difference between the present and perfect stem is in the length of the stem vowel, which is short in the present and long in the perfect.

---

[1] Some books, including this one, give a fourth principal part in -*um*; this is technically the supine, a form that is not really translatable. Others give the fourth principal part in -*us*; this is technically the perfect passive participle, e.g. 'done', 'ruled' (see chapter 6.2).

Since in most texts vowel length is not indicated, some forms of these verbs will be for all practical purposes ambiguous between the present and the perfect; in other forms the endings are different.

4.3 Perfect

The perfect is the basic past tense in Latin. To form it, you start with the third principal part, drop the -*ī*, and to the resulting stem (in the case of our paradigm verb this stem is *rēx-*) add the endings -*ī*, -*istī*, -*it*, -*imus*, -*istis*, -*ērunt*.

rēxī	'I ruled', 'I have ruled', 'I did rule'
rēxistī	'you (singular) ruled', 'you (singular) have ruled', 'you (singular) did rule'
rēxit	'he/she/it ruled', 'he/she/it has ruled', 'he/she/it did rule', 'ruled', 'has ruled', 'did rule'
rēximus	'we ruled', 'we have ruled', 'we did rule'
rēxistis	'you (plural) ruled', 'you (plural) have ruled', 'you (plural) did rule'
rēxērunt	'they ruled', 'they have ruled', 'they did rule', 'ruled', 'have ruled', 'did rule'

There is an alternative form *rēxēre* in the third person plural: writers may use either *rēxērunt* or *rēxēre*. In verbs where there is ambiguity between present and perfect stems this form can sometimes be confused with the present infinitive. This alternative form will not generally be used in this book, but it is worth remembering.

Practice

D Conjugate in the perfect active indicative:

1 currō	5 mittō
2 dūcō	6 petō
3 emō	7 pōnō
4 legō	8 scrībō

E Translate, assuming ambiguous forms are perfects:

1 cucurristi	7 posuerunt
2 duxerunt	8 scripsit
3 emistis	9 vici
4 legimus	10 cucurrerunt
5 misi	11 duximus
6 petivit	12 emisti

13 legit
14 miserunt

15 petivi
16 posuimus

F Translate into Latin:

1 they wrote
2 we have conquered
3 he ran
4 I led
5 you (singular) bought
6 you (plural) have read

7 we have sent
8 they sought
9 he has put
10 you (plural) have written
11 you (singular) conquered
12 I have run

G Translate (past, present, and future tenses mixed together):

1 agricolae equos magnos
  duxerunt.
2 agricolas bonos deae ducent.
3 servos novos agricolae ement.
4 deae bonae agricolas non
  duxerunt.
5 duxeruntne deae bonae
  agricolam?
6 amice, petesne tuum oppidum?
7 servus tuus verba mea non legit
  (2 ways).
8 dei bella nova mittent.
9 oppidum meum petivi.
10 servum meum poetae non
  ducent.
11 poetae boni agricolam ducunt.
12 duxeruntne poetas bonos
  agricolae?
13 verba bona agricola non scripsit.
14 puella, petivistine servos tuos?
15 poeta bona verba scribet.
16 dei oppidum bonum regent.
17 servum tuum agricolae petunt.
18 servi novi agricolas petent.
19 petivitne servus tuus agricolas?
20 agricolae, emistisne servos
  bonos?

21 servine vicerunt oppidum tuum?
22 oppidum novum petivimus.
23 servi, duxistisne equos meos?
24 servum novum poeta petet.
25 poetae bonos agricolas petunt.
26 petiveruntne poetam boni
  agricolae?
27 agricola bonum equum emet.
28 poeta nova verba scribet.
29 servum novum agricola non
  emit (2 ways).
30 puellae meum servum emerunt.
31 emetne poeta bonos servos?
32 emeruntne servos boni poetae?
33 puella, petivistine servos tuos?
34 agricolae equos meos non
  emerunt.
35 puellas bonas non petemus.
36 emistine servum bonum?
37 puellae magnae equum magnum
  duxerunt.
38 equos tuos duxit puella.
39 poetae oppidum tuum petunt.
40 serve, duxistine equos meos?
41 puellae equos tuos petent.
42 agricola, emesne servos novos?
43 amice, scripsistine nova verba?

44 equum magnum puella non emet.

45 equos novos agricolae emerunt.

46 amici, petetisne puellas bonas?

47 amice, petisne nova bella?

48 servum tuum non emam.

49 amice, misistine tuum servum?

50 poetae boni verba non scripserunt.

51 agricolae verba mea non legerunt.

52 bone serve, cucurristine?

H Translate into Latin:

1 The new slave ran.

2 He sought new slaves.

3 Your slaves sought your horse.

4 Slave, you will not rule the town.

5 I shall write (down) your words.

6 Friends, you led my horse.

7 Will the gods rule your town?

8 They will seek a new town.

9 The good poet did not write.

10 The gods sent good words.

11 He will read your words.

12 The good farmers bought good horses.

13 Friend, will you seek a new horse?

14 We sought good poets.

15 Farmers ruled my town.

16 You (plural) will not rule the towns.

4.4 Vocabulary to Learn

Since principal parts need to be learned for each verb before one can form all its tenses, it is now necessary to re-learn the chapter 1 vocabulary.

Verbs

currō, currere, cucurrī, cursum	'run'
dūcō, dūcere, dūxī, ductum	'lead'
emō, emere, ēmī, ēmptum	'buy'
legō, legere, lēgī, lēctum	'read'
mittō, mittere, mīsī, missum	'send'
petō, petere, petīvī, petītum	'seek'
pōnō, pōnere, posuī, positum	'put'
regō, regere, rēxī, rēctum	'rule'
scrībō, scrībere, scrīpsī, scrīptum	'write'
vincō, vincere, vīcī, victum	'conquer'

5 | Genitive Case, *Sum*

5.1 Genitive

The nominative, vocative, and accusative are only three of the six cases in Latin. Another is the genitive, whose singular endings you have already seen in the vocabulary entries. The genitive is traditionally used in dictionary entries because it was the second case (after the nominative) in the order that the Romans themselves used, and many modern Classicists (especially in North America) follow this ancient order.[1] British Classicists, however, tend to learn the cases in a revised order that puts similar endings together and therefore makes the paradigms easier to learn. In order to accommodate both traditions, this book will give all declensions twice, first in the British order and then in the ancient order. It is recommended that any given class choose one order and stick to it consistently throughout the course, to avoid confusion.

In the British order, the first four cases of the nouns are as follows:

British Case Order

	First declension		Second declension masculine		Second declension neuter	
	Singular	Plural	Singular	Plural	Singular	Plural
Nominative	puella	puellae	servus	servī	bellum	bella
Vocative	puella	puellae	serve	servī	bellum	bella
Accusative	puellam	puellās	servum	servōs	bellum	bella
Genitive	*puellae*	*puellārum*	*servī*	*servōrum*	*bellī*	*bellōrum*

The adjectives form their genitives in the same way.

---

[1] For the fascinating story of the history of the different orders of the cases see W. S. Allen and C. O. Brink, 'The Old Order and the New: A Case History', *Lingua* 50 (1980), pp. 61–100.

	Singular			Plural		
	Masculine	Feminine	Neuter	Masculine	Feminine	Neuter
Nominative	bonus	bona	bonum	bonī	bonae	bona
Vocative	bone	bona	bonum	bonī	bonae	bona
Accusative	bonum	bonam	bonum	bonōs	bonās	bona
Genitive	*bonī*	*bonae*	*bonī*	*bonōrum*	*bonārum*	*bonōrum*

In the ancient order, these are arranged as follows:

Ancient Case Order

	First declension		Second declension masculine		Second declension neuter	
	Singular	Plural	Singular	Plural	Singular	Plural
Nominative	puella	puellae	servus	servī	bellum	bella
Genitive	*puellae*	*puellārum*	*servī*	*servōrum*	*bellī*	*bellōrum*
Accusative	puellam	puellās	servum	servōs	bellum	bella
Vocative	puella	puellae	serve	servī	bellum	bella

And the adjectives have a similar pattern:

	Singular			Plural		
	Masculine	Feminine	Neuter	Masculine	Feminine	Neuter
Nominative	bonus	bona	bonum	bonī	bonae	bona
Genitive	*bonī*	*bonae*	*bonī*	*bonōrum*	*bonārum*	*bonōrum*
Accusative	bonum	bonam	bonum	bonōs	bonās	bona
Vocative	bone	bona	bonum	bonī	bonae	bona

Practice

A Decline the following, in these four cases of the forms indicated:

1 *agricola*, plural
2 *amīcus*, singular
3 *novus*, neuter plural
4 *meus*, feminine singular
5 *verbum*, plural
6 *equus*, singular
7 *tuus*, masculine plural
8 *magnus*, neuter singular
9 *dea*, plural
10 *oppidum*, singular
11 *poēta*, plural
12 *novus*, feminine singular
13 *agricola*, singular
14 *amīcus*, plural

15 *novus*, neuter singular

16 *meus*, feminine plural

17 *verbum*, singular

18 *equus*, plural

19 *tuus*, masculine singular

20 *magnus*, neuter plural

21 *dea*, singular

22 *oppidum*, plural

23 *poēta*, singular

24 *novus*, feminine plural

5.2 Use of the Genitive

The genitive case is used for possession. It is the only case that survives with distinctive endings in English nouns: words ending in an apostrophe + *s*, or *s* + apostrophe, are normally genitives in English. Thus *girl's* in 'that girl's book is on the desk' is a genitive, as is *girls'* in 'those girls' books are on the desk';[2] *puellae servī* is 'the girl's slaves' and *puellārum servī* is 'the girls' slaves'. A genitive phrase of this sort can be the subject or the object of a sentence: *puellae servus currit* 'The girl's slave is running' versus *puellae servum dūcō* 'I lead the girl's slave'. Notice that in these two sentences the case of 'slave' changes according to whether the slave is the subject or the object, but 'girl' remains in the genitive case in both, since in both sentences the girl is neither subject nor object, but the possessor of the slave. There is sometimes a temptation to mix up which word in a phrase is the genitive, i.e. to mistranslate *puellae servus* as 'the slave's girl'. To avoid this temptation, remember that the word that gets the apostrophe in English is the *same word* as the one that gets the genitive ending in Latin.

Sometimes a Latin genitive is best translated with English 'of'; thus *puellae servus* can mean 'the slave of the girl' as well as 'the girl's slave'. Here as well there is a temptation to mix up which word is the genitive, and to mistranslate *puellae servus* as 'the girl of the slave'. That temptation can be avoided by remembering that the word *after* the 'of' in English is the genitive in Latin.

Some English 'of' phrases are not possessive, but these too are normally translated with a genitive in Latin; for example 'one of the slaves' and 'some of the horses' are phrases using partitive genitives (for which see chapter 12.1). Generally speaking you should translate any English 'of' with a genitive unless there is a particular reason not to do so.

---

[2] The following distinctions apply in correct written English but are not always observed in practice; you will need to follow them if you want to translate Latin correctly:

> *girl* = one girl, nominative or accusative
> *girl's* = one girl, genitive
> *girls* = two or more girls, nominative or accusative
> *girls'* = two or more girls, genitive

Thus: 'The girls saw me', 'I saw the girls', 'I saw the girl's book' (one girl owns it), 'I saw the girls' book' (two girls own it jointly). But note also that apostrophe + *s* can sometimes be short for 'is', as in 'He's not here.' With the word 'it', an apostrophe is used before 's' when 'it's' stands for 'it is', but no apostrophe is used when 'its' is a genitive.

A genitive normally stands next to the noun that it relates to, but if a genitive falls between two nouns the sentence may be ambiguous: *servus puellae equum ēmit* could mean either 'The girl's slave bought a horse' or 'A slave bought the girl's horse'. This type of ambiguity was as perplexing to the Romans as it is to us, so they usually avoided it: in a real text the context will normally make it clear which is intended.

Since adjectives agree with the nouns they modify in gender, number, and case, any adjectives modifying nouns in the genitive will also be in the genitive case. Thus *servī bonī equus* 'the good slave's horse'.

The possessive adjectives *meus* 'my' and *tuus* 'your' are not genitives, but a different way of expressing possession.

Practice

B Identify the words in the following English sentences that would be genitives in Latin:

1 John's house is enormous.
2 I've never met Mary's brother.
3 The laws of the gods are immutable.
4 Two of the wooden chairs are broken.
5 The big chair's legs are uneven.
6 I can't find the problem with its legs.
7 Jim has one of the books.
8 The father of the bride will not attend.
9 It's dreadful to see Roger's injuries.
10 He's bringing Jane's dictionary.
11 John's got one of them.
12 The mother of those little boys is overworked.
13 Peter's wearing Mike's shoes.
14 Those cars' tyres are all rotten.
15 Every single one of the neighbours is delighted.
16 Who is the owner of this dog?
17 Peter's cat just had kittens.
18 The father of a dozen children has a hard life.

C Translate:

1 Marci equum emam.
2 verba Iuliae scripsi.
3 servus poetae equum duxit.
4 servus Quinti cucurrit.
5 agricolarum servos petemus.
6 puellarum verba legemus.
7 poetarum amicus equum emit.
8 amicus Marci oppidum meum petit.
9 verba dei scripsimus.
10 legistine deorum verba?
11 Mariae servus amicos petit.
12 servi puellarum Quintum petiverunt.
13 poetarum equos emi.
14 Marci servum mittemus.
15 equum Iuliae ducit.
16 servum poetae misit.

17 agricolae servos ducunt.

18 amici equos emerunt.

19 servus poetae boni equum duxit.

20 servum poetae novi misit.

D Translate into Latin:

1 I have bought Julia's slave.

2 I shall write Marcus' words.

3 The girl's slave will lead the horses.

4 The poets' slaves are running.

5 We sought the farmers' horses.

6 We have read the poet's words.

7 The poet's friend will buy your horse.

8 Julia's friends are seeking the slave.

9 He will write the words of the gods.

10 Will you (singular) read the god's words?

11 Quintus' slaves are seeking your horse.

12 The farmer's slave sought the horse.

13 Will you (plural) buy the poets' slaves?

14 I sent Maria's slaves.

5.3 *Sum*

The verb *sum* 'be' is irregular in Latin as in English; its principal parts are *sum, esse, fuī,* and *futūrus.*[3] It is conjugated as follows:

Present active indicative		Future active indicative		Perfect active indicative	
sum	'I am'	erō	'I will be', 'I shall be'	fuī	'I have been', 'I was'
es	'you (singular) are'	eris	'you (singular) will be', 'you (singular) shall be'	fuistī	'you (singular) have been', 'you (singular) were'
est	'he/she/it is', 'is'	erit	'he/she/it will be', 'he/she/it shall be', 'will be', 'shall be'	fuit	'he/she/it has been', 'he/she/it was', 'has been', 'was'
sumus	'we are'	erimus	'we will be', 'we shall be'	fuimus	'we have been', 'we were'
estis	'you (plural) are'	eritis	'you (plural) will be', 'you (plural) shall be'	fuistis	'you (plural) have been', 'you (plural) were'
sunt	'they are', 'are'	erunt	'they will be', 'they shall be', 'will be', 'shall be'	fuērunt	'they have been', 'they were', 'have been', 'were'

---

[3] The fourth principal part ends in *-s* because it is a different kind of form from other fourth parts you have seen; this will be explained in chapter 24.

The verb *sum* 'be' does not take an object, because 'be' does not indicate any action; it shows that the two words it joins are the same thing. So a form of *sum* takes a word in the same case as its subject, which of course is normally nominative: 'The girl is a poet' is *puella poēta est* (or *puella est poēta*, etc.).[4] This is sometimes called a 'predicate nominative'. Notice that because Latin does not have words for 'the' or 'a', and because both nouns are nominative, there is no clear distinction between 'The girl is a poet' and 'The poet is a girl'; if a Roman wanted to make such a distinction, he needed to use additional words such as *hic* 'this'. Similarly a sentence like *poēta est* can mean either 'He is a poet' or (less likely, but in certain contexts not impossible) 'The poet is.'

Practice

E Translate:

1 poeta non sum.	14 deus magnus est.
2 agricola eris.	15 servus Marci novus est.
3 estisne agricolae?	16 agricolae boni sunt.
4 agricola non sum.	17 agricolarum equi magni sunt.
5 poetae sumus.	18 servus meus bonus est.
6 esne poeta?	19 servus puellae non ero.
7 esne servus?	20 servus novus bonus non erit.
8 equus tuus bonus non est.	21 Iuliae equus bonus est.
9 poeta bonus fuit.	22 agricolae fuimus.
10 amici tui fuimus.	23 servus dei sum.
11 servi tui erimus.	24 dei agricolarum boni sunt.
12 equus meus bonus fuit.	25 poetae equus magnus non fuit.
13 dei boni sunt.	26 servi poetae boni non sunt.

F Translate into Latin:

1 I am a farmer.	9 The girls' horses are not big.
2 Are you a goddess?	10 The gods of the town are good.
3 We are gods.	11 We are the slaves of the gods.
4 I shall be a good poet.	12 Were you a farmer's slave?
5 The goddesses are good.	13 Are you a new slave?
6 Were you slaves?	14 I shall be a friend of the farmer.
7 The farmer's horse is big.	15 We are friends of the poet.
8 The poet's words will be good.	16 He has been a farmer.

---

[4] The rule that '*sum* takes the nominative' is an oversimplification but will work until chapter 19.

5.4 Additional Exercises

The sentences below provide extra practice in distinguishing predicate nominatives from accusatives.

Practice

G Identify all words in these sentences that would be nominatives or accusatives in Latin:[5]

1 I would like some cabbage.
2 He is a prince.
3 You are a saint!
4 Jack detests fish.
5 Who are you?
6 Mary saw us at the theatre.
7 Where did you put the mustard?
8 What is your name?
9 The king is now a prisoner.
10 Scholars like to write books.
11 They are desperately hungry.
12 My name is Michael.
13 Julia can carry the canoe.
14 Sally was a baby.
15 My little darling is now a politician!
16 I love you.
17 You are beautiful.
18 This is Christopher.
19 I have bought a new bicycle.
20 Whom did you see yesterday?
21 I shall be rich in ten years' time.
22 Who is that man?
23 He is the Prime Minister.
24 Why did you do that?
25 What did he want?
26 I shall never be a traitor.

5.5 Vocabulary to Learn

Verb

sum, esse, fuī, futūrus   'be'

Nouns

cōnsilium, cōnsiliī (n.)   'advice', 'plan'
epistula, epistulae (f.)   'letter'
pecūnia, pecūniae (f.)   'money'

---

[5] If you have difficulty with this exercise, first try the ones on the same point in chapter 63.3–5, which have an answer key.

6 | First and Second Conjugations, Perfect Participles

6.1 First and Second Conjugations

So far all the verbs we have seen belong to the third conjugation. The first and second conjugations function somewhat differently.

Present active indicative

First conjugation		Second conjugation		Third conjugation	
amō	'I love' etc.	moneō	'I advise' etc.	regō	'I rule' etc.
amās	'you love' etc.	monēs	'you advise' etc.	regis	'you rule' etc.
amat	'he loves' etc.	monet	'he advises' etc.	regit	'he rules' etc.
amāmus	'we love' etc.	monēmus	'we advise' etc.	regimus	'we rule' etc.
amātis	'you love' etc.	monētis	'you advise' etc.	regitis	'you rule' etc.
amant	'they love' etc.	monent	'they advise' etc.	regunt	'they rule' etc.

Future active indicative

First conjugation		Second conjugation		Third conjugation	
amābō	'I shall love' etc.	monēbō	'I shall advise' etc.	regam	'I shall rule' etc.
amābis	'you will love' etc.	monēbis	'you will advise' etc.	regēs	'you will rule' etc.
amābit	'he will love' etc.	monēbit	'he will advise' etc.	reget	'he will rule' etc.
amābimus	'we shall love' etc.	monēbimus	'we shall advise' etc.	regēmus	'we shall rule' etc.
amābitis	'you will love' etc.	monēbitis	'you will advise' etc.	regētis	'you will rule' etc.
amābunt	'they will love' etc.	monēbunt	'they will advise' etc.	regent	'they will rule' etc.

Perfect active indicative

First conjugation		Second conjugation		Third conjugation	
amāvī	'I loved' etc.	monuī	'I advised' etc.	rēxī	'I ruled' etc.
amāvistī	'you loved' etc.	monuistī	'you advised' etc.	rēxistī	'you ruled' etc.
amāvit	'he loved' etc.	monuit	'he advised' etc.	rēxit	'he ruled' etc.
amāvimus	'we loved' etc.	monuimus	'we advised' etc.	rēximus	'we ruled' etc.
amāvistis	'you loved' etc.	monuistis	'you advised' etc.	rēxistis	'you ruled' etc.
amāvērunt	'they loved' etc.	monuērunt	'they advised' etc.	rēxērunt	'they ruled' etc.

To a large extent one simply has to memorize these different forms. However, there are some tips that can reduce the burden of memorization. In the present and future the first and second conjugations take largely the same endings as each other, except that the second conjugation has a stem vowel *e* where the first conjugation has *a*: first conjugation *-ō, -ās, -at, -āmus, -ātis, -ant* and *-ābō, -ābis, -ābit, -ābimus, -ābitis, -ābunt* versus second conjugation *-eō, -ēs, -et, -ēmus, -ētis, -ent* and *-ēbō, -ēbis, -ēbit, -ēbimus, -ēbitis, -ēbunt*. In the perfect the endings are exactly the same in all three conjugations (as well as in the irregular verb *sum*): *-ī, -istī, -it, -imus, -istis, -ērunt*. Thus in the perfect the three conjugations are not useful categories; in order to know how to conjugate a verb in the perfect one simply needs to find the perfect stem from its principal parts. The principal parts of these verbs are as follows:

First conjugation paradigm verb: *amō, amāre, amāvī, amātum* 'love'
Second conjugation paradigm verb: *moneō, monēre, monuī, monitum* 'advise', 'warn'
Third conjugation paradigm verb: *regō, regere, rēxī, rēctum* 'rule'

These principal parts also illustrate how to identify which conjugation a verb belongs to: the second principal part ends in *-āre* for first-conjugation verbs,[1] in *-ēre* for second-conjugation verbs, and in *-ere* with a short *e* for third-conjugation verbs. (Notice the partial correlation between the middle vowel of each infinitive and the stem vowel of that conjugation, which is *-ā-* or *-a-* in the first conjugation, *-ē-* or *-e-* in the second conjugation, and *-i-* in the third conjugation.) It is therefore very important to learn the quantity of the *e* of the second principal part when memorizing principal parts. The second principal part can also be used as a key to forming the present and future: take the second principal part, drop the last three letters, and add the endings that in these paradigms follow the *am-*, *mon-*, and *reg-*. Similarly the third principal part is the key to forming the perfect: take the third principal part, drop the *-ī*, and add the perfect endings given above.

Practice

A Identify the conjugations to which these verbs belong:

1 laudō, laudāre, laudāvī, laudātum 'praise'

2 videō, vidēre, vīdī, vīsum 'see'

3 iuvō, iuvāre, iūvī, iūtum 'help'

4 dīcō, dīcere, dīxī, dictum 'say'

5 doceō, docēre, docuī, doctum 'teach'

6 dō, dare, dedī, datum 'give'

7 habeō, habēre, habuī, habitum 'have'

8 stō, stāre, stetī, statum 'stand'

---

[1] The *a* is occasionally short, as in *dare*.

B Conjugate in the forms indicated:

1 *iuvō*, present active indicative
2 *videō*, present active indicative
3 *laudō*, future active indicative
4 *doceō*, future active indicative
5 *dō*, perfect active indicative
6 *habeō*, perfect active indicative
7 *laudō*, perfect active indicative
8 *dīcō*, perfect active indicative

9   *dō*, present active indicative
10 *videō*, future active indicative
11 *stō*, perfect active indicative
12 *habeō*, present active indicative
13 *iuvō*, future active indicative
14 *doceō*, perfect active indicative
15 *stō*, present active indicative
16 *dīcō*, future active indicative

C Translate:

1   deum laudamus.
2   servum meum video.
3   servos poetae laudavit.
4   equum non habuit.
5   equum agricolae laudabit.
6   servum poetae docebimus.
7   servum agricolae amo.
8   amasne amicum meum?
9   servi tui deos laudant.
10 vidistisne equos agricolae?
11 deos laudavimus.
12 verba bona dixit.
13 amicus tuus iuvabit.
14 verba poetarum puellas
    docuerunt.
15 amicus puellae poetam iuvit.

16 agricolarum equos non vidimus.
17 servus poetae puellam amavit.
18 amicus tuus equum habebit.
19 verba poetae laudaverunt.
20 servos agricolarum videbimus.
21 amice, vidistine servum meum?
22 serve, habesne equum?
23 poeta verba bona dicet.
24 habuitne servus poetae equum?
25 deos oppidi laudabimus.
26 poeta verba deorum laudavit.
27 consilium poetae bonum est.
28 amicorum tuorum consilium
    bonum non est.
29 vidistine epistulam meam?
30 habesne pecuniam?

D Translate into Latin:

1 The farmer praised my horse.
2 You (plural) will have new horses.
3 We saw the farmers' war.
4 I shall teach the farmer's new
   horse.
5 Did the poets teach the girls?
6 Friend, do you have a new slave?
7 Your slave said good words.
8 The poets will help the good
   farmers.

9   We helped Maria's slaves.
10 They will see my town.
11 Slaves, have you seen my horse?
12 Marcus will see Julia's town.
13 Have you (singular) seen
    Quintus' slaves?
14 Marcus praised Quintus' words.
15 We praised the poet's advice.
16 Your money helped the girl.

6.2 Perfect Participle

The fourth principal parts of many verbs function as adjectives; that is, from *amātum* one can get a verbal adjective *amātus, -a, -um*. These verbal adjectives are passive (receiving the action of a verb rather than performing it) and have the meaning of a past participle, so *amātus* means 'loved' or 'beloved', as in *puella amāta* 'the beloved girl', and *doctus* means 'having been taught', 'learned' (in the sense of 'educated'), as in *puella docta* 'the learned girl'. Similarly *verba scrīpta* means 'written words' and *servus ēmptus* 'bought slave'. Sometimes it works better in English to substitute a relative clause with a passive verb for the participle: 'words that were written', 'slave that was bought'. **But note that most Latin perfect participles cannot be used in this way with a form of *sum*: 'The girl is loved' is a periphrastic present passive in English that needs to be translated with a one-word verb in Latin (*puella amātur*, see chapter 32) and cannot be expressed with *puella amāta est* (in fact *puella amāta est* means something else, as we shall see in chapter 32).**

Practice

E Translate these phrases:

1	verba dicta	8	verba lecta
2	servus amatus	9	servi missi
3	poeta laudatus	10	puella petita
4	agricola doctus	11	deus victus
5	oppida visa	12	equus emptus
6	deae doctae	13	epistulae scriptae
7	equus ductus	14	consilium datum

F Translate into Latin:

1	a conquered goddess	8	a learned poet
2	a written word	9	a beloved friend
3	the horse that was sought	10	a spoken word
4	the girl who was sent	11	the horse that was seen
5	the word that was read	12	the poet who was praised
6	a friend who was bought	13	the advice that was praised
7	the girl who was led	14	the money that was seen

G Translate:

1	puellam amatam laudavit.	3	verba scripta legemus.
2	servus doctus poetam iuvit.	4	servum doctum emam.

6.3 Vocabulary to Learn

Verbs

amō, amāre, amāvī, amātum	'love'
dīcō, dīcere, dīxī, dictum	'say'
dō, dare, dedī, datum	'give'
doceō, docēre, docuī, doctum	'teach'
habeō, habēre, habuī, habitum	'have'
iuvō, iuvāre, iūvī, iūtum	'help'
laudō, laudāre, laudāvī, laudātum	'praise'
moneō, monēre, monuī, monitum	'advise', 'warn'
stō, stāre, stetī, statum	'stand'
videō, vidēre, vīdī, vīsum	'see'

7.1 Dative

The fifth case is the dative. With it added, the noun and adjective paradigms look like this:

British Case Order

Nouns

	First declension		Second declension masculine		Second declension neuter	
	Singular	Plural	Singular	Plural	Singular	Plural
Nominative	puella	puellae	servus	servī	bellum	bella
Vocative	puella	puellae	serve	servī	bellum	bella
Accusative	puellam	puellās	servum	servōs	bellum	bella
Genitive	puellae	puellārum	servī	servōrum	bellī	bellōrum
Dative	*puellae*	*puellīs*	*servō*	*servīs*	*bellō*	*bellīs*

Adjectives

	Singular			Plural		
	Masculine	Feminine	Neuter	Masculine	Feminine	Neuter
Nominative	bonus	bona	bonum	bonī	bonae	bona
Vocative	bone	bona	bonum	bonī	bonae	bona
Accusative	bonum	bonam	bonum	bonōs	bonās	bona
Genitive	bonī	bonae	bonī	bonōrum	bonārum	bonōrum
Dative	*bonō*	*bonae*	*bonō*	*bonīs*	*bonīs*	*bonīs*

Ancient Case Order

Nouns

	First declension		Second declension masculine		Second declension neuter	
	Singular	**Plural**	**Singular**	**Plural**	**Singular**	**Plural**
Nominative	puella	puellae	servus	servī	bellum	bella
Genitive	puellae	puellārum	servī	servōrum	bellī	bellōrum
Dative	*puellae*	*puellīs*	*servō*	*servīs*	*bellō*	*bellīs*
Accusative	puellam	puellās	servum	servōs	bellum	bella
Vocative	puella	puellae	serve	servī	bellum	bella

Adjectives

	Singular			Plural		
	Masculine	**Feminine**	**Neuter**	**Masculine**	**Feminine**	**Neuter**
Nominative	bonus	bona	bonum	bonī	bonae	bona
Genitive	bonī	bonae	bonī	bonōrum	bonārum	bonōrum
Dative	*bonō*	*bonae*	*bonō*	*bonīs*	*bonīs*	*bonīs*
Accusative	bonum	bonam	bonum	bonōs	bonās	bona
Vocative	bone	bona	bonum	bonī	bonae	bona

Practice

A Decline the following, in these five cases of the forms indicated:

1 *agricola*, singular
2 *amīcus*, plural
3 *novus*, neuter singular
4 *meus*, feminine plural
5 *verbum*, singular
6 *equus*, plural
7 *tuus*, masculine singular
8 *magnus*, neuter plural
9 *dea*, singular
10 *oppidum*, plural
11 *poēta*, singular
12 *novus*, feminine plural

7.2 Use of the Dative

The dative has a variety of uses, including the indirect object; that is, the additional object found with a verb meaning 'give'. With such a verb, the gift itself is the direct object and is in the accusative case; the person to whom it is given is the indirect object and is in the dative case. In English there are two constructions used for indirect objects: the indirect object can come before the direct object, or it can come after the direct object with the preposition 'to'. The indirect objects in these sentences are underlined: 'I gave <u>Mary</u> the book', 'I gave the book <u>to Mary</u>', 'We gave <u>them</u> candy', 'He gave candy <u>to the children</u>'. Adjectives that agree with dative nouns are also in the dative case.

Practice

B Identify the words in the following sentences that would be datives in Latin:

1 He gave it to me.
2 She will give us the new books.
3 I gave it to the boss's wife.
4 Give the poor dog that piece of meat.
5 The boss gave most of the employees a holiday.
6 We want to give this to him.
7 Did they give that poor man anything?
8 He gave it to the father of the bride.
9 Give that to John's older brother.
10 I'll give it to the unemployed workers.
11 Will she give it to us?
12 They gave Mary's father a watch.
13 He didn't even give her a greeting!
14 We'll give it to the victim's family.
15 He wanted to give us this.
16 Mark gave that boy's dog a bone.
17 Jane gave him a new car.
18 Give this to Mike's younger sister.

C Translate:

1 equum meum agricolae non dabo.
2 poetae consilium bonum dedit.
3 poetae consilium bonum servo dederunt.
4 pecuniam servo tuo dedimus.
5 puellis doctis pecuniam do.
6 Marci servum Quinto dedi.
7 dedistine consilium poetis doctis?
8 pecuniam servorum dedit puellis.
9 agricolae pecuniam dant. (2 ways)
10 dabitisne pecuniam Iuliae?
11 bono agricolae pecuniam dant.
12 consilium puellae dabo.
13 epistulam puellae dedit poeta.
14 dedistisne epistulam Marco?
15 servo tuo epistulam scriptam dederunt.
16 amico bono epistulam scriptam dabimus.
17 pecuniam puellae dant. (2 ways)
18 dabisne equum tuum Mariae?
19 pecuniam servi agricolis dedit.
20 puellae doctae epistulam servo dedit.
21 bono agricolae pecuniam dat dea.
22 boni agricolae pecuniam dant deis.
23 poetae epistulam scriptam dabit.
24 equos agricolarum poetis doctis dabit.

D Translate into Latin:

1 I am giving the poet money.
2 The girl will give money to the goddess.
3 Julia is giving Marcus a letter.
4 The farmer will give the girls' money to a learned poet.
5 Gods give words to poets.
6 A god gave slaves to the girl.
7 Quintus will give Maria money.
8 I gave the poet's money to a learned girl.
9 We gave your horse to the farmer.
10 The farmers gave the poets' horses to the girls.
11 Marcus gave the farmer a horse that was bought.
12 Farmers do not give advice to poets who are learned.
13 Did you give my slave a horse that was bought?
14 I gave Maria's money to the slaves who were sent.

7.3 *Possum*

The verb *possum* (principal parts *possum, posse, potuī, –*) means 'be able to' or 'can'; it is a compound of *potis* and *sum* and therefore is conjugated like *sum* with *pot-* or *pos-* in front of each form.

Present active indicative		Future active indicative		Perfect active indicative	
possum	'I am able to', 'I can'	poterō	'I will be able to', 'I shall be able to'	potuī	'I have been able to', 'I could'
potes	'you (singular) are able to', 'you can'	poteris	'you (singular) will be able to', 'you (singular) shall be able to'	potuistī	'you (singular) have been able to', 'you (singular) could'
potest	'he/she/it is able to', 'he/she/it can', 'is able to', 'can'	poterit	'he/she/it will be able to', 'he/she/it shall be able to', 'will be able to', 'shall be able to'	potuit	'he/she/it has been able to', 'he/she/it could', 'has been able to', 'could'
possumus	'we are able to', 'we can'	poterimus	'we will be able to', 'we shall be able to'	potuimus	'we have been able to', 'we could'
potestis	'you (plural) are able to', 'you can'	poteritis	'you (plural) will be able to', 'you (plural) shall be able to'	potuistis	'you (plural) have been able to', 'you (plural) could'
possunt	'they are able to', 'they can', 'are able to', 'can'	poterunt	'they will be able to', 'they shall be able to', 'will be able to', 'shall be able to'	potuērunt	'they have been able to', 'they could', 'have been able to', 'could'

Because of its meaning *possum* is usually accompanied by another verb, like English 'can' as in 'I can run' (= 'I am able to run'). In Latin this additional verb is in the infinitive, that is, the second principal part. So *possum currere* (or *currere possum*) is 'I can run', 'I am able to run', and *scrībere potest* (or *potest scrībere*) is 'he can write', 'he is able to write'.

Practice

E Translate:

1   currere possumus.
2   potest vincere.
3   puellas doctas agricolae amare possunt.
4   puellae laudatae agricolas amare possunt.
5   servus meus stare non potest.
6   pecuniam puellae dare potero.
7   potesne agricolam laudatum amare?
8   poeta doctus deam amare non potest.
9   oppidum tuum regere poteris.
10 servum emptum mittere potuit.
11 servum tuum docere non potui.
12 amico epistulam scriptam dare potuimus.
13 equus tuus currere non potuit.
14 amice, potesne videre servum meum?
15 amici tui vincere possunt.
16 agricola poetae consilium dare non poterit.
17 poetae verba bona dicere poterunt.
18 deos tuos laudare non possumus.
19 potestisne equum meum videre?
20 equum meum amico dare non possum.
21 amicos monere poteritis.
22 poterimus iuvare amicos tuos.
23 amicis consilium dare potuit.
24 poterisne equum emere?
25 puellam amatam videre possum.
26 verba scripta legere non possumus.

F Translate into Latin:

1 She will be able to advise the farmer.
2 He cannot write.
3 I could not give the learned girl advice.
4 The girl will not be able to teach the poet who was praised.
5 They cannot see the poet's horse.
6 Friend, I shall be able to write your letter.
7 Friends, will you be able to conquer the town?
8 The poet's slave could write.
9 I cannot love a farmer.
10 We shall not be able to give the learned girl money.
11 The girls could not see the farmers' horses.
12 Could they lead the poet's horse?

7.4 Additional Exercises

The sentences below provide extra practice distinguishing different cases.

Practice

G Identify all words in these sentences that would be nominatives, accusatives, genitives, and datives in Latin:[1]

1 She will give us a rebate.
2 We saw Jane's mother.
3 He gave it to her.
4 The members of that choir are very young.
5 He didn't even give me a kiss!
6 The father of the bride was absent.
7 The boy gave the dog a bone.
8 We'll give most of the workers a rest.
9 The boys' clothes are shabby.
10 I want to give this to you.
11 Did you give her anything?
12 Give that to the mother of the bride.

13 Where is the owner of that dog?
14 I'll give it to John's brother.
15 Which of the boys did that?
16 The king gives money to the soldiers.
17 She will give it to us.
18 He gave Jane's father a book.
19 We want to give you this.
20 Have you seen John's coat?
21 Where is the dog's collar?
22 They gave her flowers.
23 John's father is a fireman.
24 How many of them are here?
25 Did he take Martha's hat?
26 Give that to Jane's sister.

7.5 Vocabulary to Learn

Verbs

possum, posse, potuī, –	'can', 'be able to'

Nouns

aqua, aquae (f.)	'water'
castra, castrōrum (n. plural)	'camp' (in the military sense)
gladius, gladiī (m.)	'sword'
saxum, saxī (n.)	'rock', 'stone'
silva, silvae (f.)	'forest'

Vocabulary continues overleaf.

---

[1] Another exercise of this type, with an answer key, can be found in chapter 63.6.

Adverbs

bene	'well'
crās	'tomorrow'
cūr	'why?'
herī	'yesterday'
hīc	'here'
hodiē	'today'
male	'badly'
nunc	'now'
paene	'almost'
ubi	'where'

Conjunctions

quia	'because'
sed	'but'

8 | Second Declension in *-r* and *-ius*, Substantivization

8.1 Second Declension in *-r* and *-ius*

Most second-declension nouns are declined like *servus* or like *bellum*, but there are some common words that have slight variations on these paradigms. Words with a nominative in *-r* use it for the vocative as well and then decline on a stem that is not predictable from the nominative, only from the genitive. Words with a nominative in *-ius*[1] have different forms for the vocative and genitive.[2]

The paradigms are as follows:

British Case Order

| | *puer, puerī* (m.) 'boy' | | *magister, magistrī* (m.) 'teacher' | |
	Singular	Plural	Singular	Plural
Nom.	puer	puerī	magister	magistrī
Voc.	puer	puerī	magister	magistrī
Acc.	puerum	puerōs	magistrum	magistrōs
Gen.	puerī	puerōrum	magistrī	magistrōrum
Dat.	puerō	puerīs	magistrō	magistrīs

| | *vir, virī* (m.) 'man' | | *fīlius, fīliī* (m.) 'son' | |
	Singular	Plural	Singular	Plural
Nom.	vir	virī	fīlius	fīliī
Voc.	vir	virī	fīlī	fīliī
Acc.	virum	virōs	fīlium	fīliōs
Gen.	virī	virōrum	fīlī/fīliī	fīliōrum
Dat.	virō	virīs	fīliō	fīliīs

---

[1] Neuter nouns such as *cōnsilium*, which we have already seen, can also take a genitive with one *-ī*.

[2] The genitive with one *-ī* is the older form and found up through the first century BC; from the time of Augustus onwards the genitive in *-iī* is used. Adjectives in *ius/-ium* always have the genitive in *-iī*.

Ancient Case Order

| | *puer, puerī* (m.) 'boy' | | *magister, magistrī* (m.) 'teacher' | |
	Singular	**Plural**	**Singular**	**Plural**
Nom.	puer	puerī	magister	magistrī
Gen.	puerī	puerōrum	magistrī	magistrōrum
Dat.	puerō	puerīs	magistrō	magistrīs
Acc.	puerum	puerōs	magistrum	magistrōs
Voc.	puer	puerī	magister	magistrī

| | *vir, virī* (m.) 'man' | | *filius, filiī* (m.) 'son' | |
	Singular	**Plural**	**Singular**	**Plural**
Nom.	vir	virī	filius	filiī
Gen.	virī	virōrum	filī/filiī	filiōrum
Dat.	virō	virīs	filiō	filiīs
Acc.	virum	virōs	filium	filiōs
Voc.	vir	virī	filī	filiī

8.2 Adjectives in *-r*

Adjectives of the first and second declensions may also have masculine forms with nominatives in *-er*; in such cases genitives are not normally given as part of dictionary entries, but the stem on which the other cases of the masculine are built can be deduced from the feminine and neuter. The stem will retain, in all cases singular and plural, the *e* that appears before the *r* in the masculine nominative singular if that *e* is retained in the feminine and neuter nominative singulars – but it will drop the *e* from all cases singular and plural if the *e* is dropped in the feminine and neuter nominative singulars. This distinction can be illustrated from *niger*, which drops the *e*, and *tener*, which retains it, though otherwise both these adjectives take the regular endings.

British Case Order

niger, nigra, nigrum 'black'

| | **Singular** | | | **Plural** | | |
	Masculine	**Feminine**	**Neuter**	**Masculine**	**Feminine**	**Neuter**
Nom.	niger	nigra	nigrum	nigrī	nigrae	nigra
Voc.	niger	nigra	nigrum	nigrī	nigrae	nigra
Acc.	nigrum	nigram	nigrum	nigrōs	nigrās	nigra
Gen.	nigrī	nigrae	nigrī	nigrōrum	nigrārum	nigrōrum
Dat.	nigrō	nigrae	nigrō	nigrīs	nigrīs	nigrīs

tener, tenera, tenerum 'tender'

	Singular			Plural		
	Masculine	Feminine	Neuter	Masculine	Feminine	Neuter
Nom.	tener	tenera	tenerum	tenerī	tenerae	tenera
Voc.	tener	tenera	tenerum	tenerī	tenerae	tenera
Acc.	tenerum	teneram	tenerum	tenerōs	tenerās	tenera
Gen.	tenerī	tenerae	tenerī	tenerōrum	tenerārum	tenerōrum
Dat.	tenerō	tenerae	tenerō	tenerīs	tenerīs	tenerīs

Ancient Case Order

niger, nigra, nigrum 'black'

	Singular			Plural		
	Masculine	Feminine	Neuter	Masculine	Feminine	Neuter
Nom.	niger	nigra	nigrum	nigrī	nigrae	nigra
Gen.	nigrī	nigrae	nigrī	nigrōrum	nigrārum	nigrōrum
Dat.	nigrō	nigrae	nigrō	nigrīs	nigrīs	nigrīs
Acc.	nigrum	nigram	nigrum	nigrōs	nigrās	nigra
Voc.	niger	nigra	nigrum	nigrī	nigrae	nigra

tener, tenera, tenerum 'tender'

	Singular			Plural		
	Masculine	Feminine	Neuter	Masculine	Feminine	Neuter
Nom.	tener	tenera	tenerum	tenerī	tenerae	tenera
Gen.	tenerī	tenerae	tenerī	tenerōrum	tenerārum	tenerōrum
Dat.	tenerō	tenerae	tenerō	tenerīs	tenerīs	tenerīs
Acc.	tenerum	teneram	tenerum	tenerōs	tenerās	tenera
Voc.	tener	tenera	tenerum	tenerī	tenerae	tenera

Practice

A Decline in these five cases of the forms indicated:

1 *liber, librī* (m.) 'book', singular
2 *līber, lībera, līberum* 'free', neuter singular
3 *ager, agrī* (m.) 'field', plural
4 *noster, nostra, nostrum* 'our', neuter plural
5 *vester, vestra, vestrum* 'your' (plural 'you'), feminine singular
6 *miser, misera, miserum* 'miserable', masc. singular
7 *pulcher, pulchra, pulchrum* 'beautiful', feminine plural

8 *asper, aspera, asperum* 'rough',
   masculine plural

9 *gladius*, plural

10 *Lūcius, -ī* (m.) 'Lucius', singular

B Translate:

1 puer, ubi est liber tuus?
2 Luci, cur magistro docto
   pecuniam non dedisti?
3 liberi non sumus, quia servi
   empti sumus.
4 puero misero librum dabimus.
5 saxa aspera sunt.
6 possuntne viri teneri esse?
7 magister noster doctus est, sed
   pulcher non est.
8 fili, cur gladios pueris dedisti?
9 vestrum oppidum heri vidimus.
10 equum nigrum nunc emam.
11 libros pueris cras dabo.
12 equos vestros viris liberis dedi,
   non servis.
13 magister vester hodie male docet.
14 equus fili nostri niger est.
15 agricola agros hic habet.

16 possuntne agricolae pulchri
   esse?
17 gladios nostros filiis vestris
   dedimus.
18 magister noster librum
   laudatum scripsit.
19 filii vestri liberi sunt.
20 filii, dedistisne consilium
   puellae miserae?
21 agri asperi hic sunt.
22 Luci, potesne librum scribere?
23 agros vestros videre non
   possum.
24 gladios pueris dare non
   possumus.
25 magistros nostros laudamus
   quia bene docent.
26 agricolae equum meum dare
   non possum.

C Translate into Latin:

1 The boys sent written letters
   yesterday.
2 Our sons will see the new teacher
   tomorrow.
3 You (plural) can buy the farmers'
   fields today.
4 Son, where are our swords?
5 He is not a bought slave, but a free
   man.
6 I cannot help, because I do not
   have a sword.

7 We almost gave our horses to
   a slave.
8 Now the boys have new books.
9 Beautiful girls conquer rough
   men.
10 The black horse runs badly.
11 Teacher, why can't you help?
12 Your (plural) sons are here.
13 The boys who were praised read
   well.
14 The farmer cannot buy a big field.

8.3 Substantivization

Latin adjectives are sometimes substantivized; that is, they can act like nouns. In such circumstances they are in essence agreeing with a noun that is not present in the sentence. Most often that noun is 'man' (for a masculine singular adjective), 'men' (for a masculine plural), 'woman' (for a feminine singular), 'women' (for a feminine plural), 'thing' (for a neuter singular), or 'things' (for a neuter plural).[3] Occasionally, however, a more specific noun can be understood from the context; these more specific nouns should only be supplied in translation when the context clearly provides them. Thus if Marcus says to Lucius *vīdistīne fīliōs meōs?* 'Have you seen my sons?' and Lucius responds *meōs vīdī, sed tuōs nōn vīdī*, the response can be translated 'I have seen my sons, but I have not seen yours', since it is clear from the context that the men are talking about their sons. (The same response would be translated 'I have seen my horses, but I have not seen yours' if the preceding question had been *vīdistīne equōs meōs?* 'Have you seen my horses?') But in the absence of such positive indications a sentence like *vīdistīne nostrōs?* should be translated 'Have you seen our men?', not 'Have you seen our sons?' nor 'Have you seen our horses?'

English adjectives can also be substantivized: for example 'Only the brave deserve the fair' means 'Only brave (men) deserve (to get) fair (women)'. But the phenomenon is much more common in Latin, and this discrepancy causes difficulties in translation: sometimes a Latin substantivized adjective can be translated with an English substantivized adjective, but more often one needs to supply in English the noun that is understood in the Latin. For example, *nostrī vīcērunt* has to be translated 'Our men conquered', since 'Ours conquered' would be difficult to understand. But from the adjective *Rōmānus, -a, -um* one can get *Rōmānī*, as in *Rōmānī vīcērunt*, which can easily be translated with an English substantivized adjective: 'the Romans conquered' (though 'the Roman men conquered' is also possible).

To find out whether a Latin adjective has been substantivized in a particular sentence, first work out its gender, number, and case, and then look to see whether there is a noun nearby with that gender, number, and case. If there is such a noun, the adjective agrees with it and is not substantivized. If there is no such noun, the adjective is substantivized and should normally be translated with the addition of 'man', 'men', 'woman', 'women', 'thing', or 'things', as appropriate.

---

[3] Like many ancient peoples the Romans were profoundly sexist, an attitude that can be seen even in their grammar. The masculine gender takes precedence over the feminine, so that if a group of people includes both men and women, the masculine gender is used to refer to it. So a substantivized masculine adjective like *bonī* can actually mean either 'good men' or 'good people', depending on the context. For now it will be easiest to ignore this problem and assume that all masculines in fact refer to males and therefore can be translated with 'men' in English, but occasionally a situation arises in which 'people' will work much better.

servōs nostrōs vīdērunt 'they saw our slaves' (*Nostrōs* is masculine accusative plural, and so is *servōs*, so *nostrōs* agrees with *servōs* and has its regular translation 'our'.)

servī nostrōs vīdērunt 'the slaves saw our men' (*Nostrōs* is masculine accusative plural, and there is no other accusative in the sentence, so it has nothing to agree with and must be substantivized. We add 'men' because *nostrōs* is masculine plural.)

Likewise

verba bona dīxit 'he said good words' (*Bona* is neuter accusative plural, and so is *verba*, so *bona* agrees with *verba* and has its regular translation 'good'. It would be theoretically possible to take *bona* as feminine nominative singular, in which case it would have nothing to agree with and would result in a substantivized translation 'the good woman said words', but in practice Roman writers do not usually play tricks like that: an adjective that can agree with a nearby noun should be assumed to do so unless the results of that assumption do not make sense.)

poēta bona dīxit 'the poet said good things' (*Bona* is neuter accusative plural, and there is nothing for it to agree with (*poēta*, despite ending in -*a*, is masculine nominative singular, so this time there is no possibility of taking *bona* as a feminine nominative singular), so it must be substantivized. We add 'things' because *bona* is neuter plural.)

Practice

D Translate (n.b. *Rōmānus, -a, -um* 'Roman', *Graecus, -a, -um* 'Greek'):

1. dei bona dederunt Romanis.
2. Romani bona dant poetis bonis.
3. vidistine servum meum? meum vidi, sed tuum non vidi.
4. miseri pecuniam non habent.
5. Romanos vincere non possumus.
6. dei bona dant bonis.
7. cur Graeci liberi non sunt?
8. nostri gladios non habuerunt.
9. Graecae pulchrae sunt.
10. pulchras amant viri.
11. ubi sunt equi nostri? meus hic est.
12. nostros Graeci hodie vicerunt.
13. oppidum Graecorum pulchrum est.
14. castra Romanorum videre non potuimus.
15. filios meos peto; tuos non peto.
16. gladios nostris cras dabo.
17. nostri Graecos videre non possunt.
18. equos nostrorum cras ducemus.
19. fili, ubi sunt nostri?
20. possuntne Graeci Romanos vincere?
21. amici, dedistisne bona filiis vestris?

22 pulchras petimus; ubi sunt?

23 servos meos vidi, sed tuos non vidi.

24 bona nunc habemus, quia Romani hic sunt.

25 miseris pecuniam dedi.

26 nostri Romanos vincent.

27 Romanos laudare non potuerunt.

28 castra Romanorum petivit.

E Translate into Latin:

1 Goddesses give good things to good girls.

2 The Romans' camp is big.

3 Our men praised the gods.

4 Good men give money to miserable men.

5 We shall give good things to the boys.

6 The Greeks had slaves.

7 Boy, where are the Romans?

8 Our men will help the Greeks.

9 I cannot give the Romans horses.

10 The good goddess gives good things to boys.

11 We are seeking the Romans' camp; where is it?

12 The gods are leading our men.

13 We have good things, because we praise the gods.

14 A goddess helped our men yesterday.

8.4 Vocabulary to Learn

Nouns

ager, agrī (m.)	'field'
fīlius, fīliī (m.)	'son'
liber, librī (m.)	'book'
magister, magistrī (m.)	'teacher'
puer, puerī (m.)	'boy'
vir, virī (m.)	'man'

Adjectives

asper, aspera, asperum	'rough'
Graecus, Graeca, Graecum	'Greek'
līber, lībera, līberum	'free'
miser, misera, miserum	'miserable'
niger, nigra, nigrum	'black'
noster, nostra, nostrum	'our'
pulcher, pulchra, pulchrum	'beautiful'
Rōmānus, Rōmāna, Rōmānum	'Roman'
tener, tenera, tenerum	'tender'
vester, vestra, vestrum	'your' (plural 'you')

9 | Ablative Case, Prepositions, *Eō*

9.1 Ablative

The last case is the ablative. In the declensions we have so far seen, the ablative endings are the same as those of the dative except in the singular of the first declension and in the feminine singular of adjectives: in those forms it ends in a long -*ā*. The length of the -*ā* is important because it serves to distinguish the ablative from the nominative. With the ablative added, the paradigms we have seen can be completed; words ending in -*r* and in -*ius* have the same ablative forms as other second-declension words, so the paradigms seen in chapter 8 pose no additional difficulties.

British Case Order

Nouns in -*a*, -*us*, and –*um*

	First declension		Second declension masculine		Second declension neuter	
	Singular	Plural	Singular	Plural	Singular	Plural
Nom.	puella	puellae	servus	servī	bellum	bella
Voc.	puella	puellae	serve	servī	bellum	bella
Acc.	puellam	puellās	servum	servōs	bellum	bella
Gen.	puellae	puellārum	servī	servōrum	bellī	bellōrum
Dat.	puellae	puellīs	servō	servīs	bellō	bellīs
Abl.	*puellā*	*puellīs*	*servō*	*servīs*	*bellō*	*bellīs*

Adjectives in -*us*, -*a*, -*um*

	Singular			Plural		
	Masculine	Feminine	Neuter	Masculine	Feminine	Neuter
Nom.	bonus	bona	bonum	bonī	bonae	bona
Voc.	bone	bona	bonum	bonī	bonae	bona
Acc.	bonum	bonam	bonum	bonōs	bonās	bona
Gen.	bonī	bonae	bonī	bonōrum	bonārum	bonōrum
Dat.	bonō	bonae	bonō	bonīs	bonīs	bonīs
Abl.	*bonō*	*bonā*	*bonō*	*bonīs*	*bonīs*	*bonīs*

British Case Order (*continued*)

Nouns in -*r* and -*ius*

	Singular	Plural	Singular	Plural	Singular	Plural	Singular	Plural
Nom.	puer	puerī	magister	magistrī	vir	virī	fīlius	fīliī
Voc.	puer	puerī	magister	magistrī	vir	virī	fīlī	fīliī
Acc.	puerum	puerōs	magistrum	magistrōs	virum	virōs	fīlium	fīliōs
Gen.	puerī	puerōrum	magistrī	magistrōrum	virī	virōrum	fīlī/fīliī	fīliōrum
Dat.	puerō	puerīs	magistrō	magistrīs	virō	virīs	fīliō	fīliīs
Abl.	*puerō*	*puerīs*	*magistrō*	*magistrīs*	*virō*	*virīs*	*fīliō*	*fīliīs*

Adjectives in -*r*

	Singular			Plural		
	Masculine	Feminine	Neuter	Masculine	Feminine	Neuter
Nom.	niger	nigra	nigrum	nigrī	nigrae	nigra
Voc.	niger	nigra	nigrum	nigrī	nigrae	nigra
Acc.	nigrum	nigram	nigrum	nigrōs	nigrās	nigra
Gen.	nigrī	nigrae	nigrī	nigrōrum	nigrārum	nigrōrum
Dat.	nigrō	nigrae	nigrō	nigrīs	nigrīs	nigrīs
Abl.	*nigrō*	*nigrā*	*nigrō*	*nigrīs*	*nigrīs*	*nigrīs*

	Singular			Plural		
	Masculine	Feminine	Neuter	Masculine	Feminine	Neuter
Nom.	tener	tenera	tenerum	tenerī	tenerae	tenera
Voc.	tener	tenera	tenerum	tenerī	tenerae	tenera
Acc.	tenerum	teneram	tenerum	tenerōs	tenerās	tenera
Gen.	tenerī	tenerae	tenerī	tenerōrum	tenerārum	tenerōrum
Dat.	tenerō	tenerae	tenerō	tenerīs	tenerīs	tenerīs
Abl.	*tenerō*	*tenerā*	*tenerō*	*tenerīs*	*tenerīs*	*tenerīs*

Ancient[1] Case Order

Nouns in -*a*, -*us*, and –*um*

	First declension		Second declension masculine		Second declension neuter	
	Singular	Plural	Singular	Plural	Singular	Plural
Nom.	puella	puellae	servus	servī	bellum	bella
Gen.	puellae	puellārum	servī	servōrum	bellī	bellōrum
Dat.	puellae	puellīs	servō	servīs	bellō	bellīs
Acc.	puellam	puellās	servum	servōs	bellum	bella
Abl.	*puellā*	*puellīs*	*servō*	*servīs*	*bellō*	*bellīs*
Voc.	puella	puellae	serve	servī	bellum	bella

Adjectives in -*us*, -*a*, -*um*

	Singular			Plural		
	Masculine	Feminine	Neuter	Masculine	Feminine	Neuter
Nom.	bonus	bona	bonum	bonī	bonae	bona
Gen.	bonī	bonae	bonī	bonōrum	bonārum	bonōrum
Dat.	bonō	bonae	bonō	bonīs	bonīs	bonīs
Acc.	bonum	bonam	bonum	bonōs	bonās	bona
Abl.	*bonō*	*bonā*	*bonō*	*bonīs*	*bonīs*	*bonīs*
Voc.	bone	bona	bonum	bonī	bonae	bona

Nouns in -*r* and –*ius*

	Singular	Plural	Singular	Plural	Singular	Plural	Singular	Plural
Nom.	puer	puerī	magister	magistrī	vir	virī	fīlius	fīliī
Gen.	puerī	puerōrum	magistrī	magistrōrum	virī	virōrum	fīlī/fīliī	fīliōrum
Dat.	puerō	puerīs	magistrō	magistrīs	virō	virīs	fīliō	fīliīs
Acc.	puerum	puerōs	magistrum	magistrōs	virum	virōs	fīlium	fīliōs
Abl.	*puerō*	*puerīs*	*magistrō*	*magistrīs*	*virō*	*virīs*	*fīliō*	*fīliīs*
Voc.	puer	puerī	magister	magistrī	vir	virī	fīlī	fīliī

---

[1] Strictly speaking, this is a slightly modified version of the ancient order: the actual ancient order was nominative, genitive, dative, accusative, vocative, ablative, but now the vocative is usually positioned after the ablative by adherents of this case order. Many words either have no vocative at all or have no vocative separate from the nominative; with this case order the vocative line is usually omitted in such forms. When using the British order, however, it is unsafe to leave out the vocative line as doing so can lead to uncertainty about which case labels attach to which lines of a paradigm that one has memorized.

Adjectives in *-r*

	Singular			Plural		
	Masculine	Feminine	Neuter	Masculine	Feminine	Neuter
Nom./Voc.	niger	nigra	nigrum	nigrī	nigrae	nigra
Gen.	nigrī	nigrae	nigrī	nigrōrum	nigrārum	nigrōrum
Dat.	nigrō	nigrae	nigrō	nigrīs	nigrīs	nigrīs
Acc.	nigrum	nigram	nigrum	nigrōs	nigrās	nigra
Abl.	*nigrō*	*nigrā*	*nigrō*	*nigrīs*	*nigrīs*	*nigrīs*

	Singular			Plural		
	Masculine	Feminine	Neuter	Masculine	Feminine	Neuter
Nom./Voc.	tener	tenera	tenerum	tenerī	tenerae	tenera
Gen.	tenerī	tenerae	tenerī	tenerōrum	tenerārum	tenerōrum
Dat.	tenerō	tenerae	tenerō	tenerīs	tenerīs	tenerīs
Acc.	tenerum	teneram	tenerum	tenerōs	tenerās	tenera
Abl.	*tenerō*	*tenerā*	*tenerō*	*tenerīs*	*tenerīs*	*tenerīs*

Practice

A Decline in all six cases of the forms indicated:

1 *poēta*, singular
2 *līber* 'free', neuter plural
3 *meus*, masculine plural
4 *liber* 'book', singular
5 *pulcher*, feminine plural

6 *oppidum*, singular
7 *ager*, singular
8 *miser*, feminine singular
9 *vester*, feminine plural
10 *asper*, neuter singular

9.2 Prepositions

The ablative is used in a variety of ways, including after many prepositions. Prepositions in Latin always govern a particular case or cases; for example *cum*, which means 'with' (in the sense of accompaniment, as 'John came with Mark'), is always followed by a word in the ablative, whereas *ad* 'to' (in the sense of motion towards, as 'we went to the beach') is always followed by a word in the accusative. Some of the most important prepositions and the cases they take are the following:

ā, ab + ablative 'from', 'away from'
cum + ablative 'with' (accompaniment)
dē + ablative 'from', 'about'
ē, ex + ablative 'out of'

sine + ablative 'without'

in + ablative 'in', 'on' (without motion towards, as 'He was swimming in the water')

in + accusative 'into', 'onto' (with motion towards, as 'He dived into the water')

ad + accusative 'to' (with motion towards)

per + accusative 'through'

trāns + accusative 'across'

The basic principle is that motion towards takes the accusative, motion from takes the ablative, and lack of motion also takes the ablative. Nevertheless, some prepositions always take the same case regardless of the particular context in which they occur.

Practice

B Translate:

1 nostri in castris nunc sunt.

2 filius tuus cum pueris est.

3 boni epistulas scriptas ad servos non mittunt.

4 equos trans agros heri duxerunt.

5 nostros in castra duxit.

6 servum ad oppidum vestrum cras mittet.

7 pulchrae per castros currere non possunt.

8 sine consilio tuo vincere non possumus.

9 filios nostros per castra duxit poeta laudatus.

10 servus meus ex oppido cucurrit.

11 miseros iuvare possumus.

12 Luci, scribesne librum de bello?

13 Romani pulchras amaverunt.

14 servus tuus a castris cucurrit.

15 agricolae in agro stant.

16 dei Romanos in bellum miserunt.

17 sine deo regere paene non potuerunt.

18 nostri Graecos sine bello vicerunt.

19 servos vestros ad castra hodie mittent.

20 magister pueros trans oppidum hodie duxit.

21 per silvam equos ad aquam ducemus.

22 Graeci epistulas scriptas ad Romanos miserunt.

23 nunc equi e silva currunt.

24 legesne librum meum de equis?

25 pueri ab agricola magno cucurrerunt.

26 ubi sunt pueri? cum magistro nunc stant.

27 Graeci per agros cucurrerunt.

28 sine gladio vincere non potuit.

29 equi in silva non sunt.

30 equos in silvam ducent agricolae.

31 verba tua de silvis in libro meo scripsi.

32 cum servis a castris cucurrimus.

33 sine servis e castris cucurrimus.

C Translate into Latin:

1 Son, will you lead the horses through rough stones?
2 I wrote a book about wars.
3 Where is my son? Here, with the learned poets.
4 Is your son in the camp?
5 Did you lead our men into the camp?
6 Without money I am miserable.
7 The boys ran away from the teacher yesterday.
8 The Greeks ran out of the camp.
9 I shall not lead my horse across the field.
10 The boys ran to the good teacher.
11 The Romans ran through the camp.
12 The Greeks conquered our men in the town.
13 The miserable men are standing with the poet.
14 Son, did you lead the Greeks to our town?
15 The beautiful women sent slaves to the camp of the Romans.
16 Our men saw Greeks in the fields.

9.3 *Eō*

The Latin verb 'go', like 'be' and 'can', is irregular. It is *eō, īre, iī/īvī, itum*, conjugated as follows:

Present active indicative		Future active indicative		Perfect active indicative	
eō	'I go', 'I am going'	ībō	'I will go', 'I shall go'	iī, īvī	'I went', 'I have gone'
īs	'you (singular) go', 'you (singular) are going'	ībis	'you (singular) will go', 'you (singular) shall go'	īstī, īvistī	'you (singular) went', you (singular) have gone'
it	'he/she/it goes', 'he/she/it is going', 'goes', 'is going'	ībit	'he/she/it will go', 'he/she/it shall go', 'will go', 'shall go'	iit, īvit	'he/she/it went', 'he/she/it has gone', 'went', 'has gone'
īmus	'we go', 'we are going'	ībimus	'we will go', 'we shall go'	iimus, īvimus	'we went', 'we have gone'
ītis	'you (plural) go', 'you (plural) are going'	ībitis	'you (plural) will go', 'you (plural) shall go'	īstis, īvistis	'you (plural) went', 'you (plural) have gone'
eunt	'they go', 'they are going', 'go', 'are going'	ībunt	'they will go', 'they shall go', 'will go', 'shall go'	iērunt, īvērunt	'they went', 'they have gone', 'went', 'have gone'

Practice

D Translate:

1 ibimus	9 it	17 ivimus
2 iit	10 ibis	18 eo
3 is	11 ii	19 ibo
4 ibit	12 ibunt	20 itis
5 ivisti	13 istis	21 ivisti
6 eunt	14 imus	22 ivit
7 ibitis	15 isti	23 ierunt
8 iimus	16 ivi	24 iverunt

E Translate into Latin:

1 they will go	11 I went
2 he will go	12 I shall go
3 she is going	13 you (singular) go
4 they go	14 you (plural) will go
5 it has gone	15 you (plural) went
6 they went	16 you (singular) went
7 I am going	17 you (plural) go
8 we shall go	18 you (singular) will go
9 we are going	19 they have gone
10 we have gone	20 he goes

F Translate:

1 agricolae ad agros ierunt.	10 pueri, ibitisne trans silvas?
2 agricola trans agros iit.	11 per silvas ibo.
3 agricolae, ivistisne per agros?	12 a silva ibimus.
4 agricola, istine ex agro?	13 puellae in aquam eunt.
5 ab agris ivimus.	14 puella ad aquam it.
6 in agrum ii.	15 puellae, itisne trans aquam?
7 puer in silvam ibit.	16 puella, isne per aquam?
8 pueri ad silvas ibunt.	17 ab aqua imus.
9 puer, ibisne e silva?	18 ex aqua eo.

G Translate into Latin:

1 I shall go to the town tomorrow.
2 We are going away from the camp.
3 Are you (singular) going into the water?
4 Did you (plural) go out of the town?
5 Boys do not go into war.
6 The horses went across the forest.
7 I went away from the town.
8 We went through the camp.
9 Will you (singular) go into the camp?
10 The miserable girl is going to the rock.

9.4 Vocabulary to Learn

Verb

eō, īre, iī/īvī, itum   'go'

Prepositions

ā, ab (+ ablative)	'from', 'away from'
ad (+ accusative)	'to'
cum (+ ablative)	'with'
dē (+ ablative)	'from', 'about'
ē, ex (+ ablative)	'out of'
in (+ ablative)	'in', 'on'
in (+ accusative)	'into', 'onto'
per (+ accusative)	'through'
sine (+ ablative)	'without'
trāns (+ accusative)	'across'

10 | Demonstratives and Imperatives

10.1 Demonstratives

Words for 'this' and 'that' (or, in the plural, 'these' and 'those') are known as demonstratives. Latin has several, including *hic* 'this, these' and *ille* 'that, those'; such words agree with nouns in gender, number, and case as adjectives do. They are declined irregularly.

British Case Order						
	Singular ('this')			**Plural ('these')**		
	Masculine	**Feminine**	**Neuter**	**Masculine**	**Feminine**	**Neuter**
Nom.	hic	haec	hoc	hī	hae	haec
Voc.	–	–	–	–	–	–
Acc.	hunc	hanc	hoc	hōs	hās	haec
Gen.	huius	huius	huius	hōrum	hārum	hōrum
Dat.	huic	huic	huic	hīs	hīs	hīs
Abl.	hōc	hāc	hōc	hīs	hīs	hīs
	Singular ('that')			**Plural ('those')**		
	Masculine	**Feminine**	**Neuter**	**Masculine**	**Feminine**	**Neuter**
Nom.	ille	illa	illud	illī	illae	illa
Voc.	–	–	–	–	–	–
Acc.	illum	illam	illud	illōs	illās	illa
Gen.	illīus	illīus	illīus	illōrum	illārum	illōrum
Dat.	illī	illī	illī	illīs	illīs	illīs
Abl.	illō	illā	illō	illīs	illīs	illīs

Ancient Case Order

	Singular ('this')			Plural ('these')		
	Masculine	Feminine	Neuter	Masculine	Feminine	Neuter
Nom.	hic	haec	hoc	hī	hae	haec
Gen.	huius	huius	huius	hōrum	hārum	hōrum
Dat.	huic	huic	huic	hīs	hīs	hīs
Acc.	hunc	hanc	hoc	hōs	hās	haec
Abl.	hōc	hāc	hōc	hīs	hīs	hīs

	Singular ('that')			Plural ('those')		
	Masculine	Feminine	Neuter	Masculine	Feminine	Neuter
Nom.	ille	illa	illud	illī	illae	illa
Gen.	illīus	illīus	illīus	illōrum	illārum	illōrum
Dat.	illī	illī	illī	illīs	illīs	illīs
Acc.	illum	illam	illud	illōs	illās	illa
Abl.	illō	illā	illō	illīs	illīs	illīs

Practice

A Translate each of the following phrases and identify its gender, number, and case:

1 hic poeta
2 hoc poeta
3 ille poeta
4 illo poeta
5 hi poetae
6 huic poetae
7 huius poetae
8 illi poetae (2 ways)
9 illius poetae
10 has deas
11 hunc poetam
12 illa dea (2 ways)
13 hanc deam
14 illarum dearum
15 hos poetas
16 illas deas
17 his deis (4 ways)
18 illum poetam
19 haec dea
20 hac dea
21 huius deae
22 huic deae
23 hae deae
24 illi deae
25 illae deae
26 harum dearum
27 illam deam
28 horum poetarum
29 illis poetis (2 ways)
30 illorum poetarum
31 his poetis (2 ways)
32 illis deis (4 ways)

B Give the form of *hic* that agrees with each of these nouns, and translate the resulting phrase:

1 puellam	6 equi (2 ways)	11 amicis
2 puero (2 ways)	7 servum	12 agricolarum
3 silva (2 ways)	8 libros	13 epistularum
4 bellum	9 oppida	14 magister
5 epistulae (3 ways)	10 agricolam	

C Give the form of *ille* that agrees with each of these nouns, and translate the resulting phrase:

1 puellam	6 equi (2 ways)	11 amicis
2 puero (2 ways)	7 servum	12 agricolarum
3 silva	8 libros	13 epistularum
4 bellum	9 oppida	14 magister
5 epistulae (3 ways)	10 poetam	

10.2 Demonstrative Pronouns

When *hic* and *ille* are attached to nouns, they function as adjectives. But like any other adjectives they can be substantivized (see chapter 8.3); indeed such use is particularly common with *hic* and *ille*, and for that reason they are often referred to as demonstrative pronouns. Thus very often *hic* means 'this man', *haec* 'this woman', and *hoc* 'this thing' (or just 'this'); all three can also mean 'this one' with an understood noun in the appropriate context. Thus *vidēsne hunc?* could mean 'Do you see this man?' but could also, in a conversation about fields (since *ager* is masculine), mean 'Do you see this one?', referring to a particular field. Consider the following examples:

hoc illī dabō. 'I shall give this to that man.'
lēgistīne hunc librum? nōn, sed illum lēgī. 'Did you read this book?' 'No, but I read that one.'
haec illī laudāvērunt. 'Those men praised these things.'
illīus verba bona sunt. 'That man's words are good.'

Practice

D Translate, taking forms of *hic* and *ille* as adjectives:

1 illa puella ad silvam ivit.
2 haec puella dea est.
3 possum amare hunc poetam.
4 equum illius puellae in silva
   viderunt.
5 hanc pecuniam habere potes.
6 illas puellas amavimus.

7 illae puellae poetam amaverunt.
8 haec puella agricolam amare
   potest.
9 hos poetas puellae amabunt.
10 illi agricolae poetae sunt.
11 in hoc agro Romani steterunt.
12 in illis agris nostri fuerunt.

E Translate, taking forms of *hic* and *ille* as pronouns:

1 hi puellas amant.
2 poeta bonus illas amavit.
3 horum pecuniam amicis tuis
   dedimus.
4 illae sunt deae.
5 illi fuerunt agricolae boni.
6 hunc non amo.

7 laudasne illam?
8 hos amare possumus.
9 huic pecuniam dabit filius
   noster.
10 illis pecuniam dederunt.
11 haec laudavi.
12 illa laudare possum.

F Translate, taking forms of *hic* and *ille* as adjectives or pronouns according to
the context:

1 illae sunt Graecae.
2 huius puellae servum
   laudaverunt.
3 illae puellae deae sunt.
4 hi puellas bonas laudabunt.
5 amamus hanc puellam.
6 illi pecuniam dare potero.
7 horum libros laudavit.
8 illarum pecuniam habemus.
9 ille puellam pulchram amavit.
10 hic agricola equum puellae emit.

11 illam amo.
12 huius epistulam laudavit.
13 hi agricolae teneri sunt.
14 illum amare non potui.
15 haec puella amat agricolam.
16 laudabunt illum poetam.
17 illi poetae pecuniam dabit.
18 horum pecuniam poetae dabo.
19 illius pecuniam puellae
   dederunt.
20 huic poetae vitam dedit dea.

G Translate into Latin:

1 These poets are farmers.
2 Those men are poets.
3 I am giving money to these men.
4 We sought that girl's money.

5 I gave those things to the girl.
6 He can read those men's books.
7 The goddess loved this man.
8 The girl praised that goddess.

9   Is this woman a goddess?

10   You are standing in that man's field.

11   We gave that man money.

12   This farmer has been a poet.

13   He will be able to give this girl a horse.

14   You (plural) give money to those girls.

15   This woman wrote a book.

16   I can see that.

17   This man loves the Romans.

18   We sought these farmers.

19   The goddess gives these things to farmers.

20   Did you say those things?

10.3 Imperative

So far the verbs we have seen have been in the indicative mood; this is the normal form of a verb, used for making simple statements and asking direct questions. Verbs also have several other moods, including the imperative, used for issuing orders. Thus in English 'go away!', 'come in!', and 'please close the window' use the imperative. In Latin the formation of the imperative is simple: the singular imperative is the bare verb stem (drop -*re* from the infinitive), and the plural imperative is the same as the second person plural indicative with the final -*is* replaced by -*e* (notice that in the third conjugation this not the same form as one would get by adding -*te* to the singular imperative).

	First conjugation	Second conjugation	Third conjugation
Singular imperative	amā 'love!'	monē 'advise!'	rege 'rule!'
Plural imperative	amāte 'love!'	monēte 'advise!'	regite 'rule!'

A few verbs are irregular in the imperative; thus the singular imperative of *dūcō* is *dūc* (not *dūce*), the singular imperative of *dīcō* is *dīc* (not *dīce*), the singular imperative of *eō* is *ī*; the plural imperative of *eō* is *īte*, the singular imperative of *sum* is *estō*, and the plural imperative of *sum* is *este*.[1]

When a Latin verb is in the imperative, it does not come at the end of the sentence but rather at or near the beginning.

---

[1] Officially *sum* has two singular imperatives, *es* and *estō*, and two plural ones, *este* and *estōte*; the second form in each of these pairs is called a future imperative, and in fact other verbs also have a future imperative (e.g. *amātō* and *amātōte* from *amō*). But in practice the future imperative is rarely used except in the case of *estō* (and a few other verbs we have not yet seen), and the present imperative *es* is very rarely used, being effectively replaced by *estō*. There are some other irregular imperatives, which we shall see in later chapters.

Practice

H Conjugate in the present active imperative:

1 currō	6 dīcō	11 eō
2 laudō	7 habeō	12 videō
3 doceō	8 dūcō	13 vincō
4 mittō	9 scrībō	14 petō
5 dō	10 iuvō	15 stō

I Translate:

1 servi, currite ad illam silvam.
2 magister, doce illos pueros.
3 amici, laudate hos deos.
4 duc equum meum in illum agrum.
5 servi vestri non sunt boni: emite hos.
6 pueri, nunc iuvate hunc agricolam.
7 serve, i ex hoc oppido.
8 amice, mitte filium tuum ad hoc magistrum.
9 hic state.
10 fili, scribe nunc illam epistulam.
11 mone amicum tuum de illis agricolis.
12 da pecuniam illi puellae miserae.
13 amice, rege bene oppidum nostrum.
14 petite oppidum novum: hoc nunc nostrum est.

15 pueri, date hunc librum magistro.
16 dic illi haec.
17 puer, curre in illud oppidum.
18 amice, iuva nostros.
19 ducite equos vestros trans hos agros.
20 ite ad castra Romanorum.
21 eme hunc servum; bonus est.
22 da illi librum meum.
23 lege hoc.
24 scribe de illis deis.
25 mittite nunc pecuniam ad amicos nostros.
26 pete equum tuum in illo agro, non hic.
27 puellae, legite hodie hunc librum.
28 docete hos pueros de illo bello.

J Translate into Latin:

1 Friend, praise our gods.
2 Poet, teach these boys.
3 Men, conquer the Romans.
4 Give (singular) those men money.
5 Slave, lead this horse out of the forest.
6 Boys, write those letters now.

7 Gods and goddesses, help our friends!

8 Son, write a letter about your teacher.

9 Look (plural) at that! (= See that!)

10 Send (singular) that letter to my son.

10.4 Vocabulary to Learn

Irregular Imperatives

dīc	'say!' (singular)
dūc	'lead!' (singular)
estō	'be!' (singular)
este	'be!' (plural)
ī	'go!' (singular)
īte	'go!' (plural)

Adjectives/Pronouns

hic, haec, hoc	'this', 'these'
ille, illa, illud	'that', 'those'

Reading longer passages is different from reading isolated sentences. When dealing with a connected passage it is necessary to choose carefully between the different English translations available for each word or phrase, any of which might have been acceptable when reading the sentence in isolation, in order to produce a coherent translation that hangs together. Sometimes one has to go beyond the translation possibilities already learned and come up with synonyms, or be creative in re-arranging words, in order to get a translation that makes sense and is grammatical in English. So reading connected passages is a special skill that needs to be developed separately, just like knowledge of the case system or a good vocabulary. Ultimately, good passage-reading skills are probably the most important component of knowledge of Latin, so it is worth devoting some care to their development.

Almost always, a passage of Latin makes sense: that is, the author intended the different sentences to relate to one another in a coherent fashion. But that fact is of less use to beginners than it might be, because often something that made perfect sense in an ancient Roman context does not appear to make any sense today. So when reading passages it is often useful to apply one's knowledge of Roman history and mythology, and to be alert to cultural differences. The more one understands how the Romans thought, the easier it is to understand what they said.

Another type of understanding crucial for reading passages of ancient literature is that of the ways in which the rules and translations already learned can and cannot be bent in order to produce a coherent translation. Roughly speaking, it is permissible to substitute another English word or phrase for the translation you have learned if and only if the other word or phrase is roughly equivalent to the one you learned originally, not only in meaning but also grammatically. So for example you have learned the translation 'your' for *tuus, -a, -um*, but if you found *tuus* agreeing with a word meaning 'nothing', that translation would not work in English: 'your nothing' makes no sense. There might be a temptation to try substituting 'you' for 'your', but that would make matters worse: 'your' is an adjective and 'you' is a pronoun, so the two forms are never grammatically equivalent. (Like all adjectives, *tuus* can be substantivized and thus come to function a bit more like a pronoun, but the substantivized form of *tuus* would mean 'your man', not 'you'.) If you think carefully about what 'your' plus 'nothing' ought to mean, however, you might be able to come up with another way of expressing the idea 'your' that preserves the essentially adjectival function of *tuus*, for example 'of yours'. (Compare English 'your book' with 'a book of yours', or 'He's not my son' with 'He's no son of mine': 'my' and 'your' are equivalent to 'of mine' and 'of yours' in a range of contexts in English.) Indeed 'nothing of yours' would work as a translation of *nihil tuum*, but alternatives like 'nothing is yours' or 'you are nothing' would not work, because they are not equivalent to the basic translation you know for *tuus*.

Both these types of understanding usually take time to develop: some people come to the study of Latin equipped with an extensive background knowledge of the ancient Romans and/or with a fully developed instinct for finding equivalent phrases, but for most people some experience of reading is necessary to produce these skills. They come with practice.

One important skill that can be mastered at once, however, is that of making the best use of any help given. For example, when unfamiliar vocabulary is glossed, it is necessary to pay attention to all the information in the gloss, grammatical as well as lexical. Suppose you are faced with the words *voluit iūdex* and the following vocabulary help: *volō, velle, voluī,* – 'want'; *iūdex, iūdicis* (m.) 'judge'. If you simply extracted the English translations from these glosses you might be tempted to produce a translation such as 'he wanted to judge'; this would be especially likely since *iūdex* clearly belongs to a category that you have not yet encountered, and therefore the information on how to inflect it does not appear to be very helpful. But if you look more closely at the vocabulary, you will see that *iūdex* has to be a noun, not a verb, and moreover that it is nominative: even if it belongs to a declension you are not familiar with, you know the nominative and genitive forms from the gloss. Likewise, although the verb is an irregular one that you have not yet encountered, you can tell that the form in this sentence is the perfect active indicative. You thus have all the information you need to work out the correct translation, namely 'the judge wanted'.

11.1 *Colloquium Harleianum* 27a–e (adapted)

How a Roman might appeal to a neglectful friend (second or third century AD):

I ad fratrem et dic ei: 'Quid tibi fecimus, ut neglegas nos? te diligimus, te amamus, per deum, per caelum, per terram. et ipse hoc scis, quoniam amicus noster es.'

Vocabulary (in order of first appearance; words that appear more than once are in bold)

frātrem 'brother' (accusative) (here probably used metaphorically of a friend)	nōs 'us' (accusative)
	tē **'you' (accusative)**
	dīligō, dīligere, dīlēxī, dīlēctum 'like'
eī 'to him'	**per (+ accusative) 'by'**
quid 'what?' (accusative)	caelum, caelī (n.) 'heaven'
tibi 'to you'	terra, terrae (f.) 'earth'
faciō, facere, fēcī, factum 'do'	ipse 'yourself' (nominative)
ut 'so that'	scīs 'you know'
neglegās 'you neglect' (subjunctive)	quoniam 'since'

11.2 *Colloquium Leidense–Stephani* 10a–e (adapted)

Winning belief by taking an oath (probably third or fourth century AD):

Dixit mihi, 'Si periurus non es, iura mihi.' et iuravi simpliciter, et non periuravi: 'per deum optimum, per deum maximum, sic mihi sit deus propitius: periurus in hoc sacramento non inveniar.' tunc mihi credidit.

Vocabulary (in order of first appearance; words that appear more than once are in bold, and those in bold in the preceding vocabulary list are omitted)

mihi 'to me', 'for me' (dative)
sī 'if'
periūrus, -a, -um 'perjured' (swearing falsely)
iūrō, iūrāre, iūrāvī, iūrātum 'swear'
simpliciter 'frankly'
periūrō, periūrāre, periūrāvī, periūrātum 'swear falsely'
optimus, optima, optimum 'best'
maximus, maxima, maximum 'greatest'
sīc 'thus' (i.e. only if I am telling the truth)

sit 'may (he) be' (third person singular verb in the subjunctive)
propitius, propitia, propitium 'favourable'
sacrāmentum, sacrāmentī (n.) 'oath'
inveniar 'I shall be found' (future passive)
tunc 'then'
crēdō, crēdere, crēdidī, crēditum 'believe' (takes object in the dative)

11.3 *Colloquium Harleianum* 23a–i (adapted)

An unsuccessful attempt to obtain repayment of a debt (second or third century AD):

MARCUS: nonne est ille Lucius, qui meam pecuniam habet? est. accedens ergo salutabo illum.
MARCUS: ave, paterfamilias! possumne accipere meam pecuniam, quam mihi tam diu debes?
LUCIUS: quid dicis? insanis!
MARCUS: faeneravi tibi pecuniam, et dicis 'insanis?' fraudator, nonne cognoscis me?
LUCIUS: duc te, quaere cui faeneravisti: ego enim nihil tuum habeo.
MARCUS: iura mihi.
LUCIUS: iurabo ubi velis.
MARCUS: eamus. iura in templo.
LUCIUS: per deum hunc, nihil mihi dedisti.
MARCUS: modo bene.

Vocabulary (in order of first appearance; words that appear more than once are in bold, and those in bold in the preceding vocabulary lists are omitted)

nōnne = nōn + -ne

quī 'who' (nominative)

accēdēns 'approaching' (nominative)

ergō 'therefore' (translate one word
    earlier than where it appears in
    Latin)

salūtō, salūtāre, salūtāvī, salūtātum
    'greet'

avē 'hello'

paterfamiliās 'sir' (literally 'master of
    a household')

accipiō, accipere, accēpī, acceptum
    'receive'

quam 'which' (accusative)

tam diū 'for so long'

dēbeō, dēbēre, dēbuī, dēbitum 'owe'

quid 'what?' (accusative)

īnsānīs 'you are insane'

**faenerō, faenerāre, faenerāvī,
    faenerātum 'lend'**

tibi 'you' (dative)

fraudātor, fraudātōris (m.) 'cheater'

cognōscō, cognōscere, cognōvī,
    cognitum 'recognize'

mē 'me' (accusative)

dūc tē 'get out of here!' (literally 'lead
    yourself [away]')

quaerō, quaerere, quaesīvī, quaesītum
    'find out'

cui 'to whom' (dative)

ego 'I' (nominative)

enim 'for' (in the sense of 'because';
    translate one word earlier than
    where it appears in Latin)

nihil (n.) 'nothing'

tuus *can also mean* 'of yours'

velīs 'you may wish' (subjunctive)

eāmus 'let's go!' (subjunctive)

templum, templī (n.) 'temple'

modo bene 'very well'

11.4 *Colloquium Montepessulanum* 20a–f (adapted)

The end of a Roman's day (probably third century AD):

MARCUS: nunc sero est; eamus domum.

MARCUS: domina ubi est?

IULIA: hic sum.

MARCUS: habemus quid cenare?

IULIA: habemus omnia.

MARCUS: impone mensam, da panem, praecide caseum, da poma . . . quot horae
    sunt noctis?

IULIA: nunc tres.

MARCUS: pone matellam et tolle lucernam. dormire volo, ut mane vigilem.

Vocabulary

sērō 'late'

eāmus 'let's go' (subjunctive)

domum '(to) home'

domina, dominae (f.) 'mistress of the house'

quid 'something' (accusative)

cēnō, cēnāre, cēnāvī, cēnātum 'eat for dinner'

omnia 'everything' (n. plural accusative)

impōnō (like *pōnō*) 'set up'

mēnsa, mēnsae (f.) 'table'

pānem 'bread' (accusative)

praecīdō, praecīdere, praecīdī, praecīsum 'cut up'

cāseus, cāseī (m.) 'cheese'

pōmum, pōmī (n.) 'fruit'

quot 'how many?'

hōra, hōrae (f.) 'hour'[1]

nox, noctis, *gen. pl.* noctium (f.) 'night'

trēs 'three'

pōnō *can also mean* 'set out'

matella, matellae (f.) 'chamber pot'[2]

tollō, tollere, sustulī, sublātum 'remove'

lucerna, lucernae (f.) 'lantern'

dormiō, dormīre, dormīvī, dormītum 'sleep'

volō, velle, voluī, – 'want'

ut māne vigilem 'so that I can wake up in the morning'

11.5 Translate into Latin

Use vocabulary and forms from the passages above as well as the words you already know.

'What have you done to that man, so that he neglects you?'

'I have done nothing to him.'

'Swear to me, in the temple.'

'I shall swear: by this god, by the greatest god, by heaven, by earth, I have done nothing to him.'

'Are you perjured?'

'I have not sworn falsely: see, the god knows, since he has received my oath.'

'Now I shall believe you.'

---

[1] The Romans calculated time on a system whereby the hours of daylight and the hours of darkness were each divided into twelve equal hours; the first hour of the night would be at sunset and the sixth at our midnight, so the third might have been around our 9 pm, depending on the season.

[2] Unlike many ancient peoples, the Romans had good plumbing, but nevertheless they did not expect to walk to the toilet at night and so preferred to use a chamber pot.

PART II

12 | Personal Pronouns, Partitive and Objective Genitives

12.1 Partitive and Objective Genitives

The genitive case can be used for purposes other than possession. A partitive genitive is used to indicate the whole from which a part is taken: 'some of the men', 'one of the boys', and 'half (of) the pie' are partitive genitives in English. Objective genitives are used with a noun or adjective to indicate the kind of relationship to that noun or adjective that an object would have to a verb: thus 'fear of falling' (one fears falling) and 'love of music' (one loves music) are objective genitives.[1]

In Latin these relationships are also expressed with the genitive, particularly with words like:

> odium, -ī (n.) 'hatred' (*odium Rōmānōrum* 'hatred of Romans')
> paucī, -ae, -a 'few' (*paucī Rōmānōrum* 'a few of the Romans')
> multī, -ae, -a 'many' (*multī Rōmānōrum* 'many of the Romans')
> quattuor 'four' (*quattuor Rōmānōrum* 'four of the Romans')
> quīnque 'five'
> sex 'six'
> septem 'seven'

When the word on which the genitive depends is declinable, it declines as usual and the case of the whole genitive phrase is apparent: *paucī Rōmānōrum* is 'a few of the Romans' as the subject of a sentence, but *paucōs Rōmānōrum* is 'a few of the Romans' as the object of a sentence. But with the numbers, which are indeclinable, the phrase as a whole becomes ambiguous as to case: *quattuor Rōmānōrum* could be either the subject or the object of a sentence.

Practice

A Translate:

1 multi Graecorum miseri sunt.

2 multos Graecorum rexit.

3 multae illarum puellarum hic sunt.

---

[1] There is also a subjective genitive, which has the relationship to a noun that a subject would have to a verb, and some English phrases can be either subjective or objective: 'the love of God' is a subjective genitive when it refers to the love that God feels for humans and an objective genitive when it refers to the love that humans feel for God.

4 multas illarum puellarum in oppido vidimus.

5 quattuor illorum ad silvam ibunt.

6 nostri quattuor illorum vicerunt.

7 horum servorum sex in agris sunt.

8 horum servorum sex in agros mittam.

9 pauci nostrorum hic sunt.

10 illarum epistularum paucas scripsi.

11 quinque horum libros scripserunt.

12 septem horum in castris vidimus.

13 odium poetarum bonum non est.

B Translate into Latin:

1 Many of the Romans are in the camp.

2 You will lead many of the Romans.

3 A few of our men ran across the fields.

4 He saw a few of our men.

5 Seven of the boys love this girl.

6 That man is teaching seven of the boys.

7 Five of the girls are standing in that field.

8 We saw five of the girls in the forest.

9 Four of the slaves can write.

10 He will teach four of the slaves.

12.2 Personal Pronouns

The pronouns for the first and second persons are words meaning 'I', 'you', 'we', etc. In Latin these are as follows:

British Case Order	First person singular	First person plural	Second person singular	Second person plural
Nom.	ego 'I'	nōs 'we'	tū 'you'	vōs 'you'
Voc.	–	–	–	–
Acc.	mē 'me'	nōs 'us'	tē 'you'	vōs 'you'
Gen.	meī 'of me'	nostrī/nostrum 'of us'	tuī 'of you'	vestrī/vestrum 'of you'
Dat.	mihi 'to/for me'	nōbīs 'to/for us'	tibi 'to/for you'	vōbīs 'to/for you'
Abl.	mē 'me'	nōbīs 'us'	tē 'you'	vōbīs 'you'

Ancient Case Order

	First person singular	First person plural	Second person singular	Second person plural
Nom.	ego 'I'	nōs 'we'	tū 'you'	vōs 'you'
Gen.	meī 'of me'	nostrī/nostrum 'of us'	tuī 'of you'	vestrī/vestrum 'of you'
Dat.	mihi 'to/for me'	nōbīs 'to/for us'	tibi 'to/for you'	vōbīs 'to/for you'
Acc.	mē 'me'	nōs 'us'	tē 'you'	vōs 'you'
Abl.	mē 'me'	nōbīs 'us'	tē 'you'	vōbīs 'you'

In the accusative and dative these pronouns are used like other words so far encountered, but in the other cases they are somewhat different.

1) The nominatives of the personal pronouns are normally omitted, as we have seen, but can be used for emphasis: *amō* means 'I love', and *ego amō* means '*I* love'.

2) The genitives of personal pronouns are not used as possessives (the English words 'my', 'your', and 'our' are expressed in Latin with the adjectives *meus, tuus, noster,* and *vester*), but only for other uses of the genitive such as the partitive and objective genitives. In English these other uses are normally expressed with 'of me', 'of you', or 'of us' rather than with 'my', 'your', and 'our': *quīnque nostrum* 'five of us', *odium nostrī* 'hatred of us'. The partitive genitive uses the forms *nostrum* and *vestrum*, and the objective genitive uses the forms *nostrī* and *vestrī*.

3) When the ablative of a personal pronoun is used with the preposition *cum*, it forms a compound with *cum: mēcum* 'with me', *tēcum* 'with you' (singular), *nōbīscum* 'with us', *vōbīscum* 'with you' (plural).

Be careful not to confuse the partitive genitive forms *nostrum* and *vestrum* with the *nostrum* and *vestrum* that are the neuters and accusatives of *noster* and *vester*: in *quattuor nostrum* the word is a pronoun in the genitive, so the phrase means 'four of us', but in *servum nostrum* it is an adjective in the accusative, so the phrase means 'our slave'. In *quattuor nostrōrum* we have the adjective (substantivized) in the genitive plural, so the phrase means 'four of our men'.

Practice

C Translate (n.b. *odium, -ī* (n.) 'hatred'; *quīnque* 'five'; *septem* 'seven'):

1 ego, non ille, hunc equum emi.   3 mitte servum tuum nobiscum.
2 petisne me?   4 odium mei bonum non est.

5 hic equum mihi dedit.

6 quinque puerorum mecum stant.

7 tune me vidisti?

8 odium tui non habeo.

9 possumus te iuvare.

10 tecum ad magistrum nostrum ibo.

11 septem vestrum in castris nostris vidi.

12 nos, non dei, te iuvimus.

13 quinque nostrum in oppido erunt.

14 sine nobis vincere non poteritis.

15 hi nos iuvabunt.

16 ille nobis pecuniam heri dedit.

17 vosne docuisti illos pueros?

18 septem vestrum ad castra mittam.

19 fuitne vobiscum magister noster?

20 illud vobis dabimus.

21 vosne amant hae puellae?

22 amice, curre mecum ad oppidum.

23 nos, non vos, illum servum emimus.

24 tu, non ego, hos pueros docebis.

25 vosne me iuvare potestis?

26 quinque nostrorum cum Graecis sunt.

27 hoc tibi non dabo.

28 septem nostrorum in castris vidi.

29 libros bonos tibi dabit.

30 estne filius meus vobiscum?

31 hae nos amant.

32 duc hunc servum tecum.

33 nostri tecum ibunt.

34 Romani nos vicerunt.

35 Romanos nos vicimus.

36 illos mecum duxi.

D Translate into Latin, expressing subject pronouns where italicized only:

1 I love you (singular).

2 Do you (singular) love me?

3 He will give us books.

4 We saw you (plural) in the fields.

5 Are *you* a poet?

6 I seek my son: is he with you (singular)?

7 They will give you (plural) a horse.

8 Did *you* (plural) stand in that field?

9 Seven of us will go to the town.

10 *We* wrote these letters, not *you* (plural)!

11 I shall send a slave with you (singular).

12 Are you giving me this book?

13 *I* can help you (singular).

14 I shall write a letter about you (plural).

15 *We* conquered you (plural).

16 Did *you* (singular) teach these girls?

17 Five of the girls are with us.

18 Those boys are seeking you (singular).

19 We shall send five of you to the teacher.

20 The teacher gave me those books.

21 I shall help you (singular).

22 We will give you (singular) money.

23 I am not able to help you (plural).

24 Are *you* (plural) giving us money?

25 We cannot see you (plural).

26 I am giving you (plural) good horses.

27 These men cannot see us.

28 These men can give you (singular) money.

29 The gods are helping us.

30 This girl loves me.

31 Seven of us are teachers.

32 Go (plural) with us to the town.

33 Lead (singular) this boy with you to the camp.

34 Those men will give us horses.

35 Those men's slaves will go with you (plural).

36 Our slaves do not love us.

12.3 Reading Practice

Colloquium Harleianum 13a–b (adapted): an encounter in a temple (second or third century AD).

MARCUS: salutavi te nudius tertius sursum in templo, sed me non salutavisti.
GAIUS: ego adorabam.
MARCUS: et amicum tuum tecum vidi.

Vocabulary

salūtō, salūtāre, salūtāvī, salūtātum 'greet'

nudius tertius (indeclinable) 'two days ago'

sūrsum 'up'

templum, templī (n.) 'temple'

adōrābam (imperfect tense of *adōrō* 'worship') 'I was worshipping'

12.4 Vocabulary to Learn

Verbs

abeō, abīre, abiī/abīvī, abitum (conjugated like *eō*)	'go away'
absum, abesse, āfuī, āfutūrus (conjugated like *sum*)	'be absent'
adsum, adesse, adfuī, adfutūrus (conjugated like *sum*)	'be present'
exeō, exīre, exiī/exīvī, exitum (conjugated like *eō*)	'go out'
timeō, timēre, timuī, –	'fear', 'be afraid of' (object is in accusative despite 'of')

Vocabulary continues.

Nouns

odium, odiī (n.)	'hatred'
vīta, vītae (f.)	'life'

Adjectives

malus, mala, malum	'bad'
multī, multae, multa	'many'
paucī, paucae, pauca	'few'

Numbers

quattuor	'four'
quīnque	'five'
sex	'six'
septem	'seven'

13 | Present Subjunctive, *Quis*

13.1 Present Subjunctive

Like the indicative and the imperative, the subjunctive is a mood. Latin subjunctives can be difficult to deal with because they have no fixed translation in English: they occur in a variety of different constructions, and their meanings depend on the constructions in which they are used. In Latin the subjunctive, like the indicative, can have different forms. One of these is the present active subjunctive, which is formed as follows.

First conjugation	Second conjugation	Third conjugation	*Sum*	*Possum*	*Eō*
amem	moneam	regam	sim	possim	eam
amēs	moneās	regās	sīs	possīs	eās
amet	moneat	regat	sit	possit	eat
amēmus	moneāmus	regāmus	sīmus	possīmus	eāmus
amētis	moneātis	regātis	sītis	possītis	eātis
ament	moneant	regant	sint	possint	eant

Practice

A Conjugate in the present active subjunctive:

1 currō	8 abeō	15 pōnō
2 dō	9 legō	16 iuvō
3 dīcō	10 laudō	17 scrībō
4 absum	11 mittō	18 exeō
5 dūcō	12 doceō	19 vincō
6 videō	13 petō	20 habeō
7 timeō	14 adsum	

13.2 **Hortatory and Deliberative Subjunctives**

One use of the present subjunctive is to express wishes or suggestions; subjunctives with this meaning are usually translated with 'let's' (in the first person plural) or with 'may' before the subject (in other forms), and the construction is known as the hortatory subjunctive.[1] Thus *videāmus* can mean 'let's see', *videās* can mean 'may you see' (not 'you may see'), and *videat* can mean 'may he see' (not 'he may see'). When such expressions are negative, they use *nē* rather than *nōn* as the negative: *nē scrībāmus* 'let's not write', *nē scrībat* 'may he not write'.

Another use of the present subjunctive is in questions in which the speaker wonders what to do; these subjunctives are always in the first person and are known as deliberative subjunctives. They are usually translated with 'should' or 'am I to' / 'are we to'; thus *scrībamne?* means 'should I write?', 'am I to write?', and *scrībāmusne* means 'should we write?', 'are we to write?'. It is therefore necessary to work out whether a subjunctive is hortatory or deliberative before translating it; as the deliberative subjunctive occurs only in questions and the hortatory subjunctive cannot be used in questions this task is not very difficult.

Practice

B Identify the construction and translate; note *nē* 'not':

1 curramus ad silvam.
2 curramusne in silvam?
3 dei nobis dent multos filios.
4 ne ducamus equos in agros.
5 ne magister nos male doceat.
6 demusne hoc tibi?
7 ducamne ad te equum tuum?
8 puellae, amicos meos iuvetis.
9 pecuniam nobis dent.
10 equi in agro hodie stent.
11 ubi stemus?
12 oppidum nostrum bene regat.
13 mittas mecum servum tuum.
14 adsimusne vobiscum?
15 abeamusne ab hoc oppido?
16 laudemus deos nostros.
17 pueri boni hodie sitis.
18 ubi petam filium meum?
19 eamus ad castra cum illis.
20 illamne laudem?
21 ne mittat ad illos pecuniam.
22 scribamusne hoc?
23 amemus vitam, quia vita bona est.
24 exeamne e castris Romanorum?
25 iuvemne illos pueros?
26 dei vobis vitam dent.

---

[1] Different scholars use different terminology for the hortatory subjunctive: 'jussive' and 'optative' are also found. According to some classifications these three terms apply to slightly different uses of the present subjunctive: when it is a command (e.g. 'let there be light') it is called jussive, when it is a wish (e.g. 'may the gods be propitious') it is called optative, and when it is an exhortation (a first-person plural command, e.g. 'let's go') it is hortatory. But there are also other ways of using these terms.

C Translate into Latin:

1 Should we teach those boys?
2 Let's teach these boys.
3 May the gods give you (singular) a good life.
4 Should we send a slave to you (plural)?
5 Why should I help you?
6 May the slaves go out!
7 May you (singular) be present with us!
8 Should I say that?
9 Where should we put this?
10 Let's give money to those boys.
11 Should we write letters to our teacher?
12 May he write a good book!
13 Let's say a few words.
14 Should I help those girls?
15 Should I go out of the camp without a sword?
16 Let's help that man.
17 Should I read these books?
18 Should we praise the Romans?

13.3 Interrogative Pronoun

The interrogative pronoun *quis, quid* is the Latin equivalent of '**who?**' and '**what?**'; the genitive can therefore be the equivalent of '**whose?**' and the accusative the equivalent of '**whom?**'. It is declined as follows:

British Case Order

	Singular			Plural		
	Masculine	Feminine	Neuter	Masculine	Feminine	Neuter
Nom.	quis	quis	quid	quī	quae	quae
Voc.	–	–	–	–	–	–
Acc.	quem	quam	quid	quōs	quās	quae
Gen.	cuius	cuius	cuius	quōrum	quārum	quōrum
Dat.	cui	cui	cui	quibus/quīs	quibus/quīs	quibus/quīs
Abl.	quō	quā	quō	quibus/quīs	quibus/quīs	quibus/quīs

Ancient Case Order

	Singular			**Plural**		
	Masculine	**Feminine**	**Neuter**	**Masculine**	**Feminine**	**Neuter**
Nom.	quis	quis	quid	quī	quae	quae
Gen.	cuius	cuius	cuius	quōrum	quārum	quōrum
Dat.	cui	cui	cui	quibus/quīs	quibus/quīs	quibus/quīs
Acc.	quem	quam	quid	quōs	quās	quae
Abl.	quō	quā	quō	quibus/quīs	quibus/quīs	quibus/quīs

There is also an interrogative adjective, the Latin equivalent of 'which?' in contexts such as 'Which book do you want?'. This is declined very similarly to the pronoun, but not identically; the forms that differ are in bold in the paradigm below.

British Case Order

	Singular			**Plural**		
	Masculine	**Feminine**	**Neuter**	**Masculine**	**Feminine**	**Neuter**
Nom.	**quī**	**quae**	**quod**	quī	quae	quae
Voc.	–	–	–	–	–	–
Acc.	quem	quam	**quod**	quōs	quās	quae
Gen.	cuius	cuius	cuius	quōrum	quārum	quōrum
Dat.	cui	cui	cui	quibus/quīs	quibus/quīs	quibus/quīs
Abl.	quō	quā	quō	quibus/quīs	quibus/quīs	quibus/quīs

Ancient Case Order

	Singular			**Plural**		
	Masculine	**Feminine**	**Neuter**	**Masculine**	**Feminine**	**Neuter**
Nom.	**quī**	**quae**	**quod**	quī	quae	quae
Gen.	cuius	cuius	cuius	quōrum	quārum	quōrum
Dat.	cui	cui	cui	quibus/quīs	quibus/quīs	quibus/quīs
Acc.	quem	quam	**quod**	quōs	quās	quae
Abl.	quō	quā	quō	quibus/quīs	quibus/quīs	quibus/quīs

Because most forms are identical for the pronoun and the adjective, one normally has to keep both possibilities in mind and decide between them based on the context, as with the pronominal and adjectival meanings of *hic* and *ille*. When the interrogative word agrees with another word in the sentence, it is normally best translated with 'which?': *quae puella adest?* 'Which girl is present?', *quod verbum scrīpsistī?* 'Which word did you write?'. When it does not agree with anything it is translated with 'what?' in the neuter (*quid dīxit?* 'What did he say?') and with 'who?', 'whom?', or 'whose?' in the masculine and feminine: *quis est?* 'Who is it?', *quem vīdistī?* 'Whom did you see?', *cuius pecūnia est?* 'Whose money is it?' As these examples suggest, questions introduced by forms of *quis* or *quī* do not have *-ne* as well.

Practice

D Translate:

1 quid dicam?
2 quis adest?
3 cuius filius es?
4 qui servi adsunt?
5 cuius servi estis?
6 cum quibus in silvam ivisti?
7 cuius sunt illi equi?
8 quae puellae in oppido erunt?
9 cuius est hic ager?
10 quibus illam pecuniam dabis?
11 cuius poetae es filius?
12 quae oppida sunt Graeca?
13 cuius est hic liber?
14 qui sunt illi viri?
15 cui hunc librum demus?
16 quos pueros doceam?
17 de quo scribes?
18 poeta, quam puellam amas?
19 quos in castris vidistis?
20 quae verba dixit poeta?
21 in quo agro est equus meus?
22 quorum sunt hae epistulae?
23 cui puero hoc dem?
24 quis bellum timet?
25 puella, quem poetam amas?
26 quas deas laudemus?
27 quis poeta te amat?
28 cuius agricolae est hic ager?
29 cuius est illa pecunia?
30 in quibus agris sunt equi?
31 quorum puerorum magister es?
32 quibus puellis illud demus?

E Translate into Latin:

1 Who is afraid of the Romans?
2 What do you see, son?
3 In which field is my horse?
4 Which horses are in that field?
5 Who is leading these men?
6 Whom (plural) do you rule?
7 What are you writing?
8 Whose servant are you?
9 To whom will you give the book?
10 With whom did they stand?
11 Whose is that horse?
12 Who can help us?
13 To which boy are you (plural) giving the books?
14 What should I teach?

13.4 Reading Practice

Colloquium Harleianum 3a–d (adapted): a boy goes to school (perhaps first century AD).

Surge, puer: cur sedes? tolle libros Latinos, membranas et locellum et praeductal, atramentum et cannas. eamus, magistrum salutemus.

Vocabulary

surgō, surgere, surrēxī, surrēctum   locellus, locellī (m.) 'casket'
   'get up'   praeductal, praeductālis (n.) 'ruler'
sedeō, sedēre, sēdī, sessum 'sit'   ātrāmentum, ātrāmentī (n.) 'ink'
tollō, tollere, sustulī, sublātum 'pick up'   canna, cannae (f.) 'pen'
membrāna, membrānae (f.) 'parchment'   salūtō, salūtāre, salūtāvī, salūtātum 'greet'

13.5 Vocabulary to Learn

Pronoun
quis, quid   'who?', 'what?'

Adjective
quī, quae, quod   'which?'

Adverb
nē   'not' (with many types of subjunctive)

14 | Third Declension

14.1 Third Declension

In addition to the first and second declensions, Latin has a third declension. Nouns of the third declension can be masculine, feminine, or neuter, and all three genders decline similarly, except that in the neuter the nominative, vocative, and accusative are always the same as each other. The nominatives singular of third-declension nouns are unpredictable: the first form in the vocabulary entry will always be the nominative and vocative (and accusative in the case of neuter nouns) singular, but there is no reliable way of predicting what the relationship between that form and the other forms in the paradigm will be. The stem on which these other forms are based can only be found by dropping the -*is* ending of the genitive singular: thus for a noun with a vocabulary entry *mīles, mīlitis* (m.), the stem is *mīlit-*. To this stem are added the following endings: in the singular accusative -*em*, genitive -*is*, dative -*ī*, ablative -*e* or -*ī* depending on the paradigm; in the plural nominative and vocative -*ēs*, accusative -*ēs* or -*īs* depending on the paradigm, genitive -*um* or -*ium* depending on the paradigm, dative and ablative -*ibus*. Therefore the full declension of *mīles* is as follows:

British Case Order

	Singular	Plural
Nom.	mīles	mīlit-ēs
Voc.	mīles	mīlit-ēs
Acc.	mīlit-em	mīlit-ēs
Gen.	mīlit-is	mīlit-um
Dat.	mīlit-ī	mīlit-ibus
Abl.	mīlit-e	mīlit-ibus

Ancient Case Order

	Singular	Plural
Nom./Voc.	mīles	mīlit-ēs
Gen.	mīlit-is	mīlit-um
Dat.	mīlit-ī	mīlit-ibus
Acc.	mīlit-em	mīlit-ēs
Abl.	mīlit-e	mīlit-ibus

Third-declension nouns belong to two types: consonant stems and *i*-stems. Nouns in the latter category take a slightly different set of endings; these have an additional form given in the vocabulary, the genitive plural. The forms that differ in the *i*-stem paradigm are in bold font below.

British Case Order

Consonant stems

| | Masculine and feminine *mīles, mīlitis* 'soldier' | | Neuter *opus, operis* 'work' | |
	Singular	Plural	Singular	Plural
Nom.	mīles	mīlitēs	opus	opera
Voc.	mīles	mīlitēs	opus	opera
Acc.	mīlitem	mīlitēs	opus	opera
Gen.	mīlitis	mīlitum	operis	operum
Dat.	mīlitī	mīlitibus	operī	operibus
Abl.	mīlite	mīlitibus	opere	operibus

I-stems

| | Masculine and feminine *cīvis, cīvis, cīvium* 'citizen' | | Neuter *animal, animālis, animālium* 'animal' | |
	Singular	Plural	Singular	Plural
Nom.	cīvis	cīvēs	animal	**animālia**
Voc.	cīvis	cīvēs	animal	**animālia**
Acc.	cīvem	cīvēs/**cīvīs**	animal	**animālia**
Gen.	cīvis	**cīvium**	animālis	**animālium**
Dat.	cīvī	cīvibus	animālī	animālibus
Abl.	cīve/**cīvī**	cīvibus	**animālī**	animālibus

Ancient Case Order

Consonant stems

| | Masculine and feminine *mīles, mīlitis* 'soldier' | | Neuter *opus, operis* 'work' | |
	Singular	Plural	Singular	Plural
Nom./Voc.	mīles	mīlitēs	opus	opera
Gen.	mīlitis	mīlitum	operis	operum
Dat.	mīlitī	mīlitibus	operī	operibus
Acc.	mīlitem	mīlitēs	opus	opera
Abl.	mīlite	mīlitibus	opere	operibus

I-stems

| | Masculine and feminine *cīvis, cīvis, cīvium* 'citizen' | | Neuter *animal, animālis, animālium* 'animal' | |
	Singular	Plural	Singular	Plural
Nom./Voc.	cīvis	cīvēs	animal	**animālia**
Gen.	cīvis	**cīvium**	animālis	**animālium**
Dat.	cīvī	cīvibus	animālī	animālibus
Acc.	cīvem	cīvēs/**cīvīs**	animal	**animālia**
Abl.	cīve/**cīvī**	cīvibus	**animālī**	animālibus

Practice

A Determine whether the following third-declension nouns are consonant-stems or *i*-stems, and state what the stem of each noun is:

1 classis, classis, classium (f.) 'fleet'
2 corpus, corporis (n.) 'body'
3 flūmen, flūminis (n.) 'river'
4 frāter, frātris (m.) 'brother'
5 hostēs, hostium (m. plural) 'enemy'
6 māter, mātris (f.) 'mother'
7 nōmen, nōminis (n.) 'name'

8 ovis, ovis, ovium (f.) 'sheep'
9 pater, patris (m.) 'father'
10 rēx, rēgis (m.) 'king'
11 soror, sorōris (f.) 'sister'
12 urbs, urbis, urbium (f.) 'city'
13 moenia, moenium (n. plural) 'walls'

B Decline the nouns in exercise A according to the relevant paradigm.

14.2 Agreement

When a first/second-declension adjective like *bonus* modifies a third-declension noun such as *mīles*, the endings of noun and adjective are usually completely different, but the adjective nevertheless agrees with the noun in gender, number, and case: *bonus mīles* nominative singular, *bonī mīlitēs* nominative plural, *bonī mīlitis* genitive singular, *bonō mīlitī* dative singular, etc.

Practice

C Translate:

1 fratres tui in flumine stant.
2 quis classem hostium vicit?

3 nostri flumen videre non poterunt.
4 abeamusne ab urbe?

5 mater, quis est pater meus?

6 frater, quid mihi dabis?

7 multas ovis habuit ille agricola.

8 nostri regem non timebunt.

9 abeant Romani ab urbe nostra.

10 quis pecuniam huic regi dedit?

11 quod nomen dedit mater filio?

12 quis ovis in agrum duxit?

13 absint hostes a moenibus nostris.

14 cuius pecunia in hoc flumine est?

15 matrem tuam amamus.

16 fratrem iuvare non potui.

17 exeamusne ex urbe cum militibus?

18 frater meus non erit cum hostibus.

19 cuius opera vidisti?

20 miles, ubi est flumen?

21 ubi est equus fratris tui?

22 absit rex ab urbe nostra; liberi sumus.

23 classis nostra hostes vincet.

24 quid est nomen matris vestrae?

25 videsne fratrem regis?

26 exeamus e castris; eamus ad flumen; videamus classem hostium.

27 milites hunc regem non amant.

28 rex bonus civis amat.

29 sorores nostrae cum rege sunt.

30 rex hostium classem duxit.

31 puer miser est; adsint pater et mater.

32 patri tuo equum dabo.

33 oves magnae in illo agro sunt.

34 stabisne cum sororibus meis?

35 opera matris meae bona sunt.

36 adsimus in urbe; iuvemus cives.

37 multi cives liberi sunt.

38 moenia urbis videre non possumus.

39 quis timet illos hostis?

40 suntne equi animalia?

41 timeat rex cives bonos.

42 consilium illorum civium bonum est.

43 servus animalia trans agros duxit.

44 agricola, quid petis? – peto animalia mea.

45 moenia urbium Romanarum magna fuerunt.

46 timeamusne regem?

47 multi hostes in classe sunt, sed nostri non timent.

48 hostis non timemus: urbs nostra non sine moenibus est.

D Translate into Latin:

1 Whose brother do you love?

2 We loved the good king.

3 Did you (singular) see the river?

4 Should we help our sisters?

5 Brother, where is our mother?

6 We are standing with the king.

7 The king will give horses to the soldiers.

8 May the good gods go away from the cities of the enemy!

9 Can *you* (plural) help our king?

10 Good men do not fear kings.

11 This king's work will not be good.

12 Should I praise our brothers?

13 My brother is not afraid of soldiers.

14 Do *you* (singular) love your brothers?

15 Why were you afraid of those soldiers?

16 May the enemy fear our king and our soldiers.

17 This king will have many soldiers.

18 The king's slaves are miserable.

19 I saw that man with the king.

20 Let's give our animals to the king.

21 Your king gave money to my sisters.

22 Sheep are animals.

23 What are the names of your animals?

24 Can you see the walls of the city?

25 Let's praise the king and the king's father.

26 Can you see the cities of the enemy?

27 Do you fear the enemy?

28 The enemy's fleet is in our river!

29 Should we praise the name of god?

30 Those boys were afraid of sheep.

31 We wrote about Roman walls.

32 Our men see the fleet.

33 The citizens of this city love their fathers and mothers.

14.3 Reading Practice

1 *Colloquium Harleianum* 4a–e (adapted): continuation of the school scene in the preceding chapter.

PUPIL: ave, domine magister, bene tibi sit. ab hodie studere volo. rogo te ergo, doce me Latine loqui.

TEACHER: docebo te, si me attendes.

PUPIL: ecce, attendo.

TEACHER: bene dixisti, ut decet ingenuitatem tuam.

Vocabulary

avē 'hello'
dominus, dominī (m.) 'sir'
sit: *the subject is an impersonal 'it'*
studeō, studēre, studuī, – 'work hard'
volō, velle, voluī, – 'want'
rogō, rogāre, rogāvī, rogātum 'ask'
ergō 'therefore'
Latīnē 'in Latin'
loquī 'to speak' (infinitive)

attendō, attendere, attendī, attentum 'pay attention (to)'
ecce 'look!'
ut 'as'
decet 'suits', 'befits' (impersonal verb, no subject – see chapter 45)
ingenuitās, ingenuitātis (f.) 'free birth', 'noble character'

2 *Corpus Inscriptionum Latinarum* x.877: a mosaic from Pompeii (first century A D).

Cave canem!

Vocabulary

caveō, cavēre, cāvī, cautum (+ accusative) 'beware of'
canis, canis (m.) 'dog'

14.4 Vocabulary to Learn

Nouns

animal, animālis, animālium (n.)	'animal'
cīvis, cīvis, cīvium (m.)	'citizen'
classis, classis, classium (f.)	'fleet'
corpus, corporis (n.)	'body'
flūmen, flūminis (n.)	'river'
frāter, frātris (m.)	'brother'
hostēs, hostium (m. plural)	'enemy'
māter, mātris (f.)	'mother'
mīles, mīlitis (m.)	'soldier'
moenia, moenium (n. plural)	'walls'
nōmen, nōminis (n.)	'name'
opus, operis (n.)	'work'
ovis, ovis, ovium (f.)	'sheep'
pater, patris (m.)	'father'
rēx, rēgis (m.)	'king'
soror, sorōris (f.)	'sister'
urbs, urbis, urbium (f.)	'city'

15 | Subordination, Imperfect Subjunctive, Purpose Clauses

15.1 Subordination

So far we have discussed only what grammarians call simple sentences: sentences with only one verb. Latin sentences can, and usually do, have more than one verb, and one of the greatest challenges of translating Latin is working out how to break down the long sentences that result.

Latin sentences are composed of clauses: a clause is a verb plus the words that depend on or otherwise go with that verb. English has clauses as well; in 'He said that she would win, but they denied it' there are three clauses: 'He said', 'she would win', and 'they denied it'. (You can consider the words 'that' and 'and' to be part of the clauses that follow them, or to be part of no clause; it makes no practical difference.) In this sentence the clauses are joined by 'that' and 'and', which are conjunctions. It is common for clauses to be joined by conjunctions, in both English and Latin, but sometimes there is no conjunction, as in 'He said she would win.'

Every sentence contains at least one main clause: that is, a clause that can be understood without any of the others and is not grammatically dependent on any of the others. Many sentences have more than one main clause. It is also possible for a sentence to have subordinate clauses; that is, clauses that require the presence of another clause in the sentence for one reason or another. For example, in 'He said that she would win, but they denied it', there are two main clauses ('He said' and 'they denied it') and one subordinate clause ('she would win'). The main clauses could have stood by themselves: 'He said' and 'they denied it' are perfectly possible sentences, though the first of them does not convey much information. The subordinate clause, however, uses a verb form that would not have been used on its own: what the speaker actually said was 'She will win', and the 'would' in 'she would win' (a sentence very unlikely to be uttered by itself) results from the grammatical subordination of this sentence to the main clause 'He said'. Verb forms that cannot be used without another verb, such as infinitives or participles, are always subordinate: in 'He wanted to leave Rome' the main clause is 'He wanted' and 'to leave Rome' is subordinate, while in 'Going along the road he met a fox' the main clause is 'he met a fox' and 'going along the road' is subordinate.[1]

---

[1] In English, word groups for which the verb is an infinitive or a participle are often considered phrases rather than clauses. But this distinction is not helpful for dealing with Latin, since often English has an

In English the easiest way to tell main clauses apart from subordinate clauses is to do the following: (1) look for infinitives (verbs preceded by 'to') and participles (verbs ending in '-ing'), as these are always subordinate, (2) look at the conjunctions by which the other clauses are joined. The conjunctions 'and', 'but', and 'or' always join two items of the same status, that is, either two main clauses or two subordinate clauses. For this reason they are called co-ordinating conjunctions. All other English conjunctions, including 'when', 'if', 'because', 'since', 'in order to', 'as soon as', 'although', 'that', and 'while', are called subordinating conjunctions, because they introduce subordinate clauses. Some words that are not conjunctions (e.g. the relative pronouns 'who' and 'which') also introduce clauses, and the clauses introduced by such other words are usually subordinate clauses. Sometimes a conjunction is implied rather than expressed; in those circumstances it is necessary to work out which conjunction is implied. Thus 'He said he wasn't feeling well' contains the implied conjunction 'that' (the same sentence could be expressed as 'He said that he wasn't feeling well'), and 'He opened the door, looked at the rain, and shut it again' contains the implied conjunction 'and' (the sentence could be expressed as 'He opened the door, and looked at the rain, and shut it again').

Practice

A Divide each of the following sentences into clauses and identify the conjunctions, the main clauses, and the subordinate clauses:

1 Cicero was a candidate for the consulship, and Catiline was a candidate too.

2 When Catiline canvassed for votes, people were rude to him, because they thought he was disreputable.

3 Cicero was elected, and Catiline was not elected.

4 Because he felt humiliated by that outcome, Catiline plotted a revolution.

5 Catiline said that he would give the slaves their freedom if they helped him.

6 He did this in order to gather a big army and conquer everyone else.

7 When Catiline promised freedom to slaves, he broke a Roman taboo and gave Cicero the opportunity to expel him.

8 Cicero told the senate that Catiline would kill everyone in Rome, and he told Catiline to leave Rome immediately.

9 Catiline left Rome, went to his army, and announced open rebellion against Rome.

infinitive or participle where Latin has another kind of verb, or vice versa, so it will be easier if you consider infinitive and participle phrases to be clauses when dealing with translation into and out of Latin.

10 If he had not done that, he might have survived, but as soon as he had joined a hostile army he was doomed.

11 Catiline had friends in Rome who were on his side, and he asked them to instigate riots and arson in the city.

12 Someone sent Cicero a letter saying who Catiline's friends were and what they planned to do, and Cicero had them arrested on the spot.

13 He executed them without a trial, because if he had waited for a trial their friends would have rescued them.

14 Catiline's army was defeated in a great battle, in which everyone including Catiline was killed.

15 When this had happened the Catilinarian Conspiracy was over, and everyone lost interest in it except Cicero, who kept reminding people that he had saved the state.

16 The praise of Cicero, which was described as being not without reason but alas without end, irritated everyone else.

17 Because the other Romans were jealous and annoyed, Cicero soon had many enemies.

18 In Rome it was a serious crime to execute a citizen without a trial, and eventually Cicero's enemies accused him of this crime, because he had killed Catiline's Roman co-conspirators without a trial.

19 They drove him into exile, confiscated his house, and burned it to the ground.

20 While he was in exile, Cicero was completely miserable; he wished that he were dead.

21 After his friends lobbied hard for his return, Cicero was invited back to Rome.

22 His house was rebuilt at public expense, and the senate expressed gratitude for everything he had done.

15.2 Purpose Clauses

In Latin, as in English, subordinate clauses often use verb forms that would not be used in the same way in a main clause, and they are often introduced by special conjunctions. One such special subordinating conjunction is *ut*, which cannot be translated into English but which alerts the reader that a subordinate clause with subjunctive verb is coming up. *Ut* can introduce several different kinds of subordinate clause; one of these is the type known as purpose or final clauses. These clauses always have a verb in the subjunctive and are translated in English with an infinitive or with a clause beginning 'in order to', 'in order that ... will' or 'so that ... will'. (The infinitive and 'in order to' translations can be used only if the subject of the subjunctive is the same as the subject of the sentence's main verb.) If the subordinate clause is negative, *nē* is used instead of *ut*. For example:

ad urbem ībit ut rēgem videat. 'He will go to the city to see the king.' / 'He will go to the city in order to see the king.'
ad urbem ībit nē rēgem videat. 'He will go to the city in order not to see the king.'
rēgem laudāmus ut bene regat. 'We praise the king so that he will rule well.'
puerō pecūniam dant nē miser sit. 'They are giving money to the boy so that he will not be miserable.'

When translating such clauses from English into Latin, one often needs to turn an infinitive into a subjunctive; normally that subjunctive should have the same subject as the main verb.

'They will go to the city to see the king.' → *ad urbem ībunt ut rēgem videant.* (They are the ones who will see the king, so the subject of 'see' must be 'they'.)
'We shall go to the city to see the king.' → *ad urbem ībimus ut rēgem videāmus.* (We are the ones who will see the king, so the subject of 'see' must be 'we'.)

Practice

B Translate:

1 ad urbem ibit ut patrem petat.
2 deos laudat ut bona nobis dent.
3 illi nos iuvabunt ne hostes nos vincant.
4 illos iuvamus ut nos iuvent.
5 ad urbem ibo ne in silva sim.
6 laudasne deos ut te iuvent?
7 deos laudabimus ne hostes ad urbem nostram ducant.
8 ad urbem eunt ut matrem iuvent.
9 illi nos iuvabunt ut hostes vincamus.
10 illos iuvamus ut nos laudent.
11 ibisne ad urbem ne patrem meum videas?
12 deos laudo ut mihi bona dent.
13 illi nos iuvabunt ne ad regem eamus.
14 ad urbem non eunt ne fratrem videant.
15 laudabisne deos ut tibi bona dent?
16 illi nos iuvant ne miseri simus.
17 ad urbem ibimus ut magistrum nostrum videamus.
18 illos iuvamus ne ad hostes eant.

C Translate into Latin:

1 I shall run in order to help my brother.
2 He is running in order to help us.
3 She will send you the letter so that you will read (it).
4 We are sending you this so that you will read (it).
5 They will praise the horse so that we will buy (it).
6 She is praising the slave so that you will buy (him).
7 We praise the boys so that they will love us.
8 Are you praising the girls so that they won't fear you?
9 The big farmer is going away so that the boys will not be afraid.
10 I shall warn those men so that they won't buy that horse.
11 He is warning the girls so that they will not seek the money.

15.3 Imperfect Subjunctive

As well as a present subjunctive, Latin has an imperfect subjunctive. The imperfect active subjunctive is easy to form: simply take the present active infinitive (second principal part), drop the final -*e*, and add the endings -*em*, -*ēs*, -*et*, -*ēmus*, -*ētis*, -*ent*. All verbs follow this pattern without exception, no matter how irregular they are in other moods and tenses.

First conjugation	Second conjugation	Third conjugation	*Sum*	*Possum*	*Eō*
amārem	monērem	regerem	essem	possem	īrem
amārēs	monērēs	regerēs	essēs	possēs	īrēs
amāret	monēret	regeret	esset	posset	īret
amārēmus	monērēmus	regerēmus	essēmus	possēmus	īrēmus
amārētis	monērētis	regerētis	essētis	possētis	īrētis
amārent	monērent	regerent	essent	possent	īrent

Practice

D Conjugate in the imperfect active subjunctive:

1 laudō
2 doceō
3 dīcō
4 dō
5 mittō
6 habeō
7 adsum
8 exeō
9 legō
10 iuvō
11 videō
12 stō
13 currō
14 abeō
15 absum
16 timeō

15.4 Reading Practice

Colloquium Harleianum, 5a–d (adapted): continuation of the school scene in the preceding chapter.

TEACHER: porrige mihi, puer, manuale. cito ergo porrige librum, revolve, lege cum voce magna, aperi os. nunc bene fac locum, ut scribas dictatum.

Vocabulary

porrigō, porrigere, porrēxī, porrēctum
  'hand', 'pass'
manuāle, manuālis (n.) 'book stand'
cito 'quickly'
ergō 'therefore' (translate one word
  earlier than where it appears in Latin)
revolvō, revolvere, revolvī, revolūtum
  'turn to the right place'

vōx, vōcis (f.) 'voice'
aperī 'open!' (imperative singular)
ōs, ōris (n.) 'mouth'
fac 'mark!' (imperative singular of *faciō*)
locus, locī (m.) 'place'
dictātum, dictātī (n.) 'exercise'

15.5 Vocabulary to Learn

Verbs

accipiō, accipere, accēpī, acceptum	'receive'
agō, agere, ēgī, āctum	'drive', 'do'
audiō, audīre, audīvī, audītum	'hear'
capiō, capere, cēpī, captum	'take', 'capture'
faciō, facere, fēcī, factum	'do', 'make'

16.1 Sequence of Tenses

The imperfect subjunctive, like the present subjunctive, does not have a fixed translation; its meaning depends on its construction. One construction in which the imperfect subjunctive is often used is the purpose clauses discussed in chapter 15.2: these use either present or imperfect subjunctive for the subordinate clause depending on the tense of the main verb. This relationship between the tense of the main verb and the tense of the subjunctive is called 'sequence of tenses' and is one of the most important rules of Latin syntax. Indicative tenses fall into two groups, primary and historic (also called primary and secondary); primary tenses in the main verb result in present subjunctives in the subordinate clause, and historic tenses in the main verb result in imperfect subjunctives in the subordinate clause. Of the tenses we have so far seen, the present and future are primary; the imperative, deliberative subjunctive, and hortatory subjunctive (though not strictly speaking tenses at all) also function as primary tenses. The only historic tense we have so far seen is the perfect.[1] Therefore:

Main verb		Subordinate verb
Present indicative, future indicative, imperative, subjunctive	→	Present subjunctive
Perfect indicative	→	Imperfect subjunctive

The tense of the subordinate verb can sometimes help resolve an ambiguous main verb. For example, in a text where long vowels are not marked *librum emit* might mean either 'he is buying the book' (*emit* with short *e*) or 'he bought the book' (*ēmit*), but *librum emit ut nobis daret* has to mean 'he bought the book to give it to us' (*daret* is an imperfect subjunctive, so the main verb must be a perfect indicative).

English also has a sequence of tenses, though it does not work quite like the Latin sequence, and therefore when a purpose clause has a historic main verb and an imperfect subjunctive the translation pattern is different from that seen in the last chapter: such purpose clauses are translated with an infinitive or with a clause beginning 'in order to', 'in order that . . . would', or 'so that . . . would', rather than with 'will'.

---

[1] This is an oversimplification, for sometimes the perfect can function as a primary tense. This occurs only in contexts where it would be translated with 'have' in English (e.g. 'I have ruled'); such situations will not arise in this book.

The infinitive and 'in order to' can be used only if the subject of the subjunctive is the same as the subject of the sentence's main verb. For example:

ad urbem īvit ut rēgem vidēret. 'He went to the city to see the king.' / 'He went to the city in order to see the king.'
ad urbem īvit nē rēgem vidēret. 'He went to the city in order not to see the king.'
haec scrīpsit ut legerēmus. 'He wrote these things so that we would read them.'
puerō pecūniam dedērunt nē miser esset. 'They gave money to the boy so that he would not be miserable.'

Practice

A Translate (all have historic main verbs):

1 ad urbem ivit ut patrem peteret.
2 deos laudavit ut bona nobis darent.
3 illi nos iuverunt ne hostes nos vincerent.
4 illos iuvimus ut nos iuvarent.
5 ad urbem ivi ne in silva essem.
6 laudavistisne deos ut vos iuvarent?
7 deos laudavimus ne hostes ad urbem nostram ducerent.
8 ad urbem iverunt ut matrem iuvarent.
9 illi nos iuverunt ut hostes vinceremus.
10 illos iuvimus ut nos laudarent.
11 ivistine ad urbem ne patrem meum videres?
12 deos laudavi ut mihi bona darent.
13 illi nos iuverunt ne ad regem iremus.
14 ad urbem non iverunt ne fratrem viderent.
15 laudavistine deos ut tibi bona darent?
16 illi nos iuverunt ne miseri essemus.
17 ad urbem ivimus ut magistrum nostrum videremus.
18 illos iuvimus ne ad hostes irent.

B Translate (mixture of primary and historic main verbs):

1 rex milites e castris duxit ut hostes vincerent.
2 rex milites e castris ducit ut hostes vincant.
3 rex milites e castris ducet ut hostes vincant.
4 rex milites e castris ducat ut hostes vincant.
5 ad flumen ibo ut classem hostium videam.
6 ad flumen imus ut classem hostium videamus.
7 ad flumen ivit ut classem hostium videret.
8 ad flumen eamus ut classem hostium videamus.
9 ad flumen non eo ne classem hostium videam.
10 ad flumen non ibunt ne classem hostium videant.

11 ne eamus ad flumen ne classem hostium videamus.

12 ad flumen non iverunt ne classem hostium viderent.

13 ex oppido non imus ne hostes nos videant.

14 ex oppido non ii ne hostes me viderent.

15 ex oppido ne eamus ne hostes nos videant.

16 ex oppido non ibitis ne hostes vos videant.

17 ex oppido ibunt ut hostes videant.

18 ex oppido ivit ut hostes videret.

19 ex oppido eamus ut hostes videamus.

20 ex oppido eat ut hostes videat.

21 ite in silvam ne hostes vos videant.

C Without translating, state which verb in each sentence would be subjunctive in a purpose clause, whether it would be present or imperfect, and what its subject would be.

1 Next month I shall go to Rome to see the games.

2 We opened the box to see what was inside.

3 Are they coming to ask us questions?

4 Speak loudly so that we can all hear.

5 He worked so that his children would have food.

6 Marcus, do you want to have a chariot so that you can ride in style?

7 Let's hide so that the enemy scouts won't see us.

8 Last winter I went to Rome to see the games.

9 These men will fight so that we can be free.

10 You spoke loudly so that we could all hear.

11 Let's go to Rome to see the games.

12 He works so that his children will have food.

13 They died in order to save us.

14 Let's open the box to see what's inside.

15 Will you speak loudly so that we can all hear?

16 Soldiers, hide so that the enemy scouts will not see you.

17 They all came to help.

18 He will work so that his children have food.

19 These men fought so that we could be free.

20 Let's fight for ourselves so that these men do not have to do so yet again.

21 Should we hide so that the enemy scouts won't see us?

22 Let's speak loudly so that everyone can hear.

23 Brother, please go to Rome to see the games!

24 Did they come to ask us questions?

25 May these men fight so that we can be free!

26 We left the party early in order to get home on time.

27 We're opening the box to see what's inside.

28 We hid so that the enemy scouts would not see us.

29 Marcus wants to have a chariot so that he can ride in style.

30 He got up early in order to study before class.

31 I am going to Rome to see the games.

32 He speaks loudly so that we can all hear.

33 Will they come to ask us questions?

34 We shall hide so that the enemy scouts won't see us.

35 The boys all left in order not to get in trouble.

36 Marcus wanted to have a chariot so that he could ride in style.

37 Shall we open the box to see what's inside?

38 We are hiding so that the enemy scouts will not see us.

D Translate into Latin:

1   The king went to the camp to see the soldiers.

2   The king will go to the camp to see the soldiers.

3   The king is going to the camp in order to see the soldiers.

4   The king went to the camp so that he would see the soldiers.

5   The king will go to the camp so that he will see the soldiers.

6   The king is going to the camp so that he will see the soldiers.

7   May the king go to the camp to see the soldiers!

8   King, go to the camp in order to see the soldiers!

9   We wrote a letter to the king so that he would give us money.

10 We are writing a letter to the king so that he will give us money.

11 We shall write a letter to the king so that he will give us money.

12 Let's write a letter to the king so that he will give us money.

13 Write a letter to the king so that he will give you money!

14 Our brother ran to the farmer to buy a black horse.

15 Our brother will run to the farmer in order to buy a black horse.

16 Our brother is running to the farmer to buy a black horse.

17 Let our brother run to the farmer to buy a black horse.

18 Brother, run to the farmer to buy a black horse.

19 The slave led the sheep away from the river so that they would not run into the water.

20 The slave will lead the sheep away from the river so that they will not run into the water.

21 Let the slave lead the sheep away from the river so that they will not run into the water.

22 The slave is leading the sheep away from the river so that they will not run into the water.

23 Slave, lead the sheep away from the river so that they will not run into the water!

16.2 Reading Practice

Colloquium Harleianum 6a–c (adapted): continuation of the school scene in the preceding chapter.

TEACHER: nonne mercedem attulisti?

PUPIL: petivi patrem, et dixit, 'ego ipse ad scholam hodie veniam cum pecunia. volo enim et experimentum accipere.'

Vocabulary

nōnne = nōn + ne

mercēs, mercēdis (f.) 'tuition payment'

afferō, afferre, attulī, allātum 'bring'

petō *can also mean* 'ask'

ipse 'myself' (nominative)

schola, scholae (f.) 'school'

veniam 'I shall come'

volō, velle, voluī, – 'want'

enim 'for' (in the sense of 'because'; translate one word earlier than where it appears in Latin)

et 'also'

experīmentum, -ī (n.) 'demonstration (of your progress)'

16.3 Vocabulary to Learn

Verbs

impediō, impedīre, impedīvī, impedītum	'hinder'
interficiō, interficere, interfēcī, interfectum	'kill'
inveniō, invenīre, invēnī, inventum	'find'
reficiō, reficere, refēcī, refectum	'repair'
sentiō, sentīre, sēnsī, sēnsum	'perceive', 'feel'
sepeliō, sepelīre, sepelīvī, sepultum	'bury'
vendō, vendere, vendidī, venditum	'sell'
veniō, venīre, vēnī, ventum	'come'
vīvō, vīvere, vīxī, vīctum	'live'

17.1 Fourth and Mixed Conjugations

Latin verbs are divided into five conjugations; in addition to the three that you have already learned there is a fourth conjugation and a 'mixed' conjugation with characteristics of both third and fourth conjugations. The mixed conjugation is also called 'third conjugation in -iō' or 'third conjugation i-stems'. These verbs are conjugated as follows:

	Third conjugation *regō, regere, rēxī, rēctum* 'rule' (for comparison)	Fourth conjugation *audiō, audīre, audīvī, audītum* 'hear'	Mixed conjugation *capiō, capere, cēpī, captum* 'take', 'capture'
Present active indicative	regō	audiō	capiō
	regis	audīs	capis
	regit	audit	capit
	regimus	audīmus	capimus
	regitis	audītis	capitis
	regunt	audiunt	capiunt
Future active indicative	regam	audiam	capiam
	regēs	audiēs	capiēs
	reget	audiet	capiet
	regēmus	audiēmus	capiēmus
	regētis	audiētis	capiētis
	regent	audient	capient
Perfect active indicative	rēxī	audīvī	cēpī
	rēxistī	audīvistī	cēpistī
	rēxit	audīvit	cēpit
	rēximus	audīvimus	cēpimus
	rēxistis	audīvistis	cēpistis
	rēxērunt	audīvērunt	cēpērunt
Imperative	rege	audī	cape[1]
	regite	audīte	capite

[1] The imperative of *faciō* is irregular: *fac, facite.*

	Third conjugation *regō, regere, rēxī,* *rēctum* 'rule' (for comparison)	Fourth conjugation *audiō, audīre, audīvī,* *audītum* 'hear'	Mixed conjugation *capiō, capere, cēpī,* *captum* 'take', 'capture'
Present	regam	audiam	capiam
active	regās	audiās	capiās
subjunctive	regat	audiat	capiat
	regāmus	audiāmus	capiāmus
	regātis	audiātis	capiātis
	regant	audiant	capiant
Imperfect	regerem	audīrem	caperem
active	regerēs	audīrēs	caperēs
subjunctive	regeret	audīret	caperet
	regerēmus	audīrēmus	caperēmus
	regerētis	audīrētis	caperētis
	regerent	audīrent	caperent

As with the first and second conjugations, in the perfect indicative and imperfect subjunctive these verbs take exactly the same endings as the third-conjugation verbs. In the present and future indicative and in the present subjunctive they also take the same endings, with the addition of an *-i-* wherever there is not already an *-i-*.

Like verbs of the first three conjugations, fourth-conjugation verbs can be identified by their second principal parts: their infinitives end in *-īre*. Mixed-conjugation verbs are trickier to spot, since their second principal parts end in *-ere* like those of third-conjugation verbs: one has to use the combination of a first principal part in *-iō* (which third-conjugation verbs never have, though fourth-conjugation ones do) and a second principal part in *-ere* (which fourth-conjugation verbs never have, though third-conjugation ones do) to identify verbs of the mixed conjugation.

Practice

A Identify the conjugations to which each of these verbs belongs:

1 veniō, venīre, vēnī, ventum 'come'
2 accipiō, accipere, accēpī, accep-tum 'receive'
3 agō, agere, ēgī, āctum 'drive', 'do'
4 impediō, impedīre, impedīvī, impedītum 'hinder'
5 interficiō, interficere, interfēcī, interfectum 'kill'
6 inveniō, invenīre, invēnī, inven-tum 'find'
7 vīvō, vīvere, vīxī, vīctum 'live'
8 reficiō, reficere, refēcī, refectum 'repair'

9 sentiō, sentīre, sēnsī, sēnsum
   'perceive', 'feel'
10 sepeliō, sepelīre, sepelīvī, sepultum 'bury'

11 vendō, vendere, vendidī, venditum 'sell'
12 faciō, facere, fēcī, factum 'do',
   'make'

B Conjugate in the form indicated:

1 *veniō*, present active indicative
2 *faciō*, future active indicative
3 *impediō*, perfect active indicative
4 *interficiō*, present active
   subjunctive
5 *inveniō*, imperative active
6 *accipiō*, future active indicative
7 *reficiō*, imperfect active
   subjunctive
8 *sentiō*, present active subjunctive
9 *sepeliō*, present active indicative
10 *vendō*, future active indicative
11 *veniō*, perfect active indicative
12 *vīvō*, present active subjunctive

13 *agō*, present active indicative
14 *audiō*, future active indicative
15 *faciō*, imperative active
16 *impediō*, imperfect active
   subjunctive
17 *interficiō*, present active indicative
18 *inveniō*, present active
   subjunctive
19 *accipiō*, imperative active
20 *reficiō*, future active indicative
21 *sentiō*, perfect active indicative
22 *sepeliō*, present active subjunctive
23 *vendō*, present active subjunctive
24 *veniō*, future active indicative

C Translate:

1 moenia reficiamus ne hostes
   urbem capiant.
2 moenia refecimus ne hostes
   urbem caperent.
3 moenia reficiemus ne hostes
   urbem capiant.
4 quis oves bonas vendit?
5 quem interfecit frater
   illius?
6 cuius nomen audivisti?
7 frater meus multas oves vendidit
   ut pecuniam haberet.
8 frater meus multas oves vendet
   ut pecunicam habeat.
9 frater, oves vende ut pecuniam
   habeas!

10 oves vendamus ut pecuniam
   habeamus.
11 quid invenisti?
12 cui dedit rex hanc urbem?
13 cum quibus regem audivisti?
14 ad quod flumen venimus?
15 ille ad urbem venit ut sororem
   inveniat.
16 ille ad urbem venit ut sororem
   inveniret.
17 hic ad urbem veniet ut sororem
   inveniat.
18 hic ad urbem veniat ut sororem
   inveniat.
19 veniamus ad urbem ut sororem
   inveniamus.

20 veni ad urbem ut sororem
   invenias!
21 quid audivistis?
22 qui hostes veniunt?
23 cui demus has ovis?
24 quos interfecerunt hostes?
25 cuius verba audivisti?
26 quae moenia refecit ille?

27 cuius fratrem in urbe invenisti?
28 hi ad oppidum veniunt ut
   patrem sepeliant.
29 hi ad oppidum venerunt ut
   patrem sepelirent.
30 in quo agro sepelivistis patrem?
31 has oves in agrum agamus.
32 illas oves ex agro agat.

D Translate into Latin:

1 The citizens came to the city to
  hear the king's words.
2 The citizens will come to the city
  in order to hear the king's
  words.
3 The citizens are coming to the
  city to hear the king's words.
4 Let the citizens come to the city
  to hear the king's words.
5 Citizens, come to the city to hear
  the king's words!
6 Who has repaired the walls?
  Let's praise that man!
7 What are you selling?
8 To whom should I give those
  animals?
9 Whose father did they bury?
10 The soldiers repaired our walls
   to hinder the enemy.
11 Let the soldiers repair our walls
   in order to hinder the enemy.

12 The soldiers will repair our walls
   so that they will hinder the
   enemy.
13 Who killed this soldier?
14 Which soldier did he kill?
15 Whose mother heard you?
   yours? mine?
16 The enemy came across the river
   to conquer our men.
17 The enemy is coming across the
   river to conquer our men.
18 The enemy will come across the
   river in order to conquer our
   men.
19 To which brother did you give
   my book? You have five
   brothers!
20 What have you buried in my
   field?

17.2 Reading Practice

Colloquium Harleianum 6d–f (adapted): continuation of the school scene in the preceding chapter.

TEACHER: age ergo diligenter, ut paratus sis.
PUPIL: paratus sum; incendi enim lucernam et nocte legi.
TEACHER: bene fecisti; te laudo.

Vocabulary

ergō 'therefore' (translate one word
    earlier than where it appears in Latin)
dīligenter 'diligently'
parātus, parāta, parātum 'ready'
incendō, incendere, incendī, incēnsum
    'light'

enim 'for' (in the sense of 'because';
    translate one word earlier than
    where it appears in Latin)
lucerna, lucernae (f.) 'lamp'
nocte 'at night'

18.1 *Colloquia Monacensia–Einsidlensia* 2g–l (adapted)

A boy goes to school (perhaps first century AD):

Veni in scholam. intravi, dixi: 'Ave, magister', et ipse me osculatus est et resalutavit.
porrexit mihi puer meus scriniarius tabulas, thecam graphiariam, praeductorium. loco
meo sedens delevi. praeduxi ad praescriptum; postquam scripsi, ostendi magistro;
emendavit. iussit me legere; legi. iussus librum alii puero dedi. didici interpretamenta,
reddidi. sed statim dictavit mihi condiscipulus. 'Et tu', dixit, 'dicta mihi'. dixi ei: 'Redde
primo'. et dixit mihi: 'Nonne vidisti, cum redderem prior te?' et dixi: 'Mentiris, non
reddidisti.' 'Non mentior.' 'Si verum dicis, dictabo tibi.'

Vocabulary (in order of first appearance; words that appear more than once are in bold)

schola, scholae (f.) 'school'
intrō, intrāre, intrāvī, intrātum 'enter'
avē 'hello!'
ipse 'himself' (masculine nominative)
ōsculātus est 'he kissed'
resalūtō, -āre, -āvī, -ātum 'return the
  greeting'
porrigō, porrigere, porrēxi, porrēctum
  'hand', 'pass'
scrīniārius, -a, -um 'in charge of
  carrying writing materials' (a
  Roman schoolboy often had
  a personal slave boy to carry his
  things to and from school)
tabula, tabulae (f.) 'writing tablet' (made
  of wax-coated wood; one could write
  on the wax using a sharp-pointed
  stylus and then erase the writing by
  smoothing out the wax with the flat
  end of the same stylus)
thēca, thēcae (f.) 'case'
graphiārius, -a, -um 'for styluses'

praeductōrium, -ī (n.) 'ruler'
locō 'in place'
sedēns 'sitting'
dēleō, dēlēre, dēlēvī, dēlētum 'erase' (the
  previous day's work)
praedūcō (like *dūcō*) 'rule lines'
ad (+ accusative) 'following'
praescrīptum, -ī (n.) 'model'
postquam 'after'
ostendō, ostendere, ostendī, ostentum
  'show'
ēmendō, -āre, -āvī, -ātum 'correct'
iubeō, iubēre, iussī, iussum 'order'
  (therefore *iussus* = 'ordered' (see
  chapter 6.2), but here it is best
  translated 'when ordered', i.e.
  when the teacher asked him)
alius, alia, aliud 'another', 'other' (*alii*
  is a dative singular)
dedī: *there is only one book in the
  classroom, and different boys read
  from it in turn.*

disco, discere, didici, – 'learn'

interpretāmentum, -ī (n.) 'elementary
  language textbook'

**reddō, reddere, reddidī, redditum
  'produce' (from memory), 'recite'**

statim 'at once'

**dictō, dictāre, dictāvī, dictātum 'give
  dictation practice'**

condiscipulus, condiscipulī (m.) 'fellow
  student'

et 'too'

eī 'to him'

prīmō 'first'

nōnne = nōn + -ne

cum redderem 'when I recited'

prior tē 'before you'

mentīris 'you are lying'

mentior 'I am lying'

sī 'if'

vērus, vēra, vērum 'true'

18.2 *Colloquia Monacensia–Einsidlensia* 2m–u (adapted)

Continuation of passage 18.1:

Inter haec iubente magistro surgunt pusilli ad elementa, et syllabas praebet eis unus
maiorum. alii ad subdoctorem ordine reddunt, nomina scribunt, versus scribunt, et
ego in prima classe dictatum excipio. deinde postquam sedimus, pertranseo commen-
tarium, lexicon, artem. vocatus ad lectionem audio expositiones et sensus. interrogatus
artificia respondeo: 'Ad quem dicit?' et 'Quae pars orationis?'. declino nomina, partior
versum. postquam haec egimus, magister nos ad prandium dimittit. dimissus venio
domum. muto, accipio panem candidum, olivas, caseum, caricas, nuces. bibo aquam
frigidam. pransus revertor iterum in scholam. invenio magistrum perlegentem, et
dicit: 'Incipite ab initio.'

> **Vocabulary** (in order of first appearance; words that appear more than once are in bold, and
> those in bold in the preceding vocabulary list are omitted)

inter (+ accusative) 'during'

iubente magistrō 'when the teacher
  orders'

surgō, surgere, surrēxī, surrēctum 'rise'

pusillus, pusilla, pusillum 'little'
  (substantivized here)

**ad (+ accusative) 'for' (i.e. 'to recite',
  'to do')**

elementum, elementī (n.) 'letter' (of the
  alphabet)

syllaba, syllabae (f.) 'syllable'

praebeō, praebēre, praebuī, praebitum
  'give' (The idea is that once the
  children can read the individual
  letters, they practise reading
  syllables such as 'ba' or 'mo', which

the older child writes down for them
  to read aloud. Only after learning to
  read syllables did ancient children
  progress to reading whole words.)

eīs 'to them'

ūnus, ūna, ūnum 'one'

maiōrēs, maiōrum (m. plural) 'bigger
  children'

subdoctor, subdoctōris (m.) 'teacher's
  assistant'

ōrdine 'in order'

**versus, versūs (m.) 'verse' (accusative
  plural *versūs*)**

prīmus, prīma, prīmum 'first'

classis, classis, classium (f.) 'class'

dictātum, dictātī (n.) 'exercise'

excipiō, excipere, excēpī, exceptum 'receive' (as an assignment)

deinde 'then'

sedeō, sedēre, sēdī, sessum 'sit down'

pertrānseō (like eō) 'go through'

commentārius, commentāriī (m.) 'commentary'

lexicon, lexicī (n.) 'dictionary'

ars, artis, artium (f.) 'grammar book'

vocō, vocāre, vocāvī, vocātum 'call' (translate vocātus following the pattern of iussus in extract 18.1)

lēctiō, lēctiōnis (f.) 'reading (aloud)'

expositiō, expositiōnis (f.) 'explanation'

sēnsūs 'meanings' (accusative plural)

interrogō, -āre, -āvī, -ātum 'ask' (translate interrogātus following the pattern of iussus in extract 18.1)

artificium, artificiī (n.) 'grammatical question'

respondeō, respondēre, respondī, respōnsum 'answer'

pars, partis (f.) 'part'

ōrātiō, ōrātiōnis (f.) 'speech'

dēclīnō, dēclīnāre, dēclīnāvī, dēclīnātum 'decline'

nōmen can also mean 'noun'

partior, partīrī, partītus sum 'parse' (i.e. find the subject, verb, object, etc.) (the imperative would be partire)

prandium, prandiī (n.) 'lunch'

dīmittō (like mittō) 'dismiss' (translate dīmissus following the pattern of iussus in extract 18.1)

domum '(to) home'

mūtō, mūtāre, mūtāvī, mūtātum 'change (clothes)'

pānis, pānis, pānium (m.) 'bread'

candidus, candida, candidum 'white'

olīva, olīvae (f.) 'olive'

cāseus, cāseī (m.) 'cheese'

cārica, cāricae (f.) 'dried fig'

nux, nucis (f.) 'nut'

bibō, bibere, bibī, – 'drink'

frīgidus, frīgida, frīgidum 'chilled'

prānsus, prānsa, prānsum 'having eaten lunch'

revertor 'I return'

iterum 'again'

perlegēns, gen. perlegentis 'reading (something) over'

incipiō (like capiō) 'begin'

initium, initiī (n.) 'beginning'

18.3 Translate into Latin

Use the story above as a model, making adjustments for differences as needed.

I entered into the school and said, 'Hello, teacher! Hello, fellow students!' I sat in my place and received[1] from my boy in-charge-of-carrying-writing-materials a tablet and a ruler. I wrote words on (= in) the tablet, I wrote a verse. I showed my tablet to the teacher; he corrected (it). When the teacher ordered,[2] the bigger children rose for readings. They answered grammatical questions: 'Decline this!' 'Parse this verse!' One of those boys gave us little ones letters and syllables. Then we went home to lunch. I changed, I received bread and cheese from my slave. Having eaten lunch I went to school again.

[1] Use *accipiō* not *excipiō* here (and for the other instance of 'receive' in this passage).

[2] Use the phrase translated above with 'when the teacher orders'; this takes its tense in English from the surrounding context and will therefore mean 'when the teacher ordered' here.

19 | Infinitives and Indirect Statement

19.1 **Indirect Statement**

In both Latin and English words may be reported either in direct or in indirect speech: direct speech is the type that uses quotation marks and repeats the exact words of the original statement, and indirect speech does not use quotation marks, is often introduced by 'that', and does not repeat the original words exactly.

> Direct: 'He said, "I will come soon."'
> Indirect: 'He said that he would come soon.' or 'He said he would come soon.'

In Latin, indirect statement (which can be used not only with verbs meaning 'say', but also with verbs having related meanings such as 'hear') is expressed with a subject in the accusative and a verb in the infinitive. The subject must always be expressed, since an infinitive does not provide any information on what the subject is; the reason indicative and subjunctive verbs often do not have expressed subjects in Latin is that their endings convey all the necessary information.

> *dīcit hostēs venīre.* 'He says (that) the enemy is coming.'
> *dīcit rēgem adesse.* 'He says (that) the king is present.'
> *dīcunt illam puellam pulchram esse.* 'They say (that) that girl is beautiful.'

Notice that in this last example *pulchram* is accusative despite being associated with a form of *sum*. In chapter 5.3 we saw that *sum* takes the same case as its subject, and that therefore in most circumstances *sum* effectively takes the nominative, since subjects are usually nominative. But when a subject is accusative, any word linked to that subject by *sum* will also be accusative.

When an indirect statement contains two accusatives, either may in theory be the subject, though in practice one often works better than the other in the role of subject.

dīcit tē rēgem laudāre. 'He says (that) you praise the king.' / 'He says (that) the king praises you.'

dīcit tē equum laudāre. 'He says (that) you praise the horse.'

Practice

A Translate:

1 dicit puerum venire.
2 dicit puellam scribere.
3 audio nostros vincere hostes. (2 ways)
4 dicit te me amare. (2 ways)
5 dicit vos deos laudare.
6 audio magistrum pueros docere.
7 dicit nos bonos esse.
8 dicit equum magnum esse.
9 dicit agricolam pecuniam habere.
10 dicit saxa in agro esse.
11 audio regem in urbe esse.
12 audio milites in castris esse.
13 dicit consilium tuum bonum esse.
14 dicit te pulchrum esse.

19.2 Tenses of the Infinitive

When the original statement was not in the present tense but in the past or the future, a perfect or future infinitive needs to be used. The perfect infinitive is formed by adding *-isse* to the perfect stem (the third principal part without its final *-ī*), and the future infinitive is formed by replacing the *-um* of the fourth principal part with *-ūrus* (*-ūra, -ūrum*) *esse*. (If the fourth principal part already ends in *-ūrus*, no change is necessary.)

	Present infinitive	**Perfect infinitive**	**Future infinitive**
First conjugation	amāre	amāvisse	amātūrus, -a, -um esse
Second conjugation	monēre	monuisse	monitūrus, -a, -um esse
Third conjugation	regere	rēxisse	rēctūrus, -a, -um esse
Fourth conjugation	audīre	audīvisse	audītūrus, -a, -um esse
Mixed conjugation	capere	cēpisse	captūrus, -a, -um esse
Sum	esse	fuisse	futūrus, -a, -um esse
Possum	posse	potuisse	–
Eō	īre	īvisse/īsse	itūrus, -a, -um esse

Practice

B Give these infinitives:

1 *currō*, perfect infinitive
2 *laudō*, future infinitive
3 *habeō*, present infinitive
4 *interficiō*, future infinitive
5 *exeō*, perfect infinitive
6 *agō*, future infinitive
7 *dō*, present infinitive
8 *reficiō*, future infinitive
9 *doceō*, perfect infinitive
10 *adsum*, future infinitive

11 *faciō*, present infinitive	19 *audiō*, present infinitive
12 *sentiō*, future infinitive	20 *vīvō*, future infinitive
13 *iuvō*, perfect infinitive	21 *absum*, perfect infinitive
14 *videō*, future infinitive	22 *accipiō*, future infinitive
15 *abeō*, present infinitive	23 *timeō*, present infinitive
16 *sepeliō*, future infinitive	24 *vendō*, perfect infinitive
17 *inveniō*, perfect infinitive	25 *veniō*, future infinitive
18 *impediō*, future infinitive	

19.3 Agreement of the Future Infinitive

The future infinitive agrees with its subject in gender, number, and case; the case in an indirect statement, of course, is always accusative.

> *dīcunt puellam rēgem amatūram esse.* 'They say that the girl will love the king.'
> *dīcunt puellam rēgem amatūrum esse.* 'They say that the king will love the girl.'
> *dīcit illum nōs vīsūrum esse.* 'He says that that man will see us.'
> *dīcit illum nōs vīsūrōs esse.* 'He says that we shall see that man.'

This agreement means that indirect statements with a future infinitive are less likely to be ambiguous than those with present or past infinitives.

Practice

C Translate:

1 dicit nos te visuros esse.
2 dicit nos te visurum esse.
3 audio illum vos petiturum esse.
4 audio illum vos petituros esse.
5 dicunt hanc illum amaturum esse.
6 dicunt hanc illum amaturam esse.
7 audimus puellas viros laudaturos esse.
8 audimus puellas viros laudaturas esse.
9 dicisne agricolam animalia ducturum esse?
10 dicisne agricolam animalia ductura esse?

19.4 Use of Infinitive Tenses

In formal written English, sequence of tenses applies to indirect statements: if the verb of saying is in the past, the verb of the subordinate clause is usually not in the same form as it would have been in the original direct statement. Thus an indirect statement 'He said that they had already arrived' means that what the messenger actually said was 'They have already arrived', and 'He said that they would arrive soon' means that the original statement was 'They will arrive soon.' The English tense changes are as follows:

Original sentence	Indirect speech after present tense	Indirect speech after past tense
I ate a fish.	He says he ate a fish.	He said he **had eaten** a fish.
I eat fish.	He says he eats fish.	He said he **ate** fish.
I am eating a fish.	He says he is eating a fish.	He said he **was eating** a fish.
I shall eat a fish.	He says he will eat a fish.	He said he **would eat** a fish.

In Latin the tense of the infinitive is the same as the tense of the original direct statement; in other words, the tense of the infinitive is *relative* to that of the main verb. The present infinitive is used for an original present tense, while the perfect and future infinitives are used for original perfect and future tenses.

ille tē amat. 'That man loves you.' → *dīxī illum tē amāre.* 'I said that that man loved you.' (English uses a past tense in the subordinate verb, but Latin uses a present.)

ille tē amāvit. 'That man loved you.' → *dīxī illum tē amāvisse.* 'I said that that man had loved you.' (English uses a pluperfect in the subordinate verb, but Latin uses a perfect.)

ille tē amābit. 'That man will love you.' → *dīxī illum tē amātūrum esse.* 'I said that that man would love you.' (English uses 'would' in the subordinate verb, but Latin uses a future.)

Therefore when translating in either direction it is usually necessary to adjust the tenses of the subordinate verb(s) if the main verb is in a past tense.

Practice

D For each of the indirect statements below, reconstruct the original direct sentence. Be sure to change the verb tense if the main verb is past. Example: 'He said he was coming' has an original sentence 'I am coming.'

1 He said it was raining.
2 He says it will rain.
3 He said it had rained.
4 He said it would rain.
5 He says it rains a lot here.
6 They say he has lost his shield.
7 They said he would lose his shield.
8 They said he was losing his shield.
9 They say he will lose his shield.
10 They said he had lost his shield.
11 She says they are brave.
12 She said they had been brave.
13 She said they would be brave.
14 She says they were brave.
15 She says they will be brave.
16 She said they were brave.

E Translate:

1 dicit te currere.
2 dixit te currere.
3 dicit te cucurrisse.
4 dixit te cucurrisse.
5 dicit te cursurum esse.
6 dixit te cursurum esse.

7 audio te currere.
8 audivi te currere.
9 audio te cucurrisse.
10 audivi te cucurrisse.
11 audio te cursurum esse.
12 audivi te cursurum esse.

F Translate:

1 dixit illos venisse.
2 audivi patrem meum hic esse.
3 dixi me posse.
4 dixistine deos nos ituros esse?
5 dixisti te illud nobis daturum esse.
6 dixerunt illam matrem tuam esse.
7 audivimus vos reges fuisse.
8 dixit vos moenia refecturos esse.
9 audivi te hunc librum scripsisse.
10 dixit haec verba mala esse.
11 dixistine te hoc legere posse?
12 dixi me milites ducere.
13 dixit nos magistros futuros esse.
14 dixi me poetam esse.
15 dixit nos hostes victuros esse.
16 dixistine illos posse nos audire?

17 audivimus te librum scripturum esse.
18 dixi hunc equum meum fuisse.
19 dixisti te nos iuvare posse.
20 diximus nos te visuras esse.
21 dixit matrem tuam te petere.
22 audivit nos equum bonum habere.
23 audivi te agricolam fuisse.
24 dixistine te poetam futurum esse?
25 dixerunt vos in agro stetisse.
26 dixerunt nos in agro stare.
27 dixerunt illam puellam pulchram esse.
28 audivi te nobiscum venturam esse.

G Translate into Latin:[1]

1 I said that that man had come yesterday.
2 I said that that man would come today.
3 They said this woman was beautiful.
4 They said this woman had been beautiful.

5 He said you (singular) would read the book tomorrow.
6 He said you (singular) had read the book.
7 He said you (plural) were reading the book yesterday.
8 He said that the soldiers were seeking us.

---

[1] For exercises offering practice at identifying indirect statement in English sentences and distinguishing it from other constructions, with an answer key, see chapter 63.8.

9 He said that the soldiers had sought us.

10 He said the book was good.

11 She said that the book was big.

12 She said that the book would be big.

13 They said you (singular) had buried (your) father.

14 They said you (plural) would bury (your) father.

15 We said that the horses were in the forest.

16 We said that the horses had been in the forest.

17 Did you say that that farmer had sold the sheep?

18 Did you say that that farmer was selling the sheep?

19 Did you say that that farmer would sell the sheep?

20 Did he say that the enemies' camp was without water?

21 Did she say that the enemies' camp had been without water?

19.5 Reading Practice

Colloquium Montepessulanum, 4a–g (adapted): an early-morning messenger (probably third century A D).

LUCIUS' SLAVE: quis pulsat ostium?

GAIUS' SLAVE (*outside*): nuntius a Gaio ad Lucium. si hic est, nuntia me.

LUCIUS' SLAVE (*to Lucius*): venit a Gaio.

LUCIUS: roga illum. (*to Gaius' slave*) quid est, puer? omnia recte?

GAIUS' SLAVE: etiam, domine. misit tibi epistulam signatam.

LUCIUS: da, legam. . . . scripsit mihi de negotio. vade, puer, et nuntia me venturum esse. (*to his own slaves*) date mihi calceamenta, affer aquam ad faciem, da tunicam, cinge me, da togam, operi me, da paenulam et anulos. cur stas, amice? tolle haec et veni mecum. festino ad amicum antiquum, senatorem populi Romani, qui a Romulo deducit genus, a Troianis Aeneadis.

Vocabulary (in order of first appearance; words that appear more than once are in bold)

pulsō, pulsāre, pulsāvī, pulsātum 'knock on'

ōstium, ōstiī (n.) 'door'

nūntius, nūntiī (m.) 'messenger'

nūntiō, nūntiāre, nūntiāvī, nūntiātum 'announce'

rogō, rogāre, rogāvī, rogātum 'invite inside'

omnia rēctē 'is everything okay?'

etiam 'yes'

dominus, dominī (m.) 'sir'

signō, signāre, signāvī, signātum 'seal'

negōtium, negōtiī (n.) 'business'

vādō, vādere, –, – 'go'

calceāmentum, calceāmentī (n.) 'shoe'

affer 'bring!' (imperative singular)

ad faciem 'for washing my face'

tunica, tunicae (f.) 'tunic'

cingō, cingere, cīnxī, cīnctum 'put the belt on'

toga, togae (f.) 'toga'

operiō, operīre, operuī, opertum 'drape'

paenula, paenulae (f.) 'cape'
ānulus, ānulī (m.) 'ring'
tollō, tollere, sustulī, sublātum
     'pick up'
festīnō, festīnāre, festīnāvī, festīnātum
     'hasten to the aid of', 'hasten to help'
antīquus, antīqua, antīquum 'old'
senātor, senātōris (m.) 'senator'

populus, populī (m.) 'people'
Rōmulus, Rōmulī (m.) *name of the*
     legendary founder of Rome
dēdūcō (like *dūcō*) 'trace'
genus, generis (n.) 'ancestry'
Troiānus, Troiāna, Troiānum 'Trojan'
Aeneadae, Aeneadārum (m. plural)
     'descendants of Aeneas'

19.6 Vocabulary to Learn

Verbs
vocō, vocāre, vocāvī, vocātum   'call'

Nouns
caput, capitis (n.)	'head'
homō, hominis (m.)	'human being'
laus, laudis (f.)	'praise'

Adjectives
longus, longa, longum	'long'
parvus, parva, parvum	'small'
vērus, vēra, vērum	'true'

Adverbs
diū	'for a long time'

20 | Reflexives

20.1 Reflexive Pronoun

A word that refers back to the subject of a sentence is a reflexive. In English reflexives are often indicated with '-self', as 'He saw himself in the mirror', in which the word 'himself' indicates that the person seen in the mirror is the same as the one seeing. (Compare 'He saw him in the mirror', in which the person seen is different from the one seeing.) In Latin the first- and second-person reflexives are the same as the personal pronouns we have already seen; in other words a Roman said 'me', 'you', or 'us' where we would say 'myself', 'yourself', 'ourselves'. Thus *mē videō* 'I see myself', *nōs vidēmus* 'we see ourselves'. In the third person the reflexive pronoun is *sē*, which has its own declension: it makes no distinction between singular and plural or between the three genders, but it does have distinct forms for different cases.

British Case Order	
All numbers and genders	
Nom.	–
Voc.	–
Acc.	sē/sēsē
Gen.	suī
Dat.	sibi
Abl.	sē/sēsē

Ancient Case Order	
All numbers and genders	
Nom./Voc.	–
Gen.	suī
Dat.	sibi
Acc.	sē/sēsē
Abl.	sē/sēsē

The reflexive pronoun has no nominative or vocative, because the nature of a reflexive means that it is never used in those cases. Apart from that, it bears a strong resemblance to the personal pronouns *ego* and *tū*, and that resemblance includes the peculiarities of usage of those pronouns: the genitive *suī* is not used for possession, only for other uses such as the partitive or objective genitive, and the ablative combines with *cum* to form *sēcum*.

sē docuit. 'He taught himself.' or 'She taught herself.'
sē docuērunt. 'They taught themselves.'

laus suī mala est. 'Praise of oneself is bad.'
sibi bona dedērunt. 'They gave themselves good things.'
sēcum fīlium dūxit. 'He led his son with himself.' (i.e. 'He brought his son with him.')

20.2 Reflexive Possession

Reflexive possession (that is, possession by the subject of the sentence) is indicated by the adjective *suus, sua, suum* and translated in English either with an ordinary possessive ('his', 'her', 'their') or with a reflexive possessive ('his own', 'her own', 'their own').

urbem suam amat. 'He loves his city.' / 'He loves his own city.'
nōmina sua dīxērunt. 'They said their names.' / 'They said their own names.'

But reflexive possession is not normally expressed in Latin when the word for the possessed thing implies relationship; when reflexive possession is expressed with such words, it is always emphatic.

patrem amat. 'He loves his father.' (possessive not necessary as 'father' implies
    relationship)
patrem suum interfēcit. 'He killed his own father.' (possessive used despite the fact that
    'father' implies relationship, in order to emphasize the horror of the crime)

Practice

A Translate:

1 illi se laudant.
2 illa se laudavit.
3 verba sua audire non potuit.
4 verba sua audire non possunt.
5 sese in aqua vidit.
6 sese in aqua vident.
7 gladium suum sepelivit.

8 patrem sepelivit.
9 equum novum sibi dedit.
10 equos novos sibi dabunt.
11 cives regem suum interfecerunt.
12 matrem vocavit.
13 cives liberi se regunt.
14 in agrum se duxit.

B Translate into Latin:

1 He cannot read his own book.
2 This man loves himself.
3 The sheep saw themselves in the
    river.
4 The sheep sees itself in the river.
5 They heard their own words.
6 He will not hear his own words.

7 Miserable (men) do not help
    themselves.
8 This miserable (woman) will
    help herself.
9 Our men are hindering
    themselves.
10 He will hinder himself.

20.3 Translation of the Reflexive

The Latin reflexive is not always translated with '-self' in English, because it is not always equivalent to an English reflexive. In two situations it is regularly the equivalent of English 'he'/'him', 'she'/'her', 'they'/'them': in indirect statement and in purpose clauses. In indirect statement reflexives are used when the subject of the reported statement is the same as the subject of the main verb; in other words, when the subject of the original direct statement was 'I'/'we'.

dīxit sē ad urbem īvisse. 'He said that he had gone to the city.' (original direct statement: 'I have gone to the city.')
dīxērunt sē pecūniam inventūrōs esse. 'They said that they would find the money.' (original direct statement: 'We shall find the money.')

In purpose clauses reflexives are used in the subordinate clause to refer back to the subject of the main verb.

vēnit ut sē laudārēmus. 'He came so that we would praise him.'
illī mē iūvērunt ut sē iuvārem. 'Those men helped me so that I would help them.'

Therefore it is important when translating *sē* to think about the construction in which it occurs: in a main clause it is normally equivalent to English 'himself' etc., but in a subordinate clause it is normally equivalent to English 'him' etc.

Practice

C Translate:

1 dixit se me amare.
2 dixerunt se ad urbem cucurrisse.
3 pater meus dixit se ovem interfecturum esse.
4 ad vos ivit ut se moneretis.
5 rex noster se interfecit.
6 rex dixit se bene regere.
7 venit ut se iuvaretis.
8 milites dicent se hostes vicisse.
9 multi se amant.
10 hic dicit se moenia refecturum esse.
11 deos laudavit ut se iuvarent.
12 illi se regere non possunt.
13 frater tuus dicit se oves venditurum esse.
14 milites se impediverunt.
15 servi dixerunt se capita ovium sepelivisse.
16 ad nos veniet ut se iuvemus.
17 multi homines se docere non possunt.
18 pueri dixerunt se pecuniam invenisse.
19 in silvam iverunt ne se videremus.
20 mater mea se iuvare non potuit.
21 ille dixit se magistrum bonum esse.

22 vos iuverunt ut se laudaretis.

23 hostes dixerunt se nostros victuros esse.

24 multi se laudant.

25 ad urbem venit ut se doceremus.

26 nostri dicunt se classem hostium vicisse.

27 ad nos scripserunt ne se impediremus.

28 hic epistulas sibi mittit.

29 dicit se gladium habere.

30 frater meus non me audit, sed se audit.

31 ex urbe exivit ne hostes se interficerent.

32 rex dixit se cives iuturum esse.

D Translate into Latin using forms of *sē*:

1 He said he had bought a horse.

2 They will see themselves.

3 They said that they would rule well.

4 He wrote to me so that I would write to him.

5 He is afraid of himself.

6 He said that he would help us.

7 The boys ran so that we would not capture them.

8 They said they were praising the gods.

9 Our mother did not kill herself.

10 He called (to) us so that we would not seek him.

11 They say that they are seeking (their) mother.

12 My sister does not praise herself.

13 He will say that he is seeking (his) father.

14 They gave you money so that you would teach them.

15 He said he would see us here.

16 He cannot send himself to the city.

17 He said that so that we would praise him.

18 She said she would teach those boys.

19 These men have taught themselves.

20 She said she could teach those boys.

21 They ran so that we would not see them.

22 Does God love himself?

23 They said they did not have money.

24 He gave us money so that we would help him.

25 He cannot hear himself.

26 He said that he had found this in the forest.

20.4 Reading Practice

1 Livy, *Ab urbe condita* 1.51.3–4 (adapted): a king tries to get rid of someone by means of a false accusation (written in the first century BC about a much earlier and partly mythical period).

Tarquinius paulo ante lucem accitis ad se principibus Latinorum, quasi re nova perturbatus, dicit moram suam hesternam saluti sibi et illis fuisse: Turnum se et primores interfecturum esse, ut Latinos solus regat. hunc hesterno die haec facere voluisse, sed non potuisse quia afuerit.

Vocabulary (in order of first appearance; words that appear more than once are in bold)

Tarquinius, -ī (m.) 'Tarquin' (the name of an early king of Rome)

paulō 'a little'

ante (+ accusative) 'before'

lūx, lūcis (f.) 'daylight'

accītīs prīncipibus 'when the leading men had been summoned'

Latīnus, Latīna, Latīnum 'Roman'

quasi 'as if'

rē novā 'by an attempt at revolution'

perturbō, -āre, -āvī, -ātum 'alarm'

mora, morae (f.) 'delay' (Tarquin had not appeared when he was expected)

hesternus, hesterna, hesternum 'on the previous day'

salūtī sum (+ dative) 'be the salvation of'

Turnus, -ī (m.) *the name of a man Tarquin did not like*

prīmor, prīmōris (m.) 'nobleman'

sōlus, sōla, sōlum 'by himself'

hesternō diē 'on the previous day'

volō, velle, voluī, – 'want'

āfuerit 'he (Tarquin) was absent'

2 *Colloquium Montepessulanum* 6a–b (adapted): a panegyric of a god (probably third century AD).

STUDENT: laudem scripsi.

TEACHER: cuius?

STUDENT: Iovis Capitolini.

TEACHER: lege. (*afterwards*) bene dixisti; tolle coronam. nemo tibi contradicit.

Vocabulary

laus, laudis (f.) 'praise', 'panegyric'

Iuppiter, Iovis (m.) 'Jupiter'

Capitōlīnus, -a, -um 'Capitolinus' (a title of Jupiter in Rome)

tollō, tollere, sustulī, sublātum 'take'

corōna, corōnae (f.) 'crown' (indicating victory in a competition)

nēmō (m.) 'no-one' (nominative)

contrādīcō (like *dīcō*) 'speak in opposition' (takes object in dative)

3 *Colloquium Harleianum* 26a–d (adapted): a rebuke (second or third century AD).

Quid est, frater? cur non venisti ad templum? ego te sustinui et propter te tarde prandi.

Vocabulary

templum, templī (n.) 'temple'

sustineō, sustinēre, sustinuī, sustentum
  'wait for'

propter (+ accusative) 'on account of'

tardē (adverb) 'late'

prandeō, prandēre, prandī, prānsum
  'eat lunch'

20.5 Vocabulary to Learn

Verbs

āmittō, āmittere, āmīsī, āmissum	'lose'
fugiō, fugere, fūgī, fugitūrus	'flee'
pugnō, pugnāre, pugnāvī, pugnātum	'fight'

Nouns

domina, dominae (f.)	'mistress'
dominus, dominī (m.)	'master'

Pronoun

sē	'himself', 'herself', 'themselves'

Adjective

suus, sua, suum	'his (own)', 'her (own)', 'their (own)'

Adverbs

numquam	'never'
saepe	'often'
semper	'always'

21.1 Formation of Third-Declension Adjectives

Adjectives, like nouns, can belong to the third declension, and third-declension adjectives are *i*-stems. They come in three varieties: adjectives of three terminations such as *ācer, ācris, ācre* have different forms for all three genders in the nominative singular, adjectives of two terminations such as *trīstis, trīste* have the same form for the masculine and feminine but a different form for the neuter in the nominative singular, and adjectives of one termination such as *fēlīx* have only one form for all three genders in the nominative singular. In the plural, all three types have one form for the masculine and feminine and a different form for the neuter. The stem of three-termination and two-termination adjectives can be found by dropping the *-is* from the feminine nominative singular; the stem of one-termination adjectives can be found by dropping the *-is* from the genitive singular, which will be given in the vocabulary for these adjectives only.

British Case Order

Adjectives of three terminations: *ācer, ācris, ācre* 'sharp, keen'

	Singular			Plural	
	Masculine	Feminine	Neuter	Masculine and feminine	Neuter
Nom.	ācer	ācris	ācre	ācrēs	ācria
Voc.	ācer	ācris	ācre	ācrēs	ācria
Acc.	ācrem	ācrem	ācre	ācrēs/ācrīs	ācria
Gen.	ācris	ācris	ācris	ācrium	ācrium
Dat.	ācrī	ācrī	ācrī	ācribus	ācribus
Abl.	ācrī	ācrī	ācrī	ācribus	ācribus

British Case Order (*continued*)

Adjectives of two terminations: *trīstis, trīste* 'sad'

| | Singular | | Plural | |
	Masculine and feminine	Neuter	Masculine and feminine	Neuter
Nom.	trīstis	trīste	trīstēs	trīstia
Voc.	trīstis	trīste	trīstēs	trīstia
Acc.	trīstem	trīste	trīstēs/trīstīs	trīstia
Gen.	trīstis	trīstis	trīstium	trīstium
Dat.	trīstī	trīstī	trīstibus	trīstibus
Abl.	trīstī	trīstī	trīstibus	trīstibus

Adjectives of one termination: *fēlīx*, gen. *fēlīcis* 'happy, fortunate'

| | Singular | | Plural | |
	Masculine and feminine	Neuter	Masculine and feminine	Neuter
Nom.	fēlīx	fēlīx	fēlīcēs	fēlīcia
Voc.	fēlīx	fēlīx	fēlīcēs	fēlīcia
Acc.	fēlīcem	fēlīx	fēlīcēs/fēlīcīs	fēlīcia
Gen.	fēlīcis	fēlīcis	fēlīcium	fēlīcium
Dat.	fēlīcī	fēlīcī	fēlīcibus	fēlīcibus
Abl.	fēlīcī	fēlīcī	fēlīcibus	fēlīcibus

Ancient Case Order

Adjectives of three terminations: *ācer, ācris, ācre* 'sharp, keen'

| | Singular | | | Plural | |
	Masculine	Feminine	Neuter	Masculine and feminine	Neuter
Nom./Voc.	ācer	ācris	ācre	ācrēs	ācria
Gen.	ācris	ācris	ācris	ācrium	ācrium
Dat.	ācrī	ācrī	ācrī	ācribus	ācribus
Acc.	ācrem	ācrem	ācre	ācrēs/ācrīs	ācria
Abl.	ācrī	ācrī	ācrī	ācribus	ācribus

Ancient Case Order (*continued*)

Adjectives of two terminations: *trīstis, trīste* 'sad'

	Singular		Plural	
	Masculine and feminine	Neuter	Masculine and feminine	Neuter
Nom./Voc.	trīstis	trīste	trīstēs	trīstia
Gen.	trīstis	trīstis	trīstium	trīstium
Dat.	trīstī	trīstī	trīstibus	trīstibus
Acc.	trīstem	trīste	trīstēs/trīstīs	trīstia
Abl.	trīstī	trīstī	trīstibus	trīstibus

Adjectives of one termination: *fēlīx*, gen. *fēlīcis* 'happy, fortunate'

	Singular		Plural	
	Masculine and feminine	Neuter	Masculine and feminine	Neuter
Nom./Voc.	fēlīx	fēlīx	fēlīcēs	fēlīcia
Gen.	fēlīcis	fēlīcis	fēlīcium	fēlīcium
Dat.	fēlīcī	fēlīcī	fēlīcibus	fēlīcibus
Acc.	fēlīcem	fēlīx	fēlīcēs/fēlīcīs	fēlīcia
Abl.	fēlīcī	fēlīcī	fēlīcibus	fēlīcibus

Practice

A Identify which group the following adjectives belong to and give their stems:

1 amāns, *gen.* amantis 'loving'
2 brevis, breve 'short'
3 celer, celeris, celere 'fast, swift'
4 currēns, *gen.* currentis 'running'
5 difficilis, difficile 'difficult'
6 facilis, facile 'easy'
7 fortis, forte 'strong, brave'

8 fugiēns, *gen.* fugientis 'fleeing'
9 gravis, grave 'heavy, serious'
10 immortālis, immortāle 'immortal'
11 omnis, omne 'all, every, whole'
12 pugnāns, *gen.* pugnantis 'fighting'

B Decline these adjectives in the forms indicated:

1 *omnis*, masculine singular
2 *fortis*, neuter singular

3 *celer*, masculine plural
4 *facilis*, neuter plural

5   *immortālis*, feminine singular
6   *difficilis*, neuter singular
7   *brevis*, feminine plural
8   *gravis*, neuter plural
9   *omnis*, neuter plural
10 *fortis*, masculine plural
11 *celer*, neuter singular
12 *facilis*, masculine singular

13 *immortālis*, neuter plural
14 *difficilis*, feminine plural
15 *brevis*, neuter singular
16 *gravis*, feminine singular
17 *amāns*, masculine singular
18 *pugnāns*, neuter singular
19 *currēns*, feminine plural
20 *fugiēns*, neuter plural

21.2 Use of Third-Declension Adjectives

A third-declension adjective may modify a noun of any declension; it will agree with the noun it modifies in gender, number, and case, but not necessarily in ending. Thus *equus celer* (nominative singular), *equī celerēs* (nominative plural), *equī celeris* (genitive singular), etc. Third-declension adjectives may be substantivized, i.e. used without an expressed noun (see chapter 8.3), as *omnēs illud vīdērunt* 'everyone (literally 'all the people') saw that' and *laudēmus immortālēs* 'let's praise the immortals' (i.e. the gods).

Practice

C Translate:

1   dei semper immortales sunt.
2   laudabimus immortales.
3   hoc difficile est.
4   ille difficilia numquam facit.
5   rex noster fortis fuit.
6   puellae semper fortes amant.
7   illos pugnantes audivimus.
8   pugnantes vidimus.
9   omnes deos laudamus. (2 ways)
10 omnes vitam amant.
11 omnes deos laudant. (2 ways)

12 verba tua gravia sunt.
13 servum fugientem vidimus.
14 servus currens venit.
15 liber tuus brevis est.
16 gladium acrem habeo.
17 habesne equum celerem?
18 opus facile est.
19 omnia vidimus.
20 hi pueri tristes sunt.
21 deos immortales laudat.
22 omnis equus bonus est.

D Translate into Latin:

1 This book is not short.
2 My horse is fast.
3 Your book is difficult.
4 These stones are heavy.
5 I saw you (plural) fighting.

6   He heard everything (all things).
7   She loves the immortal gods.
8   Did you see the fleeing slave?
9   They heard the slave running.
10 We saw everyone (all men).

11 Brave men always fight well.

12 I am not brave.

13 These women love that brave man.

14 Every girl here is beautiful.

15 Is your sword sharp?

16 The immortals are always happy.

17 Give these to the sad boys.

18 May you (plural) be happy!

21.3 Present Participles

The adjectives *amāns, pugnāns, fugiēns,* and *currēns* are formed from verbs; they are called present participles. (The participles you have already seen in chapter 6.2, such as *doctus*, are perfect participles.) Any verb (apart from *sum* and compounds of *sum*) can form a present participle, as follows:

First conjugation   amāns, *gen.* amantis 'loving'
Second conjugation   monēns, *gen.* monentis 'advising'
Third conjugation   regēns, *gen.* regentis 'ruling'
Fourth conjugation   audiēns, *gen.* audientis 'hearing'
Mixed conjugation   capiēns, *gen.* capientis 'taking'
Eō   iēns, *gen.* euntis 'going'

Practice

E Translate:

1 ducens

2 emens

3 legens

4 mittens

5 petens

6 scribens

7 iuvans

8 dicens

F Give the present participles of the following verbs and their translations:

1 āmittō

2 vocō

3 veniō

4 vendō

5 faciō

6 sepeliō

7 abeō

8 agō

9 impediō

10 videō

11 laudō

12 timeō

13 interficiō

14 exeō

15 dō

16 stō

17 inveniō

18 sentiō

19 accipiō

20 reficiō

G Translate into Latin:

1 the running slave (nominative)	14 the conquering soldiers (ablative)
2 the running slaves (nominative)	15 the conquering soldiers (nominative)
3 the running slaves (dative)	16 the fleeing enemy (nominative plural)
4 the teaching teacher (nominative)	17 the fleeing enemy (ablative plural)
5 the teaching teacher (accusative)	18 the fleeing enemy (genitive plural)
6 the teaching teachers (accusative)	19 the mother calling (accusative)
7 a helping god (accusative)	20 the mother calling (genitive)
8 helping gods (accusative)	21 the mother calling (ablative)
9 helping gods (genitive)	22 the fighting soldier (nominative)
10 boys fearing (nominative)	23 the fighting soldier (ablative)
11 boys fearing (dative)	24 the fighting soldier (dative)
12 boys fearing (genitive)	
13 the conquering soldiers (accusative)	

21.4 Reading Practice

Colloquium Stephani 18a–19d (adapted): the author tells teachers using his work that lessons should be individually tailored to particular students (probably first to third century AD).

Haec acta sunt per singulos iuxta unius cuiusque vires et profectum, et aetatem discipulorum. sunt enim et naturae variae studentium, et difficiles voluntates ad laborem litterarum, in quibus cum multum proficias, plus superest ut ad summum profectum venias.

Vocabulary (in order of first appearance; words that appear more than once are in bold)

acta sunt 'were done'
per singulōs 'individually'
iuxtā (+ accusative) 'according to'
ūnīus cuiusque 'of each person'
vīrēs, vīrium (f. plural) 'strength'
prōfectum, prōfectī (n.)
  'advancement'
aetās, aetātis (f.) 'age'
discipulus, discipulī (m.) 'student'
sunt 'there are'

enim 'for' (in the sense of 'because';
  translate one word earlier than where
  it appears in Latin)
et ... et 'both ... and'
nātūra, nātūrae (f.) 'nature'
varius, varia, varium 'varied'
studeō, studēre, studuī 'study'
  (substantivized adjective here, so
  add 'people')
voluntās, voluntātis (f.) 'disposition'
ad (+ accusative) 'towards'

labor, labōris (m.) 'hard work'

litterae, litterārum (f. plural) 'literary study'

cum (+ subjunctive) 'even when'

multum 'a lot'

prōficio, prōficere, prōfēcī, prōfectum 'make progress'

plūs, plūris, plūrium (n.) 'more'

supersum (like *sum*) 'be left to do'

summus, summa, summum 'greatest'

21.5 Vocabulary to Learn

Adjectives

ācer, ācris, ācre	'sharp', 'keen'
brevis, breve	'short', 'brief'
celer, celeris, celere	'fast', 'swift'
difficilis, difficile	'difficult'
facilis, facile	'easy'
fēlīx, *gen.* fēlīcis	'happy', 'fortunate'
fortis, forte	'strong', 'brave'
gravis, grave	'heavy', 'serious'
immortālis, immortāle	'immortal'
omnis, omne	'all', 'every', 'whole'
trīstis, trīste	'sad'

22.1 *Colloquia Monacensia–Einsidlensia* 6b–j (adapted)

An attempted visit to a sick friend (second or third century AD):

MARCUS: si vis, veni mecum.

GAIUS: quo?

MARCUS: ad amicum nostrum Lucium; visitemus eum.

GAIUS: quid enim habet?

MARCUS: aegrotat.

GAIUS: a quando?

MARCUS: intra paucos dies incurrit.

GAIUS: ubi habitat?

MARCUS: non longe; si vis, ambula. (*after a short walk*) haec est, puto, domus eius. haec est.

GAIUS: ecce ianitor; interroga illum num possimus intrare et videre amicum nostrum.

PORTER: quem petitis?

MARCUS: dominum tuum Lucium; de salute eius venimus.

PORTER: ascendite.

MARCUS: quot scalas?

PORTER: duas; ad dextram portam pulsate.

MARCUS: pulsemus. vide, quis est?

SLAVE (*opening door*): avete omnes.

MARCUS: dominum tuum volumus visitare. si vigilat, nuntia nos.

SLAVE: non est hic.

MARCUS: quid dicis? sed ubi est?

SLAVE: descendit ad lauretum ut ambularet.

MARCUS: gratulamur illi. cum venerit, dic illi nos ad eum venisse de salute eius gratulantes, quia omnia bona sunt.

SLAVE: sic faciam.

Vocabulary (in order of first appearance; words that appear more than once are in bold)

sī 'if'

vīs 'you want'

quō 'where', 'whither'

vīsitō, -āre, -āvī, -ātum 'go see'

eum 'him'

enim 'for' (best omitted in translation
   here)

aegrōtō, -āre, -āvī, -ātum 'be ill'

quandō 'when'

intrā paucōs diēs 'a few days ago'

incurrō (like *currō*) 'fall ill' (here
      a present where we would expect
      a past, because Latin uses the present
      for an action that began in the past
      but continues in the present)

habitō, -āre, -āvī, -ātum 'live, dwell'

longē 'far off'

**ambulō, -āre, -āvī, -ātum 'walk',
   'walk on'**

putō, putāre, putāvī, putātum 'think'

domus, domī (f.) 'house'

eius (indeclinable) 'his'

ecce 'look!'

iānitor, iānitōris (m.) 'doorman'

interrogō, -āre, -āvī, -ātum 'ask'

num (+ subjunctive) 'whether'

intrō, intrāre, intrāvī, intrātum 'enter'

salūs, salūtis (f.) 'health'

ascendō, ascendere, ascendī, ascēnsum
   'go up'

quot 'how many?'

scāla, scālae (f.) 'flight of stairs'

duās (f. accusative plural) 'two'

dexter, dextra, dextrum 'right-hand'

porta, portae (f.) 'door'

**pulsō, pulsāre, pulsāvī, pulsātum
   'knock on'**

avēte 'hello'

volumus 'we want'

vigilō, vigilāre, vigilāvī, vigilātum 'be
   awake'

nūntiō, nūntiāre, nūntiāvī, nūntiātum
   'announce'

dēscendō, dēscendere, dēscendī,
   dēscēnsum 'go down'

laurētum, laurētī (n.) 'laurel grove'

grātulāmur (+ dative) 'we congratulate'

cum vēnerit 'when he comes' (see
   chapter 47.2 for the construction)

grātulantēs *is a present participle of*
   grātulor 'congratulate'

sīc 'thus, so'

22.2 *Colloquium Harleianum* 12a–f (adapted)

A very unrealistic representation of how a lawyer finds a job (perhaps third century AD). Because many people who learned Latin did so in order to become lawyers, ancient Latin teachers painted a rosy picture of the life of a lawyer in an effort to encourage people to study Latin.

RICH FRIEND: domine, salve.

LAWYER: salvus sis semper, amice.

RICH FRIEND: quomodo sunt res tuae? omnia bene?

LAWYER: quomodo dei volunt.

RICH FRIEND: quid nunc agis?

LAWYER: agebam, nunc autem vacat mihi.

RICH FRIEND: volo tibi iniungere administrationem meae actionis. eamus; ambula et ego tibi dabo quod agas. omnium enim bonorum dignus es.

Vocabulary (in order of first appearance; words that appear more than once are in bold, and those in bold in the preceding vocabulary list are omitted)

salvē 'hello'

salvus, salva, salvum 'well'

quōmodo 'how', 'as'

rēs tuae 'your affairs' (nominative plural)

volunt '(they) want'

agēbam 'I was doing things' (imperfect tense of *agō*)

autem 'however' (translate one word earlier than where it appears in Latin)

vacat mihi 'I don't have anything to do'

volō, velle, voluī, – 'want'

iniungō, iniungere, iniūnxī, iniūnctum (+ dative and accusative) 'hand over to'

administrātiō, administrātiōnis (f.) 'management'

āctiō, āctiōnis (f.) 'court case'

quod agās 'something for you to do'

enim 'for' (in the sense of 'because'; translate one word earlier than where it appears in Latin)

dignus, digna, dignum 'worthy of'

22.3 Translate into Latin

MARCUS: Come with me in order to see Lucius.

GAIUS: Why?

MARCUS: He is ill.

GAIUS: Let's go. Where does he live?

MARCUS: He lives here; this is his house.

GAIUS: Let's knock on the door.

PORTER: Hello! Whom are you seeking?

MARCUS: We are seeking your master. We have heard that our friend Lucius is ill and we want to see him: is he awake?

PORTER: Lucius does not live here; my master's name is Titus.

PART III

| Demonstratives, Ablative of Agent

23.1 *Is, Ea, Id*

The main Latin word for 'he', 'she', 'it', 'they', etc. is the irregular pronoun *is, ea, id*.

British Case Order						
	Singular			**Plural**		
	Masculine	**Feminine**	**Neuter**	**Masculine**	**Feminine**	**Neuter**
Nom.	is 'he'	ea 'she'	id 'it'	eī/iī 'they'	eae 'they'	ea
Voc.	–	–	–	–	–	–
Acc.	eum 'him'	eam 'her'	id 'it'	eōs 'them'	eās 'them'	ea
Gen.	eius 'his'	eius 'her, hers'	eius 'its'	eōrum 'their'	eārum 'their'	eōrum
Dat.	eī 'him'	eī 'her'	eī 'it'	eīs/iīs 'them'	eīs/iīs 'them'	eīs/iīs
Abl.	eō 'him'	eā 'her'	eō 'it'	eīs/iīs 'them'	eīs/iīs 'them'	eīs/iīs

Ancient Case Order

	Singular			**Plural**		
	Masculine	**Feminine**	**Neuter**	**Masculine**	**Feminine**	**Neuter**
Nom.	is 'he'	ea 'she'	id 'it'	eī/iī 'they'	eae 'they'	ea
Gen.	eius 'his'	eius 'her, hers'	eius 'its'	eōrum 'their'	eārum 'their'	eōrum
Dat.	eī 'him'	eī 'her'	eī 'it'	eīs/iīs 'them'	eīs/iīs 'them'	eīs/iīs
Acc.	eum 'him'	eam 'her'	id 'it'	eōs 'them'	eās 'them'	ea
Abl.	eō 'him'	eā 'her'	eō 'it'	eīs/iīs 'them'	eīs/iīs 'them'	eīs/iīs

In the nominative this pronoun is not used nearly as often as its English equivalents, because the relevant information is normally conveyed in the verb endings. In the genitive *eius* and *eōrum/eārum* are used for possession freely; there is no possessive adjective for this pronoun as there are for the personal and reflexive pronouns. The genitives *eius* and *eōrum*, of course, do not agree with the nouns possessed: it is purely coincidental that one happens to end in *-us* and the other in *-um*. Thus *māter eius* means 'his/her/its mother', *māter eōrum* 'their (masculine possessors) mother', and *māter eārum* 'their (feminine possessors) mother'. Compare *māter mea* 'my mother', *māter nostra* 'our mother', and *mātres nostrae* 'our mothers': there the adjectives *meus* and *noster* are inflected to agree with 'mother' and are feminine because *māter* is feminine, regardless of the genders of 'I' or 'we'.

The neuter plural has no consistent translation, as English has no plural of 'it'; often it can be translated 'these things' or 'those things'. Like *hic* and *ille*, the forms of *is, ea, id* can be used as adjectives, meaning both 'this' and 'that', as well as pronouns.

Practice

A Translate:

1 eum audivi.	10 ei fratres sunt.
2 oppidum eorum	11 soror eius
3 pecuniam ei dedi.	12 fratres earum
4 eam amo.	13 ea pulchra est.
5 caput eius	14 eae pulchrae sunt.
6 cum eis	15 ea pulchra sunt.
7 sine eo	16 ea vidi.
8 pecuniam eis dedimus.	17 cum ea
9 id habeo.	18 pater eorum

23.2 Distinguishing *Is* from *Sē*

Since *sē* and *suus* have translations that overlap with those of *is*, it is important to distinguish carefully between them. Forms of *sē* and *suus* refer back to the subject of the sentence, while forms of *is* (unless they are nominative) refer to a person or thing that is *not* the same as the subject of the sentence. Thus *sē audit* is 'he hears himself', and *eum audit* is 'he hears him' (i.e. someone else). Similarly 'he sees his horse' is *equum suum videt* when the person who owns the horse and the person doing the seeing are the same, and *equum eius videt* when the person who owns the horse is not the same as the person doing the seeing. (Notice that *suum* is an adjective agreeing with 'horse' while *eius* is a genitive.) In indirect statement the potential for confusion between *sē* and *eum/eam* is particularly great, because English allows an ambiguity that Latin does not: *dīxit sē venīre* and *dīxit eum venīre* can both be translated 'he said he was coming', but in the first case the person doing the saying and the person doing the coming are the same (i.e. the original sentence was 'I am coming'), and in the second case the person coming is not the same as the person saying (i.e. the original sentence was 'He is coming').

Practice

B Translate:

1 dixit se me amare.	3 pater meus dixit se ovem
2 dixit eam me amare.	interfecturum esse.

4 pater meus dixit eum ovem interfecturum esse.

5 rex noster eum interfecit.

6 rex noster se interfecit.

7 venit currens ut se iuvaretis.

8 venit currens ut eam iuvaretis.

9 multi eos amant.

10 multi se amant.

11 deos laudavit ut se iuvarent.

12 deos laudavit ut eam iuvarent.

13 frater tuus dicit eum oves venditurum esse.

14 frater tuus dicit se oves venditurum esse.

15 servi dixerunt se capita ovium sepelivisse.

16 servi dixerunt eos capita ovium sepelivisse.

17 equum suum amisit.

18 equum eius amisit.

19 equum amisit.

20 matrem suam interfecit.

21 matrem eius interfecit.

22 matrem amat.

23 ad oppidum suum ivit.

24 ad oppidum eorum ivit.

25 ad oppidum ivit.

26 matrem eorum amo.

27 multi homines se docere possunt.

28 multi homines eos docere possunt.

29 in silvam iverunt ne se videremus.

30 in silvam iverunt ne equos suos videremus.

31 ille dixit eum magistrum bonum esse.

32 ille dixit se magistrum bonum esse.

33 hostes dixerunt se nostros victuros esse.

34 hostes dixerunt eos nostros victuros esse.

35 ad urbem venit ut eam doceret.

36 ad urbem venit ut se doceremus.

37 nomen suum in libro legit.

38 nomen eius in libro legit.

39 nomina in libro legit.

40 nomina eorum in libro legit.

41 pecuniam eorum invenerunt.

42 pecuniam suam invenerunt.

43 pecuniam eius invenerunt.

44 pecuniam tuam invenerunt.

C Translate into Latin:

1 He said he (same person) had bought a horse.

2 He said he (different person) had bought a horse.

3 They will see themselves.

4 They will see them (different people).

5 They said that they (different people) would rule well.

6 They said that they (same people) would rule well.

7 She is afraid of her.

8 She is afraid of herself.

9 He said that he (same person) would help us.

10 He said that he (different person) would help us.

11 He wrote to me so that I would write to him (same person).

12 He wrote to me so that I would
    write to him (different person).
13 That man lost his (own) sword.
14 That man lost his (another
    man's) sword.
15 That man lost a sword.
16 These farmers will kill their own
    sheep.
17 These farmers will kill their
    (different farmers') sheep.
18 These farmers will kill sheep.
19 The boys ran so that we would
    not capture them (same people).
20 The boys ran so that we would
    not capture them (different
    people).
21 They said that they (different
    people) were praising the gods.
22 They said that they (same
    people) were praising the gods.
23 Our mother did not kill herself.
24 Our mother did not kill her.
25 These boys love their (own)
    teacher.
26 These boys love their (other
    boys') teacher.

23.3 Ablative of Agent

The prepostion *ā* or *ab* can mean 'by' as well as 'from'. In this meaning as well it takes the ablative, and the construction is known as the ablative of agent. It is used with passive verb forms, and therefore the only forms with which you can at this stage find it are perfect participles, which as we have seen (chapter 6.2) are passive in meaning. Thus *puella ā poētā amāta* 'the girl loved by the poet', *equus ā puerō ductus* 'the horse led by the boy'. This construction can be used only when the doer is a person, god, or other animate being; for inanimate agents (e.g. 'he was killed by a landslide') a different construction is used (to be discussed in chapter 32.3).

Practice

D Translate these phrases:

1 epistula a puero scripta
2 oves ab agricola emptae
3 puer a magistro ductus
4 liber a puella lectus
5 servus a Marco missus
6 animalia ab agricola petita
7 urbes a Graecis rectae
8 hostes a nostris victi
9 puellae a deis amatae
10 verbum ab illo dictum
11 pecunia a civibus data
12 pueri a magistro docti

E Translate into Latin:

1 the king helped by the gods
2 the river praised by the poets
3 the boys advised by the teacher
4 the city seen by the farmer
5 the sheep led by the girls
6 the animals bought by the farmer
7 the girl loved by my brother
8 the letter sent by the boy

9 the book written by the king

10 the walls seen by the poet

11 the words said by the citizens

12 the boy sought by the teacher

23.4 Reading Practice

Colloquium Celtis 4–7 (adapted): a child with his own personal slave boy describes the beginning of his day (probably first to third century AD).

Mane cum coepi vigilare, surrexi de lecto et hoc primum feci: deposui dormitoria et sumpsi tunicam et reliqua vestimenta. tunc ergo excitavi meum puerum. dixi ei, 'surge, puer, et vide num iam luceat; aperi ostium et fenestram.' et ita fecit. tunc ei dixi, 'porrige mihi calceamenta.'

Vocabulary (in order of first appearance; words that appear more than once are in bold)

māne 'in the morning'

cum 'when'

coepī 'I began'

vigilō, -āre, -āvī, -ātum 'be awake'

surgō, surgere, surrēxī, surrēctum 'get up'

lectus, lectī (m.) 'bed'

prīmum 'first'

dēpōnō (like *pōnō*) 'take off'

dormītōrium, -ī (n.) 'nightgown'

sūmō, sūmere, sūmpsī, sūmptum 'take'

tunica, tunicae (f.) 'tunic'

reliquus, -a, -um 'remaining'

vestīmenta, vestīmentōrum (n. plural) 'clothes'

tunc 'then'

ergō 'so' (translate one word earlier than where it appears in Latin)

excitō, -āre, -āvī, -ātum 'wake up'

num (+ subjunctive) 'whether'

iam 'already'

lūceat 'it is light'

aperiō, aperīre, aperuī, apertum 'open'

ōstium, ōstiī (n.) 'door'

fenestra, fenestrae (f.) 'window'

ita 'thus'

porrigō, porrigere, porrēxī, porrēctum 'pass'

calceāmentum, -ī (n.) 'shoe'

23.5 Vocabulary to Learn

Prepositions

ā, ab (+ ablative)   'by'

Pronouns

is, ea, id   'he', 'she', 'it', 'they'

eius   'his', 'her', 'its' (genitive singular of *is*)

eōrum, eārum   'their' (genitive plural of *is*)

24 | Participles

24.1 Perfect, Present, and Future Participles

So far we have seen two participles: the perfect participle, which is passive (e.g. *amātus, -a, -um* 'loved' or 'having been loved', but not the active 'having loved': see chapter 6.2), and the present participle, which is active (e.g. *amāns*, gen. *amantis* 'loving': see chapter 21.3). There is also a future participle, which is active; as English does not have a future participle its translation is rather cumbersome, e.g. *amātūrus, -a, -um* '(being) about to love'. The future participle is formed by taking the fourth principal part, dropping the *-um*, and adding *-ūrus, -ūra, -ūrum* (in other words, the future participle is the future infinitive (for which see chapter 19.2) without the *esse*). When the fourth principal part already ends in *-ūrus*, as in the case of *futūrus* and *fugitūrus*, no change is necessary: for such verbs the fourth principal part is the future participle, and there is no perfect participle. The full set of participles is therefore as shown in the table below.

	Perfect participle	Present participle	Future participle
First conjugation	amātus, -a, -um 'loved', 'having been loved'	amāns, *gen.* amantis 'loving'	amātūrus, -a, -um 'being about to love'
Second conjugation	monitus, -a, -um 'advised', 'having been advised'	monēns, *gen.* monentis 'advising'	monitūrus, -a, -um 'being about to advise'
Third conjugation	rēctus, -a, -um 'ruled', 'having been ruled'	regēns, *gen.* regentis 'ruling'	rēctūrus, -a, -um 'being about to rule'
Fourth conjugation	audītus, -a, -um 'heard', 'having been heard'	audiēns, *gen.* audientis 'hearing'	audītūrus, -a, -um 'being about to hear'
Mixed conjugation	captus, -a, -um 'captured', 'having been captured'	capiēns, *gen.* capientis 'capturing'	captūrus, -a, -um 'being about to capture'
Sum	–	–	futūrus, -a, -um 'being about to be'
Eō	–	iēns, *gen.* euntis 'going'	itūrus, -a, -um 'being about to go'

Practice

A Translate:

1   pugnātūrus, -a, -um
2   fugiēns, *gen.* fugientis
3   āmissus, -a, -um
4   vocātūrus, -a, -um
5   capiēns, *gen.* capientis
6   sepultus, -a, -um
7   ventūrus, -a, -um
8   vīvēns, *gen.* vīventis
9   sēnsus, -a, -um
10 refectūrus, -a, -um
11 accipiēns, *gen.* accipientis
12 inventus, -a, -um
13 interfectūrus, -a, -um
14 impediēns, *gen.* impedientis
15 factus, -a, -um
16 audītūrus, -a, -um
17 agēns, *gen.* agentis
18 vīsus, -a, -um
19 exitūrus, -a, -um
20 timēns, *gen.* timentis
21 monitus, -a, -um
22 adfutūrus, -a, -um
23 abiēns, *gen.* abeuntis
24 datus, -a, -um

B Give the participles indicated (with feminine and neuter for the perfect and future participles, and with genitive for present participles) and translate the resulting forms:

1   *pugnō*, present
2   *vocō*, perfect
3   *āmittō*, future
4   *veniō*, present
5   *capiō*, perfect
6   *sepeliō*, future
7   *exeō*, present
8   *reficiō*, perfect
9   *sentiō*, future
10 *emō*, present
11 *interficiō*, perfect
12 *inveniō*, future
13 *legō*, present
14 *accipiō*, perfect
15 *faciō*, future
16 *mittō*, present
17 *agō*, perfect
18 *videō*, future
19 *iuvō*, present
20 *audiō*, perfect
21 *moneō*, future
22 *habeō*, present
23 *dūcō*, perfect
24 *dō*, future

24.2 Participle Usage

The literal translation of the future participle is very odd in English, so it is preferable to use a less literal translation when encountering such participles in sentences. For example, *puerōs pugnātūrōs vīdī* literally means 'I saw the being-about-to-fight boys', but since we would never say that in English, it is a good idea to use a subordinate clause with 'who' or 'when', such as 'I saw the boys <u>who were</u> about to fight' or 'I saw the boys <u>when they were</u> about to fight'. Which type of subordinate clause is best will be determined by the context. Often subordinate clauses are the best translations of perfect and present participles too (cf. chapter 6.2), because the Latin participle is frequently used in situations where English would not employ a participle.

Latin participles, despite being adjectives, retain many of the characteristics of the verbs from which they came: they can have objects in the accusative (*mīlitēs hanc puellam amantēs* 'the soldiers loving this girl', or better 'the soldiers who love this girl') or the dative (*librī puerīs datī* 'the books given to the boys', or 'the books that were given to the boys'), and they can be modified by adverbs (*puellae crās ventūrae* 'the being-about-to-come-tomorrow girls', or better 'the girls who will come tomorrow') or by prepositional phrases (*puellae ā poētīs amātae* 'the girls loved by the poets', or 'the girls who are loved by the poets').

A Latin participle normally agrees in gender, number, and case with another word in the sentence, and it is important to translate it so that that agreement is preserved. Since English often uses word order to indicate what a participle goes with, a literal translation of the Latin that does not change the word order may end up with a completely different meaning in English from that of the original Latin sentence. For example, the sentence *per silvam euntem tē vīdimus* could be literally translated 'going through the forest, we saw you', but that translation would mean that 'we' were going through the forest, whereas in Latin *euntem* agrees with *tē* and therefore it is 'you', not 'we', who were going through the forest. Therefore it would be better to translate *per silvam euntem tē vīdimus* with 'We saw you going through the forest', or 'We saw you when you were going through the forest'. If in fact it was 'we' rather than 'you' going through the forest, the Latin sentence would be *per silvam euntēs tē vīdimus*, with the participle nominative plural to agree with the understood subject of *vīdimus*, and the best English translation would be 'We saw you when we were going through the forest'.

Sometimes, however, a participle has nothing in the sentence to agree with at all; under those circumstances it must be substantivized, like any other adjective in the same situation, and in English one will normally need to add 'man', 'men', 'woman', 'women', 'thing', or 'things', depending on the participle's gender and number (cf. chapter 8.3). Thus just as *bonōs vīdī* means 'I saw the good men' and *bona vīdī* means 'I saw good things', so *currentēs vīdī* means 'I saw the running men' or 'I saw the men who were running' and *data vīdī* means 'I saw the given things', or better 'I saw the things that had been given'. The substantivized participles *dicta* and *facta* (literally 'said things' and 'done things') are usually translated 'words' and 'deeds' in English.

In Latin the tense of the participle expresses time relative to the main verb (present participle = action at same time as main verb, perfect participle = action before main verb, future participle = action after main verb). But in English, a past-tense main verb normally forces subordinate verbs in the same sentence into the past tense as well; as a result, when replacing participles with subordinate clauses in English, one must apply caution in the same way as with the tenses in indirect statement (see chapter 19.4). Thus *ovēs in agrō stantēs vīdī* 'I saw the sheep that <u>were</u> standing in the field' or 'I saw the sheep when they <u>were</u> standing in the field' (present participle in Latin, but past tense in English, because the standing happened at the same time as the seeing, both of which are now in the past) and *hostēs rēgem interfectūrōs vīdī* 'I saw the enemies when they <u>were about to</u> kill the king' or 'I saw the enemies who <u>were about to</u> kill the king'.

Practice

C Translate:

1 miles captus eos timuit.
2 vidistine captos?
3 iuti ab amicis, librum longum scripsimus.
4 vidi eum in agro stantem.
5 vidimus magistrum eos docturum.
6 verba regis audientes, cives omnia scripserunt.
7 vocantes non audivimus.
8 rex dicturus mecum stabit.
9 dominum timens, servus ex urbe fugit.
10 dominos timentes, servi ad silvam fugerunt.
11 regem visurus ille gladium mihi dedit.
12 docti libros bonos scribunt.
13 legistine scripta eorum?
14 ovem petiturus, agricola ex oppido exivit.
15 hostes timens, ad castra cum eis non veni.
16 oves vendens, agricola pecuniam accepit.
17 puella, habesne amantem?
18 eum vidimus ovem interfecturum.
19 victi servi erunt.
20 oves venditurus, agricola eas ad oppidum egit.
21 facta eorum bona sunt.
22 omnes in agro stant deos laudantes.
23 agricola oves venditurus ad urbem venit.
24 victi, hostes nostri erunt servi.
25 omnia facta eius mala sunt.
26 milites victuros e castris duxit rex.
27 vidimus eum cum patre ad oppidum euntem.
28 videsne puellam a me amatam?
29 puerum vos vocantem vidimus.
30 patrem sepulturi, fratres ad oppidum venerunt.
31 rex captum iuvit.
32 regem captum iuvit.
33 a magistro ex oppido ducti, pueri ad silvam venerunt.
34 illi vicerunt hostes nos interfecturos.
35 dabo ei librum a me scriptum.
36 scripta eius bona sunt.
37 me petentes ad urbem venerunt.

38 puero timenti pecuniam
   dedimus.
39 multi amantes mali sunt.
40 vidistine moenia refecta?
41 scripsit de factis et dictis regis
   nostri.
42 ad silvam venientes militem
   viderunt.
43 moenia urbis reficientes
   cives pecuniam amissam
   invenerunt.

D Translate into Latin using participles and omitting words in parentheses:

1 Seeing them, the boy was afraid.
2 Our king will not kill the captured
  (men).
3 Being about to sell his horse, my
  brother led it ('him' in Latin) to
  a good field.
4 (When he was) repairing the
  walls of the city, he found a lost
  sheep.
5 We will help the captured
  (women).
6 (When they were) about to repair
  the walls of the town, the citizens
  sought stones.
7 Did you see the captured soldiers?
8 Will he praise their deeds (i.e.
  things done)?
9 Being about to fight, those soldiers are miserable.
10 The immortals help lovers (i.e.
   men who love).
11 (When he) saw them, the boy
   was afraid.
12 Being about to see their (own)
   king, the citizens were afraid.
13 Having been helped by us, this
   poet praised us.
14 (When he is) about to teach girls,
   this teacher is afraid.
15 I have (i.e. possess) captured
   soldiers; will you buy them?
16 We saw a slave running out of
   the town into that forest.
17 (When they are) about to write
   books, learned men read many
   things.
18 I shall give money to the boy
   standing with him.
19 The masters found their slaves
   fleeing into the forest.
20 We found it (when we were)
   repairing their walls.

24.3 Reading Practice

1 *Colloquium Harleianum* 22a–c and 21g–h (adapted): plans for an outing (second or
  third century AD).

  GAIUS: tertio die cursus equorum erit, et postea ludi gladiatorum. communiter
     ergo spectemus et sic lavemur, cum dimittunt spectacula.
  LUCIUS: quomodo vis.
  GAIUS: frater autem meus excusavit; heri enim in balneo rixam fecit, coactus ab
     amicis ebriis, et procedere non potest, quia confunditur.

Vocabulary

tertiō diē 'on the day after tomorrow'

cursus, cursūs (m.) 'race'

posteā 'afterwards'

lūdus, lūdī (m.) 'game'

gladiātor, gladiātōris (m.) 'gladiator'

commūniter 'together'

ergō 'so' (translate one word earlier than where it appears in Latin)

spectō, spectāre, spectāvī, spectātum 'watch'

sīc 'in the same way' (i.e. *commūniter*)

lavēmur 'let's go to the baths'

cum 'when'

dīmittō (like *mittō*) 'let out'

spectāculum, -ī (n.) 'show'

quōmodo 'as'

vīs 'you wish'

autem 'however'

excūsō, -āre, -āvī, -ātum 'send excuses'

enim 'for' (in the sense of 'because'; translate one word earlier than where it appears in Latin)

balneum, balneī (n.) 'bath-house'

rixa, rixae (f.) 'brawl'

cōgō, cōgere, coēgī, coāctum 'force'

ēbrius, ēbria, ēbrium 'drunken'

prōcēdō, prōcēdere, prōcessī, prōcessum 'go out'

cōnfunditur 'he is embarrassed'

2 *Adeste fideles*: eighteenth-century Christmas carol.

Adeste, fideles, laeti triumphantes,
venite, venite in Bethlehem:
natum videte, regem angelorum.
venite adoremus, venite adoremus,
venite adoremus dominum.

Vocabulary

fidēlis, fidēle 'faithful'

laetus, laeta, laetum 'joyful'

triumphō, -āre, -āvī, -ātum 'triumph'

nātus, nātī (m.) 'baby'

angelus, angelī (m.) 'angel'

adōrō, adōrāre, adōrāvī, adōrātum 'adore'

24.4 Vocabulary to Learn

Verbs

dēfendō, dēfendere, dēfendī, dēfēnsum	'defend'
discēdō, discēdere, discessī, discessum	'leave' (in the intransive sense, i.e. 'depart')
intellegō, intellegere, intellēxī, intellēctum	'understand'
oppugnō, oppugnāre, oppugnāvī, oppugnātum	'attack'
relinquō, relinquere, relīquī, relictum	'leave behind', 'abandon'
sedeō, sedēre, sēdī, sessum	'sit'
volō, velle, voluī, –	'want', 'wish'

25 | Relative Clauses and *Volō*

25.1 Relative Pronoun

The relative pronoun is the word used for 'who', 'whom', 'whose', and 'which' when those words do not introduce questions (and for 'that' when equivalent to 'who' etc.), as 'The man who finds the gold will be rich' and 'You should have seen the one that got away.' In Latin, as in English, the relative pronoun is very similar to the interrogative pronoun, which we saw in chapter 13.3; in fact the relative pronoun is identical in form to the interrogative adjective, *quī, quae, quod*. It is therefore declined as follows:

British Case Order

	Singular			Plural		
	Masculine	Feminine	Neuter	Masculine	Feminine	Neuter
Nom.	quī	quae	quod	quī	quae	quae
Voc.	–	–	–	–	–	–
Acc.	quem	quam	quod	quōs	quās	quae
Gen.	cuius	cuius	cuius	quōrum	quārum	quōrum
Dat.	cui	cui	cui	quibus/quīs	quibus/quīs	quibus/quīs
Abl.	quō	quā	quō	quibus/quīs	quibus/quīs	quibus/quīs

Ancient Case Order

	Singular			Plural		
	Masculine	Feminine	Neuter	Masculine	Feminine	Neuter
Nom.	quī	quae	quod	quī	quae	quae
Gen.	cuius	cuius	cuius	quōrum	quārum	quōrum
Dat.	cui	cui	cui	quibus/quīs	quibus/quīs	quibus/quīs
Acc.	quem	quam	quod	quōs	quās	quae
Abl.	quō	quā	quō	quibus/quīs	quibus/quīs	quibus/quīs

25.2 Relative Clauses

A relative pronoun or adjective introduces a subordinate clause; the relative pronoun links this subordinate clause to a particular word (very often, though not always, the word just before the relative clause) in the main clause, called the antecedent. The relative pronoun agrees with the antecedent in gender and number, but it takes its case from its construction in its own (subordinate) clause.

rēx quī nōs regit bonus est. 'The king who rules us is good.' The relative pronoun is masculine and singular because it agrees with the antecedent *rēx*, but nominative because it is the subject of *regit*.

rēx quem vidēs bonus est. 'The king whom you see is good.' The relative pronoun is masculine and singular because it agrees with the antecedent *rēx*, but accusative because it is the object of *vidēs*.

pulchrae sunt puellae quās amāmus. 'The girls whom we love are beautiful.' The relative pronoun is feminine and plural because it agrees with the antecedent *puellae*, but accusative because it is the object of *amāmus*.

puellās quās vidēs amāmus. 'We love the girls whom you see.' The relative pronoun is feminine and plural because it agrees with the antecedent *puellās*, but accusative because it is the object of *vidēs*.

Notice that the relative clause in both Latin and English may come in the middle of another clause; one can identify the beginning and end of the relative clause because it begins with the relative pronoun (or with a preposition that governs the relative pronoun: *vīdī puellās cum quibus cucurristī* 'I saw the girls with whom you ran') and usually ends with the first finite verb that occurs after the relative pronoun.

Notice also that the word order is often very different in English from in Latin: in translating sentences with relative clauses from Latin to English one needs to identify the main clause, translate it, and then **translate the relative clause immediately after its antecedent**, wherever that antecedent happens to come in the English version. It is very important to keep the relative clause intact in translation; mixing words from the relative clause with ones from the main clause will nearly always produce the wrong meaning.

Practice

A In the following English sentences, find where each relative clause begins and ends; then identify each relative pronoun and its antecedent. Give the gender, number, and case that the relative pronoun would have in Latin.

1 The boy who is over there is my brother.
2 Who saw the man who stole that car?
3 We were talking with girls whom we didn't know.
4 The man that you saw is a dentist.
5 Will you give it to the boy who rescued me?
6 The things that he said are very shocking.
7 He was attacked by a lion that had a very bad temper.
8 The person whose book you stole is my best friend!
9 We did not know the women with whom we were standing.
10 The women to whom we gave the money are not actually homeless.
11 Is the girl with whom we spoke a friend of yours?
12 The men who saved him have received medals.
13 We love the boys to whom we will give these mittens.
14 The girls who attend this school are very happy.
15 Did you see the girls who stole the money?
16 Some things that go on here really should stop.
17 I know the man who found it.
18 Martha never heard the soprano (f.) whose voice she's trying to imitate.

B Identify relative clauses and antecedents, and then translate:

1 deos qui nos defendunt laudabimus.
2 dei quos laudamus bona nobis dant.
3 dei quorum facta laudamus boni sunt.
4 deos laudant homines quibus dei bona dant.
5 homines cum quibus venimus boni sunt.
6 laudamus deas quae nobis bona dederunt.
7 nos defendent deae quas laudavisti.
8 bonae sunt deae quarum nomina laudavimus.
9 homines quibus deae bona dant deas laudabunt.
10 boni sunt dei quorum nomina laudamus.
11 pulchra est puella quam monuisti.
12 videsne puellam quae me monuit?
13 ubi est puella cuius pecuniam habemus?
14 nos non amat puella cum qua sedimus.
15 docuit me magister cui librum dedi.
16 deos qui bona nobis dederunt laudabimus.
17 bona nobis dabunt dei quos laudabimus.
18 puellam quae me amat laudavi.

C Identify relative clauses and antecedents, then translate into Latin:

1 The enemy that we will attack is in that city.
2 Citizens who love the gods are happy.
3 Did you see the girls with whom we sat?
4 We loved the king who ruled us.
5 He praised the farmer whose sheep he bought.
6 They will repair the walls that defend them.
7 Where is the poet with whom you left (from) the town?
8 I shall sell the horse that you (plural) see.
9 The horse that I have is black.
10 The man to whom I gave the book is here.
11 Will you (singular) buy the sheep that I am selling?
12 The man with whom you are sitting is my father.
13 The boys to whom we gave your books will come tomorrow.
14 The farmer to whom I shall give this sheep does not have many animals.
15 The soldiers whose camp you will see never attack us.

25.3 *Volō*

The word for 'want' is *volō, velle, voluī, –*; it is irregular and conjugated as follows:

Present indicative	Future indicative	Perfect indicative	Present subjunctive	Imperfect subjunctive
volō	volam	voluī	velim	vellem
vīs	volēs	voluistī	velīs	vellēs
vult	volet	voluit	velit	vellet
volumus	volēmus	voluimus	velīmus	vellēmus
vultis	volētis	voluistis	velītis	vellētis
volunt	volent	voluērunt	velint	vellent

Infinitives: present *velle*, perfect *voluisse*, no future
Participles: present *volēns*, gen. *volentis*; no perfect or future

Volō takes a present infinitive, like *possum* and like its English equivalent 'want': *volō venīre* 'I want to come'.

Practice

D Translate:

1 eos defendere volumus.

2 dixerunt se velle eos defendere.

3 regem oppugnare volentes illi ad urbem venerunt.

4 pugnabimus ut hostes discedere velint.

5 pugnavimus ut hostes discedere vellent.

6 vultisne cum eis sedere?

7 volesne ea relinquere?

8 dixit se voluisse ab oppido discedere.

9 volui eis pecuniam dare, sed non habui.

10 magistro pecuniam dederunt ut se docere vellet.

11 magistro pecuniam dabunt ut se docere velit.

12 vidistine puerum nobiscum venire volentem?

E Translate into Latin:

1 Do you (singular) want to defend her?

2 He said he (same person) wanted to defend her.

3 He said he (different person) had wanted to attack them.

4 We will want to attack them.

5 They wanted to leave him behind.

6 Do you (plural) want to understand it?

7 He will give them money so that they will not want to attack him (same person).

8 He gave them money so that they would not want to attack him (same person).

25.4 Reading Practice

1 *Colloquium Harleianum* 7a–e (adapted): caring for one's writing tools (perhaps first century AD).

TEACHER: dealba tabulam tuam, sede et scribe. apices fac litterarum. in atramentum tuum aquam paucam mitte. ecce, nunc bonum est.

CHILD 1: porrige cannam. porrige scalpellum.

CHILD 2: quod scalpellum vis?

CHILD 1: acutum volo.

CHILD 2: acutum vis? cur?

Vocabulary

dealbō, -āre, -āvī, -ātum 'whiten' (to make a good writing surface)

tabula, tabulae (f.) 'writing tablet'

apex, apicis (m.) 'macron' (mark indicating a long vowel)

littera, litterae (f.) 'letter'

ātrāmentum, -ī (n.) 'ink'

paucus, pauca, paucum 'a little'

ecce 'look!'

porrigō, porrigere, porrēxī, porrēctum 'pass'

canna, cannae (f.) 'pen'

scalpellum, scalpellī (n.) 'pen-knife' (knife used for sharpening pens, a process necessary at frequent intervals when using a pen made from a reed or feather)

acūtus, acūta, acūtum 'sharp'

2 *Roman Inscriptions of Britain* 164 (adapted): funerary inscription from Bath (imperial period).

Dis manibus Successae Petroniae, quae vixit annos III et menses IIII et dies IX. Vettius Romulus et Victoria Sabina filiae carissimae hoc fecerunt.

Vocabulary

dīs mānibus 'to the divine spirits'

Successa Petrōnia, -ae (f.) *the name of the dead person* (possessive genitive with *mānibus*)

annōs 'for years'

III = 3

mēnsēs 'for months'

IIII = 4

diēs 'for days'

IX = 9

Vettius Rōmulus, -ī (m.) *the name of the dead person's father*

Victōria Sabīna, -ae (f.) *the name of the dead person's mother*

fīlia, fīliae (f.) 'daughter'

cārissimus, -a, -um 'dearest'

26 | Reading Practice

26.1 *Colloquia Monacensia–Einsidlensia* 7a–9o (adapted)

Having a friend over for lunch (second or third century AD):

MARCUS: Gai amice, quo vadis?

GAIUS: domum festino. cur inquisisti?

MARCUS: si tibi suave est, hodie apud me prande. vinum bonum domesticum habemus.

GAIUS: sic fiat.

MARCUS: temperi ergo veni ad nos.

GAIUS: cum me vis, mitte servum ad me; domi ero.

MARCUS: sic fiat nobis. (*to slave*) tu, puer, sequere me ad macellum; aliquid emamus ad prandium. inquire, quanti piscis.

FISHMONGER: denariis decem.

MARCUS (*having bought fish*): tu, puer, refer hoc domum, ut possimus ire ad holerarium et emere holera, quae necessaria sunt, et poma: mora, mala Persica, pira. (*to second slave*) ecce habes omnia quae emimus. refer haec domum. (*arriving home*) vocet aliquis coquum. ubi est?

SLAVE: sursum ascendit.

MARCUS: et quid ibi vult? descendat huc. (*to cook, when he comes*) tolle haec, coque diligenter. prandium bonum fiat. (*to another slave*) aperi loculum et eice clavem cellarii. profer e cellario quae necessaria sunt: salem, oleum, liquamen, acetum acre, vinum album et nigrum, ligna sicca, prunam.

SLAVE: quid aliud vis?

MARCUS: haec tantum, puer. vade ad Gaium et dic ei, 'veni, ibi prandeamus'. vade, curre, cito fac; nihil tarde, sed velociter. (*when slave returns*) fuisti apud eum?

SLAVE: fui.

MARCUS: ubi est?

SLAVE: domi sedet.

MARCUS: et quid facit?

SLAVE: legit.

MARCUS: et quid dixit?

SLAVE: amicos meos exspecto; veniunt et sequar.

MARCUS: vade iterum et dic ei, 'omnes hic sunt'. cum eo huc veni. (*to other slaves*)
vos interim componite diligenter vitreamina et aeramenta. sternite triclinium.

SLAVE: iam stravimus. omnia parata sunt.

MARCUS: nondum venit? vade, dic ei, 'sero nos facis prandere'. ecce adest; huc venit.

Vocabulary (in order of first appearance; words that appear more than once are in bold)

quō 'to where?'

vādō, vādere, –, – 'go'

domum '(to) home'

festīnō, -āre, -āvī, -ātum 'hurry'

inquīrō, inquīrere, inquīsīvī, inquīsītum 'ask'

sī 'if'

suāvis, suāve 'attractive'

apud (+ accusative) 'at the house of'

prandeō, prandēre, prandī, prānsum 'have lunch'

vīnum, vīnī (n.) 'wine'

domesticus, -a, -um 'from our own estate'

sīc 'in this way', 'thus'

fīat 'let it be (done)', 'let it become' (subjunctive)

temperī 'punctually'

ergō 'therefore' (translate one word earlier than where it appears in Latin)

cum 'when'

domī 'at home'

sequere 'follow!' (imperative)

macellum, macellī (n.) 'market'

aliquid 'something'

ad 'for'

prandium, prandiī (n.) 'lunch'

quantī 'how much' (understand 'is')

piscis, piscis, piscium (m.) 'fish'

dēnārius, dēnāriī (m.) 'denarius' (unit of money)

decem 'ten' (indeclinable)

refer 'carry' (imperative)

holerārius, holerāriī (m.) 'grocer'

holus, holeris (n.) 'vegetable'

necessārius, -a, -um 'necessary'

pōmum, pōmī (n.) 'fruit'

mōrum, mōrī (n.) 'mulberry'

mālum Persicum, mālī Persicī (n.) 'peach'

pirum, pirī (n.) 'pear'

ecce 'look!'

aliquis (like *quis*) 'someone'

coquus, coquī (m.) 'cook'

sūrsum 'upstairs'

ascendō, ascendere, ascendī, ascēnsum 'go up'

ibi 'there'

dēscendō, dēscendere, dēscendī, dēscēnsum 'come down'

hūc 'to here'

tollō, tollere, sustulī, sublātum 'take'

coquō, coquere, coxī, coctum 'cook'

dīligenter 'carefully'

aperiō, aperīre, aperuī, apertum 'open'

loculum, loculī (n.) 'casket'

ēiciō, ēicere, ēiēcī, ēiectum 'take out'

clāvis, clāvis, clāvium 'key'

cellārium, cellāriī (n.) 'cellar'

prōfer 'bring out' (imperative)

sāl, salis (m.) 'salt'

oleum, oleī (n.) 'oil'

liquāmen, liquāminis (n.) 'garum' (sauce made by leaving fish in the sun for three months)

acētum, acētī (n.) 'vinegar'

albus, alba, album 'white'

lignum, lignī (n.) 'piece of firewood'

siccus, sicca, siccum 'dry'

prūna, prūnae (f.) 'burning ember' (for
 lighting the fire)
aliud 'else' (n. singular)
tantum 'only'
cito 'quickly'
nihil 'not at all'
tardē 'slowly'
vēlōciter 'quickly'
exspectō, -āre, -āvī, -ātum 'wait for'
sequar 'I shall follow'
iterum 'again'
interim 'meanwhile'

compōnō (like *pōnō*) 'set out'
vitreāmen, vitreāminis (n.) 'glass'
aerāmentum, aerāmentī (n.) 'bronze
 utensil'
**sternō, sternere, strāvī, strātum
 'arrange'**
trīclīnium, trīclīniī (n.) 'dining room'
iam 'already'
parātus, -a, -um 'ready'
nōndum 'not yet'
sērō 'late'

26.2 *Colloquium Celtis* 42a–46a (adapted)

A schoolboy goes home for lunch with an unobservant child-minder (perhaps second or third century AD):

Dimittit nos magister; regredior domum. intro domum patris, exuo vestimenta mundiora, induo cottidiana. posco aquam ad manus. quoniam esurio, dico meo puero: 'pone mensam et mantele et mappam, et vade ad tuam dominam, ut afferas panem et pulmentarium et vinum. dic meae matri me iterum reverti debere ad domum magistri. ideo ergo festina mihi afferre prandium.' satis prandeo et bibo. sed dicit mihi meus paedagogus: 'quid pateris hodie? nihil gustavisti.'

Vocabulary (in order of first appearance; words that appear more than once are in bold, and those in bold in the preceding vocabulary list are omitted)

dīmittō (like *mittō*) 'dismiss'
regredior 'I return'
intrō, intrāre, intrāvī, intrātum 'enter'
exuō, exuere, exuī, exūtum 'take off'
vestīmenta, vestīmentōrum (n. plural)
 'clothes'
mundiōra 'finer' (neuter plural)
induō, induere, induī, indūtum 'put on'
cottīdiānus, -a, -um 'ordinary'
poscō, poscere, poposcī, – 'ask for'
ad manūs 'to wash my hands'
quoniam 'since'
ēsuriō, ēsurīre, –, – 'be hungry'
pōnō *can also mean* 'set out'
mēnsa, mēnsae (f.) 'table'

mantēle, mantēlis, mantēlium (n.)
 'tablecloth'
mappa, mappae (f.) 'napkin'
afferō, afferre, attulī, allātum 'bring'
 (third conjugation)
pānis, pānis, pānium (m.) 'bread'
pulmentārium, -ī (n.) 'relish' (i.e. tasty
 food to be eaten with bread)
iterum 'again'
revertī 'return' (infinitive)
dēbeō, dēbēre, dēbuī, dēbitum (+
 infinitive) 'have to'
ideō 'for this reason'
ergō 'therefore'
festīnō, -āre, -āvī, -ātum 'hasten'

satis 'adequately'

bibō, bibere, bibī, – 'drink'

paedagōgus, -ī (m.) 'paedagogue'
(child-minder)

pateris 'you are suffering'

nihil (n.) 'nothing'

gustō, gustāre, gustāvī, gustātum 'taste'

26.3 Translate into Latin

GAIUS: Because I had lunch at your house yesterday, have lunch at my house today.

MARCUS: Let it be thus.

GAIUS: You, boy, go with me to the grocer so that I will be able to buy fruits, which are necessary. Carry these vegetables home. Cook, come here. Take this fish and cook it carefully. Boy, open the cellar and bring out these things: good oil, wine from our own estate, garum, pieces of wood. Arrange the dining room. You, boy, go to Marcus, who is not yet here. Say 'Come! Lunch is ready!'

27 | Deponent Verbs: Forms from First Two Principal Parts

27.1 Deponent Verbs

In addition to the five conjugations of regular verbs we have so far seen, there are five conjugations of deponent verbs. Deponent verbs use a completely different set of endings, but in other respects they function exactly like the verbs we have so far seen. The paradigm verbs for the deponents are the following:

First conjugation	*vēnor, vēnārī, vēnātus sum* 'hunt'
Second conjugation	*vereor, verērī, veritus sum* (+ accusative) 'fear', 'be afraid (of)'
Third conjugation	*ūtor, ūtī, ūsus sum* (+ ablative) 'use'
Fourth conjugation	*partior, partīrī, partītus sum* 'divide'
Mixed conjugation	*morior, morī, mortuus sum* 'die'

As you can see, deponent verbs have only three principal parts, and their third principal part is periphrastic (i.e. it consists of two words, as *vēnātus sum*); this is because deponent verbs cannot be made passive and so cannot have the kind of fourth principal part that regular verbs do (see chapter 6.2). The use of the third principal part of deponent verbs will be explained in chapter 29. Deponent verbs belonging to each conjugation can be identified as follows: first-conjugation verbs have a second principal part in *-ārī*, second-conjugation verbs have a second principal part in *-ērī*, third-conjugation verbs have a second principal part in *-ī* and a first principal part that does not end in *-ior*, fourth-conjugation verbs have a second principal part in *-īrī*, and mixed-conjugation verbs have a second principal part in *-ī* and a first principal part in *-ior*. Deponents are conjugated as shown in the table below:

	First conjugation	Second conjugation	Third conjugation	Fourth conjugation	Mixed conjugation
Present indicative	vēnor	vereor	ūtor	partior	morior
	vēnāris	verēris	ūteris	partīris	moreris
	vēnātur	verētur	ūtitur	partītur	moritur
	vēnāmur	verēmur	ūtimur	partīmur	morimur
	vēnāminī	verēminī	ūtiminī	partīminī	moriminī
	vēnantur	verentur	ūtuntur	partiuntur	moriuntur

	First conjugation	Second conjugation	Third conjugation	Fourth conjugation	Mixed conjugation
Future indicative	vēnābor	verēbor	ūtar	partiar	moriar
	vēnāberis	verēberis	ūtēris	partiēris	moriēris
	vēnābitur	verēbitur	ūtētur	partiētur	moriētur
	vēnābimur	verēbimur	ūtēmur	partiēmur	moriēmur
	vēnābiminī	verēbiminī	ūtēminī	partiēminī	moriēminī
	vēnābuntur	verēbuntur	ūtentur	partientur	morientur
Perfect indicative			*in chapter 29*		
Present subjunctive	vēner	verear	ūtar	partiar	moriar
	vēnēris	vereāris	ūtāris	partiāris	moriāris
	vēnētur	vereātur	ūtātur	partiātur	moriātur
	vēnēmur	vereāmur	ūtāmur	partiāmur	moriāmur
	vēnēminī	vereāminī	ūtāminī	partiāminī	moriāminī
	vēnentur	vereantur	ūtantur	partiantur	moriāntur
Imperfect subjunctive	vēnārer	verērer	ūterer	partīrer	morerer
	vēnārēris	verērēris	ūterēris	partīrēris	morerēris
	vēnārētur	verērētur	ūterētur	partīrētur	morerētur
	vēnārēmur	verērēmur	ūterēmur	partīrēmur	morerēmur
	vēnārēminī	verērēminī	ūterēminī	partīrēminī	morerēminī
	vēnārentur	verērentur	ūterentur	partīrentur	morerentur
Imperative	vēnāre	verēre	ūtere	partīre	morere
	vēnāminī	verēminī	ūtiminī	partīminī	moriminī
Present participle	vēnāns, *gen.* vēnantis	verēns, *gen.* verentis	ūtēns, *gen.* ūtentis	partiēns, *gen.* partientis	moriēns, *gen.* morientis
Perfect participle			*in chapter 29*		
Future participle			*in chapter 29*		
Present infinitive	vēnārī	verērī	ūtī	partīrī	morī
Perfect infinitive			*in chapter 29*		
Future infinitive			*in chapter 29*		

The following observations can be made about these forms:

1) Although the deponents use a different set of personal endings from the regular verbs, they are consistent in using those forms: it is always the same set of endings.

2) The stem vowels before the endings, and indeed the entire stem apart from the endings, behave exactly as the equivalent regular paradigms would behave: it is only the endings that are different.

3) The present participles are identical to those of regular verbs.

4) The imperfect subjunctive is formed not from the actual present infinitive of a deponent verb, but from what would be the present infinitive if the verb were not deponent.

Practice

A State which conjugation each of these deponent verbs belongs to:

1 arbitror, arbitrārī, arbitrātus sum 'think'

2 loquor, loquī, locūtus sum 'speak'

3 moror, morārī, morātus sum 'delay'

4 orior, orīrī, ortus sum 'arise'

5 patior, patī, passus sum 'suffer', 'endure'

6 polliceor, pollicērī, pollicitus sum 'promise'

7 prōgredior, prōgredī, prōgressus sum 'advance'

8 sequor, sequī, secūtus sum 'follow'

B Conjugate in the forms indicated:

1 *arbitror*, present indicative

2 *loquor*, future indicative

3 *moror*, present subjunctive

4 *orior*, imperfect subjunctive

5 *patior*, imperative

6 *polliceor*, present participle

7 *sequor*, present infinitive

8 *loquor*, present indicative

9 *moror*, future indicative

10 *orior*, present subjunctive

11 *patior*, imperfect subjunctive

12 *polliceor*, imperative

13 *prōgredior*, present participle

14 *arbitror*, present infinitive

15 *moror*, present indicative

16 *orior*, future indicative

17 *patior*, present subjunctive

18 *polliceor*, imperfect subjunctive

19 *prōgredior*, imperative

20 *sequor*, present participle

C Translate:

1 loquuntur nobiscum.
2 sequemur eos.
3 polliceamur.
4 milites, progredimini!
5 multa patieris.
6 virum sequimur qui ad castra progreditur.
7 vir quem sequimur ad castra progreditur.
8 hic moremur.
9 progreditur ut loquatur.
10 arbitror eum me sequi.
11 nos sequuntur ut tecum loquantur.
12 puellae quae in urbe morantur multa patientur.
13 puellae quas ad urbem sequimur morantur.
14 tecum loquor ut me sequaris.
15 eum sequentes ad urbem progredientur.
16 morans e castris non progreditur.
17 arbitrantur nos se sequi.
18 multa patientur ut cum rege loquantur.
19 moratur ut nobiscum loquatur.
20 arbitramur eos nobiscum loqui velle.
21 arbitrarisne nos te sequi?
22 non arbitrabimini eos progredi.

D Translate into Latin:

1 We shall speak with her.
2 Are you speaking with him?
3 Let's speak with them.
4 He wants to speak with you (plural).
5 I think he is suffering.
6 He thinks that we are suffering many things.
7 Are you (singular) delaying in order to follow us?
8 They will delay in order to think.
9 We promise that we shall come.
10 He promises that he will not go away.
11 Promise that you (plural) will not hinder me!
12 (When we are) delaying, we shall not advance.
13 (When I am) promising, I do not think.
14 The man whom I am following is delaying.
15 A man who thinks well does not often promise.
16 Do you (singular) think that he will come?
17 She thinks that they are delaying.
18 They will think that I am delaying.
19 Promising that he will defend us, that man will advance to the city with us.

27.2 Reading Practice

1 *Colloquium Montepessulanum* 13g–15a (adapted): preparing for a trip to the baths (probably third century AD).

LUCIUS: quot sunt horae?

SLAVE: iam octo.

LUCIUS: eat aliquis et nuntiet me venturum esse in balneum Tigillinum. (*to servant*) sequere nos. tibi loquor, purgamentum! ego autem, donec locum invenitis nobis, unguentarium salutabo. (*to ointment-seller*) Iuli, ave: saluto te. da mihi tus et unguentum hodie quod sufficit ad homines viginti.

Vocabulary

quot 'how many'	dōnec 'until'
hōra, hōrae (f.) 'hour'[1]	locus, locī (m.) 'place' (i.e. seats in the
iam 'already'	crowded bath-house)
octō 'eight'	nōbīs 'for us'
aliquis (like *quis*) 'someone'	unguentārius, -ī (m.) 'ointment-seller'
nūntiō, nūntiāre, nūntiāvī, nūntiātum	salūtō, -āre, -āvī, -ātum 'greet'
'announce'	Iūlius, Iūliī (m.) *name of the ointment-*
balneum, balneī (n.) 'baths'	*seller*
Tigillīnus, -a, -um 'Tigilline' (i.e. named	avē 'hello'
after C. Sofonius Tigellinus, a friend	tūs, tūris (n.) 'frankincense'
of the emperor Nero)	unguentum, unguentī (n.) 'ointment'[2]
sequor, sequī, secūtus sum 'follow'	sufficiō, sufficere, suffēcī, suffectum
loquor, loquī, locūtus sum 'talk'	'suffice'
pūrgāmentum, -ī (n.) 'scum'	vīgintī (indeclinable) 'twenty'
autem 'however'	

2 *Corpus Inscriptionum Latinarum* VII.451: inscription from a dedication to the god Silvanus (imperial period; found at Stanhope, County Durham).

Silvano invicto sacrum. Gaius Tetius Veturius Micianus, praefectus alae Sebosianae, ob aprum eximiae formae captum, quem multi antecessores eius praedari non potuerunt, voto suscepto libens posuit.

---

[1] The Romans calculated time on a system whereby the hours of daylight and the hours of darkness were each divided into twelve equal hours; the first hour of the day was at sunrise and the sixth at our noon, so the eighth would have been around our 2 pm (a bit earlier or later depending on the season).

[2] As part of the bathing process, Romans were anointed with perfumed oils and other ointments.

Vocabulary

Silvānus, -ī (m.) *the name of a minor deity*

invictus, invicta, invictum 'unconquerable'

sacer, sacra, sacrum 'sacred to'

Gaius Tetius Veturius Miciānus, -ī (m.) *a man's name*

praefectus, praefectī (m.) 'prefect'

āla Sebosiāna, ālae Sebosiānae (f.) 'Sebosian cavalry regiment'

ob (+ accusative) 'on account of'

aper, aprī (m.) 'wild boar'

eximiae fōrmae 'of exceptional form'

antecessor, antecessōris (m.) 'predecessor'

praedor, praedārī, praedātus sum 'carry off'

vōtō susceptō 'in fulfilment of his vow'

libēns, *gen.* libentis 'willing(ly)'

pōnō *can also mean* 'set (this inscription) up'

27.3 Vocabulary to Learn

Verbs

morior, morī, mortuus sum	'die'
partior, partīrī, partītus sum	'divide'
ūtor, ūtī, ūsus sum (+ ablative)	'use'
vēnor, vēnārī, vēnātus sum	'hunt'
vereor, verērī, veritus sum	'fear', 'be afraid (of)' (takes accusative object despite English 'of')

28 | Indirect Commands

28.1 Indirect Commands

The imperative is used to give direct commands ('come!' 'go!'), but it is also possible for a command, like a statement, to be indirect. Indirect commands occur not only after verbs of ordering ('he ordered me to go') but also after asking ('he asked me to go') and after verbs expressing related concepts such as advising, urging, and encouraging. In English indirect commands use the infinitive, but in Latin they use *ut* with the subjunctive (or *nē* with subjunctive if negative); they are very similar to the purpose clauses seen in chapter 15.2 and chapter 16. Thus they follow the sequence of tenses rules introduced there and repeated below:

Main verb		**Subordinate verb**
Present indicative, future indicative, imperative, subjunctive	→	Present subjunctive
Perfect indicative[1]	→	Imperfect subjunctive

Examples (*rogō, rogāre, rogāvī, rogātum* 'ask'):

rogat nōs ut veniāmus 'He asks us to come.'
rogābit tē nē veniās 'He will ask you not to come.'
rogāvit mē ut venīrem 'He asked me to come.'
rogāvimus eum nē venīret. 'We asked him not to come.'

Practice

A Translate:

1 rogat eos ut nos rogent.
2 rogavit eos ut nos rogarent.
3 rogabunt eum ut te roget.
4 rogaverunt eum ut te rogaret.
5 rogo te ne eos roges.
6 rogavi te ne eos rogares.
7 rogabimus vos ne eam rogetis.
8 rogavimus vos ne eam rogaretis.
9 rogavit eam ut eos rogaret.
10 rogaverunt eas ut eam rogarent.

---

[1] But see note 1 in chapter 16.1.

28.2 Addition of Objects

The sentences above are unusual in that their main verbs all have expressed objects; more often those objects are omitted and left to be understood from the (often not expressed) subjects of the subordinate verbs. In English, most verbs of asking need to have expressed objects, so when translating Latin indirect commands into English one often needs to supply an object for the main verb.

> *rogat ut veniāmus.* 'He asks us to come.'
> *rogābit nē veniās* 'He will ask you not to come.'
> *rogāvit ut venīrem* 'He asked me to come.'
> *rogāvimus nē venīret.* 'We asked him not to come.'

Practice

B Translate:

1 rogat ut nos rogent.
2 rogavit ut nos rogarent.
3 rogabunt ut te roget.
4 rogaverunt ut te rogaret.
5 rogo ne eos roges.

6 rogavi ne eos rogares.
7 rogabimus ne eam rogetis.
8 rogavimus ne eam rogaretis.
9 rogavit ut eos rogaret.
10 rogaverunt ut eam rogarent.

C Translate into Latin without expressing italicized words:

1 I shall ask *her* to ask him.
2 I asked *her* to ask him.
3 We asked *him* to ask her.
4 We asked *him* not to ask her.
5 Are you asking *me* to ask them?
6 Did you ask *me* to ask them?

7 He will ask *you* not to ask us.
8 He asked *you* not to ask us.
9 They asked *us* not to ask you (singular).
10 They asked *us* to ask you (plural).

28.3 Identifying *Ut*-Clauses and Infinitives

We have now seen two different Latin constructions that use *ut/nē* + subjunctive: purpose clauses and indirect commands. These do not always have the same translations in English: the indirect command is nearly always translated with an infinitive, but purpose clauses cannot be translated with an infinitive if the subjects of the two verbs are different. Thus *rogāvit nōs ut venīrēmus* 'he asked us to come' is an indirect command, but *id fēcit ut venīrēmus* 'he did it so that we would come' is a purpose clause – as is *id fēcimus ut venīrēmus* 'we did it in order to come'. So it is useful to know before translating whether a subjunctive clause is a purpose clause or an indirect command. The best way to do that is to see whether the sentence's main verb indicates asking, ordering, begging, or persuading: if it does, the subjunctive clause is probably an indirect command, and if it does not, the subjunctive is probably a purpose clause. The following verbs in particular take indirect commands:

> *hortor, hortārī, hortātus sum* 'urge', 'encourage'
> *imperō, imperāre, imperāvī, imperātum* (+ dative) 'order'
> *ōrō, ōrāre, ōrāvī, ōrātum* 'beg'
> *persuādeō, persuādēre, persuāsī, persuāsum* (+ dative) 'persuade'
> *velim* (present subjunctive of *volō*) 'would like'

Note that like all forms of *volō*, *velim* takes the infinitive when the subject of the subordinate verb is the same as the subject of the main verb; it is only when the two have different subjects that an indirect command is intended and *ut* is used. Thus *velim venīre* 'I would like to come' (not a command) but *velim ut veniās* 'I would like you to come' (indirect command).

Practice

D Identify the constructions of these sentences and translate:[2]

1 hortabitur ut venemur.
2 venatur ut animalia capiat.
3 fratres oravimus ne venarentur.
4 saxis utetur ut moenia reficiat.
5 libros amissos petunt ut eos inveniant.
6 regi persuasit ut nos defenderet.
7 gladio utetur ut ovem mortuam partiatur.
8 rex milites hortabitur ut bene pugnent.
9 saxis utuntur ut moenia bene refeciant.
10 militibus imperavit ut gladiis suis uterentur.
11 omnia fecimus ne pater moreretur, et non morietur.
12 mater filio persuasit ne venaretur.
13 saxis utuntur ut moenia reficiant.
14 magister pueros hortabitur ne vereantur.
15 amicis suis persuasit ne vererentur.
16 ad pueros non ivi, ne vererentur.
17 pater filium hortatur ut venetur.
18 non potui militibus persuadere ne fugerent.
19 milites hortabimur ut nos defendant.
20 gladiis utuntur ut ovem mortuam partiantur.
21 omnia facimus ne pater moriatur.
22 dicunt se velle te sequi.

---

[2] Additional exercises on this point, with an answer key, can be found in chapter 63.9.

23 milites hortor ne fugiant, sed
fugiunt.

24 in silva venantur ut multa
animalia capiant.

25 magister pueris persuadebit ne
vereantur.

26 velim ut me iuves.

28.4 English Infinitives

When translating from English to Latin there is a further complication: while some infinitives need to be translated with *ut/nē* + subjunctive because they are indirect commands or purpose clauses, other English infinitives are equivalent to Latin infinitives. The verbs *possum* and *volō* (as well as some other verbs to be introduced later) take a 'complementary' infinitive in Latin just as they do in English. Therefore when translating an English infinitive into Latin one needs to translate first of all the verb on which the infinitive depends: if when translated into Latin that governing verb turns out to be one that takes an infinitive in Latin, then the English infinitive depending on it needs to be translated with a Latin infinitive. But if the verb on which the English infinitive depends turns out to be one that takes an indirect command in Latin, then the English infinitive needs to be translated with a Latin indirect command. And if the verb on which the English infinitive depends turns out to be one that takes neither of these constructions, then (for now – but we have not yet seen the full range of constructions) the English infinitive needs to be translated with a Latin purpose clause.

Practice

E For each of the following sentences, state whether the underlined infinitive would be translated into Latin with an indirect command, a purpose clause, or an infinitive. If the result would be an indirect command or a purpose clause, give the tense of the subjunctive that it would take.

1 Would you like us <u>to paint</u> your house?

2 No, thank you; I want <u>to paint</u> the house myself.

3 Today I need to buy supplies <u>to paint</u> the house.

4 Can we persuade you <u>to paint</u> our house too?

5 Sorry, but I am not able <u>to paint</u> your house.

6 You could order these men <u>to paint</u> it for you.

7 The sphinx asked everyone <u>to solve</u> a riddle.

8 Travellers had to answer correctly <u>to avoid</u> being killed.

9 Titus was not able <u>to solve</u> that riddle.

10 Therefore he ordered his cleverest slave <u>to solve</u> it.

11 But the slave did not want <u>to solve</u> it if Titus would get all the credit.

12 So he pretended to be unable <u>to solve</u> it.

13 But Titus knew he was pretending and begged him <u>to help</u>.

14 The slave held out <u>to get</u> a big reward.

15 Eventually Titus persuaded him <u>to reveal</u> the answer in exchange for freedom.

16 The general urged his soldiers <u>to fight</u> bravely.

17 He said that they would not be able <u>to survive</u> except by defeating their opponents,

18 for tall cliffs blocked any retreat and the enemy king wanted <u>to kill</u> them all.

19 He had ordered his men not <u>to spare</u> anyone,

20 and would do all he could <u>to make sure</u> they were all slaughtered,

21 so no-one would be able <u>to survive</u> by being taken prisoner.

22 Therefore, the general said, they should do all they could <u>to save</u> themselves by winning the battle.

23 By this speech he persuaded them <u>to fight</u> fiercely,

24 and they were all able <u>to escape</u>.

F Identify the constructions in these sentences and translate them into Latin:

1 I shall urge my brother to hunt.

2 My brother wanted to hunt.

3 I persuaded my brother not to hunt.

4 My brother came to the forest to hunt.

5 I shall beg my brother not to hunt.

6 I would like my brother to hunt.

7 Will you urge them to defend themselves?

8 They want to defend themselves.

9 They will use swords to defend themselves.

10 We ordered them not to use swords.

11 Did you (singular) ask them not to use swords?

12 I would like you not to use swords.

13 They wanted to use their swords.

14 I heard you asking the king to help you.

15 They think that the king will help them.

16 Did you see the farmer who asked us to buy these sheep?

17 I would like to buy the slave who persuaded you not to hunt.

18 Persuade that farmer to give you the dying sheep.

19 Would you like us to help you?

20 The king ordered us all to leave.

28.5 Reading Practice

1 *Colloquium Montepessulanum* 11a–12d (adapted): preparing for a dinner party
(probably third century AD).

HOST (*to caterer*): quoniam amicos ad cenam invitavi, veni ad me et para nobis
omnia quae necessaria sunt, et coquo impera ut pulmentaria bene condiat.
(*to slaves*) venite huc, excutite pulvinum, operite stragula, ducite scopam,
spargite aquam, sternite triclinium, afferte calices et argentum. tu, puer, tolle
lagenam et imple aqua, scinde ligna, exterge mensam et pone in medium. ego
vinum proferam. lavate calices.

Vocabulary (in order of first appearance; words that appear more than once are in bold)

quoniam 'since'
cēna, cēnae (f.) 'dinner'
invītō, -āre, -āvī, -ātum 'invite'
parō, parāre, parāvī, parātum 'prepare'
necessārius, -a, -um 'necessary'
coquus, coquī (m.) 'cook'
pulmentārium, pulmentāriī (n.) 'relish'
   (i.e. tasty food to be eaten with bread)
condiō, condīre, condīvī, condītum
   'season'
hūc 'here' (used instead of *hīc* when
   there is motion towards the place
   considered 'here')
excutiō, excutere, excussī, excussum
   'shake out'
pulvīnus, pulvīnī (m.) 'cushion'
operiō, operīre, operuī, opertum
   'drape', 'spread out'
strāgulum, strāgulī (n.) 'couch-cover'
dūcō *can also mean* 'pull along'
scōpa, scōpae (f.) 'broom'

spargō, spargere, sparsī, sparsum
   'sprinkle' (on the packed earth outside
   the door, to keep the dust down)
sternō, sternere, strāvī, strātum 'arrange'
trīclīnium, trīclīniī (n.) 'dining room'
afferte 'bring!' (plural imperative)
calix, calicis (m.) 'cup'
argentum, argentī (n.) 'silverware'
tollō, tollere, sustulī, sublātum 'pick up'
lagēna, lagēnae (f.) 'flask'
impleō, implēre, implēvī, implētum 'fill'
aquā 'with water'
scindō, scindere, scidī, scissum 'split'
lignum, lignī (n.) 'firewood'
extergeō, extergēre, extersī, extersum
   'wipe clean'
mēnsa, mēnsae (f.) 'table'
medium, mediī (n.) 'middle'
vīnum, vīnī (n.) 'wine'
prōferō, prōferre, prōtulī, prōlātum
   (third conjugation) 'bring out'
lavō, lavāre, lāvī, lautum 'wash'

2 *Tabulae Vindolandenses* II.250 (adapted): letter from a military officer stationed in
northern Britain to another officer (c. AD 100).

Claudius Karus Ceriali suo salutem dicit. Brigonus me rogat, domine, ut se tibi
commendarem. rogo te ergo, domine, ut des ei quod a te petit. rogo te ut eum
commendare digneris Annio Equestri centurioni regionario Luguvalio. . . . opto te
felicem esse et bene valere. vale, frater.

Vocabulary (in order of first appearance; words that appear more than once are in bold)

Claudius Kārus, -ī (m.) *name of the writer of the letter*

Ceriālis, Ceriālis (m.) *name of the recipient of the letter, a friend of the writer but not actually his brother*

salūs, salūtis (f.) 'health', 'greetings'

Brigōnus, Brigōnī (m.) *man's name*

commendō, -āre, -āvī, -ātum 'recommend'

ergō 'therefore'

dignor, dignārī, dignātus sum 'think it right'

Annius Equester, Anniī Equestrī (m.) *name of an army officer*

centuriō, centuriōnis (m.) 'centurion'

regiōnārius, -a, -um 'in charge of the region'

Luguvalius, -a, -um 'at Luguvalium'

optō, optāre, optāvī, optātum 'hope' (takes indirect statement)

valeō, valēre, valuī, valitum 'be healthy'

28.6 Vocabulary to Learn

Verbs

arbitror, arbitrārī, arbitrātus sum	'think'
hortor, hortārī, hortātus sum	'urge', 'encourage'
imperō, imperāre, imperāvī, imperātum (+ dative)	'order'
loquor, loquī, locūtus sum	'speak'
moror, morārī, morātus sum	'delay'
orior, orīrī, ortus sum	'arise'
ōrō, ōrāre, ōrāvī, ōrātum	'beg'
patior, patī, passus sum	'suffer', 'endure'
persuādeō, persuādēre, persuāsī, persuāsum (+ dative)	'persuade'
polliceor, pollicērī, pollicitus sum	'promise'
prōgredior, prōgredī, prōgressus sum	'advance'
rogō, rogāre, rogāvī, rogātum	'ask'
sequor, sequī, secūtus sum	'follow'

29 | Deponent Verbs: Perfect-Stem Forms

29.1 Perfect Indicative of Deponent Verbs

The perfect forms of deponent verbs, like those of regular verbs, are formed from the third principal part. But in the case of deponent verbs these are periphrastic; that is, each verb form is made up of two separate words, a participle and a form of *sum*, as in *vēnātus sum* from *vēnor*. Conjugating periphrastic verbs in Latin is trickier than conjugating one-word verbs, because both parts inflect. The form of *sum* is conjugated as usual, while the participle changes as necessary to agree with the subject in gender and number. The form of a deponent verb in a perfect tense therefore reflects whether the subject is masculine, feminine, or neuter, as well as whether it is singular or plural and whether it is first, second, or third person. So the complete conjugation of the perfect of *vēnor* is as follows:

Masculine subject

vēnātus sum	'I (masculine) hunted', 'I (masculine) have hunted', 'I (masculine) did hunt'
vēnātus es	'you (masculine singular) hunted', 'you (masculine singular) have hunted', 'you (masculine singular) did hunt'
vēnātus est	'he hunted', 'he has hunted', 'he did hunt', 'hunted', 'has hunted', 'did hunt'
vēnātī sumus	'we (masculine) hunted', 'we (masculine) have hunted', 'we (masculine) did hunt'
vēnātī estis	'you (masculine plural) hunted', 'you (masculine plural) have hunted', 'you (masculine plural) did hunt'
vēnātī sunt	'they (masculine) hunted', 'they (masculine) have hunted', 'they (masculine) did hunt', 'hunted', 'have hunted', 'did hunt'

Feminine subject

vēnāta sum	'I (feminine) hunted', 'I (feminine) have hunted', 'I (feminine) did hunt'
vēnāta es	'you (feminine singular) hunted', 'you (feminine singular) have hunted', 'you (feminine singular) did hunt'
vēnāta est	'she hunted', 'she has hunted', 'she did hunt', 'hunted', 'has hunted', 'did hunt'

vēnātae sumus	'we (feminine) hunted', 'we (feminine) have hunted', 'we (feminine) did hunt'
vēnātae estis	'you (feminine plural) hunted', 'you (feminine plural) have hunted', 'you (feminine plural) did hunt'
vēnātae sunt	'they (feminine) hunted', 'they (feminine) have hunted', 'they (feminine) did hunt', 'hunted', 'have hunted', 'did hunt'

Neuter subject

vēnātum sum	'I (neuter) hunted', 'I (neuter) have hunted', 'I (neuter) did hunt'
vēnātum es	'you (neuter singular) hunted', 'you (neuter singular) have hunted', 'you (neuter singular) did hunt'
vēnātum est	'it hunted', 'it has hunted', 'it did hunt', 'hunted', 'has hunted', 'did hunt'
vēnāta sumus	'we (neuter) hunted', 'we (neuter) have hunted', 'we (neuter) did hunt'
vēnāta estis	'you (neuter plural) hunted', 'you (neuter plural) have hunted', 'you (neuter plural) did hunt'
vēnāta sunt	'they (neuter) hunted', 'they (neuter) have hunted', 'they (neuter) did hunt', 'hunted', 'have hunted', 'did hunt'

In giving verb conjugations one normally represents this range of possibilities in an abbreviated version, as follows:

First conjugation	Second conjugation	Third conjugation	Fourth conjugation	Mixed conjugation
vēnātus, -a, -um sum	veritus, -a, -um sum	ūsus, -a, -um sum	partītus, -a, -um sum	mortuus, -a, -um sum
vēnātus, -a, -um es	veritus, -a, -um es	ūsus, -a, -um es	partītus, -a, -um es	mortuus, -a, -um es
vēnātus, -a, -um est	veritus, -a, -um est	ūsus, -a, -um est	partītus, -a, -um est	mortuus, -a, -um est
vēnātī, -ae, -a sumus	veritī, -ae, -a sumus	ūsī, -ae, -a sumus	partītī, -ae, -a sumus	mortuī, -ae, -a sumus
vēnātī, -ae, -a estis	veritī, -ae, -a estis	ūsī, -ae, -a estis	partītī, -ae, -a estis	mortuī, -ae, -a estis
vēnātī, -ae, -a sunt	veritī, -ae, -a sunt	ūsī, -ae, -a sunt	partītī, -ae, -a sunt	mortuī, -ae, -a sunt

Practice

A Translate:

1 venati sumus	6 veritum est	11 partitae sumus
2 venata es	7 usi estis	12 partitum est
3 venata sunt	8 usa sum	13 mortui sunt
4 veritus est	9 usa sunt	14 mortua est
5 veritae sunt	10 partitus sum	15 mortua sunt

B Translate into Latin:

1 you (masculine singular) hunted
2 we (feminine) have hunted
3 it did not hunt
4 they (masculine) have hunted
5 did you (feminine singular) hunt?
6 they (neuter) hunted
7 he did not fear
8 they (feminine) feared
9 it was afraid
10 were you (masculine plural) afraid?
11 she was afraid
12 they (neuter) did not fear
13 I (masculine) have used it
14 did you (feminine plural) use it?
15 they (neuter) used it
16 we (masculine) did not use it
17 I (feminine) have used it
18 it used it
19 did you (masculine singular) divide it?
20 she has divided it
21 they (neuter) divided it
22 they (masculine) have divided it
23 we (feminine) did not divide it
24 it has died
25 he did not die
26 did they (feminine) die?
27 they (neuter) have died

C Conjugate in the perfect:

1 arbitror, arbitrārī, arbitrātus sum 'think'
2 loquor, loquī, locūtus sum 'speak'
3 moror, morārī, morātus sum 'delay'
4 orior, orīrī, ortus sum 'arise'
5 patior, patī, passus sum 'suffer', 'endure'
6 polliceor, pollicērī, pollicitus sum 'promise'
7 prōgredior, prōgredī, prōgressus sum 'advance'
8 sequor, sequī, secūtus sum 'follow'

29.2 Other Perfect-Stem Forms

The perfect system involves not only the perfect indicative, but also the perfect and future participles and infinitives. The perfect participle of deponent verbs is simply the first half of the third principal part, with feminine and neuter endings added as an indication that it is an adjective and must agree with something. The perfect infinitive is this participle plus *esse*. The future infinitive and participle are formed just like the perfect ones, but with an ending *-ūrus* instead of *-us*.

	Perfect participle	Perfect infinitive
First conjugation	vēnātus, -a, -um 'having hunted'	vēnātus, -a, -um esse
Second conjugation	veritus, -a, -um 'having been afraid', 'fearing'[1]	veritus, -a, -um esse
Third conjugation	ūsus, -a, -um 'having used'	ūsus, -a, -um esse
Fourth conjugation	partītus, -a, -um 'having divided'	partītus, -a, -um esse
Mixed conjugation	mortuus, -a, -um 'having died', 'dead'	mortuus, -a, -um esse

	Future participle	Future infinitive
First conjugation	vēnātūrus, -a, -um 'being about to hunt'	vēnātūrus, -a, -um esse
Second conjugation	veritūrus, -a, -um 'being about to fear'	veritūrus, -a, -um esse
Third conjugation	ūsūrus, -a, -um 'being about to use'	ūsūrus, -a, -um esse
Fourth conjugation	partītūrus, -a, -um 'being about to divide'	partītūrus, -a, -um esse
Mixed conjugation	moritūrus, -a, -um 'being about to die'[2]	moritūrus, -a, -um esse

The perfect and future infinitives of deponent verbs are used in the same way as those infinitives of other verbs: *dīxit sē vēnātum esse* 'he said that he had hunted', *dīxērunt eam vēnātūram esse* 'they said that she would hunt' (as usual, the infinitive agrees with its accusative subject: see chapter 19.3). The future participle also behaves like other future participles (see chapter 24.2). But the perfect participle is different: whereas the perfect participles of other verbs are passive in meaning (*amātus* = 'having been loved', not 'having loved': see chapter 6.2), the participles of deponent verbs are active (*ūsus* = 'having used', not 'having been used').

---

[1] *Vereor* is unusual in that the perfect participle can be translated with '-ing' in English; normally this translation is reserved for present participles.

[2] The future participle and future infinitive of *morior* are irregular: we would expect **mortuūrus (esse)*. Other mixed-conjugation verbs are not irregular.

Practice

D Give the perfect participles of the verbs listed in exercise C above, and their meanings.

E Give the future participles of the verbs listed in exercise C above, and their meanings.

F Translate:

1 locutae sunt nobiscum.
2 orti, secuti sumus eos.
3 bene arbitratus, pollicitus est.
4 progressane es?
5 multa passi estis.
6 multa passi, hic morati sunt.
7 progressa est ut loqueretur.
8 arbitrata sum eum me secutum esse.
9 ortae, secutae sunt nos ut tecum loquerentur.
10 pollicitus est se omnia nobiscum passurum esse.
11 tecum locutus sum ut me sequereris.
12 arbitrata est nos secum locuturos esse.
13 eum secuti ad urbem progressi sunt.
14 pollicitusne es te mecum progressuram esse?

15 moratus, e castris progressus non est.
16 arbitrati sunt nos se secutos esse.
17 multa passi sunt ut cum rege loquerentur.
18 pollicita sum me te secuturam esse.
19 pollicita, morata est ut nobiscum loqueretur.
20 arbitrati sumus eos nobiscum loqui velle.
21 virum secuti sumus qui ad castra progressus est.
22 vir quem secuti sumus ad castra progressus est.
23 puellae quae in urbe moratae sunt multa passae sunt.
24 puellae quas ad urbem secuti sumus moratae sunt.
25 esne arbitrata nos te sequi?
26 arbitrati non sumus eos progressuros esse.

G Translate into Latin:

1 We spoke with her.
2 Did you speak with him?
3 He spoke with them.
4 They have spoken with us.
5 I thought he had suffered.
6 We thought they were suffering.

7 He thought that we had suffered many things.
8 They thought that you would suffer many things.
9 Did you (singular) delay in order to follow us?

10 They delayed in order to think.

11 We promised that we would not delay.

12 He promised that he would not speak.

13 You (plural) promised that you would follow me!

14 Having delayed, we did not advance.

15 Having promised, I did not think about it.

16 The man whom I followed delayed.

17 Having thought well, he did not promise.

18 Did you (singular) think that we had delayed?

19 She thought that they had delayed.

20 They thought that I was delaying.

21 Having promised that he would not delay, that man advanced to the city with us.

29.3 Reading Practice

1 *Colloquia Monacensia–Einsidlensia* 2c–f (adapted): a boy describes getting dressed in the morning (perhaps first century AD).

Deposui dormitoria, accepi tunicam, praecinxi me, unxi caput meum et pectinavi, indui paenulam. processi de cubiculo cum paedagogo ut salutarem patrem et matrem. ambos salutavi et osculatus sum, et descendi de domo.

Vocabulary (in order of first appearance; words that appear more than once are in bold)

dēpōnō (like *pōnō*) 'take off'
dormītōrium, -ī (n.) 'nightgown'
tunica, -ae (f.) 'tunic'
praecingō, praecingere, praecīnxī, praecīnctum 'put a belt on'
unguō, unguere, ūnxī, ūnctum 'anoint with oil'
pectinō, -āre, -āvī, -ātum 'comb'
induō, induere, induī, indūtum 'put on'
paenula, -ae (f.) 'cape'

prōcēdō, prōcēdere, prōcessī, prōcessum 'go out'
cubiculum, -ī (n.) 'bedroom'
paedagōgus, -ī (m.) 'child-minder'
salūtō, -āre, -āvī, -ātum 'greet'
ambōs 'both' (accusative)
ōsculor, -ārī, -ātus sum 'kiss'
dēscendō, dēscendere, dēscendī, dēscēnsum 'go down'
domō 'house' (ablative)

2 *Roman Inscriptions of Britain* 1064: funerary inscription from northern England (imperial period).

Dis manibus Victoris natione Maurum annorum XX libertus Numeriani equitis alae I Asturum qui pientissime prosecutus est.

Vocabulary

dīs mānibus 'to the divine spirits'

Victor, Victōris (m.): *name of the dead man* (possessive genitive with *mānibus*)

nātiōne 'from the nation'

Maurum 'Moors' (genitive plural) (an African people)

annōrum 'aged'

XX '20'

lībertus, lībertī (m.) 'freedman'

Numeriānus, Numeriānī (m.): *name of the man responsible for the tomb*

eques, equitis (m.) 'cavalryman'

ālae I Asturum 'of the first regiment of Asturians'

pientissimē 'very devotedly'

prōsequor (like *sequor*) 'follow him to the tomb' (i.e. conduct a funeral procession for him)

30.1 Fear Clauses

Verbs expressing fear, such as *timeō* and *vereor*, take several different constructions in Latin. As in English, they can take an infinitive; this occurs in exactly the same circumstances in both languages. They can also take a subjunctive clause using present or imperfect subjunctive according to the rules of sequence discussed in chapters 16 and 28. Such clauses are introduced by *nē*, which is translated in English by 'that' or 'lest'.

timeō venīre. 'I am afraid to come.'
veritus est venīre. 'He was afraid to come.'
timeō nē veniat. 'I am afraid that he will come.' / 'I fear lest he come.'
veritus est nē venīrent. 'He was afraid that they would come.' / 'He feared lest they come.'

The fact that fear clauses are introduced by *nē* when the subordinate clause is positive means that when the subordinate clause is negative one cannot simply signal that by replacing the initial *ut* with *nē*, as is done with purpose clauses and indirect commands. Instead a negative fear clause can be expressed either by adding *nōn* to it, or by changing *nē* to *ut*.

timeō nē nōn veniat. 'I am afraid that he will not come.' / 'I fear lest he not come.'
timeō ut veniat. 'I am afraid that he will not come.' / 'I fear lest he not come.'
veritus est nē nōn venīrent. 'He was afraid that they would not come.' / 'He feared lest they not come.'
veritus est ut venīrent. 'He was afraid that they would not come.' / 'He feared lest they not come.'

Practice

A Translate:

1 timet ne moriatur.
2 timet mori.
3 timuit ne moreretur.
4 timuit ut moreretur.
5 vereor pati.
6 vereor ne patiar.
7 veritus sum ne paterer.
8 timent sequi.
9 timent ne sequatur.
10 timent ut sequatur.

11 timuerunt ne non sequeretur.
12 veremur ut loquantur.
13 veriti sumus ne loquerentur.
14 veremur loqui.
15 veriti sumus ne non loquerentur.
16 timui ne venaretur.
17 timeo ut venentur.
18 timui venari.

19 milites veriti sunt progredi.
20 milites veriti sunt ne hostes
    progrederentur.
21 milites verentur ut hostes
    progrediantur.
22 milites verebuntur ne hostes
    progrediantur.

B Translate into Latin:

1 He is afraid that they will use
   swords.
2 He was afraid that they would use
   swords.
3 He is afraid that they will not use
   swords.
4 He was afraid to use his sword.
5 They were afraid that we would
   delay.
6 They are afraid that we shall not
   delay.

7 They were afraid that we would
   not delay.
8 They are afraid to delay.
9 We are afraid that he will not
   promise.
10 We are afraid to promise.
11 We were afraid that he would
   promise.
12 We were afraid that he would
   not promise.

30.2 Long Sentences

Latin sentences are often very long. When dealing with a long sentence, the first step is to identify the different clauses of which it is composed (see chapter 15.1 for clauses) and where they begin and end. Conjunctions often provide good clues to the location of clause boundaries, since conjunctions usually come at the start of clauses, but many constructions, particularly those involving infinitives and participles, are not introduced by conjunctions. Verbs can also be helpful, because verbs often come at the end of their clauses, but verbs do not *always* come at the ends of their clauses. Punctuation, when present, should always be used to the maximum; usually it comes not from the original author but from an editor trying to make the sentence intelligible to modern readers. Most of the time, the words for each clause will be grouped together (though one clause may 'nest' inside another); it is rare for the words belonging to one clause to be interspersed randomly with those belonging to another clause (except in poetry, for which see the next chapter). Remember that normally speaking each clause has one verb, so you should expect to end up with as many clauses as you have verbs.

The second step in translating a long sentence is to identify the constructions in the various clauses. Because the same verb form can have radically different translations according to which construction is being used, it is essential to avoid translating verbs until you have identified their constructions.

Practice

C Divide the following sentences into clauses and identify the construction of each clause, then translate:

1 veniens ad urbem, frater meus gladium amisit quem filio dare voluit, et veritus est ut eum inveniret.
2 veritus ne se interficeremus, ille pollicitus est se omnia facturum esse quae volumus.
3 milites hortatus ut bene pugnarent, sed veritus ne fugerent, rex eos e castris ad hostium oppidum duxit.
4 frater meus ad urbem cras ibit quia servos malos quos heri emit vendere vult.
5 euntes ad castra hostium ut ea oppugnarent, milites nos persuaserunt ut secum veniremus.

30.3 Dividing Sentences

When reading real Latin texts, you will often find that there are many words you do not know and have to look up in a dictionary; when you look them up, you discover that each of them has several different meanings, and it is necessary to choose the right one. In order to do that successfully it is usually necessary to have divided the sentence up correctly *before* looking up the words, and therefore it is important to be able to divide up sentences even when you do not know what the words in them mean. If you think carefully about the grammar, this is usually not difficult as long as you know the words that provide the clues to the constructions.

Practice

D Divide the following sentences into clauses and identify the construction of each clause, without translating:

1 arbitrans me aurum ad se laturum esse, mercator me expectavit in taberna ubi aurum semper accipit.
2 quia duci persuasimus ut nuntios ad urbem mitteret, cives gratias agentes nobis argentum dederunt.
3 veritus ne inimici se culparent, consul in senatu orationem habuit et negavit se haec fecisse.

4 pollicitus se me uxorem ducere,
Theseus me dormientem in
insula reliquit et ad patriam
navigavit.

5 puerum poma in arbore edentem
vidimus et ei persuasimus ut
descenderet et pretium pomorum
agricolae daret cuius in fundo
arbor est.

E Translate:

1 quia multa mala de rege nostro
diximus, et arbitramur regem
omnia audivisse, veremur ne
mala patiamur.

2 hostes e castris progressi ad nos
venerunt, et veriti ne nos
oppugnarent in silvam fugimus.

3 regi persuasi ut milites ex urbe
duceret quia veritus sum ne
patrem meum interficerent ut
pecuniam eius haberent.

4 pollicitus se nobis pecuniam
nostram daturum esse, sed
pecuniam non habens, ille
moratur ut eam inveniat.

5 quia pollicita sum eis me in
oppido moraturam non esse, et id

quod pollicita sum non feci,
vereor ne amici mala de me
arbitrentur.

6 verentes ne hostes se
interficerent, nostri regem
oraverunt ne se e castris duceret
et dixerunt se cum amicis morari
velle.

7 servos heri emptos malos esse
arbitrans, pater meus hodie ad
oppidum ire voluit ut eos
venderet; sed ei persuasi ut
moraretur et cras iret.

8 te rogo ut equum nigrum quem
emisti mihi des, quia vereor ut
sine equo amicos meos in urbem
sequi possim.

F Translate into Latin:

1 Fearing that those boys would
follow us, we said that we were
advancing to the enemy in order
to attack them.

2 The boys, who were the sons of
many of us, thought that we
would conquer the enemy and
begged us to take (lead) them
with us so that they could see us
fighting.

3 Because we feared that the enemy
would conquer us, we did not
want to attack them, but we did

not want to say to our sons that
we were afraid.

4 We ordered them not to follow
us, and we persuaded their
mothers to hinder them, so that
we could go away without them.

5 But the boys fled from their
mothers and followed us to the
town, where we bought slaves and
horses.

6 We did not see the boys who
followed us, and we thought that

they were sitting with their mothers and reading books.

7 We ordered the slaves whom we had bought to say that we had captured them fighting, and they did this, but our sons said that they had seen us buying them.

8 Now we are sad, and we fear that our sons will think that we are not brave, because we aren't.

30.4 Reading Practice

1 *Colloquia Monacensia–Einsidlensia*, 1b–q (adapted): the author's preface to the work (perhaps first century AD).

Quoniam video multos velle Latine loqui et Graece, neque facile posse propter difficultatem et multitudinem verborum, meo labori et industriae non peperci, ut in tribus libris interpretamentorum omnia verba scriberem. multos enim video conatos esse, non pro dignitate sicut ipsa res postulat, sed suae cupiditatis et exercitationis causa. propter quam causam non audeo plura verba facere, sed volo omnibus palam facere, neminem melius neque exquisitius interpretatum esse quam me in tribus libris quos scripsi; quorum hic liber primus erit.

 Quoniam parvis pueris incipientibus doceri necessariam vidi esse auditionem interpretamentorum sermonis cottidiani, ut facillime Latine et Graece loqui discant: idcirco paucis verbis de sermone cottidiano scripsi haec quae subiecta sunt.

Vocabulary (in order of first appearance; words that appear more than once are in bold)

quoniam 'since'
Latīnē 'in Latin'
Graecē 'in Greek'
neque 'and . . . not', 'nor'
facile 'easily'
propter (+ accusative) 'on account of'
difficultās, -tātis (f.) 'difficulty'
multitūdō, -tūdinis (f.) 'large number'
labor, labōris (m.) 'effort'
industria, industriae (f.) 'industry'
parcō, parcere, pepercī, parsūrus 'spare'
  (takes object in dative)
tribus 'three' (ablative)
**interpretāmentum, -ī (n.) 'language
  textbook'**
enim 'for' (in the sense of 'because';
  translate one word earlier than
  where it appears in Latin)
cōnor, cōnārī, cōnātus sum 'try'

prō (+ ablative) 'in accordance with'
dignitās, dignitātis (f.) 'worth'
sīcut 'as'
ipsa rēs 'the matter itself' (nominative)
postulō, -āre, -āvī, -ātum 'demand'
cupiditās, cupiditātis (f.) 'gratification'
exercitātiō, -ōnis (f.) 'practice'
causā (+ preceding genitive) 'for the
  sake of'
causa, causae (f.) 'reason'
audeō, audēre, ausus sum 'dare'
plūra 'more' (neuter plural)
palam 'clear' (indeclinable)
nēminem 'no-one' (accusative)
melius 'better' (adverb)
exquīsītius 'more meticulously'
interpretor, -ārī, -ātus sum 'produce
  translations'
quam (+ accusative) 'than'

incipiō (like *capiō*) 'begin'
necessārius, -a, -um 'necessary'
audītiō, audītiōnis (f.) 'hearing'
sermō, sermōnis (m.) 'speech'
cottīdiānus, -a, -um 'daily'

facillimē 'very easily'
discō, discere, didicī, – 'learn'
idcircō 'for that reason'
subiectus, -a, -um 'below'

2 Cicero, *In Catilinam* 3.1: Cicero explains to the Roman populace that he has saved them from a revolutionary plot and they should be grateful to him (beginning of a speech delivered in 63 BC).

Rem publicam, Quirites, vitamque omnium vestrum, bona, fortunas, coniuges liberosque vestros atque hoc domicilium clarissimi imperi, fortunatissimam pul-cherrimamque urbem, hodierno die deorum immortalium summo erga vos amore, laboribus, consiliis, periculis meis e flamma atque ferro ac paene ex faucibus fati ereptam et vobis conservatam ac restitutam videtis.

Vocabulary (in order of first appearance; words that appear more than once are in bold)

rem pūblicam 'state' (accusative
    singular)
Quirītēs, Quirītum (m. plural)
    'Romans'
-que 'and' (translate *before* the word to
    which it is attached)
fortūna, fortūnae (f.) 'fortune'
coniūnx, coniugis (f.) 'wife'
līberī, līberōrum (m. plural) 'children'
atque 'and'
domicilium, domiciliī (n.) 'seat'
clārissimus, -a, -um 'most glorious'
imperium, imperiī (n.) 'empire'
fortūnātissimus, -a, -um 'most
    fortunate'
pulcherrimus, -a, -um 'most beautiful'
hodiernō diē = hodiē

(*translate the ablatives with 'by'*)
summus, summa, summum 'very great'
ergā (+ accusative) 'towards'
amor, amōris (m.) 'love'
labor, labōris (m.) 'labour'
perīculum, perīculī (n.) 'danger'
flamma, flammae (f.) 'fire'
ferrum, ferrī (n.) 'sword'
ac 'and'
faucēs, faucium (f.) 'jaws'
fātum, fātī (n.) 'fate'
ēripiō, ēripere, ēripuī, ēreptum 'snatch
    away'
cōnservō, -āre, -āvī, -ātum 'preserve',
    'save'
restituō, restituere, restituī, restitūtum
    'restore'

Note: with this speech began a praise of Cicero's actions that contemporaries found so wearying that his consulship was called *nōn sine causā sed sine fīne laudātus* (causa, -ae (f.) 'reason'; fīnis, -is, -ium (f.) 'end').

31 | Reading Poetry

31.1 Tips for Reading Latin Poetry

Latin poetry is different from the type of writing we have so far seen. It uses a wider range of vocabulary and grammatical forms (including some borrowed from Greek) and an even freer word order than prose. Adjectives are often some distance from the nouns with which they agree, and the words of one clause may be interspersed with those of another clause. The extracts below come from the beginning of Virgil's *Aeneid* (first century B C); they have not been altered in any way. See whether you can translate them using the vocabulary below and being imaginative with the word order; if you get stuck, try looking at the version below each vocabulary, where the words have been rearranged into an order more like that of prose.

In order to appreciate Latin poetry fully, one needs to learn how its metrical structure works. This information is provided in chapter 66.

31.2 Sample Passages

1 Virgil, Aeneid 1.1–7: the beginning of the epic.

> Arma virumque cano, Troiae qui primus ab oris
> Italiam fato profugus Laviniaque venit
> litora, multum ille et terris iactatus et alto
> vi superum, saevae memorem Iunonis ob iram,
> multa quoque et bello passus, dum conderet urbem
> inferretque deos Latio; genus unde Latinum
> Albanique patres atque altae moenia Romae.

Vocabulary (in order of first appearance; words that appear more than once are in bold)

arma, armōrum (n. plural) 'weapons', 'arms'

-que 'and' (translate *before* the word to which it is attached)

canō, canere, cecinī, cantum 'sing of'

Troia, Troiae (f.) 'Troy'

prīmus, prīma, prīmum 'first'

ōra, ōrae (f.) 'shore'

Italia, Italiae (f.) 'Italy' (translate here as if it were *ad Italiam*; the first vowel can be either long or short)

fātō 'by fate'

profugus 'banished'

Lāvīnius, -a, -um 'of Lavinium' (an old settlement in Italy)

lītus, lītoris (n.) 'coast' (translate as if it were *ad lītora*) multum 'much' (adverbial)

et ... et 'both ... and'

terra, terrae (f.) 'land' (translate here as
  if it were *in terrīs*)

iactō, iactāre, iactāvī, iactātum 'throw
  around'

altō 'on the seas'

vī superum 'by the force of the gods'

saevus, saeva, saevum 'savage'

memor, *gen.* memoris 'implacable'

Iūnō, Iūnōnis (f.) 'Juno'

ob (+ accusative) 'on account of'

īra, īrae (f.) 'anger'

quoque 'also'

bellō: *translate as if it were* in bellō

dum (+ subjunctive) 'until (he) could'

**condō, condere, condidī, conditum
  'found'**

īnferō, īnferre, intulī, illātum 'bring in'

Latiō 'to Latium' (the region of Italy
  around Rome)

genus, generis (n.) 'race'

unde 'from which (came)'

Latīnus, -a, -um 'Latin' (i.e. Roman)

Albānus, -a, -um 'Alban' (i.e. from the
  town of Alba Longa, which provided
  some of Rome's first settlers)

atque 'and'

altus, alta, altum 'high', 'lofty'

Rōma, Rōmae (f.) 'Rome'

A possible prose order of the above would be:

arma virumque cano, qui primus ab oris Troiae fato profugus Italiam Laviniaque litora venit, ille multum iactatus et terris et alto vi superum, ob iram memorem Iunonis saevae, et multa quoque bello passus, dum urbem conderet inferretque deos Latio; unde genus Latinum Albanique patres atque moenia Romae altae.

2 Virgil, *Aeneid* 1.8–11: continuation of passage 1.

Musa, mihi causas memora, quo numine laeso
quidve dolens regina deum tot volvere casus
insignem pietate virum, tot adire labores
impulerit. tantaene animis caelestibus irae?

Vocabulary (in order of first appearance; words that appear more than once are in bold, and words in bold in the preceding vocabulary are not included)

mūsa, mūsae (f.) 'muse' (goddess of song)

causa, causae (f.) 'reason'

memorō, -āre, -āvī, -ātum 'declare'

quō nūmine laesō 'through what slight
  to her divinity'

-ve 'or' (translate *before* the word to
  which it is attached)

doleō, dolēre, doluī, dolitum 'be upset
  about'

rēgīna, rēgīnae (f.) 'queen'

deum: *for* deōrum

tot 'so many'

volvō, volvere, volvī, volūtum 'undergo'

cāsūs 'hardships' (accusative plural!)

īnsignis, īnsigne 'outstanding'

pietāte 'for piety'

adeō (like *eō*) 'undertake'

labor, labōris (m.) 'labour'

impulerit 'compelled'

tantus, tanta, tantum 'so great'

animīs 'spirits' (dative of possession:
  nominative X + dative Y can have
  the same meaning as nominative
  Y + *habeō* + accusative X)

caelestis, caeleste 'heavenly'

A possible prose order of the above would be:

musa, causas mihi memora, quo numine laeso quidve dolens regina deum impulerit virum insignem pietate tot volvere casus, tot adire labores. tantaene (sunt) irae animis caelestibus?

3 Virgil, *Aeneid* 1.12–18: continuation of passage 2.

Urbs antiqua fuit (Tyrii tenuere coloni)
Carthago, Italiam contra Tiberinaque longe
ostia, dives opum studiisque asperrima belli,
quam Iuno fertur terris magis omnibus unam
posthabita coluisse Samo. hic illius arma,
hic currus fuit; hoc regnum dea gentibus esse,
si qua fata sinant, iam tum tenditque fovetque.

Vocabulary (in order of first appearance; words that appear more than once are in bold, and words in bold in the preceding vocabularies are not included)

antīquus, antīqua, antīquum 'ancient'
Tyrius, Tyria, Tyrium 'from Tyre' (a Phoenician city)
tenuēre: *for* tenuērunt, *from* teneō, tenēre, tenuī, tentum 'hold'
colōnus, colōnī (m.) 'colonist'
Carthāgō, Carthāginis (f.) 'Carthage' (a city the Romans hated)
contrā (+ accusative) 'opposite'
Tiberīnus, -a, -um 'of the Tiber' (the river of Rome)
longē 'far'
ōstia, ōstiōrum (n. plural) 'mouth'
dīves, *gen.* dīvitis 'rich'
opum 'in resources'
studiīs (+ genitive) 'in eagerness for'
asperrimus, -a, -um 'very keen'
fertur 'is said' (takes nominative and infinitive)

magis 'more than'
ūnus, ūna, ūnum 'alone'
posthabitā Samō 'with even Samos coming second'
colō, colere, coluī, cultum 'cherish'
currus, currūs (m.) 'chariot'
rēgnum, rēgnī (n.) 'kingdom'
gentibus 'for the world'
sī 'if'
quā 'somehow'
fātum, fātī (n.) 'fate'
sinant 'might allow' (subjunctive)
iam 'already'
tum 'then'
tendō, tendere, tetendī, tentum 'intend'
-que . . . -que 'both . . . and'
foveō, fovēre, fōvī, fōtum 'nurture'

A possible prose order of the above would be:

Carthago urbs antiqua fuit (Tyrii coloni tenuere), longe contra Italiam Tiberinaque ostia, dives opum asperrimaque studiis belli, quam unam Iuno fertur coluisse magis terris omnibus, posthabita Samo: hic illius arma fuit, hic currus; hoc dea iam tum tenditque fovetque esse regnum gentibus, si qua fata sinant.

4 Virgil, *Aeneid* 1.19–22: continuation of passage 3.

Progeniem sed enim Troiano a sanguine duci
audierat Tyrias olim quae verteret arces;
hinc populum late regem belloque superbum
venturum excidio Libyae; sic volvere Parcas.

> **Vocabulary** (in order of first appearance; words in bold in the preceding vocabularies are not included)

prōgeniēs, prōgeniēī (f.) 'offspring'
    (here accusative plural)
enim 'indeed'
Troiānus, -a, -um 'Trojan'
sanguis, sanguinis (n.) 'blood'
dūcī: *present passive infinitive of* dūcō *in indirect statement; translate* 'was being established'
audierat 'she had heard (that)'
ōlim 'some day'
vertō, vertere, vertī, versum 'overturn'
    (subjunctive; translate with 'would')
arx, arcis, arcium (f.) 'citadel'
hinc 'from this (race)'

populus, populī (m.) 'people'
lātē 'widely'
rēgem 'ruling' (literally 'being king')
bellō 'in war'
superbus, -a, -um 'proud'
ventūrum: *for* ventūrum esse
excidiō 'for the ruin'
Libya, Libyae (f.) 'Libya' (an ancient name for the region where Carthage was located, though in modern terms the site of the city is in Tunisia)
sīc 'thus'
volvō, volvere, volvī, volūtum 'decree'
Parcae, Parcārum (f. plural) 'Fates'

A possible prose order of the above would be:

sed enim audierat progeniem a sanguine Troiano duci quae Tyrias arces olim verteret; hinc populum late regem belloque superbum venturum excidio Libyae; sic volvere Parcas.

5 Virgil, *Aeneid* 1.23–33: continuation of passage 4.

Id metuens veterisque memor Saturnia belli,
prima quod ad Troiam pro caris gesserat Argis
(necdum etiam causae irarum saevique dolores
exciderant animo; manet alta mente repostum
iudicium Paridis spretaeque iniuria formae
et genus invisum et rapti Ganymedis honores) –
his accensa super iactatos aequore toto
Troas, reliquias Danaum atque immitis Achilli,
arcebat longe Latio, multosque per annos
errabant acti fatis maria omnia circum.
tantae molis erat Romanam condere gentem.

Vocabulary (in order of first appearance; words in bold in the preceding vocabularies are not included)

metuō, metuere, metuī, – 'dread'

vetus, *gen.* veteris 'former'

memor, *gen.* memoris (+ genitive) 'mindful of'

Sāturnia, Sāturniae (f.) 'daughter of Saturn' (i.e. Juno)

prō (+ ablative) 'on behalf of'

cārus, cāra, cārum 'dear'

gesserat '(she) had waged'

Argus, Arga, Argum 'Argive' (i.e. Greek)

necdum 'nor yet'

etiam 'indeed'

dolor, dolōris (m.) 'grief'

exciderant (+ ablative) 'had departed from'

animus, animī (m.) 'mind' (referring here to Juno's mind)

maneō, manēre, mānsī, mānsum 'remain'

altā mente repostum 'stored deep in her mind' (agrees with *iūdicium*)

iūdicium, iūdiciī (n.) 'judgement'

Paris, Paridis (m.) *name of a Trojan prince*

spernō, spernere, sprēvī, sprētum 'slight', 'insult'

iniūria, iniūriae (f.) 'injury'

fōrma, fōrmae (f.) 'beauty' (referring here to Juno's beauty, implicitly insulted by Paris when he judged Venus the most beautiful goddess)

invīsus, -a, -um 'hateful' (i.e. the Trojans, whom Juno hated)

rapiō, rapere, rapuī, raptum 'snatch away'

Ganymēdēs, -is (m.) 'Ganymede' (a Trojan boy whom Jupiter abducted and kept as a lover, to the annoyance of his wife Juno)

honor, honōris (m.) 'honour'

accendō, accendere, accendī, accēnsum 'enrage'

super (+ ablative) 'across'

iactō, -āre, -āvī, -ātum 'drive', 'toss'

aequor, aequoris (n.) 'sea'

tōtus, tōta, tōtum 'whole'

Trōas 'Trojans' (m. plural accusative)

reliquiae, reliquiārum (f. plural) 'remnants from (the attacks of)' (scans as *relliquiae*)

Danaum 'Greeks' (genitive plural)

immītis, immīte 'pitiless'

Achillī 'Achilles' (genitive singular)

arcēbat 'she was pursuing' (imperfect of *arceō*)

Latiō 'from Latium' (the region of Rome)

annus, annī (m.) 'year'

errābant 'they were wandering' (imperfect of *errō*)

fātīs 'by the fates'

mare, maris, marium (n.) 'sea'

circum (+ accusative) 'around'

mōlēs, mōlis, mōlium (f.) 'effort'

gēns, gentis, gentium (f.) 'nation'

A possible prose order of the above would be:

Saturnia, id metuens memorque veteris belli, quod prima ad Troiam pro caris Argis gesserat (necdum etiam causae irarum saevique dolores exciderant animo; manet alta mente repostum iudicium Paridis iniuriaque spretae formae et genus invisum et honores rapti Ganymedis) – his accensa Troas, reliquias Danaum atque immitis Achilli, iactatos super aequore toto arcebat longe Latio, perque multos annos, acti fatis, circum maria omnia errabant. tantae molis gentem Romanam condere erat.

PART IV

32.1 Active Versus Passive

So far almost all the verb forms we have seen have been in the active voice; that is, they have indicated action done by the subject. It is also possible for a verb to be passive; that is, to indicate action done *to* the subject (we have seen this with the perfect participles in chapters 6.2, 23.3, and 24). Compare the following:

Active: He loves. He will love. He loved. He has loved.
Passive: He is loved. He will be loved. He was loved. He has been loved.

In all these pairs of sentences the same person is the subject of the same verb in the same tense, but because one element of the pair is active and the other is passive, the meaning is very different.

32.2 Verb Endings for the Passive

In Latin regular verbs form their passives by conjugating like deponent verbs; deponent verbs do not have any passives at all. Another way of thinking about this situation is that the endings you have already learned for the deponent verbs are the passive endings, and that deponent verbs are verbs that take passive endings in the active and that therefore cannot have a passive. So the passive system of the tenses we have so far seen is as shown in the tables on the following pages:

	First conjugation	Second conjugation	Third conjugation	Fourth conjugation	Mixed conjugation
Present passive indicative	amor	moneor	regor	audior	capior
	amāris	monēris	regeris	audīris	caperis
	amātur	monētur	regitur	audītur	capitur
	amāmur	monēmur	regimur	audīmur	capimur
	amāminī	monēminī	regiminī	audīminī	capiminī
	amantur	monentur	reguntur	audiuntur	capiuntur
Future passive indicative	amābor	monēbor	regar	audiar	capiar
	amāberis	monēberis	regēris	audiēris	capiēris
	amābitur	monēbitur	regētur	audiētur	capiētur
	amābimur	monēbimur	regēmur	audiēmur	capiēmur
	amābiminī	monēbiminī	regēminī	audiēminī	capiēminī
	amābuntur	monēbuntur	regentur	audientur	capientur
Perfect passive indicative	amātus, -a, -um sum	monitus, -a, -um sum	rēctus, -a, -um sum	audītus, -a, -um sum	captus, -a, -um sum
	amātus, -a, -um es	monitus, -a, -um es	rēctus, -a, -um es	audītus, -a, -um es	captus, -a, -um es
	amātus, -a, -um est	monitus, -a, -um est	rēctus, -a, -um est	audītus, -a, -um est	captus, -a, -um est
	amātī, -ae, -a sumus	monitī, -ae, -a sumus	rēctī, -ae, -a sumus	audītī, -ae, -a sumus	captī, -ae, -a sumus
	amātī, -ae, -a estis	monitī, -ae, -a estis	rēctī, -ae, -a estis	audītī, -ae, -a estis	captī, -ae, -a estis
	amātī, -ae, -a sunt	monitī, -ae, -a sunt	rēctī, -ae, -a sunt	audītī, -ae, -a sunt	captī, -ae, -a sunt
Present passive subjunctive	amer	monear	regar	audiar	capiar
	amēris	moneāris	regāris	audiāris	capiāris
	amētur	moneātur	regātur	audiātur	capiātur
	amēmur	moneāmur	regāmur	audiāmur	capiāmur
	amēminī	moneāminī	regāminī	audiāminī	capiāminī
	amentur	moneantur	regantur	audiantur	capiantur

	First conjugation	Second conjugation	Third conjugation	Fourth conjugation	Mixed conjugation
Imperfect passive subjunctive	amārer amārēris amārētur amārēmur amārēminī amārentur	monērer monērēris monērētur monērēmur monērēminī monērentur	regerer regerēris regerētur regerēmur regerēminī regerentur	audīrer audīrēris audīrētur audīrēmur audīrēminī audīrentur	caperer caperēris caperētur caperēmur caperēminī caperentur
Imperative passive	amāre amāminī	monēre monēminī	regere regiminī	audīre audīminī	capere capiminī
Present passive participle	–	–	–	–	–
Perfect passive participle	amātus, -a, -um	monitus, -a, -um	rēctus, -a, -um	audītus, -a, -um	captus, -a, -um
Future passive participle	–	–	–	–	–
Present passive infinitive	amārī	monērī	regī	audīrī	capī
Perfect passive infinitive	amātus, -a, -um esse	monitus, -a, -um esse	rēctus, -a, -um esse	audītus, -a, -um esse	captus, -a, -um esse
Future passive infinitive	amātum īrī	monitum īrī	rēctum īrī	audītum īrī	captum īrī

This chart does not include quite the same forms we saw in the active, because Latin verbs are not evenly balanced between active and passive: some forms exist only in the active, and others exist only in the passive. Present and future participles exist only in the active, and therefore there are no such participles in this list. Perfect participles, on the other hand, exist only in the passive (except in the case of deponent verbs), and therefore the perfect participles listed above are ones we have seen already. For the infinitives, the present and perfect infinitives are forms we have already seen with the deponent verbs, but the future infinitive has a different form: the fourth principal part (always ending in -*um* regardless of the gender or number or case of the subject, i.e. not agreeing with anything) plus *īrī* (which is the present passive infinitive of *eō* 'go').

The irregular verbs *sum, possum,* and *volō* have no passives. The verb *eō* does have a passive, used largely with compound forms, but as it is not common it will not be discussed here.

The translations of the passive forms of *amō* are as follows:

Present passive indicative

amor	'I am loved', 'I am being loved'
amāris	'you (singular) are loved', 'you (singular) are being loved'
amātur	'he is loved', 'she is loved', 'it is loved', 'he is being loved', 'she is being loved', 'it is being loved', 'is loved', 'is being loved'
amāmur	'we are loved', 'we are being loved'
amāminī	'you (plural) are loved', 'you (plural) are being loved'
amantur	'they are loved', 'they are being loved', 'are loved', 'are being loved'

Future passive indicative

amābor	'I will be loved', 'I shall be loved'
amāberis	'you (singular) will be loved', 'you (singular) shall be loved'
amābitur	'he will be loved', 'she will be loved', 'it will be loved', 'he shall be loved', 'she shall be loved', 'it shall be loved', 'will be loved', 'shall be loved'
amābimur	'we will be loved', 'we shall be loved'
amābiminī	'you (plural) will be loved', 'you (plural) shall be loved'
amābuntur	'they will be loved', 'they shall be loved', 'will be loved', 'shall be loved'

Perfect passive indicative

Note: There is a strong temptation to translate perfect passives as presents. This temptation must be resisted, because although *amātus* means 'loved' and *est* means 'he is', *amātus est* does not mean 'he is loved' (that is *amātur*), but rather 'he was loved'.

amātus sum	'I (masculine) was loved', 'I (masculine) have been loved'
amāta sum	'I (feminine) was loved', 'I (feminine) have been loved'
amātum sum	'I (neuter) was loved', 'I (neuter) have been loved'

amātus es	'you (masculine singular) were loved', 'you (masculine singular) have been loved'
amāta es	'you (feminine singular) were loved', 'you (feminine singular) have been loved'
amātum es	'you (neuter singular) were loved', 'you (neuter singular) have been loved'
amātus est	'he was loved', 'he has been loved', 'was loved', 'has been loved'
amāta est	'she was loved', 'she has been loved', 'was loved', 'has been loved'
amātum est	'it was loved', 'it has been loved', 'was loved', 'has been loved'
amātī sumus	'we (masculine) were loved', 'we (masculine) have been loved'
amātae sumus	'we (feminine) were loved', 'we (feminine) have been loved'
amāta sumus	'we (neuter) were loved', 'we (neuter) have been loved'
amātī estis	'you (masculine plural) were loved', 'you (masculine plural) have been loved'
amātae estis	'you (feminine plural) were loved', 'you (feminine plural) have been loved'
amāta estis	'you (neuter plural) were loved', 'you (neuter plural) have been loved'
amātī sunt	'they (masculine) were loved', 'they (masculine) have been loved', 'were loved', 'have been loved'
amātae sunt	'they (feminine) were loved', 'they (feminine) have been loved', 'were loved', 'have been loved'
amāta sunt	'they (neuter) were loved', 'they (neuter) have been loved', 'were loved', 'have been loved'

Present passive subjunctive

Translation of the present subjunctive depends on the context and construction and cannot be given in isolation, but the following are examples:

amētur	'may he be loved!' (hortatory subjunctive)
amēmur	'let's be loved!' (hortatory subjunctive)
veniet ut amētur.	'He will come in order to be loved.' / ' He will come so that he will be loved.' (purpose clause)
timeō nē amētur.	'I am afraid that he will be loved.' (fear clause)

Imperfect passive subjunctive

Translation of the imperfect subjunctive depends on the context and contruction and cannot be given in isolation, but the following are examples:

vēnit ut amārētur.	'He came in order to be loved.' / 'He came so that he would be loved.' (purpose clause)
timuī nē amārētur.	'I was afraid that he would be loved.' (fear clause)

Imperative passive

amāre   'be loved!' (singular)

amāminī   'be loved!' (plural)

Perfect passive participle

amātus, -a, -um   'having been loved', 'loved'

Present passive infinitive

amārī   'to be loved'

But after certain introductory words the 'to' is omitted. Compare:

vult amārī.   'He wants to be loved.'

potest amārī.   'He can be loved.' / 'He is able to be loved.'

In indirect statement the present infinitive is translated with a present or past indicative, as in these examples:

dīcit eam amārī.   'He says that she is loved.'

dīxit sē amārī.   'He said that he was loved.'

Perfect passive infinitive

In indirect statement the perfect infinitive is translated with a past or pluperfect indicative, as in these examples:

dīcit eam amātam esse.   'He says that she was loved.'

dīxit sē amātum esse.   'He said that he had been loved.'

Future passive infinitive

In indirect statement the future infinitive is translated with a future indicative or with 'would', as in these examples:

dīcit eam amātum īrī.   'He says that she will be loved.'

dīxit sē amātum īrī   'He said that he would be loved.'

Practice

A Translate:

1 regitur	5 capiuntur	9 monemur
2 regetur	6 capientur	10 monebimur
3 rectus est	7 capti sunt	11 moniti sumus
4 recta	8 captae	12 monitae

13 audiris

14 audieris

15 auditus es

16 audita

17 regor

18 regar

19 recta sum

20 capimini

21 capiemini

22 capti estis

23 monetur

24 monebitur

25 monitus est

26 audiuntur

27 audientur

28 auditi sunt

B Translate into Latin:

1   they are ruled

2   they were ruled

3   they will be ruled

4   he was heard

5   he will be heard

6   she is being heard

7   we have been captured

8   we shall be captured

9   we are being captured

10 you (singular) have been warned

11 you (singular) will be warned

12 you (singular) are being warned

13 you (plural) are ruled

14 you (plural) will be ruled

15 you (plural) were ruled

16 I shall be heard

17 I was heard

18 I am heard

19 they were captured

20 they are being captured

21 they will be captured

22 she has been warned

23 she will be warned

24 she is being warned

25 I was ruled

26 I shall be ruled

27 I am ruled

32.3 Expressions of Agency and Means

A passive verb often, but by no means always, has an agent, that is, an indication of who does the action (usually expressed with 'by' in English). The agent in the passive construction is in some ways equivalent to the subject in the active construction, for the following pairs of sentences have very similar meanings:

Active: He loves her.   He will love her.   He loved her.

Passive: She is loved by him.   She will be loved by him.   She was loved by him.

We have already seen (in chapter 23.3) the main agent construction in Latin, *ā* or *ab* + ablative (*amātus ab eō* = 'loved by him'). This construction is used when the agent is a person or other animate being (that is, a deity, a personification, or sometimes an animal), so the pairs of sentences above could be expressed in Latin as follows:

Active: *eam amat.* 'He loves her.'
Passive: *amātur ab eō.* 'She is loved by him.'

Active: *eam amābit.* 'He will love her.'
Passive: *amābitur ab eō.* 'She will be loved by him.'

Active: *eam amāvit.* 'He loved her.'
Passive: *amāta est ab eō.* 'She was loved by him.'

But when the action is caused by an inanimate object, the ablative is used without *ā/ab* where English would use 'by'; this construction is known as the ablative of means.

mīlitēs saxīs impedītī sunt. 'The soldiers were hindered by the stones.'
hī puerī pecūniā nostrā iuvantur. 'These boys are being helped by our money.'

Practice

C Translate:

1   mater a filio amatur.
2   a matre filius amatus est.
3   quis ab hac puella amatus est?
4   cives a rege regentur.
5   hostes flumine impedientur.
6   a magistro liber legitur.
7   haec epistula ab amico nostro scripta est.
8   a poeta dicentur pauca verba.
9   moenia urbis a civibus reficientur.
10 saxis impediti sumus.
11 classis hostium a nobis videbitur.
12 hostium classis a nostris visa est.
13 qui servi a domino vocantur?
14 regis milites flumine impediuntur.
15 urbs nostra ab hostibus oppugnata est.
16 a servo animalia ex aqua acta sunt.
17 dicit te ab omnibus amari.
18 dixit se a puella pulchra amatum esse.
19 ad vos venio ut a vobis defendar.
20 ad regem venerunt ut ab eo defenderentur.
21 quis timuit ne ab hostibus interficeretur?
22 qui timent ne a nobis oppugnantur?
23 dixerunt patrem a se sepultum iri.
24 dixit pecuniam a se inventam esse.
25 milites a rege ducti sunt.
26 ab omnibus vita amatur.
27 soror mea ab agricola amata est.

D Translate into Latin:

1 The gods are praised by everyone.
2 These gods will be praised by them.
3 The god was praised by all the citizens.

4   We shall not be hindered by these stones.

5   Good things will be given to us by the goddess.

6   Good things have been given by our gods.

7   Good things are given to humans by the gods.

8   Were you hindered by the river?

9   I was not hindered by those stones.

10   We went to the teacher in order to be taught.

11   We will go to the teacher in order to be taught.

12   Our men were not hindered by the river.

13   Are you afraid that we will be seen by the enemy?

14   Were you afraid that we would be seen?

15   He says that the money will be found.

16   He said that the money would be found.

17   He will say that the money was found.

18   He said that the money had been found.

32.4 Reading Practice

1 *Colloquium Stephani*, 3a–6a (adapted): an unusually clean Roman boy describes the start of his day (probably first to third century AD). Immediately after this passage he leaves for school: what crucial element of the usual morning routine has he omitted?

Surrexi mane expergefactus, et vocavi puerum. imperavi ut fenestram aperiret; aperuit cito. poposci calceamenta et ocreas; erat enim frigus. calceatus ergo accepi linteum: porrectum est mundum. allata est aqua in urceolo, qua primum manus, deinde faciem lavi. dentes fricui et gingivas; exspui inutilia et emunxi me. tersi manus, deinde bracchia et faciem, ut mundus procederem.

Vocabulary

surgō, surgere, surrēxī, surrēctum 'get up'
māne 'in the morning'
expergēfaciō (like *faciō*) 'awaken'
fenestra, fenestrae (f.) 'window'
aperiō, aperīre, aperuī, apertum 'open'
cito 'quickly'
poscō, poscere, poposcī, – 'ask for'
calceāmentum, -ī (n.) 'shoe'
ocrea, ocreae (f.) 'legging'
erat 'it was'

enim 'for' (in the sense of 'because'; translate one word earlier than where it appears in Latin)
frīgus, frīgoris (n.) 'cold'
calceō, calceāre, calceāvī, calceātum 'shoe' (i.e. put shoes on)
ergō 'so' (translate one word earlier than where it appears in Latin)
linteum, linteī (n.) 'linen towel'
porrigō, porrigere, porrēxī, porrēctum 'pass'
mundus, munda, mundum 'clean'

afferō, afferre, attulī, allātum 'bring'
urceolus, urceolī (m.) 'little jug'
quā 'with which'
prīmum 'first'
manūs 'hands' (accusative plural)
deinde 'then'
faciem 'face' (accusative)
lavō, lavāre, lāvī, lautum 'wash'
dēns, dentis, dentium (m.) 'tooth'
fricō, fricāre, fricuī, frictum 'brush'
gingīva, gingīvae (f.) 'gum'

exspuō, exspuere, exspuī, exspūtum
  'spit out'
inūtilis, inūtile 'useless'
ēmungō, ēmungere, ēmūnxī,
  ēmūnctum 'blow or wipe the nose'
  (with accusative of person whose
  nose is blown or wiped)
tergō, tergere, tersī, tersum 'dry'
bracchium, bracchiī (n.) 'arm'
prōcēdō, prōcēdere, prōcessī,
  prōcessum 'go out'

2 Caesar, *De bello Gallico* 1.1.1–2: the geography of Gaul (first century BC). Some words are left implied: can you supply them from nearby clauses?

Gallia est omnis divisa in partes tres, quarum unam incolunt Belgae, aliam Aquitani, tertiam qui ipsorum lingua Celtae, nostra Galli appellantur. hi omnes lingua, institutis, legibus inter se differunt. Gallos ab Aquitanis Garumna flumen, a Belgis Matrona et Sequana dividit. horum omnium fortissimi sunt Belgae.

Vocabulary

Gallia, Galliae (f.) 'Gaul'
dīvidō, dīvidere, dīvīsī, dīvīsum
  'divide'
pars, partis, partium (f.) 'part'
trēs, tria 'three'
ūnus, ūna, ūnum 'one'
incolō, incolere, incoluī, – 'inhabit'
Belgae, Belgārum (m. plural) *the*
  name of a Gaulish people
alius, alia, aliud 'another'
Aquītānī, -ōrum (m. plural) *the name*
  of a Gaulish people
tertius, tertia, tertium 'third'
ipsōrum = suā (here, but not usually)
lingua, linguae (f.) 'language',
  'tongue'

Celtae, Celtārum (m. plural) *the name*
  of a Gaulish people
Gallī, Gallōrum (m. plural) *the name*
  of a Gaulish people
appellō, -āre, -āvī, -ātum 'call'
  (*translate the ablatives here with 'in'*)
īnstitūtum, -ī (n.) 'custom'
lēx, lēgis (f.) 'law'
inter (+ accusative) 'between', 'among'
differō, differre, distulī, dīlātum (third
  conjugation) 'differ'
Garumna, -ae (f.) *the name of a river*
Mātrona, -ae (f.) *the name of a river*
Sēquana, -ae (f.) *the name of a river*
fortissimus, -a, -um 'bravest'

3 *Corpus Inscriptionum Latinarum* VI.889: inscription from Rome (AD 12).

Gaius Caesar, Germanici Caesaris filius, hic crematus est.

Vocabulary

Caesar, Caesaris (m.) *was at this period
an inherited name of the imperial
family*

Germānicus, -ī (m.) *the individual
name of a member of the imperial
family*

cremō, cremāre, cremāvī, cremātum
'cremate'

4 Martial 14.42: in praise of a wax candle (first century AD).

Hic tibi nocturnos praestabit cereus ignis:
  subducta est puero namque lucerna tuo.

Vocabulary

nocturnus, -a, -um 'at night'
praestō, -stāre, -stitī, -stitum 'provide'
cēreus, cēreī (m.) 'wax candle'
ignis, ignis, ignium (m.) 'light' (here
  accusative plural)

subdūcō (like *dūcō*) 'steal from'
  (+ ablative)
namque 'for' (translate at start
  of second line)
lucerna, lucernae (f.) 'lamp'

5 *Puer nobis nascitur* (verses 1–3): medieval Christmas carol.

Puer nobis nascitur, rector angelorum;
in hoc mundo panditur dominus dominorum.

In praesepe positum, sub faeno asinorum,
cognoverunt dominum Christum regem caelorum.

Hunc Herodes timuit magno cum tremore;
in infantes irruit, hos caedens in furore.

Vocabulary

nāscor, nāscī, nātus sum 'be born'
rēctor, rēctōris (m.) 'ruler'
angelus, angelī (m.) 'angel'
mundus, mundī (m.) 'world'
pandō, pandere, pandī, pānsum 'reveal'
praesēpe, praesēpis (n.) 'stall'
faenum, faenī (n.) 'hay'
asinus, asinī (m.) 'donkey'
cognōscō, cognōscere, cognōvī,
  cognitum 'recognize'

Chrīstus, -ī (m.) 'Christ'
caelum, caelī (n.) 'heaven'
Hērōdēs, Hērōdis (m.) 'king Herod'
cum: *translate before* magnō
tremor, tremōris (m.) 'trembling'
īnfāns, īnfantis (m.) 'little child'
irruō, irruere, irruī, – (+ *in* + accusative)
  'attack'
caedō, caedere, cecīdī, caesum 'kill'
furor, furōris (m.) 'fury'

33 | Result Clauses

33.1 Result Clauses

So far we have seen three types of subordinate clause taking the subjunctive: purpose clauses, indirect commands, and fear clauses. A fourth type is the result clause, which indicates the result of the action expressed in the main verb. Like the three types of subjunctive clause already seen, result clauses follow sequence of tenses: the present subjunctive is used if the main verb is in a primary tense, and the imperfect subjunctive if it is in a historic tense.[1] (So far, the only historic tense we have seen is the perfect.) Result clauses are introduced by *ut*; if the result is negative, the *ut* does not change to *nē*, but instead a *nōn* is added to the verb of the subordinate clause. Most result clauses can be translated with English 'that' and a normal indicative verb, but there are also other possibilities.

Result clauses are almost always signalled by the presence of one of these words in the main clause: *tot* 'so many'; *tantus, -a, -um* 'so great', 'so big'; *tālis, -e* 'such'; *ita* 'so', in such a way'; *tam* 'so'; *adeō* 'so', 'to such an extent'.

mīlitēs adeō timuērunt ut fugerent. 'The soldiers were so frightened that they fled.'
classis hostium tanta est ut timeāmus. 'The enemy's fleet is so big that we are frightened.'
nostrī tam fortēs sunt ut nōn fugiant. 'Our men are so brave that they are not fleeing.'

Practice

A Translate:

1 tot hostes visi sunt ut nostri timerent.
2 soror mea tam pulchra est ut ab omnibus ametur.
3 classis hostium tanta est ut nostri vincantur.
4 haec puella adeo laudatur ut semper felix sit.
5 talis est ut numquam vincatur.
6 hic magister tam bonus est ut omnes pueri ab eo doceri velint.
7 milites adeo timuerunt ut e castris duci non possent.

---

[1] Although this rule will suffice for most occurrences, it is not strictly speaking complete, as result clauses sometimes take a perfect subjunctive (see chapter 46).

8 moenia illius urbis tanta sunt ut capi non possit.

9 tot libri scripti sunt ut legi non possent.

B Translate into Latin:

1 The new king is so brave that now all the soldiers want to fight.

2 The farmer bought so many sheep that he did not have money.

3 I was praised to such an extent that I wanted to flee.

4 That animal is so big that we cannot bury it.

5 Our king is such (a person) that he is always defeated.

33.2 Distinguishing Different Types of Subjunctive Clauses

The four types of subordinate clause with subjunctive that we have so far seen are distinguished by the following features:

Construction	Syntactic clues in main clause	Subordinate clause introduced by (if no negative in subordinate clause)	(if negative in subordinate clause)
Result clause	*tantus, tam*, etc.	*ut*	*ut ... nōn*
Fear clause	verb of fearing	*nē*	*ut* (or *nē ... nōn*)
Indirect command	verb of asking, etc.	*ut*	*nē*
Purpose clause	none	*ut*	*nē*

Their translations are different as follows (only the most common translations are listed here; many others are possible):

Construction	Translation	Example
Result clause	1. 'that' + present indicative (if in primary sequence)	*adeō timet ut fugiat.* 'He is so frightened that he is fleeing.'
	2. 'that' + past indicative (if in historic sequence)	*adeō timuit ut fugeret.* 'He was so frightened that he fled.' historic sequence
Fear clause	3. 'that' + future indicative (if in primary sequence)	*timeō nē veniat.* 'I am afraid that he will come.'
	4. 'that' + 'would' (if in historic sequence)	*timuī nē venīret.* 'I was afraid that he would come.'
Indirect command	5. infinitive	*rogō eum ut veniat.* 'I am asking him to come.'
Purpose clause	6. infinitive (if both clauses have the same subject)	*discēdit ut veniat.* 'He is leaving (e.g. home) to come.'
	7. 'in order to' + infinitive (if both clauses have the same subject)	*discēdit ut veniat.* 'He is leaving in order to come.'
	8. 'so that' + future indicative (if in primary sequence)	*vocō eum ut veniat.* 'I am calling him so that he will come.'
	9. 'so that' + 'would' (if in historic sequence)	*vocāvī eum ut venīret.* 'I called him so that he would come.'

The result of all this is that it is essential to look for the clues provided in the first table above before translating one of these subordinate clauses: one can only choose between the translations provided in the second table after working out which construction is present.

Practice

C Identify the constructions of the subordinate clauses and translate:

1 saxis hostes adeo impediti sunt ut vinci possent.

2 milites capti timuerunt ne interficerentur.

3 quis servos hortatus est ut nobiscum venirent?

4 tot hostes videntur ut nostri timeant.

5 haec saxa tam gravia sunt ut eis uti non possimus.

6 quis pecuniam patri dedit ne amitteretur?

7 milites orati sunt ne fugerent, sed fugerunt.

8 rex veretur ne ab hostibus capiatur.

9 moenia nostra tanta sunt ut omnes hostes vincantur.

10 pueri veriti sunt ut ab hoc magistro docerentur.

11 rex ab omnibus civibus rogabitur ut nos iuvet.

12 nobiscum locutus est ut intellegeretur.

13 hanc puellam amo adeo ut cum ea sepeliri velim.

14 ad vos venio ne interficiar.

15 tot milites fugerunt ut nostri vincerentur.

16 rex veritus est ne ab hostibus caperetur.

17 soror mea tam pulchra fuit ut ab omnibus amaretur.

18 vobiscum loquor ut intellegar.

19 rex ab omnibus civibus rogatus est ut nos iuvaret.

20 classis hostium tanta fuit ut nostri vincerentur.

21 pueri verentur ut ab hoc magistro doceantur.

22 quis pecuniam patri dabit ne amittatur?

23 tot hostes oppugnaverunt ut nostri vincerentur.

24 haec saxa hostes adeo impedient ut vinci possint.

25 milites capti timent ne interficiantur.

26 tot libri scribuntur ut legi non possint.

27 illa puella adeo laudata est ut semper felix esset.

28 servosne hortaberis ut tecum veniant?

29 illam puellam adeo amavit ut cum ea sepeliri vellet.

30 ad nos venerunt ne interficerentur.

31 liber a te scriptus tam longus est ut eum legere non possimus.

32 hoc oppidum tantum est ut a nostris oppugnari non possit.

33 ille magister tam bonus fuit ut omnes pueri ab eo doceri vellent.

34 milites adeo timent ut e castris duci non possint.

35 moenia illius urbis tanta fuerunt ut capi non posset.

D Identify the constructions of the subordinate clauses and translate:

1 He was afraid that the money would be lost.

2 I was asked not to hunt.

3 They are so small that they cannot be seen.

4 He came so that he would be helped.

5 So many of our men came that the enemy fled.

6 She is afraid that she will not be loved.

7 The walls are so big that we cannot see the river.

8 Who persuaded them to hear us?

9 They were so frightened that they fled into the forest.

10 He gave us money in order to be praised.

33.3 **Reading Practice**

1 *Colloquium Celtis* 66c–68b (adapted): coming home to a scolding after a party (probably second or third century AD).

WIFE: itane decet sapientem patremfamilias, qui aliis consilia dat, se regere? non potest turpius nec ignominiosius agere quam heri egisti.

HUSBAND: me certe valde pudet.

WIFE: quid dicunt alii in absentia tua? infamiam maximam tibi cumulavisti. rogo te ne postea talia facias.

HUSBAND: nescio quid dicam; ita enim perturbatus sum ut rationem nulli possim reddere.

Vocabulary

decet 'it is fitting (for)'
sapiēns, *gen.* sapientis 'wise'
paterfamiliās (declines like *pater + familiās*) 'head of a household'
alius, alia, aliud 'other'
potest 'it is possible'
turpius 'more shamefully'
nec 'nor'
ignōminiōsius 'more ignominiously'
quam 'than'

certē 'certainly'
valdē 'very much'
pudet 'it embarrasses'
absentia, absentiae (f.) 'absence'
īnfāmia, īnfāmiae (f.) 'infamy', 'bad reputation'
maximus, maxima, maximum 'enormous'
cumulō, -āre, -āvī, -ātum 'accumulate'
posteā 'in the future'

nesciō, nescīre, nescīvī, nescītum 'not
    know'
perturbātus, -a, -um 'upset'
ratiō, ratiōnis (f.) 'explanation'

nūllī 'to no-one' (dative)
reddō, reddere, reddidī, redditum
    'give'

2 Cicero, *Epistulae ad familiares* 15.1.5: Cicero informs the Senate of the problems with Rome's allies in Cilicia (part of a letter written in 51 BC).

Nam sociorum auxilia propter acerbitatem atque iniurias imperi nostri aut ita imbecilla sunt, ut non multum nos iuvare possint, aut ita alienata a nobis, ut neque exspectandum ab iis neque committendum iis quicquam esse videatur.

Vocabulary

nam 'for'
socius, sociī (m.) 'ally'
auxilia, auxiliōrum (n. plural)
    'auxiliary troops'
propter (+ accusative) 'on
    account of'
acerbitās, acerbitātis (f.) 'harshness'
atque 'and'
iniūria, iniūriae (f.) 'injustice'
imperium, imperiī (n.) 'rule'
aut . . . aut 'either . . . or'
imbēcillus, -a, -um 'feeble'

multum 'much' (adverb)
aliēnātus, -a, -um 'alienated'
neque . . . neque 'neither . . . nor'
exspectandus, -a, -um 'able to be
    expected'
committendus, -a, -um (+ dative) 'able
    to be entrusted to'
quicquam 'anything' (neuter
    nominative singular; needs
    to be translated twice
    in English)
videor (passive of *videō*) 'seem'

3 Cicero, *Tusculan Disputations* 2.11.27 (adapted): praise of Plato's *Republic* (first century BC).

Sed videsne, poetae quid mali adferant? lamentantes inducunt fortissimos viros, molliunt animos nostros, ita sunt deinde dulces, ut non legantur modo, sed etiam ediscantur. . . . recte igitur a Platone eiciuntur ex ea civitate, quam finxit ille cum optimos mores et optimum rei publicae statum exquireret.

Vocabulary

quid malī 'what trouble' (literally
    'what of trouble')
adferant '(they) produce'
lāmentor, -ārī, -ātus sum
    'lament'
indūcō (like *dūcō*) 'portray'
fortissimus, -a, -um 'the bravest'

molliō, mollīre, mollīvī, mollītum
    'soften'
animus, animī (m.) 'spirit'
deinde 'finally'
dulcis, dulce 'sweet'
nōn . . . modo 'not only'
etiam 'even'

ēdiscō, ēdiscere, ēdidicī, – 'learn by
    heart'
rēctē 'rightly'
igitur 'therefore'
Platō, Platōnis (m.) *name of a Greek
    philosopher*
ēiciō, ēicere, ēiēcī, ēiectum 'expel'
cīvitās, cīvitātis (f.) 'state'

fingō, fingere, fīnxī, fictum 'invent'
cum … exquīreret 'when he was
    investigating'
optimus, optima, optimum 'best'
mōs, mōris (m.) 'customs'
reī pūblicae 'of a state'
statum 'condition' (accusative
    singular)

33.4 Vocabulary to Learn

Nouns

cornū, cornūs (n.)	'horn'
diēs, diēī (m.)	'day'
domus, domūs/domī (f.)	'house', 'home'
exercitus, exercitūs (m.)	'army'
fidēs, fideī (f.)	'faith', 'trust'
genū, genūs (n.)	'knee'
gradus, gradūs (m.)	'step'
manus, manūs (f.)	'hand'
metus, metūs (m.)	'fear'
rēs, reī (f.)	'matter', 'affair', 'thing'
senātus, senātūs (m.)	'senate'
spēs, speī (f.)	'hope'
versus, versūs (m.)	'verse'

Adjectives

tālis, -e	'such', 'of such a sort'
tantus, -a, -um	'so great', 'so big'
tot (indeclinable)	'so many'

Adverbs and Conjunctions

adeō	'so', 'to such an extent' (used with verbs)
aut	'or'
autem (postpositive)	'however'
enim (postpositive)	'for' (the conjunction 'for' in 'for he's a jolly good fellow', not the preposition 'for' in 'he stayed for two days')
ergō	'therefore'
ibi	'there'
igitur (postpositive)	'therefore'

Vocabulary continues.

ita	'so', 'thus', 'in such a way' (used with adjectives, adverbs, and verbs)
nam	'for' (the conjunction 'for' in 'for he's a jolly good fellow', not the preposition 'for' in 'he stayed for two days')
-que (postpositive)	'and'
sī	'if'
tam	'so' (i.e. to such a degree, used with adjectives and adverbs)
tamen	'nevertheless'

Note: 'postpositive' means that the word in question does not come first in a clause or phrase and usually needs to be translated in English one word earlier than where it appears. Thus *puerī enim vēnērunt* means 'for the boys came', not 'the boys for came', and *puerī puellaeque* means 'boys and girls', not 'boys girls and'. *Autem* and *igitur* can be translated either where they appear in Latin or one place to the left, depending on one's English style: *puerī autem vēnērunt* = 'The boys, however, came' or 'However, the boys came'; *puerī igitur vēnērunt* = 'The boys, therefore, came' or 'Therefore, the boys came'.

34 | Fourth and Fifth Declensions, Uses of the Ablative

34.1 Fourth and Fifth Declensions

So far we have seen three declensions, but there are also two more. The fourth declension includes nouns of all three genders, while the fifth includes only masculine and feminine nouns; neither includes any adjectives. In both these declensions masculine and feminine nouns are declined identically to each other.

British Case Order

Fourth declension

	Masculine and feminine *gradus, gradūs* (m.) 'step'		Neuter *genū, genūs* (n.) 'knee'	
	Singular	Plural	Singular	Plural
Nom.	gradus	gradūs	genū	genua
Voc.	gradus	gradūs	genū	genua
Acc.	gradum	gradūs	genū	genua
Gen.	gradūs	graduum	genūs	genuum
Dat.	graduī	gradibus	genū	genibus
Abl.	gradū	gradibus	genū	genibus

Fifth declension

	rēs, reī (f.) 'matter', 'affair', 'thing'		*diēs, diēī* (m.) 'day'	
	Singular	Plural	Singular	Plural
Nom.	rēs	rēs	diēs	diēs
Voc.	rēs	rēs	diēs	diēs
Acc.	rem	rēs	diem	diēs
Gen.	reī	rērum	diēī	diērum
Dat.	reī	rēbus	diēī	diēbus
Abl.	rē	rēbus	diē	diēbus

Ancient Case Order

Fourth declension

| | Masculine and feminine *gradus, gradūs* (m.) 'step' | | Neuter *genū, genūs* (n.) 'knee' | |
	Singular	Plural	Singular	Plural
Nom./Voc.	gradus	gradūs	genū	genua
Gen.	gradūs	graduum	genūs	genuum
Dat.	graduī	gradibus	genū	genibus
Acc.	gradum	gradūs	genū	genua
Abl.	gradū	gradibus	genū	genibus

Fifth declension

| | *rēs, reī* (f.) 'matter', 'affair', 'thing' | | *diēs, diēī* (m.) 'day' | |
	Singular	Plural	Singular	Plural
Nom./Voc.	rēs	rēs	diēs	diēs
Gen.	reī	rērum	diēī	diērum
Dat.	reī	rēbus	diēī	diēbus
Acc.	rem	rēs	diem	diēs
Abl.	rē	rēbus	diē	diēbus

Notice that in the paradigm of *gradus* the *-us* ending has a short *u* in the nominative and vocative singular, but a long *ū* everywhere else. The dative singular *genū* is surprising; we would expect *genuī*.

34.2 *Domus*

The word for 'home' and 'house' (*domus, domūs/domī* (f.)) combines forms from the second and the fourth declensions.

British Case Order

	Singular	Plural
Nom.	domus	domūs
Voc.	domus	domūs
Acc.	domum	domōs/domūs
Gen.	domūs/domī	domōrum
Dat.	domuī/domō	domibus
Abl.	domō	domibus

Ancient Case Order

	Singular	Plural
Nom./Voc.	domus	domūs
Gen.	domūs/domī	domōrum
Dat.	domuī/domō	domibus
Acc.	domum	domōs/domūs
Abl.	domō	domibus

Practice

A Identify the paradigms to which the following belong and decline them:

1 cornū, cornūs (n.) 'horn'
2 exercitus, exercitūs (m.) 'army'
3 fidēs, fideī (f.) 'faith', 'trust' (singular only)
4 manus, manūs (f.) 'hand'

5 metus, metūs (m.) 'fear' (singular only)
6 senātus, senātūs (m.) 'senate' (singular only)
7 spēs, speī (f.) 'hope' (singular only)
8 versus, versūs (m.) 'verse'

B Translate:

1 genua mea fortia non sunt.
2 suntne acria, cornua ovium ad nos currentium?
3 nunc dies longi sunt.
4 exercitus noster progrediens ab hostibus visus est.
5 hi agri senatui Romano dabuntur.
6 pecunia tua amissa in manibus eius inventa est.
7 domus nostros reficiemus.
8 hanc rem non intellego.
9 versus a poetis scribuntur.
10 nostri sine metu hostes oppugnaverunt.
11 fides omnium in te posita est.

12 deus, qui bona hominibus dat, spes nostra est.
13 domus regum a multis videntur.
14 verba tua a senatu audientur.
15 quis ovem sine cornibus emere vult?
16 gladii ab eo facti exercitui dati sunt.
17 manus dei a poeta laudatur.
18 multos versus scripsit hic poeta.
19 domus mea ab eo reficietur.
20 haec res mea est, non tua.
21 hi versus ab illo poeta scripti sunt.
22 liber de his rebus ab eo scriptus est.

C Translate into Latin:

1 Who wants to repair our houses?
2 Do you see the enemy's army advancing?
3 Our senate is praised by everyone.
4 The girl's knees were seen by the poet.
5 My affairs do not have themselves well. (= are not in good shape)
6 Horses do not have hands.
7 All the sheep without horns have now been sold.
8 We shall always have hope.

9 The verses written by this poet are not good.
10 Whose houses were sold yesterday?
11 The faith of Greeks who speak well is bad.
12 The soldiers advanced without fear into the forest.
13 I would like to buy your (singular) house.
14 A book about the senate will not be read.
15 Is your (plural) house big?

34.3 Ablative of Means with Active Verbs

We have seen (chapter 32.3) the ablative of means, namely the ablative used without a preposition to designate a thing that carries out the action of a passive verb, as *mīlitēs saxīs impediuntur* 'the soldiers are hindered by the stones' (recall that this ablative of means is different from the ablative of agent with *ā/ab*, which is used when a person carries out the action of a passive verb: *mīlitēs ab hostibus impediuntur* 'the soldiers are hindered by the enemy'). The ablative of means construction can also be used with an active verb, but in those circumstances the English translation is normally 'with' rather than 'by', as *mīlitēs saxīs impedīvimus* 'we hindered the soldiers with stones' (or 'we hindered the soldiers by means of stones').

Practice

D Translate these ablatives of means, using 'with' or 'by' as appropriate:

1 agricola animalia gladio interfecit.

2 nostros gladiis vincere non potestis.

3 haec omnia manibus nostris facta sunt.

4 amicos pecunia iuvare possumus.

5 nostri metu non impedientur.

6 manibus suis domum refecit.

7 exercitu magno urbem defendemus.

8 hostes saxis impedivimus.

9 fide tua victi sumus.

10 oves se defendunt cornibus suis.

11 magister pueros verbis scriptis docuit.

12 discedens flumine impeditus sum.

13 hostes metu victi sunt.

14 multis versibus deos laudavit.

34.4 Ablative of Accompaniment

When translating from English to Latin it is important to distinguish this use of 'with' to identify the means by which something is done (normally an object, e.g. 'I fixed it with string') from the use of 'with' for accompaniment (normally a person, e.g. 'I came with my friends'); this latter 'with' is Latin *cum* + ablative (the 'ablative of accompaniment') rather than the ablative of means. Thus *cum amicīs hostēs gladiīs oppugnāvimus* can be translated '(along) with (our) friends we attacked the enemy with swords'. Note in particular the difference between *cum eō pugnāvī* 'I fought with him' (i.e. he and I had a fight) versus *gladiō pugnāvī* 'I fought with a sword' (i.e. I used a sword to fight). If a Roman had said *cum gladiō pugnāvī*, he would have been implying that his sword had come to life and fought on its own. Of course, it is also necessary to distinguish the 'by' that would be an ablative of means (one followed by an inanimate object) from the 'by' that would be an ablative of agent and therefore require *ā/ab* in Latin (one followed by a word indicating a person or other animate agent). A simple rule that will work almost all the time is that 'with' and 'by' are equivalent to the Latin ablative without a preposition when their object is a thing, but when their object is a person they are equivalent to *cum* or *ā/ab* (+ ablative).

Practice

E State whether the underlined words in each sentence should be translated into Latin with *ā/ab* (+ ablative), *cum* (+ ablative), or an ablative without a preposition.

1   He came with his brother.
2   They tricked him with a fake ID.
3   Did you work with Mike?
4   We work by stealth.
5   We shall not be defeated by the Parthians.
6   The temple was buried by a landslide.
7   Our men fought with javelins.
8   Our men fought with the enemy.
9   I like to chat with Jim.
10 I bought it with the money he gave me.
11 We are saddened by his early death.
12 She was mistreated by her husband.
13 He is over there with the soldiers.
14 She struck me with her fist.
15 May I come with you?
16 Jane lives with John.
17 We were seen by everyone.
18 They won by trickery.
19 With your help we can do it.
20 Our son always plays with Jimmy.
21 I sewed it up with a shoelace.
22 She's walking with Mary.
23 The police caught him with a hidden camera.
24 The police caught him with his accomplice.
25 We shall win by hook or by crook.
26 These poems will be read by posterity.

34.5 Reading Practice

1 Cicero, *Epistulae ad Atticum* 7.13.1 (adapted): Cicero writes to his friend T. Pomponius Atticus about the dangers posed by Caesar (part of a letter written in 49 BC).

Amo etiam Pisonem, cuius iudicium de genero suspicor visum iri grave – quamquam genus belli vides. ita civile est ut non ex civium dissensione, sed ex unius perditi civis audacia natum sit. is autem valet exercitu, tenet multos spe et promissis, omnia omnium concupivit.

Vocabulary

etiam 'even'	dissēnsiō, dissēnsiōnis (f.)
Pīsō, Pīsōnis (m.) *name of Caesar's*	'disagreement'
father-in-law	ūnīus 'one' (genitive singular)
iūdicium, iūdiciī (n.) 'judgement'	perditus, -a, -um 'abandoned' (i.e. lost
gener, generī (m.) 'son-in-law'	to all good sense)
suspicor, suspicārī, suspicātus sum	audācia, audāciae (f.) 'audacity'
'suspect'	nātus, nāta, nātum 'born from'
videor (passive of *videō*) 'be seen as'	valeō, valēre, valuī, valitum 'be strong
gravis *can also mean* 'important'	in' (+ ablative)
quamquam 'although'	teneō, tenēre, tenuī, tentum 'hold'
genus, generis (n.) 'type'	prōmissum, prōmissī (n.) 'promise'
cīvīlis, cīvīle 'civil'	concupīscō, -pīscere, -pīvī, -pītum
	'desire'

2 St Thomas Aquinas, first verse of hymn *Pange lingua*: the saint speaks to his own tongue (thirteenth century). The 'king of peoples' refers to Christ.

Pange, lingua, gloriosi corporis mysterium,
sanguinisque pretiosi quem in mundi pretium
fructus ventris generosi rex effudit gentium.

Vocabulary

pangō, pangere, pepigī, pāctum 'fix',	mundus, mundī (m.) 'world'
'celebrate in poetry'	pretium, pretiī (n.) 'price'
lingua, linguae (f.) 'tongue'	frūctus, frūctūs (m.) 'produce'
glōriōsus, -a, -um 'glorious'	venter, ventris (m.) 'womb'
mystērium, -ī (n.) 'mystery'	generōsus, -a, -um 'noble'
sanguis, sanguinis (m.) 'blood'	effundō, effundere, effūdī, effūsum
pretiōsus, -a, -um 'precious'	'pour out'
in (+ accusative) 'as'	gēns, gentis, gentium (f.) 'people'

3 Apicius, *De re coquinaria* 7.7.1 (adapted): from an ancient cookbook, the recipe for cooking a pig's stomach (perhaps fifth century AD).

Ventrem porcinum bene evacuas, lavas aceto et sale et postea aqua, et hanc impensam imples: pulpam porcinam tonsam et ita tritam ut enervata commisceas cerebella tria et ova cruda, cui nucleos infundis et piper integrum mittis et hoc iure temperas: teris piper, silphium, anisum, zingiberi, rutam modicam, liquamen optimum, et oleum modicum. ventrem ita reples ut laxamentum habeat, ne dissiliat in coctura. surculas ambas et in ollam bullientem mittis. levas et pungis acu, ne crepet. cum ad

dimidias coctum fuerit, levas et in fumum suspendis ut coloretur, et denuo eum
perelixabis ut coqui possit. deinde liquamen, merum, oleum modicum mittis, et
cultello aperis et cum liquamine apponis.

Vocabulary

venter, ventris (m.) 'stomach'
porcīnus, -a, -um 'of a pig', 'pork'
ēvacuō, -āre, -āvī, -ātum 'empty'
lavō, lavāre, lāvī, lautum 'wash'
acētum, acētī (n.) 'vinegar'
sāl, salis (m.) 'salt'
posteā 'afterwards'
impēnsa, impēnsae (f.) 'stuffing'
impleō, implēre, implēvī, implētum
    'stuff into it'
pulpa, pulpae (f.) 'meat'
tondeō, tondēre, totondī, tōnsum 'cut up'
terō, terere, trīvī, trītum 'pound'
ēnervō, -āre, -āvī, -ātum 'remove the
    sinews of'
commisceō, -miscēre, -miscuī, -mixtum
    'mix in'
cerebellum, cerebellī (n.) 'brain'
trēs, tria 'three'
ōvum, ōvī (n.) 'egg'
crūdus, crūda, crūdum 'raw'
nucleus, nucleī (m.) 'nut'
īnfundō, īnfundere, īnfūdī, īnfūsum (+
    dative) 'pour in to'
piper, piperis (n.) 'peppercorn'
integer, integra, integrum 'whole', 'intact'
mittō *can also mean* **'put in'**
iūs, iūris (n.) 'juice', 'sauce'
temperō, -āre, -āvī, -ātum 'blend'
silphium, silphiī (n.) 'silphium' (a plant)
anīsum, anīsī (n.) 'anise'
zingiberi, zingiberis (n.) 'ginger'
rūta, rūtae (f.) 'rue'
modicus, -a, -um 'a little'
liquāmen, liquāminis (n.) 'garum'
    (sauce made by leaving fish in the
    sun for 3 months)

optimus, optima, optimum 'best-
    quality'
oleum, oleī (n.) 'olive oil'
repleō, replēre, replēvī, replētum 'fill up'
laxāmentum, laxāmentī (n.) 'spare
    space'
dissiliō, dissilīre, dissiluī, dissultum
    'burst'
coctūra, coctūrae (f.) 'cooking'
surculō, -āre, -āvī, -ātum 'tie up'
ambās 'both ends' (accusative)
ōlla, ōllae (f.) 'pot'
bulliō, -īre, -īvī, -ītum 'boil'
levō, levāre, levāvī, levātum 'lift it out'
pungō, pungere, pupugī, pūnctum
    'puncture'
acus, acūs (f.) 'needle'
crepō, crepāre, crepuī, crepitum 'rattle'
    (from bubbles of air)
cum ad dīmidiās coctum fuerit 'when it
    is half cooked'
fūmus, fūmī (m.) 'smoke'
suspendō, -pendere, -pendī, -pēnsum
    'hang up'
colōrō, -āre, -āvī, -ātum 'colour'
dēnuō 'once again'
perēlixō, -āre, -āvī, -ātum 'boil
    thoroughly'
coquō, coquere, coxī, coctum 'cook'
deinde 'then'
merum, merī (n.) 'pure wine' (i.e. not
    mixed with water)
cultellus, cultellī (m.) 'small knife'
aperiō, aperīre, aperuī, apertum 'open'
appōnō (like *pōnō*) 'serve' (understood
    object: the stomach)

35 | Time and Place

35.1 Locative

In addition to the six regular cases, Latin has a locative case. The locative is used instead of *in* + ablative to express location (i.e. the place where someone or something is, when no motion to or from is involved), but only with certain words, including *domus* and the names of cities and towns.[1] Because the locative has no endings that are uniquely its own, and because most words do not have a locative case, the locative is not traditionally learned as part of noun paradigms. Nevertheless, it is necessary to know how to recognize and to form locatives for those words that have them. The rule of formation is that for words of the first and second declensions the locative is the same as the genitive in the singular and the same as the ablative in the plural; for words of other declensions the locative is always the same as the ablative.

> *Rōma, -ae* (f.) 'Rome': locative *Rōmae* 'at Rome', 'in Rome'
> *Londinium, -ī* (n.) 'London': locative *Londiniī* 'at London', 'in London'
> *Athēnae, -ārum* (f. plural) 'Athens': locative *Athēnīs* 'at Athens', 'in Athens'
> *Carthāgō, -ginis* (f.) 'Carthage': locative *Carthāgine* 'at Carthage', 'in Carthage'
> *domus, domūs/domī* (f.) 'home': locative *domī* (not *domūs*) 'at home'

35.2 Omission of *Ad* and *Ab*

Words that take a locative instead of *in* + ablative (i.e. *domus* and the names of cities and towns) also take the accusative without a preposition to express motion towards, and the ablative without a preposition to express motion from. So 'to Rome' is *Rōmam* rather than *ad Rōmam*, and 'from Rome' is *Rōmā* rather than *ā Rōmā* (even though 'to the city' is *ad urbem* and 'from the city' is *ab urbe*).[2] Similarly 'to home' (or just 'home' in expressions like 'He went home') is *domum* rather than *ad domum*, and 'from home' is *domō* rather than *ā domō*.

---

[1] The full list is: *domus, rūs* ('country'), *humus* ('ground'), and the names of cities, towns, and small islands.
[2] Actually Roman authors do not always follow this rule in the case of *ā: ā Rōmā* does occur, especially in Livy. But overall omission of *ā* is more usual.

Practice

A Translate, on the assumption that each of these words is used in a way discussed in this chapter:

1	Romam	7	Londinium
2	Romae	8	Londinio
3	Roma	9	Athenas
4	Carthaginem	10	Athenis (2 ways)
5	Carthagine (2 ways)	11	domi
6	Londinii	12	domo

B Translate into Latin, noting in addition to the place-names above *Syrācūsae, -ārum* (f. plural) 'Syracuse', *Delphī, -ōrum* (m. plural) 'Delphi', and *Corinthus, -ī* (f.) 'Corinth':

1	in Athens	7	from Syracuse
2	to Athens	8	in Syracuse
3	from Athens	9	to Syracuse
4	to Corinth	10	in Delphi
5	from Corinth	11	to Delphi
6	in Corinth	12	from Delphi

35.3 Accusative of Extent

The accusative can also be used without a preposition in a completely different function, to express an extent in time or space; in this usage it is often translatable with 'for' in English. Unlike the locative and other prepositionless constructions just discussed, this one is not restricted to particular words; it can be used with any expression.

> *paucōs diēs Rōmae erō.* 'I shall be in Rome for a few days.'
> *multōs annōs rēxit.* 'He ruled for many years.' (*annus, annī* (m.) 'year')

35.4 Ablative of Time

Similarly the ablative can be used without a preposition to indicate the time when or within which something happens; again there are no restrictions to particular words. These ablatives are usually translated 'on' (when indicating time when) or 'in' or 'within' (when indicating time within which).

> *illō diē Rōmam ībō.* 'I shall go to Rome on that day.'
> *paucīs diēbus Rōmam ībō.* 'I shall go to Rome in a few days.' / 'I shall go to Rome within a few days.'

Practice

C Translate, noting the following vocabulary: *annus, annī* (m.) 'year'; *maneō, manēre, mānsī, mānsum* 'remain', 'stay', 'wait'; *hōra, -ae* (f.) 'hour'; *quārtus, -a, -um* 'fourth'; *quīntus, -a, -um* 'fifth'; *sextus, -a, -um* 'sixth'; *septimus, -a, -um* 'seventh':

1 quarto die Athenas ivit.
2 filius meus quattuor dies Athenis moratus est.
3 pater noster quattuor diebus ad oppidum veniet.
4 Londinii sex annos ero.
5 sexto anno Londinium veni.
6 sex annis ad urbem veniam.
7 quinque horis domo discedent.
8 quinta hora domo discedent.
9 quinque horas domi erunt.
10 illo die Athenis Corinthum iverunt.
11 multos annos hic ero.
12 septima hora e castris progressi sunt.
13 quis paucos dies Romae manebit?
14 quattuor annos Corinthi mansit.
15 cur tot annos Syracusis mansisti?
16 cur sexto die Delphis discessistis?
17 manebisne multos annos Carthagine?
18 discedetisne Syracusis quinto die?
19 veniesne Delphos quarto die?
20 Carthaginem sexto die veniemus.

D Translate into Latin:

1 On the seventh day he departed from Carthage.
2 In seven days he will depart from the city.
3 He will be in Carthage for seven days.
4 That king ruled in Syracuse for four hours.
5 The king left Syracuse at the fourth hour.
6 Within four hours the king will come to the city.
7 The boys ran home.
8 My son has left home.
9 Is your father at home?
10 On that day we came to Rome.
11 We shall stay in Syracuse for five days.
12 They stayed in Rome for six years.
13 My father will stay in Athens for a few years.
14 Why did you delay for so many days in Delphi?
15 I shall leave Athens on the sixth day.
16 Will they go to London on the fourth day?
17 They delayed for many years in Corinth.
18 He left Rome in the seventh year.

35.5 Distinguishing Different Ablatives

We have now seen a number of different constructions in which the ablative, or a locative identical in form to the ablative, is employed without a preposition. (There are also further constructions using prepositions, such as the ablatives of agent and accompaniment, but these are much easier to identify because of the preposition.) The constructions taking an ablative (or apparent ablative) without a preposition are:

Name	Distinguishing characteristics	Translation
Locative having the same form as an ablative	The word that appears to be ablative is the name of a city or town, and is plural and/or belongs to the third declension; no motion is indicated.	'in', 'at'
Ablative of motion from	The word in the ablative is *domus* or the name of a city or town; the verb indicates motion.	'from'
Ablative of time	The word in the ablative indicates a date or time.	'in', 'on', 'at', 'within'
Ablative with verbs	The word in the ablative is near a verb known to take the ablative case (at present, only *ūtor*).	translate as a direct object (no preposition in English)
Ablative of means	The word in the ablative is something that could be the means by which the action of the verb happened.	'by' (if passive verb) or 'with' (if active verb)

Practice

E Identify the ablatives (and apparent ablatives) and translate:

1 Carthagine discedentes flumine impediti sumus.
2 Carthagine gladiis nostris usi sumus.
3 quinto anno domo discessit.
4 pecuniam meam Delphis amisi.
5 Athenis pueri gladiis non pugnant.
6 quarta hora domum veniam.
7 Syracusis moenia saxis reficimus.
8 septima hora libris non utemur.
9 hostes sexto die vicit.
10 Athenis multi multis verbis utuntur.
11 moenia reficientes saxis utuntur.
12 domo discedens saxo impeditus sum.
13 amici me pecunia iuverunt Delphis.
14 frater meus quarto die interfectus est gladio suo.
15 captos gladio interfecit.
16 Athenis discessit septimo die.

35.6 Roman Numerals

When Romans used signs for numbers rather than writing out the names of the numbers, they used Roman numerals.

I	1	IX or VIIII	9	XVII	17
II	2	X	10	XVIII	18
III	3	XI	11	XIX or XVIIII	19
IV or IIII	4	XII	12	XX	20
V	5	XIII	13	XXX	30
VI	6	XIV or XIIII	14	XL	40
VII	7	XV	15	L	50
VIII	8	XVI	16	C	100

These numerals are strung together in order from largest to smallest. Thus 236 is CCXXXVI, and 349 is CCCXLIX.

35.7 Reading Practice

1 *Corpus Inscriptionum Latinarum* IV.3881, 1190, 7994, and 3884 (all adapted): signs advertising gladiatorial shows, from the walls of Pompeii (first century AD).

Gladiatorum paria XX Quinti Monni Rufi pugnabunt Nolae Kalendis Maiis, et venatio erit.

Auli Suetti Certi aedilis familia gladiatoria pugnabit Pompeis pridie Kalendas Iunias; venatio et vela erunt.

Gladiatorium paria XLIX familiae Capiniae muneribus Augustorum pugnabunt Puteolis ante diem XVII et XV Kalendas Iunias; vela erunt. Magus hoc scripsit.

Decimi Lucreti Satri Valentis, flaminis Neronis Caesaris, gladiatorum paria XX, et Decimi Lucreti Valentis, filii, gladiatorum paria X pugnabunt Pompeis pridie Idus Apriles; venatio et vela erunt. scripsit Aemilius Celer singulus ad lunam.

Vocabulary

gladiātor, gladiātōris (m.) 'gladiator'
pār, paris, parium (n.) 'pair'
Quīntus Monnius Rūfus, -ī (m.) *name of an owner of gladiators*
Nōla, Nōlae (f.) *name of a town*
Kalendae Maiae, Kalendārum Maiārum (f. plural) 'the first of May' (literally 'the Kalends of May')

vēnātiō, vēnātiōnis (f.) 'hunt'
Aulus Suēttius Certus, -ī (m.) *name of an owner of gladiators*
aedīlis, aedīlis, aedīlium (m.) 'aedile' (an elected official)
familia, familiae (f.) 'troupe', 'family'
gladiātōrius, -a, -um 'gladiatorial'

Pompeiī, Pompeiōrum (m. plural)
   name of a town
prīdiē Kalendās Iūniās 'on the last day
   of May' (literally the day before the
   Kalends (first) of June)
vēlum, vēlī (n.) 'awning' (over the
   spectators at the games, to keep off
   hot sun or rain)
Capinius, -a, -um 'Capinian' (i.e.
   belonging to Capinius)
mūneribus Augustōrum 'at the games
   of the Augusti'
Puteolī, Puteolōrum (m. plural) *name*
   of a town
ante diem + (number) + Kalendās
   Iūniās '(number) days before the
   Kalends (first) of June' (i.e. 16 and
   18 May, as the Romans counted
   inclusively and May had 31 days)

Magus, Magī (m.) *name of a*
   sign-painter
Decimus Lucrētius Satrius Valēns,
   Decimī Lucrētiī Satriī Valentis (m.)
   name of a priest
flāmen, flāminis (m.) 'priest'
Nerō, Nerōnis (m.) *name of the emperor*
Caesar, Caesaris (m.) 'emperor'
Decimus Lucrētius Valēns, Decimī
   Lucrētiī Valentis (m.) *name of the*
   priest's son
prīdiē Īdūs Aprīlēs 'on 12 April'
   (literally the day before the Ides
   (13th) of April)
Aemilius Celer, Aemiliī Celeris (m.):
   name of a sign-painter
singulus, singula, singulum 'alone', 'by
   himself'
ad lūnam 'by moonlight'

2 Cicero, *Epistulae ad Atticum* 8.11c: a letter from Pompey to Cicero preserved with Cicero's correspondence (written in 49 BC).

Cn. Magnus proconsul salutem dicit M. Ciceroni imperatori. si vales, bene est. tuas litteras libenter legi; recognovi enim tuam pristinam virtutem etiam in salute communi. consules ad eum exercitum, quem in Apulia habui, venerunt. magno opere te hortor pro tuo singulari perpetuoque studio in rem publicam, ut te ad nos conferas, ut communi consilio rei publicae afflictae opem atque auxilium feramus. censeo, via Appia iter facias et celeriter Brundisium venias.

Vocabulary

Cn. Magnus = Gnaeus Pompeius Magnus
   (Pompey, the writer of the letter; the
   use of first and last names while
   omitting the middle one was an
   aristocratic convention also applied
   here to M(arcus) (Tullius) Cicero)
prōcōnsul, prōcōnsulis (m.) 'proconsul'
   (a Roman official)
salūs, salūtis (f.) 'greetings', 'welfare'
imperātor, imperātōris (m.) 'man with
   military authority', 'general'
litterae, litterārum (f. plural) 'letter'

libenter 'with pleasure'
recognōscō, -nōscere, -nōvī, -nitum
   'recognize'
prīstinus, -a, -um 'former'
virtūs, virtūtis (f.) 'excellent
   disposition'
etiam 'still'
in *can also mean* 'for'
commūnis, commūne 'shared' (i.e. 'of
   us all')
cōnsul, cōnsulis (m.) 'consul' (the
   leaders of the Roman Republic)

Āpulia, Āpuliae (f.) 'Apulia'
(a region of Italy)
prō 'by'
singulāris, singulāre 'outstanding'
perpetuus, -a, -um 'unchanging'
studium, studiī (n.) 'zeal'
in (+ accusative) 'for'
rēs pūblica, reī pūblicae (f.) 'state'
tē ... cōnferās (present subjunctive)
'come' (literally 'bring yourself')
afflīgō, afflīgere, afflīxī, afflīctum
'batter', 'afflict'

ops, opis (f.) 'help'
atque 'and'
auxilium, auxiliī (n.) 'support'
ferō, ferre, tulī, lātum (third
conjugation) 'bring'
cēnseō, cēnsēre, cēnsuī, cēnsum 'think
it best' (parenthetical here)
viā Appiā 'on the Appian way'
iter, itineris (n.) 'journey'
celeriter 'quickly'
Brundisium, -ī (n.) 'Brundisium' (a port
town)

3 Cicero, *Epistulae ad Atticum* 7.24 (adapted): Cicero sends Atticus news about the progress of the civil wars in 49 B C.

Cicero Attico salutem dicit. Philotimi litterae me quidem non nimis, sed eos, qui in his locis erant, admodum delectaverunt. ecce postridie intelleximus de litteris missis Capua a Lucretio Nigidium a Domitio Capuam venisse. ... idem scripsit Capua consules discessisse. non dubito quin Gnaeus in fuga sit: modo effugiat.

Vocabulary

Cicerō, Cicerōnis (m.) *name of the writer*
Atticus, Atticī (m.) *name of a friend*
salūs, salūtis (f.) 'greetings'
Philotīmus, -ī (m.) *name of another correspondent*
litterae, litterārum (f. plural) 'letter'
quidem 'indeed'
nimis 'too much'
erant 'were'
locus, locī (m.) 'place'
admodum 'very much'
dēlectō, -āre, -āvī, -ātum 'delight'
ecce 'look!'
postrīdiē 'on the next day'
Capua, Capuae (f.) *name of a town*

Lucrētius, -ī (m.) *name of a person currently in Capua*
Nigidius, -ī (m.) *name of an envoy*
Domitius, -ī (m.) *name of the commander of some of Pompey's forces*
īdem 'the same man' (nominative singular)
cōnsul, cōnsulis (m.) 'consul' (the leaders of the Roman Republic)
dubitō, -āre, -āvī, -ātum 'doubt'
quīn (+ subjunctive) 'that'
Gnaeus, Gnaeī (m.) 'Pompey' ('Gnaeus' was his first name)
fuga, fugae (f.) 'retreat'
modo 'only'
effugiō (like *fugiō*) 'escape'

4 *Corpus Inscriptionum Latinarum* IV.1136 (adapted): a notice from a wall in Pompeii about property for rent (first century AD).

In praediis Iuliae Spuri filiae Felicis locantur balneum, tabernae, pergulae, cenacula; ex Idibus Augustis primis in Augustas sextas, annos continuos quinque. si quis desiderabit, locatrici dicat.

Vocabulary

praedium, praediī (n.) 'estate'
Iūlia Fēlīx, Iūliae Fēlīcis (f.) *name of a property owner* (the two names should be put next to each other in English)
Spurius, Spuriī (m.) *man's name*
fīlia, fīliae (f.) 'daughter'
locō, locāre, locāvī, locātum 'offer to be rented'
balneum, balneī (n.) 'bath-house'
taberna, tabernae (f.) 'shop'

pergula, pergulae (f.) 'balcony'
cēnāculum, cēnāculī (n.) 'dining room'
Īdibus Augustīs 'Ides (13th) of August'
prīmus *can also mean* 'next'
Augustās sextās '(Ides of) the sixth August (from now)'
continuus, -a, -um 'continuous'
quis 'anyone'
dēsīderō, -āre, -āvī, -ātum 'desire (this property)'
locātrīx, locātrīcis (f.) 'landlady'

35.8 Vocabulary to Learn

Verbs

maneō, manēre, mānsī, mānsum	'remain', 'stay', 'wait'
rapiō, rapere, rapuī, raptum	'seize', 'grab', 'carry off'
valeō, valēre, valuī, valitum	'be well', 'be healthy'

Nouns

annus, annī (m.)	'year'
Athēnae, Athēnārum (f. plural)	'Athens'
Carthāgō, Carthāginis (f.)	'Carthage'
Corinthus, Corinthī (f.)	'Corinth'
Delphī, Delphōrum (m. plural)	'Delphi'
hōra, hōrae (f.)	'hour'
locus, locī (m., also n. in plural)	'place'
Londinium, Londiniī (n.)	'London'
pēs, pedis (m.)	'foot'
Rōma, Rōmae (f.)	'Rome'
Syrācūsae, Syrācūsārum (f. plural)	'Syracuse'

Vocabulary continues.

Adjectives

prīmus, prīma, prīmum	'first'
quārtus, quārta, quārtum	'fourth'
quīntus, quīnta, quīntum	'fifth'
sextus, sexta, sextum	'sixth'
septimus, septima, septimum	'seventh'

Prepositions

propter (+ accusative)	'on account of'

36.1 *Colloquia Monacensia–Einsidlensia* 10a–u (adapted)

A family visit to the public baths (second or third century AD):

FATHER (*to slaves*): deferte sabana ad balneum, strigilem, faciale, pedale, ampullam, aphronitrum. antecedite, occupate locum.

SLAVES: quo imperas ut eamus? ad thermas aut ad privatum?

FATHER: quo vultis. antecedite tantum; vobis loquor, qui hic estis. (*to son*) surge, eamus. (*on arriving at public toilets located at entrance to baths*) visne venire ad secessum?

SON: bene me admonuisti: venter me cogit. nunc eamus.

FATHER (*to son, on arriving at changing rooms*): exspolia te, (*to slave*) discalcea me, compone vestimenta, cooperi, serva bene, noli obdormire propter fures. (*to son*) rape nobis pilam; ludamus in sphaeristerio.

SON: exercere volo in ceromate. veni luctemur uno momento.

FATHER: nescio num possim; olim enim cessavi luctari. tamen temptabo num possim. (*shortly afterwards*) leviter fatigatus sum. introeamus in cellam primam, tepidarium. da balneatori nummos; recipe reliquum. (*once in the tepidarium*) unge te.

SON: unxi me.

FATHER (*sceptically*): unxistine te?

SON: ungo me.

FATHER: frica. (*later*) veni ad sudatorium. sudas?

SON: sudo; lassus sum. introeamus ad solium.

FATHER: descende.

SON: utamur assis et sic descendamus ad solium.

FATHER: descende, fomenta me. exi iam. mitte te in piscinam subdivalem. nata.

SON: natavi.

FATHER accede ad luterem, perfunde te.

SON: perfudi, resumpsi. porrige strigilem.

FATHER (*back in changing room, to slaves*): deterge me. cinge sabana. terge caput meum et pedes. da mihi caligulas, calcea me. porrige mihi dalmaticam et pallium. colligite vestimenta et omnia nostra. sequimini nos domum, et emite nobis minutalia et lupinos et fabas acetatas. (*to bath attendant*) bene nos lavisti, bene tibi sit.

Vocabulary

dēferte (imperative plural) 'carry down'

sabanum, sabanī (n.) 'towel'

balneum, balneī (n.) 'bath'

strigilis, strigilis, strigilium (f.)
   'strigil' (scraper for removing dirt,
   oil, and sweat from skin)

faciāle, faciālis, faciālium (n.) 'face-cloth'

pedāle, pedālis, pedālium (n.) 'foot-cloth'

ampulla, ampullae (f.) 'flask of oil'

aphronitrum, aphronitrī (n.) 'soap'

antecēdō, -cēdere, -cessī, -cessum 'go
   ahead'

occupō, -āre, -āvī, -ātum 'occupy', i.e.
   'get us'

quō 'where' (with verbs of motion
   towards)

thermae, thermārum (f. plural) 'public
   baths'

prīvātum (i.e. balneum), prīvātī (n.)
   'private bathing establishment'
   (open to the public but privately
   owned and run)

tantum 'just'

surgō, surgere, surrēxī, surrēctum 'get
   up'

sēcessus, sēcessūs (m.) 'toilet'

admoneō, -ēre, -uī, -itum 'advise'

venter, ventris (m.) 'belly'

cōgō, cōgere, coēgī, coāctum 'compel'

exspoliō, -āre, -āvī, -ātum 'undress'

discalceō, -āre, -āvī, -ātum 'take off the
   shoes of'

compōnō (like pōnō) 'put together'

vestīmentum, vestīmentī (n.) 'clothes'

cooperiō, -perīre, -peruī, -pertum
   'cover'

servō, servāre, servāvī, servātum 'watch'

nōlī obdormīre 'don't doze off'

fūr, fūris (m.) 'thief'

pila, pilae (f.) 'ball'

lūdō, lūdere, lūsī, lūsum 'play'

sphaeristērium, -ī (n.) 'ball-court'

exerceō, -cēre, -cuī, -citum 'train'

cērōma, cērōmatis (n.) 'wrestling-
   ground'

luctor, luctārī, luctātus sum 'wrestle'

ūnō mōmentō 'just a moment'

nesciō, nescīre, nescīvī, nescītum 'not
   know'

num (+ subjunctive) 'whether'

ōlim 'long ago'

cessō, cessāre, cessāvī, cessātum 'cease'

temptō, temptāre, temptāvī, temptātum
   'try'

leviter 'easily'

fatīgō, fatīgāre, fatīgāvī, fatīgātum 'tire
   out'

introeō (like eō) 'go in'

cella, cellae (f.) 'room'

tepidārium, tepidāriī (n.) 'warm room'

balneātor, balneātōris (m.) 'bath
   attendant'

nummus, nummī (m.) 'coin' (there was
   a small admission charge to the
   public baths, which was often paid
   not at the entrance to the whole
   complex but at the entrance to the
   heated rooms)

recipiō (like capiō) 'take', 'get'

reliquum, reliquī (n.) 'change'

ungō, ungere, ūnxī, ūnctum 'anoint'
   (= put oil on)

fricō, fricāre, fricuī, frictum 'rub'

sūdātōrium, -ī (n.) 'sweat room'

sūdō, sūdāre, sūdāvī, sūdātum 'sweat'

lassus, lassa, lassum 'exhausted'

solium, soliī (n.) 'hot pool'

dēscendo, dēscendere, dēscendī,
   dēscēnsum 'go down'

assa, assōrum (n. plural) 'dry heat
   room'

sīc 'that way' (i.e. using that route)

fōmentō, -āre, -āvī, -ātum 'pour hot water over'

iam 'now'

mittō *can also mean* 'throw'

piscīna, piscīnae (f.) 'swimming pool'

subdīvālis, subdīvāle 'open-air'

natō, natāre, natāvī, natātum 'swim'

accēdō, accēdere, accessī, accessum 'go over'

lūtēr, lūtēris (m.) 'shower' (for washing off grime from dirty communal bath water; it may not have been very effective, as the bathers still need to use the strigil to scrape off the remaining grime before drying themselves)

perfundō, -fundere, -fūdī, -fūsum 'pour water over'

resūmō, resūmere, resūmpsī, resūmptum 'hang (it) up'

porrigō, porrigere, porrēxī, porrēctum 'pass'

dētergō, dētergere, dētersī, dētersum 'dry off'

cingō, cingere, cīnxī, cīnctum 'wrap around (me)'

tergō, tergere, tersī, tersum 'dry'

caligula, caligulae (f.) 'shoe', 'boot'

calceō, calceāre, calceāvī, calceātum 'put on shoes'

dalmatica, dalmaticae (f.) 'Dalmatian tunic'

pallium, palliī (n.) 'mantle' (a type of outer garment consisting of a large square of cloth)

colligō, colligere, collēgī, collēctum 'gather up'

minūtālia, minūtālium (n. plural) 'chopped food'

lupīnus, lupīnī (m.) 'lupin seed'

faba, fabae (f.) 'bean'

acētātus, -a, -um 'served in vinegar'

lavō, lavāre, lāvī, lautum 'bathe'

36.2 **Translate into Latin**

FATHER: Son, come! Grab a towel and soap: let's go to the bath.

SON: To the public baths or to the private one?

FATHER: We are not in Rome, where (there) are many public baths; we are in London, where (there) are not public baths. We shall go to the private bath.

SON: Why did we leave Rome and come to London? A private bath is small; I want to go to public baths with a big ball-court and an open-air pool! I want to go to Rome! I want to go home!

FATHER: You are at home: your home is now in London. We shall be here for many days, and we cannot be always dirty. The bath in London is so small that it does not have a ball-court. But it has water, and we are dirty. Let's go!

Additional Vocabulary

sordidus, -a, -um 'dirty'

36.3 Virgil, *Aeneid* 1.34–8

Juno gets cross (continuation of passages in chapter 31):

Vix e conspectu Siculae telluris in altum
vela dabant laeti et spumas salis aere ruebant,
cum Iuno aeternum servans sub pectore vulnus
haec secum: 'mene incepto desistere victam
nec posse Italia Teucrorum avertere regem?'

Vocabulary

vix 'scarcely'

cōnspectus, cōnspectūs (m.) 'sight'

Siculus, -a, -um 'Sicilian'

tellūs, tellūris (f.) 'land'

altum, altī (n.) 'open sea'

vēlum, vēlī (n.) 'sail'

dabant '(they) were setting'

laetus, laeta, laetum 'joyful'

spūma, spūmae (f.) 'foam'

sāl, salis (m.) 'salt sea'

aes, aeris (n.) 'bronze (prows of the ships)'

ruēbant 'they were churning up'

cum 'when'

Iūnō, Iūnōnis (f.) 'Juno'

aeternus, -a, -um 'eternal'

servō, servāre, servāvī, servātum 'keep'

sub (+ ablative) 'deep inside' (literally 'under')

pectus, pectoris (n.) 'heart'

vulnus, vulneris (n.) 'wound', 'grievance'

haec secum: *supply* dīxit *here*

mēne = mē + -ne (the *mē* is the accusative subject of the following infinitives, as this quotation is in accusative and infinitive, though not in indirect statement)

inceptum, inceptī (n.) 'undertaking'

dēsistō, dēsistere, dēstitī, dēstitum (+ ablative) 'desist from' (translate the infinitive as if it were a deliberative subjunctive)

nec 'and not'

Italia, Italiae (f.) 'Italy' (supply *ab* here; the first vowel of *Italia* can be either long or short)

āvertō, āvertere, āvertī, āversum 'turn away'

Teucrī, Teucrōrum (m. plural) 'Trojans'

A possible prose order of the above would be:

Vix e conspectu Siculae telluris, laeti in altum vela dabant et spumas salis aere ruebant, cum Iuno aeternum vulnus sub pectore servans haec secum: 'mene victam incepto desistere nec posse regem Teucrorum Italia avertere?'

37.1 Forms of Nōlō and Mālō

The verb *volō* ('wish', 'want': see chapter 25.3) has two compounds. *Nōlō* is formed from *nōn + volō* and means 'I do not want', and *mālō* is formed from *magis* 'more' + *volō* and means 'I prefer' (i.e. 'I want more'). Like *volō*, they have no passive. These verbs are conjugated as follows (*volō* is given for comparison):

	Volō, velle, voluī, –	*Nōlō, nōlle, nōluī, –*	*Mālō, mālle, māluī, –*
Present active indicative	volō	nōlō	mālō
	vīs	nōn vīs	māvīs
	vult	nōn vult	māvult
	volumus	nōlumus	mālumus
	vultis	nōn vultis	māvultis
	volunt	nōlunt	mālunt
Future active indicative	volam	nōlam	mālam
	volēs	nōlēs	mālēs
	volet	nōlet	mālet
	volēmus	nōlēmus	mālēmus
	volētis	nōlētis	mālētis
	volent	nōlent	mālent
Perfect active indicative	voluī	nōluī	māluī
	voluistī	nōluistī	māluistī
	voluit	nōluit	māluit
	voluimus	nōluimus	māluimus
	voluistis	nōluistis	māluistis
	voluērunt	nōluērunt	māluērunt
Present active subjunctive	velim	nōlim	mālim
	velīs	nōlīs	mālīs
	velit	nōlit	mālit
	velīmus	nōlīmus	mālīmus
	velītis	nōlītis	mālītis
	velint	nōlint	mālint

	Volō, velle, voluī, –	*Nōlō, nōlle, nōluī, –*	*Mālō, mālle, māluī, –*
Imperfect active subjunctive	vellem	nōllem	māllem
	vellēs	nōllēs	māllēs
	vellet	nōllet	māllet
	vellēmus	nōllēmus	māllēmus
	vellētis	nōllētis	māllētis
	vellent	nōllent	māllent
Imperative active	–	nōlī	–
		nōlīte	
Present active participle	volēns, *gen.* volentis	nōlēns, *gen.* nōlentis	–
Perfect participle	–	–	–
Future participle	–	–	–
Present active infinitive	velle	nōlle	mālle
Perfect active infinitive	voluisse	nōluisse	māluisse
Future infinitive	–	–	–

37.2 Use of *Nōlō* and *Mālō*

Like *volō*, the verbs *nōlō* and *mālō* normally take a present infinitive: *nōlō venīre* 'I do not want to come', *mālō venīre* 'I prefer to come'. *Mālō* often takes a construction with *quam* 'than', 'rather than': *mālō venīre quam hīc sedēre* 'I prefer to come rather than to sit here'. The imperatives *nōlī* and *nōlīte* are used with infinitives to make negative commands; originally this was a polite construction, but in Classical Latin it is simply a negative command and not noticeably polite.

> *nōlī venīre* 'do not come!' (literally 'do not want to come!')
> *nōlīte scrībere* 'do not write!' (literally 'do not want to write!')

Practice

A Translate:

1 noluimus cum Romanis pugnare.
2 mavultisne Roma discedere?
3 puer epistulam longam scribere non vult.
4 illi servi vendi maluerunt quam hic manere.
5 illi currentes a nobis vocari nolent.
6 hic poeta mavult docere quam doceri.
7 amice, noli ab hostibus capi.
8 quis dixit se a te defendi malle?
9 mecum loquens dixit se nolle Londinii relinqui.
10 quis mavult ab illa quam ab hac amari?
11 milites capti interfici nolunt.
12 malunt te sequi quam nos.
13 discedens, pecuniam puellae dedit ut secum Romam ire mallet.
14 a puella pulchra ita amatus est, ut cum ea Romae manere mallet.

15 haec puella, a viro non pulchro amata, cum eo sedere noluit.
16 noli regem rogare ut tibi pecuniam det!
17 maluimus magistro persuadere ne cum patribus de nobis loqueretur.
18 quis septem dies Athenis manere maluit?
19 hic puer, nolens exercitum Romanum videre, maluit domi manere.
20 nolentes ab exercitu Romano oppugnari, fugimus.
21 multos annos Londinii manere nolumus.
22 interfici nolo, sed malo a te interfici quam ab eo.
23 dicit se poetam esse, sed versus scribere non vult.
24 maluntne puellae pulchrae manus pulchras habere quam genua pulchra?
25 noluit a nobis defendi, quia se defendere potuit.

B Translate into Latin:

1 Who does not want to go home?
2 They preferred to go to Athens rather than to Corinth.
3 Do not stay (singular) in Rome!
4 We preferred to give this town to the Roman senate rather than to the Greeks.
5 The soldiers did not want to be led to Carthage.

6 The king did not want to leave Corinth.
7 Son, do not go to Corinth!
8 The enemy's army is so big that our men do not want to go out from the camp.
9 My brother will prefer to stay in Delphi for a few days.
10 The boys' fear is so great that they do not want to be seen by us.

11 So many men now want to write verses that all men are poets today.

12 My sister preferred to leave home rather than to be seen by that farmer.

13 We prefer to stay at home and be defended by you (singular).

14 Friends, do not hunt in this forest; (there) are not animals.

15 I do not want to write verses in Athens; I prefer to go to Syracuse with our army!

37.3 Reading Practice

1 Cicero, *Epistulae ad Familiares* 16.25 (adapted): Cicero's son (also named Cicero) writes to his father's secretary (44 BC).

Cicero filius Tironi suo salutem dicit. etsi iusta et idonea usus es excusatione intermissionis epistularum tuarum, tamen id ne saepius facias rogo. nam etsi de re publica rumoribus et nuntiis certior fio, et semper ad me perscribit pater, tamen de quavis minima re scripta a te ad me epistula semper fuit gratissima. quare cum in primis tuas desiderem epistulas, noli committere, ut excusatione potius expleas officium scribendi, quam assiduitate epistularum. vale.

Vocabulary

Cicerō, Cicerōnis (m.) *name of the writer*
Tīrō, Tīrōnis (m.) *name of the addressee*
salūs, salūtis (f.) 'greetings'
etsī 'although'
iūstus, iūsta, iūstum 'fair'
idōneus, idōnea, idōneum 'suitable'
excūsātiō, excūsātiōnis (f.) 'excuse'
intermissiō, intermissiōnis (f.) 'stopping'
saepius 'more often'
rēs pūblica, reī pūblicae (f.) 'state'
rūmor, rūmōris (m.) 'rumour'
nūntium, nūntiī (n.) 'message'
certior fīō 'I am informed'

perscrībō (like *scrībō*) 'write thoroughly'
quāvīs (ablative) 'any'
minimus, minima, minimum 'tiny'
grātissimus, -a, -um 'very pleasing'
quārē 'for which reason'
cum ... dēsīderem 'since I desire'
in prīmīs 'above all'
committō (like *mittō*) 'commit (the offence)'
potius ... quam 'rather ... than'
expleō, explēre, explēvī, explētum 'fulfill'
officium, officiī (n.) 'duty'
scrībendum, scrībendī (n.) 'writing'
assiduitās, assiduitātis (f.) 'frequency'

2 Vulgate version of the Bible, Luke 2:1–10 (adapted): the Christmas story (translated in the fourth century AD from an earlier Greek version).

Diebus illis exiit edictum a Caesare Augusto ut describerentur omnes homines, et iverunt omnes ut profiterentur, singuli in suam urbem. ascendit igitur Ioseph a Galilaea de urbe Nazareth in Iudaeam, in urbem David quae vocatur Bethleem, quia erat de familia David, ut profiteretur cum Maria desponsa sibi uxore praegnante. et cum essent ibi impleti sunt dies ut pareret, et peperit filium suum primogenitum, et pannis eum involvit, et reclinavit eum in praesepio, quia non erat eis locus in deversorio. et pastores erant in illa regione vigilantes et custodientes oves suas, ad quos venit angelus domini. lux dei circumfulsit eos, et timuerunt timore magno, sed dixit eis angelus 'nolite timere!'

Vocabulary

ēdictum, ēdictī (n.) 'edict'

Caesar Augustus, Caesaris Augustī (m.) 'the emperor'

dēscrībō (like *scrībō*) 'register'

profiteor, profitērī, professus sum 'enrol oneself'

singulus, singula, singulum 'each one'

ascendō, ascendere, ascendī, ascēnsum 'go up'

Iōsēph (indeclinable) 'Joseph'

Galilaea, Galilaeae (f.) 'Galilee' (a region)

Nāzareth (indeclinable) 'Nazareth'

Iūdaea, Iūdaeae (f.) 'Judea' (a region)

Dāvīd (indeclinable) 'of David' (an earlier king)

Bēthleem (indeclinable) 'Bethlehem'

erat '(he) was'

familia, familiae (f.) 'family'

Marīa, Marīae (f.) 'Mary'

dēspondeō, dēspondēre, dēspondī, dēspōnsum 'engage' (to marry)

uxor, uxōris (f.) 'wife'

praegnāns, *gen.* praegnantis 'pregnant'

cum essent 'when they were'

impleō, implēre, implēvī, implētum 'fulfil' (i.e. come to the end of)

pariō, parere, peperī, partum 'give birth (to)', 'bear'

prīmōgenitus, -a, -um 'first-born'

pannus, pannī (m.) 'rag', 'swaddling cloth'

involvō, involvere, involvī, involūtum 'wrap up'

reclīnō, -āre, -āvī, -ātum 'lay'

praesēpium, praesēpiī (n.) 'manger'

dēversōrium, dēversōriī (n.) 'inn'

pāstor, pāstōris (m.) 'shepherd'

erant 'there were'

regiō, regiōnis (f.) 'region'

vigilō, -āre, -āvī, -ātum 'stay awake'

custōdiō, -īre, -īvī, -ītum 'watch over'

angelus, angelī (m.) 'angel'

lūx, lūcis (f.) 'light'

circumfulgeō, -fulgēre, -fulsī, -fulsum 'shine around'

timor, timōris (m.) 'fear'

3 Martial 9.81: the poet responds to criticism of his work by comparing it to a dinner party (first century A D).

Lector et auditor nostros probat, Aule, libellos,
    sed quidam exactos esse poeta negat.
non nimium curo: nam cenae fercula nostrae
    malim convivis quam placuisse cocis.

Vocabulary

lēctor, lēctōris (m.) 'reader'

audītor, audītōris (m.) 'hearer'

probō, probāre, probāvī, probātum
    'approve'

Aulus, -ī (m.) *a man's name*

libellus, libellī (m.) 'little book'

quīdam, quaedam, quoddam
    (declines like *quī*) 'a certain'

exāctus, exācta, exāctum 'polished'

negō, negāre, negāvī, negātum 'say
    that . . . not'

nimium 'very much'

cūrō, cūrāre, cūrāvī, cūrātum
    'care'

cēna, cēnae (f.) 'dinner'

ferculum, ferculī (n.) 'course'
    (of a meal)

convīva, convīvae (m.)
    'dinner guest'

placeō, placēre, placuī, placitum
    (+ dative) 'please'

cocus, cocī (m.) 'cook'

37.4 Vocabulary to Learn

Verbs

mālō, mālle, māluī, – 'prefer'

nōlō, nōlle, nōluī, – 'not want'

Conjunction

quam   'than', 'rather than'

38 | Regular Comparison

38.1 Comparison of Adjectives

Adjectives have three degrees of comparison: the positive, which we have already seen (indicating that a noun has a certain quality), the comparative (indicating that a noun has more of that quality), and the superlative (indicating that a noun has most of that quality). In English these three degrees are formed with '-er'/'-est' or (for long words) with 'more'/'most', as follows:

Positive	Comparative	Superlative
long	longer	longest
short	shorter	shortest
beautiful	more beautiful	most beautiful

In Latin the comparative ends in *-ior* (masculine nominative singular) and can be translated not only like the English comparative, but also with 'rather' when it is used in an absolute sense, rather than being used to compare two things. The superlative ends in *-issimus* or *-errimus* and can be translated not only like the English superlative, but also with 'very' (when it is used in an absolute sense). So from *fortis* 'strong' we have the comparatives *fortior*, which would be translated 'stronger' in a context like 'This horse is *fortior* than that one' but 'rather strong' in a context like 'This horse is *fortior*.' Likewise the superlative *fortissimus* would be translated 'strongest' in a context like 'This horse is *fortissimus* of all the ones we have seen' but 'very strong' in a context like 'This horse is *fortissimus*' (when no comparison with others was implied by the larger context).

Practice

A Give both possible translations of each of these forms:

1 novissimus
2 miserior
3 acerrimus
4 tenerior
5 acrior
6 celerrimus

7 gravissimus
8 facilior
9 miserrimus
10 celerior
11 tenerrimus
12 gravior

38.2 Formation of Regular Comparatives and Superlatives

In Latin the comparative is formed by adding *-ior, -ius* to the stem of the adjective (the stem is found by dropping the ending of the genitive singular or the feminine nominative singular: see chapters 8.2 and 21.1). This means that the comparative is a third-declension adjective (even when the positive was a first/second-declension adjective) ending in *-ior* in the masculine and feminine and *-ius* in the neuter. The superlative is formed by adding *-issimus, -issima, -issimum* to the stem of the adjective; this means that the superlative is a first/second-declension adjective (even when the positive was a third-declension adjective).

Positive	Comparative	Superlative
longus, -a, -um	longior, longius	longissimus, -a, -um
'long'	'longer', 'rather long'	'longest', 'very long'
brevis, breve	brevior, brevius	brevissimus, -a, -um
'short'	'shorter', 'rather short'	'shortest', 'very short'

But adjectives with a masculine singular in *-er* (whether second or third declension) have superlatives in *-errimus, -errima, -errimum*. In this superlative the *e* of the original *-er* remains regardless of whether it is part of the stem or not, but the comparatives of such adjectives contain the *e* only if it is part of the stem.

Positive	Comparative	Superlative
tener, tenera, tenerum	tenerior, tenerius	tenerrimus, -a, -um
ācer, ācris, ācre	ācrior, ācrius	ācerrimus, -a, -um

Practice

B Find the stems of these adjectives:

1 asper, aspera, asperum
2 fortis, forte
3 turpis, turpe 'shameful'
4 trīstis, trīste
5 pulcher, pulchra, pulchrum
6 līber, lībera, līberum
7 niger, nigra, nigrum
8 fēlīx, *gen.* fēlīcis
9 certus, certa, certum 'certain', 'reliable'
10 stultus, stulta, stultum 'foolish'
11 dulcis, dulce 'sweet'
12 grātus, grāta, grātum 'pleasing', 'grateful'
13 sapiēns, *gen.* sapientis 'wise'
14 dūrus, dūra, dūrum 'hard', 'harsh'
15 potēns, *gen.* potentis 'powerful'
16 clārus, clāra, clārum 'bright', 'famous'

C Give the comparatives of the adjectives in exercise B, and all translations of the resulting forms.

D Give the superlatives of the adjectives in exercise B, and all translations of the resulting forms.

38.3 Declension of Comparatives

The genitive of comparative adjectives ends in *-iōris*, so their stem ends in *-iōr-*. Unlike most other third-declension adjectives (see chapter 21.1), comparatives are not *i*-stems: they therefore decline like *mīles* and *flūmen* (cf. chapter 14.1).

British Case Order

	Singular Masculine and feminine	Neuter	Plural Masculine and feminine	Neuter
Nom.	trīstior	trīstius	trīstiōrēs	trīstiōra
Voc.	trīstior	trīstius	trīstiōrēs	trīstiōra
Acc.	trīstiōrem	trīstius	trīstiōrēs	trīstiōra
Gen.	trīstiōris	trīstiōris	trīstiōrum	trīstiōrum
Dat.	trīstiōrī	trīstiōrī	trīstiōribus	trīstiōribus
Abl.	trīstiōre	trīstiōre	trīstiōribus	trīstiōribus

Ancient Case Order

	Singular Masculine and feminine	Neuter	Plural Masculine and feminine	Neuter
Nom./Voc.	trīstior	trīstius	trīstiōrēs	trīstiōra
Gen.	trīstiōris	trīstiōris	trīstiōrum	trīstiōrum
Dat.	trīstiōrī	trīstiōrī	trīstiōribus	trīstiōribus
Acc.	trīstiōrem	trīstius	trīstiōrēs	trīstiōra
Abl.	trīstiōre	trīstiōre	trīstiōribus	trīstiōribus

Practice

E Decline in the forms indicated:

1 *celerior*, masculine singular
2 *longior*, neuter singular
3 *brevior*, feminine plural

4 *tenerior*, neuter plural
5 *ācrior*, feminine singular
6 *gravior*, masculine plural

7 *celerior*, neuter singular

8 *longior*, feminine plural

9 *brevior*, masculine singular

10 *tenerior*, feminine singular

11 *ācrior*, masculine plural

12 *gravior*, neuter plural

38.4 Use of Comparatives and Superlatives

Comparatives and superlatives are involved in a variety of constructions, of which the most common are the following:

1) The comparative with *quam* 'than'. The word after *quam* needs to be in the same case as the noun to which it is being compared: *hic liber longior est quam ille* 'this book is longer <u>than that one</u>' (*ille* is nominative because *hic liber* is), *vīdī virum fortiōrem quam tē* 'I saw a man stronger <u>than you</u>' (*tē* is accusative because *virum* is).

2) The ablative of comparison. With this construction there is no separate word for 'than'; the noun compared is put into the ablative. Thus *hic liber longior est illō* 'this book is longer <u>than that one</u>' (the 'than' is expressed by the ablative case of *illō*).

3) The partitive genitive with the superlative. This genitive, as usual for partitives, is normally translated with 'of', but 'among' is another possibility: *hic liber longissimus est omnium* 'this book is the longest <u>of all</u>', *vīdī (virum) fortissimum Graecōrum* 'I saw the strongest <u>of the Greeks</u>', 'I saw the strongest man <u>among the Greeks</u>'.

4) The superlative with *quam*. This construction means 'as . . . as possible', and the Latin superlative is translated with the English positive, not the English superlative: *liber quam longissimus* 'a book <u>as long as possible</u>', *vir quam fortissimus* 'a man <u>as strong as possible</u>'.

Practice

F Translate:

1 haec puella pulchrior est quam ea.

2 illa puella pulcherrima omnium est.

3 gladium acriorem emere volo.

4 gladium acerrimum emere malo.

5 dei immortales feliciores sunt hominibus.

6 dei semper quam felicissimi sunt.

7 pueri qui non docentur tristiores sunt quam ei qui a magistro bono docentur, sed feliciores quam ei qui a magisro malo docentur.

8 epistula mea longior est quam tua.

9 epistula eius quam brevissima est.

10 pater noster fortissimus est omnium militum.

11 potestne homo fortior esse equo?
12 hic equus nigrior est quam ille.
13 hic equus nigerrimus est
   omnium.
14 equi eorum quam celerrimi sunt.

15 equi eius celeriores sunt quam
   vestri.
16 haec saxa gravissima sunt.
17 haec saxa graviora sunt.

G Translate into Latin:

1 That man is happier than I.
2 That woman is rather happy.
3 Those men are very happy.
4 Those women are as happy as
  possible.
5 These girls are happiest of all.
6 This is the happiest of the girls.
7 I do not want to read a very long
  book.
8 He wants to read the longest of all
  books.
9 They wanted to read a book as
  long as possible.

10 She didn't want to read a longer
   book.
11 Did you want to read a book
   longer than this one?
12 He preferred to buy a more
   beautiful horse.
13 Do you prefer to buy a very
   beautiful horse?
14 We prefer to buy the most
   beautiful horse of all.
15 They preferred to sell the rather
   beautiful horse.
16 I prefer my horse to be as beautiful as possible.

38.5 Reading Practice

1 *Tabulae Vindolandenses* 11.291 (adapted): from the letters of soldiers stationed in
  northern Britain and their families, an invitation to a birthday party (*c.* AD 100).

Claudia Severa Lepidinae suae salutem dicit. III Idus Septembres, soror, die sollemne natale meo, rogo ut venias ad nos, iucundiorem mihi diem interventu tuo
factura. Cerialem tuum saluta. Aelius meus et filiolus te salutant. sperabo te, soror.
vale, soror, anima mea carissima.

Vocabulary

Claudia Sevēra, Claudiae Sevērae (f.)
   name of the writer of the letter
Lepidīna, Lepidīnae (f.) *name of the*
   recipient of the letter, a friend of the
   writer but probably not actually her
   sister
salūs, salūtis (f.) 'greetings'

III Īdūs Septembrēs 'On 11 September'
   (literally 'on the third day before the
   Ides (13th) of September' – Romans
   counted inclusively)
sollemnis, sollemne 'of celebration'
nātālis, nātāle 'of birthday'
iūcundus, -a, -um 'pleasant'

interventus, interventūs (m.) 'arrival'

Ceriālis, Ceriālis (m.) *name of Lepidina's husband*

salūtō, -āre, -āvī, -ātum 'greet'

Aelius, Aeliī (m.) *name of Claudia Severa's husband*

fīliolus, fīliolī (m.) 'little son'

spērō, spērāre, spērāvī, spērātum 'expect'

anima, animae (f.) 'soul' (a term of endearment)

cārus, cāra, cārum 'dear'

2 *Tabulae Vindolandenses* III.628: an officer stationed in northern Britain sends requests to a superior (*c.* AD 100).

Masclus Ceriali regi suo salutem dicit. rogo te, domine, ut praecipias quid velis ut cras faciamus. . . . cervesiam milites non habent, quam rogo ut iubeas mitti. felicissimus sis et mihi propitius. vale.

Vocabulary

Masclus, Masclī (m.) *name of the writer*

Ceriālis, Ceriālis (m.) *name of the recipient of the letter*

rēx *can also mean* 'patron'

praecipiō, -cipere, -cēpī, -ceptum 'send instructions'

cervēsia, cervēsiae (f.) 'beer'

iubeō, iubēre, iussī, iussum 'order' (takes accusative and infinitive rather than the usual indirect command construction)

propitius, -a, -um (+ dative) 'well disposed towards'

3 Vulgate version of the Bible, Genesis 3:1–3 (adapted): Adam and Eve meet the serpent (translated in the fourth century AD from an earlier Greek version).

Sed serpens, qui erat callidior omnibus animalibus terrae quae fecerat dominus deus, dixit mulieri, 'cur imperavit vobis deus ne comederetis de arboribus in paradiso?' cui respondit mulier, 'de fructu arborum quae sunt in paradiso licet nobis comedere, sed de fructu huius arboris imperavit nobis deus ne comederemus et ne tangeremus, ne moreremur.'

Vocabulary

erat 'was'

callidus, -a, -um 'clever'

terra, terrae (f.) 'earth'

fēcerat 'had made' (pluperfect)

mulier, mulieris (f.) 'woman'

comedō, comedere, comēdī, comēsum 'eat'

arbor, arboris (f.) 'tree'

paradīsus, paradīsī (m.) 'paradise'

respondeō, respondēre, respondī, respōnsum 'reply'

frūctus, frūctūs (m.), 'fruit'

licet 'it is allowed'

tangō, tangere, tetigī, tāctum 'touch'

4 *Corpus Inscriptionum Latinarum* VI.1136: inscription from Rome recording the restoration of baths (fourth century AD).

Domina nostra Helena venerabilis domini nostri Constantini Augusti mater et avia beatissimorum et florentissimorum Caesarum nostrorum thermas incendio destructas restituit.

Vocabulary

Helena, Helenae (f.) *name of the*
   emperor's mother
venerābilis, venerābile 'venerable'
   (here nominative)
Cōnstantīnus, -ī (m.)
   'Constantine'
Augustus, -ī (m.) *was at this period the*
   title of the senior emperor
avia, aviae (f.) 'grandmother'
beātus, beāta, beātum
   'blessed'

flōrēns, *gen.* flōrentis
   'flourishing'
Caesar, Caesaris (m.) *was at this period*
   the title of the emperor's son(s)
thermae, thermārum (f. plural) 'public
   baths'
incendium, incendiī (n.) 'fire'
dēstruō, dēstruere, dēstrūxī,
   destrūctum 'destroy'
restituō, restituere, restituī, restitūtum
   'restore'

5 Martial 13.76: the taste of meat depends on its price (first century AD).

Rustica sim an perdix quid refert, si sapor idem est?
   carior est perdix: sic sapit illa magis.

Vocabulary

rūstica, rūsticae (f.) 'woodcock'
   (an edible bird)
an 'or'
perdīx, perdīcis (f.) 'partridge'
quid rēfert (+ subjunctive) 'what
   difference does it make whether'
sapor, sapōris (m.) 'taste'

īdem, eadem, idem (declined like *is*)
   'same'
cārus, cāra, cārum 'expensive'
sīc 'that is how'
sapiō, sapere, sapīvī, – 'taste good'
magis 'more' (adverb)

38.6 Vocabulary to Learn

Adjectives

cārus, cāra, cārum	'dear', 'expensive'
certus, certa, certum	'certain', 'reliable'
clārus, clāra, clārum	'bright', 'famous'
dulcis, dulce	'sweet'
dūrus, dūra, dūrum	'hard', 'harsh'

Vocabulary continues.

grātus, grāta, grātum	'pleasing', 'grateful'
potēns, *gen.* potentis	'powerful'
sapiēns, *gen.* sapientis	'wise'
similis, simile (+ dative)	'like', 'similar'
stultus, stulta, stultum	'foolish'
turpis, turpe	'shameful'

Adverb

| quam | 'as . . . as possible' |

39 | Imperfect Tense

39.1 Imperfect Indicative of Regular Verbs

So far we have seen only one past indicative tense, the perfect, but Latin has an imperfect indicative as well. The imperfect is used to describe actions as ongoing in the past, such as 'I was doing' or 'I used to do'. It is relatively simple to form, because all the different conjugations take exactly the same endings, and the only differences between them come from the stem vowels used before those endings.

	First conjugation	Second conjugation	Third conjugation	Fourth conjugation	Mixed conjugation
Active	amābam	monēbam	regēbam	audiēbam	capiēbam
	amābās	monēbās	regēbās	audiēbās	capiēbās
	amābat	monēbat	regēbat	audiēbat	capiēbat
	amābāmus	monēbāmus	regēbāmus	audiēbāmus	capiēbāmus
	amābātis	monēbātis	regēbātis	audiēbātis	capiēbātis
	amābant	monēbant	regēbant	audiēbant	capiēbant
Passive	amābar	monēbar	regēbar	audiēbar	capiēbar
	amābāris	monēbāris	regēbāris	audiēbāris	capiēbāris
	amābātur	monēbātur	regēbātur	audiēbātur	capiēbātur
	amābāmur	monēbāmur	regēbāmur	audiēbāmur	capiēbāmur
	amābāminī	monēbāminī	regēbāminī	audiēbāminī	capiēbāminī
	amābantur	monēbantur	regēbantur	audiēbantur	capiēbantur
Deponent	vēnābar	verēbar	ūtēbar	partiēbar	moriēbar
	vēnābāris	verēbāris	ūtēbāris	partiēbāris	moriēbāris
	vēnābātur	verēbātur	ūtēbātur	partiēbātur	moriēbātur
	vēnābāmur	verēbāmur	ūtēbāmur	partiēbāmur	moriēbāmur
	vēnābāminī	verēbāminī	ūtēbāminī	partiēbāminī	moriēbāminī
	vēnābantur	verēbantur	ūtēbantur	partiēbantur	moriēbantur

39.2 Imperfect Indicative of Irregular Verbs

Even the irregular verbs are mostly regular in the imperfect: *eō*, *volō*, *nōlō*, and *mālō* are completely regular, and *sum* and *possum* take the regular endings without the characteristic *-b-*.

Sum	Possum	Eō	Volō	Nōlō	Mālō
eram	poteram	ībam	volēbam	nōlēbam	mālēbam
erās	poterās	ībās	volēbās	nōlēbās	mālēbās
erat	poterat	ībat	volēbat	nōlēbat	mālēbat
erāmus	poterāmus	ībāmus	volēbāmus	nōlēbāmus	mālēbāmus
erātis	poterātis	ībātis	volēbātis	nōlēbātis	mālēbātis
erant	poterant	ībant	volēbant	nōlēbant	mālēbant

Practice

A Conjugate in the imperfect indicative:

1 *currō*, active
2 *laudō*, passive
3 *absum*
4 *faciō*, active
5 *loquor*
6 *abeō*
7 *arbitror*
8 *sentiō*, passive
9 *prōgredior*
10 *adsum*
11 *vendō*, active
12 *orior*
13 *doceō*, passive
14 *dō*, active
15 *exeō*
16 *dūcō*, passive
17 *polliceor*
18 *patior*

39.3 Translation of the Imperfect Indicative

The imperfect has two main translations, both of them periphrastic (involving more than one word in English). It is important to be able to recognize these English forms as equivalents of the Latin imperfect, as otherwise there is a temptation to translate 'was doing' with a form of *sum* and the present participle in Latin (which would not be correct), and to translate 'used to do' with a form of *ūtor* and the infinitive (which would be even more incorrect). For most verbs, actives and deponents are translated like *amābam*, and passives are translated like *amābar*.

Active

amābam 'I was loving', 'I used to love'
amābās 'you (singular) were loving', 'you (singular) used to love'
amābat 'he was loving', 'she was loving', 'it was loving', 'was loving', 'he used to love', 'she used to love', 'it used to love', 'used to love'
amābāmus 'we were loving', 'we used to love'
amābātis 'you (plural) were loving', 'you (plural) used to love'
amābant 'they were loving', 'they used to love', 'were loving', 'used to love'

Passive

> *amābar* 'I was being loved', 'I used to be loved'
> *amābāris* 'you (singular) were being loved', 'you (singular) used to be loved'
> *amābātur* 'he was being loved', 'she was being loved', 'it was being loved', 'was being loved', 'he used to be loved', 'she used to be loved', 'it used to be loved', 'used to be loved'
> *amābāmur* 'we were being loved', 'we used to be loved'
> *amābāminī* 'you were being loved', 'you used to be loved'
> *amābantur* 'they were being loved', 'they used to be loved', 'were being loved', 'used to be loved'

For a few verbs these English translations do not work; for example 'I was being' would usually be unfortunate as a translation of *eram*, as would 'I was being able' as a translation of *poteram*. For such verbs, in situations where the 'used to' translation does not work either, one has to use the simple past in English; thus 'I was' can be the translation either of *fuī* or of *eram*. In fact *eram* is more common than *fuī* in situations where an English speaker would say 'I was'; the action of 'being' is one that is naturally continuous and so lends itself to the use of the imperfect tense.

The imperfect is a historic tense for the purposes of sequence of tenses (see chapter 16.1): if it is used in a main clause on which a subordinate clause with a subjunctive verb depends, the subjunctive in that clause is imperfect rather than present.

Practice

B Translate, giving all possible meanings:

1	audiebat	15	monebamini
2	audiebatur	16	verebamur
3	regebant	17	ibat
4	regebantur	18	volebam
5	utebamur	19	nolebatis
6	nolebas	20	partiebar
7	eras	21	ibas
8	capiebas	22	audiebam
9	eratis	23	capiebant
10	ibam	24	audiebar
11	regebamur	25	volebamus
12	capiebaris	26	regebamus
13	monebatis	27	erant
14	eram		

C Translate into Latin:

1 I used to capture
2 I used to be captured
3 I used to hunt
4 we were hearing
5 we were being heard
6 we were dying

7 he used to warn
8 he used to be warned
9 he used to be able
10 they were ruling
11 they were being ruled
12 they were wanting

D Translate:

1 ille poeta libros longissimos vendebat.
2 illa puella turpissima omnium erat.
3 tot viri pugnabant ut multi interficerentur.
4 Athenas venturi, paucos dies Corinthi manebant.
5 quis milites hortabatur ut bene pugnarent?
6 dei Romani semper quam felicissimi erant.
7 exercitus hostium progrediens a nostris impediebatur.
8 arbitrabar me sapientissimum esse.
9 pueri et puellae a patribus defendebantur.
10 ille vir clarissimus mecum loquebatur.

11 domus nostrae a servis reficiebantur.
12 servus stultissimus ab equo fugiebat.
13 quis dicebat eum potentissimum esse?
14 tantus erat exercitus ut nostri fugerent.
15 hic equus nigrior erat quam ille.
16 Romam ibamus ut patrem sepeliremus.
17 arbitrabantur nos durissimos esse.
18 Athenas ibant ut viros sapientiores invenirent.
19 dicebamus filios tuos dulcissimos esse.
20 tam turpis erat ut numquam laudaretur.

E Translate into Latin:

1 I was calling you for many hours.
2 The Roman senate was very powerful.
3 We were being defended by many soldiers.
4 The Greeks were wiser than the Romans.

5 That rather foolish man used to think that we were very famous.
6 That girl was so sweet that she was loved by all men.
7 We used to beg him to come to Syracuse, but he never came.
8 My sister was so happy in Athens that she stayed there for many years.

9   You used to say that I was as sweet as possible.

10 We were hunting for so many hours that we killed many animals.

11 The king was ordering the soldiers to go to London.

12 Whom were you calling?

39.4 Reading Practice

1 *Colloquium Harleianum* 8a–9d (adapted): a boy refutes an accusation of truancy (perhaps first century AD).

SCHOOL OFFICIAL: heri cessabas et meridie domi ludebas. quaesivi te et audivi omnia quae fecisti a nutrice tua.

BOY: mentitur qui illud tibi dixit! duxit enim me pater secum in praetorium. salutatus est a magistratibus et epistulas accepit a domino meo imperatore; et statim ascendit in templum et immolavit pro aeterna victoria imperatoris.

Vocabulary

cessō, cessāre, cessāvī, cessātum 'slack off'

merīdiēs (like *diēs*) (m.) 'midday'

lūdō, lūdere, lūsī, lūsum 'play'

quaerō, quaerere, quaesīvī, quaesītum 'look for'

nūtrīx, nūtrīcis (f.) 'nurse'

mentior, mentīrī, mentītus sum 'lie'

praetōrium, praetōriī (n.) 'town hall'

salūtō, -āre, -āvī, -ātum 'greet'

magistrātus, magistrātūs (m.) 'magistrate'

imperātor, imperātōris (m.) 'emperor'

statim 'immediately'

ascendō, ascendere, ascendī, ascēnsum 'go up'

templum, templī (n.) 'temple'

immolō, -āre, -āvī, -ātum 'offer a sacrifice'

prō (+ ablative) 'for'

aeternus, -a, -um 'eternal'

victōria, victōriae (f.) 'victory'

2 St Augustine (fourth century AD), *Confessions* 1.9 (adapted): the saint describes his early school years.

Inde in scholam missus sum, ut discerem litteras, in quibus quid utilitatis esset ignorabam miser. et tamen, si segnis in discendo eram, vapulabam. laudabatur enim hoc a maioribus, et multi ante nos vitam agentes praestruxerant aerumnosas vias, per quas vitam transire cogebamur multiplicato labore et dolore.

Vocabulary

inde 'then'	ante (+ accusative) 'before'
schola, scholae (f.) 'school'	praestrūxerant 'had built'
discō, discere, didicī, – 'learn'	(pluperfect tense)
littera, litterae (f.) 'letter' (of the	aerumnōsus, -a, -um 'painful'
alphabet)	via, viae (f.) 'road', 'route'
quid ūtilitātis esset 'what the point was'	trānseō (like *eō*) 'go across'
ignōrō, -āre, -āvī, -ātum 'be ignorant'	cōgō, cōgere, coēgī, coāctum
sēgnis, sēgne 'lazy'	'compel'
discendum, discendī (n.) 'learning'	multiplicō, -āre, -āvī, -ātum 'multiply'
vāpulō, -āre, -āvī, -ātum 'be beaten'	labor, labōris (m.) 'toil'
maior *can also mean* 'adult', 'grown up'	dolor, dolōris (m.) 'pain'

3 Martial 5.82: the poet complains about someone who does not deliver on his promises (first century AD).

Quid promittebas mihi milia, Gaure, ducenta,
   si dare non poteras milia, Gaure, decem?
an potes et non vis? rogo: non est turpius istud?
   i tibi, dispereas, Gaure: pusillus homo es.

Vocabulary

quid 'why'	an 'can it be that?'
prōmittō (like *mittō*) 'promise'	istud (neuter nominative singular)
mīlia ducenta 'two hundred thousand	'that'
(sesterces)'	ī tibi 'away with you!'
Gaurus, Gaurī (m.) *a man's name*	dispereō (like *eō*) 'perish'
mīlia decem 'ten thousand (sesterces)'	pusillus, -a, -um 'of no account'

40.1 Irregular Comparison

So far we have not mentioned the comparatives or the superlatives of the most common adjectives, such as *bonus, malus, magnus,* and *parvus.* Just as the most common verbs tend to have irregular conjugations, so the most common adjectives have irregular comparisons. The most important irregular comparatives and superlatives in Latin are the following:

Positive	Comparative	Superlative
bonus, -a, -um 'good'	melior, melius 'better', 'rather good'	optimus, -a, -um 'best', 'very good'
malus, -a, -um 'bad'	peior, peius 'worse', 'rather bad'	pessimus, -a, -um 'worst', 'very bad'
magnus, -a, -um 'big'	maior, maius 'bigger', 'rather big'	maximus, -a, -um 'biggest', 'very big'
parvus, -a, -um 'small'	minor, minus 'smaller', 'rather small'	minimus, -a, -um 'smallest', 'very small'
multī, -ae, -a 'many'	plūrēs, plūra 'more', 'rather many'	plūrimī, -ae, -a 'most', 'very many'
facilis, -e 'easy'	facilior, facilius 'easier', 'rather easy'	facillimus, -a, -um 'easiest', 'very easy'
difficilis, -e 'difficult'	difficilior, difficilius 'more difficult', 'rather difficult'	difficillimus, -a, -um 'most difficult', 'very difficult'
similis, -e 'like'	similior, similius 'more like', 'rather like'	simillimus, -a, -um 'most like', 'very like'

All these comparatives decline like *trīstior* (see chapter 38.3), except *plūrēs* which declines as follows:

British Case Order

| | Singular | | Plural | |
| | Masculine and | | Masculine and | |
	feminine	Neuter	feminine	Neuter
Nom.	–	plūs	plūrēs	plūra
Voc.	–	plūs	plūrēs	plūra
Acc.	–	plūs	plūrēs	plūra
Gen.	–	plūris	plūrium	plūrium
Dat.	–	–	plūribus	plūribus
Abl.	–	plūre	plūribus	plūribus

Ancient Case Order

| | Singular | | Plural | |
| | Masculine and | | Masculine and | |
	feminine	Neuter	feminine	Neuter
Nom./Voc.	–	plūs	plūrēs	plūra
Gen.	–	plūris	plūrium	plūrium
Dat.	–	–	plūribus	plūribus
Acc.	–	plūs	plūrēs	plūra
Abl.	–	plūre	plūribus	plūribus

Notice that the genitive plural *plūrium* has an *i*-stem form, but the other forms are not *i*-stems (neuter nominative plural *plūra* not **plūria*, ablative singular *plūre* not **plūrī*). (* is used to indicate words that do not exist.)

Practice

A Translate:

1 ille agricola plures equos habebat quam nos.

2 quis dicebat me quam pessimum esse?

3 plurima verba Athenis audiebamus.

4 liber a clarissimo poeta scriptus minor erat.

5 cives nostri ab exercitu optimo defendebantur.

6 puer minimus domum a matre ducebatur.

7 equus maximus ad agrum ab agricola ductus est.

8 fides eius quam optima erat.

9 exercitus noster melior erat quam exercitus illorum.

10 moenia minora Corinthi reficiebantur.

11 domus minima refecta non est.

12 libri facillimi scribebantur.

13 libri difficillimi a poetis
   doctissimis scripti sunt.
14 ille puer similis est tibi, sed hic
   similior.

15 arbitrabatur nos optimos
   omnium esse.
16 plurimos dies Athenis
   manebo.

40.2 *Nēmō* and *Nihil*

The normal words for 'no-one' (*nēmō*), 'nothing' (*nihil*), and adjectival 'no' (as in 'no king is humble', Latin *nūllus*) are also irregular in Latin.

British Case Order

	'No-one' (singular only)	'Nothing' (singular only)
Nom.	nēmō	nihil/nīl
Voc.	–	–
Acc.	nēminem	nihil/nīl
Gen.	–	–
Dat.	nēminī	–
Abl.	–	–

Ancient Case Order

	'No-one' (singular only)	'Nothing' (singular only)
Nom.	nēmō	nihil/nīl
Gen.	–	–
Dat.	nēminī	–
Acc.	nēminem	nihil/nīl
Abl.	–	–

British Case Order

'No'

	Singular Masculine	Feminine	Neuter	Plural Masculine	Feminine	Neuter
Nom.	nūllus	nūlla	nūllum	nūllī	nūllae	nūlla
Voc.	–	–	–	–	–	–
Acc.	nūllum	nūllam	nūllum	nūllōs	nūllās	nūlla
Gen.	nūllīus	nūllīus	nūllīus	nūllōrum	nūllārum	nūllōrum
Dat.	nūllī	nūllī	nūllī	nūllīs	nūllīs	nūllīs
Abl.	nūllō	nūllā	nūllō	nūllīs	nūllīs	nūllīs

Ancient Case Order

'No'

	Singular			Plural		
	Masculine	Feminine	Neuter	Masculine	Feminine	Neuter
Nom.	nūllus	nūlla	nūllum	nūllī	nūllae	nūlla
Gen.	nūllīus	nūllīus	nūllīus	nūllōrum	nūllārum	nūllōrum
Dat.	nūllī	nūllī	nūllī	nūllīs	nūllīs	nūllīs
Acc.	nūllum	nūllam	nūllum	nūllōs	nūllās	nūlla
Abl.	nūllō	nūllā	nūllō	nūllīs	nūllīs	nūllīs

Like other adjectives, *nūllus* can be substantivized with *vir* understood; then it means 'no man' or 'no person' and as such is very similar to *nēmō*. In fact substantivized forms of *nūllus* effectively supply the missing forms of *nēmō*, so that one could (and many people do) say that *nēmō* has a genitive *nūllīus* and an ablative *nūllō*.

40.3 Use of Negatives

The three negative words *nēmō*, *nihil*, and *nūllus* are used in circumstances when an ordinary negative would be *nōn* rather than *nē*. In constructions where *nē* would be found instead of *nōn*, a completely different set of words is used: *nēmō* is replaced by *nē quis* 'no-one', *nihil* is replaced by *nē quid* 'nothing', and *nūllus* is replaced by *nē ūllus* 'no'. Declension of these terms is straightforward: *quis* and *quid* decline like the *quis* and *quid* we have already seen meaning 'who?' (chapter 13.3), and *ūllus* is identical to *nūllus* without the initial *n-*.

nēmō vēnit. 'No-one came.' (ordinary direct statement, negative *nōn*)

nē quis veniat. 'May no-one come.' (hortatory subjunctive, negative *nē*)

tālia dīxit ut nēmō venīre vellet. 'He said such things that no-one wanted to come.' (result clause, negative *nōn*)

haec dīxit nē quis venīre vellet. 'He said these things so that no-one would want to come.' (purpose clause, negative *nē*)

nūllōs hostēs in silvā vīdit. 'He saw no enemies in the forest.' (ordinary direct statement, negative *nōn*)

nē ūllōs hostēs in silvā videat. 'May he see no enemies in the forest!' (hortatory subjunctive, negative *nē*)

English also has two-word negatives that look similar to *nē quis*, *nē quid*, and *ne ūllus*: 'not … anyone', 'not … anything', and 'not … any'. Indeed structurally the English and Latin forms are very similar, because in certain contexts *quis*, *quid*, and *ūllus* can also be used without *nē* to mean 'anyone', 'anything', and 'any'. But the principles governing the use of such two-word negatives in English are different from those applying to the Latin ones, so depending on the particular sentence either type of English negative may be used to translate either type of Latin negative.

nēminem vīdit. 'He did not see anyone.' / 'He saw no-one.'
nihil facere potuit. 'He could not do anything.' / 'He could do nothing.'
nūllōs hostēs in silvā vīdit. 'He did not see any enemies in the forest.' / 'He saw no enemies in the forest.'
hoc dīximus nē quid facere posset. 'We said this so that he would not be able to do anything.' (purpose)
tālia dīximus ut nihil facere posset. 'We said such things that he was not able to do anything.' (result)

When translating from Latin to English, therefore, one needs to choose between the English one-word negatives ('no-one' etc.) and two-word negatives ('not … anyone' etc.) according to what sounds best in English; it is not a good idea to try to translate Latin one-word negatives (*nēmō* etc.) only with English one-word negatives and Latin two-word negatives (*nē quis* etc.) only with English two-word negatives. When translating from English to Latin it is vital to be ready to translate either type of English negative with either type of Latin negative, according to what is needed in Latin: the Latin one-word negatives are used in contexts where the simple negative would be *nōn*, and the two-word negatives in contexts where the simple negative would be *nē*.

Practice

B Translate:

1. arbitrabatur neminem se amare.
2. arbitrabantur nihil bonum esse.
3. tu equum optimum habebas, et ego nullum.
4. nihil peius erat quam consilium eius.
5. nemo equum minorem malebat.
6. nullus exercitus Athenis aderat.
7. hic puer tam malus erat ut nemo eum docere vellet.
8. puer pessima faciebat ne quis se docere vellet.
9. exercitus in castris manebat ne ullus miles caperetur.
10. nemo versus difficillimos a poeta scriptos legebat.
11. nihil melius quam hoc inventum est.
12. fugiens Corinthum ivit ne quis se inveniret.
13. puer minor a patre domum ductus est ne quid facere posset.
14. puer minimus domum a matre ductus nihil facere poterat.
15. nullus liber tam difficile est ut eum legere non possim.
16. librum difficillimum scripsi ne quis eum legere vellet.
17. hic liber tam difficile erat ut nemo eum legere vellet.

C Translate into Latin:

1 I did not see anyone (when I was) coming home.
2 We were not doing anything.
3 The bigger boy is better, and the smaller boy is worse.
4 No-one was reading the easier book.
5 Rather many poets used to write rather difficult verses.
6 No verse of this poet is very difficult.
7 No-one bought my very small sheep.
8 My sheep was so small that no-one bought it.
9 I was leading a rather small sheep, in order that no-one would want to buy it.
10 (When I was) driving rather many small sheep, I did not lose any sheep.
11 Who bought the very small sheep that no-one used to want?
12 No river could hinder our army.
13 Our army was not being hindered by any enemies.
14 That river was so small that it did not hinder any army.
15 Coming to a rather large river, our army was hindered.
16 No-one was advancing, because everyone was hindered by the enemies.

40.4 Reading Practice

1 Catullus 49: the poet praises Cicero (first century BC).

Disertissime Romuli nepotum,
quot sunt quotque fuere, Marce Tulli,
quotque post aliis erunt in annis,
gratias tibi maximas Catullus
agit pessimus omnium poeta,
tanto pessimus omnium poeta,
quanto tu optimus omnium patronus.

Vocabulary

disertus, -a, -um 'eloquent'
Rōmulus, Rōmulī (m.) *name of an ancestor of the Romans*
nepōs, nepōtis (m.) 'descendant'
quot (indeclinable) 'as many as'
fuēre = fuērunt
Mārcus Tullius, Mārcī Tulliī (m.) 'Cicero' (his full name was Mārcus Tullius Cicerō)

post 'later'
alius, alia, aliud 'other' (i.e. future)
grātiae, grātiārum (f. plural) 'thanks'
Catullus, Catullī (m.) *name of the poet*
agō *can also mean* 'give'
tantō . . . quantō 'by as much . . . as'
patrōnus, patrōnī (m.) 'patron' (supply *es* with this)

2 Martial 3.9: the poet disparages a rival (first century AD).

> Versiculos in me narratur scribere Cinna.
> non scribit, cuius carmina nemo legit.

Vocabulary

versiculus, versiculī (m.) 'little verse'
in *can also mean* 'against'
narrō, narrāre, narrāvī, narrātum 'say'

Cinna, Cinnae (m.) *name of a poet*
carmen, carminis (n.) 'poem'

3 Martial 3.61: further disparagement (first century AD).

> Esse nihil dicis quidquid petis, improbe Cinna:
> si nil, Cinna, petis, nil tibi, Cinna, nego.

Vocabulary

quidquid 'whatever' (neuter accusative
    singular)
improbus, -a, -um 'reprobate'

Cinna, Cinnae (m.) *name of a poet*
negō, negāre, negāvī, negātum 'refuse'

4 Martial 8.35: a bad marriage (first century AD).

> Cum sitis similes paresque vita,
> uxor pessima, pessimus maritus,
> miror non bene convenire vobis.

Vocabulary

cum (+ subjunctive) 'since'
păr, *gen.* paris 'equal'
vītā 'in your life'
uxor, uxōris (f.) 'wife'

marītus, marītī (m.) 'husband'
mīror, mīrārī, mīrātus sum 'be amazed
    that'
convenīre vōbīs '(you) suit each other'

5 Martial, *De spectaculis* 36: the thoughts of a loser at the games (first century AD).

> Cedere maiori virtutis fama secunda est.
> illa gravis palma est, quam minor hostis habet.

Vocabulary

cēdō, cēdere, cessī, cessum (+ dative)
    'yield to'
maior *can also mean* 'superior'
virtūtis (f. genitive) 'in excellence'
fāma, fāmae (f.) 'glory'

secundus, -a, -um 'second-best' (i.e. the
    next best thing after winning)
gravis *can also mean* 'difficult to bear'
palma, palmae (f.) 'prize'
minor *can also mean* 'inferior'
hostis, hostis (m.) 'competitor'

40.5 Vocabulary to Learn

Nouns

nēmō (m.)	'no-one', 'not . . . anyone'
nē quid (n.)	'nothing', 'not . . . anything'
nē quis (m.)	'no-one', 'not . . . anyone'
nihil (n.)	'nothing', 'not . . . anything'

Adjectives

difficilior, difficilius	'more difficult', 'rather difficult'
difficillimus, difficillima, difficillimum	'most difficult', 'very difficult'
facilior, facilius	'easier', 'rather easy'
facillimus, facillima, facillimum	'easiest', 'very easy'
maior, maius	'bigger', 'rather big'
maximus, maxima, maximum	'biggest', 'very big'
melior, melius	'better', 'rather good'
minimus, minima, minimum	'smallest', 'very small'
minor, minus	'smaller', 'rather small'
nē ūllus, nē ūlla, nē ūllum	'no', 'none'
nūllus, nūlla, nūllum	'no', 'none'
optimus, optima, optimum	'best', 'very good'
peior, peius	'worse', 'rather bad'
pessimus, pessima, pessimum	'worst', 'very bad'
plūrēs, plūra	'more', 'rather many'
plūrimī, plūrimae, plūrima	'most', 'very many'
similior, similius	'more like', 'rather like'
simillimus, simillima, simillimum	'most like', 'very like'

41.1 Formation of the Gerundive

In addition to the participles, another kind of adjective can be formed from a verb. This is the gerundive, a form that expresses obligation. Gerundives are formed by adding *-ndus*, *-nda*, *-ndum* to the stem of the verb (the same base as is used to form the imperfect indicative: see chapter 39.1); they are regular first/second-declension adjectives and therefore decline like *bonus*.

First conjugation	amandus, -a, -um 'having to be loved'
Second conjugation	monendus, -a, -um 'having to be warned'
Third conjugation	regendus, -a, -um 'having to be ruled'
Fourth conjugation	audiendus, -a, -um 'having to be heard'
Mixed conjugation	capiendus, -a, -um 'having to be captured'
First conjugation deponent	vēnandus, -a, -um 'having to be hunted'
Second conjugation deponent	verendus, -a, -um 'having to be feared'
Third conjugation deponent	ūtendus, -a, -um 'having to be used'
Fourth conjugation deponent	partiendus, -a, -um 'having to be divided'
Mixed conjugation deponent	moriendus, -a, -um (no literal translation available)
Sum	–
Possum	–
Eō	eundus, -a, -um (no literal translation available)
Volō	volendus, -a, -um 'having to be wanted'
Nōlō	nōlendus, -a, -um 'having to be not wanted'
Mālō	–

The translations are provided only as an indication of the basic meaning of these forms; in practice such translations are almost never used, because a number of more idiomatic English expressions work better in different contexts (see below). It is not possible to give a literal translation of the gerundives of verbs that are intransitive in English.

Practice

A Give the gerundives of these verbs:

1 loquor	7 prōgredior	13 videō
2 impediō	8 vendō	14 agō
3 mittō	9 sepeliō	15 patior
4 doceō	10 polliceor	16 pugnō
5 laudō	11 vocō	
6 emō	12 arbitror	

41.2 Use of Gerundives of Transitive Verbs

Gerundives of transitive verbs (verbs that take a direct object in the accusative) agree with the nouns they modify in gender, number, and case: *puella amanda* 'a having-to-be-loved girl', i.e. a girl who must be loved; *liber legendus* 'a having-to-be-read book', i.e. a book that must be read. Most often the gerundive is used with a form of *sum* and in English is best translated with 'must' or 'have to': *haec puella amanda est* 'this girl must be loved', 'this girl has to be loved' (literally 'this girl is having-to-be-loved'); *ille liber legendus est* 'that book must be read', 'that book has to be read' (literally 'that book is having-to-be-read').[1] Often there is an agent, i.e. an indication of who must do the action that is necessary. The agent is in the dative case (this is known as the 'dative of agent'), not in the ablative as for ordinary passives, and there is no *ā/ab*: *haec puella amanda est mihi* 'this girl must be loved by me', 'this girl has to be loved by me' (literally 'this girl is having-to-be-loved by me'); *ille liber legendus est mihi* 'that book must be read by me', 'that book has to be read by me' (literally 'that book is having-to-be-read by me').

Although ordinary Latin passives are normally translated into English with English passives, gerundives are usually translated into English with active verbs if there is an agent. (This is partly because the gerundive construction is the most common way of saying 'must' in Latin, whereas in English the active construction is much more common than the passive, and partly because of the difficulties caused by the gerundives of intransitive verbs, for which see chapter 45.2.) So the normal way to translate *haec puella amanda est mihi* is 'I must love this girl' or 'I have to love this girl', and the normal way to translate *ille liber legendus est mihi* is 'I must read that book' or 'I have to read that book', even though these translations are much less literal than others we normally use.

---

[1] This construction is sometimes called the 'passive periphrastic'. That term is not ideal, because the gerundive is no more periphrastic than many other passive verb forms (e.g. *amātus est* 'he was loved'). The gerundive itself is sometimes called the 'future passive participle'; again this is not ideal, as the gerundive behaves differently from the participles.

Therefore the translation possibilities are as follows, in declining order of attractiveness in English:

With agent: *haec dīcenda sunt tibi.*   'You must say these things.'
                                           'You have to say these things.'
                                           'These things must be said by you.'
                                           'These things have to be said by you.'

Without agent: *haec dīcenda sunt.*   'These things must be said.'
                                           'These things have to be said.'

Practice

B Translate, giving all possibilities:

1 dei laudandi sunt.
2 dei laudandi sunt omnibus.
3 timendus est rex noster.
4 timendus est tibi rex noster.
5 hi pueri docendi sunt.
6 hi pueri docendi sunt magistro.
7 Carthago oppugnanda est.
8 Carthago nobis oppugnanda est.
9 equi ad aquam ducendi sunt.
10 servis equi ad aquam ducendi sunt.
11 liber scribendus est.
12 liber mihi scribendus est.
13 Athenae defendendae sunt.
14 nostris defendendae sunt Athenae.
15 haec domus reficienda est.
16 haec domus ei reficienda est.
17 vincendi sunt hostes.
18 nostris vincendi sunt hostes.

C Translate into Latin:

1 Our friends must be helped.
2 We must help our friends.
3 That city has to be seen.
4 You (singular) have to see that city.
5 The soldiers must be encouraged.
6 The king must encourage the soldiers.
7 That man has to be sent to Rome.
8 I have to send that man to Rome.
9 Your (plural) sheep have to be driven to the field.
10 You (plural) must drive the sheep to the field.
11 His son must be sought.
12 The father has to seek his son.
13 Our walls have to be repaired.
14 We have to repair our walls.
15 The enemies' king must be captured.
16 You must capture the enemies' king.
17 The money must be found.
18 They have to find the money.
19 Our city has to be defended.
20 We have to defend our city.
21 His words must be heard.
22 She must hear his words.

41.3 **Tenses**

The gerundive can also be used in a past or future tense, by changing the tense of *sum*: *ille liber legendus erit mihi* means 'I will have to read that book' and *ille liber legendus erat mihi* means 'I had to read that book'. Notice that in English 'must' cannot be used in the past or future, so only 'have to' is available to translate such sentences.

Practice

D Translate, giving all possibilities:

1 dei laudandi erant.
2 dei laundandi erant omnibus.
3 timendus erat rex noster.
4 timendus erat nobis rex noster.
5 hi pueri docendi erunt.
6 hi pueri docendi erunt magistro.
7 Carthago oppugnanda erit.
8 Carthago nobis oppugnanda erit.
9 equi ad aquam ducendi erant.
10 servis equi ad aquam ducendi erant.

11 liber scribendus erit.
12 liber mihi scribendus erit.
13 Athenae defendendae erant.
14 nostris defendendae erant Athenae.
15 haec domus reficienda erit.
16 haec domus ei reficienda erit.
17 vincendi erant hostes.
18 nostris vincendi erant hostes.

E Translate into Latin:

1 Our friends will have to be helped.
2 We had to help our friends.
3 That city had to be seen.
4 Did you (singular) have to see that city?
5 The soldiers had to be encouraged.
6 The king will have to encourage the soldiers.
7 That man will have to be sent to Rome.
8 I shall have to send that man to Rome.
9 Did your (plural) sheep have to be driven to the field?
10 Did you (plural) have to drive the sheep to the field?

11 His son had to be sought.
12 The father will have to seek his son.
13 Our walls will have to be repaired.
14 We had to repair our walls.
15 The enemies' king will have to be captured.
16 You will have to capture the enemies' king.
17 The money had to be found.
18 They had to find the money.
19 Our city will have to be defended.
20 We shall have to defend our city.
21 His words had to be heard.
22 She had to hear his words.

41.4 Reading Practice

1 Terence, *Andria* 252–7 (adapted): a youth complains of his father's treatment of him (second century BC).

Nam quid ego dicam de patre? tantam rem tam neglegenter agit! praeteriens modo mihi in foro dixit 'uxor tibi ducenda est, Pamphile, hodie: para, abi domum.' visus est mihi dicere 'abi cito et suspende te.' obstupui. arbitrarisne me verbum potuisse ullum loqui? aut ullam causam, ineptam saltem falsam iniquam? obmutui.

Vocabulary

neglegenter 'casually'	suspendō, suspendere, suspendī,
praetereō (like *eō*) 'go past'	suspēnsum 'hang'
modo 'just now'	obstupēscō, obstupēscere, obstupuī, –
forum, forī (n.) 'forum', 'marketplace'	'be struck dumb'
uxor, uxōris (f.) 'wife'	**ūllus, ūlla, ūllum 'any'**
dūcō *can also mean* 'marry'	causa, causae (f.) 'excuse'
Pamphilus, Pamphilī (m.) *name of the*	ineptus, inepta, ineptum 'inadequate'
youth who speaks these lines	saltem 'even'
parō, parāre, parāvī, parātum 'get ready'	falsus, falsa, falsum 'false'
videor (passive of *videō*) 'seem'	inīquus, inīqua, inīquum 'unjust'
cito 'at once'	obmūtēscō, obmūtēscere, obmūtuī, –
	'be silent'

2 Cicero, *Epistulae ad familiares* 14.14.1: Cicero writes to his wife and daughter about whether they should flee Rome at Caesar's approach (part of a letter written in 49 BC).

Si vos valetis, nos valemus. vestrum iam consilium est, non solum meum, quid sit vobis faciendum. si ille Romam modeste venturus est, recte in praesentia domi esse potestis; sin homo amens diripiendam urbem daturus est, vereor ut Dolabella ipse satis nobis prodesse possit. . . . etiam illud verendum est, ne brevi tempore fames in urbe sit.

Vocabulary

iam 'now'	dīripiendam 'to be plundered'
cōnsilium *can also mean* 'decision'	Dolābella, -ae (m.) *name of Cicero's*
sōlum 'only'	*daughter's husband, a close friend of*
sit: *translate as indicative*	*Caesar*
modestē 'with moderation'	ipse, ipsa, ipsum 'himself'
rēctē 'all right'	satis 'adequately'
praesentia, praesentiae (f.) 'present	prōsum, prōdesse (like *sum*) 'be of help'
circumstances'	etiam 'also'
sīn 'but if'	tempus, temporis (n.) 'time'
āmēns, *gen.* āmentis 'reckless'	famēs, famis (f.) 'famine'

3 Terence, *Heauton timorumenos* 322–6: advice for a young man in love (second century BC).

Vis amare, vis potiri, vis quod des illi effici;
tuum esse in potiundo periclum non vis: haud stulte sapis,
siquidem id sapere est, velle te id quod non potest contingere.
aut haec cum illis sunt habenda, aut illa cum his mittenda sunt.
harum duarum condicionum nunc utram malis vide.

Vocabulary

potior, potīrī, potītus sum 'possess (the girl you love)'
quod dēs illī efficī 'to have something to give her'
potiundum, potiundī (n.) 'getting possession'
perīc(u)lum, perīc(u)lī (n.) 'danger'
haud 'not'
stultē 'foolishly'

sapiō, sapere, sapīvī, – 'think'
siquidem 'if indeed'
possum *can also mean* 'be possible'
contingō, -tingere, -tigī, -tāctum 'get'
aut ... aut 'either ... or'
mittō *can also mean* 'let go', 'pass up'
duo, duae, duo 'two'
condiciō, condiciōnis (f.) 'condition'
uter, utra, utrum 'which?'

41.5 Vocabulary to Learn

Verbs

ascendō, ascendere, ascendī, ascēnsum	'go up'
dēscendō, dēscendere, dēscendī, dēscēnsum	'go down'
discō, discere, didicī, –	'learn'
ingredior, ingredī, ingressus sum	'enter'
salūtō, salūtāre, salūtāvī, salūtātum	'greet'

Nouns

advocātus, advocātī (m.)	'advocate' (i.e. lawyer)
argentum, argentī (n.)	'silver'
aurum, aurī (n.)	'gold'
causa, causae (f.)	'case', 'reason'
fāma, fāmae (f.)	'fame', 'reputation', 'rumour'
fīnis, fīnis, fīnium (f.)	'end'
iūdex, iūdicis (m.)	'judge'
salūs, salūtis (f.)	'health', 'greetings'
vōx, vōcis (f.)	'voice'

42.1 *Colloquium Celtis* 73a–77b (adapted)

Watching the trials in a Roman courtroom (probably fourth century AD). One of the main reasons Greek students learned Latin was to become lawyers: note the emphasis on the role of the lawyers. Torture of both defendants and witnesses was common during the later imperial period, when this piece was written.

Fit hora tertia. ingrediuntur advocati, causidici, scholastici. agunt plures causas, quisque quomodo potest secundum litterarum facundiam. sunt et causae in fine temporum, quae hodie terminandae sunt. exinde ascendit praeses ad tribunal sessurus. conscendit iudex tribunal, et sic voce praeconis imperat ut rei sistantur. reus sistitur latro, qui interrogatur secundum merita (torquetur, quaestionarius eum pulsat, suspenditur, flagellatur, fustibus vapulat), et adhuc negat se id fecisse. puniendus est: ducitur ad gladium. deinde alter sistitur, innocens, cui adest magnum patrocinium, et viri docti stant cum eo. hic habet bonum eventum: absolvitur. testes in illa causa sine iniuria absoluti sunt. haec causa habuit idoneam defensionem, et viri docti multos denarios acceperunt.

Vocabulary

fit 'arrives' (third person singular verb, followed by a subject in the nominative)

tertius, tertia, tertium 'third'[1]

causidicus, causidicī (m.) 'barrister'

scholasticus, scholasticī (m.) 'legal expert'

quisque 'each one' (nominative singular)

quōmodo 'as'

secundum (+ accusative) 'in accordance with'

litterae, litterārum (f. plural) 'literacy'

fācundia, fācundiae (f.) 'skill'

sunt 'there are'

et 'also'

in (+ ablative) 'at'

tempus, temporis (n.) 'time limit'

terminō, -āre, -āvī, -ātum 'finish'

exinde 'then'

praeses, praesidis (m.) 'presiding official'

tribūnal, tribūnālis, tribūnālium (n.) 'speaker's platform'

cōnscendō, cōnscendere, cōnscendī, cōnscēnsum 'ascend'

---

[1] See note 1 in chapter 27.2 for the Roman method of reckoning time. What time would the third hour be in our reckoning?

sīc 'thus', 'in this way'

praecō, praecōnis (m.) 'herald'

reus, rea, reum 'accused'

**sistō, sistere, stitī, statum 'cause to
   stand up'**

latrō, latrōnis (m.) 'bandit'

interrogō, -āre, -āvī, -ātum 'interrogate'

merita, meritōrum (n. plural) 'deserts'
   (i.e. things he has deserved)

torqueo, torquēre, torsī, tortum
   'torture'

quaestiōnārius, -ī (m.) 'torturer'

pulsō, -āre, -āvī, -ātum 'beat'

suspendō, suspendere, suspendī,
   suspēnsum 'hang up'

flagellō, -āre, -āvī, -ātum 'whip'

fūstis, fūstis, fūstium 'stick'

vāpulō, -āre, -āvī, -ātum 'be beaten'

adhūc 'still'

negō, negāre, negāvī, negātum 'deny'

pūnio, pūnīre, pūnīvī, pūnītum 'punish'

deinde 'then'

alter, altera, alterum 'another'

innocēns, *gen.* innocentis 'innocent'

patrōcinium, patrōciniī (n.) 'crowd of
   supporters'

ēventus, ēventūs (m.) 'outcome'

**absolvō, absolvere, absolvī, absolūtum
   'acquit', 'dismiss'**

testis, testis, testium (m.) 'witness'

iniūria, iniūriae (f.) 'injury'

idōneus, -a, -um 'suitable'

dēfēnsiō, dēfēnsiōnis (f.) 'defence'

dēnārius, dēnāriī (m.) 'denarius' (unit
   of money)

42.2 Translate into Latin

At the fifth hour an accused man entered with his advocate in order to defend himself.
He was (use imperfect) innocent, but another man said that he (i.e. the accused man)
was a bandit, so (*ergō*) he had to find money in order to have an advocate. He testified,
denying that he had been a bandit; the other man testified; the advocate spoke; and
then the judge ordered the torturer to torture the accused man. He was beaten (use
imperfect) and said (use perfect) nothing, because he was very (use imperfect) brave.
Then he was acquitted. He gave the advocate seven denarii, and the advocate was (use
imperfect) very happy.

Additional Vocabulary

testor, testārī, testātus sum 'testify'

42.3 Virgil, *Aeneid* 1.39–49

Juno finds it unfair that she is not allowed by the fates to kill the Trojan refugees led by
Aeneas, especially given what Athena can get away with (continuation of the passage in
chapter 36):

'Quippe vetor fatis. Pallasne exurere classem
Argivum atque ipsos potuit summergere ponto
unius ob noxam et furias Aiacis Oilei?

ipsa Iovis rapidum iaculata e nubibus ignem
disiecitque rates evertitque aequora ventis,
illum exspirantem transfixo pectore flammas
turbine corripuit scopuloque infixit acuto;
ast ego, quae divum incedo regina Iovisque
et soror et coniunx, una cum gente tot annos
bella gero. et quisquam numen Iunonis adorat
praeterea aut supplex aris imponet honorem?'

Vocabulary

quippe 'but of course'
vetō, vetāre, vetuī, vetitum 'forbid'
fātum, fātī (n.) 'fate'
Pallas, Palladis (f.) 'Athena'
exūrō, exūrere, exussī, exustum 'burn up'
Argīvum 'Greeks' (genitive plural)
atque 'and'
ipsōs '(the men) themselves'
summergō, -mergere, -mersī, -mersum
   'drown'
pontus, pontī (m.) 'sea' (supply *in*)
ūnius: *genitive of* ūnus 'alone'
ob (+ accusative) 'on account of'
noxa, noxae (f.) 'crime'
furiae, furiārum (f. plural) 'fury'
Aiāx Oīleus, Aiācis Oīlei (m.) 'Ajax son
   of Oileus'
ipsa 'she herself' (Athena)
Iuppiter, Iovis (m.) 'Jupiter'
rapidus, -a, -um 'swift'
iaculor, -ārī, -ātus sum 'hurl'
nūbēs, nūbis, nūbium (f.) 'cloud'
ignis, ignis, ignium (m.) 'fire'
disiciō, disicere, disiēcī, disiectum
   'break up' (the first syllable is long)
-que . . . -que 'both . . . and'
ratis, ratis, ratium (f.) 'ship'
ēvertō, ēvertere, ēvertī, ēversum
   'overturn'
aequor, aequoris (n.) 'sea'
ventus, ventī (m.) 'wind'

exspīrō, -āre, -āvī, -ātum 'breathe out'
trānsfīgō, -fīgere, -fīxī, -fīxum 'pierce'
pectus, pectoris (n.) 'chest'
flamma, flammae (f.) 'flame' (i.e.
   breaths that hurt him like fire)
turbō, turbinis (m.) 'whirlwind'
corripiō, corripere, corripuī, correptum
   'snatch up'
scopulus, scopulī (m.) 'rock'
īnfīgō, īnfīgere, īnfīxī, īnfīxum (+
   accusative and ablative) 'impale on'
acūtus, acūta, acūtum 'sharp'
ast 'but'
dīvum = deōrum
incēdō, incēdere, incessī, incessum 'go
   about as'
rēgīna, rēgīnae (f.) 'queen'
coniūnx, coniugis (m. or f.) 'spouse'
ūnus, ūna, ūnum 'one'
gēns, gentis, gentium (f.) 'people'
gerō, gerere, gessī, gestum 'wage'
quisquam, quicquam 'anyone'
nūmen, nūminis (n.) 'divine power'
Iūnō, Iūnōnis (f.) 'Juno'
adōrō, -āre, -āvī, -ātum 'worship'
praetereā 'besides'
supplex, *gen.* supplicis 'suppliant'
āra, ārae (f.) 'altar'
impōnō (like *pōnō*) (+ accusative and
   ablative) 'put on'
honor, honōris (m.) 'offerings'

A possible prose order of the above would be:

'Quippe vetor fatis. Pallasne classem Argivum exurere potuit atque ipsos ponto summergere ob noxam et furias unius Aiacis Oilei? ipsa Iovis ignem rapidum e nubibus iaculata ratesque disiecit aequoraque ventis evertit, (et) illum transfixo pectore flammas exspirantem turbine corripuit scopuloque acuto infixit; ast ego, quae regina divum Iovisque et soror et coniunx incedo, cum una gente tot annos bella gero. et quisquam numen Iunonis praeterea adorat aut supplex honorem aris imponet?'

43 | Adverbs

43.1 Meanings of Adverbs

Adverbs are words that modify verbs and adjectives. In English they are often formed by adding *-ly* to the stem of an adjective, as 'badly' from 'bad', but many of the most common English adverbs are formed in other ways: 'well', 'always', and 'very' are also adverbs. We have already seen a number of Latin adverbs as independent vocabulary items, including *diū* 'for a long time', *numquam* 'never', *bene* 'well', and *saepe* 'often'; as in English, these common adverbs are not formed regularly, but most others are derived from adjectives via a regular process. We have already seen one (almost-) regular adverb, *male* 'badly' from *malus, -a, -um* 'bad'.[1]

Because many English adverbs end in *-ly*, many Latin adverbs can be translated by adding *-ly* to the translation of the corresponding adjective: *malus* 'bad', so *male* 'badly'. But sometimes there is no English adverb in *-ly*, and then it is necessary to use a periphrasis that gets the adverbial meaning across: *Rōmānus* 'Roman', but *Rōmānē* clearly not '*Romanly*', so 'in a Roman fashion', etc. Similarly *longus* 'long', but *longē* clearly not '*longly*', so '(by) a long way', '(by) far'. (* is used to indicate words that do not exist.)

Practice

A Translate these adverbs:

1 male	4 Romane	7 certe
2 longe	5 dure	8 stulte
3 vere	6 Graece	

43.2 Formation of Adverbs

As one can see from the above, adjectives of the first and second declensions form adverbs by adding *-ē* to the stem. In writing there is often ambiguity between the adverb and the masculine singular vocative, but in Roman pronunciation there was no such ambiguity, because the vocative ending is *-ĕ* and the adverb ending (usually) *-ē*. Adjectives of the third declension form adverbs by adding *-iter* to the stem; thus the adverb of *fortis*

---

[1] *Male* is not quite regular because it has a short *-e* rather than the *-ē* of most adverbs of its type.

'brave' is *fortiter* 'bravely'. With both types of adjective some care must be taken if the masculine nominative singular ends in *-er*: not only may such adjectives belong to either declension, but the *-e-* may or may not disappear in the stem. As we have seen (chapters 8.2, 21.1, and 38.2), it is necessary to know the feminine nominative singular or the masculine genitive singular in order to find the stem. Thus the adverb of *celer* 'swift' is *celeriter* 'swiftly', because the stem is *celer-* (dictionary entry *celer, celeris, celere*), but the adverb of *ācer* 'keen' is *ācriter* 'keenly', because the stem is *ācr-* (dictionary entry *ācer, ācris, ācre*).

Practice

B Form and translate the adverbs corresponding to the following adjectives:

1 fortis	6 miser	11 turpis
2 celer	7 brevis	12 gravis
3 ācer	8 līber	13 tener
4 clārus	9 fēlīx	14 pulcher
5 similis	10 asper	

43.3 Irregular Adverbs

The relationship between adjectives and adverbs is not always completely straightforward. Some adverbs, such as *numquam*, do not have corresponding adjectives, and some adjectives, such as *tuus*, do not have corresponding adverbs. Also, some adverbs are formed irregularly, including the following:

Adverb		Adjective	
bene	'well'	bonus, bona, bonum	'good'
facile	'easily'	facilis, facile	'easy'
magnopere	'greatly'	magnus, magna, magnum	'great'
multum	'much'	multī, multae, multa	'many'
paulum	'little'	parvus, parva, parvum	'small'

43.4 Comparison of Adverbs

Like adjectives, adverbs have a comparative and superlative. In English the comparative and superlative of adverbs are normally formed with 'more' and 'most': 'He won easily / more easily / most easily' (cf. 'The task is easy/easier/easiest' for the corresponding adjective). Sometimes, however, English comparative and superlative adverbs have the same forms as the adjectives: 'He ran fast/faster/fastest' (cf. 'This runner is fast/faster/fastest' for the adjective). In Latin, the comparative adverb is almost always the neuter accusative singular of the comparative adjective, and the superlative adverb is the superlative adjective with the adverbial -ē ending. Thus the following are examples of adverbs corresponding to adjectives with a regular comparison:

Positive		Comparative		Superlative	
longē	'(by) far' (adjective *longus, -a, -um* 'long')	**longius**	'(by) farther' (adjective *longior, longius* 'longer', 'rather long')	**longissimē**	'(by) farthest' (adjective *longissimus, -a, -um* 'longest', 'very long')
breviter	'briefly' (adjective *brevis, -e* 'short')	**brevius**	'more briefly', 'rather briefly' (adjective *brevior, -ius* 'shorter', 'rather short')	**brevissimē**	'most briefly', 'very briefly' (adjective *brevissimus, -a, -um* 'shortest', 'very short')
tenerē	'tenderly' (adjective *tener, -era, -erum* 'tender')	**tenerius**	'more tenderly', rather tenderly' (adjective *tenerior, -ius* 'tenderer', 'rather tender')	**tenerrimē**	'most tenderly', 'very tenderly' (adjective *tenerrimus, -a, -um* 'tenderest', 'very tender')
ācriter	'keenly' (adjective *ācer, ācris, ācre* 'keen')	**ācrius**	'more keenly', 'rather keenly' (adjective *ācrior, -ius* 'keener', 'rather keen')	**ācerrimē**	'most keenly', 'very keenly' (adjective *ācerrimus, -a, -um* 'keenest', 'very keen')

Practice

C Translate these adverbs:

1 turpius
2 stultissime
3 sapientius
4 gratissime
5 turpissime
6 stultius
7 sapientissime
8 gratius
9 durius
10 dulcissime
11 clarius
12 certissime
13 durissime
14 dulcius
15 clarissime
16 certius

D Translate into Latin:

1 more truly	9 more roughly
2 rather swiftly	10 rather beautifully
3 most bravely	11 most recently (= newly)
4 very seriously	12 very freely
5 most truly	13 most roughly
6 very swiftly	14 very beautifully
7 more bravely	15 more recently (= newly)
8 rather seriously	16 rather freely

43.5 Irregular Comparison

The same principle applies for most adverbs corresponding to irregular adjectives, but some additional irregularities can be found.

Positive		Comparative		Superlative	
bene	'well' (adjective *bonus, -a, -um* 'good')	**melius**	'better', 'rather well' (adjective *melior, melius* 'better', 'rather good')	**optimē**	'excellently', 'very well' (adjective *optimus, -a, -um* 'best', 'very good')
male	'badly' (adjective *malus, -a, -um* 'bad')	**peius**	'more badly', 'rather badly' (adjective *peior, peius* 'worse', 'rather bad')	**pessimē**	'worst', 'very badly' (adjective *pessimus, -a, -um* 'worst', 'very bad')
magnopere	'greatly' (adjective *magnus, -a, -um* 'big')	**magis**	'more greatly', 'rather greatly' (adjective *maior, maius* 'bigger', 'rather big')	**maximē**	'most greatly', 'very greatly' (adjective *maximus, -a, -um* 'biggest', 'very big')
paulum	'little' (adjective *parvus, -a, -um* 'small')	**minus**	'less', 'rather little' (adjective *minor, minus* 'smaller', 'rather small')	**minimē**	'least', 'very little' (adjective *minimus, -a, -um* 'smallest', 'very small')
multum	'much' (adjective *multī, -ae, -a* 'many')	**plūs**	'more' (adjective *plūres, plūra* 'more', 'rather many')	**plūrimum**	'most', 'very much' (adjective *plūrimī, -ae, -a* 'most', 'very many')
facile	'easily' (adjective *facilis, -e* 'easy')	**facilius**	'more easily', 'rather easily' (adjective *facilior, facilius* 'easier', 'rather easy')	**facillimē**	'most easily', 'very easily' (adjective *facillimus, -a, -um* 'easiest', 'very easy')
similiter	'similarly' (adjective *similis, -e* 'like')	**similius**	'more similarly', 'rather similarly' (adjective *similior, similius* 'more like', 'rather like')	**simillimē**	'most similarly', 'very similarly' (adjective *simillimus, -a, -um* 'most like', 'very like')

43.6 Use of Comparative Adverbs

Comparative adverbs can take most of the constructions used by comparative adjectives (see chapter 38.4).

tū celerius currēbās quam ego. 'You were running faster than I.'
celerrimē omnium cucurrī. 'I ran the fastest of all.'
quam celerrimē cucurrit. 'He ran as fast as possible.'

Practice

E Translate:

1 nemo melius pugnabat quam tu.
2 illi milites quam optime pugnabant.
3 ille pulchre locutus est, sed tu pulchrius.
4 tu pulcherrime omnium locutus es.
5 haec moenia melius reficienda sunt nobis.
6 frater meus hodie certissime domum veniet.
7 pueri ab illo magistro pessime docebantur.
8 nos peius docti sumus quam vos.
9 regem habemus qui quam sapientissime reget.
10 rex vester sapientius regebat.
11 illos hostes nostri facilius vicerunt.
12 hos libros facile legam.
13 verba eius facillime intelleximus.
14 haec epistula quam optime scribenda est.
15 rex noster diu et feliciter vivat!
16 ille felicissime vixit.
17 milites orabat ut acrius pugnarent.
18 militem adeo laudavit ut acerrime pugnaret.
19 pecuniam militibus dabo ut acriter pugnent.
20 nemo acrius pugnavit quam ille.

F Translate into Latin:

1 These citizens must be ruled as well as possible.
2 He spoke most truly.
3 This horse runs faster than that one.
4 We shall fight as bravely as possible.
5 Were you (plural) fighting more bravely than we (were)?
6 Urge (singular) these men to fight bravely.
7 The teacher spoke very briefly.
8 That horse is by far the best.
9 Those men praised the gods more than we (did).
10 The boys departed from home very sadly.
11 Those shameful girls spoke rather foolishly.
12 We shall speak more wisely than they.

43.7 Reading Practice

1 *Colloquium Stephani* 16a–17d (adapted): lessons at school (probably first to third century AD).

Consedi meo loco; librum accepi et scripsi cottidiana. interrogavi, et responso accepto legi lectionem meam, quam mihi magister diligenter exposuit, donec intellegerem et personas et sensum verborum auctoris. deinde ab oculo celeriter legi versus ignotos qui rare leguntur.

Vocabulary

cōnsedeō (like *sedeō*) 'sit down'
cottīdiānum, cottīdiānī (n.)
   'conversational phrase'
interrogō, -āre, -āvī, -ātum 'ask
   questions'
respōnsō acceptō 'when I had received
   the answer'
lēctiō, lēctiōnis (f.) 'reading assignment'
dīligenter 'carefully'
expōnō (like *pōnō*) 'explain'
dōnec (+ subjunctive) 'until'

et ... et 'both ... and'
persōna, persōnae (f.) 'speaker' (i.e. who
   speaks which lines of a dramatic
   text)
sēnsus, sēnsūs (m.) 'meaning'
auctor, auctōris (m.) 'author'
deinde 'then'
ab oculō 'at sight' (i.e. without
   preparation)
ignōtus, -a, -um 'unfamiliar'
rārus, rāra, rārum 'infrequent'

2 Livy, *Ab urbe condita* 1.23.88 (adapted): the leader of the Albans warns the king of Rome about the dangers posed by the Etruscans (written in the first century BC about a much earlier and partly mythical period).

Illud te, Tulle, monere velim. Etruscam rem periculosam esse nobis vobisque maxime, magis scitis quam nos quo propiores estis. multum illi terra, plurimum mari pollent.

Vocabulary

Tullus, -ī (m.) *name of a Roman king*
Etrūscus, -a, -um 'Etruscan'
rēs *can also mean* 'state'
perīculōsus, -a, -um (+ dative)
   'dangerous (to)'

quō 'in proportion as'
propior, propius 'nearer' (i.e. to the
   Etruscans)
marī 'on the sea' (i.e. with their navy)
polleō, pollēre, –, – 'be powerful'

3 Martial 7.85: the difficulty of poetry (first century AD).

Quod non insulse scribis tetrasticha quaedam,
   disticha quod belle pauca, Sabelle, facis,
laudo nec admiror. facile est epigrammata belle
   scribere, sed librum scribere difficile est.

Vocabulary

quod 'because'	Sabellus, Sabellī (m.) *name of a rival*
īnsulsus, -a, -um 'without wit'	*poet*
tetrastichum, -ī (n.) 'four-line poem'	nec 'but not'
quīdam, quaedam, quoddam 'some'	admīror, -ārī, -ātus sum 'be surprised'
distichum, -ī (n.) 'two-line poem'	epigramma, epigrammatis (n.)
bellus, bella, bellum 'pretty'	'epigram' (a kind of short poem)

4 Martial 14.49: the poet's contempt for those who exercise instead of doing useful work with their muscles (first century AD).

> Quid pereunt stulto fortes haltere lacerti?
> exercet melius vinea fossa viros.

Vocabulary

quid 'why'	exerceō, -cēre, -cuī, -citum 'provides
pereō (like *eō*) 'be wasted'	exercise for'
haltēr, haltēris (m.) 'weight-lifting'	vīnea, vīneae (f.) 'vineyard'
lacertus, lacertī (m.) 'arm'	fodiō, fodere, fōdī, fossum 'dig up' (i.e.
	cultivate)

5 Plautus, *Bacchides* 408–10 (adapted): a tolerant father reacts to a negative report on his teenage son's activities (second century BC).

> heia, Lyde, leniter qui saeviunt sapiunt magis. minus mirandum est si illa aetate haec facit quam si non facit. feci ego talia itidem in adulescentia.

Vocabulary

heia 'come on!'	mīrandum est 'it is surprising'
Lȳdus, -ī (m.) *name of the speaker's slave*	aetās, aetātis (f.) 'age'
lēnis, lēne 'mild'	itidem 'exactly the same way'
saeviō, saevīre, saeviī, saevītum 'get	adulēscentia, -ae (f.) 'youth', 'time of
angry'	being young'
sapiō, sapere, sapīvī, – 'be wise'	

43.8 Vocabulary to Learn

Adverbs

facile	'easily'
facilius	'more easily', 'rather easily'
facillimē	'most easily', 'very easily'
magis	'more greatly', 'rather greatly'
magnopere	'greatly'
maximē	'most greatly', 'very greatly'
melius	'better', 'rather well'
minimē	'least', 'very little'
minus	'less', 'rather little'
multum	'much'
optimē	'excellently', 'very well'
paulum	'little'
peius	'more badly', 'rather badly'
pessimē	'worst', 'very badly'
plūrimum	'most', 'very much'
plūs	'more'
similiter	'similarly'
similius	'more similarly', 'rather similarly'
simillimē	'most similarly', 'very similarly'

44.1 Pluperfect Indicative Tense

In addition to the two past indicative tenses we have so far seen, the perfect ('he did, he has done') and the imperfect ('he was doing, he used to do'), Latin has a pluperfect ('he had done'). In the active, the pluperfect is formed by attaching an ending formed like the imperfect of *sum* to the perfect stem of the verb (third principal part minus *-ī*). In the passive, it is formed by adding the imperfect of *sum* to the perfect participle (fourth principal part). See the table on the next page.

The translations of these forms follow the pattern of *amāveram* and *amātus eram*:

Active

amāveram 'I had loved'
amāverās 'you (singular) had loved'
amāverat 'he had loved', 'she had loved', 'it had loved', 'had loved'
amāverāmus 'we had loved'
amāverātis 'you (plural) had loved'
amāverant 'they had loved', 'had loved'

Passive

amātus, -a, -um eram 'I had been loved'
amātus, -a, -um erās 'you (singular) had been loved'
amātus, -a, -um erat 'he had been loved', 'she had been loved', 'it had been loved', 'had been loved'
amātī, -ae, -a erāmus 'we had been loved'
amātī, -ae, -a erātis 'you (plural) had been loved'
amātī, -ae, -a erant 'they had been loved', 'had been loved'

Deponent verbs, as usual, have passive forms with active meanings: *vēnātus eram* 'I had hunted', *veritus eram* 'I had feared', *ūsus eram* 'I had used', *partītus eram* 'I had divided', *mortuus eram* 'I had died'. All irregular verbs are regular in the pluperfect: *fueram* 'I had been' from *sum*, *potueram* 'I had been able to' from *possum*, *īveram* and *ieram* 'I had gone' from *eō*, *volueram* 'I had wanted' from *volō*, etc.

Active

First conjugation	Second conjugation	Third conjugation	Fourth conjugation	Mixed conjugation
amāveram	monueram	rēxeram	audīveram	cēperam
amāverās	monuerās	rēxerās	audīverās	cēperās
amāverat	monuerat	rēxerat	audīverat	cēperat
amāverāmus	monuerāmus	rēxerāmus	audīverāmus	cēperāmus
amāverātis	monuerātis	rēxerātis	audīverātis	cēperātis
amāverant	monuerant	rēxerant	audīverant	cēperant

Passive

First conjugation	Second conjugation	Third conjugation	Fourth conjugation	Mixed conjugation
amātus, -a, -um eram	monitus, -a, -um eram	rēctus, -a, -um eram	audītus, -a, -um eram	captus, -a, -um eram
amātus, -a, -um erās	monitus, -a, -um erās	rēctus, -a, -um erās	audītus, -a, -um erās	captus, -a, -um erās
amātus, -a, -um erat	monitus, -a, -um erat	rēctus, -a, -um erat	audītus, -a, -um erat	captus, -a, -um erat
amātī, -ae, -a erāmus	monitī, -ae, -a erāmus	rēctī, -ae, -a erāmus	audītī, -ae, -a erāmus	captī, -ae, -a erāmus
amātī, -ae, -a erātis	monitī, -ae, -a erātis	rēctī, -ae, -a erātis	audītī, -ae, -a erātis	captī, -ae, -a erātis
amātī, -ae, -a erant	monitī, -ae, -a erant	rēctī, -ae, -a erant	audītī, -ae, -a erant	captī, -ae, -a erant

44.2 Future Perfect Tense

The future perfect tense ('he will have done') is formed very similarly to the pluperfect, but substituting the future of *sum* for the imperfect – except that in the active the third person plural ends in *-erint* rather than *-erunt*. See the table on the next page.

The translations of these forms follow the pattern of *amāverō* and *amātus erō*:

Active

amāverō 'I will have loved', 'I shall have loved'

amāveris 'you (singular) will have loved', 'you (singular) shall have loved'

amāverit 'he will have loved', 'she will have loved', 'it will have loved', 'will have loved', 'he shall have loved', 'she shall have loved', 'it shall have loved', 'shall have loved'

amāverimus 'we will have loved', 'we shall have loved'

amāveritis 'you (plural) will have loved', 'you (plural) shall have loved'

amāverint 'they will have loved', 'they shall have loved', 'will have loved', 'shall have loved'

Passive

amātus, -a, -um erō 'I will have been loved', 'I shall have been loved'

amātus, -a, -um eris 'you (singular) will have been loved, 'you (singular) shall have been loved'

amātus, -a, -um erit 'he will have been loved', 'she will have been loved', 'it will have been loved', 'will have been loved', 'he shall have been loved', 'she shall have been loved', 'it shall have been loved', 'shall have been loved'

amātī, -ae, -a erimus 'we will have been loved', 'we shall have been loved'

amātī, -ae, -a eritis 'you (plural) will have been loved', 'you (plural) shall have been loved'

amātī, -ae, -a erunt 'they will have been loved', 'they shall have been loved', 'will have been loved', 'shall have been loved'

Deponent and irregular verbs all form future perfects regularly, following the same pattern.

Active

First conjugation	Second conjugation	Third conjugation	Fouth conjugation	Mixed conjugation
amāverō	monuerō	rēxerō	audīverō	cēperō
amāveris	monueris	rēxeris	audīveris	cēperis
amāverit	monuerit	rēxerit	audiverit	cēperit
amāverimus	monuerimus	rēxerimus	audīverimus	cēperimus
amāveritis	monueritis	rēxeritis	audīveritis	cēperitis
amāverint	monuerint	rēxerint	audiverint	cēperint

Passive

First conjugation	Second conjugation	Third conjugation	Fourth conjugation	Mixed conjugation
amātus, -a, -um erō	monitus, -a, -um erō	rēctus, -a, -um erō	audītus, -a, -um erō	captus, -a, -um erō
amātus, -a, -um eris	monitus, -a, -um eris	rēctus, -a, -um eris	audītus, -a, -um eris	captus, -a, -um eris
amātus, -a, -um erit	monitus, -a, -um erit	rēctus, -a, -um erit	audītus, -a, -um erit	captus, -a, -um erit
amātī, -ae, -a erimus	monitī, -ae, -a erimus	rēctī, -ae, -a erimus	audītī, -ae, -a erimus	captī, -ae, -a erimus
amātī, -ae, -a eritis	monitī, -ae, -a eritis	rēctī, -ae, -a eritis	audītī, -ae, -a eritis	captī, -ae, -a eritis
amātī, -ae, -a erunt	monitī, -ae, -a erunt	rēctī, -ae, -a erunt	audītī, -ae, -a erunt	captī, -ae, -a erunt

Practice

A Conjugate:

1 *laudō*, pluperfect active indicative
2 *emō*, pluperfect passive indicative
3 *doceō*, future perfect active indicative
4 *faciō*, future perfect passive indicative

5 *veniō*, pluperfect active indicative
6 *loquor*, pluperfect indicative
7 *arbitror*, future perfect indicative
8 *adsum*, future perfect indicative
9 *exeō*, pluperfect indicative
10 *nōlō*, pluperfect indicative

B Translate:

1 duxeramus
2 emptum erat
3 dixerant
4 visus eram
5 miserit
6 ortus ero

7 viceritis
8 scripti erunt
9 egerant
10 mortua erat
11 dederamus
12 interfecti erant

13 invenero
14 petitus erit
15 legeris
16 pollicita erat

C Translate into Latin:

1 I shall have followed
2 we shall have fled
3 it will have been sold
4 he will have repaired
5 they had advanced
6 you (singular) had not wanted
7 she had been called
8 I had fled

9 he will have spoken
10 we shall have sat
11 they (neuter) will have been found
12 had you (plural) delayed?
13 they had attacked
14 he had been left
15 they had lived

44.3 Sequence of Tenses

The pluperfect is a historic tense like the perfect and imperfect, but the future perfect is a primary tense, since it refers to actions that will take place in the future. Thus a subjunctive subordinated to a main verb in the pluperfect indicative will be an imperfect subjunctive, but a subjunctive subordinated to a main verb in the future perfect indicative will be a present subjunctive (cf. chapters 16.1 and 28.1).

> *ōrāverat nōs ut pugnārēmus* 'he had begged us to fight'
> *ōrāverit nōs ut pugnēmus* 'he will have begged us to fight'

Practice

D Translate:

1 multos annos Romae feliciter manserant.
2 maxime timuerint ne nos se interficiamus.
3 illum secuti erant quia verba eius audienda erant.
4 illud turpissime fecerant.
5 militibus imperaverit ut quam optime pugnent.
6 discesserat stultissime ut hostes oppugnaret.
7 gladius meus dandus erat ei quia ab eo mihi datus erat.
8 multos annos Romae feliciter manserit.
9 hostes certissime vincendi erant quia nos oppugnaverant.
10 sex diebus id fecerint.
11 militibus imperaverat ut quam optime pugnarent.
12 discesserit stultissime ut hostes oppugnet.
13 verba eius sapientissima ab omnibus audita erant.

14 magistrum rogaverimus ut melius doceat.
15 petiveramus te quia equus celerior nobis emendus erat.
16 tot pueri venerint ut minores videre non possint.
17 maxime timuerant ne nos se interficeremus.
18 magistrum rogaveramus ut melius doceret.
19 tot pueri venerant ut minores videre non possent.
20 servis imperaveram ut deos laudarent.
21 dei immortales ab omnibus laudati erant.
22 quattuor horis pecunia amissa inventa erit.
23 amici celeriter iuvandi erant nobis quia nos celerrime iuverant.
24 sex horis hostes victi erunt.

E Translate into Latin:

1 We had wanted to go to Athens for many years.
2 No-one will have fought more bravely than I.
3 The city had to be defended because it had been attacked.
4 Within four days our father will have been buried.
5 Had you ordered the slaves to repair the house?
6 My brother had sold (his) sheep in order to buy a better horse.
7 Who had said that we were very brave?
8 Will they have come in five days?
9 The king had spoken so fast that we understood nothing.
10 The lost money had easily been found by our slaves.

44.4 Reading Practice

1 *Colloquium Leidense-Stephani* 7a–e (adapted): a schoolboy's lunch hour (probably second or third century AD).

Nunc didici versus quos acceperam. magistrum rogavi ut me dimitteret domum ad prandium, et me dimisit. 'bene vale' ei dixi et resalutatus discessi. postquam pranderam, reversus reddidi quod didiceram.

Vocabulary

dīmittō (like *mittō*) 'dismiss'	prandeō, prandēre, prandī, prānsum
prandium, prandiī (n.) 'lunch'	'eat lunch'
resalūtō, -āre, -āvī, -ātum 'greet in	revertor, revertī, reversus sum 'return'
return'	reddō, reddere, reddidī, redditum
postquam 'after'	'recite'

2 Cicero, *Epistulae ad familiares* 13.51: a request for help for a friend (first century BC).

Cicero Publio Caesio salutem dicit. P. Messienum, equitem Romanum, omnibus rebus ornatum meumque perfamiliarem, tibi commendo ea commendatione, quae potest esse diligentissima. peto a te et pro nostra et pro paterna amicitia, ut eum in tuam fidem recipias eiusque rem famamque tuearis. virum bonum tuaque amicitia dignum tibi adiunxeris mihique gratissimum feceris.

Vocabulary

Cicerō, Cicerōnis (m.) *name of the writer*	et . . . et 'both . . . and'
Pūblius Caesius, -ī (m.) *name of the addressee*	prō (+ ablative) 'by'
	paternus, -a, -um 'of our fathers'
Pūblius Messiēnus, -ī (m.) *name of the writer's friend*	**amīcitia, amīcitiae (f.) 'friendship'**
	fidēs *can also mean* 'confidence'
eques, equitis (m.) 'knight'	recipiō, recipere, recēpī, receptum
ōrnō, ōrnāre, ōrnāvī, ōrnātum 'honour'	'receive'
perfamiliāris, -e 'very close friend'	rēs *can also mean* 'welfare'
commendō, -āre, -āvī, -ātum	tueor, tuērī, tuitus sum (+ accusative)
'recommend'	'take care of'
commendātiō, commendātiōnis (f.)	dignus, digna, dignum (+ ablative)
'recommendation'	'worthy of'
dīligēns, *gen.* dīligentis 'particular'	adiungō, adiungere, adiūnxī,
	adiūnctum 'attach'

3 Martial 12.73: the poet accuses Catullus (not the famous poet of that name, but a later figure) of lying about what he has put in his will (first century AD). Because a Roman's will was read only after the death of its writer, the ending suggests that Martial is impatient for Catullus' death.

Heredem tibi me, Catulle, dicis.
non credo nisi legero, Catulle.

Vocabulary

hērēs, hērēdis (m.) 'heir'   crēdō, crēdere, crēdidī, crēditum 'believe'
(*understand* esse *in the first line*)   nisi 'unless'

45.1 Impersonal Verbs

Some verbs are impersonal; that is, they have no meaningful subject. In English, where the structure of the language requires that verbs have expressed subjects, impersonal verbs have a grammatical subject 'it', as in 'it is raining' or 'it is important to do the right thing'. In Latin impersonal verbs have no expressed subject, but they appear in the third person singular, and in forms where the gender of the subject is specified they are neuter: thus in many ways the Latin impersonal subject is not unlike the English 'it'. Some verbs are only used impersonally and therefore do not occur in forms other than the third person singular, as is signalled by their principal parts. For example:

pluit, pluere, pluit, – 'it is raining'
decet, decēre, decuit, – 'it is fitting' (+ accusative and infinitive)
licet, licēre, licuit, – 'it is allowed' (+ dative and infinitive)
oportet, oportēre, oportuit, – 'it is right' (+ accusative and infinitive)
paenitet, paenitēre, paenituit, – 'it repents' (+ accusative of person and genitive of cause)
pudet, pudēre, puduit, – 'it shames' (+ accusative of person and genitive of cause)

These verbs are sometimes tricky to translate into English, as English does not always have equivalent impersonal constructions. Often it is best not to use the literal, impersonal translation but to turn the sentence around and make the Latin object the subject.

licet tibi venīre 'you may come', 'you are allowed to come' (literally 'it is allowed to you to come')
oportet tē venīre 'you ought to come' (literally 'it is right for you to come')
paenitet mē factī 'I repent of (my) deed', 'I am sorry for my deed' (literally 'it repents me of the deed')
pudet mē factī 'I am ashamed of (my) deed' (literally 'it shames me of the deed')

Practice

A Translate:

1 heri pluebat et hodie pluit.
2 decet nos adesse.
3 licetne nobis discedere?
4 paenitueratne eum facti?
5 puduit me filiorum.
6 nos oportet ire.

7 licebit tibi nobiscum venire.
8 paenitet me illius consilii.
9 pudebitne te nostrum?
10 licuit mihi abesse.
11 vos oportet Romae manere.
12 decuit eam iuvari.

B Translate into Latin:

1 It is fitting for girls and boys to be loved.
2 May I come with you?
3 We ought to leave Rome.
4 I am ashamed of my brother.
5 I'm sorry!
6 They were ashamed of (their) mother.
7 Did it rain in Rome yesterday?

8 It was fitting for us to depart.
9 You may not see the god.
10 We have repented of our deeds.
11 It is right for all people to praise the gods.
12 Is it raining in Athens today?
13 He ought to come to Rome.
14 The boys will not be allowed to leave.

45.2 **Impersonal Gerundives**

Ordinary verbs can also be used impersonally on occasion. This impersonal construction is particularly important with gerundives, as it allows intransitive verbs (ones that do not take an object in the accusative) to be used in the gerundive. When a gerundive is used intransitively, it has nothing to agree with, so it becomes neuter singular by default; the agent remains in the dative. The best way to translate these constructions is to turn them around so that the dative is the subject and the verb is preceded by 'must' or 'have to' (see chapter 41); it is, however, also possible to translate them impersonally with English 'it is necessary'.

eundum est mihi 'I must go', 'I have to go', 'it is necessary for me to go' (literally 'it is having-to-be-gone by me')
iuvandum erat nōbīs 'we had to help', 'it was necessary for us to help' (literally 'it was having-to-be-helped by us')

Compare the personal construction *illī iuvandī erant nōbīs* 'we had to help those men' (literally 'those men had to be helped by us').

If there is no agent expressed, impersonal gerundives can be translated with 'it is necessary' or with the generic English 'one'.

bene vīvendum est 'it is necessary to live well', 'one must live well' (literally 'it is having-to-be-lived well')

nunc timendum est 'now it is necessary to fear', 'now one must fear' (literally 'now it is having-to-be-feared')

Verbs that take an object in a case other than the accusative use the impersonal construction for the gerundive as well; the object remains in its usual case.

aquā nōbīs ūtendum erit 'we shall have to use water', 'it will be necessary for us to use water' (literally 'it will be having-to-be-used water by us')

persuādendum est rēgī 'the king must be persuaded', 'the king has to be persuaded', 'it will be necessary to persuade the king' (literally 'it will be having-to-be-persuaded the king'); in the right context this sentence could also mean 'the king must persuade'.[1]

Practice

C Translate:

1 illi celeriter veniendum est domum.
2 vobiscum veniendum erat.
3 omnibus hominibus moriendum erit.
4 moriendum est.
5 celerrime progrediendum est nobis.
6 e castris progrediendum erat.
7 regibus quam optime vivendum est.
8 bene vivendum erit.
9 gladio mihi utendum erat.
10 manibus tibi utendum est.
11 verissime loquendum est mihi.
12 sapientius loquendum erat.
13 multos annos Athenis manendum est ei.
14 Londinii paucos dies manendum erit.
15 nobis celerius eundum erit Romam.
16 Carthaginem eundum est.
17 hic nobiscum sedendum est vobis.
18 cum agricolis sedendum erat.
19 ovibus in agro paucas horas standum est.
20 diu standum erat.
21 sapientissime regendum erit tibi.
22 quam sapientissime regendum est.
23 patri nostro hodie persuadendum est.
24 matri tuae persuadendum erit.
25 celerrime pollicendum erit tibi.
26 nunc pollicendum est.

---

[1] If a verb taking an object in the dative appears as an impersonal gerundive with both an object and an agent, ambiguity can be avoided by putting the agent into the ablative with *ā/ab* (the regular agent construction for non-gerundive verbs). Thus 'I must persuade the king' would be *rēgī ā mē persuādendum est*, not **rēgī mihi persuādendum est*. But this solution is only used when both object and agent are present; if only one is present, the ambiguity of the dative is tolerated.

D Translate into Latin:

1 I shall have to go home in five days.
2 It was necessary to go home.
3 You will have to fight more bravely.
4 One must fight bravely.
5 We had to depart from London rather fast.
6 It is necessary to depart from Rome.
7 One must love tenderly.
8 All men must suffer.
9 We shall have to run more swiftly.
10 It is necessary to run as fast as possible.
11 Do I have to promise?
12 A brave man must hunt.

45.3 Reading Practice

1 *Colloquium Stephani* 9a–10a (adapted): a boy's arrival at school (probably first to third century AD).

Ergo cum venissem ad scalas, ascendi per gradus, otio, sicut oportebat. et in proscholio deposui birrum, et demulsi capillos. tum elevato centone ingressus sum, et primum salutavi magistros et condiscipulos.

Vocabulary

cum vēnissem 'when I had come'
scālae, scālārum (f. plural) 'stairs'
per gradūs 'one step at a time' (i.e. not running)
ōtium, ōtiī (n.) 'leisure'
sīcut 'as'
proscholium, -ī (n.) 'school vestibule'
dēpōnō (like *pōnō*) 'take off'

birrus, birrī (m.) 'cloak'
dēmulceō, dēmulcēre, dēmulsī, dēmulsum 'smooth down'
capillus, capillī (m.) 'hair'
ēlevātō centōne 'lifting the curtain (that served as a door)'
prīmum (here an adverb) 'first'
condiscipulus, -ī (m.) 'fellow student'

2 Martial 14.12: praise of ivory cashboxes (first century AD).

Hos nisi de flava loculos implere moneta
    non decet: argentum vilia ligna ferant.

Vocabulary

nisi 'except'
flāvus, flāva, flāvum 'golden'
loculus, loculī, (m.) 'cashbox'
impleō, implēre, implēvī, implētum 'fill'
monēta, monētae (f.) 'money'

vīlis, vīle 'cheap'
lignum, lignī (n.) 'wooden box' (unusually)
ferō (third conjugation) 'hold'

3 Martial 9.53: the poet suggests to his friend Quintus an agreement over birthday presents (first century AD).

Natali tibi, Quinte, tuo dare parva volebam
    munera; tu prohibes: imperiosus homo es.
parendum est monitis; fiat quod uterque volemus
    et quod utrumque iuvat: tu mihi, Quinte, dato.

Vocabulary

nātālis, nātālis, nātālium (m.) 'birthday'
mūnus, mūneris (n.) 'gift'
prohibeō, -bēre, -buī, -bitum 'forbid'
imperiōsus, -a, -um 'imperious'
pāreō, pārēre, pāruī, – (+ dative) 'obey'
moneō *can also mean* 'order'

fiat 'may it happen', 'let us do'
uterque, utraque, utrumque 'both' (singular in form but plural in meaning, so the nominative singular can be the subject of a plural verb)
datō 'give a gift' (imperative)

45.4 Vocabulary to Learn

Verbs

decet, decēre, decuit, – (+ accusative and infinitive)	'it is fitting'
ignōscō, ignōscere, ignōvī, ignōtum (+ dative)	'forgive'
licet, licēre, licuit, – (+ dative and infinitive)	'it is allowed', 'may' (in the sense of 'is allowed to')
nesciō, nescīre, nescīvī/nesciī, nescītum	'not know', 'be ignorant (of)'
oportet, oportēre, oportuit, – (+ accusative and infinitive)	'it is right', 'ought to'
paenitet, paenitēre, paenituit, – (+ accusative of person and genitive of cause)	'it repents', 'sorry'
pluit, pluere, pluit, –	'it is raining'
pudet, pudēre, puduit, – (+ accusative of person and genitive of cause)	'it shames', 'be ashamed'
sciō, scīre, scīvī/sciī, scītum	'know'

Vocabulary continues.

Nouns

lingua, linguae (f.)	'tongue', 'language'
nox, noctis, noctium (f.)	'night'
patria, patriae (f.)	'homeland', 'fatherland'
rēgīna, rēgīnae (f.)	'queen'

Adjectives

dignus, digna, dignum (+ ablative)	'worthy (of)'
idōneus, idōnea, idōneum	'suitable'
secundus, secunda, secundum	'second'
tertius, tertia, tertium	'third'

Adverbs and Conjunctions

atque	'and'
deinde	'then'
et	'also', 'even'
et ... et	'both ... and'
nec	'neither', 'nor', 'and ... not'
neque	'neither', 'nor', 'and ... not'
sīc	'thus', 'in this way'
statim	'at once'

46 | Perfect and Pluperfect Subjunctives

46.1 Formation of Perfect and Pluperfect Subjunctives

In addition to the present and imperfect tenses, the subjunctive also has perfect and pluperfect tenses. Like all subjunctive forms, these have no fixed translations but rather a variety of meanings depending on the constructions in which they are found. In formation the perfect subjunctive is very similar to the future perfect indicative, particularly in the active. See the tables on the following pages.

Deponents and irregular verbs are entirely regular in both these subjunctive forms. The deponents form perfect subjunctives *vēnātus sim*, *veritus sim*, etc. and pluperfect subjunctives *vēnātus essem*, *veritus essem*, etc. The irregulars form perfect subjunctives *fuerim* from *sum*, *potuerim* from *possum*, etc. and pluperfect subjunctives *fuissem* from *sum*, *potuissem* from *possum*, etc.

Practice

A Conjugate in the forms indicated:

1 *vocō*, pluperfect subjunctive active
2 *sequor*, pluperfect subjunctive
3 *volō*, perfect subjunctive active
4 *petō*, perfect subjunctive passive
5 *stō*, pluperfect subjunctive active
6 *loquor*, pluperfect subjunctive
7 *pugnō*, perfect subjunctive active
8 *faciō*, perfect subjunctive passive
9 *impediō*, pluperfect subjunctive active
10 *inveniō*, pluperfect subjunctive passive
11 *timeō*, perfect subjunctive active
12 *arbitror*, perfect subjunctive
13 *videō*, pluperfect subjunctive active
14 *sepeliō*, pluperfect subjunctive passive

Active

First conjugation	Second conjugation	Third conjugation	Fourth conjugation	Mixed conjugation
amāverim	monuerim	rēxerim	audīverim	cēperim
amāverīs	monuerīs	rēxerīs	audīverīs	cēperīs
amāverit	monuerit	rēxerit	audīverit	cēperit
amāverīmus	monuerīmus	rēxerīmus	audīverīmus	cēperīmus
amāverītis	monuerītis	rēxerītis	audīverītis	cēperītis
amāverint	monuerint	rēxerint	audīverint	cēperint

Passive

First conjugation	Second conjugation	Third conjugation	Fourth conjugation	Mixed conjugation
amātus, -a, -um sim	monitus, -a, -um sim	rēctus, -a, -um sim	audītus, -a, -um sim	captus, -a, -um sim
amātus, -a, -um sīs	monitus, -a, -um sīs	rēctus, -a, -um sīs	audītus, -a, -um sīs	captus, -a, -um sīs
amātus, -a, -um sit	monitus, -a, -um sit	rēctus, -a, -um sit	audītus, -a, -um sit	captus, -a, -um sit
amātī, -ae, -a sīmus	monitī, -ae, -a sīmus	rēctī, -ae, -a sīmus	audītī, -ae, -a sīmus	captī, -ae, -a sīmus
amātī, -ae, -a sītis	monitī, -ae, -a sītis	rēctī, -ae, -a sītis	audītī, -ae, -a sītis	captī, -ae, -a sītis
amātī, -ae, -a sint	monitī, -ae, -a sint	rēctī, -ae, -a sint	audītī, -ae, -a sint	captī, -ae, -a sint

The pluperfect subjunctive is formed from the perfect infinitive, to which are added the standard endings.

Active

First conjugation	Second conjugation	Third conjugation	Fourth conjugation	Mixed conjugation
amāvissem	monuissem	rēxissem	audīvissem	cēpissem
amāvissēs	monuissēs	rēxissēs	audīvissēs	cēpissēs
amāvisset	monuisset	rēxisset	audīvisset	cēpisset
amāvissēmus	monuissēmus	rēxissēmus	audīvissēmus	cēpissēmus
amāvissētis	monuissētis	rēxissētis	audīvissētis	cēpissētis
amāvissent	monuissent	rēxissent	audīvissent	cēpissent

Passive

First conjugation	Second conjugation	Third conjugation	Fourth conjugation	Mixed conjugation
amātus, -a, -um essem	monitus, -a, -um essem	rēctus, -a, -um essem	audītus, -a, -um essem	captus, -a, -um essem
amātus, -a, -um essēs	monitus, -a, -um essēs	rēctus, -a, -um essēs	audītus, -a, -um essēs	captus, -a, -um essēs
amātus, -a, -um esset	monitus, -a, -um esset	rēctus, -a, -um esset	audītus, -a, -um esset	captus, -a, -um esset
amātī, -ae, -a essēmus	monitī, -ae, -a essēmus	rēctī, -ae, -a essēmus	audītī, -ae, -a essēmus	captī, -ae, -a essēmus
amātī, -ae, -a essētis	monitī, -ae, -a essētis	rēctī, -ae, -a essētis	audītī, -ae, -a essētis	captī, -ae, -a essētis
amātī, -ae, -a essent	monitī, -ae, -a essent	rēctī, -ae, -a essent	audītī, -ae, -a essent	captī, -ae, -a essent

46.2 Sequence of Tenses

Sequence of tenses, the Latin principle whereby the choice of which subjunctive to use in a subordinate clause is determined by the tense of the main verb (see chapter 16.1), also applies to perfect and pluperfect subjunctives. The perfect subjunctive appears after primary tenses, like the present subjunctive, and the pluperfect subjunctive appears after historic tenses, like the imperfect subjunctive. The details are:

Main verb		Subordinate verb
Primary tense (present indicative, future indicative, future perfect indicative, subjunctive, imperative)	→	Present subjunctive or perfect subjunctive
Historic tense (perfect indicative,[1] imperfect indicative, pluperfect indicative)	→	Imperfect subjunctive or pluperfect subjunctive

But there is also a difference of meaning between the present and perfect subjunctives and between the imperfect and pluperfect subjunctives: the present and imperfect refer to things that happen at the same time as or after the main clause, while the perfect and pluperfect refer to things that happen before the main clause.[2] In a sentence such as 'When they were together they were blissfully happy', the action of the subordinate clause ('they were together') takes place at the same time as the action of the main clause ('they were blissfully happy'). In a sentence such as 'When he had eaten he went to bed', the action of the subordinate clause ('he had eaten') takes place before the action of the main clause ('he went to bed'). And in a sentence such as 'She brought food so that everyone could eat', the action of the subordinate clause ('everyone could eat') takes place after the action of the main clause ('she brought food'). The distinction among these four subjunctives therefore involves *both* the tense of the main verb *and* the time of the subordinate clause relative to that main verb, and a diagram explaining their use needs to have four parts:

Relative time of **subordinate** clause

		Before the action of the main clause	After or at the same time as the action of the main clause
Tense of **main** verb	Primary	**Subordinate verb is** *perfect* **subjunctive**	**Subordinate verb is** *present* **subjunctive**
	Historic	**Subordinate verb is** *pluperfect* **subjunctive**	**Subordinate verb is** *imperfect* **subjunctive**

---

[1] But see note 1 in chapter 16.   [2] In chapter 54.2 we shall see that this rule is a slight oversimplification.

The subordinate subjunctive constructions we have seen so far (purpose clauses, indirect commands, fear clauses, and result clauses) are all ones in which the action of the subordinate clause naturally tends to be after the action of the main clause: purpose, commands, and result all involve the future by their very nature. Hence these constructions normally use only two of the four subjunctives.

46.3 Causal *Cum* Clauses

One construction that uses all four subjunctives is the causal *cum* clause. In this construction *cum* is a conjunction meaning 'since' or 'because' (as well as some other meanings, which will be discussed in the next chapter); this is a completely different word from the preposition *cum* 'with'.

cum fortis sit, bene pugnat. 'Since he is brave, he fights well.' (subordinate clause at same time as main clause, primary sequence, therefore present subjunctive)

cum fortis esset, bene pugnāvit. 'Since he was brave, he fought well.' (subordinate clause at same time as main clause, historic sequence, therefore imperfect subjunctive)

cum mē vocāverint, veniam. 'Since they have called me, I shall come.' (subordinate clause before main clause, primary sequence, therefore perfect subjunctive)

cum mē vocāvissent, vēnī. 'Since they (had) called me, I came.' (subordinate clause before main clause, historic sequence, therefore pluperfect subjunctive)

As can be seen from the above examples, the subjunctives in *cum* clauses are translated with indicatives in English. And there is a shortcut available when translating this type of *cum* clause into English: a correct translation can usually be obtained simply by converting the Latin subjunctive to the corresponding English indicative tense (present = present, perfect = perfect, imperfect = imperfect, pluperfect = pluperfect). But this shortcut does not work for many other types of clause, some of which will be encountered very soon, so it is important to understand the sequence rules. The shortcut is best used in this chapter to check that one has obtained the right answer by applying the sequence rules, and then discarded in later chapters.

When a *cum* clause is negative, the negative used is *nōn* (and therefore *nēmō*, *nihil*, *nūllus*) rather than *nē*. A *cum* clause can occur either before or after the main clause.

Practice

B Translate:

1 cum nox venerit, statim domum eamus.
2 statim domum ivimus cum nox venisset.
3 cum nox veniat, statim domum ibimus.
4 statim domum ivimus cum nox veniret.
5 cum aurum invenissem, equum meliorem emi.
6 equum meliorem emam cum aurum invenerim.
7 cum manendum sit nobis, non discedemus.
8 non discessimus cum manendum esset nobis.
9 cum mortuus esset, pater vester sepeliendus erat.
10 pater vester sepeliendus est cum mortuus sit.
11 cum patriam ament, hi milites optime pugnant.
12 ille bene pugnabat cum patriam amaret.
13 cum rex optime hortatus esset, milites acerrime pugnabant.
14 milites acerrime pugnant cum rex optime hortatus sit.
15 cum rex optime hortetur milites acerrime pugnabunt.
16 milites acerrime pugnabant cum rex optime hortaretur.
17 cum Roma discessissimus, regem milites hortantem non vidimus.
18 regem milites hortantem non videbimus cum Roma discesserimus.
19 cum linguam Graecam nesciam, Athenas ire nolo.
20 Athenas ire nolui cum linguam Graecam nescirem.
21 cum illos versus scripserit, poeta laudabitur.
22 poeta laudatus est cum illos versus scripsisset.

C Translate into Latin:

1 Since he had asked me, I helped him. (do not use *sē*)
2 Since he has asked me, I shall help him.
3 Since they were good, we praised them.
4 Since they are good, we are praising them.
5 Since he has repented, we shall forgive him.
6 Since he had repented, we forgave him.
7 I cannot give you silver since I do not have any (silver).
8 Since I did not have silver, I could not give (it) to you.
9 We did it since we had promised.
10 Since we have promised, we shall do it.
11 Since he was allowed to read the letter, he read (it).
12 I am reading the letter, since I am allowed to.

46.4 Reading Practice

1 Cicero, *Epistulae ad familiares* 13.77.3 (adapted): Cicero asks for help in capturing a runaway slave (part of a letter written in 46 BC).

Dionysius, servus meus, qui meam bibliothecam pretiosam tractavit, cum multos libros surripuisset nec se impune laturum esse putaret, aufugit. is est in provincia tua. eum et Marcus Bolanus, familiaris meus, et multi alii Naronae viderunt. ... hunc tu si mihi restituendum curaris, non possum dicere, quam mihi gratum futurum sit.

Vocabulary

Dionȳsius, Dionȳsiī (m.) *name of*
  a slave
bibliothēca, bibliothēcae (f.) 'library'
pretiōsus, -a, -um 'valuable'
tractō, tractāre, tractāvī, tractātum
  'manage'
surripiō, surripere, surripuī, surreptum
  'steal'
impūne 'with impunity'
ferō, ferre, tulī, lātum 'carry off (the
  thefts)'
putō, putāre, putāvī, putātum 'think'

aufugiō (like *fugiō*) 'run away'
prōvincia, prōvinciae (f.) 'province'
Mārcus Bōlānus, -ī (m.) *name of the*
  writer's friend
familiāris, familiāris, familiārium (m.)
  'acquaintance'
Narōna, Narōnae (f.) *name of a town*
restituendum cūrāris 'take care of
  restoring'
quam 'how'
futūrum sit 'it will be'

2 *Tabulae Vindolandenses* 11.248 (adapted): soldiers stationed in northern Britain wish each other good luck (*c.* AD 100).

Niger et Brocchus Ceriali suo salutem dicit. optamus, frater: id quod ages, felicissi-mum sit. erit autem, cum et votis nostris conveniat hoc pro te precari et tu sis dignissimus. optamus, domine frater, te bene valere.

Vocabulary

Niger, Nigrī (m.) *name of one of the*
  writers
Brocchus, Brocchī (m.) *name of one of*
  the writers
Ceriālis, Ceriālis (m.) *name of the*
  addressee, not actually a brother of
  the writers

optō, optāre, optāvī, optātum 'hope'
  (can take indirect statement)
fēlīx *can also mean* 'successful'
vōtum, vōtī (n.) 'wish'
conveniō (like *veniō*) 'agree'
prō (+ ablative) 'on behalf of'
precor, precārī, precātus sum 'pray for'

3 Martial 3.56: a water shortage at Ravenna (first century AD). Note the dative of possession: *sit mihi* + nominative = *habeam* + accusative. The subjunctive *sit* is dependent on *mālō*: 'I prefer that . . . '

Sit cisterna mihi quam vinea malo Ravennae,
   cum possim multo vendere pluris aquam.

Vocabulary

cisterna, cisternae (f.) 'water
   tank'
vīnea, vīneae (f.) 'vineyard'

Ravenna, Ravennae (f.) *name of a town
   in northern Italy*
multō plūris 'for much more (than wine)'

47 | More Subordinate Clauses

47.1 Concessive *Cum* Clauses

In addition to meaning 'since' or 'because', *cum* can mean 'although'. As there is considerable potential for confusion when a word can mean both 'since' and 'although', Roman authors usually took care to make it clear from the context when *cum* meant 'although'; often they did this by adding *tamen* 'nevertheless' to the main clause. In this meaning, just as when it means 'since', *cum* takes a subjunctive, with the choice among subjunctives determined by sequence of tenses and the English translations of those subjunctives being indicatives (see chapter 46.3).

cum crās paeniteat, tamen hodiē hoc faciam. 'Although I shall be sorry tomorrow,
  nevertheless I shall do this today'.
hoc hodiē faciam cum crās paeniteat. 'I shall do this today although I'll be sorry
  tomorrow.'

Notice that in these examples the translation shortcut mentioned in the last chapter does not work, because the Latin present subjunctive has to be translated with an English future indicative. One can work out that a future indicative is needed by thinking about what sequence of tenses tells us about the actual relationship of the two clauses: the present subjunctive means that the action of the subordinate clause happens after or at the same time as the action of the main clause. The main clause is in the future, and a subordinate clause describing action that happens after or at the same time as an action in the future is also future.

47.2 Temporal *Cum* Clauses

Cum can also mean 'when', and in this meaning it takes a slightly different construction. In historic sequence (i.e. with a main verb in a past tense), clauses in which *cum* means 'when' usually function like the other *cum* clauses and take a verb in the subjunctive (translated with the indicative in English), but in primary sequence (i.e. with a main verb in a primary tense) they take a verb in the indicative.[1]

cum in urbe essem, multa ēmī. 'When I was in the city I bought many things.'
cum in urbe sum, multa emō. 'When I am in the city I buy many things.'

---

[1] This is something of an oversimplification, and moreover there are several other types of *cum* clause in addition to the three presented here – but the rules given here will work for all the material in this book.

When the main verb is in the future, English normally uses a present tense for a 'when' clause. But Latin makes a distinction between actions that happen at the same time as the main clause and ones that happen before the main clause: the former take the future indicative and the latter the future perfect indicative.

cum in urbe erō, multa emam. 'When I am in the city I shall buy many things.' (literally 'When I shall be in the city I shall buy many things.' The being in the city and the buying happen at the same time, and that time is future, so Latin uses the future for both.)
cum ad urbem īverō, multa emam. 'When I go to the city I shall buy many things.' (literally 'When I shall have gone to the city I shall buy many things.' The going to the city happens before the buying, so Latin uses the future perfect.)
cum amābit, amābitur. 'When he loves, he will be loved.' (literally 'When he will love, he will be loved.')
cum mortuus erit, sepeliētur. 'When he dies he will be buried.' (literally 'When he will have died he will be buried.')

This distinction is effectively the same one that in past time is made using sequence of tenses.

cum ad urbem īvissem, multa ēmī. 'When I had gone (or 'when I went') to the city, I bought many things.' (The going to the city happens before the buying, and this is reflected in the use of the pluperfect subjunctive; see chapter 46.3.)
cum in urbe essem, multa ēmī. 'When I was in the city I bought many things.' (The being in the city and the buying happen at the same time, and this is reflected in the use of the imperfect subjunctive; see chapter 46.3.)

47.3 Distinguishing Types of *Cum* Clause

It is necessary to be able to distinguish these three types of *cum* clause in order to know whether any given instance of *cum* should be translated 'when', 'since', or 'although'. The first place to look is at the verb of the *cum* clause: if that verb is indicative, *cum* must mean 'when', and if that verb is present or perfect subjunctive, *cum* must mean 'since' or 'although'. (Present and perfect subjunctives occur only in primary sequence, and in primary sequence *cum* meaning 'when' does not take a subjunctive.) If the verb is imperfect or pluperfect subjunctive, all three translations of *cum* are possible and the reader needs to pick the one that best fits the context; often there is more than one possibility. With all three types of *cum* clause a subjunctive verb will always be translated with an indicative in English: it is the translation of the conjunction *cum*, not the translation of the verb, that reflects in English whether the Latin verb is subjunctive.

cum māter abest, puer timet. 'When his mother is away, the boy is afraid.' (The verb of the *cum* clause is indicative, so *cum* must mean 'when'.)

cum māter absit, tamen puer nōn timet. 'Although his mother is away, nevertheless the boy is not afraid.' (The verb of the *cum* clause is present subjunctive, so *cum* must mean 'since' or 'although'; the context indicates 'although'.)

cum māter absit, puer timet. 'Since his mother is away, the boy is afraid.' (The verb of the *cum* clause is present subjunctive, so *cum* must mean 'since' or 'although'; the context indicates 'since'.)

cum bene locūtus esset, laudātus est. 'Since he spoke (had spoken) well, he was praised.' or 'When he spoke (had spoken) well, he was praised.' (The verb of the *cum* clause is pluperfect subjunctive, so all three possibilities are available, and two of them fit the context.)

Practice

A Translate:

1. cum pecuniam habebo, meliorem domum emam.
2. meliorem domum emam cum pecuniam habeam.
3. cum pecuniam habeam, tamen meliorem domum non emam.
4. cum pecuniam invenerim, meliorem domum emam.
5. meliorem domum emam cum pecuniam invenero.
6. amicos vidit cum Romam ivisset.
7. cum Romam ivisset tamen amicos non vidit.
8. amicos videt cum Romae sit.
9. amicos videbit cum Romae erit.
10. cum illi patriam optime defendissent, laudati sunt.
11. cum illi patriam optime defendissent, tamen laudati non sunt.
12. cum illi patriam optime defenderint, laudabuntur.
13. cum e castris progressi essent, nostri classem hostium viderunt.
14. nostri classem hostium videbunt cum e castris progressi erunt.
15. cum e castris progressi sint, nostri classem hostium nunc videbunt.
16. nostri classem hostium viderunt cum e castris progrederentur.
17. cum e castris progressi essent, tamen nostri classem hostium non viderunt.
18. Athenas ibo cum mihi licebit.
19. cum mihi liceat, Athenas ibo.
20. Athenas ivi cum mihi liceret.
21. cum mihi liceret tamen Athenas non ivi.
22. cum omnes fugiunt, pudet omnes.
23. puduit omnes cum omnes fugerent.
24. cum omnes fugissent puduit omnes.
25. cum omnes fugissent tamen puduit neminem.
26. pudebit omnes cum omnes fugerint.

B Translate into Latin:

1 When we sell the house we shall have money.
2 We have money since we have sold the house.
3 Although we have sold the house, nevertheless we have no money.
4 When he goes to Carthage he will see the queen.
5 I shall see the queen when I am in Carthage.
6 They saw the queen when they were in Carthage.
7 Did you see the queen when you went to Carthage?
8 Although I went to Carthage, nevertheless I did not see the queen.
9 My father forgave me when I lost the horse.
10 Although I lost the horse, nevertheless my father forgave me.
11 When you order these slaves to follow you, they will follow.
12 When you have to sell this horse, come to me!
13 I went to that farmer when I had to sell my horse.

47.4 **Other Temporal Clauses**

Clauses in which a word for 'when', 'while', 'before', or 'after' occurs are known as temporal clauses, because they indicate the time at which an action occurred. There are other words besides *cum* that introduce Latin temporal clauses, including:

> *dum* 'while', 'until'
> *antequam* 'before'
> *postquam* 'after'

These other temporal conjunctions normally take indicative verbs;[2] the tenses are generally the same as in English, except that if the main verb is future the subordinate verb must be future or future perfect (as in temporal *cum* clauses).

postquam Londinium vēnī rēgīnam vīdī. 'After I came to London I saw the queen.'
antequam Londiniō discesserō rēgīnam vidēbō. 'Before I leave London I shall see the queen.'

But *dum* takes a present indicative (regardless of the time of the main verb) when it indicates a span of time at one point in which the action of the main verb takes place.

dum Londiniī sum rēgīnam vīdī. 'While I was in London I saw the queen.' (The seeing of the queen did not occupy the whole of my time in London but happened at one point during it, so *dum* takes the present tense.)

---

[2] There are a number of circumstances in which these conjunctions take the subjunctive, but these rules will suffice for now.

dum Londiniī eram fēlīcissimus eram. 'While I was in London I was very happy.'
(The being happy occurred throughout the whole of my time in London, so *dum* takes whatever tense is logical, in this case the imperfect.)

Closely related to *dum* is *dummodo*, which takes the subjunctive (tenses determined by sequence of tenses as in chapter 46.2) and means 'provided that'; its negative is *nē* (and therefore *nē quis, nē quid, nē ūllus*) rather than *nōn*.

dummodo nē discēdās, rēgīnam vidēbis. 'Provided that you don't leave, you will see the queen.'

Practice

C Translate:

1 dummodo mecum maneas nemo te impediet.
2 dum mecum manebat nemo eum impediebat.
3 dum mecum manet regem vidit.
4 postquam illud feci, puduit me.
5 Romam ivit antequam scivit nos ibi futuros esse.
6 dum Carthagine sum pecuniam meam amisi.
7 dum Athenis sum a magistris doctissimis doceor.
8 tecum veniam postquam patri persuasero.
9 dummodo deceat, Carthaginem ire velim.
10 polliciti sumus nos illum secuturos esse antequam scivimus te adesse.
11 dum venor animalia numquam video; dum non venor semper adsunt.
12 postquam victi sunt, interfecti sunt.
13 illud faciam dummodo pollicearis te me iuturum esse.
14 nunc faciamus, dum licet.
15 antequam domum venero amici iuvandi erunt mihi.
16 dummodo patri persuadere possim, Athenas ire volo.

D Translate into Latin:

1 We shall be very happy here provided that we are not attacked.
2 While the king was speaking everyone was listening.
3 While I was in Rome I heard the king.
4 After I forgave him he thought I was the best.
5 We must hinder the enemy while we can, for tomorrow they will advance to the city.
6 I shall help you provided that you give me money.
7 He lost his horse before we came to Rome.

8 After those enemies were conquered no-one attacked us.

9 While we were away the slaves fled.

10 Before you leave London you must see the queen.

47.5 Reading Practice

1 *Colloquium Stephani* 13a–15 (adapted): a boy does his schoolwork (probably first to third century AD).

Cum vocatus essem, ad praeceptorem accessi et tabulam, in qua erat lectio mea, ei dedi. et coepi reddere memoria quae acceperam ut discerem: versus ad numerum et distinctum et clausulam, cum aspiratione ubi oportebat, et versuum metaphrasin dedi. dum reddo emendatus sum a praeceptore, ut vocem praeparem bonam.

Vocabulary

praeceptor, praeceptōris (m.) 'instructor'

accēdō, accēdere, accessī, accessum 'approach'

tabula, tabulae (f.) 'writing-tablet'

lēctiō, lēctiōnis (f.) 'reading assignment'

coepī 'I began'

reddō, reddere, reddidī, redditum 'recite'

memoria, memoriae (f.) 'memory'

ad numerum 'in their proper rhythm'

(ad) distīnctum 'with pauses at the ends of sentences'

(ad) clausulam 'with pauses for commas'

aspīrātiō, aspīrātiōnis (f.) 'pronunciation of *h*' (uneducated Romans often did not pronounce this letter)

metaphrasin (accusative) 'paraphrase' (i.e. the boy summarizes the verses in his own words to show that he has understood them)

ēmendō, -āre, -āvī, -ātum 'correct'

vōx, vōcis (f.) 'style of speaking'

praeparō, -āre, -āvī, -ātum 'develop'

2 *Gaudeamus igitur* (verses 1–4): medieval students' song.

Gaudeamus igitur, iuvenes dum sumus!
post iucundam iuventutem, post molestam senectutem,
nos habebit humus.

Ubi sunt qui ante nos in mundo fuere?
vadite ad superos, transite in inferos,
hos si vis videre.

Vita nostra brevis est, brevi finietur.
venit mors velociter, rapit nos atrociter,
nemini parcetur.

Vivat academia, vivant professores!
vivat membrum quodlibet, vivant membra quaelibet,
semper sint in flore.

Vocabulary

gaudeō, gaudēre, gāvīsus sum 'rejoice'
iuvenis, iuvenis (m.) 'young man'
post (+ accusative) 'after'
iūcundus, -a, -um 'pleasant'
iuventūs, iuventūtis (f.) 'youth'
molestus, -a, -um 'unpleasant'
senectūs, senectūtis (f.) 'old age'
humus, humī (f.) 'earth' (i.e. the grave)
ante (+ accusative) 'before'
mundus, mundī (m.) 'world'
fuēre = fuērunt
vādō, vādere, –, – 'go'
superī, superōrum (m. plural) 'those
    above' (i.e. the dead who have gone
    to heaven)
trānseō (like *eō*) 'cross over'

īnferī, īnferōrum (m. plural) 'those
    below' (i.e. the dead who have gone
    to hell)
brevī 'in a short time'
fīniō, fīnīre, fīnīvī, fīnītum 'finish'
mors, mortis, mortium (f.) 'death'
vēlōx, *gen.* vēlōcis 'swift'
atrōx, *gen.* atrōcis 'dreadful'
nēminī parcētur 'no-one will be spared'
    (literally 'it will be spared to no-one')
acadēmīa, acadēmīae (f.) 'university'
professor, professōris (m.) 'professor'
membrum, membrī (n.) 'member'
quīlibet, quaelibet, quodlibet 'any one
    you please'
flōs, flōris (m.) 'flower', 'prime of life'

3 Martial 12.12: a frustrating drinking companion (first century AD).

Omnia promittis cum tota nocte bibisti;
    mane nihil praestas. Pollio, mane bibe.

Vocabulary

prōmittō (like *mittō*) 'promise'
tōtus, tōta, tōtum 'whole'
bibō, bibere, bibī, – 'drink'
māne 'in the morning'

praestō, -stāre, -stitī, -stitum 'fulfil'
Pōlliō, Pōlliōnis (m.) *name of the poem's
    addressee*

4 Martial 14.6: praise of a three-leaved writing tablet (first century AD).

Tunc triplices nostros non vilia dona putabis,
    cum se venturam scribet amica tibi.

Vocabulary

tunc 'then'

triplicēs 'three leaves' (accusative
  plural)

vīlis, vīle 'poor'

dōnum, dōnī (n.) 'gift'

putō, putāre, putāvī, putātum 'think'

ventūram = ventūram esse

amīca, amīcae (f.) 'girlfriend'

5 Martial 6.72: the adventures of a garden thief, as told to Fabullus (first century AD).
   Dum here has a causal implication ('since, because'); this is unusual.

Fur notae nimium rapacitatis
compilare Cilix volebat hortum,
ingenti sed erat, Fabulle, in horto
praeter marmoreum nihil Priapum.
dum non vult vacua manu redire,
ipsum surripuit Cilix Priapum.

Vocabulary

fūr, fūris (m.) 'thief'

nōtae nimium rapācitātis 'of well-
  known extreme rapacity'

compīlō, -āre, -āvī, -ātum 'pillage'

Cilix, Cilicis (m.) *a man's name*

hortus, hortī (m.) 'garden'

ingēns, *gen.* ingentis 'enormous'

praeter (+ accusative) 'except for'

marmoreus, -a, -um 'made of marble'

Priāpus, Priāpī (m.) 'statue of Priapus'
  (a god)

vacuus, vacua, vacuum 'empty'

redeō (like *eō*) 'return'

ipsum 'himself' (masculine accusative
  singular)

surripiō, surripere, surripuī, surreptum
  'snatch secretly'

47.6 **Vocabulary to Learn**

Verbs

adveniō, advenīre, advēnī, adventum — 'arrive'

egeō, egēre, eguī, – (+ genitive or ablative) — 'need', 'lack'

reddō, reddere, reddidī, redditum — 'give back', 'return' (in the sense of 'give back')

redeō, redīre, rediī, reditum (like *eō*) — 'go back', 'come back', 'return' (in the sense of 'go back')

surgō, surgere, surrēxī, surrēctum — 'get up'

tollō, tollere, sustulī, sublātum — 'lift', 'pick up'

Vocabulary continues overleaf.

Adjectives

dīligēns, *gen.* dīligentis	'careful'
Latīnus, Latīna, Latīnum	'Latin'
ūtilis, ūtile	'useful'

Conjunctions

antequam	'before'
cum	'since', 'although', 'when'
dum	'while', 'until'
dummodo	'provided that'
postquam	'after'

48.1 *Colloquia Monacensia–Einsidlensia* 4a–p (adapted)

Winning a court case (second or third century AD):

LUCIUS: ave, Gai.

GAIUS: bene valeas, Luci.

LUCIUS: quid agis?

GAIUS: omnia recte se habent. quomodo te habes?

LUCIUS: gratulor tibi sicut mihi. sed iudicium habeo.

GAIUS: ad quem? ad quaestorem?

LUCIUS: non ibi.

GAIUS: sed ubi? ad proconsulem?

LUCIUS: ibi.

GAIUS: quale est ipsa res?

LUCIUS: non valde magnum; est enim pecuniarium, ut omne videas. si vacat tibi, veni nobiscum; iudices diem nobis dederunt, quae hodie est, et sententia dicetur. quare volo te praesente de causa cum advocatis tractare.

GAIUS: adhibuistine advocatos?

LUCIUS: adhibui.

GAIUS: quos?

LUCIUS: tuos amicos.

GAIUS: bene fecisti. constituistine? circa quam horam? in quo loco?

LUCIUS: in foro, in porticu, iuxta stoam Victoriae.

GAIUS: post modicum ad te veniam.

LUCIUS: sed rogo ut hoc in mente habeas.

GAIUS: securus esto; mihi pertinet.

LUCIUS (*to son*): eamus nos ad nummularium; accipiamus ab eo denarios centum; demus eos causidico et advocatis et iuris peritis, ut quam optime defendant nos. hic est. accipe ab eo denarios et sequere. (*on arrival at court*) sicut constituimus, adest Gaius. convocemus eum in consilium. hic habemus instrumenta.

GAIUS: denuntiavistine illi?

LUCIUS: denuntiavi.

GAIUS: testatusne es?

LUCIUS: testatus sum. tace, audiamus sententiam. audivistine nos vicisse, Gai?

Vocabulary

avē 'hello'

quid 'how'

rēctē 'rightly', 'as it should'

habeō *with a reflexive is equivalent to* **'be'**

quōmodo 'how'

grātulor, -ārī, -ātus sum (+ dative) 'rejoice for'

sīcut 'just as'

iūdicium, iūdiciī (n.) 'court case'

ad (+ accusative) 'before' (i.e. in the court of)

quaestor, quaestōris (m.) 'quaestor' (kind of official)

prōcōnsul, prōcōnsulis (m.) 'proconsul' (kind of official)

quāle 'what sort of thing?'

ipse, ipsa, ipsum 'itself'

valdē 'very'

pecūniārius, -a, -um 'financial'

vacat tibi 'you have leisure' (literally 'it is vacant to you')

diēs, diēī (f.) 'appointed date' (note gender in this meaning!)

sententia, sententiae (f.) 'verdict'

quārē 'for which reason'

tē praesente 'in your presence'

tractō, tractāre, tractāvī, tractātum 'discuss'

adhibeō, adhibēre, adhibuī, adhibitum 'call in'

cōnstituō, -ere, cōnstituī, cōnstitūtum 'agree about a meeting'

circā (+ accusative) 'around'

forum, forī (n.) 'forum', 'marketplace'

porticus, porticūs (f.) 'colonnade'

iuxtā (+ accusative) 'next to'

stoa, stoae (f.) 'stoa' (a building)

Victōria, Victōriae (f.) 'Victory' (personified)

post (+ accusative) 'after'

modicum, modicī (n.) 'a little while'

mēns, mentis, mentium (f.) 'mind'

sēcūrus, -a, -um 'free from worry'

pertinet (+ dative) 'it matters to'

nummulārius, nummulāriī (m.) 'banker'

dēnārius, dēnāriī (m.) 'denarius' (a coin)

centum (indeclinable) 'hundred'

causidicus, causidicī (m.) 'barrister', 'lawyer'

iūris perītus, iūris perītī (m.) 'legal expert' (literally 'skilled in law')

convocō (like *vocō*) 'call together'

cōnsilium, cōnsiliī (n.) 'consultation'

īnstrūmentum, īnstrūmentī (n.) 'evidence'

dēnūntiō, -āre, -āvī, -ātum (+ dative) 'serve a summons to'

testor, testārī, testātus sum 'testify'

taceō, tacēre, tacuī, tacitum 'keep silent'

48.2 Translate into Latin

GAIUS: Hello, Lucius.

LUCIUS: How are you doing, Gaius?

GAIUS: Very badly: I must go to the forum today to help my friend Marcus.

LUCIUS: Why?

GAIUS: He has a court case before the quaestor, since he owes many denarii.

LUCIUS: But Marcus bought a new house yesterday.

GAIUS: He did (*Latin 'he bought'*), although he has no money, and now that house will have to be given to his creditors, provided that the judge is wise. But I must not say such things, for he is my friend. When he loses his house, he will have to live with me.

LUCIUS: You are a good friend; therefore it is fitting for you to be praised.

Additional Vocabulary

dēbeō, dēbēre, dēbuī, dēbitum 'owe'
crēditor, crēditōris (m.) 'creditor'
habitō, -āre, -āvī, -ātum 'live' (in the sense of 'dwell'; *vīvō* means 'be alive')

48.3   Virgil, *Aeneid* 1.50–9

Juno visits the god of the winds (continuation of the passage in chapter 42):

Talia flammato secum dea corde volutans
nimborum in patriam, loca feta furentibus Austris,
Aeoliam venit. hic vasto rex Aeolus antro
luctantis ventos tempestatesque sonoras
imperio premit ac vinclis et carcere frenat.
illi indignantes magno cum murmure montis
circum claustra fremunt; celsa sedet Aeolus arce
sceptra tenens mollitque animos et temperat iras;
ni faciat, maria ac terras caelumque profundum
quippe ferant rapidi secum verrantque per auras.

Vocabulary

flammō, -āre, -āvī, -ātum 'inflame'
cor, cordis (n.) 'heart'
volūtō, -āre, -āvī, -ātum 'turn over'
nimbus, nimbī (m.) 'stormcloud'
fētus, fēta, fētum (+ ablative) 'breeding',
   'teeming with'
furō, furere, –, – 'rage'
Auster, Austrī (m.) 'storm-wind'
Aeolia, Aeoliae (f.) *name of a place*
vāstus, vāsta, vāstum 'vast'
Aeolus, Aeolī (m.) *name of the god of*
   the winds
antrum, antrī (n.) 'cave' (supply *in*)
luctor, luctārī, luctātus sum 'struggle'

ventus, ventī (m.) 'wind'
tempestās, tempestātis (f.) 'tempest'
sonōrus, -a, -um 'noisy'
imperium, imperiī (n.) 'rule', 'power'
premō, premere, pressī, pressum
   'oppress'
ac 'and'
vinclum, vinclī (n.) 'chain'
carcer, carceris (m.) 'prison'
frēnō, -āre, -āvī, -ātum 'restrain'
indignor, -ārī, -ātus sum 'be angry'
murmur, murmuris (n.) 'growl'
mōns, montis, montium (m.)
   'mountain'

circum (+ accusative) 'around'

claustra, claustrōrum (n. plural)
   'defences'

fremō, fremere, fremuī, fremitum 'roar'

celsus, celsa, celsum 'lofty'

arx, arcis, arcium (f.) 'citadel' (supply *in*)

scēptrum, scēptrī (n.) 'sceptre'

teneō, tenēre, tenuī, tentum 'hold'

molliō, mollīre, mollīvī, mollītum
   'soften'

animus, animī (m.) 'spirit'

temperō, -āre, -āvī, -ātum 'moderate'

īra, īrae (f.) 'anger'

nī 'if not'

mare, maris, marium (n.) 'sea'

terra, terrae (f.) 'land'

caelum, caelī (n.) 'heaven'

profundus, -a, -um 'boundless'

quippe 'indeed'

rapidus, -a, -um 'swift'

verrō, verrere, –, versum 'sweep'

aura, aurae (f.) 'air'

A possible prose order of the above would be:

Talia flammato corde secum volutans dea in patriam nimborum, loca feta furentibus Austris, Aeoliam venit. hic vasto antro rex Aeolus ventos luctantis tempestatesque sonoras imperio premit ac vinclis et carcere frenat. illi indignantes cum magno murmure circum claustra montis fremunt; celsa arce sedet Aeolus sceptra tenens mollitque animos et iras temperat; ni faciat, maria ac terras caelumque profundum quippe rapidi secum ferant perque auras verrant.

PART V

49.1 *Ferō*

The word for 'carry' is irregular, both in its principal parts (*ferō, ferre, tulī, lātum*) and in its conjugation (note the forms in bold below); unlike other irregular verbs we have seen so far, it has passive as well as active forms. Essentially *ferō* is a third-conjugation verb with some contractions, including the shortening of the infinitive *ferre* from **ferere*. (* is used to indicate words that do not exist.)

| | Indicative | | Subjunctive | |
	Active	Passive	Active	Passive
Present	ferō	feror	feram	ferar
	fers	**ferris**	ferās	ferāris
	fert	**fertur**	ferat	ferātur
	ferimus	ferimur	ferāmus	ferāmur
	fertis	feriminī	ferātis	ferāminī
	ferunt	feruntur	ferant	ferantur
Future	feram	ferar		
	ferēs	ferēris		
	feret	ferētur		
	ferēmus	ferēmur		
	ferētis	ferēminī		
	ferent	ferentur		
Perfect	tulī	lātus, -a, -um sum	tulerim	lātus, -a, -um sim
	tulistī	lātus, -a, -um es	tulerīs	lātus, -a, -um sīs
	tulit	lātus, -a, -um est	tulerit	lātus, -a, -um sit
	tulimus	lātī, -ae, -a sumus	tulerīmus	lātī, -ae, -a sīmus
	tulistis	lātī, -ae, -a estis	tulerītis	lātī, -ae, -a sītis
	tulērunt	lātī, -ae, -a sunt	tulerint	lātī, -ae, -a sint
Imperfect	ferēbam	ferēbar	ferrem	ferrer
	ferēbās	ferēbāris	ferrēs	ferrēris
	ferēbat	ferēbātur	ferret	ferrētur
	ferēbāmus	ferēbāmur	ferrēmus	ferrēmur
	ferēbātis	ferēbāminī	ferrētis	ferrēminī
	ferēbant	ferēbantur	ferrent	ferrentur

	Indicative		Subjunctive	
	Active	Passive	Active	Passive
Pluperfect	tuleram	lātus, -a, -um eram	tulissem	lātus, -a, -um essem
	tulerās	lātus, -a, -um erās	tulissēs	lātus, -a, -um essēs
	tulerat	lātus, -a, -um erat	tulisset	lātus, -a, -um esset
	tulerāmus	lātī, -ae, -a erāmus	tulissēmus	lātī, -ae, -a essēmus
	tulerātis	lātī, -ae, -a erātis	tulissētis	lātī, -ae, -a essētis
	tulerant	lātī, -ae, -a erant	tulissent	lātī, -ae, -a essent
Future perfect	tulerō	lātus, -a, -um erō		
	tuleris	lātus, -a, -um eris		
	tulerit	lātus, -a, -um erit		
	tulerimus	lātī, -ae, -a erimus		
	tuleritis	lātī, -ae, -a eritis		
	tulerint	lātī, -ae, -a erunt		

	Active	Passive
Imperative	**fer**	**ferre**
	ferte	feriminī
Present infinitive	**ferre**	**ferrī**
Future infintive	lātūrus, -a, -um esse	lātum īrī
Perfect infinitive	tulisse	lātus, -a, -um esse
Present participle	ferēns, *gen.* ferentis	
Future participle	lātūrus, -a, -um	
Perfect participle		lātus, -a, -um
Gerundive		ferendus, -a, -um

Practice

A Conjugate these compounds of *ferō* in the forms indicated: *afferō, afferre, attulī, allātum* 'bring' (from *ad + ferō*), *auferō, auferre, abstulī, ablātum* 'carry off' (from *ab + ferō*).

1 *afferō*, present active indicative
2 *auferō*, present passive indicative
3 *afferō*, present active subjunctive
4 *auferō*, future active indicative
5 *afferō*, present passive subjunctive
6 *auferō*, future passive indicative
7 *afferō*, imperfect active subjunctive
8 *auferō*, imperfect active indicative
9 *afferō*, imperfect passive subjunctive

10 *auferō*, imperfect passive
   indicative
11 *afferō*, perfect active indicative
12 *auferō*, pluperfect active indicative
13 *afferō*, perfect passive indicative
14 *auferō*, pluperfect passive
   indicative

15 *afferō*, imperative active
16 *auferō*, imperative passive
17 *afferō*, perfect active infinitive
18 *auferō*, present participle
19 *afferō*, gerundive
20 *auferō*, present passive
   infinitive

B Translate:

1 servus multa fert.
2 hostes cum discederent aurum
   nostrum abstulerunt.
3 cum servus sim, tamen nolo hos
   libros ferre.
4 servi, afferte aquam.
5 miles mortuus ab amicis fertur.
6 nihil ferens domum venit.
7 cum hostes adsint, affer mihi
   gladium.
8 noli argentum meum auferre.
9 cum fugere non posset, tamen ab
   amicis ferri noluit.

10 liber a fratre meo allatus
   pessimus erat.
11 quid mihi afferes?
12 cum domum reficiam, haec saxa
   mihi ferenda erunt.
13 timeo ne nihil mihi afferat.
14 dixit se multa abstulisse.
15 cum amici pecuniam attulissent,
   equum maiorem emit.
16 dum puer saxa ferebat miser erat.
17 aurum ad te afferam cum illi
   mihi dederint.
18 servo imperavit ut libros ferret.

C Translate into Latin:

1 Bring us the books!
2 They asked me to bring this to
   you.
3 Did you carry off my gold?
4 The slaves will bring the books.
5 We must carry this letter to
   London.
6 That silver will have to be
   brought to Rome.
7 The farmer does not want to carry
   a dead sheep.
8 Are you carrying that with your
   own hands?
9 The dead soldier is being carried
   by his friends.

10 She never carries money with her.
11 The gold has been carried off by
   the enemy.
12 Your letter was brought by a very
   small boy.
13 I shall order the slaves to carry
   everything.
14 We brought this in order to use it.
15 You said that you would bring
   a sword.
16 Let's carry off that gold; no-one
   will see us.
17 Are we to carry these things?
18 Since we brought the book, let's
   read it.

49.2 Roman Names

Roman names are declinable and fit into the Latin grammatical system; men's names are masculine (and usually belong to the second or third declension), while women's names are feminine (and usually belong to the first or third declension). Women are usually referred to by one name (in the Republic this is nearly always a first-declension word ending in *-ia* in the nominative), occasionally by two. Men are more often referred to by multiple names, to the point where it can be difficult to work out how many men are under discussion and which names go with whom. It is therefore useful to understand something of Roman male nomenclature.

A Roman man's first name or *praenōmen* was drawn from an extremely small pool of traditional names, most notably *Decimus, Gaius, Gnaeus, Lūcius, Mārcus, Pūblius, Quīntus,* and *Titus*. These were usually abbreviated by their first letters (with *C* used for *Gaius* and *Cn* for *Gnaeus*, as the abbreviations predated the invention of the letter *G*). The second name or *gentīlicium* was inherited and almost always ended in *-ius* in the nominative; common *gentīlicia* include *Claudius, Iūlius,* and *Aurēlius*. The third name or *cognōmen* could be either given or inherited and was unpredictable in form; third-declension names are nearly always *cognōmina*, but there are also many *cognōmina* belonging to the second declension. Some men had more than one *cognōmen*;[1] in the imperial period this was the most used of the three names and could appear before rather than after the *gentīlicium*. Non-Romans and slaves usually had only one name, of unpredictable form and sometimes (particularly in the case of Jewish names found in the Bible) indeclinable.

Names should always be put into the nominative case when translating into English.

49.3 Reading Practice

1 *Oxyrhynchus Papyri* VII.1022.1–23 (adapted): a letter to a cohort of the Roman army in Egypt, enrolling six new soldiers (AD 103).

C. Minicius Italus Celsiano suo salutem dicit. tirones sex probatos a me in cohorte cui praees in numeros referri iube ex XI Kalendas Martias. nomina eorum et iconismos huic epistulae subieci. vale, frater carissime.
C. Veturium Gemellum, annorum XXI, sine iconismo
C. Longium Priscum, annorum XXII, iconismus supercilio sinistro

[1] For example, Pūblius Cornēlius Scīpiō Aemiliānus Āfricānus had three, with different origins: born with the *gentīlicium* Aemilius, he was adopted into a different family and therefore (as was usual in Roman adoptions) took a complete new name from his new family, Pūblius Cornēlius Scīpiō. To commemorate his original family, he formed the second *cognōmen* Aemiliānus out of his original *gentīlicium* Aemilius (again this was standard practice in adoptions). Then upon conquering Carthage he received the third *cognōmen* Āfricānus.

C. Iulium Maximum, annorum XXV, sine iconismo

M. Lucium Secundum, annorum XX, sine iconismo

C. Iulium Saturninum, annorum XXIII, iconismus manu sinistra

M. Antonium Valentem, annorum XXII, iconismus frontis parte dextra.

Vocabulary

tīrō, tīrōnis (m.) 'recruit' (i.e. new
entrant to the army)

probō, probāre, probāvī, probātum
'approve'

cohors, cohortis (f.) 'cohort' (a unit
of the Roman army)

praesum (like *sum*) (+ dative) 'be in
charge of'

referō (like *ferō*) in numerōs 'enrol'

iubeō, iubēre, iussī, iussum 'order'
(takes accusative and infinitive
rather than the usual indirect
command construction)

ex 'starting from'

XI Kalendās Mārtiās '19 February'
(literally '11 days before the Kalends

(first) of March': February had 28
days and the Romans counted
inclusively)

īconismus, īconismī (m.)
'distinguishing mark'
(e.g. a birthmark)

subiciō, subicere, subiēcī, subiectum
'append to' (+ accusative of thing
appended and dative of thing to
which appended)

annōrum 'aged' (literally 'of years')

superciliō (ablative) 'on his eyebrow'

sinister, sinistra, sinistrum 'left'

frōns, frontis, frontium (f.) 'forehead'

parte (ablative) 'on the side'

dexter, dextra, dextrum 'right'

2 *Corpus Inscriptionum Latinarum* IV.429 and IV.3640 (both adapted): Campaign
notices from Pompeii (first century AD).

C. Iulium Polybium oro ut vos aedilem faciatis: panem bonum affert.

Cn. Helvium Sabinum oro ut vos aedilem faciatis. Thyrsus hoc fecit.

Vocabulary

ōrō, ōrāre, ōrāvī, ōrātum 'beg'

aedīlis, aedīlis, aedīlium (m.) 'aedile' (an
elected official)

faciō *can also mean* 'vote for', 'elect'

pānis, pānis, pānium (m.) 'bread'

3 *Roman Inscriptions of Britain* 10, 959, 934, 560, 363, 369, 594 (all adapted): inscriptions on imperial-period tombstones found in Britain.

a. M. Aurelio Eucarpo filio piissimo, qui vixit annos XV et menses VI, Aurelia
Eucarpia mater hoc posuit.

b. Dis manibus. Aurelia Aureliana vixit annos XXXXI. Ulpius Apollinaris coniugi
carissimae hoc posuit.

c. Dis manibus. Crotilo Germanus vixit annos XXVI. Graeca vixit annos IIII. Vindicianus frater titulum posuit.

d. Dis manibus. Atiliana annorum I, Atilianus annorum X, Protus annorum XII. Pompeius Optatus dominus titulum posuit.

e. Dis manibus. Iulius Valens, veteranus legionis II, vixit annos C. Iulia Secundina coniunx et Iulius Martinus filius hanc memoriam posuerunt.

f. Dis manibus. Tadia Vallaunia vixit annos LXV, et Tadius Exuperatus filius vixit annos XXXVII, defunctus in expeditione Germanica. Tadia Exuperata filia piissima matri et fratri hoc prope tumulum patris posuit.

g. His terris tegitur Aelia Matrona, quae vixit annos XXVIII menses II dies VIII, et M. Iulius Maximus filius, qui vixit annos VI menses III dies XX, et Campania Dubitata mater, quae vixit annos LIII. Iulius Maximus, singularis consularis alae Sarmatarum, coniunx, coniugi incomparabili et filio piissimo et socrui tenacissimae hanc memoriam posuit.

Vocabulary

pius, pia, pium 'devoted'
mēnsis, mēnsis (m.) 'month'
pōnō *can also mean* **'set up'**
dīs mānibus 'to the divine spirits'
coniūnx, coniugis (m. or f.) 'spouse'
titulus, titulī (m.) 'inscription'
annōrum 'aged' (literally 'of years')
veterānus, veteranī (m.) 'veteran'
legiō, legiōnis (f.) 'legion'
memoria, memoriae (f.) 'memorial'
dēfungor, dēfungī, dēfūnctus sum 'die'
expedītiō, expedītiōnis (f.) 'expedition'
Germānicus, -a, -um 'German' (i.e to
    Germany)

prope (+ accusative) 'near'
tumulus, tumulī (m.) 'tomb'
terrae, terrārum (f. plural) 'earth'
tegō, tegere, tēxī, tēctum 'cover'
singulāris cōnsulāris (nominative)
    'officer'
āla, ālae (f.) 'cavalry regiment'
Sarmatae, Sarmatārum (m. plural)
    'Sarmatians' (a people living in the
    eastern empire, near the Black Sea)
incomparābilis, -e 'incomparable'
socrus, socrūs (f.) 'mother in law'
tenāx, *gen.* tenācis
    'steadfast'

49.4 Vocabulary to Learn

Verbs

afferō, afferre, attulī, allātum	'bring'
auferō, auferre, abstulī, ablātum	'carry off'
ferō, ferre, tulī, lātum	'carry'

50.1 English Conditional Clauses

Clauses containing a word for 'if' (Latin *sī*) are known as 'conditional clauses' because they indicate the conditions under which something is or would be true: 'If the weather is good we shall have a picnic' or 'If he had come sooner it would have been a disaster.' In order to translate Latin conditional sentences successfully it is necessary to understand how conditionals work in formal written English, though many spoken varieties of English diverge from this system significantly.

In formal English, some types of conditional sentence present a condition without saying anything about whether it is or has been fulfilled:

Past simple:	1a) 'If John went to Rome, he had a great time.' (We do not know whether John went to Rome.)
	1b) 'If John was in Rome yesterday, he missed seeing the queen.' (We do not know where John was.)
	1c) 'If they were in Rome yesterday, they missed seeing the queen.' (We do not know where they were.)
Present simple:	2) 'If John is in Rome, he is having a great time.' (We do not know where John is.)
Future more vivid:	3) 'If John goes to Rome, he will have a great time.' (We do not know whether John will go to Rome.)

But the following types tell us that the condition has *not* been fulfilled and that therefore the statement in the main clause is *not* true:

Past contrary to fact:	4a) 'If John had gone to Rome, he would have had a great time.' (John did not go to Rome.)
	4b) 'If John had been in Rome yesterday, he would have missed seeing the queen.' (John was not in Rome.)
Present contrary to fact:	5a) 'If John were in Rome, he would be having a great time.' (John is not in Rome.)
	5b) 'If they were in Rome, they would be having a great time.' (They are not in Rome.)

5c) 'If she loved him, she would not be treating him like that.' (She does not love him.)

5d) 'If Martha were doing her job properly, we would not have this problem.' (Martha is not doing her job properly.)

For the future one cannot say positively that a condition has not been fulfilled, since the fulfilment or non-fulfilment has not yet happened, but it is still possible to indicate that it is unlikely to be fulfilled, as follows:

Future less vivid:

6a) 'If John should[1] go to Rome, he would have a great time.' (John might go to Rome, but it is not likely.)

6b) 'If John were to go to Rome, he would have a great time.' (John might go to Rome, but it is not likely.)

There is much more consistency in the main clauses than in the subordinate clauses: in English most of the meaning of a conditional sentence is carried by the verb of the main clause, so that for example sentences 4–6 (the ones in which fulfilment of the condition is impossible or doubtful) all have 'would' in the main clause, while sentences 1–3 (the ones in which fulfilment of the conditional is left open) do not have 'would'. There is a distinction between the use of 'was' (past indicative) in sentence 1b and singular 'were' (subjunctive) in sentence 5a: 'if he was ...' means that he may have been, whereas 'if he were ...' using the subjunctive indicates that he is not. But in the plural (cf. sentences 1c and 5b) there is no distinction: 'if they were ...' can be used both when they may have been (indicative) and when they are not (subjunctive). Sentences 6a–b are largely absent from modern spoken English and are now fairly rare even in writing, but because their Latin equivalents are common it is worth learning these elements of a slightly older type of English in order to be able to make the same distinctions as the Romans did.

In many informal varieties of English the subjunctive has disappeared, so the similarity between sentences 1c and 5b is carried over into sentences 1b and 5a; thus it is possible in those informal varieties (but not in standard written English) to produce sentences like 'If John was in Rome, he would be having a great time' (meaning that John is not in Rome). Some varieties of spoken English also admit sentences like 'If John went to Rome he would have had a great time' (meaning that John did not go to Rome), 'If John would've gone to Rome he would've had a great time' (meaning that John did not go to Rome) or even 'If John is in Rome he would be having a great time' (meaning that John is not in Rome). These formulations, which are usually considered grammatically incorrect in formal written English, cause difficulties for translating Latin, so it is a good idea to avoid them and stick to the formulations given in 1–6 above.

---

[1] The use of 'should' in if-clauses does not imply obligation; it is different from the 'should' in main clauses, such as 'You really should wait for the green light before crossing the road.'

Practice

A Take the following sentences and change their tenses to express the circumstances given in formal English. Example: given the sentence 'If Mary is there, she is protesting' and asked to change it to the past, under the circumstances that we do not know whether Mary was there, one would say 'If Mary was there, she was protesting' or 'If Mary was there, she protested'; if asked to change it to the past, under the circumstances that Mary was not there, one would say 'If Mary had been there, she would have protested.' If you find this exercise difficult, use the sentences whose numbers are given in parentheses as models.[2]

'If Jim is in charge everything is going well.'

1 past: we don't know whether Jim was in charge (1)
2 past: Jim was not in charge (4)
3 present: we don't know whether Jim is in charge (2)
4 present: Jim is not in charge (5)
5 future: we don't know whether Jim will be in charge (3)
6 future: Jim is unlikely to be in charge (6)

'If Jane goes to the shop she buys a paper.'

7 past: we don't know whether Jane went to the shop (1)
8 past: Jane did not go to the shop (4)
9 future: we don't know whether Jane will go to the shop (3)
10 future: Jane is unlikely to go to the shop (6)
11 present: we don't know whether Jane is going to the shop (2)
12 present: Jane is not going to the shop (5)

50.2 Latin Conditional Clauses

In Latin, sentences in which nothing is indicated about the fulfilment of the condition have their verbs in the indicative in both the if-clause and the main clause; such sentences are the equivalents of 1–3 above, the simple conditions and the future more vivid. Sentences indicating that the fulfilment of the condition is doubtful (future) or impossible (past and present) have their verbs in the subjunctive in both the if-clause and the main clause; these are the equivalent of 4–6 above, the contrary-to-fact conditions and the future less vivid. In other words, if the English main clause contains the word 'would', the Latin has the subjunctive in *both* clauses; otherwise the Latin has the indicative in both clauses. In the indicative the tenses are self-evident, except that in

---

[2] Another exercise of this type, with an answer key, can be found in chapter 63.11, exercise O.

future conditions Latin uses the future in both clauses[3] where English uses the present in the if-clause; in the subjunctive Latin uses the pluperfect to express past time, the imperfect for present time, and the present for future time. Therefore:

1) Indicative condition, past (= **past simple**): any past indicative tense(s)
   sī Rōmae erat, fēlīx erat. 'If he was in Rome, he was happy.'
   sī rēx locūtus est, cīvēs audīvērunt. 'If the king spoke, the citizens listened.'

2) Indicative condition, present (= **present simple**): present indicative
   sī Rōmae est, fēlīx est. 'If he is in Rome, he is happy.'
   sī rēx loquitur, cīvēs audiuntur. 'If the king speaks, the citizens listen.' / 'If the king is speaking, the citizens are listening.'

3) Indicative condition, future (= **future more vivid**): future indicative in *both* clauses
   sī Rōmae erit, fēlīx erit. 'If he is in Rome, he will be happy.' (literally 'If he will be in Rome, he will be happy.')
   sī rēx loquētur, cīvēs audientur. 'If the king speaks, the citizens will listen.' (literally 'If the king will speak, the citizens will listen.')

4) Subjunctive condition, past (= **past contrary to fact**): pluperfect subjunctive in *both* clauses
   sī Rōmae fuisset, fēlīx fuisset. 'If he had been in Rome, he would have been happy.'
   sī rēx locūtus esset, cīvēs audīvissent. 'If the king had spoken, the citizens would have listened.'

5) Subjunctive condition, present (= **present contrary to fact**): imperfect subjunctive in *both* clauses
   sī Rōmae esset, fēlīx esset. 'If he were in Rome, he would be happy.'
   sī rēx loquerētur, cīvēs audīrent. 'If the king were speaking, the citizens would be listening.'

6) Subjunctive condition, future (= **future less vivid**): present subjunctive in *both* clauses
   sī Rōmam eat, fēlīx sit. 'If he should go to Rome, he would be happy.' / 'If he were to go to Rome, he would be happy.'
   sī rēx loquātur, cīvēs audiant. 'If the king should speak, the citizens would listen.' / 'If the king were to speak, the citizens would listen.'

---

[3] But see the next chapter for the use of the future perfect.

Practice

B For each sentence, state which mood (indicative or subjunctive) and tense each verb would take in Latin.

1 If I had been Menelaus, I would not have bothered to pursue Helen.
2 If ancient heroes were insulted, they got extremely angry.
3 If we were ancient Romans, we would know Virgil's poetry by heart.
4 If this thing is your coat, you need a new one.
5 If you spend the summer in Rome you will learn all about the city.
6 If we were to do these sentences for the next two hours, we would all fall asleep.
7 If I were you I would not be doing that.
8 If swimmers go into these waters, they get eaten by sharks.
9 If we sit in the sun it will be too hot.
10 If this building should collapse, we would be squashed.
11 If people were rude to Roman emperors, they were executed.
12 If he had not been injured he would have won the race.
13 If Louise stays with us over the holidays, there will be eight people using one bathroom.
14 If we were to be asked to translate these sentences into Latin, we would have trouble.
15 If Lucy were older she would be able to join the army.
16 If ever a man rendered great services to the Athenians, they banished him.
17 If Ariadne thinks Theseus will make her happy, she's making a big mistake.
18 If we had lived in the last years of the Roman republic we would not have been very happy.
19 If Zeus wanted a woman's love, he had to disguise himself to get it.
20 If a person gets his head chopped off, he dies.
21 If I were a Frenchman I would speak French with a much better accent than the one I've got.
22 If we spend the winter in Switzerland we shall do a lot of skiing.
23 If she had been a citizen she would have voted in the election.
24 If a penguin should walk into this room we would all be surprised.
25 If you were to spend the next four hours doing these sentences you would get very good at them.

C Translate (using vocabulary from 50.4 as necessary):

1 si milites in castris manserunt, non pugnaverunt.
2 si milites in castris mansissent, non pugnavissent.
3 si milites in castris manent, non pugnant.
4 si milites in castris manerent, non pugnarent.
5 si milites in castris manebunt, non pugnabunt.
6 si milites in castris maneant, non pugnent.
7 si rex in urbe fuisset, interfectus esset.
8 si rex in urbe erit, interficietur.
9 si rex in urbe erat, interfectus est.
10 si rex in urbe sit, interficiatur.
11 si exercitum vidit, veritus est.
12 si exercitum vidisset, veritus esset.
13 si exercitum videbit, verebitur.
14 si eam amavisset, iuvisset.
15 si eam amaret, iuvaret.
16 si eam amat, iuvat.
17 si eam amabit, iuvabit.
18 si rex eum Romam misisset, ivisset.
19 si rex eum Romam mittat, eat.

20 si rex eum Romam misit, ivit.
21 si milites essemus, pugnaremus.
22 si milites fuissemus, pugnavissemus.
23 si librum scribas, legam.
24 si librum scripsisses, legissem.
25 si servos haberem, liberarem.
26 si servos habuissem, liberavissem.
27 si servos habeam, liberem.
28 si regem videam, de te loquar.
29 si regem vidissem, de te locutus essem.
30 si illud feras, pecuniam tibi dem.
31 si illud tulisses, pecuniam tibi dedissem.
32 si illud feres, pecuniam tibi dabo.
33 si equo usus esses, aurum ferre potuisses.
34 si equo utereris, aurum ferre posses.
35 si equo uteris, aurum ferre poteris.
36 si equo utaris, aurum ferre possis.
37 si ille domum tuum refecit, bene refecta est.
38 si ille domum tuum refecisset, bene refecta non fuisset.

D Translate into Latin:

1 If he is loved he is happy.
2 If he is loved he will be happy.
3 If he had been loved he would have been happy.
4 If he were loved he would be happy.
5 If he were to be loved he would be happy.
6 If our men are happy they will fight well.

7 If our men were happy they fought well.
8 If our men were happy they would be fighting well.
9 If our men had been happy they would have fought well.
10 If our men are happy they fight well.
11 If our men should be happy they would fight well.

50.3 Reading Practice

1 Cicero, *Epistulae ad familiares* 14.17: Cicero (M. Tullius Cicero) writes to his wife, mentioning their daughter Tullia, in 48 BC. Three verbs (*scrīberem, sint, sim affectus*) are subjunctive for reasons we have not yet discussed; the first can be translated 'I might write' and the second two with indicatives.

Tullius Terentiae suae salutem dicit. si vales bene est; ego valeo. si quid haberem, quod ad te scriberem, facerem id et pluribus verbis et saepius. nunc quae sint negotia vides. ego autem quomodo sim affectus, ex Lepta et Trebatio poteris cognoscere. tu fac ut tuam et Tulliae valetudinem cures. vale.

Vocabulary

quid 'anything' (neuter accusative)
negōtia, negōtiōrum (n. plural)
  'business'
quōmodo 'how'
afficiō, afficere, affēcī, affectum
  'affect'

cognōscō, -nōscere, -nōvī, -nitum
  'find out'
faciō (+ *ut* + subjunctive) *can also mean*
  'see to it that'
valētūdō, valētūdinis (f.) 'health'
cūrō, cūrāre, cūrāvi, cūrātum 'take care of'

2 Martial 13.45: the poet sends a humble gift of chickens (first century AD). Note the dative of possession in the first line: *nōbīs essent* + nominative = *habērēmus* + accusative

Si Libycae nobis volucres et Phasides essent,
    acciperes; at nunc accipe chortis aves.

Vocabulary

Libycus, -a, -um 'Libyan' (the 'Libyan
  bird' was a guinea fowl)
volucer, volucris (f.) 'bird'
Phāsis, *gen.* Phāsidis 'Colchian' (the
  'Colchian bird' was a pheasant)

at 'but'
chōrs, chōrtis (f.) 'farmyard'
avis, avis, avium (f.) 'bird'

3 Martial 6.30: a delayed gift earns the giver no gratitude (first century AD). In line 6 note the omission of *ut*: thus *vīs dīcam* = *velīs ut dīcam* (cf. chapter 28.3).

Sex sestertia si statim dedisses,
cum dixti mihi 'sume, tolle, dono',
deberem tibi, Paete, pro ducentis.
at nunc cum dederis diu moratus,
post septem, puto, vel novem Kalendas,
vis dicam tibi veriora veris?
sex sesteria, Paete, perdidisti.

Vocabulary

sēstertia, sēstertiōrum (n. plural)
  'thousand sesterces'
dīxtī = dīxistī
sūmō, sūmere, sūmpsī, sūmptum 'take'
tollō *can also mean* 'carry away'
dōnō, dōnāre, dōnāvī, dōnātum 'give'
dēbeō, dēbēre, dēbuī, dēbitum
  'owe', 'feel gratitude'
prō (+ ablative) 'for'
ducentī, ducentae, ducenta
  'two hundred' (thousand sesterces)

at 'but'
post (+ accusative) 'after'
putō, putāre, putāvī, putātum 'think'
novem (indeclinable) 'nine'
vel 'or'
Kalendae, Kalendārum (f. plural)
  'festival on the first day of the
  month' (here effectively 'month')
perdō, perdere, perdidī, perditum
  'waste'

50.4 Vocabulary to Learn

Verbs

cōgitō, cōgitāre, cōgitāvī, cōgitātum   'think'
cūrō, cūrāre, cūrāvī, cūrātum   'take care (of)' (object in accusative despite English 'of')
līberō, līberāre, līberāvī, līberātum   'free'
putō, putāre, putāvī, putātum   'think'
servō, servāre, servāvī, servātum   'save'

Nouns

dīvitiae, dīvitiārum (f. plural)   'wealth'
dōnum, dōnī (n.)   'gift'
inimīcus, inimīcī (m.)   'enemy' (*inimīcus* is a personal enemy; *hostēs* are a public enemy, the other side in a war)

Adjective

summus, summa, summum   'very great'

Conjunctions

nisī   'if not', 'unless'
sī   'if'
vel   'or'

51.1 Conjugation of *Fīō*

The verb *fīō* is in effect the passive of *faciō* in the present, future, and imperfect tenses (i.e. those tenses formed from the first two principal parts); its principal parts are therefore *fīō, fierī, factus sum*. Strictly speaking *fīō* is not very irregular, for nearly all its forms can be formed regularly from the principal parts if one classes it as a mixed conjugation partially deponent verb. Nevertheless this formation process is tricky enough that *fīō* is normally classed with the irregular verbs.

	Indicative	Subjunctive
Present	fīō	fīam
	fīs	fīās
	fit	fīat
	fīmus	fīāmus
	fītis	fīātis
	fīunt	fīant
Future	fīam	
	fīēs	
	fīet	
	fīēmus	
	fīētis	
	fīent	
Perfect	factus, -a, -um sum	factus, -a, -um sim
	factus, -a, -um es	factus, -a, -um sīs
	factus, -a, -um est	factus, -a, -um sit
	factī, -ae, -a sumus	factī, -ae, -a sīmus
	factī, -ae, -a estis	factī, -ae, -a sītis
	factī, -ae, -a sunt	factī, -ae, -a sint
Imperfect	fīēbam	fierem
	fīēbās	fierēs
	fīēbat	fieret
	fīēbāmus	fierēmus
	fīēbātis	fierētis
	fīēbant	fierent

	Indicative	Subjunctive
Pluperfect	factus, -a, -um eram	factus, -a, -um essem
	factus, -a, -um erās	factus, -a, -um essēs
	factus, -a, -um erat	factus, -a, -um esset
	factī, -ae, -a erāmus	factī, -ae, -a essēmus
	factī, -ae, -a erātis	factī, -ae, -a essētis
	factī, -ae, -a erant	factī, -ae, -a essent
Future perfect	factus, -a, -um erō	
	factus, -a, -um eris	
	factus, -a, -um erit	
	factī, -ae, -a erimus	
	factī, -ae, -a eritis	
	factī, -ae, -a erunt	

Imperative	–
Present infinitive	fierī
Future infinitive	factum īrī
Perfect infinitive	factus, -a, -um esse
Present participle	–
Future participle	–
Perfect participle	factus, -a, -um
Gerundive	faciendus, -a, -um

51.2 Use of *Fīō*

In addition to the 'be made', 'be done' meanings that come with being the passive of *faciō*, *fīō* can mean 'become' or 'come to be'; when it has these meanings it takes a complement in the nominative, like the verb 'be'.

rēgīna fiet 'she will become queen'
cīvis factus est 'he became a citizen'
fiat lūx 'let there be light' (*lūx, lūcis* (f.) 'light') (literally 'may light come to be')

Practice

A Translate:

1 hic puer magister aut poeta fiet.
2 ergo volo rex fieri.
3 heri autem factus sum pater.
4 agricola fieri nolo.
5 si ille rex fiat, bene regamur.
6 cum victi essent, servi facti sunt.
7 si ille rex esset, bene regeremur.
8 si ille rex factus esset, bene recti essemus.

B Translate into Latin:

1 Humans, however, do not become gods.
2 Therefore my brother has become a farmer.
3 The captured men will become slaves or be killed.
4 I want to become a poet.
5 These boys, however, are becoming men.

6 Therefore his writings will become immortal.
7 May our town become a big city!
8 I shall never become king.
9 May the walls of the town become big.
10 The king has become a god.

51.3 Conditional Clauses Continued

The straightforward conditional sentences seen in the last chapter are not very common in Latin, for there are a number of complications that frequently occur. The most common of these are the following:

Order of Clauses
The if-clause does not necessarily come before the main clause of a conditional sentence; in both English and Latin the main clause often precedes.

fēlīx esset sī Rōmae esset. 'He would be happy if he were in Rome.'

Negatives
A negative in the main clause of a conditional sentence is expressed with *nōn* in all types of condition. But a negative in the subordinate clause (the if-clause) combines with the *sī* to produce *nisī* 'if not', which is often best translated 'unless'.

fēlīx numquam est nisī Rōmae est. 'He is never happy unless he is in Rome.' / 'He is never happy if he is not in Rome.'

Mixed Conditions
Sometimes, both in English and Latin, a conditional sentence has one clause in present time and the other in past time; this can occur with either indicative or subjunctive conditions.

sī Rōmam īvit, nōn est hīc. 'If he has gone to Rome, he is not here.' (indicative mixed: past + present simple)
sī hīc est, Rōmam nōn īvit. 'If he is here, he has not gone to Rome.' (indicative mixed: present + past simple)
sī Rōmam īvisset, nōn esset hīc. 'If he had gone to Rome, he would not be here.' (subjunctive mixed: past + present contrary to fact)
sī hīc esset, Rōmam nōn īvisset. 'If he were here, he would not have gone to Rome.' (subjunctive mixed: present + past contrary to fact)

Future Perfect

If the action of the if-clause of a future indicative (= future more vivid) condition logically occurs before the action of the main clause, the future perfect is used in the if-clause. This is the same phenomenon we have seen in temporal clauses; see chapter 47.

sī Rōmam īverit, diū manēbit. 'If he goes to Rome, he will stay a long time.'

Imperatives

Sometimes the main clause of a future indicative (= future more vivid) condition does not actually have a future indicative, but rather an imperative, since imperatives inherently refer to future time.

cape illum sī vēnerit. 'Capture that man if he comes.' (future more vivid condition composed of imperative + future perfect indicative)

Practice

C Without translating, indicate the following for each sentence: whether the if-clause comes first or second, whether it would be introduced by *sī* or by *nisi* in Latin, and what mood and tense would be used for each verb in Latin.[1]

1 He would have told the police if he had seen the robbery.
2 Do be sensible if you look for the treasure.
3 If you were not involved in the robbery, why did you confess?
4 We would have arrested him today if he weren't already in custody on other charges.
5 If Martha were to say that, she would undoubtedly have a good reason.
6 If you see something, say something!
7 No-one would have known that unless he had seen the murder happen.
8 The children do not play outside unless they have finished their homework.
9 If it were to rain tomorrow, we would have to change our plans.
10 I shall only believe that if I see it.
11 I can never sleep unless it is completely dark.
12 They would have arrested him if he hadn't handed himself in.
13 If Martha is saying that, she has a good reason.
14 If I hadn't seen the robbery, I wouldn't be here to report it.
15 Do not try to move to a foreign country unless you are prepared to do a lot of paperwork.
16 If we had not made a mess last night we would not be cleaning it up now.
17 If I were to succeed in getting a driving licence, I would throw a huge party.
18 If we weren't so old and dignified we would be playing with those toys right now.

[1] Another exercise of this type, with an answer key, can be found in chapter 63.11, exercise P.

D Translate:

1 ille non esset factus rex nisi vir fortis esset.
2 si multi ad oppidum nostrum venerint, urbs fiet.
3 oppidum nostrum non factus esset urbs nisi multi venissent.
4 nisi hostes vicisset, rex noster non factus esset magnus.
5 rex noster magnus non fiet nisi hostes vicerit.
6 iuva nos si rex factus eris.
7 si reges facti erimus, cives bene regemus.
8 numquam te laudabo nisi me iuveris.
9 numquam te laudavissem nisi me iuvisses.
10 voca me si illum videris.
11 nisi multos libros legisses, non factus esses magister.
12 magister non esses nisi multos libros legisses.
13 non fies magister nisi multos libros legeris.
14 nisi mihi pecuniam dederis, equus meus non fiet tuus.
15 si equum meum inveneris, dic mihi.

16 nisi ab hostibus victi essemus, servi non facti essemus.
17 servus non fies nisi ab hostibus victus eris.
18 nisi immortalis factus esset, mortuus esset.
19 nisi immortales facti erimus, moriemur.
20 nisi morati essent Romae, domi essent.
21 nisi morati essent Romae, domum ivissent.
22 nisi morati sunt Romae, domi sunt.
23 nisi morantur Romae, domi sunt.
24 eum non audires nisi loqueretur.
25 eum non audivisses nisi locutus esset.
26 moenia refecissemus si saxa ferre potuissemus.
27 moenia reficeremus si saxa ferre possemus.
28 nisi milites hortatus eris, hostes non vincent.
29 nisi milites hortatus esses, hostes non vicissent.

E Translate into Latin:

1 Unless he becomes a teacher he will not be happy.
2 If he had not become a teacher he would not have been happy.
3 I would love my brother if he had not carried off my wealth.
4 I shall never love my brother unless he returns my wealth.

5 I would not love you if you were not my brother.
6 We would follow him if he were our king.
7 We shall follow him if he becomes our king.
8 We would follow him if he should become our king.

9 We would have followed him if he had been our king.

10 I would not be helping you if you were not helping me.

11 I would not have helped you if you had not helped me.

12 I shall not help you if you do not help me.

13 Unless that man leads the soldiers, they will be defeated.

14 If that man had not led the soldiers, they would have been defeated.

15 Unless that man should lead the soldiers, they would be defeated.

16 If that man weren't leading the soldiers, they would be being defeated.

17 The soldiers were always defeated, unless that man led them.

18 Unless the farmer has sold the sheep, they are in this field.

19 If the farmer hadn't sold the sheep, they would have been in this field.

20 If the farmer hadn't sold the sheep, they would be in this field.

51.4 Reading Practice

1 Cicero, *Epistulae ad familiares* 16.13 (adapted): Cicero (M. Tullius Cicero) writes to his secretary Tiro, who is ill (53 BC).

Tullius Tironi salutem dicit. omnia a te data esse mihi putabo, si te valentem videro. summa cura exspectabam adventum Andrici, quem ad te miseram. si me diligis, cura ut valeas et ad nos venias cum te bene confirmaris. vale.

Vocabulary

cūra, cūrae (f.) 'anxiety'	dīligō, dīligere, dīlēxī, dīlēctum
exspectō, -āre, -āvī, -ātum 'wait for'	'be fond of'
adventus, adventūs (m.) 'arrival'	cōnfirmāris = cōnfirmāveris, *from*
Andrīcus, Andrīcī (m.) *name*	cōnfirmō, -āre, -āvī, -ātum 'recover'
of the letter carrier	

2 Cicero, *Epistulae ad familiares* 14.8 (adapted): Cicero writes to his wife in 47 BC.

Tullius Terentiae suae salutem dicit. si vales, bene est; ego valeo. valetudinem tuam velim ut cures diligentissime. nam mihi et scriptum et nuntiatum est, te in febrem subito incidisse. quia celeriter me fecisti de Caesaris epistula certiorem, fecisti mihi gratum. item posthac, si quid opus erit, si quid acciderit novi, cura ut sciam. cura ut valeas. vale.

Vocabulary

valētūdō, valētūdinis (f.) 'health'

nūntio, nūntiāre, nūntiāvī, nūntiātum
  'report orally'

febris, febris, febrium (f.) 'fever'

subitō 'suddenly'

incidō, incidere, incidī, – 'fall into'

certiōrem faciō 'inform' (literally 'make
  more certain')

item 'also'

posthāc 'afterwards'

**quid (neuter nominative singular)
  'any', 'anything'**

opus, operis (n.) 'need'

accidō, accidere, accidī, – 'happen'

novī *translate as if it were* novum

3 Vulgate version of the Bible, Genesis 1:1–5 (adapted): the creation of the world
(translated in the fourth century AD from a much earlier Hebrew version).

In principio creavit deus caelum et terram; terra autem erat inanis et vacua, et
tenebrae erant super faciem abyssi, et spiritus dei ferebatur super aquas, dixitque
deus 'fiat lux' et facta est lux, et vidit deus lucem quod esset bona, et divisit lucem ac
tenebras, appellavitque lucem diem et tenebras noctem, factusque est dies unus
vespere et mane.

Vocabulary

prīncipium, prīncipiī (n.) 'beginning'

creō, creāre, creāvī, creātum 'create'

caelum, caelī (n.) 'heaven'

terra, terrae (f.) 'earth'

inānis, ināne 'empty'

vacuus, vacua, vacuum 'vacant'

**tenebrae, tenebrārum (f. plural)
  'darkness'**

super (+ accusative) 'upon'

faciēs, faciēī (f.) 'face', 'surface'

abyssus, abyssī (f.) 'abyss'

spīritus, spīritūs (m.) 'spirit'

lūx, lūcis (f.) 'light'

quod esset 'that it was'

dīvidō, dīvidere, dīvīsī, dīvīsum 'divide'

ac 'and'

appellō, -āre, -āvī, -ātum 'call'

ūnus, ūna, ūnum 'one'

vesper, vesperis (m.) 'evening'

māne (indeclinable) 'morning'

4 Catullus 13.1–8: an invitation to a poor man's dinner (first century BC). 'Full of
cobwebs' implies 'empty of anything else'.

Cenabis bene, mi Fabulle, apud me
paucis, si tibi di favent, diebus,
si tecum attuleris bonam atque magnam
cenam, non sine candida puella
et vino et sale et omnibus cachinnis.
haec si, inquam, attuleris, venuste noster,
cenabis bene; nam tui Catulli
plenus sacculus est aranearum.

Vocabulary

cēnō, cēnāre, cēnāvī, cēnātum 'dine'

mī *is the vocative of* meus

apud (+ accusative) 'at the house of'

dī = dei

faveō, favēre, fāvī, fautum (+ dative)
   'favour'

cēna, cēnae (f.) 'dinner'

candidus, -a, -um 'pretty'

vīnum, vīnī (n.) 'wine'

sāl, salis (m.) 'salt'

cachinnus, cachinnī (m.) 'laugh'

inquam 'I tell you'

venustus, -a, -um 'charming'

plēnus, -a, -um 'full'

sacculus, sacculī (m.) 'purse'

arānea, arāneae (f.) 'cobweb'

51.5 Vocabulary to Learn

Verb

fīō, fierī, factus sum   'become', 'be made', 'be done'

52.1 Declension of *Iste* and *Ipse*

Latin has a relatively large group of words that can function either as adjectives or as pronouns. We have seen *quis* 'who?', 'which?', *hic* 'this', *ille* 'that', and *is* 'he', 'this', 'that', but there are also a number of others, including *iste* 'that of yours' and *ipse* '-self'. These two are declined as follows; note the similarity to the declension of *ille*.

British Case Order

Iste	Singular			Plural		
	Masculine	Feminine	Neuter	Masculine	Feminine	Neuter
Nom.	iste	ista	istud	istī	istae	ista
Voc.	–	–	–	–	–	–
Acc.	istum	istam	istud	istōs	istās	ista
Gen.	istīus	istīus	istīus	istōrum	istārum	istōrum
Dat.	istī	istī	istī	istīs	istīs	istīs
Abl.	istō	istā	istō	istīs	istīs	istīs

Ipse	Singular			Plural		
	Masculine	Feminine	Neuter	Masculine	Feminine	Neuter
Nom.	ipse	ipsa	ipsum	ipsī	ipsae	ipsa
Voc.	–	–	–	–	–	–
Acc.	ipsum	ipsam	ipsum	ipsōs	ipsās	ipsa
Gen.	ipsīus	ipsīus	ipsīus	ipsōrum	ipsārum	ipsōrum
Dat.	ipsī	ipsī	ipsī	ipsīs	ipsīs	ipsīs
Abl.	ipsō	ipsā	ipsō	ipsīs	ipsīs	ipsīs

Ancient Case Order

Iste	Singular			Plural		
	Masculine	Feminine	Neuter	Masculine	Feminine	Neuter
Nom.	iste	ista	istud	istī	istae	ista
Gen.	istīus	istīus	istīus	istōrum	istārum	istōrum
Dat.	istī	istī	istī	istīs	istīs	istīs
Acc.	istum	istam	istud	istōs	istās	ista
Abl.	istō	istā	istō	istīs	istīs	istīs

Ipse	Singular			Plural		
	Masculine	Feminine	Neuter	Masculine	Feminine	Neuter
Nom.	ipse	ipsa	ipsum	ipsī	ipsae	ipsa
Gen.	ipsīus	ipsīus	ipsīus	ipsōrum	ipsārum	ipsōrum
Dat.	ipsī	ipsī	ipsī	ipsīs	ipsīs	ipsīs
Acc.	ipsum	ipsam	ipsum	ipsōs	ipsās	ipsa
Abl.	ipsō	ipsā	ipsō	ipsīs	ipsīs	ipsīs

52.2 Use of *Iste* and *Ipse*

Iste can be used for something connected with the addressee, and/or for something about which a disparaging comment is made: *iste equus* 'that horse of yours', *istud* 'that thing of yours'.

Ipse is usually translated with English 'himself', 'herself', 'themselves', 'myself', 'yourself', 'ourselves', 'yourselves', but nevertheless it is sharply distinct from *sē*. *Ipse* is intensive, meaning that it emphasizes the word to which it is attached; *sē* is reflexive, meaning that it refers back to the subject of the sentence. *Ipse* can be used for any of the three grammatical persons ('I/we', 'you', 'he/she/it/they'), while *sē* belongs exclusively to the third person ('him', 'her', 'them') – for reflexive 'myself', 'ourselves', 'yourself' and 'yourselves' the ordinary personal pronouns *mē, nōs, tē, vōs* are used. *Ipse* can be either a pronoun or an adjective, with the same translation in either case, but *sē* can only be a pronoun. The possessive of *ipse* is the genitive *ipsīus* ('of himself' etc.), but the possessive of *sē* is the adjective *suus, -a, -um* ('his own', 'her own', 'their own'). *Ipse* always means '-self'; *sē* is sometimes (in indirect statement) equivalent to English 'he' etc. rather than 'himself' etc.

Reflexive	Intensive
sē vīdērunt. 'They saw themselves.'	*ipsī vīdērunt.* 'They themselves saw (it).' *ipsum vidērunt.* 'They saw (the man) himself.'
rēx sē vīdit. 'The king saw himself.'	*rēx ipse vīdit.* 'The king himself saw (it).' *rēgem ipse vīdit.* 'He himself saw the king.' *rēgem ipsum vīdit.* 'He saw the king himself.'
rēgem suum vīdērunt. 'They saw their own king.'	*rēgem ipsum vīdērunt.* 'They saw the king himself.'
fīliōs suōs docet. 'He teaches his own sons.'	*fīliōs ipsōs docet.* 'He teaches the sons themselves.' *fīliōs ipsīus docet.* 'He teaches the sons of that man himself.' *fīliōs ipse docet.* 'He teaches his sons himself.'
dīxit sē āfuisse. 'He said he had been away.' (man away is same as speaker)	*dīxit ipsum āfuisse.* 'He said that that man himself had been away' (man away is *not* the same as the speaker)
in aquā mē vīdī. 'I saw myself in the water.'	*ipse aquam vīdī.* 'I myself saw the water.'
vīdistīne tē? 'Did you see yourself?'	*vīdistīne ipsum?* 'Did you see the man himself?' *vīdistīne ipse?* 'Did you yourself see (it)?'

Practice

A State whether the underlined words are reflexives or intensives and whether they would be expressed in Latin with *sē, ipse,* or a personal pronoun.

1 She loved herself dearly.
2 She came herself to see it.
3 I love myself.
4 I myself discovered this.
5 They made it all themselves.
6 They admired themselves greatly.
7 He wrote this himself.
8 The baby cannot feed itself.
9 If you want more food, help yourself!
10 Do not kill yourself!
11 They expressed themselves well.
12 They said so themselves.
13 We saw the king himself.
14 The king saw it himself.
15 The king saw himself.
16 We helped ourselves.
17 We ourselves helped them.
18 I heard the man himself.
19 I myself shall do it.
20 I want to do it myself.
21 She knew herself very well.
22 She knew it herself.
23 The queen gave it to me herself.
24 I got this dress from the queen herself.
25 The queen herself gave it to me.
26 The queen cannot dress herself.

B Translate:

1 dominam suam amat.
2 dominam ipsam amat.
3 ipsam amat.
4 se amat.
5 ipse amat.
6 istam amat.
7 iste amat.
8 ipsos regunt.

9   se regunt.
10 ipsi regunt.
11 isti regunt.
12 urbes suas regunt.
13 urbem ipsam regunt.
14 istos regunt.
15 donum ipsi dederunt. (2 ways)
16 donum sibi dederunt.

C Translate into Latin:

1 They themselves praised us with many verses.
2 They praised themselves with many verses.
3 They praised the king himself with many verses.
4 They praised the man himself with many verses.
5 They praised that man of yours with many verses.
6 That man of yours praised us with many verses.
7 They praised their own king with many verses.

8   With swords we shall defend the queen ourselves.
9   With swords we shall defend ourselves.
10 With swords we shall defend the queen herself.
11 The king himself gave me this horse.
12 I myself gave this horse to the king.
13 I gave that horse of yours to the king himself.
14 I gave the horse to that man of yours.

D Translate:

1 si aurum ipsi attulerint, ab omnibus laudabuntur.
2 si aurum isti attulissent, ab omnibus laudati essent.
3 ab omnibus laudemini si aurum ipsi afferatis.
4 a nullo laudabor nisi aurum ipse attulero.
5 si servus Romani civis liberatus est, civis Romanus ipse factus est.
6 si servi istius liberati erunt, cives Romani fient.

7   ipse civis Romanus numquam factus essem nisi servus fuissem.
8   si servus esses, civis Romanus ipse fieri posses.
9   si iste fiat servus, civis Romanus fieri possit.
10 servi vestri cives Romani non fient nisi ipsi cives Romani facti eritis.
11 ipsi dixerunt se argentum abstulisse.

12 isti dixerunt se argentum regis ipsius abstulisse.

13 iste dixit magistrum ipsum argentum auferre.

14 ipse dixi istum argentum auferre, sed me non audivisti.

E Translate into Latin:

1 If we do that thing of yours, our friends themselves will become (our personal) enemies.

2 If you had not done that, you yourself would have become our (personal) enemy.

3 Slaves carry our books. If we ourselves were slaves, we would carry books.

4 Unless that man of yours becomes a slave, he will not carry books.

5 Slaves do not carry their own books; they carry the books of their masters.

6 That man of yours carries not his own book but the book of the master himself.

52.3 Reading Practice

1 *Corpus Inscriptionum Latinarum* IV.8364 (adapted): graffiti from the walls of Pompeii (first century AD).

Secundus Primae suae ubique ipse salutem dicit. rogo, domina, ut me ames.

Vocabulary

ubīque 'everywhere'

2 Vulgate version of the Bible, John 1:1–5 (adapted): a metaphysical account of creation (translated in the fourth century AD from an earlier Greek version).

In principio erat verbum, et verbum erat apud deum, et deus erat verbum. sic erat in principio apud deum: omnia ab ipso facta sunt, et sine ipso factum est nihil quod factum est; in ipso vita erat, et vita erat lux hominum, et lux in tenebris lucebat, et tenebrae eam non conprehenderunt.

Vocabulary

prīncipium, prīncipiī (n.) 'beginning'
apud (+ accusative) 'with'
sīc 'thus', 'in this way'
lūx, lūcis (f.) 'light'

tenebrae, tenebrārum (f. plural) 'darkness'
lūceō, lūcēre, lūxī, – 'shine'
comprehendō, -hendere, -hendī, -hēnsum 'comprehend', 'grasp', 'contain'

3   Catullus 14.1–7: the poet is not grateful for the gift of a book of bad poetry (first century BC). To love someone more than one's own eyes was in Latin an expression of great affection.

Ni te plus oculis meis amarem,
iucundissime Calve, munere isto
odissem te odio Vatiniano:
nam quid feci ego quidve sum locutus,
cur me tot male perderes poetis?
isti di mala multa dent clienti
qui tantum tibi misit impiorum.

Vocabulary

nī = nisī

oculus, oculī (m.) 'eye'

iūcundus, -a, -um 'pleasant'

mūnus, mūneris (n.) 'gift'

ōdī, ōdisse, ōsum 'hate' (perfect
   in form but present in
   meaning)

Vatīniānus, -a, -um 'like that of
   Vatinius' (i.e. in this case, very
   great)

-ve 'or' (translate before the word to
   which it is attached)

cūr perderēs 'to justify your destroying
   me'

istī *goes with* clientī

dī = dei

cliēns, clientis (m.) 'inferior friend'

tantum impiōrum 'so much shameless
   writing' (literally 'so much of
   shameless (poets)')

4   Martial 8.40: the poet threatens a wooden statue of the god Priapus that protects the grove from which he takes his firewood (first century AD).

Non horti neque palmitis beati
sed rari nemoris, Priape, custos,
ex quo natus es et potes renasci,
furaces moneo manus repellas
et silvam domini focis reserves:
si defecerit haec, et ipse lignum es.

Vocabulary

hortus, hortī (m.) 'garden'

palmes, palmitis (m.) 'vineyard'

beātus, beāta, beātum 'fertile'

rārus, rāra, rārum 'sparse'

nemus, nemoris (n.) 'grove',
   'wood-lot'

custōs, custōdis (m.) 'guardian'

nāscor, nāscī, nātus sum
   'be born'

renāscor (like *nāscor*) 'be reborn'

fūrāx, *gen.* fūrācis 'thieving'

moneō: *supply* tē *and* ut *here*

repellō, repellere, reppulī, repulsum
   'repel', 'keep off'

focus, focī (m.) 'hearth'
reservō, -āre, -āvī, -ātum
   'preserve'

dēficiō, dēficere, dēfēcī, dēfectum 'run
  out'
lignum, lignī (n.) 'wood'

52.4 Vocabulary to Learn

Adjectives/Pronouns
ipse, ipsa, ipsum   '-self'
iste, ista, istud   'that of yours'

53.1 *Colloquia Monacensia–Einsidlensia* 5a–6a (adapted)

Two visits to a banker (second or third century AD):

BANKER: domine, quid velis?

LUCIUS: habesne pecuniam vacuam?

BANKER: quid vis mutuari?

LUCIUS: si habes, da mihi quinque sestertia.

BANKER: etsi non habuissem, undecumque explicavissem.

LUCIUS: pignusne vis?

BANKER: absit, nihil tibi dandum est. cave autem, scribens te accepisse.

LUCIUS: sic faciam; quibus usuris?

BANKER: usuris quas vis.[1]

LUCIUS: cavi.

BANKER: gratias tibi ago; signa.

LUCIUS: signavi.

BANKER: numero numera.

LUCIUS: numeravi.

BANKER: proba.

LUCIUS: probavi.

BANKER: sicut pecuniam accepisti, probam reddas.

LUCIUS: cum eam tibi reddidero, satisfaciam.

    (*later*)

BANKER: bono die venisti.

LUCIUS: sic veni.

BANKER: attulistine pecuniam? dedistine servo meo?

LUCIUS: dedi.

BANKER: caruisti.

LUCIUS: estne aliud mihi faciendum?

BANKER: valendum est tibi.

---

[1] This startling flexibility is not to be taken at face value; it may be a display of politeness when a standard interest rate was known to both parties, or an indication to the original user of this book that he needed to fill in a number here.

Vocabulary

vacuus, vacua, vacuum 'available'

mūtuor, mūtuārī, mūtuātus sum
'borrow'

sēstertia, sēstertiōrum (n. plural)
'thousand sesterces'

etsī 'even if' (*et* 'even' + *sī*)

undecumque 'from somewhere or other'

explicō, -āre, -āvī, -ātum 'sort out'

pignus, pignoris (n.) 'security'
(something valuable kept by the
lender to ensure repayment)

absit 'heaven forbid!' (literally 'may (the
thought) be absent!')

**caveō, cavēre, cāvī, cautum 'give
a guarantee'**

ūsūrae, ūsūrārum (f. plural) 'rate of
interest'

grātiae, grātiārum (f. plural) 'thanks'

agō *can also mean* 'give'

signō, signāre, signāvī, signātum 'seal'
(i.e. impress a personal sealing ring
on melted wax to identify the
agreement as yours)

numerus, numerī (m.) 'number'

**numerō, -āre, -āvī, -ātum 'count it
out'**

**probō, probāre, probāvī, probātum
'examine and approve'** (i.e. check
that the coins are not counterfeit or
debased)

sīcut 'just as'

probus, proba, probum 'correct', 'in
good coins'

satisfaciō (like *faciō*) 'give satisfaction'

bonus 'auspicious'

careō, carēre, caruī, – 'be discharged'

aliud (n.) 'something else', 'anything
else'

53.2 Translate into Latin

GAIUS: Lucius, I need money; unless I am allowed to borrow from you yourself,
I shall have to go to a banker.

LUCIUS: What would you like to borrow?

GAIUS: I need four or five thousand sesterces.

LUCIUS: Heaven forbid! Even if I had that (sum of money) of yours, I would not be
giving (it) to you. Are you not (*attach the* -ne *to the* nōn) ashamed when you ask
such things?

GAIUS: I cannot do anything else; I have to find the money, since I want to become
quaestor. When I become quaestor I shall have wealth, and I shall return the
money to you at (= *with*) a great rate of interest, and I shall give satisfaction.

LUCIUS: Will you give a guarantee and seal (it)? Will you return the money in good
coins?

GAIUS: Yes (*literally 'I shall do in this way'*), provided that you give me the money now.

LUCIUS: I will not do (it), since I do not think (*use* arbitror *not* cōgitō) that you will
become quaestor.

GAIUS: You have become my enemy, and you will be sorry when I am quaestor!

Additional Vocabulary

nummulārius, nummulāriī (m.) 'banker'
quaestor, quaestōris (m.) 'quaestor'

53.3 Virgil, *Aeneid* 1.60–75

Continuation of the passage in chapter 48, where it is explained what damage the winds do when free. Note the repeated use of the *-īs* accusative plural ending of third-declension *i*-stem nouns.

Sed pater omnipotens speluncis abdidit atris
hoc metuens molemque et montis insuper altos
imposuit, regemque dedit qui foedere certo
et premere et laxas sciret dare iussus habenas.
ad quem tum Iuno supplex his vocibus usa est:
'Aeole, namque tibi divum pater atque hominum rex
et mulcere dedit fluctus et tollere vento,
gens inimica mihi Tyrrhenum navigat aequor
Ilium in Italiam portans victosque penatis:
incute vim ventis summersasque obrue puppis,
aut age diversos et dissice corpora ponto.
sunt mihi bis septem praestanti corpore Nymphae,
quarum quae forma pulcherrima Deiopea,
conubio iungam stabili propriamque dicabo,
omnis ut tecum meritis pro talibus annos
exigat et pulchra faciat te prole parentem.'

Vocabulary

omnipotēns, *gen.* omnipotentis 'all-powerful'
spēlunca, spēluncae (f.) 'cave'
abdō, abdere, abdidī, abditum 'confine' (understood object is 'the winds')
āter, ātra, ātrum 'black'
metuō, metuere, metuī, – 'fear'
mōlēs, mōlis, mōlium (f.) 'massive structure'
-que . . . -que 'both . . . and'
mōns, montis, montium (m.) 'mountain'
īnsuper 'on top (of the winds)'

altus, alta, altum 'high'
impōnō (like *pōnō*) 'put'
foedere certō 'under fixed rules'
premō, premere, pressī, pressum 'tighten'
laxās dare 'loosen'
iubeō, iubēre, iussī, iussum 'order'
habēna, habēnae (f.) 'reins' (treating the winds as horses)
tum 'then'
Iūnō, Iūnōnis (f.) 'Juno'
supplex, *gen.* supplicis 'as a suppliant'
vōx, vōcis (f.) 'word'

Aeolus, Aeolī (m.) *name of the king of*
  the winds
namque '(I speak to you) since'
dīvum = deōrum
mulceō, mulcēre, mulsī, mulsum 'soothe'
dō *can also mean* 'grant'
flūctus, flūctūs (m.) 'wave'
tollō *can also mean* 'stir up'
ventus, ventī (m.) 'wind'
gēns, gentis, gentium (f.) 'clan, people'
inimīcus, -a, -um 'hateful'
Tyrrhēnus, -a, -um 'near Rome'
nāvigō, -āre, -āvī, -ātum 'sail'
aequor, aequoris (n.) 'sea'
Īlium, Īliī (n.) 'Troy'
Italia, Italiae (f.) 'Italy'
portō, portāre, portāvī, portātum 'carry'
penātēs, penātium (m. plural) 'gods'
incutiō, incutere, incussī, incussum
  'instil (something in accusative) into
  (something in dative)'
vim 'force' (accusative singular)
summersās obrue 'overwhelm and
  submerge' (imperative)

puppis, puppis, puppium (f.) 'ship'
dīversōs agō 'drive apart'
dis(s)iciō, disicere, disiēcī, disiectum
  'scatter'
corpus *can also mean both* 'corpse'
  and 'physical beauty'
pontō 'on the sea'
sunt mihi + nominative = *habeō* +
  accusative
bis septem 'fourteen' (literally 'twice
  seven')
praestāns, *gen.* praestantis 'outstanding'
nympha, nymphae (f.) 'nymph'
fōrmā (ablative) 'in form'
cōnubiō 'in marriage'
iungō, iungere, iūnxī, iūnctum 'join'
stabilis, stabile 'stable', 'long-lasting'
propriam dicābō 'I shall declare her to
  be your own'
meritum, meritī (n.) 'merit'
prō (+ ablative) 'in recompense for'
exigō, exigere, exēgī, exāctum 'pass'
prōlēs, prōlis, prōlium (f.) 'offspring'
parēns, parentis (m.) 'father'

A possible prose order of the above would be:

Hoc metuens (Iuppiter) molemque et montis altos insuper (ventis) imposuit, regemque (eis) dedit qui foedere certo sciret et premere habenas (eorum) et (habenas) laxas dare iussus. ad quem Iuno supplex his vocibus tum usa est: 'Aeole, namque tibi pater divum atque rex hominum dedit et fluctus mulcere et (fluctus) vento tollere, gens inimica mihi Tyrrhenum aequor navigat, Ilium victosque penatis in Italiam portans: vim ventis incute summersasque puppis obrue, aut age (illos) diversos et corpora (eorum) ponto dissice. sunt mihi bis septem nymphae praestanti corpore, quarum (illa) quae forma pulcherrima (est, est) Deiopea: (illam tibi) conubio stabili iungam, propriamque dicabo, ut pro (tuis) talibus meritis omnis annos (suos) tecum exigat et pulchra prole te parentem faciat.'

54 | Indirect Questions

54.1 Indirect Questions

We have so far seen two kinds of indirect speech: indirect statement (accusative + infinitive) and indirect commands (*ut* + subjunctive). There is also a third type of indirect speech, indirect questions. Indirect questions take the subjunctive like indirect commands, but they are introduced by an interrogative word rather than by *ut* or *nē*; if they are negative *nōn* is used. The Latin subjunctive is translated with an English indicative (usually in the same tense; see 54.3 below).

Direct	Indirect
quis adest? 'Who is present?'	*rogāvī quis adesset.* 'I asked who was present.'
cūr Rōmam īvit? 'Why did he go to Rome?'	*rogāvī cūr Rōmam īvisset.* 'I asked why he had gone to Rome.'

Practice

A Translate:

1 isti rogaverunt quis venisset.
2 isti rogabunt quis venerit.
3 ipsi rogant quis veniat.
4 ipsi rogabant quis veniret.
5 iste rogat cur discesserimus.
6 iste rogavit cur discessissemus.
7 ipse rogabit cur discedamus.
8 ipse rogabat cur discederemus.
9 ipse rogavisti ubi essemus.
10 ipsi rogavistis ubi fuissemus.
11 iste rogabit ubi fuerimus.
12 iste rogabit ubi simus.

54.2 Sequence of Tenses

The tense of a subordinate verb in Latin is determined by sequence of tenses, but the sequence rules we have seen need one modification in the case of indirect questions. In chapter 46 we saw the following diagram, which applies to all types of sequence *except* that of indirect questions:

Relative time of **subordinate** clause

		Before the action of the main clause	After or at the same time as the action of the main clause
Tense of **main** verb	Primary	**Subordinate verb is** *perfect* **subjunctive**	**Subordinate verb is** *present* **subjunctive**
	Historic	**Subordinate verb is** *pluperfect* **subjunctive**	**Subordinate verb is** *imperfect* **subjunctive**

But for indirect questions it is crucial to be able to distinguish between present and future, that is between actions at the same time as the main clause and actions later than the main clause: the difference between an original 'Is he here?' and 'Will he be here?' needs to be preserved even when the questions become indirect ('We asked whether he was there' versus 'We asked whether he would be there'). So for indirect questions an original future is indicated with the future participle and a subjunctive of *sum*, necessitating a third column in the diagram:

Relative time of **subordinate** clause

		Before the action of the main clause (original past)	At the same time as the action of the main clause (original present)	After the action of the main clause (original future)
Tense of **main** verb	Primary	**Subordinate verb is** *perfect* **subjunctive**	**Subordinate verb is** *present* **subjunctive**	**Subordinate verb is future participle +** *sim, sīs, sit* . . .
	Historic	**Subordinate verb is** *pluperfect* **subjunctive**	**Subordinate verb is** *imperfect* **subjunctive**	**Subordinate verb is future participle +** *essem, essēs, esset* . . .

Therefore:

Direct	Indirect
quis aderit? 'Who will be present?'	*rogō quis adfutūrus sit.* 'I am asking who will be present.' / 'I am asking who is going to be present.'
	rogāvī quis adfutūrus esset. 'I asked who would be present.' / 'I asked who was going to be present.'
cūr Rōmam veniet? 'Why will he come to Rome?'	*rogō cūr Rōmam ventūrus sit.* 'I am asking why he will come to Rome.' / 'I am asking why he is going to come to Rome.'
	rogāvī cūr Rōmam ventūrus esset. 'I asked why he would come to Rome.' / 'I asked why he was going to come to Rome.'

54.3 English Tenses

The tense of the verb of an indirect question in English is usually the same as the Latin tense, because English shifts the tense of the subordinate verb back when the introductory verb is in the past. This is the same shift that we saw with indirect statement in chapter 19.4, and the diagram of English usage seen there (and reproduced with modifications below) can also be applied to questions. But whereas this feature of English can cause difficulty in translating indirect statements, it is an advantage for indirect questions, where the sequence rules of the two languages largely match.

Original sentence	Indirect question after present tense	Indirect question after past tense
Who ate the fish?	He asks who ate the fish.	He asked who **had eaten** the fish.
Who eats fish?	He asks who eats fish.	He asked who **ate** fish.
Who is eating the fish?	He asks who is eating the fish.	He asked who **was eating** the fish.
Who will eat the fish?	He asks who will eat the fish.	He asked who **would eat** the fish.
Who is going to eat the fish?	He asks who is going to eat the fish.	He asked who **was going** to eat the fish.

Practice

B Translate:

1 rogaverunt quis venturus esset.
2 rogabunt quis venturus sit.
3 rogat cur discessuri simus.
4 rogabat cur discessuri essemus.
5 rogat ubi futura sis.

6 rogavit ubi futura esses.
7 rogabant quem visurus essem.
8 rogant quem visurus sim.
9 rogabit quid facturi simus.
10 rogavit quid facturi essemus.

54.4 *Num*

When the direct version of the question begins with an interrogative word, as in the examples seen so far, the same interrogative word also begins the indirect question. But some direct questions begin with *-ne* rather than an interrogative word, and *-ne* is not used in indirect questions; it has to be replaced by *num*, which is translated with 'whether' or 'if' in English. (Care is needed with the 'if' translation, as this 'if' is completely different from the 'if' that introduces conditional clauses: compare 'I asked him if it had rained' (indirect question) with 'We would have stayed home if it had rained' (conditional).)

Direct	Indirect
cucurritne? 'Did he run?'	*rogāvī num cucurrisset.* 'I asked whether he had run.' / 'I asked if he had run.'
curritne? 'Is he running?'	*rogāvī num curreret.* 'I asked whether he was running.' / 'I asked if he was running.'
curretne? 'Will he run?'	*rogāvī num cursūrus esset.* 'I asked whether he would run.' / 'I asked if he would run.' / 'I asked whether he was going to run.' / 'I asked if he was going to run.'

Practice

C Translate:

1 rogaverunt num venisses.
2 rogant num veneris.
3 rogabant num venturus esses.
4 rogabunt num venias.
5 rogat num discessuri simus.
6 rogavit num discederemus.
7 rogabit num discesserimus.

8 rogabat num discessissemus.
9 rogavi num Romae esset.
10 rogo num Romae futurus sit.
11 rogabam num Romae futurus esset.
12 rogavi num Romae fuisset.

54.5 Other Interrogative Words

We have already seen a range of interrogative words, all of which can be used in indirect questions as well as in direct questions:

-ne (indirect version *num*): used for questions answerable with 'yes' or 'no'
quis 'who?'
quid (neuter of *quis*) 'what?'
quī, quae, quod (adjective) 'which?'
cūr 'why?'
ubi 'where?' (when motion is not involved: *ubi est* 'Where is he?')

There are also a number of other interrogative words not seen so far, including the following:

quō 'to where?', 'where?' (when motion towards a place is involved: *quō currit?* 'Where
    is he running to?', *quō īvit?* 'Where did he go?')
unde 'from where?' (*unde vēnit?* 'Where did he come from?')
quot 'how many?'
quandō 'when?' (only usable in questions and to be clearly distinguished from *cum*
    'when', which is only used in temporal clauses)
quōmodo 'how?'
quantus, -a, -um 'how big?'
utrum . . . an (used for double questions, where *utrum* has no translation and *an* is
    equivalent to 'or': *utrum hoc an illud vīs?* 'Do you want this or that?')

54.6 Introductory Verbs

Indirect questions occur not only after verbs of asking such as *rogō* (and *quaerō, quaerere, quaesīvī, quaesītum*, which also means 'ask') but also after verbs expressing related concepts such as wondering or not knowing. Thus *nesciō num currat* 'I don't know whether he is running' / 'I don't know if he is running' is also an indirect question.

Practice

D Translate:

1 rex quaesivit quot hostes essent.
2 rex quaerit ubi hostes futuri sint.
3 rex quaerebat quanta esset classis
   hostium.
4 quaesivimus quo irent.
5 quaerimus unde venerint.
6 quaerebamus num valeretis.
7 nesciunt quando venturi simus.

8 nesciebant quid faciendum esset.

9 nescient quomodo faciendum sit.

10 nesciverunt ubi essent.

11 quaerit num venire volueris.

12 quaesivit num venire voluisses.

13 quaerit num venire velis.

14 quaesivit num venire velles.

15 rogaverunt quot essemus.

16 rogaverunt quot futuri essemus.

17 rogabunt quot fuerimus.

18 rogabunt quot simus.

19 quaerimus cui id des.

20 quaesivimus cui id daturus esses.

21 quaerimus cui id dederis.

22 quaesivimus cui id dares.

23 quaesivimus cui id dedisses.

24 quaerimus cui id daturus sis.

25 rogavit utrum manere an discedere vellemus.

26 rogabit utrum manere an discedere velimus.

E Translate into Latin:

1 He did not know where we were.

2 He does not know where we were.

3 He did not know where we had come from.

4 He will not know where we have come from.

5 They did not know where we were carrying it to.

6 They will ask where we are carrying it to.

7 They do not know how many sheep we will sell.

8 They asked how many sheep we had sold.

9 I do not know how big your house is.

10 I asked how big his house was going to be.

11 You do not know how the gods must be praised.

12 We shall ask how the gods must be praised.

13 We do not know when the queen will arrive.

14 He asked when the queen would arrive.

15 He does not know whether the slaves have been freed.

16 He asked whether the slaves were being freed.

17 They will ask whether we want to buy or to sell.

18 They asked whether we wanted to buy or to sell.

54.7 Reading Practice

1 *Colloquium Montepessulanum* 7a–b (adapted): setting up a visit to a friend (probably third century AD).

MASTER (*to slave*): scis ubi habitet amicus meus Lucius, vir fortis: antecede me, disce num domi sit, rursus veni, dic mihi ubi sit.

Vocabulary

habitō, -āre, -āvī, -ātum 'live, dwell'
antecēdō, -cēdere, -cessī, -cessum 'go ahead of'
rūrsus 'back'

2 Cicero, *Epistulae ad familiares* 14.9 (adapted): Cicero writes to his wife about his worries in 48 BC. Dolabella (a first-declension masculine, like *agricola*) was the husband of their daughter Tullia. Note that *faciam* is an original deliberative question (*quid faciam?* 'What should I do?').

Tullius Terentiae suae salutem plurimam dicit. ad ceteras meas miserias accessit dolor et de Dolabellae valetudine et de Tulliae. omnino de omnibus rebus quid faciam nescio. tu velim ut tuam et Tulliae valetudinem cures. vale.

Vocabulary

cēterus, -a, -um 'other'	dolor, dolōris (m.) 'sorrow'
miseria, miseriae (f.) 'misery'	**valētūdō, valētūdinis (f.) 'health'**
accēdō, accēdere, accessī, accessum 'be added'	omnīnō 'entirely'

3 Cicero, *Epistulae ad familiares* 14.23 (adapted): Cicero writes to his wife about Caesar in 47 BC. Note that *prōgrediar* and *exspectem* are original deliberative questions ('whether I should advance', etc.)

Tullius Terentiae suae salutem dicit. si vales bene est; ego valeo. reddita mihi tandem est a Caesare epistula satis liberalis, et ipse opinione celerius venturus esse dicitur; cum constituero utrum obviam ei progrediar an hic eum exspectem, faciam te certiorem. velim ut tabellarios mihi quam primum remittas. valetudinem tuam cura diligenter. vale.

Vocabulary

tandem 'finally'	exspectō, -āre, -āvī, -ātum 'wait for'
satis 'reasonably'	certiōrem faciō 'inform'
līberālis, -e 'generous'	tabellārius, tabellāriī (m.) 'letter carrier'
opīniōne celerius 'sooner than (previously) thought'	(one of Cicero's slaves)
cōnstituō, -stituere, -stituī, -stitūtum 'decide'	quam prīmum 'as soon as possible'
obviam (+ dative) 'to meet'	remittō (like *mittō*) 'send back'
	valētūdō, valētūdinis (f.) 'health'

4 Catullus 7 (extract): the poet expresses his love for Lesbia (first century BC).

Quaeris, quot mihi basiationes
tuae, Lesbia, sint satis superque.
. . . quam sidera multa, cum tacet nox,
furtivos hominum vident amores,
tam te basia multa basiare
vesano satis et super Catullost.

Vocabulary

bāsiātiō, bāsiātiōnis (f.) 'kiss'
satis superque 'enough and more than
     enough'
quam multa 'as many . . . as'
sīdus, sīderis (n.) 'star'
taceō, tacēre, tacuī, tacitum 'be silent'
fūrtīvus, -a, -um 'secret'

amor, amōris (m.) 'love affair'
tam multa 'so many'
bāsium, bāsiī (n.) 'kiss'
bāsiō, bāsiāre, bāsiāvī, bāsiātum 'kiss'
vēsānus, -a, -um 'mad (with love)'
Catullōst = Catullō est

5 Catullus 85: the poet reflects on his emotions (first century BC).

Odi et amo. quare id faciam, fortasse requiris:
    nescio, sed fieri sentio et excrucior.

Vocabulary

ōdī, ōdisse, ōsum (perfect in form but
     present in meaning) 'hate'
quārē = cūr
fortasse 'perhaps'

requīrō, requīrere, requīsīvī, requīsītum
     'ask'
excruciō, -āre, -āvī, -ātum 'torture'

6 Martial 9.77 (extract): the best kind of dinner party for a hater of music (first
   century AD).

Quod optimum sit disputat convivium
    facunda Prisci pagina . . .
quod optimum sit quaeritis convivium?
    in quo choraules non erit.

Vocabulary

disputō, -āre, -āvī, -ātum 'discuss'
convīvium, convīviī (n.) 'dinner party'
fācundus, -a, -um 'eloquent'

pāgina, pāginae (f.) 'page' (i.e. writings)
choraulēs, choraulae (m.) 'flute player'

54.8 Vocabulary to Learn

Verbs

audeō, audēre, ausus sum	'dare' (semideponent, i.e. deponent in perfect tenses but not in present, future, or imperfect tenses)
crēdō, crēdere, crēdidī, crēditum (+ dative)	'believe', 'trust'
quaerō, quaerere, quaesīvī, quaesītum	'ask', 'seek'

Nouns

ars, artis, artium (f.)	'art', 'skill'
iūs, iūris (n.)	'right', 'law'

Adjectives

quantus, quanta, quantum	'how big?'
quot (indeclinable)	'how many?'

Adverbs

iterum	'again'
quandō	'when?'
quō	'to where?', 'where?' (with motion towards)
quōmodo	'how?'
unde	'from where?'

Conjunctions

num	'whether', 'if' (in indirect questions)
utrum . . . an	'or' (in double questions)

55 | Numbers

55.1 Declinable Numbers

We have so far seen several numbers, such as *quattuor* 'four' and *quīnque* 'five'. These are indeclinable, so that the same form is used regardless of the gender, number, or case of the items being counted: *quattuor virī vēnērunt* 'four men came', *quattuor puellās vīdī* 'I saw four girls'. But the numbers 'one', 'two', and 'three' inflect: 'one' follows the pronominal declension like *ipse*, 'three' is a third-declension adjective, and 'two' is irregular (it is one of the few Latin remnants of the dual number, which was originally used when referring to two things, with the plural restricted to three or more things).

British Case Order

| | 'One'[1] | | | 'Two' | | | 'Three' | |
	Masc.	Fem.	Neuter	Masc.	Fem.	Neuter	M./F.	Neuter
Nom.	ūnus	ūna	ūnum	duo	duae	duo	trēs	tria
Voc.	–	–	–	–	–	–	–	–
Acc.	ūnum	ūnam	ūnum	duōs/duo	duās	duo	trēs	tria
Gen.	ūnīus	ūnīus	ūnīus	duōrum	duārum	duōrum	trium	trium
Dat.	ūnī	ūnī	ūnī	duōbus	duābus	duōbus	tribus	tribus
Abl.	ūnō	ūnā	ūnō	duōbus	duābus	duōbus	tribus	tribus

Ancient Case Order

| | 'One' | | | 'Two' | | | 'Three' | |
	Masc.	Fem.	Neuter	Masc.	Fem.	Neuter	M./F.	Neuter
Nom.	ūnus	ūna	ūnum	duo	duae	duo	trēs	tria
Gen.	ūnīus	ūnīus	ūnīus	duōrum	duārum	duōrum	trium	trium
Dat.	ūnī	ūnī	ūnī	duōbus	duābus	duōbus	tribus	tribus
Acc.	ūnum	ūnam	ūnum	duōs/duo	duās	duo	trēs	tria
Abl.	ūnō	ūnā	ūnō	duōbus	duābus	duōbus	tribus	tribus

---

[1] 'One' also has a plural; this is not common and inflects regularly: *ūnī, ūnae, ūna*, etc.

Practice

A Translate:

1 duas oves amissas quaero.
2 duobus vel tribus pueris dona dedit.
3 rogavit num tres puellae adessent.
4 duobus gladiis se defendit.
5 argentum unius militis amissum est.
6 uno saxo magno hostem interfecit.
7 cum duabus sororibus hic maneamus.

8 rogaverunt num tria dona haberemus.
9 uni servo imperabo ut te iuvet, non duobus.
10 domus duorum vel trium agricolarum refectae sunt.
11 tres annos Carthagine manebimus.
12 duobus annis Londinio domum veniet.
13 cum tribus amicis advenit.
14 sit unum ius omnibus civibus.

B Translate into Latin:

1 I shall free two or three slaves.
2 How many gifts do you have? – Three.
3 Within three years he will go to Athens.
4 Give that to one of the slaves.
5 The city is defended by two large walls.
6 Come (plural) with two or three girls.

7 How many sisters do you have, one or two?
8 The books of two girls have been found.
9 We stayed in Rome for two years.
10 I persuaded three men with one gift.
11 One of my friends has become a (personal) enemy.
12 When will your two brothers arrive?

55.2 *Alius* and *Alter*

Latin has two words for 'other': in most circumstances *alius* is used, but when 'other' means the other of two (usually 'the other' in English), *alter* is used. Both these words can be pronouns or adjectives; *alius* declines similarly to *iste*, and *alter* similarly to *ipse*.

British Case Order

Alius	Singular			Plural		
	Masculine	**Feminine**	**Neuter**	**Masculine**	**Feminine**	**Neuter**
Nom.	alius	alia	aliud	aliī	aliae	alia
Voc.	–	–	–	–	–	–
Acc.	alium	aliam	aliud	aliōs	aliās	alia
Gen.	alīus²	alīus	alīus	aliōrum	aliārum	aliōrum
Dat.	aliī	aliī	aliī	aliīs	aliīs	aliīs
Abl.	aliō	aliā	aliō	aliīs	aliīs	aliīs

Alter	Singular			Plural		
	Masculine	**Feminine**	**Neuter**	**Masculine**	**Feminine**	**Neuter**
Nom.	alter	altera	alterum	alterī	alterae	altera
Voc.	–	–	–	–	–	–
Acc.	alterum	alteram	alterum	alterōs	alterās	altera
Gen.	alterīus	alterīus	alterīus	alterōrum	alterārum	alterōrum
Dat.	alterī	alterī	alterī	alterīs	alterīs	alterīs
Abl.	alterō	alterā	alterō	alterīs	alterīs	alterīs

Ancient Case Order

Alius	Singular			Plural		
	Masculine	**Feminine**	**Neuter**	**Masculine**	**Feminine**	**Neuter**
Nom.	alius	alia	aliud	aliī	aliae	alia
Gen.	alīus²	alīus	alīus	aliōrum	aliārum	aliōrum
Dat.	aliī	aliī	aliī	aliīs	aliīs	aliīs
Acc.	alium	aliam	aliud	aliōs	aliās	alia
Abl.	aliō	aliā	aliō	aliīs	aliīs	aliīs

Alter	Singular			Plural		
	Masculine	**Feminine**	**Neuter**	**Masculine**	**Feminine**	**Neuter**
Nom.	alter	altera	alterum	alterī	alterae	altera
Gen.	alterīus	alterīus	alterīus	alterōrum	alterārum	alterōrum
Dat.	alterī	alterī	alterī	alterīs	alterīs	alterīs
Acc.	alterum	alteram	alterum	alterōs	alterās	altera
Abl.	alterō	alterā	alterō	alterīs	alterīs	alterīs

---

[2] The genitive of *alter, alterīus*, is often used instead of *alīus* as genitive singular of *alius*.

Examples:

> *quid dīxit alter?* 'What did the other man say?'
> *quid dīcunt aliī?* 'What are the others saying?'

When two forms of *alius* occur together, they often mean 'one ... another' or, in the plural, 'some ... others'; similarly two forms of *alter* can mean 'one ... the other'.

> *aliī volunt, aliī nōlunt.* 'Some want (it, and) others do not (want it).'
> *alter puer magnus est, alter parvus.* 'One boy (of the two) is big, the other little.'

But if two forms of *alius* are in different genders, numbers, or cases, each must be translated twice in English; usually one can also translate this construction with 'different' and a plural.

> *alius aliam amat.* 'One man loves one woman, and another loves another
>   woman.' / 'Different men love different women.'
> *aliī alia dīxērunt.* 'Some people said some things, and others said other things.' /
>   'Different people said different things.'

Practice

C Translate:

1 duo libri mihi legendi sunt; alter longior est, alter brevior.

2 rogaverunt unde aliae puellae venissent.

3 alii gladiis se defendebant, alii saxis.

4 alii alia fecerunt.

5 harum duarum artium altera facilis est, altera difficilis.

6 tria dona accepi, quorum unum bonum est et alia mala.

7 alii pueri a magistro docentur, alii domi manent.

8 illo die alius aliud vidit.

9 illum Athenis vidi, alios Corinthi.

10 hoc nescio, sed multa alia scio.

11 quaesivit ubi alias puellas vidissemus.

12 aliae alia emerunt.

13 nihil aliud invenire poteram.

14 pecunia mea inventa est, sed pecunia omnium aliorum amissa est.

15 alter magister nunc adest, alter duobus diebus veniet.

16 rogaverunt num alios servos liberaturus essem.

17 nescivit quando adventuri essent alii.

18 aliae alia invenerunt.

19 duo servi sumus; dominus alterius bonus est, alterius malus.

20 si alii hostes venissent, nostri victi essent.

21 horum duorum alter nos verbis iuvit, alter factis.

22 alii poetae versus pessimos scribunt, sed ego versus optimos.

23 hic servus doctissimus est, sed alii nihil sciunt.

24 alia oppida moenibus defenduntur, sed nostrum nulla habet.

25 tres equi mortui sunt, sed alii valent.

D Translate into Latin:

1 I have two good horses; the others are very bad.

2 This man has said nothing, but the other will ask where we found these three books.

3 One of you will be allowed to depart; the others must wait here.

4 The others asked whether I had given gifts to the three sisters.

5 The slaves of three citizens have fled, but the slaves of the others have remained.

6 I myself will give money to one boy; you will have to give money to the others.

7 I love one of my two brothers, but I cannot love the other.

8 He said nothing else (= other), but he knows more.

9 The other men do not know how many names Roman men had.

10 I can persuade the other men with gifts, but those two will not accept money.

11 The other man asked whether I had fought with two swords or with one.

55.3 Reading Practice

1 Livy, *Ab urbe condita* 1.21.6: comparison of two early kings of Rome, Romulus and Numa (written in the first century BC about a much earlier and partly mythical period).

Ita duo deinceps reges, alius alia via, ille bello hic pace, civitatem auxerunt. Romulus septem et triginta regnavit annos, Numa tres et quadraginta. cum valida tum temperata et belli et pacis artibus erat civitas.

Vocabulary

deinceps 'in succession'
via, viae (f.) 'way'
pāx, pācis (f.) 'peace'
cīvitās, cīvitātis (f.) 'state'
augeō, augēre, auxī, auctum 'cause to grow'

trīgintā (indeclinable) 'thirty'
quadrāgintā (indeclinable) 'forty'
cum ... tum 'not only ... but also'
validus, -a, -um 'strong'
temperātus, -a, -um 'well organized'

2 St Augustine, *Confessions* 1.13 (adapted): as a child, the saint preferred Virgil to mathematics, an opinion he later considered sinful (fourth century AD).

Peccabam ergo puer, cum illa inania his utilioribus amore praeponerem – vel potius haec oderam, illa amabam. iam vero 'unum et unum sunt duo, duo et duo sunt quattuor' odiosa cantio mihi erat, et dulcissima erant spectacula vanitatis: equus ligneus plenus armatis, et Troiae incendium, atque ipsius umbra Creusae.

Vocabulary

peccō, -āre, -āvī, -ātum 'sin'	vānitās, vānitātis (f.) 'vanity,
puer 'being a boy', 'when I was a boy'	uselessness'
inānis, ināne 'vain', 'empty'	ligneus, lignea, ligneum 'wooden'
amōre 'in my affections'	plēnus, plēna, plēnum (+ ablative)
praepōnō (like *pōnō*) (+ X accusative	'full of'
and Y ablative) 'put X before Y'	armātus, armātī (m.) 'armed man'
potius 'rather'	Troia, Troiae (f.) 'Troy'
ōdī, ōdisse, ōsum (perfect in form but	incendium, incendiī (n.) 'burning'
present in meaning) 'hate'	umbra, umbrae (f.) 'ghost'
iam vērō 'indeed'	Creūsa, Creūsae (f.) *name of Aeneas'*
odiōsus, -a, -um 'hateful'	*dead wife, who appears as a ghost*
cantiō, cantiōnis (f.) 'chant'	*in the Aeneid*
spectāculum, spectāculī (n.) 'spectacle'	

3 Martial 3.8: bad taste in love (first century AD).

Thaida Quintus amat. 'quam Thaida?' Thaida luscam.
    unum oculum Thais non habet, ille duos.

Vocabulary

Thāida *is accusative of the woman's name* Thāis
luscus, lusca, luscum 'one-eyed'
oculus, oculī (m.) 'eye'

4 Martial 7.65: the undesirability of long lawsuits (first century AD).

Lis te bis decimae numerantem frigora brumae
    conterit una tribus, Gargiliane, foris.
ah miser et demens! viginti litigat annos
    quisquam cui vinci, Gargiliane, licet?

Vocabulary

līs, lītis, lītium (f.) 'lawsuit'

bis 'twice', 'two times'

decimus, -a, -um 'tenth'

numerō, -āre, -āvī, -ātum 'count'

frīgus, frīgoris (n.) 'cold weather'

brūma, brūmae (f.) 'winter solstice'

conterit 'has been wearing you out'

forum, -ī (n.) 'court' (here)

āh 'oh!'

dēmēns, *gen.* dēmentis 'mad'

vīgintī (indeclinable) 'twenty'

lītigō, -āre, -āvī, -ātum 'litigate'

quisquam (nominative singular) 'anyone'

55.4 Vocabulary to Learn

Adjectives/Pronouns

alius, alia, aliud   'other' (of more than two)

alter, altera, alterum 'other' (of two)

Numbers

ūnus, ūna, ūnum   'one'

duo, duae, duo   'two'

trēs, tria   'three'

56 | Relative Clauses with the Subjunctive, Participle Overview

56.1 Relative Clauses of Characteristic

In chapter 25 we saw relative clauses that use the relative pronoun (*quī, quae, quod*) and an indicative verb, such as these examples.

vir quem vidēs rēx est. 'The man whom you see is the king.'
librum quem legis scrīpsī. 'I wrote the book that you are reading.'

Sometimes, however, relative clauses have verbs in the subjunctive (the tense is determined by normal sequence of tenses: see chapter 46.2, not chapter 54). These subjunctives can have a variety of meanings, which must be distinguished primarily by context. The most important of these meanings is a generalizing function known as the 'relative clause of characteristic'; this is used to indicate that the subject has the characteristics that would cause the action of the verb, rather than that the subject necessarily does cause the action of the verb.

is nōn est quī illud faciat. 'He is not a person who would do that.' / 'He is not the sort of person who does that.'
nēmō est quī hoc crēdat. 'There is no-one who would believe this.'
sunt quī hoc crēdant. 'There are those who would believe this.'
ille liber est quem omnēs Rōmānī legant. 'That is a book that all the Romans would read.' / 'That is the sort of book that all the Romans read.'
versus
ille liber est quem omnēs Rōmānī legunt. 'That is the book that all the Romans are reading.'

Practice

A Translate:

1 nemo est qui istum laudet.
2 sunt qui pugnare nolint.
3 is est qui omnia audeat.
4 hi sunt versus quos omnes legant.
5 erant qui dicerent alios non advenisse.
6 nihil erat quod facere possemus.
7 quis est qui hoc credat?
8 libros scripsit quos nemo legeret.
9 sunt qui inimicis ignoverint.
10 nemo erat qui bene pugnaret.

B Translate into Latin using relative clauses with subjunctive verbs:

1 There is nothing that others can do now.

2 There were those who would give the queen gifts.

3 He is the sort of man who frees his slaves.

4 There was no-one who would have wanted to go.

5 There are those who would always fear other men.

6 He said the sort of words that persuade everyone.

7 He is not the sort of person who carries off other men's money.

8 He was the sort of person who helps others.

56.2 Relative Clauses of Purpose and Cause

Sometimes a relative clause with subjunctive verb is equivalent to a purpose clause; this occurs only with certain types of main verb, including ones meaning 'send', 'go', and 'come'.

mīlitēs mīsit quī oppidum dēfenderent. 'He sent soldiers to defend the town.'
trēs virī vēnērunt quī rēgī persuādērent. 'Three men came to persuade the king.'

Alternatively, a relative clause with subjunctive can express cause; under these circumstances the particle *quippe* is often placed in front of the relative pronoun.

mīlitēs quippe quī fūgissent interfectī sunt. 'The soldiers were killed because they had fled.'
hanc puellam quippe quae pulcherrima sit maximē amō. 'I greatly love this girl because she is very beautiful.'

Practice

C Translate:

1 Athenas iverunt alii qui nostros captos invenirent et liberarent.

2 iuvandus mihi est ille quippe qui vitam meam servaverit.

3 nemo erat qui nihil regi afferret.

4 Syracusas misit duos milites qui pecuniam amissam invenirent.

5 alter, quippe qui nesciret, rogavit unde missi essemus.

6 is non est qui uni amico donum magnum det et aliis nihil.

7 Londinium venerunt multi qui reginam novam viderent.

8 alii, quippe qui servi sint, haec domum ferent.

9 sunt qui dicant te servos tuos liberavisse.

10 servum Romam mittam qui epistulam tuam mihi afferat.

374 Relative Clauses with the Subjunctive, Participles

D Translate into Latin using relative clauses with subjunctive verbs:

1 We sent slaves to the river to drive the sheep out of the water.
2 My father, because he knew these things, spoke with the king.
3 There is nothing that that man does not know.
4 Soldiers of the king came to lead us to Corinth.
5 Our mother, because she is at home, will persuade our father to forgive us.
6 He is the sort of man who fears nothing.
7 Other men will go to Carthage to persuade the queen.

56.3 Participles: Summary of Formation

Before embarking on the next chapter it will be useful to look again at participles, which we saw in chapters 6.2, 21.3, 24, and 32. The available participle forms are:

	Perfect passive participle	Perfect active participle	Present active participle	Future active participle
First conjugation	amātus, -a, -um '(having been) loved'	–	amāns, amantis 'loving'	amātūrus, -a, -um '(being) about to love'
First conjugation deponent	–	vēnātus, -a, -um 'having hunted'	vēnāns, vēnantis 'hunting'	vēnātūrus, -a, -um '(being) about to hunt'
Second conjugation	monitus, -a, -um '(having been) advised'	–	monēns, monentis 'advising'	monitūrus, -a, -um '(being) about to advise'
Second conjugation deponent	–	veritus, -a, -um 'having feared'	verēns, verentis 'fearing'	veritūrus, -a, -um '(being) about to fear'
Third conjugation	rēctus, -a, -um '(having been) ruled'	–	regēns, regentis 'ruling'	rēctūrus, -a, -um '(being) about to rule'
Third conjugation deponent	–	ūsus, -a, -um 'having used'	ūtēns, ūtentis 'using'	ūsūrus, -a, -um '(being) about to use'

	Perfect passive participle	Perfect active participle	Present active participle	Future active participle
Fourth conjugation	audītus, -a, -um '(having been) heard'	–	audiēns, audientis 'hearing'	audītūrus, -a, -um '(being) about to hear'
Fourth conjugation deponent	–	partītus, -a, -um 'having divided'	partiēns, partientis 'dividing'	partītūrus, -a, -um '(being) about to divide'
Mixed conjugation	captus, -a, -um '(having been) captured'	–	capiēns, capientis 'capturing'	captūrus, -a, -um '(being) about to capture'
Mixed conjugation deponent	–	mortuus, -a, -um 'having died'	moriēns, morientis 'dying'	moritūrus, -a, -um '(being) about to die'
Sum	–	–	–	futūrus, -a, -um '(being) about to be'
Eō	–	–	iēns, euntis 'going'	itūrus, -a, -um '(being) about to go'
Volō	–	–	volēns, volentis 'wanting'	–
Nōlō	–	–	nōlēns, nōlentis 'not wanting'	–
Ferō	lātus, -a, -um '(having been) carried'	–	ferēns, ferentis 'carrying'	lātūrus, -a, -um '(being) about to carry'

The perfect participles, being first/second-declension adjectives, are declined as follows; future participles are declined the same way but have -*ūr*- before the ending.

British Case Order

	Singular Masculine	Feminine	Neuter	Plural Masculine	Feminine	Neuter
Nom.	amātus	amāta	amātum	amātī	amātae	amāta
Voc.	amāte	amāta	amātum	amātī	amātae	amāta
Acc.	amātum	amātam	amātum	amātōs	amātās	amāta
Gen.	amātī	amātae	amātī	amātōrum	amātārum	amātōrum
Dat.	amātō	amātae	amātō	amātīs	amātīs	amātīs
Abl.	amātō	amātā	amātō	amātīs	amātīs	amātīs

Ancient Case Order

	Singular Masculine	Feminine	Neuter	Plural Masculine	Feminine	Neuter
Nom.	amātus	amāta	amātum	amātī	amātae	amāta
Gen.	amātī	amātae	amātī	amātōrum	amātārum	amātōrum
Dat.	amātō	amātae	amātō	amātīs	amātīs	amātīs
Acc.	amātum	amātam	amātum	amātōs	amātās	amāta
Abl.	amātō	amātā	amātō	amātīs	amātīs	amātīs
Voc.	amāte	amāta	amātum	amātī	amātae	amāta

The present participles are third-declension adjectives, with a variation in the ablative singular that has not hitherto been relevant to us.

British Case Order

	Singular Masculine/Feminine	Neuter	Plural Masculine/Feminine	Neuter
Nom.	amāns	amāns	amantēs	amantia
Voc.	amāns	amāns	amantēs	amantia
Acc.	amantem	amāns	amantēs/amantīs	amantia
Gen.	amantis	amantis	amantium	amantium
Dat.	amantī	amantī	amantibus	amantibus
Abl.	amantī/amante	amantī/amante	amantibus	amantibus

Ancient Case Order

	Singular Masculine/ Feminine	**Neuter**	**Plural** Masculine/ Feminine	**Neuter**
Nom./Voc.	amāns	amāns	amantēs	amantia
Gen.	amantis	amantis	amantium	amantium
Dat.	amantī	amantī	amantibus	amantibus
Acc.	amantem	amāns	amantēs/amantīs	amantia
Abl.	amantī/amante	amantī/amante	amantibus	amantibus

Practice

E Translate:

1 vidi servos aurum ferentes.
2 rex dicturus reginam miseram vidit.
3 servi liberati felices erunt.
4 a nostris servati, milites domum venerunt.
5 milites capti, timentes ne interficerentur, miseri erant.
6 Athenas te petens veni.
7 domi manentes nihil vidimus.
8 milites hortatus rex e castris discessit.

56.4 Reading Practice

1 Livy, *Ab urbe condita* 1.9.1–2: the historian explains the problems that led the early Romans to steal the Sabine women (written in the first century BC about a much earlier and partly mythical period).

Iam res Romana adeo erat valida, ut cuilibet finitimarum civitatum bello par esset; sed penuria mulierum hominis aetatem duratura magnitudo erat, quippe quibus nec domi spes prolis nec cum finitimis conubia essent. tum ex consilio patrum Romulus legatos circa vicinas gentes misit, qui societatem conubiumque novo populo peterent.

Vocabulary

iam 'at that time'
rēs can also mean 'state'
validus, -a, -um 'strong'
quīlibet, quaelibet, quidlibet (declines like *quī*) 'any one'
fīnitimus, -a, -um 'neighbouring'
cīvitās, cīvitātis (f.) 'state'
pār, *gen.* paris 'equal'

pēnūria, pēnūriae (f.) 'scarcity'
mulier, mulieris (f.) 'woman'
aetās, aetātis (f.) 'lifespan'
dūrō, dūrāre, dūrāvī, dūrātum 'endure'
magnitūdō, magnitūdinis (f.) 'greatness'
prōlēs, prōlis (f.) 'children'
cōnūbium, cōnūbiī (n.) 'marriage'

tum 'then'

pater *can also mean* 'senator'

lēgātus, lēgātī (m.) 'envoy'

circā (+ accusative) 'around'

vīcīnus, -a, -um 'neighbouring'

gēns, gentis, gentium (f.) 'tribe'

societās, societātis (f.) 'alliance'

populus, populī (m.) 'people' (i.e. the
  Romans)

2 Martial 2.20: another way to become a poet (first century AD).

> Carmina Paulus emit. recitat sua carmina Paulus.
> nam quod emas possis iure vocare tuum.

Vocabulary

carmen, carminis (n.) 'poem'

recitō, -āre, -āvī, -ātum 'recite'

possīs 'you may'

iūre 'rightly'

3 Cicero, *Epistulae ad Atticum* 10.3 (adapted): Cicero asks his friend Atticus anxious questions about the war between Caesar and Pompey in 49 BC.

Cicero Attico salutem dicit. cum quod scriberem plane nihil haberem, haec autem reliqua essent quae scire cuperem: num Caesar profectus esset, quo in statu urbem reliquisset, in ipsa Italia quem cuique regioni aut negotio praefecisset, ecqui essent ad Pompeium et ad consules ex senatus consulto de pace legati – cum igitur haec scire cuperem dedita opera has ad te litteras misi. feceris igitur commode mihique gratum si me de his rebus et si quid erit aliud quod scire opus sit feceris certiorem. ego in Arcano opperior dum ista cognosco.

Vocabulary

plānē 'absolutely'

reliquus, -a, -um 'remaining'

cupiō, cupere, cupīvī, cupītum 'desire'

proficīscor, proficīscī, profectus sum
  'set out'

status, statūs (m.) 'condition'

cuique 'each' (dative singular adjective)

regiō, regiōnis (f.) 'region'

negōtium, negōtiī (n.) 'task'

praeficiō, praeficere, praefēcī,
    praefectum (+ X accusative and
    Y dative) 'put X in charge of Y'

ecquī 'whether any' (agrees with *lēgātī*)

cōnsul, cōnsulis (m.) 'consul'

cōnsultum, cōnsultī (n.) 'decree'

pāx, pācis (f.) 'peace'

lēgātus, lēgātī (m.) 'envoy'

dēditā operā 'by special messenger'

litterae, litterārum (f. plural) 'letter'

commodē 'conveniently'

opus est (+ infinitive) 'it is necessary to'

certiōrem faciō 'inform'

Arcānum, Arcānī (n.) *name of Cicero's
    brother's estate*

opperior, opperīrī, oppertus sum 'wait'

cognōscō, -nōscere, -nōvī, -nitum 'find
  out'

4 Martial 11.50: the reputation of Virgil in the later first century AD. Silius Italicus was
an important composer of imperial-period Latin epic.

Iam prope desertos cineres et sancta Maronis
    nomina qui coleret pauper et unus erat.
Silius orbatae succurrere censuit umbrae,
    et vatem vates non minor ipse colit.

Vocabulary

iam 'now'

prope 'almost'

dēserō, dēserere, dēseruī, dēsertum
    'desert, abandon'

cinis, cineris (m.) 'ashes'

sānctus, -a, -um 'holy'

Marō, Marōnis (m.) *was the cognomen
    of P. Vergilius Maro, now known as
    'Virgil'*

colō, colere, coluī, cultum 'honour'

pauper et ūnus erat 'there was only one
    man, a pauper'

orbō, orbāre, orbāvī, orbātum 'make
    destitute'

succurrō (like *currō*) (+ dative) 'come to
    the help of'

cēnseo, cēnsēre, cēnsuī, cēnsum 'decide'

umbra, umbrae (f.) 'ghost'

vātēs, vātis, vātium (m.) 'poet'

57 | Ablative Absolute

57.1 Ablative Absolute

All the participles we have seen so far have a clear grammatical relationship to the rest of the sentence. Sometimes they agree with the subject (expressed or understood), as *mīlitēs captī timēbant* 'the captured soldiers were afraid' or *captī timēbant* 'the captured men were afraid'; sometimes they agree with the direct object (expressed or understood), as *mīlitēs captōs vīdī* 'I saw the captured soldiers' or *captōs vīdī* 'I saw the captured men'; and sometimes they have other functions that cause them to end up in a variety of cases, as *mīlitibus captīs aquam dedit* 'He gave water to the captured soldiers', *cum captīs stat* 'He is standing with the captured men', etc.

But in Latin it is also possible for a participle and the word it modifies to have no grammatical relationship to the rest of the sentence; this is called an 'absolute' construction because it is not relative to anything else. When this occurs the participle and the word it modifies are put into the ablative, and the construction is therefore known as the 'ablative absolute'. The ablative in question has one declensional peculiarity: present participles have an ablative singular in *-e* rather than *-ī* when used in the ablative absolute construction.

English can also use absolute constructions to a limited extent, and therefore some Latin ablatives absolute can be translated literally into English.

patre mortuō, frātrēs Rōmā discessērunt. 'Their father having died, the brothers left Rome.'
aurō inventō, omnēs fēlīcēs erant. 'The gold having been found, everyone was happy.'

More often, however, the literal English equivalent of a Latin ablative absolute construction sounds peculiar, ungrammatical, or even nonsensical.

patre vēnante, frātrēs Rōmā discessērunt. '*Their father hunting, the brothers left Rome.' (* is used to indicate an impossible sentence.)

Under these circumstances one can add 'with' in English ('With their father hunting ... ') or one can translate the ablative absolute with an English clause introduced by a conjunction such as 'when' or 'since' ('When their father was hunting ... '). Such translations can also be used for other ablatives absolute.

patre mortuō, frātrēs Rōmā discessērunt. 'With their father having died, the brothers
   left Rome.' / 'When their father (had) died, the brothers left Rome.'
aurō inventō, omnēs fēlīcēs erant 'With the gold having been found, everyone was
   happy.' / 'When the gold was found, everyone was happy.'

In dealing with an ablative absolute, one needs to understand the word that the
participle agrees with as the subject of the verb that the participle comes from: thus
in *patre mortuō* one needs to take the ablative *patre* as the subject of *mortuō* (which
needs to be translated as a verb when using the 'when' translation: 'when their father
(had) died'). The tense of the participle is relative to that of the main verb, so because
this ablative absolute uses a perfect participle, it means that the father died before the
brothers left Rome. In the sentence *patre mortuō frātrēs Rōmā discēdent* the same
ablative absolute would mean 'When their father dies (or 'has died') the brothers will
leave Rome': the translation of the ablative absolute depends on the tense of the main
verb. Likewise the sentence *patre moriente frātrēs Rōmā discēdunt* means 'Since their
father is dying the brothers are leaving Rome', but *patre moriente frātrēs Rōmā
discessērunt* means 'When their father was dying, the brothers left Rome' (or 'With
their father dying, the brothers left Rome'): the present participle means that the two
actions occurred at the same time, but because of the English sequence of tenses (cf.
chapters 19.4 and 24.2) it is translated with a past tense in English.

Practice

A Translate, using 'when/since' rather than 'with' for the ablatives absolute and
making sure the tense of the main verb is reflected in your translation of the
ablative absolute:

1 amico veniente puer felix erat.
2 amico veniente puer felix erit.
3 auro ablato nihil habuimus.
4 auro ablato nihil habemus.
5 cives felices erunt illo regente.
6 cives felices erant illo regente.
7 urbe visa celerius cucurrimus.
8 celerius curremus urbe visa.
9 domum celeriter reficiemus amicis iuvantibus.
10 amicis iuvantibus domum celeriter refecimus.
11 hostibus victis urbs nostra servata est.
12 urbs nostra servabitur hostibus victis.
13 rege ipso ducente milites acrius pugnabant.
14 milites acrius pugnabunt rege ipso ducente.
15 servis liberatis dominus ipse saxa feret.
16 dominus ipse saxa ferebat servis liberatis.

57.2 Additional Words Attached to an Ablative Absolute

An ablative absolute does not have to consist of only two words; other words that depend on those two can also be part of the construction. Often such words are also in the ablative case, because they are adjectives agreeing with the ablative absolute.

iūvistī mē patre meō moriente. 'You helped me when <u>my</u> father was dying.'
illō aurō inventō omnēs fēlīcēs erant. 'When <u>that</u> gold was found everyone was happy.'

But often the words depending on an ablative absolute are in other cases, if they are the objects of the participle (see chapter 24.2 for the tendency of participles to take objects), a possessive genitive with the noun, or even a prepositional phrase.

rēge mīlitēs hortātō ē castrīs prōgressī sumus. 'When the king had encouraged <u>the soldiers</u> we advanced out of the camp.'
patre eius moriente nihil facere poteram. 'When <u>his</u> father was dying I was unable to do anything.'
rēge ab hostibus interfectō miserrimī erāmus. 'When the king was killed <u>by the enemy</u> we were very miserable.'

Very often, as in these examples, the additional words come between the two ablative words; words that belong to the main sentence rather than to the ablative absolute phrase are not normally found in this position. This positioning is therefore useful because it allows the reader to work out easily which extra words go with the ablative absolute and which with the main sentence, but it is also tricky because it makes the ablative absolute itself harder to spot in the first place. It is also possible for words that belong to the ablative absolute construction to occur before or after the two main words.

rēge interfectō ab hostibus miserrimī erāmus. 'When the king was killed <u>by the enemy</u> we were very miserable.'

Practice

B Translate:

1 his verbis dictis omnes discesserunt.

2 his verbis dictis omnes discedent.

3 militibus e castris progressis hostes visi sunt.

4 militibus e castris progressis hostes oppugnabunt.

5 matre domum veniente pueros malos paenituit.

6 matre domum veniente vos paenitebit.

7 multis libris scriptis magister clarissimus factus est.

8 multis libris scriptis ipse clarissimus fies.

9 patre ab hostibus capto filius
   aurum afferet.

10 patre capto ab hostibus filius
   aurum attulit.

11 auro nostro ab illis ablato
   tristissimi eramus.

12 tristes sumus auro nostro ablato
   ab illis.

13 ovibus in agrum actis,
   agricola ad nos venit. (2 ways)

14 omnes tristes erant his verbis
   auditis.

15 hostibus visis a nostris, rex
   milites e castris duxit.

16 quis aurum feret servis ab eo
   venditis?

17 hostes urbem defendebant
   nostris oppugnantibus.

18 oppido nostro relicto, quo
   eamus?

19 rege ipso interfecto omnes
   regere volebant.

20 deos laudemus moenibus
   nostris refectis.

21 pater tuus haec verba dixit
   omnibus in agro sedentibus.

22 his verbis scriptis vir doctus
   mortuus est.

23 auro nostro invento te iuvare
   poterimus.

24 patre vivente haec omnia
   fecerat.

C Translate into Latin using ablatives absolute for the underlined clauses:

1 When the money was found
   everyone was happy.

2 When the money is found
   everyone will be happy.

3 Since everyone is afraid, we shall
   go home.

4 Since everyone was afraid, we
   went home.

5 Everyone was present when the
   king was dying.

6 When the king had died everyone
   departed.

7 When my father was speaking
   those words I was in Rome.

D Translate into Latin using ablatives absolute where possible:

1 Since the enemy was advancing,
   our men were afraid.

2 The enemy was advancing since
   our men were afraid.

3 The king died after this letter was
   written.

4 This letter was written after the
   king had died.

5 When our men were defeated that
   city was abandoned.

6 When that city had been
   abandoned our men were
   defeated.

7 We shall come home when the
   walls have been repaired.

8 I saw it when the boys were
   speaking.

9 Since his father was coming to
   Rome, Marcus departed.

57.3 Reading Practice

1 *Colloquium Stephani* 38a–d: a schoolboy does an advanced Greek exercise (probably first to third century AD).

Sumptis ergo pugillaribus scripsi de oratione Demosthenis dictante praeceptore, quod sufficiebat et hora permittebat; et distinxi ut oportebat.

Vocabulary

sūmō, sūmere, sūmpsī, sūmptum 'take up'

pugillāris, pugillāris, pugillārium (m.) 'writing-tablet'

ōrātiō, ōrātiōnis (f.) 'speech'

Dēmosthenēs, Dēmosthenis (m.) *name of a famous Greek orator*

dictō, dictāre, dictāvī, dictātum 'dictate'

praeceptor, praeceptōris (m.) 'instructor'

sufficiō, sufficere, suffēcī, suffectum 'suffice'

hōra *can also mean* 'time'

permittō (like *mittō*) 'permit'

distinguō, distinguere, distīnxī, distīnctum 'put in punctuation marks'

ut (+ indicative) 'as'

2 *Colloquium Stephani* 7a–8c (adapted): how a model child with his own personal slave boy goes to school (probably first to third century AD).

Graphium requisivi et membranam, et haec tradidi meo puero. paratus ergo in omnia, progressus sum domo sequente me paedagogo, recte per porticum quae ducebat ad scholam. cum mihi noti occurrissent, salutavi eos; et illi me resalutaverunt.

Vocabulary

graphium, graphiī (n.) 'stylus'

requīrō, requīrere, requīsīvī, requīsītum 'ask for'

membrāna, membrānae (f.) 'parchment'

trādō, trādere, trādidī, trāditum 'hand over'

parō, parāre, parāvī, parātum 'prepare'

in (+ accusative) *can also mean* 'for'

paedagōgus, paedagōgī (m.) 'child-minder'

rēctē 'straight', 'directly'

porticus, porticūs (f.) 'colonnade'

schola, scholae (f.) 'school'

nōtus, nōtī (m.) 'acquaintance'

occurrō (like *currō*) (+ dative) 'meet'

resalūtō, -āre, -āvī, -ātum 'greet in return'

3 *Corpus Inscriptionum Latinarum* VII.273: an inscription on a bath-house in Yorkshire (second century AD).

Deae Fortunae. Virius Lupus, legatus Augusti pro praetore, balineum vi ignis exustum cohorti I Thracum restituit, curante Valerio Frontone praefecto equitum alae Vettonum.

Vocabulary

Fortūna, Fortūnae (f.) 'fortune'
  (a minor goddess)
lēgātus, lēgātī (m.) 'legate'
Augustus, Augustī (m.) 'emperor'
prō praetōre 'propraetorian' (i.e. having
  the powers of a *praetor*)
balineum, balineī (n.) 'bath-house'
vī (ablative singular) 'violence'
ignis, ignis, ignium (m.) 'fire'
exūrō, exūrere, exussī, exustum 'burn
  down'
cohortī I Thrācum 'for the First Cohort
  of Thracians' (the army unit who
  used that bath-house)

restituō, restituere, restituī, restitūtum
  'rebuild' (i.e. pay to have something
  rebuilt)
cūrō *can also mean* 'have charge of the
  work'
praefectus, -a, -um 'prefect' (a grade of
  officer)
equitēs, equitum (m. plural) 'cavalry'
āla, ālae (f.) 'squadron'
Vettōnēs, Vettōnum 'Vettonians' (i.e.
  men from what is now Bettona in
  Italy)

4 *Corpus Inscriptionum Latinarum* IV.1842 (adapted): graffito from a wall in Pompeii
(first century AD).

C. Pumidius Dipilus hic fuit, ante diem V Nonas Octobres M. Lepido et Q. Catulo
consulibus.

Vocabulary

ante diem V 'five days before'
Nōnae, Nōnārum 'Nones' (a festival
  that in October fell on the
  seventh day of the month)
Octōber, -bris, -bre 'of October'
cōnsulibus 'being consuls' (with the
  preceding names this forms an

ablative absolute with the participle
  of *sum* understood; as *sum* has no
  participle this is the only way to
  form an ablative absolute involving
  'be', and it is a very common way of
  giving dates)

5 Apicius, *De re coquinaria* 7.13.1 (adapted): from a Roman cookbook, a recipe for
sweets made from dates (perhaps fifth century AD).

Dulcia domestica: palmulas vel dactilos excepto semine nucibus vel nucleis vel
pipere trito infercies. sal foris continges, friges in melle cocto, et inferes.

Vocabulary

domesticus, -a, -um 'home-made'
palmula, palmulae (f.) 'palm date'
dactilus, dactilī (m.) 'date'
excipiō, excipere, excēpī, exceptum
  'take out'

sēmen, sēminis (n.) 'pit, stone'
nux, nucis (f.) 'nut'
nucleus, nucleī (m.) 'pine nut'
piper, piperis (n.) 'pepper'
terō, terere, trīvī, trītum 'grind'

īnferciō, īnfercīre, īnfersī, īnfersum
    'stuff'
sāl, salis (m.) 'salt'
forīs 'on the outside'
contingō, -tingere, -tigī, -tāctum
    'sprinkle'

frīgō, frīgere, frīxī, frīctum 'fry'
mel, mellis (n.) 'honey'
coquō, coquere, coxī, coctum 'cook'
īnferō (like *ferō*) 'serve'

6 Apicius, *De re coquinaria* 4.3.6 (adapted): a recipe for apricot stew (perhaps fifth century AD).

Minutal ex armeniacis: adicies in caccabum oleum, liquamen, vinum; concides cepam ascaloniam aridam; spatulam porcinam coctam tessellatim concides. his omnibus coctis teres piper, cuminum, mentam aridam, anethum; suffundes mel, liquamen, passum, acetum modice; temperabis. armeniaca enucleata adicies, facies ut ferveant donec percoquantur. piper asperges et inferes.

Vocabulary

minūtal, minūtālis (n.) 'stew'
armeniacum, armeniacī (n.) 'apricot'
adiciō, adicere, adiēcī, adiectum 'put in'
caccabus, caccabī (m.) 'pot'
oleum, oleī (n.) 'olive oil'
liquāmen, liquāminis (n.) 'garum'
vīnum, vīnī (n.) 'wine'
concīdō, -cīdere, -cīdī, -cīsum 'cut up'
cēpa, cēpae (f.) 'onion'
ascalōnius, -a, -um 'Ascalonian' (a variety of onion)
āridus, -a, -um 'dried'
spatula, spatulae (f.) 'wide piece'
porcīnus, -a, -um 'of pork'
coquō, coquere, coxī, coctum 'cook'
tessellātim 'in little squares'
terō, terere, trīvī, trītum 'grind'
piper, piperis (n.) 'pepper'

cumīnum, cumīnī (n.) 'cumin'
menta, mentae (f.) 'mint'
anēthum, anēthī (n.) 'dill'
suffundō, suffundere, suffūdī, suffūsum 'pour in'
mel, mellis (n.) 'honey'
passum, passī (n.) 'raisin wine'
acētum, acētī (n.) 'vinegar'
modicē 'a little'
temperō, -āre, -āvī, -ātum 'blend'
ēnucleātus, -a, -um 'with the pit/stone removed'
ferveō, fervēre, ferbuī, – 'boil'
dōnec (+ subjunctive) 'until'
percoquō (like *coquō*) 'cook thoroughly'
aspergō, aspergere, aspersī, aspersum 'sprinkle on'
īnferō (like *ferō*) 'serve'

57.4 Vocabulary to Learn

Verbs

cadō, cadere, cecidī, cāsum	'fall'
cēnō, cēnāre, cēnāvī, cēnātum	'dine', 'have dinner'
dēleō, dēlēre, dēlēvī, dēlētum	'destroy'
dormiō, dormīre, dormīvī, dormītum	'sleep'
fugō, fugāre, fugāvī, fugātum	'cause to flee', 'put to flight'
gerō, gerere, gessī, gestum	'wear', 'wage (war)', 'conduct'
iaceō, iacēre, iacuī, –	'lie' (i.e. be horizontal)
iaciō, iacere, iēcī, iactum	'throw'

Nouns

canis, canis (m., f.)	'dog'
cēna, cēnae (f.)	'dinner'
dux, ducis (m.)	'leader'
fīlia, fīliae (f.)	'daughter'
ignis, ignis, ignium (m.)	'fire'

Adjectives

altus, alta, altum	'high', 'deep'
antīquus, antīqua, antīquum	'ancient'
dīves, *gen.* dīvitis	'rich'
laetus, laeta, laetum	'joyful'

Pronouns

aliquis, aliquid (declines like *quis*)	'someone', 'anyone' (in neuter 'something', 'anything')

58.1 *Īdem*

The Latin for 'same' is formed by adding *-dem* to the forms of *is, ea, id*. The results look strange but are almost entirely regular (final *-m* changes to *-n* before the *-dem*, final *-s* and *-d* are lost in the nominative and accusative singular only).

British Case Order

	Singular			Plural		
	Masculine	Feminine	Neuter	Masculine	Feminine	Neuter
Nom.	īdem	eadem	idem	eīdem	eaedem	eadem
Voc.	–	–	–	–	–	–
Acc.	eundem	eandem	idem	eōsdem	eāsdem	eadem
Gen.	eiusdem	eiusdem	eiusdem	eōrundem	eārundem	eōrundem
Dat.	eīdem	eīdem	eīdem	eīsdem/īsdem	eīsdem/īsdem	eīsdem/īsdem
Abl.	eōdem	eādem	eōdem	eīsdem/īsdem	eīsdem/īsdem	eīsdem/īsdem

Ancient Case Order

	Singular			Plural		
	Masculine	Feminine	Neuter	Masculine	Feminine	Neuter
Nom.	īdem	eadem	idem	eīdem	eaedem	eadem
Gen.	eiusdem	eiusdem	eiusdem	eōrundem	eārundem	eōrundem
Dat.	eīdem	eīdem	eīdem	eīsdem/īsdem	eīsdem/īsdem	eīsdem/īsdem
Acc.	eundem	eandem	idem	eōsdem	eāsdem	eadem
Abl.	eōdem	eādem	eōdem	eīsdem/īsdem	eīsdem/īsdem	eīsdem/īsdem

Practice

A Translate:

1 eandem ovem iterum amisi.
2 eosdem libros videre velim.
3 nolumus eundem ducem sequi; alium volumus.
4 illi ad eandem urbem iverunt.

5 idem canis iterum oves interfecit.

6 eadem nocte ille bene dormivit.

7 aliquis eundem librum ad me iterum attulit.

8 eadem hora regina mortua est.

9 ille Mariam filiam Marci amat; ego eiusdem filiam alteram amo.

10 cum eisdem Romam ibo.

11 rogavit utrum alius canis an idem pueros fugavisset.

12 eidem filiae pecuniam dedi, non alteri.

B Translate into Latin:

1 Do we have to read the same book again?

2 Let's give this to the same boy.

3 We shall have to sit with the same girls again.

4 The same man's dogs have put me to flight again.

5 When the enemies had been put to flight, our men returned to the same camp. (2 ways)

6 You must give the same gift to all your sons; if you don't do this they will fight.

7 His two daughters died on the same night.

8 Do not give me the same advice again; I want to hear something new.

9 Those three boys were all taught by the same teacher, but these two by a different teacher.

10 We don't know where we are, since we have arrived again at (= to) the same forest.

58.2 Expressions of Price and Value

To express a price, Latin uses the ablative without a preposition: *tribus dēnāriīs hoc ēmī* 'I bought this for three denarii.' For value, however, the genitive is normally used rather than the ablative: *illum magnī aestimō* 'I value him greatly.' The distinction between price and value is not absolute, but price expressed in monetary terms is nearly always ablative, while indefinite expressions like *quantī* 'how much?', *magnī* 'greatly', and *parvī* 'a little' are normally genitive. Also, verbs of buying and selling (e.g. *emō* and *vendō*) are more likely to take the ablative and verbs of valuing (e.g. *aestimō*) to take the genitive. Note the following vocabulary:

dēnārius, -ī (m.) 'denarius' (a coin of significant value)

sēstertius, -ī (m.) 'sestertius' (English plural 'sesterces') (a coin worth a quarter of a denarius)

as, assis (m.) 'as' (a coin worth one-tenth or, later, one-sixteenth of a denarius)

aestimō, -āre, -āvī, -ātum 'value'

faciō 'value'

(nōn) floccī faciō 'I consider to be of no value' (literally 'I (don't) value at the rate of a tuft of wool').

Practice

C Translate:

1 donum tuum magni aestimat.
2 donum tuum tribus denariis vendidit.
3 quanti emisti hunc canem?
4 canem meum duobus sestertiis emi.
5 consilium nostrum flocci non facit.
6 cenam nobis emi quattuor assibus.
7 quanti venditus est equus tuus?
8 oves meae venditae sunt multis denariis.
9 canem suum parvi aestimavit.
10 domum tribus sestertiis emere non potes.

D Translate into Latin:

1 I value your advice greatly.
2 I have sold the black horse for five denarii.
3 You cannot buy a slave for two sesterces.
4 We shall sell our fields for many denarii.
5 He considers their life to be of no value.
6 How much will you sell this field (for)?
7 They value us greatly.
8 How much do you value your fatherland?
9 We bought a sheep for three sesterces.
10 I bought this little book for two asses.

E Translate, paying particular attention to participles:

1 reginae filia domum rediens in idem flumen cecidit.
2 eidem saxis iactis canes fugaverunt.
3 ignis oppidum delevit militibus dormientibus.
4 his rebus gestis regina discedere ausa non est.
5 filiam tuam in eodem agro iacentem invenimus.
6 filiam regis cenantem vidimus.
7 hostibus iterum fugatis, dux nostros laudavit.
8 igne domo deleta pater laetus non erat.
9 aurum nostrum inimicis divitibus dantes laeti non sumus.
10 bello gesto domum redibimus.
11 oves in agro iacentes interfecit canis tuus.
12 pueri saxa iacientes mali sunt.
13 canibus fugatis progredi ausi sumus.
14 eosdem canes domi dormientes vidi.
15 castris igne deletis milites domum redierunt.
16 patre cenante filiae aurum abstulerunt.
17 matre legente puer in flumen cecidit.
18 hoc duce mortuo nemo milites ducere potuit.

F Translate, using the vocabulary for this chapter as well as words you already know:

1 tribus filiis natis, domus maior patri emenda erat.
2 pater, quippe qui senex esset, in lecto iacebat.
3 his rebus nuntiatis, rogavimus ubi aliae naves essent.
4 si conatus esses, ipse opus perfecisses.
5 duos nuntios Athenas misi qui haec nuntiarent.
6 filiae raptae patribus quaerendae erunt.
7 classe nostra ostenta, rex ipse rogavit quot naves adessent.
8 si castra bene paraveritis, nocte bene dormietis.
9 ab hostibus coacti, nostri in flumen ceciderunt.
10 sunt qui senes fieri nolint, sed nisi mortui erunt senes fient.
11 omnibus navibus hostium amissis, bellum perfectum est.
12 senex aquam attulisset si iste puer ignem ei ostendisset.
13 si mecum cenare vis, cena tibi ipsi afferenda est.
14 filia ducis quaesivit quid nuntius nuntiavisset.

G Translate into Latin, using vocabulary from this chapter as needed:

1 With the old man having died, we reported these things to (his) daughters.
2 I do not know what we will accomplish, but we have to try.
3 If you show me the place, I shall bring dinner myself.
4 When his daughter was born the old man was very joyful. (2 ways)
5 We ourselves do not know what that leader of yours is trying to accomplish.
6 There is nothing that that man cannot accomplish.
7 If I were sleeping, I would be lying in bed.
8 When the enemies' ships had been driven together our men conquered easily. (2 ways)
9 You must prepare the ships so that we can show them to the queen.

58.3 Reading Practice

1 *Colloquium Montepessulanum* 13b–f (adapted): shopping for clothes (probably third century AD).

Ego duco me ad vestiarium.
BUYER: quanti pallium?
SELLER: centum denariis.
BUYER: quanti paenula?

SELLER: ducentis denariis.

BUYER: multum dicis; accipe centum denarios.

SELLER: non potest tanti; tanti constat de infertoribus.

BUYER: udones emam. quid dabo?

SELLER: quod vis.

BUYER (*to servant carrying his purse*): da illi XXV denarios. eamus et ad lintearium. confer et illi.

SERVANT (*to seller*): da nobis quattuor lintea. quanti omnia?

SELLER: trecentis denariis.

Vocabulary

dūcō mē = eō	cōnstat 'it costs'
vestiārius, vestiāriī (m.) 'garment seller'	īnfertor, īnfertōris (m.) 'importer'
pallium, palliī (n.) 'mantle' (a type of outer garment consisting of a large square of cloth)	ūdō, ūdōnis (m.) 'sock'
	linteārius, linteāriī (m.) 'linen seller'
	cōnferō (like *ferō*) (+ dative) 'bargain with'
centum (indeclinable) 'one hundred'	
paenula, paenulae (f.) 'hooded cape'	linteum, linteī (n.) 'linen towel'
ducentī, -ae, -a 'two hundred'	trecentī, -ae, -a 'three hundred'
potest *can also mean* 'it is possible'	

2 *Corpus Inscriptionum Latinarum* IV.1679 (adapted): sign advertising prices at a tavern in Pompeii (first century AD).

Hedone dicit: assibus hic bibitur; dupondium si dederis, meliora bibes; quattuor si dederis, vina Falerna bibes.

Vocabulary

Hēdonē (nominative singular) *is the Greek word for 'pleasure' and perhaps the name of the tavern owner*	bibitur 'one can have drinks' (impersonal passive, so literally 'it is drunk')
	dupondius, dupondiī (m.) 'two *asses*'
assibus: *the plural goes with the multiple drinks suggested by* bibitur, *so the price given is just one as*	**bibō, bibere, bibī, – 'drink'**
	vīnum, vīnī (n.) 'wine'
	Falernus, -a, -um 'Falernian' (a particularly good kind of wine)

3 Catullus 5: the joys of love (first century BC).

Vivamus, mea Lesbia, atque amemus,
rumoresque senum severiorum
omnes unius aestimemus assis.
soles occidere et redire possunt:
nobis, cum semel occidit brevis lux,
nox est perpetua una dormienda.
da mi basia mille, deinde centum,
dein mille altera, dein secunda centum,
deinde usque altera mille, deinde centum.
dein, cum milia multa fecerimus,
conturbabimus illa, ne sciamus,
aut ne quis malus invidere possit,
cum tantum sciat esse basiorum.

Vocabulary

rūmor, rūmōris (m.) 'calumny'	bāsium, bāsiī (n.) 'kiss'
senex, senis (m.) 'old man'	**mīlle (n., indeclinable in singular,**
sevērus, -a, -um 'strict'	**plural *mīlia, mīlium*) 'thousand'**
sōl, sōlis (m.) 'sun'	**dein/deinde 'then'**
occidō, occidere, occidī, occāsum	**centum (indeclinable) 'a hundred'**
'set', 'die'	usque 'as much as'
semel 'once'	conturbō, -āre, -āvī, -ātum 'mix up'
lūx, lūcis (f.) 'light'	invideō, invidēre, invīdī, invīsum 'be
perpetuus, -a, -um 'eternal'	envious'
mī = mihi	

4 Martial 12.46: the difficulties of love (first century AD).

Difficilis facilis, iucundus acerbus es idem:
nec tecum possum vivere nec sine te.

Vocabulary

iūcundus, -a, -um 'pleasant'
acerbus, -a, -um 'bitter'

5 Martial 8.10: how to get rich by buying fancy clothes (first century AD).

Emit lacernas milibus decem Bassus
Tyrias coloris optimi. lucri fecit.
'adeo bene emit?' inquis. immo non solvit.

Vocabulary

lacerna, lacernae (f.) 'cloak'

mīlia, mīlium (n. plural) 'thousands'

decem (indeclinable) 'ten'

Tyrius, Tyria, Tyrium 'purple'

colōris optimī 'of excellent colour'

lucrī faciō 'make a profit'

inquis 'you say'

immō 'yes indeed'

solvō, solvere, solvī, solūtum 'pay'

58.4 Vocabulary to Learn

Verbs

aestimō, aestimāre, aestimāvī, aestimātum   'value'

cōgō, cōgere, coēgī, coāctum   'force', 'drive together'

cōnor, cōnārī, cōnātus sum   'try'

nāscor, nāscī, nātus sum   'be born'

nūntiō, nūntiāre, nūntiāvī, nūntiātum   'announce', 'report'

ostendō, ostendere, ostendī, ostentum   'show'

parō, parāre, parāvī, parātum   'prepare'

perficiō, perficere, perfēcī, perfectum   'accomplish'

Nouns

as, assis (m.)   'as' ($\frac{1}{10}$ or $\frac{1}{16}$ denarius)

dēnārius, dēnāriī (m.)   'denarius'

floccus, floccī (m.)   'tuft of wool'

lectus, lectī (m.)   'bed'

nāvis, nāvis, nāvium (f.)   'ship'

nūntius, nūntiī (m.)   'messenger'

senex, senis (m.)   'old man'

sēstertius, sēstertiī (m.)   'sestertius' (¼ denarius)

Adjective/Pronoun

īdem, eadem, idem   'same'

59.1 *Colloquia Monacensia–Einsidlensia* 11a–12d (adapted)

Giving a dinner party (second or third century AD):

(*As the guests gather in the library before dinner*)

LUCIUS (*to slaves*): date hic cathedras, sellas, cervicalia. (*to Gaius*) sede.

GAIUS: sedeo.

LUCIUS (*to Quintus*): cur stas? (*to slaves*) lava calicem et vinum aqua calida tempera; valde enim sitio. misce omnibus. (*to guests*) quis quid vult? conditum aut carenum? (*to slave, after getting an answer from a guest*) illud ei misce. (*to Gaius*) tu, quid vis? (*to slave*) lava calicem.

GAIUS: misce mihi calidum, noli miscere ferventem neque tepidum, sed temperatum. (*after tasting it*) mitte aquam. (*after tasting it again*) adice merum.

(*As the guests move into the dining room*)

LUCIUS: cur statis? sedete, si vultis.

GAIUS: discumbamus. ubi imperas ut discumbam?

LUCIUS: in primo loco discumbe. (*to slaves*) date nobis liquamen. da nobis malvas ferventes. porrige mihi mappam. mitte impensam in acetabulum. partire ungellas. concide aqualiculum et chordam ex aqua. da ficatum tenerum, turdos, lactucas. unus vestrum panem frangat et in canistellum inferat. (*to guests*) cenate. (*to slaves*) da sardinas, cymam cum liquamine, rapatum, gallinam assam, porcellum assum. pone discum cum radicibus, menta, olivis albis et caseo salso, fungis. (*to stewards, after all the guests have been fed*) ministrantibus et coquo date cenam; et date bellaria, quia bene ministraverunt. date nobis aquam manibus. (*in preparation for the last part of the evening*) terge mensam. da calicem, da merum.

GAIUS: bibamus aquam de gillone.

QUINTUS: misce calidum.

SLAVE: in maiore calice?

QUINTUS: in minore.

SLAVE: libenter.

QUINTUS (*to Lucius*): si mihi permittis, propino tibi; bene accipis?

LUCIUS: a te, libenter. (*to Marcus*) cur non bibis? bibe, Marce.

MARCUS: rogavi et nemo mihi dedit.

GAIUS: sufficit nobis. nunc eamus. (*to slave*) accende lampadem.

SLAVE: accipe.

GAIUS (*to Lucius*): bene nos accepisti.

(*After guests have left*)

LUCIUS (*to slave*): puer, veni. collige haec omnia et suis locis repone. diligenter sterne lectum.

SLAVES: stravimus.

LUCIUS: cur igitur durus est?

SLAVES: excussimus et pulvinum commollivimus.

LUCIUS: si cuius vocem audiero, non ei parcam. recipite vos, dormite et galli cantu excitate me, ut excurram.

Vocabulary

cathedra, cathedrae (f.) 'chair'

sella, sellae (f.) 'seat'

cervīcal, cervīcālis (n.) 'cushion'

lavō, lavāre, lāvī, lautum 'rinse out'

calix, calicis (m.) 'cup'

vīnum, vīnī (n.) 'wine'

calidus, -a, -um 'hot'

temperō, -āre, -āvī, -ātum 'mix'

valdē 'extremely'

sitiō, sitīre, –, – 'be thirsty'

misceō, miscēre, miscuī, mixtum 'mix'

condītum, condītī (n.) 'spiced wine'

carēnum, carēnī (n.) 'sweet boiled wine'

calidum, calidī (n.) 'hot drink'

fervēns, *gen.* ferventis 'boiling'

tepidus, -a, -um 'lukewarm'

temperātus, -a, -um 'the right temperature'

mittō *can also mean* 'add' *and* 'pour'

adiciō, adicere, adiēcī, adiectum 'add'

merum, merī (n.) 'unmixed wine'

discumbō, -cumbere, -cubuī, -cubitum 'recline'

liquāmen, liquāminis (n.) 'garum'

malva, malvae (f.) 'mallow'

porrigō, porrigere, porrēxī, porrēctum 'pass'

mappa, mappae (f.) 'napkin'

impēnsa, impēnsae (f.) 'fish oil sauce'

acētābulum, acētābulī (n.) 'vinegar cup'

ungella, ungellae (f.) 'pig's foot'

concīdō, -cīdere, -cīdī, -cīsum 'cut up'

aquāliculum, aquāliculī (n.) 'paunch'

chorda, chordae (f.) 'tripe'

ex aquā 'boiled'

fīcātum, fīcātī (n.) 'liver'

turdus, turdī (m.) 'thrush'

lactūca, lactūcae (f.) 'lettuce'

pānis, pānis, pānium (m.) 'bread'

frangō, frangere, frēgī, frāctum 'break'

canistellum, canistellī (n.) 'basket'

īnferō (like *ferō*) 'serve'

sardīna, sardīnae (f.) 'pilchard'

cȳma, cȳmae (f.) 'cabbage-sprout'

rāpātum, rāpātī (n.) 'meat in grated turnip'

gallīna, gallīnae (f.) 'chicken'

assus, assa, assum 'roasted'

porcellus, porcellī (m.) 'suckling pig'

pōnō *can also mean* 'set out'

discus, discī (m.) 'platter'

rādīx, rādīcis (f.) 'radish'

menta, mentae (f.) 'mint'

olīva, olīvae (f.) 'olive'

albus, alba, album 'white'

cāseus, cāseī (f.) 'cheese'

salsus, salsa, salsum 'salted'

fungus, fungī (m.) 'mushroom'

ministrāns, ministrantis (m.) 'waiter'

coquus, coquī (m.) 'cook'

bellārium, bellāriī (n.) 'dessert'

ministrō, -āre, -āvī, -ātum 'serve'

tergō, tergere, tersī, tersum 'wipe off'

mēnsa, mēnsae (f.) 'table'

bibō, bibere, bibī, – 'drink'

gillō, gillōnis (m.) 'cooler'

libenter 'gladly'

permittō (like *mittō*) 'allow'

propīnō, propīnāre, –, – 'drink a toast'

sufficiō, sufficere, suffēcī, suffectum 'be enough'

accendō, accendere, accendī, accēnsum 'light'

lampas, lampadis (f.) 'torch'

colligō, colligere, collēgī, collēctum 'gather up'

repōnō (like *pōnō*) 'put back'

dīligenter 'carefully'

sternō, sternere, strāvī, strātum 'spread out'

lectus, lectī (m.) 'bed'

excutiō, excutere, excussī, excussum 'shake out'

pulvīnus, pulvīnī (m.) 'pillow'

commolliō, -īre, -īvī, -ītum 'soften up'

cuius = alicuius (after *sī*)

parcō, parcere, pepercī, parsūrus (+ dative) 'spare'

recipiō mē 'take myself away'

gallus, gallī (m.) 'rooster'

cantus, cantūs (m.) 'song'

excitō, -āre, -āvī, -ātum 'wake up'

excurrō (like *currō*) 'run out'

59.2 Translate into Latin

GAIUS: Lucius, we dined very well yesterday; you received us well.

LUCIUS: I give you thanks. But I am sad since Marcus is saying bad things about my dinner.

GAIUS: What? There is nothing bad that you could say about that dinner; it must be praised. We had very good pigs' feet, very good liver, very good pilchards, a very good cabbage sprout, very good fish sauce. If your cook is a slave, free him!

LUCIUS: But Marcus had nothing; he asked and no-one gave (anything) to him. I am ashamed. The waiters served so badly that I must sell them all.

Additional Vocabulary

agō *can also mean* 'give' (and is so used in 'give thanks')

grātiae, grātiārum (f. plural) 'thanks'

59.3 Virgil, *Aeneid* 1.76–91

Aeolus, king of the winds, responds to Juno's request that he destroy Aeneas' fleet with a storm (continuation of the passage in chapter 53):

Aeolus haec contra: 'tuus, o regina, quid optes
explorare labor; mihi iussa capessere fas est.

tu mihi quodcumque hoc regni, tu sceptra Iovemque
concilias, tu das epulis accumbere divum
nimborumque facis tempestatumque potentem.'
haec ubi dicta, cavum conversa cuspide montem
impulit in latus; ac venti velut agmine facto,
qua data porta, ruunt et terras turbine perflant.
incubuere mari totumque a sedibus imis
una Eurusque Notusque ruunt creberque procellis
Africus, et vastos volvunt ad litora fluctus.
insequitur clamorque virum stridorque rudentum;
eripiunt subito nubes caelumque diemque
Teucrorum ex oculis; ponto nox incubat atra;
intonuere poli et crebris micat ignibus aether
praesentemque viris intentant omnia mortem.

Vocabulary

contrā 'in reply'
optō, optāre, optāvī, optātum 'want'
explōrō, -āre, -āvī, -ātum 'find out'
labor, labōris (m.) 'task' (supply *est* here)
iubeō, iubēre, iussī, iussum 'order'
capessō, capessere, capessīvī,
    capessītum 'carry out'
fās (n. indeclinable) 'right'
quodcumque hoc rēgnī 'this, whatever
    kingdom (is mine)'
scēptrum, scēptrī (n.) 'royal power'
Iuppiter, Iovis (m.) 'Jupiter'
conciliō, -āre, -āvī, -ātum 'procure',
    'make favourable'
epulae, epulārum (f. plural) 'feast'
accumbō, accumbere, accubuī,
    accubitum (+ dative) 'recline at'
    (Roman banqueters reclined while
    eating, so this effectively means 'join
    in feasting')
dīvum = deōrum
nimbus, nimbī (m.) 'storm-cloud'
-que . . . -que 'both . . . and'
tempestās, tempestātis (f.) 'storm'
potēns, *gen.* potentis (+ genitive)
    'powerful over'

ubi 'when'
cavus, cava, cavum 'hollow'
convertō, -vertere, -vertī, -versum
    'reverse'
cuspis, cuspidis (f.) 'spear'
impellō, impellere, impulī, impulsum
    'strike'
latus, lateris (n.) 'side'
ac 'and'
ventus, ventī (m.) 'wind'
velut 'as if'
agmine factō 'in military formation'
quā 'where' (short for *quā viā*, so
    literally 'by which way')
porta, portae (f.) 'gateway'
ruō, ruere, ruī, rūtum 'rush out',
    'heave up'
terra, terrae (f.) 'land'
turbō, turbinis (m.) 'whirlwind'
perflō, -āre, -āvī, -ātum 'blow through'
incubuēre = incubuērunt, *from*
    incumbō, incumbere, incubuī,
    incubitum (+ ablative) 'swoop down
    on, settle on'
mare, maris, marium (n.) 'sea'
tōtus, tōta, tōtum 'whole'

sēdēs, sēdis (f.) 'bottom'

īmus, īma, īmum 'deepest'

ūnā 'together'

Eurus, Eurī (m.) 'east wind'

Notus, Notī (m.) 'south wind'

crēber, crēbra, crēbrum (+ ablative)
   'prolific in', 'frequent'

procella, procellae (f.) 'storm'

Āfricus, Āfricī (m.) 'south-west wind'

vāstus, vāsta, vāstum 'enormous'

volvō, volvere, volvī, volūtum 'turn'

lītus, lītoris (n.) 'shore'

flūctus, flūctūs (m.) 'wave'

īnsequor (like *sequor*) 'follow
   immediately'

clāmor, clāmōris (m.) 'shouting'

virum = virōrum

strīdor, strīdōris (m.) 'creaking'

rudentēs, rudentum (m. plural)
   'rigging' (on a sailing ship)

ēripiō, ēripere, ēripuī, ēreptum 'snatch
   away'

subitō 'suddenly'

nūbēs, nūbis, nūbium (f.) 'cloud'

caelum, caelī (n.) 'sky'

Teucrī, Teucrōrum (m. plural) 'Trojans'

oculus, oculī (m.) 'eye'

pontus, pontī (m.) 'sea'

incubō, incubāre, incubuī, incubitum
   'broods over'

āter, ātra, ātrum 'black'

intonō, intonāre, intonuī, intonātum
   'thunder'

polus, polī (m.) 'heaven'

micō, micāre, micuī, – 'flash'

aethēr, aetheris (m.) 'sky'

praesēns, *gen.* praesentis 'immediate'

intentō, intentāre, intentāvī, intentātum
   'threaten'

mors, mortis, mortium (f.) 'death'

A possible prose order of the above would be:

Aeolus haec (dixit) contra: 'tuus, o regina, labor (est) explorare quid optes; mihi fas est iussa capessere. tu mihi quodcumque hoc regni (concilias), tu sceptra Iovemque concilias, tu (mihi) das epulis divum accumbere, nimborumque tempestatumque potentem (me) facis.' ubi haec dicta (sunt), conversa cuspide cavum montem in latus impulit; ac venti, velut agmine facto, ruunt qua data (est) porta, et terras turbine perflant. incubuere mari, totumque (mare) a sedibus imis ruunt una Eurusque Notusque Africusque creber procellis, et vastos volvunt ad litora fluctus; insequitur clamorque virum stridorque rudentum. nubes caelum-que diemque ex oculis Teucrorum subito eripiunt; ponto nox atra incubat. intonuere poli et crebris micat ignibus aether omniaque viris praesentem mortem intentant.

60 | Gerunds I

60.1 Formation of Gerunds

The gerund is a noun formed from a verb. In English gerunds are formed by adding '-ing' to the stem of a verb; this makes them look like present participles. Nevertheless a gerund functions very differently from a participle, so it is important to be able to distinguish the two.

'I love swimming': *swimming* is a noun, a gerund.
'The boy swimming in the river is very fast': *swimming* is an adjective, a present participle.

In Latin the gerund has a neuter gender and is formed like the neuter singular of the gerundive (see chapter 41).

First conjugation	*amandum* 'loving'
Second conjugation	*monendum* 'advising'
Third conjugation	*regendum* 'ruling'
Fourth conjugation	*audiendum* 'hearing'
Mixed conjugation	*capiendum* 'capturing'
First conjugation deponent	*vēnandum* 'hunting'
Second conjugation deponent	*verendum* 'fearing'
Third conjugation deponent	*ūtendum* 'using'
Fourth conjugation deponent	*partiendum* 'dividing'
Mixed conjugation deponent	*moriendum* 'dying'
Sum	–
Possum	–
Eō	*eundum* 'going'
Volō	*volendum* 'wanting'
Nōlō	*nōlendum* 'not wanting'
Mālō	–
Ferō	*ferendum* 'carrying'
Fīō	–

60.2 Declension of Gerunds

Because the gerund is not only always neuter but also always singular, it has very few forms when declined, and their number is further reduced by the fact that the present infinitive serves as the nominative of the gerund. This makes the gerund an exceptional paradigm in that the neuter nominative and accusative are not the same.

British Case Order		Ancient Case Order	
Nom.	amāre	**Nom.**	amāre
Voc.	–	**Gen.**	amandī
Acc.	amandum	**Dat.**	amandō
Gen.	amandī	**Acc.**	amandum
Dat.	amandō	**Abl.**	amandō
Abl.	amandō		

Practice

A Give all forms of the gerunds of:

1 laudō
2 doceō
3 dīcō
4 audiō
5 faciō
6 scrībō

7 reficiō
8 habeō
9 iuvō
10 veniō
11 interficiō
12 cōgitō

60.3 Distinguishing Gerunds from Other Words Translated with '-ing' in English

The fact that the infinitive is the nominative of the gerund means that in an English sentence like 'Swimming is fun' the word in '-ing' is equivalent to a Latin infinitive. In fact the full range of Latin possibilities for English words in '-ing' is four, because some such words are part of verbs.

'Ruling well is good.' *bene regere bonum est.* (English gerund, Latin infinitive acting as gerund in the nominative)
'You will conquer by ruling well.' *bene regendō vincēs.* (English gerund, Latin gerund)
'The ruling men are happy.' (*virī*) *regentēs fēlīcēs sunt.* (English participle, Latin participle)

'You are <u>ruling</u> well.' *bene regis.* (English participle as part of a present periphrastic verb; Latin finite verb). Cf. 'you were ruling well' *bene regēbās,* 'you will be ruling well' *bene regēs.*

Practice

B State whether each underlined word is a gerund or a participle in English and whether it would be translated in Latin with an infinitive, a gerund, a participle, or a finite verb.

<u>Speaking</u> (1) to a class of <u>aspiring</u> (2) stockbrokers, Mr Smith was <u>explaining</u> (3) the basics of <u>buying</u> (4) and <u>selling</u> (5) shares. '<u>Being</u> (6) a broker isn't simple,' he said; 'you will be <u>taking</u> (7) decisions of huge magnitude, in which by <u>making</u> (8) the right move you can earn thousands in an hour and by <u>goofing</u> (9) up you can lose a fortune. So a broker is always <u>paying</u> (10) attention to everything. Is <u>selling</u> (11) an under-<u>performing</u> (12) stock the right move? Only by <u>knowing</u> (13) the factors <u>affecting</u> (14) its future performance can you be sure: next week it might be <u>going</u> (15) through the roof, and you would be <u>kicking</u> (16) yourself for <u>selling</u> (17). On the other hand there are times when <u>selling</u> (18) quickly is essential: <u>waiting</u> (19) a day could lead to <u>staggering</u> (20) losses when the price is <u>dropping</u> (21) fast. But <u>knowing</u> (22) what you need to do takes work. It takes <u>reading</u> (23) the financial sections of at least three papers each <u>working</u> (24) day, it takes <u>paying</u> (25) attention not just to the companies in which you are <u>investing</u> (26) but also to their competitors, and it takes constant <u>monitoring</u> (27) of the markets, even when you're <u>travelling</u> (28) or on vacation.' He saw one of the students <u>waving</u> (29) a hand and stopped. 'Mr Smith, what's the point of <u>making</u> (30) lots of money and <u>being</u> (31) rich if you never have time to enjoy it?' <u>Pausing</u> (32) briefly, the teacher considered. '<u>Answering</u> (33) that kind of question is really the province of the philosophy department. Our university employs <u>leading</u> (34) philosophers who are no doubt experienced in <u>thinking</u> (35) about that sort of thing. I'm not; my speciality is just <u>making</u> (36) money, not <u>enjoying</u> (37) it.'

60.4 Use of the Gerund

The Latin gerund is normally used only in particular constructions, of which the most common are the following:

***ad* + accusative of gerund**: translated 'for ... -ing', 'for the purpose of ... -ing'. Thus *veniō ad laudandum* 'I come for praising', 'I come for the purpose of praising'.

genitive of gerund + *causā* or *grātiā*: translated 'for the sake of ... -ing'. Thus *veniō laudandī causā, veniō laudandī grātiā* 'I come for the sake of praising'.

ablative of gerund with preposition: translated '-ing' with appropriate preposition.
  Thus *dē laudandō* 'about praising', *in laudandō* 'in praising'.
ablative of gerund without preposition: ablative of means, translated 'by ... -ing'.
  Thus *laudandō* 'by praising'.
nominative of gerund (infinitive) as subject: translated as gerund or as infinitive.
  Thus *laudāre bonum est* 'praising is good', 'it is good to praise'.

A gerund may be modified by an adverb and may take an object, as *bene laudandī causā* 'for the sake of praising well' or *eōs laudandī causā* 'for the sake of praising them'. But the use of objects with gerunds is rare (cf. chapter 61).

Practice

C Translate:

1 scribam de bene vivendo.
2 veni ad iuvandum.
3 petendo multa invenies.
4 bonum est alios iuvare.
5 venerunt ad hoc nuntiandum.
6 deos laudare bonum est.
7 illud feci audiendi causa.
8 multa dixit de bene dormiendo.
9 equis utendo haec saxa attulit.
10 veniam iuvandi causa.

11 discessit ad opus perficiendum.
12 bene regendo cives laetos fecit.
13 Romam ibo eos iuvandi gratia.
14 librum scripsit de pecunia egendo.
15 difficile est his saxis uti.
16 venimus hoc videndi gratia.
17 ortus est ad dicendum.
18 hoc dicendo omnibus persuasimus.

D Translate into Latin:

1 I came to Rome for the sake of showing this to you.
2 By trying you will accomplish many things.
3 He wrote a book about thinking well.
4 Carrying off other people's money is bad.
5 Humans do many things for the purpose of being well.

6 We spoke about using slaves.
7 We ran for the purpose of arriving today.
8 You will accomplish nothing by sleeping.
9 I did everything for the sake of going to Athens.
10 Freeing slaves is foolish.

E Translate, distinguishing gerunds from gerundives:

1 patre mortuo, filii iuvandi sunt.
2 pater venit filios iuvandi causa.

3 hoc feci ad manendum Romae.
4 Romae mihi manendum est.

5 nisi hunc librum de optime dicendo scripsisses, clarissimus numquam factus esses.

6 nisi nobiscum venies, cum aliis tibi eundum erit.

7 hic manendo nihil perficietis.

8 magister venit ad docendum pueris sequentibus.

9 haec tibi nuntianda erunt regi.

10 hoc opus mihi perficiendum erat.

11 omnia conabor servos liberandi causa.

12 regina nostra ab hostibus servanda est.

13 ab aliis pecunia tibi petenda est; non habeo.

14 ille Athenas venit ad patrem nostrum videndum.

15 tibi pollicendum est.

60.5 Reading Practice

1 Terence, *Adelphi* 210–14 (adapted): Sannio has a bad experience with the master of the slave Syrus (second century BC).

SYRUS: quid istud, Sannio, est quod audio te concertavisse cum ero?

SANNIO: numquam vidi certationem iniquius comparatam, quam quae hodie inter nos fuit: ego vapulando, ille verberando, usque ambo defessi sumus.

SYRUS: tua culpa.

Vocabulary

concertō, -āre, -āvī, -ātum 'quarrel'
erus, erī (m.) 'master'
certātiō, certātiōnis (f.) 'quarrel'
inīquus, inīqua, inīquum 'unequal'
comparō, -āre, -āvī, -ātum 'match'
inter (+ accusative) 'between'
vāpulō, -āre, -āvī, -ātum 'be beaten'

verberō, -āre, -āvī, -ātum 'beat'
usque 'until'
ambō (nominative) 'both'
dēfētīscor, dēfētīscī, dēfessus sum 'get tired'
culpa, culpae (f.) 'fault'

2 Terence, *Adelphi* 867–80 (adapted): an old man complains about his hard life (second century BC).

Duxi uxorem: quam ibi miseriam vidi! nati sunt filii: alia cura. heia, dum studeo ut illis quam plurimum facerem, contrivi in quaerendo vitam et aetatem meam. nunc exacta aetate hunc fructum pro labore ab eis accipio: odium. et frater meus sine labore commoda patria potitur. illum amant, me fugitant; illi credunt consilia omnia, illum diligunt, apud illum sunt ambo, ego desertus sum; illum ut uiuat optant, meam autem mortem exspectant scilicet. ita eos meo labore maximo eductos hic fecit suos parvo sumptu: ego miseriam omnem capio, hic potitur gaudia. age age, nunc experiamur contra num ego possim blande dicere aut benigne facere.

ego quoque a meis me amari et magni pendi postulo. si id fit dando atque obse-
quendo, faciam.

Vocabulary

dūcō *can also mean* 'marry'

uxor, uxōris (f.) 'wife'

miseria, miseriae (f.) 'misery'

cūra, cūrae (f.) 'care'

heia 'alas'

studeō, studēre, studuī, – 'make an
   effort'

conterō, -terere, -trīvī, -trītum 'wear
   away'

quaerō *can also mean* 'try'

aetās, aetātis (f.) 'prime of life'

exigō, exigere, exēgī, exāctum 'finish'

frūctus, frūctūs (m.) 'reward'

prō (+ ablative) 'for'

labor, labōris (m.) 'work', 'effort'

commodum, commodī (n.) 'benefit'

patrius, patria, patrium 'associated with
   fatherhood'

**potior, potīrī, potītus sum
   (+ accusative) 'get possession of'**

fugitō, -āre, -āvī, -ātum 'avoid'

crēdō, crēdere, crēdidī, crēditum
   (+ dative) 'entrust'

dīligō, dīligere, dīlēxī, dīlēctum 'esteem'

apud (+ accusative) 'at the house of'

ambō (nominative) 'both'

dēserō, dēserere, dēseruī, dēsertum
   'abandon'

optō, optāre, optāvī, optātum 'wish'

mors, mortis, mortium (f.) 'death'

exspectō, -āre, -āvī, -ātum 'look forward
   to'

scīlicet 'certainly'

ēdūcō, ēdūcere, ēdūxī, ēductum 'bring
   up'

sūmptus, sūmptūs (m.) 'expense'

gaudium, gaudiī (n.) 'joy'

age 'come on!'

experior, experīrī, expertus sum 'try'

contrā 'on the other side'

blandus, -a, -um 'flattering'

benignus, -a, -um 'kind'

quoque 'too', 'also'

pendō, pendere, pependī, pēnsum
   'value'

postulō, -āre, -āvī, -ātum (+ accusative
   and infinitive) 'ask'

obsequor (like *sequor*) 'be compliant'

3   Apicius, *De re coquinaria* 1.3: a recipe for rose-flavoured wine (perhaps fifth
century AD).

Rosatum sic facies: folia rosarum, albo sublato, lino inseres ut sutiles facias, et vino
quam plurima infundes, ut septem dies in vino sint. post septem dies, rosas de vino
tolles et alias rosas recentes similiter sutiles infundes, ut dies septem in vino
maneant, et rosas tolles. similiter et tertio facies et rosas tolles, et vinum percolabis,
et cum ad bibendum uti voles, addito melle rosatum conficies. similiter et de violis
violacium facies, et eodem modo melle temperabis.

Vocabulary

rosātum, rosātī (n.) 'rose-flavoured wine'

folium, foliī (n.) 'petal'

rosa, rosae (f.) 'rose'

albus, alba, album 'white part'

tollō *can also mean* **'remove'**

līnum, līnī (n.) 'thread'

īnserō, īnserere, īnseruī, īnsertum 'string'

sūtilis, sūtile 'strung together'

vīnum, vīnī (n.) 'wine'

īnfundō, īnfundere, īnfūdī, īnfūsum (+ dative) 'pour into'

post (+ accusative) 'after'

recēns, *gen.* recentis 'fresh'

tertiō *can also mean* 'for a third time'

percōlō, -āre, -āvī, -ātum 'strain', 'filter'

bibō, bibere, bibī, – 'drink'

addō, addere, addidī, additum 'add'

mel, mellis (n.) 'honey'

cōnficiō, -ficere, -fēcī, -fectum 'finish'

viola, violae (f.) 'violet'

violācium, violāciī (n.) 'violet-flavoured wine'

modus, modī (m.) 'way'

temperō, -āre, -āvī, -ātum 'mix'

60.6 Vocabulary to Learn

Verbs

bibō, bibere, bibī, –	'drink'
coquō, coquere, coxī, coctum	'cook', 'bake'
tangō, tangere, tetigī, tāctum	'touch'

Nouns

amor, amōris (m.)	'love'
hospes, hospitis (m.)	'guest', 'host'
īnsula, īnsulae (f.)	'island'
īra, īrae (f.)	'anger'
iter, itineris (n.)	'journey'
Iuppiter, Iovis (m.)	'Jupiter'
lūdus, lūdī (m.)	'game'
mare, maris, marium (n.)	'sea'
mōns, montis, montium (m.)	'mountain'
mulier, mulieris (f.)	'woman'
porta, portae (f.)	'gate'
tēctum, tēctī (n.)	'roof'

Adjective

| vetus, *gen.* veteris | 'old' |

61 | Gerunds II

61.1 Attraction of the Gerund

When a gerund in a case other than the nominative ought to have an accusative object, the most common Latin construction is to substitute a gerundive for the gerund.[1] The gerundive takes on the gender and number of the noun that should have been the gerund's object, and the noun takes on the case that the gerund would have had. But the meaning remains that of the gerund.

ad librōs legendum becomes *ad librōs legendōs* 'for the purpose of reading books' (not 'for books that have to be read') (* is used to indicate a phrase that would not occur).

librum legendī causā becomes *librī legendī causā* 'for the sake of reading a book' (not 'for a book that has to be read')

librōs legendō becomes *librīs legendīs* 'by reading books' (not 'by having-to-be-read books')

When the gerundive is used this way it must be translated with an English gerund, not with the 'must' or 'have to' constructions that normally translate a gerundive. The infinitive when used as a gerund does not take this construction; there are no restrictions on the kinds of objects an infinitive can take.

Practice

A Translate (all gerundives are acting as gerunds):

1 multa dixit de urbe defendenda.
2 milites progressi sunt ad hostes vincendos.
3 hostes vicit duce capiendo.
4 domum venit ad servos liberandos.
5 magister multa fecit pueri docendi gratia.
6 rex ad castra ibit ad milites hortandos.
7 Romae sumus tui iuvandi gratia.
8 Corinthum venimus dei laudandi causa.

---

[1] Normally the gerund takes an accusative object only when either (1) the object is a neuter pronoun or adjective, or (2) the gerund is genitive and the object is plural and belongs to the first or second declension (to avoid the rhyming *ōrum . . . ōrum* of the gerundive construction).

9 servis suis liberandis haec mulier
   nos laetos fecit.

10 Romam venit urbis videndae
   causa.

11 his verbis dicendis iudex nos
   omnes liberavit.

12 venietne domum ad patrem
   sepeliendum?

13 puer ad nos venit patris
   inveniendi causa.

14 librum scripsit de mulieribus
   intellegendis.

15 pecunia petenda miser factus est.

16 epistulam scripsit de urbibus
   oppugnandis.

B Take the following non-standard Latin sentences, which contain gerunds with accusative objects, and rewrite them using the gerundive construction without changing their meaning. (Hint: first put the object into the case of the gerund, then turn the gerund into a gerundive by putting it into the gender and number of the word that was originally its object. Thus **rēgīnam videndī causā* would become *rēgīnae videndae causā* 'for the sake of seeing the queen' as follows: **rēgīnam* (feminine accusative singular) *videndī* (neuter genitive singular) *causā* → **rēgīnae* (feminine genitive singular) *videndī* (neuter genitive singular) *causā* → *rēgīnae* (feminine genitive singular) *videndae* (feminine genitive singular) *causā*.)

1 *iter fecimus hanc insulam
  videndi causa.

2 *venimus ad iudices
  quaerendum.

3 *portas reficiendo urbem bene
  defendemus.

4 *librum scribam de Iovem
  laudando.

5 *hospites Romam venerunt ad
  ludos videndum.

6 *iram ostendendo te non iuvabis.

7 *hae mulieres adsunt cenam
  parandi causa.

8 *multa dixit de sepeliendo
  amorem.

C Translate into Latin, turning all gerunds into gerundives:

1 We came for the purpose of
  seeing these mountains.

2 He is writing a book about
  abandoning cities.

3 We did that for the sake of
  hearing this woman.

4 By hearing your words we
  became learned men.

5 You saved us all by repairing the
  gates.

6 He said that for the sake of
  receiving money.

7 They said many things about
  repairing houses.

8 By giving money you will not
  become rich.

9 I have come for the sake of
  returning the money.

10 The enemy placed a camp here for the purpose of hindering our men.

11 The king has come to Corinth for the purpose of encouraging the soldiers.

61.2 Distinguishing Gerundives by Attraction from Gerundives of Obligation

This construction, known as 'gerundive by attraction', is not always easy to distinguish from the gerundive of obligation construction (chapters 41 and 45.2) – but it is essential to do so, as the two have very different meanings. Useful clues for telling them apart are that in the gerundive by attraction construction the gerundive is never nominative, whereas in the obligation construction the gerundive is *usually* nominative (and usually accompanied by a form of the verb *sum*). So a rule that will work about 95 per cent of the time is that if the gerundive is nominative, it should be translated with 'must'/'have to', and if it is not nominative, it should be translated with '-ing'.

vēnit ad dōna videnda: the form *videnda* is not nominative, so 'He came for the purpose of seeing the gifts.'
urbs videnda est nōbīs: the form *videnda* is nominative, so 'We must see the city.'
vēnit rēgis audiendī causā: the form *audiendī* is not nominative, so 'He came for the sake of hearing the king.'
rēgēs audiendī erant nōbīs: the form *audiendī* is nominative, so 'We had to hear the kings.'
vēnit ad videndum: the form *videndum* is not nominative, so 'He came for the purpose of seeing.'
videndum est: the form *videndum* is nominative, so 'One must see', 'It is necessary to see.'

Practice

D Translate, watching for all types of gerundives and gerunds:

1 hostes vicit rege capiendo.
2 hae portae reficiendae sunt.
3 venietne domum ad patrem sepeliendum?
4 omnibus moriendum erit.
5 dei laudandi erant omnibus.
6 venimus tui videndi gratia.
7 multa audivimus de ovibus vendendis.
8 iter fecerunt ad illos montes videndos.
9 hi ludi videndi sunt omnibus civibus.
10 ibi ponenda erunt castra.
11 puer ad nos venit patris inveniendi causa.
12 nostris vincendi erunt hostes.
13 vobis hic sedendum est.
14 veni ad iuvandum.
15 nocte dormiendum est bonis hominibus.

16 mulieres raptae quaerendae sunt nobis.
17 multa dixit de urbe defendenda.
18 hostes adsunt ad portas nostras oppugnandas.
19 his verbis dicendis nos omnes liberavit.
20 nunc magnopere conandum est vobis.
21 nobis eundum erit Romam.
22 petendo multa invenies.
23 nostri progressi sunt ad hostes vincendos.
24 veniam iudicis videndi causa.
25 bellum illis gerendum erit.
26 cogitandum est mihi.
27 milites progressi sunt ad ducem sequendum.
28 illi veniendum est domum.
29 bene regendum erit tibi.
30 bene regendo cives laetos fecit.
31 verba dicenda erant mihi.
32 Romam ibo eos iuvandi gratia.
33 Iuppiter laudandus est iudicibus.
34 hi pueri docendi erunt magistro.
35 veniam iuvandi causa.
36 delenda erat Carthago.
37 progrediendum est nobis.
38 illi venerunt ad bellum gerendum.
39 epistulam accepi de senibus audiendis.
40 domum venit ad servos liberandos.
41 his mulieribus cena paranda erit.
42 servis liberandis nos laetos fecit.
43 librum scripsit de regibus intellegendis.
44 haec domus reficienda erit.
45 hoc feci audiendi causa.

E Translate into Latin, turning all gerunds with accusative objects into gerundives:

1 I must go home.
2 He went for the purpose of fighting.
3 By throwing stones we put the dogs to flight.
4 She had to hear his words.
5 He praises us for the sake of receiving money.
6 You will have to speak.
7 They will have to find the gold.
8 I am present for the purpose of seeing the fleet.
9 I have a book about repairing houses.
10 We shall have to defend our city.
11 You will have to see that city.
12 They had to capture the enemies' king.
13 I have come for the purpose of returning the money.
14 You saved us all by defending our city.
15 We had to think.
16 We will have to help our friends.
17 He became rich by selling horses.
18 You (plural) must go to the camp.
19 We had to depart from Rome.
20 The sheep will have to be driven to the field.
21 We shall have to repair our walls.
22 The soldiers had to be encouraged.
23 Our guest is in Rome for the purpose of hearing the senate.

61.3 Reading Practice

1 Vitruvius, *On Architecture* 2.8.19 (adapted): how to find out which bricks are strongest (first century BC).

De ipsa autem testa, utrum sit optima an vitiosa ad structuram, statim nemo potest iudicare, sed postquam in tempestatibus et aestate in tecto collocata est, tunc, si est firma, probatur; nam testa quae non erit facta ex creta bona aut parum erit cocta, ibi se ostendet esse vitiosam gelis et pruina tacta. ergo testa quae non in tectis potest pati laborem, ea non potest in structurae oneri ferendo esse firma. maxime igitur ex veteribus tegulis structa tecta et ex vetere testa structi parietes firmitatem poterunt habere.

Vocabulary

testa, testae (f.) 'brick'	parum 'insufficiently'
vitiōsus, -a, -um 'bad', 'flawed'	gelum, gelī (n.) 'frost'
strūctūra, strūctūrae (f.) 'building'	pruīna, pruīnae (f.) 'winter weather'
iūdicō, -āre, -āvī, -ātum 'determine'	labor, labōris (m.) 'exposure'
tempestās, tempestātis (f.) 'bad weather'	onus, oneris (n.) 'weight'
aestās, aestātis (f.) 'summer heat'	tēgula, tēgulae (f.) 'roof tile'
collocō, -āre, -āvī, -ātum 'place'	struō, struere, strūxī, strūctum
tunc 'then'	'construct'
firmus, firma, firmum 'sound'	pariēs, parietis (m.) 'wall'
probō, -āre, -āvī, -ātum 'approve'	firmitās, firmitātis (f.) 'strength'
crēta, crētae (f.) 'clay'	

2 Terence, *Andria* 175–80 (adapted): a slave worries about what his master is up to (second century BC).

Semper verebar quorsum eri lenitas evaderet: qui postquam audiverat non datum iri uxorem filio suo, numquam quoiquam nostrum verbum dixit neque id aegre tulit. fortasse voluit nos sic necopinantes duci falso gaudio, sperantes, iam amoto metu capi, ne esset spatium cogitandi ad disturbandas nuptias.

Vocabulary

quōrsum 'to which result?'	falsus, falsa, falsum 'false'
erus, erī (m.) 'master'	gaudium, gaudiī (n.) 'joy'
lēnitās, lēnitātis (f.) 'mildness'	spērō, spērāre, spērāvī, spērātum 'hope'
ēvādō, ēvādere, ēvāsī, ēvāsum 'end up'	iam 'already'
uxor, uxōris (f.) 'wife'	āmoveō, āmovēre, āmōvī, āmōtum
quoiquam 'to any one'	'remove'
aegrē 'badly'	spatium, spatiī (n.) (+ genitive)
fortasse 'perhaps'	'opportunity for'
necopīnāns, *gen.* necopīnantis	disturbō, -āre, -āvī, -ātum 'disrupt'
'unsuspecting'	nuptiae, nuptiārum (f. plural) 'wedding'

3   St Augustine, *Confessions* 1.14 (adapted): as a child, Augustine hated learning Greek (fourth century AD).

Cur ergo graecas etiam litteras oderam talia cantantes? nam Homerus peritus est texere tales fabulas, sed mihi tamen amarus erat puero. credo etiam graecis pueris Vergilium ita esse, cum eum sic discere coguntur ut ego Homerum. videlicet difficultas discendae linguae peregrinae quasi felle aspergebat omnes suavitates graecarum fabularum.

Vocabulary

litterae, litterārum (f. plural) 'literature'
ōdī, ōdisse, ōsum 'hate' (perfect in form,
    but present in meaning)
cantō, -āre, -āvī, -ātum (+ accusative)
    'sing of'
perītus, -a, -um (+ infinitive) 'skilled in'
texō, texere, texuī, textum 'weave',
    'compose'
fābula, fābulae (f.) 'story'

amārus, -a, -um 'bitter', 'unpleasant'
ut (without subjunctive) 'as'
vidēlicet 'indeed'
difficultās, difficultātis (f.) 'difficulty'
peregrīnus, -a, -um 'foreign'
fel, fellis (n.) 'bile', 'bitterness'
aspergō, aspergere, aspersī, aspersum
    'sprinkle'
suāvitās, suāvitātis (f.) 'sweetness'

4   Funerary inscription in the Metropolitan Museum of Art, New York: a freedwoman mourns her son (second century AD). See the cover of this volume.

Diis manibus. sacrum P. Sextilio P. lib. Fortunato, qui vixit annos XXII mensib. III. Sextilia P. lib. Isias filio karissimo fecit et sibi et suis et libertis libertabusque posterisque eorum.

Vocabulary

diīs mānibus 'to the divine spirits'
sacer, sacra, sacrum 'sacred to'
P. lib. (= Pūblī lībertō or Pūblī
    lībertae) 'freedman of Publius' or
    'freedwoman of Publius'
    (designation inserted between
    a freedman's second and third
    names or a freedwoman's first
    and second names)
mēnsib. (= mēnsibus) 'for months'
kārus = cārus
(understand *hoc* with *fēcit*)

suī, suōrum (m.) 'his/her own people',
    'his/her relatives'
lībertus, lībertī (m.) 'freedman'
līberta, lībertae (f.) 'freedwoman' (the
    dative/ablative plural ending -*ābus*
    is sometimes used in the first
    declension on feminine words that
    would otherwise have the same
    ending as masculine ones: *fīliīs*
    fīliābusque 'sons and daughters',
    deīs deābusque 'gods and
    goddesses')
posterī, posterōrum (m.) 'offspring'

61.4 Vocabulary to Learn

Verbs

negō, negāre, negāvī, negātum	'deny'
parcō, parcere, pepercī, parsūrus (+ dative)	'spare'
pāreō, pārēre, pāruī, – (+ dative)	'obey'

Nouns

adulēscēns, adulēscentis, adulēscentium (m.)	'young man'
aestās, aestātis (f.)	'summer'
aetās, aetātis (f.)	'age'
animus, animī (m.)	'soul'
āra, ārae (f.)	'altar'
arbor, arboris (f.)	'tree'
cōpia, cōpiae (f.)	'supply', (in plural) 'troops'
gaudium, gaudiī (n.)	'joy'
nauta, nautae (m.)	'sailor'
ōrātor, ōrātōris (m.)	'speaker'
perīculum, perīculī (n.)	'danger'

Adjectives

aequus, aequa, aequum	'even', 'fair'
albus, alba, album	'white'
inīquus, inīqua, inīquum	'uneven', 'unfair'
tōtus, tōta, tōtum	'whole'

APPENDICES

62 | How to Use the Appendices

The appendices are designed to help readers consolidate their grammatical skills by means of revision exercises with an answer key. The first exercises focus on helping readers become familiar with the grammatical terminology used to describe Latin; it is important to be able to understand that terminology, because otherwise one has great difficulty understanding explanations of how Latin works. Readers not already used to grammatical terminology may find the new vocabulary daunting, particularly because it is not easily translated into words that such readers already know: the terms used to describe language express concepts that are not expressed at all in non-technical language, so learning the grammatical vocabulary means learning a new set of ideas. But precisely for this reason learning grammatical terminology pays off in the long run, for the ideas described by these terms are genuinely useful – if the same ideas could be expressed in non-technical language we would not have the terminology in the first place. Learning the concepts and principles of grammatical analysis will greatly improve not only your ability to learn Latin, but also your grasp of English and your ability to learn other Indo-European languages; in fact the mastery of grammatical analysis that goes with learning Latin is generally agreed to be one of the major benefits of learning the language. Former Latin students often find that this aspect of their studies continues to pay dividends even when they have forgotten much of the Latin language itself.

Chapter 65 is an alphabetical glossary; this is designed to be used for quick reference if you have forgotten a term and just need to be reminded of it. If you are completely unfamiliar with a concept, however, it is best to start with chapter 63, a set of explanations and exercises. The way to get the most out of this section is to read the explanation and then immediately do the associated exercises, checking yourself frequently with the answer key in chapter 64. The maximum learning will occur if you write down your answer to each question in each exercise and then check every single answer against the key as soon as you have written it down (both the process of writing the answer and the immediate checking aid learning). Checking your answers at longer intervals will work as well, provided you do not let the intervals become too long: if you do all the exercises available on a given point and then check yourself, and at that point you discover that you were making a systematic mistake on some particular point, you will no longer be able to do further exercises to practise that point, and therefore you will learn much less than you could have learned if you had checked your work sooner.

63.1 Parts of Speech

Words can be classified into parts of speech; this is necessary when dealing with an inflected language like Latin as the various parts of speech behave differently from each other. The main parts of speech are verbs, nouns, adjectives, pronouns, adverbs, prepositions, and conjunctions.

Verbs are traditionally defined as action words, but the 'action' they describe can be fairly inactive: 'run', 'sit', 'sleep', and 'think' are all verbs. Another way verbs can be identified is as words that can inflect (i.e. change form) to indicate past or present action: in English 'run' changes to 'ran' to indicate past time, and similarly 'sit' becomes 'sat', 'sleep' becomes 'slept', and 'think' becomes 'thought'. Alternatively, you can think of verbs as words that become singular (referring to only one subject) when you add '-s': in the plural 'they run', 'they sit', 'they sleep', and 'they think', but in the singular 'he runs', 'he sits', 'he sleeps', and 'he thinks'. However you do it, it is essential to be able to identify verbs, as they are the most important parts of speech: there is at least one in every sentence, and the sentence is built around the verb(s). Sometimes a single verb form is made up of more than one word (see section 63.2, 'periphrastic verbs').

Nouns are traditionally defined as words that name a person, place, or thing; 'Julia', 'London', 'beauty', and 'turnip' are all nouns. In English, most nouns inflect for number: they become plural (i.e. they indicate two or more items) when an '-s' is added to them. Thus 'beauties' and 'turnips' are easily recognizable, and while you may never have seen 'Julias' or 'Londons', you can nevertheless tell that they would refer to two women named 'Julia' or two places named 'London'. Some nouns take a different plural ending, or change their vowels when they are plural: thus the plural of 'child' is 'children', the plural of 'foot' is 'feet', and the plural of 'man' is 'men'. Most English nouns also form a genitive by adding apostrophe + s: 'Julia's dog', 'London's crowds', 'beauty's disappearance', and 'the turnip's colour' are all possible possessive phrases.

Adjectives are words that modify (i.e. describe) nouns: 'big', 'many', and 'beautiful' are all adjectives. In English, adjectives do not inflect (i.e. change their form): you cannot add '-s' to them. Thus '*bigs', '*manies', and '*beautifuls' do not exist (* is used to indicate words that do not exist).

Pronouns are short words that stand for a noun; most languages have only a few different pronouns and use each one frequently. Common types of pronouns include personal pronouns such as 'I', 'we', and 'you'; demonstrative pronouns such as 'this' and 'that'; and relative pronouns such as 'who' and 'what'. English pronouns contain remnants of our language's original inflection system that are no longer visible elsewhere: they inflect for gender ('he' versus 'she'), number ('he' and 'she' versus 'they', 'I' versus 'we'), and case (nominative 'I', 'he', 'she', 'they'; accusative 'me', 'him', 'her', 'them').

Adverbs are words that modify verbs and/or adjectives; very often they describe how or when something is done. In English many adverbs end in '-ly' (e.g. 'quickly', 'kindly', 'enormously'), but this is not a secure way of identifying adverbs since some very common ones have other endings (e.g. 'very', 'tomorrow').

Prepositions are words like 'to', 'in', 'at', 'by', 'from', etc.: little words that have to be followed by nouns or pronouns. Thus 'to London', 'in consideration', 'at school', 'by Julia', 'from work', etc. are preposition + noun groups known as prepositional phrases. Sometimes adjectives and/or other modifiers come between the preposition and the noun and form part of the prepositional phrase, as 'in a red dress'.

Conjunctions are words that join other words or sentences together. They are divided into co-ordinating conjunctions ('and', 'but', and 'or') and subordinating conjunctions ('if', 'when', 'because', 'since', etc.). (For subordination see chapter 15.)

Articles are a part of speech that exists in English but not in Latin: the English articles are 'the' and 'a'. 'The' is known as the 'definite article' and 'a' as the 'indefinite article', but this distinction is irrelevant for Latin.

There are also a few words that belong to other parts of speech, including **interjections** (exclamations like 'oh!' and 'ouch!'). These parts of speech are not discussed in this book.

A difficulty with identifying parts of speech in English is that sometimes the same word can function in more than one way, depending on the context. Thus for example 'cut' can be a verb, a noun, or an adjective, but in any particular sentence it can be only one of those. In 'He cut the bread' it is a verb, in 'She has a nasty-looking cut on her finger' it is a noun, and in 'There is some cut cheese in the refrigerator' it is an adjective. Likewise 'that' is a pronoun in 'I didn't know that', an adjective in 'That house is enormous', and a conjunction in 'He said that she was away.' So it is important to work out what a word's function in a particular sentence is.

An English sentence can be broken up into different parts of speech as follows: 'Jim's friend Mike is coming to dinner tonight, and we have a huge roast in the oven.'

Jim's	noun
friend	noun
Mike	noun
is coming	verb
to	preposition

dinner	noun
tonight	adverb
and	conjunction
we	pronoun
have	verb
a	article
huge	adjective
roast	noun
in	preposition
the	article
oven	noun

Practice

A Identify the part of speech of each underlined word or group of words in the following English paragraphs:

Romulus and Remus, the founders of Rome, had a doubtful ancestry. Their father was unknown: legend has it that he was the god of war, Mars, but even in antiquity that story was viewed with suspicion. Their mother was Rhea Silvia, daughter of Numitor, rightful king of Alba Longa. Numitor's evil brother, Amulius, seized the throne from him, and in order to make sure that the legitimate king had no male heirs (female heirs did not count in antiquity, which was lucky for Rhea Silvia as otherwise Numitor would have killed her as he allegedly killed her brother), he ordered Rhea to become a Vestal Virgin.

   It was a serious crime for a Vestal Virgin to have a child, and when the twins were born, Amulius was furious. He took them away from their mother and dumped them in a river in hopes that they would drown. But they did not drown; the basket containing the twins drifted to shore, where they were rescued and fed by a wolf. Later a shepherd found the babies and took them home to his wife, who raised them until they became unruly teenagers.

   As teenagers Romulus and Remus caused more trouble than most: they not only robbed people, but also gathered a band of followers and became powerful bandits. Eventually Remus was captured and brought to the king, at which point he was recognized by his grandfather, Numitor. Romulus and his men came to rescue Remus, and with Numitor's help they killed the king. Numitor then became king of Alba, and Romulus and Remus, who were not used to the restraint and decorum required of princes in Alba, went off to found Rome.

Now an <u>ancient</u> <u>city</u> <u>can</u> <u>have</u> <u>only</u> <u>one</u> <u>founder</u>, <u>so</u> the <u>story</u> <u>was</u> bound <u>to end</u> <u>badly</u>: <u>they</u> <u>had</u> a <u>quarrel</u> over <u>who</u> <u>was</u> <u>to be</u> <u>king</u>, <u>and</u> <u>Romulus</u> <u>killed</u> <u>Remus</u>.

63.2 Periphrastic Verb Forms

Some English verbs have two parts: 'he <u>is coming</u>', 'he <u>was coming</u>', '<u>did</u> he <u>come</u>?', 'he <u>has come</u>', '<u>has</u> he <u>come</u>?', 'he <u>has been coming</u>', 'he <u>will come</u>', '<u>will</u> he <u>come</u>?', 'he <u>will</u> <u>be coming</u>', 'he wants <u>to come</u>', etc. These verb forms function as a single unit in English and must be translated with a single word in Latin, so it is important to be able to identify them. Generally speaking any form of English 'be', 'do', 'have', 'will', 'shall', or 'would' that is followed by another verb form makes up a periphrastic unit; the two elements need not be exactly next to each other. Infinitives are also periphrastic and consist of 'to' plus a verb, for example 'to be'. It is often stated that English infinitives should not be split, i.e. that nothing should come between 'to' and 'be', but in practice English infinitives are often split (e.g. 'to boldly go where no-one has gone before', where the infinitive 'to go' is split by the adverb 'boldly'), so it is useful to be alert to this possibility when trying to identify them.

Not all groups of verb forms are periphrastic units; often several different verbs are involved. If the different verb forms do not combine to express one idea, but instead express separate ideas, they are separate entities rather than a single periphrastic unit: 'he <u>came</u>, <u>saw</u>, and <u>conquered</u>' has three verbs, while 'he <u>has been conquering</u>' has one periphrastic verb form in three parts. A verb form and a following infinitive count as two separate entities: 'he <u>wants</u> <u>to come</u>', 'he <u>likes</u> <u>to argue</u>', and 'he <u>hates</u> <u>to be</u> wrong' are each composed of two verb forms. There is a grey area with verbs that take an infinitive without 'to', such as 'can' and 'could': from an English perspective one could certainly think of 'he <u>can come</u>' as a single periphrastic verb form, but that analysis would be unhelpful in dealing with Latin, where two verbs are involved. And the main advantage of the concept of periphrastic verb forms is that it allows one to identify English multi-word groupings that are equivalent to a single word in Latin (and Latin multi-word groupings that are equivalent to a single word in English). It is therefore easiest to think of 'can' and 'could' as separate verbs from what follows them, not as parts of periphrastic units.

The simplest rule to follow is that English periphrastic verb forms can only begin with forms of 'be', 'do', 'have', 'will', 'shall', and 'would' (or, for infinitives, with 'to'): when a group of verb forms starts off with any other verb ('want', 'can', 'need', etc.) two separate verbs are involved. And when punctuation intervenes, separate verbs are always involved. Thus 'he <u>was</u>, <u>is</u>, and always <u>will be</u> a scoundrel' contains three separate verbs, of which the third is periphrastic, and 'he <u>would like</u> <u>to see</u> you' contains two separate verbs, both periphrastic.

Practice

B Each of these sentences contains one periphrastic verb. Identify it and find all its parts:

1 I was giving the dog a bath.
2 He will do it.
3 We are coming as fast as we can.
4 Have you seen this?
5 I want to learn Latin.
6 Has he been doing that all day?
7 Were they carrying it up the hill?
8 Will you be staying long?
9 They did not come after all.
10 I shall never forget that.
11 They have been sitting here since noon.
12 No-one has ever seen this before.
13 They will be handling this case.
14 It is very difficult to be perfect.
15 Will they give us anything?
16 Did you really say that?
17 We were not just standing there.
18 Have you been waiting long?
19 Has he turned up yet?
20 I shall be coming next week.
21 He wants to go home.
22 He has not said anything all year.
23 He will be sitting in the back.
24 You were praising him too much.
25 We shall come next week.
26 They will be living here all year.
27 What were you doing there?
28 It is impossible not to believe her.
29 Will you look at this for me?
30 Are you going to the party?
31 Who is helping him this year?
32 No-one wants to do it.

C Some of these sentences contain periphrastic verbs; others just contain two or more separate verbs. Some contain several periphrastic verbs. Identify the periphrastic verbs and find all their parts:

1 Which of you has been sitting here the longest?
2 We are going very carefully on this cliff because many climbers have fallen off it.
3 They are not coming after all, because they did not want to wait any longer.
4 I cannot believe that the train has already arrived!
5 I came, I saw, I conquered, and then I wrote a book about it.
6 They have not done anything to deserve such an awful fate.
7 Who can tell what will happen next?
8 Robin Hood was an outlaw who lived in Sherwood forest and was kind to the poor.
9 They could not identify the man who had attacked them, because he was wearing a mask.
10 Come and see the chairman once you've settled in; you will

recognize him because he will be asleep in the lounge.

11 I would think twice before deciding to buy a used car, because many people have been tricked by car salesmen.

12 Who knows whether we shall ever see our homeland again? No-one who has come this way has ever returned to tell the tale of his adventures.

13 The captain could not see the other ship, so he did not try to steer away from it.

14 People have been learning Latin as a foreign language for more than two thousand years.

15 I can see something, but I have no idea what it is.

16 I wanted to be an Olympic swimmer, but it didn't work out, so I decided to be a writer instead.

17 No-one can be sure who will win that race, but we all know that the winner will not be Martin.

63.3 Subjects and Objects

Every sentence consists of, at a minimum, one verb and a subject for that verb, that is, an indication of who or what performs the action of the verb. In Latin the subject may be understood rather than expressed, but in English it has to be expressed (except in the case of imperatives). Subjects can be nouns or pronouns: in 'Julia runs', 'London is crowded', 'The cat wants to come in', or 'Beauty is truth', the subjects (underlined) are nouns; in 'He saw it', 'You know her', and 'They have a big dog', the subjects are pronouns.

The subject is often the first word or phrase in an English sentence, but not always. Sometimes an adverb or prepositional phrase precedes the subject, as 'Tomorrow we shall go shopping' or 'In spring this wood is full of bluebells'. In questions an interrogative word and/or a verb usually comes first, forcing the subject into a later position, as 'Do you know him?', 'Whom did you see?', 'Which one did he buy?', 'Have you seen Mary?'. (If the interrogative word happens to be the subject, then it continues to come first: 'Who saw them?')

Sometimes several verbs connected by a conjunction share the same subject, as in 'He comes and goes', where 'he' is the subject of both 'comes' and 'goes'. Some verbs depend directly on another verb and do not have expressed subjects: for example, in 'I want to go to Paris' the main verb is 'want', which has the subject 'I', but the dependent verb 'to go' does not have an expressed subject.

Many, but not all, verbs have objects. An object is a noun or pronoun that receives the action of the verb; in English objects normally come after verbs. Some verbs have more than one object. The objects are underlined in the following sentences: 'I love John', 'John loves me', 'We saw an enormous rattlesnake', 'They gave her flowers' (here 'her' is an indirect object and 'flowers' is a direct object; see chapter 7.2), 'They had cake, ice cream, and candied fruit'.

Verbs expressing identity, such as 'be', 'become', or 'be called', do not have objects since the thing that comes after them is stated to be the same thing as the subject. Thus 'He has become famous', 'We are hungry', and 'He is named Jim' are sentences without objects.

Practice

D Find the subjects of these sentences, and the objects where they exist; although a subject or object may consist of more than one word, try to identify just the one word that is the core of each.

1 I am Canadian.
2 What do you see?
3 Oliver's sister is a chemist.
4 Where is Jane going?
5 His work is very good.
6 You are brilliant.
7 Who knows that?
8 A student's life can be exhausting.
9 Whom do you choose?
10 Jane doesn't love John.
11 Martin's dog is overweight.
12 What is in the box?
13 In December the lights are lit.
14 Mark works here.
15 In which house are the children?
16 Sometimes I wonder.
17 Where are you?
18 Rarely have I been so frightened.
19 In what direction did he go?
20 Jim bought the last one.
21 That boy's father is a fireman.
22 The mother of this girl is very rich.

E For every underlined verb in the paragraphs below, find its subject or identify it as an infinitive. Work out which verbs have objects and what those objects are. Be sure to identify the actual word that is the grammatical subject or object, not the idea behind that word: for example, in the sentence 'Bob, who <u>is</u> a surgeon, <u>works</u> long hours', the subject of 'works' is 'Bob', but the subject of 'is' is 'who', not 'Bob'. Although logically 'who' is the same person as 'Bob', grammatically only 'who' can be the subject of 'is'; this point is important for some aspects of Latin.

Romulus and Remus, the founders of Rome, <u>had</u> a doubtful ancestry. Their father <u>was</u> unknown: legend <u>has</u> it that he <u>was</u> the god of war, Mars, but even in antiquity that story <u>was viewed</u> with suspicion. Their mother <u>was</u> Rhea Silvia, daughter of Numitor, rightful king of Alba Longa. Numitor's evil brother, Amulius, <u>seized</u> the throne from him, and in order <u>to make</u> sure that the legitimate king <u>had</u> no male heirs (female heirs <u>did not count</u> in antiquity, which <u>was</u> lucky for Rhea Silvia as otherwise Numitor <u>would have killed</u> her as he allegedly <u>killed</u> her brother), he <u>ordered</u> Rhea to become a Vestal Virgin.

It <u>was</u> a serious crime for a Vestal Virgin to have a child, and when the twins <u>were born</u>, Amulius <u>was</u> furious. He <u>took</u> them away from their mother and <u>dumped</u> them in a river in hopes that they <u>would drown</u>. But they <u>did not drown</u>; the basket containing the twins <u>drifted</u> to shore, where they <u>were rescued</u> and fed by a wolf. Later a shepherd <u>found</u> the babies and <u>took</u> them home to his wife, who <u>raised</u> them until they <u>became</u> unruly teenagers.

As teenagers Romulus and Remus <u>caused</u> more trouble than most: they not only <u>robbed</u> people, but also <u>gathered</u> a band of followers and <u>became</u> powerful bandits. Eventually Remus <u>was captured</u> and brought to the king, at which point he <u>was recognized</u> by his grandfather, Numitor. Romulus and his men <u>came to rescue</u> Remus, and with Numitor's help they <u>killed</u> the king. Numitor then <u>became</u> king of Alba, and Romulus and Remus, who <u>were not used</u> to the restraint and decorum required of princes in Alba, <u>went</u> off <u>to found</u> Rome.

Now an ancient city <u>can</u> have only one founder, so the story <u>was</u> bound <u>to end</u> badly: they <u>had</u> a quarrel over who was to be king, and Romulus <u>killed</u> Remus.

63.4 Nominatives and Accusatives

The subject of a sentence is in the nominative case in Latin, and the direct object is in the accusative (see section 63.3 above for subjects and objects). Words connected to the subject by a verb indicating identity, such as 'be', 'become', or 'be called', are also in the nominative: thus in these sentences the underlined words are all nominatives even though they are not subjects: 'He has become <u>famous</u>', 'We are <u>hungry</u>', and 'He is named <u>John</u>'.

Practice

F Identify all the words in these sentences that would be nominatives or accusatives in Latin:

1 Jane likes fish.
2 You are wonderful.
3 Jim doesn't eat meat.
4 I am a doctor.
5 I need a doctor.
6 What is it?
7 Mark is carrying a book.
8 The house is pink.
9 Jane wrote a book.
10 Rachel is beautiful.
11 I see you.
12 He is a prisoner.
13 I'd like oatmeal.
14 We are all hungry.
15 Where did he put it?
16 Who did it?

17 Who are you?

18 Whom did you ask?

19 How did you learn that?

20 John is a banker.

21 What do you want?

22 Who is it?

63.5 Nominatives and Accusatives Continued

Adjectives agree in case with the nouns they relate to (see chapter 3.3). Therefore if an adjective agrees with the subject of a sentence, it is nominative like the subject; if it agrees with the object, it is accusative like the object.

Practice

G Identify all the words in these sentences that would be nominatives or accusatives in Latin:

1 Jane likes fried fish.

2 This book is short.

3 True vegetarians do not eat any meat.

4 I am a good doctor.

5 I need a good doctor.

6 What is that thing?

7 The little boy is carrying a big book.

8 My house is pink.

9 These two authors wrote long books.

10 Our sister is beautiful but vain.

11 Some people cannot see certain colours.

12 This man is a model prisoner.

13 I'd like some more oatmeal.

14 The little boys are all happy.

15 Where did your brother put those glasses?

16 Who committed that dreadful murder?

17 Who is the current president?

18 Which people did you ask?

19 How did those girls learn that?

20 Many people are good workers.

21 Which piece did the little girl choose?

22 Who is that man?

H For every underlined word in the paragraphs below, state whether it would be nominative or accusative in Latin.

Romulus and Remus, the founders of Rome, had a doubtful ancestry. Their father was unknown: legend has it that he was the god of war, Mars, but even in antiquity that story was viewed with suspicion. Their mother was Rhea Silvia, daughter of Numitor, rightful king of Alba Longa. Numitor's evil brother, Amulius, seized the throne from him, and in order to make sure that the legitimate king had no male heirs (female heirs did not count in antiquity, which was lucky for Rhea Silvia as otherwise Numitor would have killed her as he allegedly killed her brother), he ordered Rhea to become a Vestal Virgin.

It was a serious crime for a Vestal Virgin to have a child, and when the twins were born, Amulius was furious. He took them away from their mother and dumped them in a river in hopes that they would drown. But they did not drown; the basket containing the twins drifted to shore, where they were rescued and fed by a wolf. Later a shepherd found the babies and took them home to his wife, who raised them until they became unruly teenagers.

As teenagers Romulus and Remus caused more trouble than most: they not only robbed people, but also gathered a band of followers and became powerful bandits. Eventually Remus was captured and brought to the king, at which point he was recognized by his grandfather, Numitor. Romulus and his men came to rescue Remus, and with Numitor's help they killed the king. Numitor then became king of Alba, and Romulus and Remus, who were not used to the restraint and decorum required of princes in Alba, went off to found Rome.

Now an ancient city can have only one founder, so the story was bound to end badly: they had a quarrel over who was to be king, and Romulus killed Remus.

63.6 Genitives and Datives

Genitives are used in Latin for words that in English have an apostrophe with 's' and for phrases beginning with 'of' (see chapter 5.2); thus 'girls' would be genitive both in 'The girls' father is over there' and in 'One of the girls has left' (but 'father' and 'one' would be nominative). Datives are used for indirect objects, that is, the recipient with the verb 'give': in 'I gave him a book', 'him' is dative and 'book', the thing actually given, is accusative (see chapter 7.2).

Practice

I Identify all the words in these sentences that would be nominatives, accusatives, genitives, or datives in Latin:

1 I shall not give him a penny.
2 Those men sell children's toys.
3 A mother of quadruplets has a busy life.
4 Who gave Martha's hat to Jane?
5 Children of rich parents often have expensive clothes.

6 Those children gave lovely presents to Mark's son.
7 In this country even the daughter of a pauper can enter politics.
8 In that country only the sons of rich men enter politics.
9 We all gave generous tips to the superb staff.

10 Are artists' houses always well
    painted?
11 Many people gave him
    something, but no-one gave him
    much.
12 The houses of famous people
    attract tourists.
13 Mike's brother gave flowers to
    Julia's sister.
14 Would you give ten dollars to
    a good cause?

15 The father of ten children needs
    a good income.
16 That man's son knew the right
    answer.
17 The son of a king should give
    generously to charity.
18 Unaccompanied minors need to
    have suitable insurance.
19 What did those women give
    you?
20 When will we see Jane's new
    baby?

63.7 Case Usage: Advanced

In addition to the case usages mentioned above, accusatives are used for the subjects of indirect statements (see chapter 19.1), for indicating an extent of time or space (see chapter 35.3), and after certain prepositions such as *ad* 'to' and *in* 'into'. Verbs meaning 'be' and 'become', since they take a word in the same case as their subjects, also take an accusative if their subjects are accusative (i.e. in indirect statement: see chapter 19.1). Although usually English words that have an apostrophe and 's' (in either order) are genitives and ones that have the 's' without an apostrophe are not genitives (unless they are part of a phrase with 'of'), two words use the apostrophe differently: 'whose' and 'its' are genitives, while 'who's' and 'it's' are not. (These latter forms are contractions of 'who is' and 'it is'.) Datives are used after verbs that take an object in the dative, such as *persuādeō* 'persuade' (see chapter 28.3). Ablatives are used after prepositions such as *cum* 'with', *ā/ab* 'by' and 'from', and *in* 'in'; after verbs that take an object in the ablative, such as *ūtor* 'use'; and in a number of other constructions (see chapter 35). Relative pronouns take their case from their own clause, not from the main clause (see chapter 25.2).

Practice

J Identify the cases that the underlined words would have in Latin, and explain the reason for each case.

1 Who saw the robbery?
2 John thinks that we will give our
   money to charity.

3 Whose coat is this?
4 I like people who love dogs.
5 Which students are ill?

6   Martha is now a neurosurgeon, but when I last saw her she was a little girl.

7   Jane said that she had come from Corinth.

8   John will never persuade Julia to leave Rome; she has lived there for twenty years.

9   What are you running away from?

10   The dog that Maria bought is eating all her socks.

11   Which books did the teacher borrow?

12   Mary thinks that poets are boring.

13   Mark has not yet used the money that his grandfather gave him for Christmas.

14   Who did you go to the play with?

15   Jane is sad because she doesn't know what to do.

16   Who did Martin give his cloak to?

17   Rome is overrun by people who write bad poetry.

18   To whom is Martha giving all that money?

19   Mary fixed the lawnmower with a rubber band that she found in the bottom drawer.

20   Who knows the answer?

21   Jim says that he is not a poet.

22   Martin's sister is a doctor who works in London.

23   Whose dissertation won the prize?

24   Joshua knows the girl whose hat that is.

25   Can Jane persuade her mother to buy her a new phone?

26   What did the fishermen catch today?

27   Jonathan saw the men who had burgled the shop.

28   Julia thinks that we will stay in Rome.

29   Whom did James see in town?

30   The father of these boys is unemployed, but he is trying hard to find a job.

31   What will Marcia use to fix the window?

32   Which beggar did you give your sandwich to?

33   Mark's father said that the boys had given him an apple.

34   Those children are always happy; all day I see them laughing.

35   Who persuaded Jim to come to the party?

63.8 Distinguishing Different Constructions I

One of the most important aspects of Latin grammar is the different constructions used; it is necessary to learn to distinguish these both in Latin and in English if one is to be able to translate successfully between the two languages. The exercise below concentrates on indirect statement and purpose clauses; as these are covered in chapters 15, 16, and 19 the exercise can be done at any point after chapter 19.

Practice

K Without translating, do the following for each underlined verb: name its construction, state whether it would be indicative, subjunctive, or infinitive in Latin; give its tense in Latin; state whether its subject would be nominative or accusative; and state whether it would be introduced by *ut*, *nē*, or no conjunction.

1   My mother said that she <u>had seen</u> a snake in the kitchen.

2   She said it <u>had slithered</u> under the refrigerator.

3   My father came to <u>find</u> the snake.

4   My mother said it <u>would go</u> away by itself if we left it alone.

5   But my father said it <u>would</u> not <u>be able</u> to get out of the house on its own.

6   My mother said she <u>didn't want</u> to find it in our bedrooms.

7   I sat down to <u>watch</u> my father look for the snake.

8   My brother arrived to <u>join</u> us.

9   My sister will be here any minute, so that she <u>won't be</u> separated from us.

10   My father asked us all to leave so that he <u>could</u> search in peace.

11   He said that we <u>were distracting</u> him.

12   We went outside to <u>look</u> through the window.

13   We hurried in order not to <u>miss</u> anything.

14   My brother said he <u>was</u> too short to see properly.

15   He said I <u>needed</u> to let him sit on my shoulders.

16   He only did it to <u>be</u> annoying, as he's nearly as tall as I am.

17   I went away in order not to <u>be</u> annoyed by him, so he watched by himself.

18   He said afterwards that my father <u>had moved</u> the table and all the chairs out of the kitchen.

19   He did that in order not to <u>have</u> to lie under the table while looking under the refrigerator.

20   Then he found a long spoon to <u>fish</u> under the refigerator with.

21   My brother says my father <u>fished</u> many things out from under the refrigerator.

22   He says among them <u>was</u> a book he lost weeks ago.

23   He says that next time he <u>will think</u> more carefully about where he leaves his books.

24   Then my father shouted, saying that the snake <u>had slithered</u> up his trouser leg.

25   We all came rushing in to <u>help</u> him.

26   Also, we ran in order not to <u>miss</u> seeing the snake.

27   When we came in, my father said the snake <u>was</u> no longer up his trousers.

28   He said it <u>had gone</u> down a hole in the floor.

29   My mother said it <u>would</u> probably <u>come</u> up again.

30   She said she <u>did not want</u> to be in the kitchen when it returned.

31   My father said it <u>would</u> not <u>come</u> up again.

32 He said it probably <u>did</u> not <u>want</u> to be in the kitchen with her either.

33 We put a brick over the hole so it <u>would</u>n't <u>return</u>.

63.9 Distinguishing Different Constructions II

Indirect commands and purpose clauses look similar to each other in Latin but mean different things and must therefore be translated differently in English. In order to distinguish them, one looks for a verb that introduces an indirect command: if such a verb is present, the following subjunctive has to be translated as an indirect command, and if not, it can be translated as a purpose clause. See chapter 28.3; this exercise is designed to be done any time after chapter 29.

Practice

L Identify the constructions (indirect command, purpose clause, indirect statement, none of the above) and translate:

1 rex militibus imperavit ut progrederentur.
2 amicos suos oravit ne morarentur.
3 servo meo imperavi ut sequeretur.
4 servum meum rogabo ne moretur.
5 amicos suos oraverunt ut pollicerentur.
6 velim ut mecum in urbe moreris.
7 pater filio imperat ut sequatur.
8 dixit se tibi persuasisse ut sequereris.
9 venati sunt ut animalia caperent.
10 velim ut me sequaris.
11 rex militibus imperavit ut sequerentur.
12 mater filium oravit ne moraretur.
13 dixerunt se voluisse te sequi.
14 regem sequentes, milites e castris progressi sunt.

15 arbitratus sum eos nobis persuadere velle ut secum loqueremur.
16 dominum sequentes, servi ex oppido progressi sunt.
17 milites e castris progressi non sunt ne hostes se caperent.
18 pollicitus sum me te oraturum non esse ut me defenderes.
19 servis imperantes ut nos sequantur, ex oppido progressi sumus.
20 milites quibus imperavit rex ut se sequerentur ex oppido progressi sunt.
21 arbitror eos nobis persuadere velle ut secum loquamur.
22 pueri quibus non persuadebo ne loquantur multa patientur.

23 filium tuum, cui imperavisti ne
   cum militibus loqueretur, in
   castris hodie vidi.

24 milites qui polliciti sunt se nos
   secuturos esse e castris non
   progrediuntur.

M Additional exercises with indirect commands, purpose clauses, indirect statements, and infinitives. Translate into Latin:

1 Her father will ask her to speak.
2 She came in order to speak with you.
3 Her father is begging her to speak.
4 Her father ordered her to speak.
5 Her father thinks that she is speaking.
6 Her father persuaded her not to speak.
7 She wants to speak.
8 I would like her to speak.
9 We order you (singular) to promise.
10 Did we persuade you (plural) to promise?
11 We thought you (singular) had promised.
12 We shall ask you (plural) not to promise.
13 We would like you (singular) to promise.
14 Do you (plural) want to promise?
15 I thought you (singular) would promise.
16 Are you (plural) able to promise?
17 We spoke often with the king, asking him to help us.
18 Having urged the king to help us, we left.
19 You (singular) think that that man will follow you, but we shall persuade him to follow us.
20 Having promised that he would help us, the king led his soldiers to our town.
21 The girl who wanted to speak with us is now asking us not to come.
22 Having promised that they would not attack us, the soldiers departed.
23 The king who urged us to come is now ordering us to leave.

63.10 Distinguishing Different Constructions III

On the following page is a chart listing the different possible constructions for Latin infinitives, participles, and subjunctives introduced in chapters 1– 35, followed by some practice exercises. If you have trouble working out how to translate such verb forms, it is recommended that you use the chart for each sentence: first identify the construction using the two left-hand columns and then translate it using the right-hand column. Practice translating this way should enable you to internalize the identification process and learn to translate these constructions without such help.

Latin Verb Form	Other words (or other types of clue) nearby	Construction and Translation
Present infinitive	*possum, volō, nōlō, mālō*	Translate with English **infinitive**. *potest Rōmam īre.* 'He is able to go to Rome.' *volō Rōmam īre.* 'I want to go to Rome.'
Infinitive (any tense)	*dīcō, arbitror*, other verb of saying or thinking	Indirect statement: translate with **indicative** verb in the tense of the infinitive. *dīcit sē Rōmam itūrum esse.* 'He says he will go to Rome.' *dīcit sē Rōmam īre.* 'He says he is going to Rome.' *dīcit sē Rōmam īvisse.* 'He says he went to Rome.'
Perfect **participle**	The participle is near a form of *sum*.	Translate the participle and the form of *sum* together as a **past indicative** (active if the verb is deponent, otherwise passive). *ille vēnātus est.* 'That man hunted.' *ille amātus est.* 'That man was loved.'
Perfect **participle**	The participle is not near a form of *sum*.	Translate with an English **past active participle** ('having loved') if the verb is deponent, otherwise with a **past passive participle** ('loved', 'having been loved'), or translate with a subordinate clause with a similar meaning. *vēnātus Rōmam īvit.* 'Having hunted, he went to Rome.' *amātus Rōmam ibit.* 'Since/if/when he is loved, he will go to Rome.' *puella amāta discessit.* 'The beloved girl has left.'

Latin Verb Form	Other words (or other types of clue) nearby	Construction and Translation
Present **participle**	–	Translate with an English **present participle** ('loving'), or with a subordinate clause with a similar meaning. *servōs dūcēns Rōmam ībit.* 'He will go to Rome leading slaves.'
Future **participle**	–	Translate with **'being about to'** or with a subordinate clause having a similar meaning. *dictūrus impedītus est.* 'Being about to speak, he was hindered.' / 'He was hindered when he was about to speak.'
Present **subjunctive**	The subjunctive is the only or main verb of the sentence, the sentence is a question, and the subjunctive is in the first person.	Deliberative subjunctive: translate with **'should . . . ?'**. *eāmusne Rōmam?* 'Should we go to Rome?'
Present **subjunctive**	The subjunctive is the only or main verb of the sentence, and the sentence is *not* a question.	Hortatory subjunctive: translate with **'let's'** if first person, otherwise with **'may'** *before* the subject. *Rōmam eāmus.* 'Let's go to Rome.' *Rōmam eat.* 'May he go to Rome.' (*not* 'He may go to Rome.') *nē Rōmam eant.* 'May they not go to Rome.' (*not* 'They may not go . . .')
Subjunctive (any tense)	Subjunctive is in a clause opened by *ut,* and in the	Result clause: translate with **'that'** and **present or past indicative** according to sequence.

	main clause there is *tantus*, *tam*, etc.	*tam fortis est ut Rōmam eat.* 'He's so brave that he's going to Rome.' *tam fortis erat ut Rōmam īret.* 'He was so brave that he went to Rome.'
Subjunctive (any tense)	Subjunctive is in a clause opened by *ut* or *nē*, dependent on a verb of fearing.	Fear clause: translate with **'that' and future indicative or 'would'**, with negative if *ut* and no negative if *nē*. *timeō ut Rōmam eat.* 'I'm afraid that he will not go to Rome.' *timuī nē Rōmam īret.* 'I was afraid that he would go to Rome.'
Subjunctive (any tense)	Subjunctive is in a clause opened by *ut* or *nē*, dependent on a verb of asking, ordering, etc.	Indirect command: translate with **infinitive**. *rogō eum ut Rōmam eat.* 'I'm asking him to go to Rome.' *imperāvī eī nē Rōmam īret.* 'I ordered him not to go to Rome.'
Subjunctive (any tense)	Subjunctive is in a clause opened by *ut* or *nē*, with none of the above clues present.	Purpose clause: translate with **'so that' or '(in order) to'**. *discessit ut Rōmam īret.* 'He left (in order) to go to Rome.' *impediam eum nē Rōmam eat.* 'I shall hinder him so that he doesn't go to Rome.'

Practice

N For each of the sentences below, identify the construction and translate the sentence.

1 pecuniam meam rapturus ille a fratre meo impeditus est.

2 defendantur nostri a deis.

3 pecuniam amissam invenire non potuimus.

4 arbitror eos visum iri.

5 adeo laudati sunt ut omnes eos amarent.

6 veritine estis ne Londinii moraremur?

7 rogaverunt nos ne Carthaginem iremus.

8 timentes domum venerunt.

9 quam urbem defendamus?

10 dixerunt se ab hostibus oppugnatos esse.

11 venantes trans silvam ibunt.

12 cum his militibus ne pugnemus.

13 nobiscum sessurum puerum mater vocavit.

14 dicit se flumine impediri.

15 Londinii manemus ne inveniamur a patribus.

16 tanta est spes nostra ut tristes non simus.

17 vocati a matre, pueri domum venerunt.

18 tantus est metus eius ut fugiat.

19 arbitratus sum pueros a magistro doceri.

20 ubi sedeam?

21 te vidimus venantem.

22 timuerunt ne hodie domi maneremus.

23 dei nos iuvent.

24 imperabimus servis ut Londinii maneant.

25 urbs a nobis defensa numquam ab hostibus capietur.

26 Athenis multos dies maneamus.

27 numquam dicent se a nobis defensos esse.

28 veritus sum ut Athenas ires.

29 moenia refecturi cives saxa petunt.

30 quid dicam?

31 domum venerunt ut matres viderent.

32 arbitrabuntur se a nobis laudari.

33 animalia ab hoc agricola vendita numquam bona sunt.

34 exercitus hostium tantus est ut nostri vincantur.

35 matri persuadeamus.

36 pecuniam in illo agro sepultam invenire volumus.

37 rogavit ut secum maneremus.

38 Athenis discessurus ab amicis impedior.

39 dixistine te a servis tuis Delphis relictum esse?

40 quem sequamur?

41 domus eorum tanta est ut multi homines in ea sint.

42 multa passi tristes sunt.

43 timebit ne Corinthum veniamus.

44 te cum rege locuturum vidi.

45 tot annos Romae mansit ut numquam domum veniret.

46 nostri Corinthum iverunt ne ab hostibus oppugnaretur.

47 hostes saxis impediti nostros oppugnare non potuerunt.

48 saxis impediti nostri hostes oppugnare non potuerunt.

49 imperavi militibus ne Athenas irent.

50 timui ne multas horas domi maneres.

51 milites ab hostibus oppugnatos iuvemus.

52 quos milites oppugnem?

53 multos dies ibi manserunt ne se videremus.

54 dixit vos regem rogaturas esse.

55 Athenis tot dies morati sunt ut Corinthum numquam irent.

56 tot horas Londinii manebimus ut cras domum veniamus.

57 Romam venimus ut senatum audiremus.

58 dicit te Delphos ire.

59 milites hortabimur ut nobiscum ad senatum veniant.

60 verentur ne Carthaginem eamus.

61 hostes Corinthum progressi a nostris impediti sunt.

62 defendamus filios nostros.

63 dixit illam puellam ab omnibus amatum iri.

64 cum hostibus pugnaturi, nostri non timent.

65 timuit ne poeta versus suos legeret.

66 domi manentes regem non videbitis.

67 pollicearne?

68 tecum locutus felix ero.

69 dixerunt se pecunia nostra usos esse.

70 timeo ne non defendar.

71 Athenis maneo ut versus scribam.

72 puellae discessurae hoc demus.

73 arbitror hunc servum cras venditum iri.

74 audiatur a rege.

75 rogatus ab amicis, pollicitus sum.

76 vereor ne multos dies hic maneant.

77 dicet se nos secuturum esse.

78 adeo amor ut semper felix sim.

79 vidi servos te sequentes.

80 vidi servos te sequentem.

81 relinquamusne hic equos nostros?

82 matri persuasi ne me Corinthum mitteret.

83 ne impediamini saxis in agro.

84 arbitrata sum te nos sequi.

85 in silva relictus a patre, puer felix non est.

86 tanti sunt gradus ut ascendere non possimus.

87 rogemne patrem ut me iuvet?

88 vos cum amicis loquentes audivimus.

89 Delphos imus ut cum deo loquamur.

90 ne pecuniam nostram amittant.

91 arbitrati sunt me Athenis mansisse.

92 pueri te secuti filii eius sunt.

93 quis tibi persuasit ut Athenas ires?

94 timeo ne liber meus a poeta legatur.

95 Athenis domum venit ut patrem sepeliret.

96 amicum tuum in silva venaturum vidimus.

97 adeo veriti sunt ut fugerent.

98 timentes ne viderentur, in silvam fugerunt.

99 ne hunc exercitum oppugnemus.

100 arbitrabitur me tibi persuasisse.

101 maneamusne Romae multos dies?

102 verebuntur ut secum eamus.

103 senatum hortatus domum ibo.

104 mater mihi persuasit ut tecum Delphos irem.

105 milites Corinthum oppugnaturi a nostris oppugnati sunt.

106 pater moriens cum filiis locutus est.

107 senatum oravimus ut nos iuvaret.

108 arbitror nos quattuor dies Romae mansuros esse.

109 Carthagine multos annos manentes multa viderunt.

110 eamus ad senatum ut a Romanis iuvemur.

111 discedamusne Athenis?

112 militem fugiturum impediverunt.

63.11 Conditional Clauses

The formation of conditional clauses is discussed in chapters 50 and 51.3. Here are some additional exercises on that topic.

Practice

O Take the following sentences and change their tenses to express, in formal English, the circumstances given. Example: given the sentence 'If Mary is there, she is protesting' and asked to change it to the past, under the circumstances that we do not know whether Mary was there, one would say 'If Mary was there, she was protesting' or 'If Mary was there, she protested'; if asked to change it to the past, under the circumstances that Mary was not there, one would say 'If Mary had been there, she would have protested.' If you find this exercise difficult, use the chapter 50 sample sentences whose numbers are given in parentheses as models.

'If they are under 18 they are not allowed to buy that.'

1 past: we don't know whether they were under 18 (1)

2 past: they were not under 18 (4)

3 future: we don't know whether they will be under 18 (3)

4 future: they are unlikely to be under 18 (6)

'No doubt Mark got job offers if he submitted applications.'

5 future: we don't know if Mark will
   submit applications (3)
6 future: Mark is unlikely to submit
   applications (6)
7 present: we don't know if Mark is
   submitting applications (2)

8 present: Mark is not submitting
   applications (5)
9 past: we don't know if Mark
   submitted applications (1)
10 past: Mark did not submit
    applications (4)

P Without translating, indicate the following for each sentence: whether the if-clause comes first or second, whether it would be introduced by *sī* or by *nisī* in Latin, and what mood and tense would be used for each verb in Latin.

1 We would not have to do this
   exercise now if we had done it
   yesterday.
2 If I forget, remind me.
3 If Julia was in Athens yesterday,
   she is probably still there.
4 If you find any problems, alert
   the supervisor.
5 Caesar will be assassinated
   unless someone warns him
   about the plot.
6 If we were Romans, we would
   have learned these constructions
   as children.
7 If your dog made that mess, you
   ought to clean it up.
8 I shall get a job as a cowherd in
   the Alps if things do not improve
   here.
9 What would happen if we
   should all fall asleep in class?
10 If the sun is shining tomorrow,
    we shall have a picnic.
11 If he learns these rules well, he
    will know them for at least
    a week.
12 I would not have done that if
    I were you.

13 You will never succeed unless
    you try.
14 If I should see anything,
    naturally I would say something.
15 If we had been sensible about our
    search we would never have
    found the treasure.
16 We would not have been so
    cold this morning if we were in
    Egypt.
17 If Troy is not destroyed Juno will
    be very sad.
18 I would be paying more
    attention if these sentences
    weren't so silly.
19 If that fire was caused by the
    match you tossed, you ought to
    be ashamed of yourself.
20 If the queen comes to town, we
    shall see her.
21 If I had not seen it myself,
    I would not believe it.
22 The Greek heroes would not
    have had such entertaining
    adventures if their gods had
    been more sensible.
23 Catiline will take over the city
    unless someone stops him.

24 They would not have drowned if they had learned to swim.

25 You will be eaten by a shark if you try to swim here.

26 I would be amazed if she should fail the exam.

27 We would be able to learn Carthaginian as well as Latin if the Romans had been less power-hungry.

28 The milk will go sour unless you put it somewhere cool.

29 Call the fire brigade at once if you see a fire.

30 If the sun is shining tomorrow, we shall definitely go to the park.

63.12 Where to Find Additional Exercises in Grammatical Analysis in This Book

Chapter 5, exercise B: identification of genitives.

Chapter 5, exercise G: identification of nominatives and accusatives (like exercises F and G above).

Chapter 7, exercise B: identification of datives.

Chapter 7, exercise G: identification of nominatives, accusatives, genitives, and datives (like exercise I above).

Chapter 15, exercise A: division of sentences into clauses; identification of conjunctions, main clauses, and subordinate clauses.

Chapter 25, exercise A: identification of relative clauses.

Chapter 28, exercise E: distinguishing the different Latin translations of English infinitives.

Chapter 30, exercises C and D: dividing long sentences into clauses.

Chapter 34, exercise E: identifying different types of ablative.

Chapter 35, exercise E: identifying different types of ablative.

Chapter 50, exercise A: manipulation of English conditional clauses (like exercise O above).

Chapter 50, exercise B, and chapter 51, exercise C: identification of conditional clauses (like exercise P above).

Exercise A

Word	Part of speech	Word	Part of speech
Romulus	noun	of	preposition
and	conjunction	Numitor	noun
Remus	noun	rightful	adjective
founders	noun	king	noun
of	preposition	of	preposition
Rome	noun	Alba	noun
had	verb	Numitor's	noun
doubtful	adjective	evil	adjective
ancestry	noun	brother	noun
father	noun	Amulius	noun
was	verb	seized	verb
unknown	adjective	throne	noun
legend	noun	from	preposition
has	verb	him	pronoun
it	pronoun	and	conjunction
that	conjunction	to make	verb
he	pronoun	that	conjunction
was	verb	legitimate	adjective
god	noun	king	noun
of	preposition	had	verb
war	noun	no	adjective
Mars	noun	male	adjective
but	conjunction	heirs	noun
in	preposition	female	adjective
antiquity	noun	heirs	noun
that	adjective	in	preposition
story	noun	antiquity	noun
was viewed	verb	which	pronoun
with	preposition	was	verb
suspicion	noun	lucky	adjective
mother	noun	for	preposition
was	verb	Rhea	noun
Rhea	noun	otherwise	adverb
daughter	noun	Numitor	noun

Word	Part of speech	Word	Part of speech
would have killed	verb	would drown	verb
her	pronoun	But	conjunction
he	pronoun	they	pronoun
allegedly	adverb	basket	noun
killed	verb	twins	noun
brother	noun	drifted	verb
he	pronoun	to	preposition
ordered	verb	shore	noun
Rhea	noun	they	pronoun
to become	verb	were rescued	verb
Vestal	adjective	and	conjunction
Virgin	noun	fed	verb
It	pronoun	by	preposition
was	verb	wolf	noun
serious	adjective	Later	adverb
crime	noun	shepherd	noun
for	preposition	found	verb
Vestal	adjective	babies	noun
Virgin	noun	and	conjunction
to have	verb	took	verb
child	noun	them	pronoun
and	conjunction	to	preposition
when	conjunction	wife	noun
twins	noun	who	pronoun
were born	verb	raised	verb
Amulius	noun	them	pronoun
was	verb	until	conjunction
furious	adjective	they	pronoun
He	pronoun	became	verb
took	verb	unruly	adjective
them	pronoun	teenagers	noun
from	preposition	teenagers	noun
mother	noun	Romulus	noun
and	conjunction	and	conjunction
dumped	verb	Remus	noun
them	pronoun	caused	verb
in	preposition	more	adjective
river	noun	trouble	noun
in	preposition	they	pronoun
hopes	noun	robbed	verb
that	conjunction	people	noun
they	pronoun	but	conjunction

Word	Part of speech	Word	Part of speech
also	adverb	Alba	noun
gathered	verb	and	conjunction
band	noun	Romulus	noun
of	preposition	and	conjunction
followers	noun	Remus	noun
and	conjunction	who	pronoun
became	verb	to	preposition
powerful	adjective	restraint	noun
bandits	noun	and	conjunction
Eventually	adverb	decorum	noun
Remus	noun	required	adjective
was captured	verb	of	preposition
and	conjunction	princes	noun
brought	verb	in	preposition
to	preposition	Alba	noun
king	noun	went	verb
at	preposition	to found	verb
which	adjective	Rome	noun
point	noun	ancient	adjective
he	pronoun	city	noun
was recognized	verb	can	verb
by	preposition	have	verb
grandfather	noun	only	adverb
Numitor	noun	one	adjective
Romulus	noun	founder	noun
and	conjunction	so	conjunction
men	noun	story	noun
came	verb	was	verb
to rescue	verb	to end	verb
Remus	noun	badly	adverb
and	conjunction	they	pronoun
with	preposition	had	verb
Numitor's	noun	quarrel	noun
help	noun	who	pronoun
they	pronoun	was	verb
killed	verb	to be	verb
king	noun	king	noun
Numitor	noun	and	conjunction
then	adverb	Romulus	noun
became	verb	killed	verb
king	noun	Remus	noun
of	preposition		

Exercise B

All parts of the periphrastic verbs are underlined.

1   I <u>was giving</u> the dog a bath.
2   He <u>will do</u> it.
3   We <u>are coming</u> as fast as we can.
4   <u>Have</u> you <u>seen</u> this?
5   I want <u>to learn</u> Latin.
6   <u>Has</u> he <u>been doing</u> that all day?
7   <u>Were</u> they <u>carrying</u> it up the hill?
8   <u>Will</u> you <u>be staying</u> long?
9   They <u>did</u> not <u>come</u> after all.
10 I <u>shall</u> never <u>forget</u> that.
11 They <u>have been sitting</u> here since noon.
12 No-one <u>has</u> ever <u>seen</u> this before.
13 They <u>will be handling</u> this case.
14 It is very difficult <u>to be</u> perfect.
15 <u>Will</u> they <u>give</u> us anything?
16 <u>Did</u> you really <u>say</u> that?
17 We <u>were</u> not just <u>standing</u> there.
18 <u>Have</u> you <u>been waiting</u> long?
19 <u>Has</u> he <u>turned</u> up yet?
20 I <u>shall be coming</u> next week.
21 He wants <u>to go</u> home.
22 He <u>has</u> not <u>said</u> anything all year.
23 He <u>will be sitting</u> in the back.
24 You <u>were praising</u> him too much.
25 We <u>shall come</u> next week.
26 They <u>will be living</u> here all year.
27 What <u>were</u> you <u>doing</u> there?
28 It is impossible not <u>to believe</u> her.
29 <u>Will</u> you <u>look</u> at this for me?
30 <u>Are</u> you <u>going</u> to the party?
31 Who <u>is helping</u> him this year?
32 No-one wants <u>to do</u> it.

Exercise C

The periphrasic verbs alone are listed.

1   has been sitting
2   are going, have fallen
3   are coming, did want, to wait
4   has arrived ('cannot believe' counts as two verbs)
5   (none: there are four separate verbs)
6   have done, to deserve
7   will happen ('can tell' counts as two verbs)
8   (none: there are three separate verbs)
9   had attacked, was wearing ('could identify' counts as two verbs)
10 've settled, will recognize, will be
11 would think, to buy, have been tricked
12 shall see, has come, has returned, to tell
13 did try, to steer ('could see' counts as two verbs)
14 have been learning
15 (none: 'can see' counts as two verbs)
16 to be, did work, to be
17 will win, will be ('can be' counts as two verbs)

Exercise D

Subjects are underlined; objects are in italics.

1   <u>I</u> am Canadian.
2   *What* do <u>you</u> see?
3   Oliver's <u>sister</u> is a chemist.
4   Where is <u>Jane</u> going?
5   His <u>work</u> is very good.
6   <u>You</u> are brilliant.
7   <u>Who</u> knows *that*?
8   A student's <u>life</u> can be exhausting.
9   *Whom* do <u>you</u> choose?
10 <u>Jane</u> doesn't love *John*.

11	Martin's <u>dog</u> is overweight.	17
12	<u>What</u> is in the box?	18
13	In December the <u>lights</u> are lit.	19
14	<u>Mark</u> works here.	20
15	In which house are the <u>children</u>?	21
16	Sometimes <u>I</u> wonder.	22

17   Where are <u>you</u>?
18   Rarely have <u>I</u> been so frightened.
19   In what direction did <u>he</u> go?
20   <u>Jim</u> bought the last <u>one</u>.
21   That boy's <u>father</u> is a fireman.
22   The <u>mother</u> of this girl is very rich.

Exercise E

Word in parentheses modify the noun or pronoun that is the subject or object; for the purposes of this exercise it is legitimate either to consider them part of the subject/object or not to do so.

Verb	Subject	Object
had	Romulus and Remus	(a doubtful) ancestry
was	(their) father	–
has	legend	it
was	he	–
was viewed	(that) story	–
was	(their) mother	–
seized	(Numitor's evil) brother (Amulius)	(the) throne
to make	– [infinitive]	–
had	(the legitimate) king	(no male) heirs
did (not) count	(female) heirs	–
was	which	–
would have killed	Numitor	her
killed	he	(her) brother
ordered	he	Rhea
was	it	–
were born	twins	–
was	Amulius	–
took	he	them
dumped	he [the one before 'took']	them
would drown	they	–
did (not) drown	they	–
drifted	(the) basket (containing the twins)	–
were rescued	they	–
found	(a) shepherd	(the) babies
took	(a) shepherd	them
raised	who	them
became	they	–
caused	Romulus (and) Remus	(more) trouble (than most)
robbed	they	people
gathered	they [the one before 'robbed']	(a) band (of followers)

Verb	Subject	Object
became	they [still the one before 'robbed']	–
was captured	Remus	–
was recognized	he	–
came	Romulus (and his) men	–
to rescue	– [infinitive]	Remus
killed	they	(the) king
became	Numitor	–
were (not) used	who	–
went	Romulus (and) Remus	–
to found	– [infinitive]	Rome
can	(an ancient) city	–
was	(the) story	–
to end	– [infinitive]	–
had	they	(a) quarrel
killed	Romulus	Remus

Exercise F

Nominatives are underlined; accusatives are in italics. Articles ('a', 'the') are not so marked because they would not appear in Latin, but it would be legitimate to consider that in principle they belong in the same case as the words they precede.

1   Jane likes *fish*.
2   You are wonderful.
3   Jim doesn't eat *meat*.
4   I am a doctor.
5   I need a *doctor*.
6   What is it?
7   Mark is carrying a *book*.
8   The house is pink.
9   Jane wrote a *book*.
10 Rachel is beautiful.
11 I see *you*.
12 He is a prisoner.
13 I'd like *oatmeal*.
14 We are all hungry.
15 Where did he put *it*?
16 Who did *it*?
17 Who are you?
18 *Whom* did you ask?
19 How did you learn *that*?
20 John is a banker.
21 *What* do you want?
22 Who is it?

Exercise G

Nominatives are underlined; accusatives are in italics. Articles ('a', 'the') are not so marked because they would not appear in Latin, but it would be legitimate to consider that in principle they belong in the same case as the words they precede.

1   Jane likes *fried fish*.
2   This book is short.
3   True vegetarians do not eat *any meat*.
4   I am a good doctor.
5   I need a *good doctor*.
6   What is that thing?
7   The little boy is carrying a *big book*.
8   My house is pink.
9   These two authors wrote *long books*.
10 Our sister is beautiful but vain.
11 Some people cannot see *certain colours*.
12 This man is a model prisoner.

13   I'd like *some more oatmeal.*
14   The <u>little boys</u> are <u>all happy.</u>
15   Where did <u>your brother</u> put *those glasses?*
16   <u>Who</u> committed *that dreadful murder?*
17   <u>Who</u> is the <u>current president?</u>

18   *Which people* did <u>you</u> ask?
19   How did <u>those girls</u> learn *that?*
20   <u>Many people</u> are <u>good workers.</u>
21   *Which piece* did the <u>little girl</u> choose?
22   <u>Who</u> is <u>that man?</u>

Exercise H

Word	Case		Word	Case
Romulus	nominative		crime	nominative
Remus	nominative		child	accusative
doubtful	accusative		twins	nominative
ancestry	accusative		Amulius	nominative
father	nominative		furious	nominative
unknown	nominative		He	nominative
legend	nominative		them	accusative
it	accusative		them	accusative
he	nominative		they	nominative
god	nominative		they	nominative
that	nominative		basket	nominative
story	nominative		they	nominative
mother	nominative		shepherd	nominative
Rhea	nominative		babies	accusative
Silvia	nominative		them	accusative
evil	nominative		who	nominative
brother	nominative		them	accusative
throne	accusative		they	nominative
legitimate	nominative		unruly	nominative
king	nominative		teenagers	nominative
no	accusative		Romulus	nominative
male	accusative		Remus	nominative
heirs	accusative		more	accusative
female	nominative		trouble	accusative
heirs	nominative		they	nominative
which	nominative		people	accusative
lucky	nominative		band	accusative
Numitor	nominative		powerful	nominative
her	accusative		bandits	nominative
he	nominative		Remus	nominative
brother	accusative		he	nominative
he	nominative		Romulus	nominative
Rhea	accusative		men	nominative
It	nominative		Remus	accusative
serious	nominative		they	nominative

Word	Case	Word	Case
king	accusative	one	accusative
Numitor	nominative	founder	accusative
king	nominative	story	nominative
Romulus	nominative	they	nominative
Remus	nominative	quarrel	accusative
who	nominative	who	nominative
Rome	accusative	king	nominative
ancient	nominative	Romulus	nominative
city	nominative	Remus	accusative

Exercise I

Nominatives are underlined, accusatives are in italics, genitives are double underlined, and datives are in bold. Articles ('a', 'the') are not so marked because they would not appear in Latin, but it would be legitimate to consider that in principle they belong in the same case as the words they precede.

1   I shall not give **him** a *penny*.
2   Those men sell children's *toys*.
3   A mother of quadruplets has a *busy life*.
4   Who gave Martha's *hat* to **Jane**?
5   Children of rich parents often have *expensive clothes*.
6   Those children gave *lovely presents* to Mark's **son**.
7   In this country even the daughter of a pauper can enter *politics*.
8   In that country only the sons of rich men enter *politics*.
9   We all gave *generous tips* to the **superb staff**.
10 Are artists' houses always well painted?

11 Many people gave **him** *something*, but no-one gave **him** *much*.
12 The houses of famous people attract *tourists*.
13 Mike's brother gave *flowers* to Julia's **sister**.
14 Would you give *ten dollars* to a **good cause**?
15 The father of ten children needs a *good income*.
16 That man's son knew the *right answer*.
17 The son of a king should give generously to **charity**.
18 Unaccompanied minors need to have *suitable insurance*.
19 *What* did those women give **you**?
20 When will we see Jane's *new baby*?

Exercise J

1   Who [nominative, subject of 'saw'] saw the robbery [accusative, object of 'saw']?
2   John [nominative, subject of 'thinks'] thinks that we [accusative, because although it is the subject of 'will give', the construction is accusative and infinitive in indirect statement] will give our money [accusative, object of 'will give'] to charity [dative, indirect object of 'will give'].
3   Whose [genitive, possession] coat [nominative, subject of 'is'] is this [nominative, because verb 'be' is followed by a word in the same case as its subject]?
4   I [nominative, subject of 'like'] like people [accusative, object of 'like'] who [nominative, because it is the subject of 'love': the relative pronoun agrees with its antecedent in gender and number but gets its case from its own clause] love dogs [accusative, object of 'love'].

5   Which [nominative, agrees with 'students'] <u>students</u> [nominative, subject of 'are'] are <u>ill</u> [nominative, because 'be' is followed by a word in the same case as its subject]?

6   <u>Martha</u> [nominative, subject of 'is'] is now a <u>neurosurgeon</u> [nominative, because 'be' is followed by a word in the same case as its subject], but when <u>I</u> [nominative, subject of 'saw'] last saw <u>her</u> [accusative, object of 'saw'] <u>she</u> [nominative, subject of 'was'] was a <u>little</u> [nominative, agrees with 'girl'] <u>girl</u> [nominative, because 'be' is followed by a word in the same case as its subject].

7   <u>Jane</u> [nominative, subject of 'said'] said that <u>she</u> [accusative, because although it is the subject of 'had come' the construction is accusative and infinitive in indirect statement] had come from <u>Corinth</u> [ablative of motion from].

8   <u>John</u> [nominative, subject of 'will persuade'] will never persuade <u>Julia</u> [dative, object of 'persuade' and *persuādeō* takes a dative] to leave <u>Rome</u> [ablative of motion from]; <u>she</u> [nominative, subject of 'has lived'] has lived there for <u>twenty</u> [accusative, agrees with 'years'] <u>years</u> [accusative, indicates extent of time].

9   <u>What</u> [ablative, object of preposition 'from' (*ab*)] are <u>you</u> [nominative, subject of 'are running'] running away from?

10 The <u>dog</u> [nominative, subject of 'is eating'] <u>that</u> [accusative, object of 'bought'] <u>Maria</u> [nominative, subject of 'bought'] bought is eating <u>all</u> [accusative, agrees with 'socks'] her <u>socks</u> [accusative, object of 'is eating'].

11 Which [accusative, agrees with 'books'] <u>books</u> [accusative, object of 'borrow'] did the <u>teacher</u> [nominative, subject of 'borrow'] borrow?

12 <u>Mary</u> [nominative, subject of 'thinks'] thinks that <u>poets</u> [accusative, because although it is the subject of 'are' the construction is accusative and infinitive in indirect statement] are <u>boring</u> [accusative, because 'be' is followed by a word in the same case as its subject].

13 <u>Mark</u> [nominative, subject of 'has used'] has not yet used the <u>money</u> [ablative, object of 'has used' and *ūtor* takes an ablative] <u>that</u> [accusative, object of 'gave'] his <u>grandfather</u> [nominative, subject of 'gave'] gave <u>him</u> [dative, indirect object of 'gave'] for Christmas.

14 <u>Who</u> [ablative, object of 'with' (*cum*)] did <u>you</u> [nominative, subject of 'go'] go to the <u>play</u> [accusative, object of 'to' (*ad*)] with?

15 <u>Jane</u> [nominative, subject of 'is'] is <u>sad</u> [nominative, because 'be' is followed by a word in the same case as its subject] because <u>she</u> [nominative, subject of 'does know'] doesn't know <u>what</u> [accusative, object of 'do'] to do.

16 <u>Who</u> [dative, indirect object of 'give'] did <u>Martin</u> [nominative, subject of 'give'] give his <u>cloak</u> [accusative, object of 'give'] to?

17 <u>Rome</u> [nominative, subject of 'is'] is overrun by <u>people</u> [ablative, object of 'by' (*ab*)] <u>who</u> [nominative, subject of 'write'] write <u>bad</u> [accusative, agrees with 'poetry'] <u>poetry</u> [accusative, object of 'write'].

18 To <u>whom</u> [dative, indirect object of 'is giving'] is <u>Martha</u> [nominative, subject of 'is giving'] giving <u>all</u> [accusative, agrees with 'money'] <u>that</u> [accusative, agrees with 'money'] <u>money</u> [accusative, object of 'is giving']?

19 <u>Mary</u> [nominative, subject of 'fixed'] fixed the <u>lawnmower</u> [accusative, object of 'fixed'] with a <u>rubber</u> [ablative, agrees with 'band'] <u>band</u> [ablative of means] <u>that</u> [accusative, object of 'found'] <u>she</u> [nominative, subject of 'found'] found in the <u>bottom</u> [ablative, agrees with 'drawer'] <u>drawer</u> [ablative, object of 'in' (*in*)].

20 <u>Who</u> [nominative, subject of 'knows'] knows the <u>answer</u> [accusative, object of 'knows']?

21   Jim [nominative, subject of 'says'] says that <u>he</u> [accusative, though subject of 'is', because the construction is accusative and infinitive in indirect statement] is not a <u>poet</u> [accusative, because 'be' is followed by a word in the same case as its subject].

22   <u>Martin</u>'s [genitive, possession] <u>sister</u> [nominative, subject of 'is'] is a <u>doctor</u> [nominative, because 'be' is followed by a word in the same case as its subject] <u>who</u> [nominative, subject of 'works'] works in <u>London</u> [locative].

23   <u>Whose</u> [genitive, possession] <u>dissertation</u> [nominative, subject of 'won'] won the <u>prize</u> [accusative, object of 'won']?

24   Joshua [nominative, subject of 'knows'] knows the <u>girl</u> [accusative, object of 'knows'] <u>whose</u> [genitive, possession] <u>hat</u> [nominative, because 'be' is followed by a word in the same case as its subject] <u>that</u> [nominative, subject of 'is'] is.

25   Can Jane [nominative, subject of 'persuade'] persuade her <u>mother</u> [dative, object of 'persuade' and *persuādeō* takes a dative] to buy her a <u>new</u> [accusative, agrees with 'phone'] <u>phone</u> [accusative, object of 'buy']?

26   <u>What</u> [accusative, object of 'did catch'] did the <u>fishermen</u> [nominative, subject of 'did catch'] catch today?

27   Jonathan [nominative, subject of 'saw'] saw the <u>men</u> [accusative, object of 'saw'] <u>who</u> [nominative, subject of 'had burgled'] had burgled the <u>shop</u> [accusative, object of 'had burgled'].

28   Julia [nominative, subject of 'thinks'] thinks that <u>we</u> [accusative, subject of 'will stay' but accusative and infinitive in indirect statement] will stay in <u>Rome</u> [locative].

29   <u>Whom</u> [accusative, object of 'see'] did James [nominative, subject of 'see'] see in <u>town</u> [ablative, object of 'in' (*in*)]?

30   The <u>father</u> [nominative, subject of 'is'] of these [genitive, agrees with 'boys'] <u>boys</u> [genitive, possession] is <u>unemployed</u> [nominative, because 'be' is followed by a word in the same case as its subject], but <u>he</u> [nominative, subject of 'is trying'] is trying hard to find a <u>job</u> [accusative, object of 'find'].

31   <u>What</u> [ablative, object of 'will use' and *ūtor* takes an ablative] will <u>Marcia</u> [nominative, subject of 'will use'] use to fix the <u>window</u> [accusative, object of 'fix']?

32   <u>Which</u> [dative, agrees with 'beggar'] <u>beggar</u> [dative, indirect object of 'give'] did <u>you</u> [nominative, subject of 'give'] give your <u>sandwich</u> [accusative, object of 'give'] to?

33   <u>Mark</u>'s [genitive, possession] <u>father</u> [nominative, subject of 'said'] said that the <u>boys</u> [accusative, subject of 'had given' but accusative and infinitive in indirect statement] had given <u>him</u> [dative, indirect object of 'had given'] an <u>apple</u> [accusative, object of 'had given'].

34   Those [nominative, agrees with 'children'] <u>children</u> [nominative, subject of 'are'] are always <u>happy</u> [nominative, because 'be' is followed by a word in the same case as its subject]; <u>all</u> [accusative, agrees with 'day'] <u>day</u> [accusative, extent of time] <u>I</u> [nominative, subject of 'see'] see <u>them</u> [accusative, object of 'see'] <u>laughing</u> [accusative, agrees with 'them'].

35   <u>Who</u> [nominative, subject of 'persuaded'] persuaded <u>Jim</u> [dative, object of 'persuaded' and *persuādeō* takes a dative] to come to the <u>party</u> [accusative, object of 'to' (*ad*)]?

Exercise K

1   indirect statement; infinitive; perfect; accusative; no conjunction
2   indirect statement; infinitive; perfect; accusative; no conjunction
3   purpose clause; subjunctive; imperfect; nominative; *ut*

4 indirect statement; infinitive; future; accusative; no conjunction
5 indirect statement; infinitive; future; accusative; no conjunction
6 indirect statement; infinitive; present; accusative; no conjunction
7 purpose clause; subjunctive; imperfect; nominative; *ut*
8 purpose clause; subjunctive; imperfect; nominative; *ut*
9 purpose clause; subjunctive; present; nominative; *nē*
10 purpose clause; subjunctive; imperfect; nominative; *ut*
11 indirect statement; infinitive; present; accusative; no conjunction
12 purpose clause; subjunctive; imperfect; nominative; *ut*
13 purpose clause; subjunctive; imperfect; nominative; *nē*
14 indirect statement; infinitive; present; accusative; no conjunction
15 indirect statement; infinitive; present; accusative; no conjunction
16 purpose clause; subjunctive; imperfect; nominative; *ut*
17 purpose clause; subjunctive; imperfect; nominative; *nē*
18 indirect statement; infinitive; perfect; accusative; no conjunction
19 purpose clause; subjunctive; imperfect; nominative (or, if 'have to' is translated with a gerundive, dative); *nē*
20 purpose clause; subjunctive; imperfect; nominative; *ut*
21 indirect statement; infinitive; perfect; accusative; no conjunction
22 indirect statement; infinitive; perfect; accusative; no conjunction
23 indirect statement; infinitive; future; accusative; no conjunction
24 indirect statement; infinitive; perfect; accusative; no conjunction
25 purpose clause; subjunctive; imperfect; nominative; *ut*
26 purpose clause; subjunctive; imperfect; nominative; *nē*
27 indirect statement; infinitive; present; accusative; no conjunction
28 indirect statement; infinitive; perfect; accusative; no conjunction
29 indirect statement; infinitive; future; accusative; no conjunction
30 indirect statement; infinitive; present; accusative; no conjunction
31 indirect statement; infinitive; future; accusative; no conjunction
32 indirect statement; infinitive; present; accusative; no conjunction
33 purpose clause; subjunctive; imperfect; nominative; *nē*

Exercise L

1 The king ordered the soldiers to advance. (indirect command)
2 He begged his friends not to delay. (indirect command)
3 I ordered my slave to follow. (indirect command)
4 I shall ask my slave not to delay. (indirect command)
5 They begged their friends to promise. (indirect command)
6 I would like you to delay in the city with me. (indirect command)
7 The father ordered his son to follow. (indirect command)
8 He said that he had persuaded you to follow. (indirect statement + indirect command)
9 They hunted in order to capture animals. (purpose clause)
10 I would like you to follow me. (indirect command)
11 The king ordered the soldiers to follow. (indirect command)

12   The mother begged her son not to delay. (indirect command)
13   They said that they had wanted to follow you. (indirect statement)
14   Following the king, the soldiers advanced out of the camp. (none of the above)
15   I thought that they wanted to persuade us to speak with them. (indirect statement + indirect command)
16   Following their master, the slaves advanced out of the town. (none of the above)
17   The soldiers did not advance out of the camp so that the enemy would not capture them. (purpose clause)
18   I promised that I would not beg you to defend me. (indirect statement + indirect command)
19   Ordering the slaves to follow us, we advanced out of the town. (indirect command)
20   The soldiers whom the king ordered to follow him advanced out of the town. (indirect command)
21   I think that they want to persuade us to speak with them. (indirect statement + indirect command)
22   The boys whom I shall not persuade not to speak will suffer many things. (indirect command)
23   In the camp today I saw your son, whom you ordered not to speak with soldiers. (indirect command)
20   The soldiers who promised that they would follow us are not advancing out of the camp. (indirect statement)

Exercise M

1   pater (eius) (eam) rogabit ut loquatur. (indirect command)
2   venit ut tecum loqueretur. (purpose clause)
3   pater (eius) (eam) orat ut loquatur. (indirect command)
4   pater (eius) ei imperavit ut loqueretur. (indirect command)
5   pater (eius) arbitratur eam loqui. (indirect statement)
6   pater (eius) ei persuasit ne loqueretur. (indirect command)
7   loqui vult.
8   velim ut loquatur. (indirect command)
9   tibi imperamus ut pollicearis. (indirect command)
10   persuasimusne vobis ut polliceremini? (indirect command)
11   arbitrati sumus te pollicitum (or pollicitam) esse. (indirect statement)
12   rogabimus (vos) ne polliceamini. (indirect command)
13   velimus ut pollicearis. (indirect command)
14   vultisne polliceri?
15   arbitratus sum te polliciturum (or pollicituram) esse. (indirect statement)
16   potestisne polliceri?
17   cum rege saepe locuti (or locutae) sumus rogantes (eum) ut nos iuvaret. (indirect command)
18   regem hortati (or hortatae) ut nos iuvaret, discessimus. (indirect command)
19   arbitraris illum te secuturum esse, sed ei persuadebimus ut nos sequatur. (indirect statement + indirect command)
20   pollicitus se nos iuturum esse, rex milites suos ad oppidum nostrum duxit. (indirect statement)
21   puella quae nobiscum loqui voluit nunc (nos) rogat ne veniamus. (indirect command)
22   polliciti se nos oppugnaturos non esse, milites discesserunt. (indirect statement)
23   rex qui nos hortatus est ut veniremus nunc imperat ut discedamus. (two indirect commands)

Exercise N

1   That man was hindered by my brother when he was about to grab my money. (future participle)

2   May our men be defended by the gods! (hortatory subjunctive)

3   We were not able to find the lost money. (perfect participle, infinitive)

4   I think that they will be seen. (indirect statement)

5   They were praised to such an extent that everyone loved them. (result clause)

6   Were you afraid that we would delay in London? (fear clause)

7   They asked us not to go to Carthage. (indirect command)

8   Being afraid (since they were afraid), they came home. (present participle)

9   Which city should we defend? / Which city are we to defend? (deliberative subjunctive)

10 They said that they had been attacked by the enemy. (indirect statement)

11 While they are hunting they will go across the forest. (present participle)

12 Let's not fight with these soldiers. (hortatory subjunctive)

13 His mother called the boy who was about to sit with us. / When the boy was about to sit with us, his mother called him. (future participle)

14 He says that he is being hindered by the river. (indirect statement)

15 We are staying in London so that we will not be found by our fathers. (purpose clause)

16 So great is our hope that we are not sad. (result clause)

17 Having been called by their mother (when they were called by their mother), the boys came home. (perfect participle)

18 His fear is so great that he is fleeing. (result clause)

19 I thought that the boys were being taught by the teacher. (indirect statement)

20 Where should I sit? / Where am I to sit? (deliberative subjunctive)

21 We saw you hunting. / We saw you when you were hunting. (present participle)

22 They were afraid that we would stay home today. (fear clause)

23 May the gods help us! (hortatory subjunctive)

24 We shall order the slaves to remain in London. (indirect command)

25 A city defended by us will never be captured by the enemy. (perfect participle)

26 Let's stay in Athens for many days. (hortatory subjunctive)

27 They will never say that they were defended by us. (indirect statement)

28 I was afraid that you would not go to Athens. (fear clause)

29 When they are about to repair the walls, the citizens look for stones. / Being about to repair the walls, the citizens are looking for stones. (future participle)

30 What should I say? / What am I to say? (deliberative subjunctive)

31 They came home to see their mothers. (purpose clause)

32 They will think that they are being praised by us. (indirect statement)

33 Animals sold by that farmer are never good. (perfect participle)

34 The enemy's army is so great that our men are being conquered. (result clause)

35 Let's persuade our mother. (hortatory subjunctive)

36 We want to find the money buried in that field. (perfect participle, infinitive)

37 He asked us to stay with him. (indirect command)

38 When I am about to leave Athens I am hindered by my friends. / Being about to leave Athens, I am hindered by my friends. (future participle)

39 Did you say that you had been left in Delphi by your slaves? (indirect statement)

40   Whom should we follow? / Whom are we to follow? (deliberative subjunctive)

41   Their house is so big that many people are in it. (result clause)

42   Having suffered many things, they are sad. (perfect participle)

43   He will be afraid that we will come to Corinth. (fear clause)

44   I saw you when you were about to speak with the king. (future participle)

45   He stayed in Rome for so many years that he never came home. (result clause)

46   Our men went to Corinth so that it would not be attacked by the enemy. (purpose clause)

47   The enemy, hindered by stones, were not able to attack our men. (perfect participle, infinitive)

48   Our men, hindered by stones, were not able to attack the enemy. (perfect participle, infinitive)

49   I ordered the soldiers not to go to Athens. (indirect command)

50   I was afraid that you would stay at home for many hours. (fear clause)

51   Let's help the soldiers attacked by the enemy. (hortatory subjunctive, perfect participle)

52   Which soldiers should I attack? / Which soldiers am I to attack? (deliberative subjunctive)

53   They remained there for many days so that we would not see them. (purpose clause)

54   He said that you (feminine plural) would ask the king. (indirect statement)

55   They delayed in Athens for so many days that they never went to Corinth. (result clause)

56   We shall stay in London for so many hours that we shall come home tomorrow. (result clause)

57   We came to Rome to hear the senate. (purpose clause)

58   He says that you are going to Delphi. (indirect statement)

59   We shall urge the soldiers to come with us to the senate. (indirect command)

60   They are afraid that we will go to Carthage. (fear clause)

61   Having advanced to Corinth, the enemy were hindered by our men. / When they had advanced to Corinth, the enemy were hindered by our men. (perfect participle)

62   Let's defend our sons. (hortatory subjunctive)

63   He said that that girl would be loved by everyone. (indirect statement)

64   When they are about to fight with the enemy, our men do not fear. (future participle)

65   He was afraid that the poet would read his verses. (fear clause)

66   You will not see the king when/if you stay at home. (present participle)

67   Should I promise? / Am I to promise? (deliberative subjunctive)

68   When I have spoken with you I shall be happy. (perfect participle)

69   They said that they had used our money. (indirect statement)

70   I fear that I shall not be defended. (fear clause)

71   I am staying in Athens to write verses. (purpose clause)

72   Let's give this to the girl who is about to leave. (hortatory subjunctive, future participle)

73   I think that this slave will be sold tomorrow. (indirect statement)

74   May he be heard by the king! (hortatory subjunctive)

75   When I was asked by my friends, I promised. (perfect participle)

76   I fear that they will stay here for many days. (fear clause)

77   He will say that he will follow us. (indirect statement)

78   I am loved to such an extent that I am always happy. (result clause)

79   I saw the slaves following you. (present participle)

80   I saw you following the slaves. (present participle)

81   Should we leave our horses here? / Are we to leave our horses here? (deliberative subjunctive)

82   I persuaded my mother not to send me to Corinth. (indirect command)

83   May you not be hindered by the stones in the field! (hortatory subjunctive)

84   I thought that you were following us. / I thought that we were following you. (indirect statement)

85   Having been left in the forest by his father, the boy is not happy. (perfect participle)

86   The steps are so big that we cannot go up. (result clause)

87   Should I ask my father to help me? (deliberative subjunctive, indirect command)

88   We heard you talking with friends. (present participle)

89   We are going to Delphi to speak with the god. (purpose clause)

90   May they not lose our money! (hortatory subjunctive)

91   They thought that I had stayed in Athens. (indirect statement)

92   The boys who followed you are his sons. (perfect participle)

93   Who persuaded you to go to Athens? (indirect command)

94   I am afraid that my book will be read by the poet. (fear clause)

95   He came home from Athens to bury his father. (purpose clause)

96   We saw your friend when he was about to hunt in the forest. (future participle)

97   They were so afraid that they fled. (result clause)

98   Fearing that they would be seen, they fled into the forest. (present participle, fear clause)

99   Let's not attack this army. (hortatory subjunctive)

100 He will think that I persuaded you. (indirect statement)

101 Should we stay in Rome for many days? / Are we to stay in Rome for many days? (deliberative subjunctive)

102 They will be afraid that we will not go with them. (fear clause)

103 When I have encouraged the senate I will go home. (perfect participle)

104 My mother persuaded me to go to Delphi with you. (indirect command)

105 The soldiers who were about to attack Corinth were attacked by our men. / When they were about to attack Corinth, the soldiers were attacked by our men. (future participle)

106 The dying father spoke with his sons. (present participle)

107 We begged the senate to help us. (indirect command)

108 I think that we will stay in Rome for four days. (indirect statement)

109 Staying in Carthage for many years, they saw many things. (present participle)

110 Let's go to the senate so that we will be helped by the Romans. (hortatory subjunctive, purpose clause)

111 Should we leave Athens? / Are we to leave Athens? (deliberative subjunctive)

112 They hindered the soldier who was about to flee. / They hindered the soldier when he was about to flee. (future participle)

Exercise O

1   If they were under 18 they were not allowed to buy that.

2   If they had been under 18 they would not have been allowed to buy that.

3   If they are under 18 they will not be allowed to buy that.

4   If they should be (were to be) under 18 they would not be allowed to buy that.

5   No doubt Mark will get job offers if he submits applications.

6   No doubt Mark would get job offers if he should submit (were to submit) applications.

7   No doubt Mark is getting job offers if he is submitting applications.

8   No doubt Mark would be getting job offers if he were submitting applications.

9   No doubt Mark got job offers if he submitted applications.
10 No doubt Mark would have got job offers if he had submitted applications.

Exercise P

The if-clause is underlined.

1   We would not have to do this exercise now if we had done it yesterday. *sī*; imperfect subjunctive + pluperfect subjunctive (mixed contrary-to-fact condition)

2   If I forget, remind me. *sī*; future perfect indicative + imperative (future more vivid condition)

3   If Julia was in Athens yesterday, she is probably still there. *sī*; imperfect indicative + present indicative (mixed simple condition)

4   If you find any problems, alert the supervisor. *sī*; future perfect indicative + imperative (future more vivid condition)

5   Caesar will be assassinated unless someone warns him about the plot. *nisī*; future indicative + future perfect indicative (future more vivid condition)

6   If we were Romans, we would have learned these constructions as children. *sī*; imperfect subjunctive + pluperfect subjunctive (mixed contrary-to-fact condition)

7   If your dog made that mess, you ought to clean it up. *sī*; perfect indicative + present indicative or gerundive (mixed simple condition)

8   I shall get a job as a cowherd in the Alps if things do not improve here. *nisī*; future indicative + future perfect indicative (future more vivid condition)

9   What would happen if we should all fall asleep in class? *sī*; present subjunctive + present subjunctive (future less vivid condition)

10 If the sun is shining tomorrow, we shall have a picnic. *sī*; future indicative + future indicative (future more vivid condition)

11 If he learns these rules well, he will know them for at least a week. *sī*; future perfect indicative + future indicative (future more vivid condition)

12 I would not have done that if I were you. *sī*; pluperfect subjunctive + imperfect subjunctive (mixed contrary-to-fact condition)

13 You will never succeed unless you try. *nisī*; future indicative + future perfect indicative (future more vivid condition)

14 If I should see anything, naturally I would say something. *sī*; present subjunctive + present subjunctive (future less vivid condition)

15 If we had been sensible about our search we would never have found the treasure. *sī*; pluperfect subjunctive + pluperfect subjunctive (past contrary-to-fact condition)

16 We would not have been so cold this morning if we were in Egypt. *sī*; pluperfect subjunctive + imperfect subjunctive (mixed contrary-to-fact condition)

17 If Troy is not destroyed Juno will be very sad. *nisī*; future perfect indicative + future indicative (future more vivid condition)

18 I would be paying more attention if these sentences weren't so silly. *nisī*; imperfect subjunctive + imperfect subjunctive (present contrary-to-fact condition)

19 If that fire was caused by the match you tossed, you ought to be ashamed of yourself. *sī*; perfect indicative + present indicative (mixed simple condition)

20 If the queen comes to town, we shall see her. *sī*; future perfect indicative + future indicative (future more vivid condition)

21 <u>If I had not seen it myself</u>, I would not believe it. *nisī*; pluperfect subjunctive + imperfect subjunctive (mixed contrary-to-fact condition)

22 The Greek heroes would not have had such entertaining adventures <u>if their gods had been more sensible</u>. *sī*; pluperfect subjunctive + pluperfect subjunctive (past contrary-to-fact condition)

23 Catiline will take over the city <u>unless someone stops him</u>. *nisī*; future indicative + future perfect indicative (future more vivid condition)

24 They would not have drowned <u>if they had learned to swim</u>. *sī*; pluperfect indicative + pluperfect indicative (past contrary-to-fact condition)

25 You will be eaten by a shark <u>if you try to swim here</u>. *sī*; future indicative + future perfect indicative (future more vivid condition)

26 I would be amazed <u>if she should fail the exam</u>. *sī*; present subjunctive + present subjunctive (future less vivid condition)

27 We would be able to learn Carthaginian as well as Latin <u>if the Romans had been less power-hungry</u>. *sī*; imperfect subjunctive + pluperfect subjunctive (mixed contrary-to-fact condition)

28 The milk will go sour <u>unless you put it somewhere cool</u>. *nisī*; future indicative + future perfect indicative (future more vivid condition)

29 Call the fire brigade at once <u>if you see a fire</u>. *sī*; imperative + future perfect indicative (future more vivid condition)

30 <u>If the sun is shining tomorrow</u>, we shall definitely go to the park. *sī*; future indicative + future indicative (future more vivid condition)

Ablative: a case used to indicate means, manner, motion from, and many other functions. See chapters 9, 34.3–4, and 35.

Ablative absolute: a construction using a noun and participle, both ablative, grammatically independent of the rest of the sentence. See chapter 57.

Accusative: the case indicating that a noun, adjective, or pronoun functions as the direct object of its sentence. There are also some other functions. See chapter 2 for the main function, and chapters 19 and 35.2–3 for other functions; identification exercises in chapter 63.4–7.

Active: of a verb, indicating that the subject performs the verb's action, as 'I love', 'you bring', 'he thought'. See chapter 32.1.

Adjective: a word that describes or modifies a noun, as 'red', 'beautiful', or 'hot'. See chapter 3.3.

Adverb: a word that modifies a verb or an adjective, as 'quickly', 'very', or 'effectively'. See chapter 43; identification exercise in chapter 63.1.

Agent: a word indicating the person performing the action of a passive verb, as 'hunter' in 'The bear was killed by a hunter.' See chapters 23.3 and 32.3.

Agree: take on the grammatical characteristics of another word in the sentence. In Latin adjectives agree with nouns by taking on their gender, number, and case, while verbs agree with their subjects by taking on the subject's person and number. See chapter 3.3.

Animate: a being that has a mind and can think, i.e. a human or divinity, as opposed to an (inanimate) object or thing. For grammatical purposes the Romans sometimes treated animals as animate beings and sometimes as inanimate things.

Antecedent: the word (usually a noun) modified by a relative clause. See chapter 25.2.

Article: the words 'a' and 'the', which do not occur in Latin. See chapter 63.1.

Case: a form of a noun that indicates its grammatical role in the sentence. The Latin cases are nominative, vocative, accusative, genitive, dative, ablative, and sometimes locative. See chapters 2, 5, 7, 9, and 35; identification exercises in chapter 63.

Causal: indicating the reason for something. A causal clause is one that begins with a word like 'because' or 'since' in English. See chapter 46.3.

Clause: part of a sentence, that is, a single verb and the other words that go with that verb. See chapter 15.

Comparative: the form of an adjective or adverb used to indicate 'more', as 'bigger' or 'more enthusiastic'. See chapters 38 and 43.4–6.

Conditional: containing a word for 'if'. See chapters 50 and 51.3.

Conjugation: inflection of a verb. The term is also used for the five groups into which regular Latin verbs are divided on the basis of their inflection. See chapters 6 and 17.

Conjunction: a word used for joining words or clauses, as 'and', 'but', 'if', 'when', 'while', or 'because'. See chapters 15.1 and 63.1.

Consonant stems: in the third declension, the largest group of nouns (those that are not *i*-stems). See chapter 14.

Consonants: letters of the alphabet other than *a, e, i, o, u*, or *y*. See 'The Pronunciation of Latin'.

Construction: a particular grammatical trick that a language uses, or a particular way of expressing a certain kind of sentence. Examples of commonly discussed Latin constructions are conditional clauses, purpose clauses, ablatives absolute, and indirect statement, but one can also describe the construction of virtually any word in a sentence by indicating what it depends on and what other words depend on it.

Dactyl: metrical unit made up of a long syllable followed by two short syllables. See chapter 66.

Dative: the case for the indirect object in Latin. See chapter 7; identification exercises in chapter 63.6–7.

Declension: inflection of a noun. The term is also used for the five groups into which Latin nouns are divided on the basis of their inflection. See chapter 2.

Degrees of comparison: the forms an adjective or adverb assumes in positive, comparative, and superlative. See chapters 38, 40, and 43.4–6.

Deliberative: used for making a decision (of a use of the subjunctive). See chapter 13.2.

Demonstrative: word meaning 'this' or 'that'. See chapter 10.

Deponent: a verb that is passive in form but active in meaning. See chapters 27 and 29.

Diphthong: a vowel made up of two vowel sounds, as *ae*. See 'The Pronunciation of Latin'.

Direct object: the word or words in a sentence that most directly receive the action of an active verb; in English the direct object normally follows the verb, like 'Jane' in 'I love Jane'. In Latin the direct object is in the accusative case. See chapter 2; identification exercises in chapter 63.3.

Direct speech: a sentence in which the speaker's original words are quoted verbatim, something that would go in quotation marks in English. See chapter 19.

Fear clause: a clause dependent on a verb meaning 'fear' or 'be afraid'. See chapter 30.

Feminine: a noun belonging to the 'feminine gender', one of three classes into which Latin nouns are divided (see also 'Masculine' and 'Neuter'); or an adjective or pronoun agreeing with a feminine noun (see 'Agree'). Some feminine words refer to actual females and some to things that from an English speaker's perspective have no gender. See chapter 3.

First person: indicating 'I' or 'we'. See chapter 1.

Future perfect: a tense indicating what will be past at some future point, as 'it will have been done by Monday'. See chapter 44.2.

Gender: the division of nouns into masculine, feminine, and neuter. See chapter 3.

Genitive: the case indicating possession and other relationships expressed by English 'of'. See chapters 5 and 12.1; identification exercises in chapter 63.6–7.

Gerund: a noun formed from a verb. See chapters 60 and 61.

Gerundive: an adjective formed from a verb and implying obligation. See chapters 41 and 45.2.

Govern: to cause another word or words in the sentence to assume particular forms. For example, prepositions govern their objects: in *ad urbem* 'to the city' *urbem* is accusative because *ad* takes the accusative.

Hexameter: a verse form used for heroic poetry such as Virgil's *Aeneid*. Each line is made up of six units, each of which is a dactyl or spondee. See chapter 66.

Historic tenses: most past tenses. See chapter 16.

Hortatory: urging someone to do something (of a use of the subjunctive). See chapter 13.2.

I-stems: words (especially nouns and adjectives of the third declension) with a stem ending in *i*. See chapters 14 and 21.1.

Imperative: the mood (form of the verb) used for giving orders. See chapter 10.3.

Imperfect: the indicative tense used for continuous action in the past; also the name of a subjunctive tense used in historic sequence. See chapters 15.3, 16 and 39.

Impersonal: of verbs, having no subject or, in English, having a vague 'it' as subject, for example 'it's raining'. See chapter 45.

Inanimate: something inert and incapable of independent action, as a rock or a piece of wood.

Indeclinable: having the same form in all the different cases.

Indicative: of verbs, the normal set of tenses, as opposed to the subjunctive, imperative, infinitive, and participle.

Indirect command: a clause reporting at second hand that something is or was ordered or requested. 'He asked me to go with him' is an indirect command presuming a direct version 'Please come with me'; the direct version, as in this example, need not be an order as opposed to a request, plea, or suggestion. See chapter 28.

Indirect object: a word indicating the person or other entity to whom something is given (the thing given being a direct object). In 'Johnny gave bread to the ducks', 'ducks' is the indirect object (and 'bread' is the direct object). The indirect object is translated with the dative case in Latin. See chapter 7; identification exercises in chapter 63.6–7.

Indirect question: a clause reporting at second hand that something is or was asked, wondered, or not known. 'He asked where everyone was' is an indirect question presuming a direct version 'Where is everyone?' See chapter 54.

Indirect speech: speech that is reported without quotation marks and without using the speaker's exact words, as 'He said he'd think about it' (where the speaker probably said 'I'll think about it') or 'We asked who was there' (where the direct question was something like 'Who's there?'). Indirect speech is a cover term including indirect statements, indirect questions, and indirect commands. See chapters 19, 28, and 54.

Indirect statement: a clause reporting at second hand what is or was said or known. 'He said that she was on her way' is an indirect statement presuming a direct version 'She is on her way.' See chapter 19.

Infinitive: the form of a verb that normally has 'to' in English, as 'to be' or 'to go'. Latin verbs have multiple infinitives (present, perfect, and future, active and passive); the most common of these is the present active infinitive, which can be found as the second principal part. See chapters 4.2, 19, and index.

Inflection: changing a word's form to indicate its grammatical function, as *learn* becoming *learns* or *learned*, or *puella* becoming *puellam*. Conjugation and declension are both types of inflection; see chapters 1 and 2.

Intensive: emphasizing the word to which something is attached. See chapter 52.2.

Interrogative: used for asking questions.

Intransitive: of verbs, not having a direct object.

Irregular verbs: verbs that do not fit predictably into any of the five conjugations, like *sum, possum*, and *eō*.

Locative: a case used (only for the names of cities, towns, and small islands and the words *domus, rūs*, and *humus*) to indicate location at a particular place. See chapter 35.

Macron: a horizontal bar written over a vowel to show that it is long, as *ā*. See 'The Pronunciation of Latin'.

Main clause: a clause that can form a complete sentence by itself; i.e. it stands on its own grammatically. See chapter 15.1.

Masculine: a noun belonging to the 'masculine gender', one of three classes into which Latin nouns are divided (see also 'Feminine' and 'Neuter'); or an adjective or pronoun agreeing with a masculine noun (see 'Agree'). Some masculine words refer to actual males and some to things that from an English speaker's perspective have no gender. See chapter 3.

Metre: the rhythmical structure of a Latin poem. See chapter 66.

Mixed conjugation: the paradigm of verbs like *capiō* that share some characteristics of the third conjugation and some of the fourth. See chapter 17.

Modify: to belong together with, in a subordinate capacity; to describe. Adjectives modify nouns, so in 'He has a big dog' the adjective 'big' modifies 'dog'; adverbs modify verbs and adjectives, so in 'He ran quickly' and 'She is very beautiful' the adverbs 'quickly' and 'very' modify 'ran' and 'beautiful'.

Mood: whether a verb is indicative, subjunctive, or imperative.

Mute and liquid: the consonant clusters that can count as a single consonant for the purposes of Latin metre. They are *c, g, t, d, p, b*, or *f* followed by *l, r, m*, or *n*; see chapter 66.

Negative: containing the word 'not', 'never', or an equivalent.

Neuter: the gender for nouns that are neither masculine nor feminine. See chapter 3.

Nominative: the case indicating that a noun, adjective, or pronoun functions as the subject of its sentence. See chapter 2; identification exercises in chapter 63.4–7.

Noun: a word for a person, place, or thing. Many words can function either as nouns or as verbs depending on context, as 'walk' (a noun in 'We had a great walk yesterday' but a verb in 'They walk to the bank'). See chapter 63.1.

Number: whether a word is singular or plural.

Object: the word or words in a sentence that receive the action of an active verb. In English the object normally follows the verb; in Latin it is normally in the accusative case. Objects can be further divided into direct and indirect objects; the direct object has no preposition in English and is in the accusative case in Latin, and the indirect object often has the preposition 'to' in English and is in the dative case in Latin. Thus in 'I gave a cake to John', the direct object is 'cake' and the indirect object 'John'. See chapters 2, 7.2, and 63.3.

Objective genitive: a genitive used with a noun or adjective to indicate the kind of relationship to that noun or adjective that an object would have to a verb. See chapter 12.1.

Paradigm: a sample set of forms that can be used as a model for inflecting a whole group of words. Thus in this book *regō* is used as a paradigm for third-conjugation verbs, and *puella* is used as a paradigm for first-declension nouns. The term 'paradigm' can also be used for the group of words so illustrated, e.g. for first-declension nouns as a group.

Participle: an adjective formed from a verb. English participles are usually made by adding either '-ing' or '-ed' to the verb, as 'loving' and 'loved'. See chapters 6.2, 21.3, 24, 56.3, and 57.

Partitive genitive: the use of the genitive case to indicate the whole of which some part is designated, as 'one of the cooks'. See chapter 12.1.

Parts of speech: the different grammatical categories into which words are divided: nouns, verbs, adjectives, pronouns, adverbs, prepositions, conjunctions. See chapter 63.1.

Passive: of a verb, indicating that the subject has an action done to it, as 'I am loved', 'you were brought', 'it had been thought'. See chapters 6.2 and 32.

Past participle: an adjective formed from a verb by adding '-ed' in English; the last principal part of English verbs when principal parts are given in the form 'sing, sang, sung' or 'do, did, done'. There is a similarity between the English past participle and the Latin perfect participle. See chapter 6.2.

Perfect: The Latin past tense corresponding to the English simple past ('he did') and English perfect ('he has done'). See chapter 4.3.

Periphrastic: a single verb form made up of two or more separate words; thus the sentence 'He is not coming' contains the periphrastic verb 'is coming'. See chapters 1, 29, and 63.2.

Person: whether a verb has as its subject 'I/we' (first person), 'you' (second person), or another word (third person). See chapter 1.

Personal pronouns: words for 'I', 'you', and 'we' (and sometimes other words). Third-person pronouns such as 'he', 'she', and 'they' are also considered personal pronouns by some scholars, but that classification is not used in this book.

Phrase: a group of words forming a meaningful syntactic unit, such as a preposition and the words it governs: e.g. 'in the blue car'. Often the term 'phrase' is restricted to word groups that do not contain a finite verb and therefore are not clauses, but this distinction is not very useful in Latin, where some word groups do not contain finite verbs but are nevertheless the exact equivalents of English clauses.

Pluperfect: a tense indicating that an action was past from the perspective of a point in the past, as 'he had already done it'. See chapters 44.1 and 46.1.

Plural: a form indicating that the word concerned designates more than one entity, as 'men' or 'things'. See chapter 1.

Positive: the basic form of an adjective, neither comparative nor superlative. See chapter 38.

Postpositive: unable to come first in a sentence or clause. Postpositive words must usually be moved when translating into English: *puellae enim vēnērunt* 'for the girls came'.

Predicate: the part of a sentence that is neither the subject nor direct modifiers of the subject, i.e. the verb and words associated with the verb.

Predicate nominative: a word that is not part of the subject of a sentence but nevertheless appears in the nominative because it is connected to the subject by a verb meaning 'be', 'become', or 'be called'. See chapters 5.3–4 and 63.4.

Preposition: a small, uninflected word that is regularly followed by a noun or pronoun, as 'of', 'in', or 'about'. See chapter 9.2.

Present participle: an adjective formed from a verb by adding '-ing' in English, or the Latin equivalent. See chapters 21.3 and 24.

Primary sequence: sequence of tenses introduced by a verb that is not in a past tense. See chapters 16 and 46.2.

Primary tenses: non-past tenses. See chapter 16.

Principal parts: a set of verb forms that tells you all the different stems a particular verb has. English verbs have three principal parts, as 'go, went, gone'; most Latin verbs have four. See chapters 4.2 and 6.2.

Pronoun: a word standing for a noun, such as 'he', 'she', 'it', 'they', 'I', 'you', 'we', 'this one', 'that one', 'who', 'which', 'that', etc. See chapter 63.1.

Purpose clause: a clause indicating the purpose of the action of the main verb. See chapter 15.2.

Quantity: whether a vowel (or syllable) is long or short. See 'The Pronunciation of Latin' and chapter 66.

Reflexive: a word referring back to the subject of the sentence, as 'himself' in 'He saw himself in the water'. See chapter 20.

Relative clause: a clause containing a relative pronoun and modifying some noun (the antecedent). See chapter 25.

Relative pronoun: a pronoun introducing a relative clause. In English the basic relative pronouns are 'who' and 'which'; in Latin the basic relative pronoun is *quī, quae, quod*. See chapter 25.

Result clause: a clause indicating the result of the action expressed in the main verb. See chapter 33.

Second person: indicating 'you'. See chapter 1.

Secondary tenses: most past tenses. See chapter 16.

Sequence of tenses: a rule for determining how to interpret the tense of a subjunctive verb in Latin. See chapters 16, 46.2, and 54.2.

Singular: a form indicating that the word concerned designates just one entity, as 'man' or 'thing'. See chapter 1.

Spondee: a metrical unit made up of two long syllables. See chapter 66.

Stem: a word without its ending, the part of a word that remains when the ending is subtracted. The stem of a noun is normally found by subtracting the ending from the genitive: thus the stem of *mīles, mīlitis* is *mīlit-*, and that of *puella, puellae* is *puell-*. The stem of an adjective is sometimes found by subtracting the ending from the genitive and sometimes from the feminine (this characteristic determines what is given in a dictionary entry): the stem of *tener, tenera, tenerum* is *tener-*, that of *niger, nigra, nigrum* is *nigr-*, and that of *fēlīx*, gen. *fēlīcis* is *fēlīc-*. Verbs have several different stems (that is why one has to learn their principal parts): with *regō*, for example, the present stem is *reg-*, but the perfect stem is *rēx-*. Sometimes it is convenient to think of the characteristic vowels of the different verb conjugations as part of the present stem (thus the present stem of *amō* is *amā-* and that of *moneō* is *monē-*).

Subject: the word(s) in a sentence designating the person or thing that performs the action described by the verb. In English the subject is usually near the beginning of the sentence. See chapters 1 and 2; identification exercises in chapter 63.3.

Subjunctive: a mood with no fixed translation into English. See chapter 13.

Subordinate clause: a clause that does not stand on its own grammatically and would not form a complete sentence without another clause, such as 'because I'd like to see him', 'when the door opens', or 'if it doesn't rain'. See chapter 15.

Substantivize: to make into a noun. See chapter 8.3.

Superlative: the form an adjective or adverb assumes to indicate 'most', as 'biggest' or 'most enthusiastic'. See chapters 38 and 43.4–6.

Syllable: a vowel (either a pure vowel or a diphthong) and the consonants associated with it. See chapter 66.

Syntax: how words are put together to make clauses and sentences, and how the relationships between different words in a sentence affects their meanings.

Temporal clause: a clause indicating time, as 'when he came back' or 'ever since she left'. See chapter 47.

Tense: whether a verb indicates past (e.g. 'he went'), present (e.g. 'he goes'), future (e.g. 'he will go'), etc.

Third person: a form indicating that the subject is anything other than 'I', 'we', or 'you'; most often indicating 'he', 'she', 'it', or 'they'. See chapter 1.

Transitive: of verbs, having a direct object.

Verb: a word indicating the action performed by or done to the subject of the sentence. See chapter 1; identification exercises in chapter 63.1.

Vocative: the case indicating that a noun or adjective is being called or directly spoken to. See chapter 2.2.

Voice: whether a verb is active (doing action, e.g. 'he does', 'they did') or passive (receiving action, e.g. 'it is being done', 'it was done').

Vowels: the letters *a, e, i, o, u*. The letter *y* is always a vowel in Latin and sometimes a vowel in English (in 'quickly' it is a vowel, but in 'you' it is a consonant); the letter *i* is always a vowel in English but only sometimes a vowel in Latin (in *in* it is a vowel, but in *iam* it is a consonant). See 'The Pronunciation of Latin'.

The *Aeneid* is poetry: the rhythm of the words is part of the art form. But Latin poetry works on different principles from English poetry, in that it is based on syllable quantity: the *Aeneid* is built on a pattern of long and short syllables.

The basic unit on which this pattern is based is a dactyl, that is, a long syllable followed by two short ones. In principle six dactyls make up each line of the *Aeneid*, which is therefore in a type of verse known as the 'dactylic hexameter'. In practice this pattern allows some variations, because a rhythm consisting entirely of dactyls would be monotonous. Therefore sometimes the two short syllables of a dactyl are replaced by one long syllable; that replacement changes the dactyl into a spondee (i.e. two long syllables). In fact the last unit of a dactylic hexameter line is always a spondee, while the next-to-last unit is almost always a dactyl.

The core of a syllable is a vowel, so each line of verse has as many syllables as it does vowels (a diphthong counts as one vowel;[1] *i* can be a vowel or a consonant). If a vowel is long, the syllable containing it is long. If a vowel is short, the syllable containing it is short if there is only one consonant between that vowel and the next vowel (except that *x* counts as two consonants), but the syllable is long if there is more than one consonant before the next vowel. For this purpose word boundaries are ignored, so the underlined units of all the following phrases result in long syllables: *est urbs, ex undīs, gaudia studiōrum, in terrīs*. So if one indicates a long syllable with the symbol -, a short syllable with the symbol ˘, and the division between one unit and the next with |, the metrical structure of the first line of Virgil's *Aeneid* can be analysed as follows:

$$ - \quad \breve{} \quad \breve{}| - \quad \breve{} \quad \breve{}| - \quad - | - \quad - \quad | - \quad \breve{} \quad \breve{} \quad | - \quad - $$

arma virumque canō, Troiae quī prīmus ab ōrīs

In this line the last unit is obviously a spondee, because both syllables are long. But the last syllable of a line always counts as long even if it ends in a syllable that ought to be short, like *vēnit* in line 2. Therefore that line can be analysed like this (unusually, the second *i* of *Lāvīniaque* functions as a consonant here).

$$ - \breve{} \breve{}| - \quad - | - \quad \breve{} \quad \breve{}| - \quad - | - \quad \breve{} \quad \breve{} \quad | - \quad - $$

Ītaliam fātō profugus Lāvīniaque vēnit

When one word ends in a vowel or a vowel followed only by -*m*, and the next begins with a vowel or a vowel preceded only by *h*-, the two syllables merge into one. (This merger happens only across word boundaries; a similar sequence within a word, for

---

[1] In addition to the common Latin diphthongs *ae, au,* and *oe,* rarer diphthongs *oi, ai, ei,* and *eu* also occur.

example in *mihi*, does not merge.) Therefore in the third line of the *Aeneid* the phrase *ille et* is only two syllables, and *multum ille et* is only three syllables. So that line has fourteen syllables rather than the sixteen one might see at first glance (the *i* of *iactatus* is a consonant), and its metrical structure is:

$$- \smile \smile \mid \ - \quad - \mid - \ - \mid - \ - \mid - \smile \smile \mid - \ -$$
lītora, multum ille et terrīs iactātus et altō

Although the above rule might suggest that final -*m* was not really a consonant, it does act as a full consonant for the purposes of determining whether a syllable with a short vowel is long or short. So does consonantal *i*, in any position (but *h* does not: the second syllable in *videt hostēs* is short). Therefore in the fourth line of the *Aeneid* the last syllables of *superum* and *memorem* are long.

$$- \ \smile \smile \mid - \quad - \mid - \ \smile \smile \mid - \ - \mid - \smile \smile \mid - \ -$$
vī superum, saevae memorem Iūnōnis ob īram

You should now be able to work out the metrical structure of lines 5 and 6 for yourself if given macrons on the long vowels.

multa quoque et bellō passus, dum conderet urbem

īnferretque deōs Latiō; genus unde Latīnum

Some clusters of consonants can count as a single consonant for metrical purposes; these clusters consist of a 'mute and liquid', i.e. *c, g, t, d, p, b,* or *f* followed by *l, r, m,* or *n*. For example, the first syllable of *patrēs* is usually short despite the two consonants following the *a*. This information allows one to work out the metrical form of line 7. (In this line *moenia* forms a dactyl: the *oe* is a diphthong and the *ia* counts as two short vowels, differently from the same combination in line 2. The treatment of *ia* seen here is the more common one; poets allowed themselves some freedom in making their words fit the metre.)

$$- \ - \mid - \ \smile \ \smile \mid - \ - \mid \quad - \ - \quad \mid - \ \smile\smile \mid - \ -$$
Albānīque patrēs atque altae moenia Rōmae

You should now be able to work out the metrical structure of lines 8–11 for yourself if given macrons on the long vowels.

mūsa, mihī causās memorā, quō nūmine laesō

quidve dolēns rēgīna deum tot volvere cāsūs

īnsignem pietāte virum, tot adīre labōrēs

impulerit. tantaene animīs caelestibus īrae?

When macrons are not provided on the long vowels it is more difficult to see the metrical structure of a verse. This is one of the main reasons to memorize the quantities of vowels when learning a word or form: most texts of Latin poetry do not provide macrons, so if you know for yourself which vowels are long, you are in a much better position to appreciate Latin poetry. But if you need a quantity that you do not know, there are two ways to proceed: looking up the word concerned to find the vowel quantity, or working it out from the rest of the verse. For example, suppose you know none of the quantities in line 23. You can start by identifying all the syllables that must be long because the vowel is followed by two consonants and/or comes at the end of the line.

$$\text{–} \qquad \text{–} \qquad \text{–} \qquad \text{–} \qquad \text{–} \qquad \text{– –}$$

id   metuens   veterisque   memor   Saturnia   belli

The metrical structure of a dactylic hexameter means that short syllables can only come in pairs, so whenever just one syllable of doubtful quantity occurs between two that must be long, the doubtful syllable must also be long. Therefore the first *a* of *Saturnia* is long.

$$\text{–} \qquad \text{–} \qquad \text{–} \qquad \text{–} \quad \text{– –} \qquad \text{– –}$$

id   metuens   veterisque   memor   Saturnia   belli

The maximum possible number of syllables that a dactylic hexameter can have (after any combining of syllables that needs to be done when words end and begin with vowels) is seventeen, and in order to have seventeen syllables the verse must consist of five dactyls and one spondee. A line with sixteen syllables must have four dactyls and two spondees, one with fifteen syllables three dactyls and three spondees, one with fourteen syllables two dactyls and four spondees, one with thirteen syllables one dactyl and five spondees, and a twelve-syllable line six spondees. This line has sixteen syllables, so it must have four dactyls, and therefore all the remaining doubtful syllables must be short. The metrical structure can be completed like this:

$$\text{–} \quad \smile \ \smile \ | \text{–} \quad \smile \ \smile | \text{–} \quad \smile \quad \smile | \ \text{–} \quad \text{–} \ | \text{–} \ \smile \smile | \ \text{–} \ \text{–}$$

id   metuens   veterisque   memor   Saturnia   belli

Line 24 is trickier. Marking the syllables that are obviously long produces this result (*oi* is a diphthong).

$$\text{–} \qquad \text{– –} \qquad \text{–} \qquad \text{–} \qquad \text{– –}$$

prima   quod   ad   Troiam   pro   caris   gesserat   Argis

The first syllable of *prima* must also be long, because the line must begin either with a dactyl or with a spondee, and both those units start with a long syllable.

$$\text{–} \qquad \text{–} \qquad \text{– –} \qquad \text{–} \qquad \text{–} \qquad \text{– –}$$

prima   quod   ad   Troiam   pro   caris   gesserat   Argis

The verse has fourteen syllables, therefore two dactyls and four spondees. But there are three places where a dactyl could in theory be placed: *prima quod, -am pro car-,* and *gesserat*; since there are two dactyls in the line only two of these places can actually hold dactyls, and the third must have long syllables. At this point a knowledge of some quantities is essential; if you do not know them, you need to look them up in the vocabulary for this book (or in any good dictionary). But it is not usually necessary to look up all the quantities, because often knowing one or two will make it possible to work out the others. For example, if you know that *prō* has a long vowel it follows that the first syllable of *caris* must also be long and that *prima quod* and *gesserat* must be the dactyls.

$$- \smile \quad \smile \mid - \quad - \mid - \quad - \mid - - \mid - \smile \smile \mid - -$$
prima quod ad Troiam pro caris gesserat Argis

This result gives you the information that the final *a* of *prima* is short, and that in turn tells you that the word is nominative; understanding the metrical structure of a line can therefore be helpful in understanding the syntax. Understanding the syntax can likewise help work out the metre, for if you can tell from the meaning of the line that *prima* is nominative, you know that this line must begin with a dactyl.

These principles will allow you to analyse almost any Latin hexameter line; only rarely do other complications arise. The Virgil extracts in this book include only three lines for which additional information is needed:

Line 16: *illius* has a short second *i* here (the usual form is *illīus*), and the last syllable of *Samō* does not merge with the following *hīc*.
Line 41: the name *Aiācis* is - - �‿ (*ai* is a diphthong), and *Oīlei* is �‿ - - (*oi* is not a diphthong here, but *ei* is). Although *ūnius* normally has a long *i*, it can be shortened in poetry.
Line 72: the name *Dēiopēā* is made up of five syllables (none of the vowels form diphthongs): - ˘ ˘ - -

English speakers often find it hard to hear rhythm based exclusively on syllable length, because we are used to poetry based on patterns of stressed and unstressed syllables. For example, English poets also sometimes use a version of the dactylic hexameter, but that version is based not on long and short syllables but on stressed and unstressed ones. Thus the opening of Longfellow's *Evangeline* ('Thís is the fórest priméval. The múrmuring pínes and the hémlocks') is made up of five dactyls and a spondee if you consider a dactyl to consist of a stressed syllable (marked ´ here) followed by two unstressed ones.

When reading Latin poetry aloud, many people place a stress on the first syllable of each dactyl or spondee. This pronunciation makes it easier for English speakers to appreciate the rhythm of the hexameter, but it necessitates changing the stress system that goes with the word accent. For example, the verb *canō* would naturally have its accent on the first syllable, but in the first line of the *Aeneid* this method of expressing the metre puts a stress on the last syllable.

Cumulative Vocabulary, Latin to English

ā, ab (+ ablative)	'by', 'from', 'away from' (chapters 9 and 23)
abeō, abīre, abiī/abīvī, abitum (conjugated like *eō*)	'go away' (chapter 12)
absum, abesse, āfuī, āfutūrus (conjugated like *sum*)	'be absent' (chapter 12)
accipiō, accipere, accēpī, acceptum	'receive', 'accept' (chapter 15)
ācer, ācris, ācre	'sharp', 'keen' (chapter 21)
ad (+ accusative)	'to' (chapter 9)
adeō	'so', 'to such an extent' (chapter 33)
adsum, adesse, adfuī, adfutūrus (conjugated like *sum*)	'be present' (chapter 12)
adulēscēns, adulēscentis, adulēscentium (m.)	'young man' (chapter 61)
adveniō, advenīre, advēnī, adventum	'arrive' (chapter 47)
advocātus, advocātī (m.)	'advocate' (i.e. lawyer) (chapter 41)
aequus, aequa, aequum	'even', 'fair' (chapter 61)
aestās, aestātis (f.)	'summer' (chapter 61)
aestimō, aestimāre, aestimāvī, aestimātum	'value' (chapter 58)
aetās, aetātis (f.)	'age' (chapter 61)
afferō, afferre, attulī, allātum	'bring' (chapter 49)
ager, agrī (m.)	'field' (chapter 8)
agō, agere, ēgī, āctum	'drive', 'do' (chapter 15)
agricola, agricolae (m.)	'farmer' (chapters 2 and 3)
albus, alba, album	'white' (chapter 61)
aliquis, aliquid (declines like *quis*)	'someone', 'anyone' (in neuter 'something', 'anything') (chapter 57)
alius, alia, aliud	'other' (of more than two) (chapter 55)
alter, altera, alterum	'other' (of two) (chapter 55)
altus, alta, altum	'high', 'deep' (chapter 57)
amīcus, amīcī (m.)	'friend' (chapters 2 and 3)

āmittō, āmittere, āmīsī, āmissum	'lose' (chapter 20)
amō, amāre, amāvī, amātum	'love' (chapter 6)
amor, amōris (m.)	'love' (chapter 60)
animal, animālis, animālium (n.)	'animal' (chapter 14)
animus, animī (m.)	'soul' (chapter 61)
annus, annī (m.)	'year' (chapter 35)
antequam	'before' (conjunction) (chapter 47)
antīquus, antīqua, antīquum	'ancient' (chapter 57)
aqua, aquae (f.)	'water' (chapter 7)
āra, ārae (f.)	'altar' (chapter 61)
arbitror, arbitrārī, arbitrātus sum	'think' (chapter 28)
arbor, arboris (f.)	'tree' (chapter 61)
argentum, argentī (n.)	'silver' (chapter 41)
ars, artis, artium (f.)	'art', 'skill' (chapter 54)
as, assis (m.)	'as' (small coin) (chapter 58)
ascendō, ascendere, ascendī, ascēnsum	'go up' (chapter 41)
asper, aspera, asperum	'rough' (chapter 8)
Athēnae, Athēnārum (f. plural)	'Athens' (chapter 35)
atque	'and' (chapter 45)
audeō, audēre, ausus sum (semideponent)	'dare' (chapter 54)
audiō, audīre, audīvī, audītum	'hear' (chapter 15)
auferō, auferre, abstulī, ablātum	'carry off' (chapter 49)
aurum, aurī (n.)	'gold' (chapter 41)
aut	'or' (chapter 33)
autem (postpositive)	'however' (chapter 33)
bellum, bellī (n.)	'war' (chapter 3)
bene	'well' (chapter 7)
bibō, bibere, bibī, –	'drink' (chapter 60)
bonus, bona, bonum	'good' (chapter 3)
brevis, breve	'short', 'brief' (chapter 21)
cadō, cadere, cecidī, cāsum	'fall' (chapter 57)
canis, canis (m., f.)	'dog' (chapter 57)
capiō, capere, cēpī, captum	'take', 'capture' (chapter 15)
caput, capitis (n.)	'head' (chapter 19)
Carthāgō, Carthāginis (f.)	'Carthage' (chapter 35)
cārus, cāra, cārum	'dear', 'expensive' (chapter 38)
castra, castrōrum (n. plural)	'camp' (in the military sense) (chapter 7)
causa, causae (f.)	'case', 'reason' (chapter 41)

celer, celeris, celere	'fast', 'swift' (chapter 21)
cēna, cēnae (f.)	'dinner' (chapter 57)
cēnō, cēnāre, cēnāvī, cēnātum	'dine', 'have dinner' (chapter 57)
certus, certa, certum	'certain', 'reliable' (chapter 38)
cīvis, cīvis, cīvium (m.)	'citizen' (chapter 14)
clārus, clāra, clārum	'bright', 'famous' (chapter 38)
classis, classis, classium (f.)	'fleet' (chapter 14)
cōgitō, cōgitāre, cōgitāvī, cōgitātum	'think' (chapter 50)
cōgō, cōgere, coēgī, coāctum	'force', 'drive together' (chapter 58)
cōnor, cōnārī, cōnātus sum	'try' (chapter 58)
cōnsilium, cōnsiliī (n.)	'advice', 'plan' (chapter 5)
cōpia, cōpiae (f.)	'supply', (in plural) 'troops' (chapter 61)
coquō, coquere, coxī, coctum	'cook', 'bake' (chapter 60)
Corinthus, Corinthī (f.)	'Corinth' (chapter 35)
cornū, cornūs (n.)	'horn' (chapter 33)
corpus, corporis (n.)	'body' (chapter 14)
crās	'tomorrow' (chapter 7)
crēdō, crēdere, crēdidī, crēditum (+ dative)	'believe', 'trust' (chapter 54)
cum (+ ablative)	'with' (chapter 9)
cum (conjunction)	'since' (chapter 46), 'when' (chapter 47), 'although' (chapter 47)
cūr	'why?' (chapter 7)
cūrō, cūrāre, cūrāvī, cūrātum (+ accusative, despite English 'of')	'take care (of)' (chapter 50)
currō, currere, cucurrī, cursum	'run' (chapters 1 and 4)
dē (+ ablative)	'from', 'about' (chapter 9)
dea, deae (f.)	'goddess' (chapters 2 and 3)
decet, decēre, decuit, – (+ accusative and infinitive)	'it is fitting' (chapter 45)
dēfendō, dēfendere, dēfendī, dēfēnsum	'defend' (chapter 24)
deinde	'then' (chapter 45)
dēleō, dēlēre, dēlēvī, dēlētum	'destroy' (chapter 57)
Delphī, Delphōrum (m. plural)	'Delphi' (chapter 35)
dēnārius, dēnāriī (m.)	'denarius' (chapter 58)
dēscendō, dēscendere, dēscendī, dēscēnsum	'go down' (chapter 41)
deus, deī (m.)	'god' (chapters 2 and 3)
dīc (imperative singular)	'say!' (chapter 10)

dīcō, dīcere, dīxī, dictum — 'say' (chapter 6)

diēs, diēī (m.) — 'day' (chapter 33)

difficilior, difficilius — 'more difficult', rather difficult' (chapter 40)

difficilis, difficile — 'difficult' (chapter 21)

difficillimus, difficillima, difficillimum — 'most difficult', 'very difficult' (chapter 40)

dignus, digna, dignum (+ ablative) — 'worthy (of)' (chapter 45)

dīligēns, *gen.* dīligentis — 'careful' (chapter 47)

discēdō, discēdere, discessī, discessum — 'leave' (in the intransive sense, i.e. 'depart') (chapter 24)

discō, discere, didicī, – — 'learn' (chapter 41)

diū — 'for a long time' (chapter 19)

dīves, *gen.* dīvitis — 'rich' (chapter 57)

dīvitiae, dīvitiārum (f. plural) — 'wealth' (chapter 50)

dō, dare, dedī, datum — 'give' (chapter 6)

doceō, docēre, docuī, doctum — 'teach' (chapter 6)

domina, dominae (f.) — 'mistress' (chapter 20)

dominus, dominī (m.) — 'master' (chapter 20)

domus, domūs/domī (f.) — 'house', 'home' (chapter 33)

dōnum, dōnī (n.) — 'gift' (chapter 50)

dormiō, dormīre, dormīvī, dormītum — 'sleep' (chapter 57)

dūc (imperative singular) — 'lead!' (chapter 10)

dūcō, dūcere, dūxī, ductum — 'lead' (chapters 1 and 4)

dulcis, dulce — 'sweet' (chapter 38)

dum — 'while', 'until' (chapter 47)

dummodo — 'provided that' (chapter 47)

duo, duae, duo — 'two' (chapter 55)

dūrus, dūra, dūrum — 'hard', 'harsh' (chapter 38)

dux, ducis (m.) — 'leader' (chapter 57)

ē, ex (+ ablative) — 'out of' (chapter 9)

egeō, egēre, eguī, – (+ genitive or ablative) — 'need', 'lack' (chapter 47)

eius (genitive singular of *is*) — 'his', 'her', 'its' (chapter 23)

emō, emere, ēmī, ēmptum — 'buy' (chapters 1 and 4)

enim (postpositive) — 'for' (chapter 33)

eō, īre, iī/īvī, itum — 'go' (chapter 9)

eōrum, eārum (genitive plural of *is*) — 'their' (chapter 23)

epistula, epistulae (f.) — 'letter' (chapter 5)

equus, equī (m.) — 'horse' (chapters 2 and 3)

ergō	'therefore' (chapter 33)
este (imperative plural)	'be!' (chapter 10)
estō (imperative singular)	'be!' (chapter 10)
et	'and' (chapter 1); 'also', 'even' (chapter 45)
et . . . et	'both . . . and' (chapter 45)
ex (+ ablative)	'out of' (chapter 9)
exeō, exīre, exiī/exīvī, exitum (conjugated like *eō*)	'go out' (chapter 12)
exercitus, exercitūs (m.)	'army' (chapter 33)
facile	'easily' (chapter 43)
facilior, facilius	'easier', 'rather easy' (chapter 40)
facilis, facile	'easy' (chapter 21)
facilius	'more easily', 'rather easily' (chapter 43)
facillimē	'most easily', 'very easily' (chapter 43)
facillimus, facillima, facillimum	'easiest', 'very easy' (chapter 40)
faciō, facere, fēcī, factum (use *fīō* for passive)	'do', 'make' (chapter 15)
fāma, fāmae (f.)	'fame', 'reputation', 'rumour' (chapter 41)
fēlīx, *gen.* fēlīcis	'happy', 'fortunate' (chapter 21)
ferō, ferre, tulī, lātum	'carry' (chapter 49)
fidēs, fideī (f.)	'faith', 'trust' (chapter 33)
fīlia, fīliae (f.)	'daughter' (chapter 57)
fīlius, fīliī (m.)	'son' (chapter 8)
fīnis, fīnis, fīnium (f.)	'end' (chapter 41)
fīō, fierī, factus sum	'become', 'be made', 'be done' (chapter 51)
floccus, floccī (m.)	'tuft of wool' (chapter 58)
flūmen, flūminis (n.)	'river' (chapter 14)
fortis, forte	'strong', 'brave' (chapter 21)
frāter, frātris (m.)	'brother' (chapter 14)
fugiō, fugere, fūgī, fugitūrus	'flee' (chapter 20)
fugō, fugāre, fugāvī, fugātum	'cause to flee', 'put to flight' (chapter 57)
gaudium, gaudiī (n.)	'joy' (chapter 61)
genū, genūs (n.)	'knee' (chapter 33)
gerō, gerere, gessī, gestum	'wear', 'wage (war)', 'conduct' (chapter 57)
gladius, gladiī (m.)	'sword' (chapter 7)
gradus, gradūs (m.)	'step' (chapter 33)
Graecus, Graeca, Graecum	'Greek' (chapter 8)
grātus, grāta, grātum	'pleasing', 'grateful' (chapter 38)
gravis, grave	'heavy', 'serious' (chapter 21)

habeō, habēre, habuī, habitum	'have' (chapter 6)
herī	'yesterday' (chapter 7)
hīc	'here' (chapter 7)
hic, haec, hoc	'this', 'these' (chapter 10)
hodiē	'today' (chapter 7)
homō, hominis (m.)	'human being' (chapter 19)
hōra, hōrae (f.)	'hour' (chapter 35)
hortor, hortārī, hortātus sum	'urge', 'encourage' (chapter 28)
hospes, hospitis (m.)	'guest', 'host' (chapter 60)
hostēs, hostium (m. plural)	'(public) enemy' (chapter 14)
ī (imperative singular)	'go!' (chapter 10)
iaceō, iacēre, iacuī, –	'lie' (i.e. be horizontal) (chapter 57)
iaciō, iacere, iēcī, iactum	'throw' (chapter 57)
ibi	'there' (chapter 33)
īdem, eadem, idem	'same' (chapter 58)
idōneus, idōnea, idōneum	'suitable' (chapter 45)
igitur (postpositive)	'therefore' (chapter 33)
ignis, ignis, ignium (m.)	'fire' (chapter 57)
ignōscō, ignōscere, ignōvī, ignōtum (+ dative)	'forgive' (chapter 45)
ille, illa, illud	'that', 'those' (chapter 10)
immortālis, immortāle	'immortal' (chapter 21)
impediō, impedīre, impedīvī, impedītum	'hinder' (chapter 16)
imperō, imperāre, imperāvī, imperātum (+ dative)	'order' (chapter 28)
in (+ ablative)	'in', 'on' (chapter 9)
in (+ accusative)	'into', 'onto' (chapter 9)
ingredior, ingredī, ingressus sum	'enter' (chapter 41)
inimīcus, inimīcī (m.)	'(personal) enemy' (chapter 50)
inīquus, inīqua, inīquum	'uneven', 'unfair' (chapter 61)
īnsula, īnsulae (f.)	'island' (chapter 60)
intellegō, intellegere, intellēxī, intellēctum	'understand' (chapter 24)
interficiō, interficere, interfēcī, interfectum	'kill' (chapter 16)
inveniō, invenīre, invēnī, inventum	'find' (chapter 16)
ipse, ipsa, ipsum	'-self' (chapter 52)
īra, īrae (f.)	'anger' (chapter 60)
is, ea, id	'he', 'she', 'it', 'they' (chapter 23)

iste, ista, istud	'that of yours' (chapter 52)
ita	'so', 'thus', 'in such a way' (chapter 33)
īte (imperative plural)	'go!' (chapter 10)
iter, itineris (n.)	'journey' (chapter 60)
iterum	'again' (chapter 54)
iūdex, iūdicis (m.)	'judge' (chapter 41)
Iuppiter, Iovis (m.)	'Jupiter' (chapter 60)
iūs, iūris (n.)	'right', 'law' (chapter 54)
iuvō, iuvāre, iūvī, iūtum	'help' (chapter 6)
laetus, laeta, laetum	'joyful' (chapter 57)
Latīnus, Latīna, Latīnum	'Latin' (chapter 47)
laudō, laudāre, laudāvī, laudātum	'praise' (chapter 6)
laus, laudis (f.)	'praise' (chapter 19)
lectus, lectī (m.)	'bed' (chapter 58)
legō, legere, lēgī, lēctum	'read' (chapters 1 and 4)
līber, lībera, līberum	'free' (chapter 8)
liber, librī (m.)	'book' (chapter 8)
līberō, līberāre, līberāvī, līberātum	'free' (chapter 50)
licet, licēre, licuit, – (+ dative and infinitive)	'it is allowed', 'may' (in the sense of 'is allowed to') (chapter 45)
lingua, linguae (f.)	'tongue', 'language' (chapter 45)
locus, locī (m., also n. in plural)	'place' (chapter 35)
Londinium, Londiniī (n.)	'London' (chapter 35)
longus, longa, longum	'long' (chapter 19)
loquor, loquī, locūtus sum	'speak' (chapter 28)
lūdus, lūdī (m.)	'game' (chapter 60)
magis	'more greatly', 'rather greatly' (chapter 43)
magister, magistrī (m.)	'teacher' (chapter 8)
magnopere	'greatly' (chapter 43)
magnus, magna, magnum	'big' (chapter 3)
maior, maius	'bigger', 'rather big' (chapter 40)
male	'badly' (chapter 7)
mālō, mālle, māluī, –	'prefer' (chapter 37)
malus, mala, malum	'bad' (chapter 12)
maneō, manēre, mānsī, mānsum	'remain', 'stay', 'wait' (chapter 35)
manus, manūs (f.)	'hand' (chapter 33)
mare, maris, marium (n.)	'sea' (chapter 60)
māter, mātris (f.)	'mother' (chapter 14)

maximē	'most greatly', 'very greatly' (chapter 43)
maximus, maxima, maximum	'biggest', 'very big' (chapter 40)
melior, melius	'better', 'rather good' (chapter 40)
melius	'better', 'rather well' (chapter 43)
metus, metūs (m.)	'fear' (chapter 33)
meus, mea, meum	'my' (chapter 3)
mīles, mīlitis (m.)	'soldier' (chapter 14)
minimē	'least', 'very little' (adverb) (chapter 43)
minimus, minima, minimum	'smallest', 'very small' (chapter 40)
minor, minus	'smaller', 'rather small' (chapter 40)
minus	'less', 'rather little' (adverb) (chapter 43)
miser, misera, miserum	'miserable' (chapter 8)
mittō, mittere, mīsī, missum	'send' (chapters 1 and 4)
moenia, moenium (n. plural)	'walls' (chapter 14)
moneō, monēre, monuī, monitum	'advise', 'warn' (chapter 6)
mōns, montis, montium (m.)	'mountain' (chapter 60)
morior, morī, mortuus sum	'die' (chapter 27)
moror, morārī, morātus sum	'delay' (chapter 28)
mulier, mulieris (f.)	'woman' (chapter 60)
multī, multae, multa	'many' (chapter 12)
multum	'much' (adverb) (chapter 43)
nam	'for' (conjunction; chapter 33)
nāscor, nāscī, nātus sum	'be born' (chapter 58)
nauta, nautae (m.)	'sailor' (chapter 61)
nāvis, nāvis, nāvium (f.)	'ship' (chapter 58)
-ne	*introduces yes/no questions* (chapter 1)
nē	'not' (with many types of subjunctive) (chapter 13)
nē quid (n.)	'nothing', 'not anything' (chapter 40)
nē quis (m.)	'no-one', 'not anyone' (chapter 40)
nē ūllus, nē ūlla, nē ūllum	'no', 'none' (chapter 40)
nec	'neither', 'nor', 'and . . . not' (chapter 45)
negō, negāre, negāvī, negātum	'deny' (chapter 61)
nēmō (m.)	'no-one', 'not . . . anyone' (chapter 40)
neque	'neither', 'nor', 'and . . . not' (chapter 45)
nesciō, nescīre, nescīvī/nesciī, nescītum (+ accusative, despite English 'of')	'not know', 'be ignorant (of)' (chapter 45)
niger, nigra, nigrum	'black' (chapter 8)
nihil	'nothing', 'not . . . anything' (chapter 40)

nisī	'if not', 'unless' (chapter 50)
nōlō, nōlle, nōluī, –	'not want' (chapter 37)
nōmen, nōminis (n.)	'name' (chapter 14)
nōn	'not' (chapter 1)
noster, nostra, nostrum	'our' (chapter 8)
novus, nova, novum	'new' (chapter 3)
nox, noctis, noctium (f.)	'night' (chapter 45)
nūllus, nūlla, nūllum	'no', 'none' (chapter 40)
num	'whether', 'if' (in indirect questions) (chapter 54)
numquam	'never' (chapter 20)
nunc	'now' (chapter 7)
nūntiō, nūntiāre, nūntiāvī, nūntiātum	'announce', 'report' (chapter 58)
nūntius, nūntiī (m.)	'messenger' (chapter 58)
odium, odiī (n.)	'hatred' (chapter 12)
omnis, omne	'all', 'every', 'whole' (chapter 21)
oportet, oportēre, oportuit, – (+ accusative and infinitive)	'it is right', 'ought to' (chapter 45)
oppidum, oppidī (n.)	'town' (chapter 3)
oppugnō, oppugnāre, oppugnāvī, oppugnātum	'attack' (chapter 24)
optimē	'excellently', 'very well' (chapter 43)
optimus, optima, optimum	'best', 'very good' (chapter 40)
opus, operis (n.)	'work' (chapter 14)
ōrātor, ōrātōris (m.)	'speaker' (chapter 61)
orior, orīrī, ortus sum	'arise' (chapter 28)
ōrō, ōrāre, ōrāvī, ōrātum	'beg' (chapter 28)
ostendō, ostendere, ostendī, ostentum	'show' (chapter 58)
ovis, ovis, ovium (f.)	'sheep' (chapter 14)
paene	'almost' (chapter 7)
paenitet, paenitēre, paenituit, – (+ accusative of person and genitive of cause)	'it repents', 'sorry' (chapter 45)
parcō, parcere, pepercī, parsūrus (+ dative)	'spare' (chapter 61)
pāreō, pārēre, pāruī, – (+ dative)	'obey' (chapter 61)
parō, parāre, parāvī, parātum	'prepare' (chapter 58)
partior, partīrī, partītus sum	'divide' (chapter 27)
parvus, parva, parvum	'small' (chapter 19)
pater, patris (m.)	'father' (chapter 14)

patior, patī, passus sum	'suffer', 'endure' (chapter 28)
patria, patriae (f.)	'homeland', 'fatherland' (chapter 45)
paucī, paucae, pauca	'few' (chapter 12)
paulum	'little' (adverb) (chapter 43)
pecūnia, pecūniae (f.)	'money' (chapter 5)
peior, peius	'worse', 'rather bad' (chapter 40)
peius	'more badly', 'rather badly' (chapter 43)
per (+ accusative)	'through' (chapter 9)
perficiō, perficere, perfēcī, perfectum	'accomplish' (chapter 58)
perīculum, perīculī (n.)	'danger' (chapter 61)
persuādeō, persuādēre, persuāsī, persuāsum (+ dative)	'persuade' (chapter 28)
pēs, pedis (m.)	'foot' (chapter 35)
pessimē	'worst', 'very badly' (chapter 43)
pessimus, pessima, pessimum	'worst', 'very bad' (chapter 40)
petō, petere, petīvī, petītum	'seek' (chapters 1 and 4)
pluit, pluere, pluit, –	'it is raining' (chapter 45)
plūrēs, plūra	'more', 'rather many' (chapter 40)
plūrimī, plūrimae, plūrima	'most', 'very many' (chapter 40)
plūrimum	'most', 'very much' (chapter 43)
plūs	'more' (chapter 43)
poēta, poētae (m.)	'poet' (chapters 2 and 3)
polliceor, pollicērī, pollicitus sum	'promise' (chapter 28)
pōnō, pōnere, posuī, positum	'put' (chapters 1 and 4)
porta, portae (f.)	'gate' (chapter 60)
possum, posse, potuī, –	'can', 'be able to' (chapter 7)
postquam	'after' (conjunction) (chapter 47)
potēns, *gen.* potentis	'powerful' (chapter 38)
prīmus, prīma, prīmum	'first' (chapter 35)
prōgredior, prōgredī, prōgressus sum	'advance' (chapter 28)
propter (+ accusative)	'on account of' (chapter 35)
pudet, pudēre, puduit, – (+ accusative of person and genitive of cause)	'it shames', 'be ashamed' (chapter 45)
puella, puellae (f.)	'girl' (chapters 2 and 3)
puer, puerī (m.)	'boy' (chapter 8)
pugnō, pugnāre, pugnāvī, pugnātum	'fight' (chapter 20)
pulcher, pulchra, pulchrum	'beautiful' (chapter 8)
putō, putāre, putāvī, putātum	'think' (chapter 50)
quaerō, quaerere, quaesīvī, quaesītum	'ask', 'seek' (chapter 54)

quam	'than', 'rather than' (chapter 37); 'as . . . as possible' (chapter 38) (also feminine accusative singular of *quī* and of *quis*)
quandō	'when?' (chapter 54)
quantus, quanta, quantum	'how big?' (chapter 54)
quārtus, quārta, quārtum	'fourth' (chapter 35)
quattuor	'four' (chapter 12)
-que (translated before the word to which it is attached: *puerī puellaeque* 'boys and girls')	'and' (chapter 33)
quī, quae, quod	'which?' (chapter 13); 'who', 'which', 'that' (chapter 25)
quia	'because' (chapter 7)
quīnque	'five' (chapter 12)
quīntus, quīnta, quīntum	'fifth' (chapter 35)
quippe quī	'because' (chapter 56)
quis, quid	'who?', 'what?' (chapter 13)
quō	'to where?', 'where?' (with motion towards) (chapter 54)
quōmodo	'how?' (chapter 54)
quot (indeclinable)	'how many?' (chapter 54)
rapiō, rapere, rapuī, raptum	'seize', 'grab', 'carry off' (chapter 35)
reddō, reddere, reddidī, redditum	'give back', 'return' (in the sense of 'give back') (chapter 47)
redeō, redīre, rediī, reditum (conjugated like *eō*)	'go back', 'come back', 'return' (in the sense of 'go back') (chapter 47)
reficiō, reficere, refēcī, refectum	'repair' (chapter 16)
rēgīna, rēgīnae (f.)	'queen' (chapter 45)
regō, regere, rēxī, rēctum	'rule' (chapters 1 and 4)
relinquō, relinquere, relīquī, relictum	'leave behind', 'abandon' (chapter 24)
rēs, reī (f.)	'matter', 'affair', 'thing' (chapter 33)
rēx, rēgis (m.)	'king' (chapter 14)
rogō, rogāre, rogāvī, rogātum	'ask' (chapter 28)
Rōma, Rōmae (f.)	'Rome' (chapter 35)
Rōmānus, Rōmāna, Rōmānum	'Roman' (chapter 8)
saepe	'often' (chapter 20)
salūs, salūtis (f.)	'health', 'greetings' (chapter 41)
salūtō, salūtāre, salūtāvī, salūtātum	'greet' (chapter 41)
sapiēns, *gen.* sapientis	'wise' (chapter 38)

saxum, saxī (n.)	'rock', 'stone' (chapter 7)
sciō, scīre, scīvī/sciī, scītum	'know' (chapter 45)
scrībō, scrībere, scrīpsī, scrīptum	'write' (chapters 1 and 4)
sē	'himself', 'herself', 'themselves' (chapter 20)
secundus, secunda, secundum	'second' (chapter 45)
sed	'but' (chapter 7)
sedeō, sedēre, sēdī, sessum	'sit' (chapter 24)
semper	'always' (chapter 20)
senātus, senātūs (m.)	'senate' (chapter 33)
senex, senis (m.)	'old man' (chapter 58)
sentiō, sentīre, sēnsī, sēnsum	'perceive', 'feel' (chapter 16)
sepeliō, sepelīre, sepelīvī, sepultum	'bury' (chapter 16)
septem	'seven' (chapter 12)
septimus, septima, septimum	'seventh' (chapter 35)
sequor, sequī, secūtus sum	'follow' (chapter 28)
servō, servāre, servāvī, servātum	'save' (chapter 50)
servus, servī (m.)	'slave' (chapters 2 and 3)
sēstertius, sēstertiī (m.)	'sestertius' (chapter 58)
sex	'six' (chapter 12)
sextus, sexta, sextum	'sixth' (chapter 35)
sī	'if' (chapter 33)
sīc	'thus', 'in this way' (chapter 45)
silva, silvae (f.)	'forest' (chapter 7)
similior, similius	'more like', 'rather like' (chapter 40)
similis, simile (+ dative)	'like', 'similar' (chapter 38)
similiter	'similarly' (chapter 43)
similius	'more similarly', 'rather similarly' (chapter 43)
simillimē	'most similarly', 'very similarly' (chapter 43)
simillimus, simillima, simillimum	'most like', 'very like' (chapter 40)
sine (+ ablative)	'without' (chapter 9)
soror, sorōris (f.)	'sister' (chapter 14)
spēs, speī (f.)	'hope' (chapter 33)
statim	'at once' (chapter 43)
stō, stāre, stetī, statum	'stand' (chapter 6)
stultus, stulta, stultum	'foolish' (chapter 38)
sum, esse, fuī, futūrus	'be' (chapter 5)

summus, summa, summum	'very great' (chapter 50)
surgō, surgere, surrēxī, surrēctum	'get up' (chapter 47)
suus, sua, suum	'his (own)', 'her (own)', 'their (own)' (chapter 20)
Syrācūsae, Syrācūsārum (f. plural)	'Syracuse' (chapter 35)
tālis, tāle	'such', 'of such a sort' (chapter 33)
tam	'so' (i.e. to such a degree) (chapter 33)
tamen	'nevertheless' (chapter 33)
tangō, tangere, tetigī, tāctum	'touch' (chapter 60)
tantus, tanta, tantum	'so great', 'so big' (chapter 33)
tēctum, tēctī (n.)	'roof' (chapter 60)
tener, tenera, tenerum	'tender' (chapter 8)
tertius, tertia, tertium	'third' (chapter 45)
timeō, timēre, timuī, – (+ accusative)	'fear', 'be afraid of' (chapter 12)
tollō, tollere, sustulī, sublātum	'lift', 'pick up' (chapter 47)
tot (indeclinable)	'so many' (chapter 33)
tōtus, tōta, tōtum	'whole' (chapter 61)
trāns (+ accusative)	'across' (chapter 9)
trēs, tria	'three' (chapter 55)
trīstis, trīste	'sad' (chapter 21)
turpis, turpe	'shameful' (chapter 38)
tuus, tua, tuum	'your' (singular 'you') (chapter 3)
ubi	'where' (chapter 7)
unde	'from where?' (chapter 54)
ūnus, ūna, ūnum	'one' (chapter 55)
urbs, urbis, urbium (f.)	'city' (chapter 14)
ūtilis, ūtile	'useful' (chapter 47)
ūtor, ūtī, ūsus sum (+ ablative)	'use' (chapter 27)
utrum . . . an	'or' (in double questions) (chapter 54)
valeō, valēre, valuī, valitum	'be well', 'be healthy' (chapter 35)
vel	'or' (chapter 50)
vendō, vendere, vendidī, venditum	'sell' (chapter 16)
veniō, venīre, vēnī, ventum	'come' (chapter 16)
vēnor, vēnārī, vēnātus sum	'hunt' (chapter 27)
verbum, verbī (n.)	'word' (chapter 3)
vereor, verērī, veritus sum (+ accusative)	'fear', 'be afraid (of)' (chapter 27)
versus, versūs (m.)	'verse' (chapter 33)
vērus, vēra, vērum	'true' (chapter 19)
vester, vestra, vestrum	'your' (plural 'you') (chapter 8)

vetus, *gen.* veteris   'old' (chapter 60)

videō, vidēre, vīdī, vīsum   'see' (chapter 6)

vincō, vincere, vīcī, victum   'conquer' (chapters 1 and 4)

vir, virī (m.)   'man' (chapter 8)

vīta, vītae (f.)   'life' (chapter 12)

vīvō, vīvere, vīxī, vīctum   'live' (i.e. 'be alive', not 'inhabit') (chapter 16)

vocō, vocāre, vocāvī, vocātum   'call' (chapter 19)

volō, velle, voluī, –   'want', 'wish' (chapter 24)

vōx, vōcis (f.)   'voice' (chapter 41)

Cumulative Vocabulary, English to Latin

'abandon'   relinquō, relinquere, relīquī, relictum
                                            (chapter 24)

'able': use verb 'be able to'   possum, posse, potuī, – (chapter 7)

'about'   dē (+ ablative) (chapter 9)

'absent': use verb 'be absent'   absum, abesse, āfuī, āfutūrus (conjugated like
                                            sum) (chapter 12)

'accept'   accipiō, accipere, accēpī, acceptum (chapter 15)

'accomplish'   perficiō, perficere, perfēcī, perfectum
                                            (chapter 58)

'account': use 'on account of'   propter (+ accusative) (chapter 35)

'across'   trāns (+ accusative) (chapter 9)

'advance'   prōgredior, prōgredī, prōgressus sum
                                            (chapter 28)

'advice'   cōnsilium, cōnsiliī (n.) (chapter 5)

'advise'   moneō, monēre, monuī, monitum (chapter 6)

'advocate' (i.e. lawyer)   advocātus, advocātī (m.) (chapter 41)

'affair' (in the sense of 'business')   rēs, reī (f.) (chapter 33)

'afraid': use verb 'be afraid of'   timeō, timēre, timuī, – (chapter 12); vereor,
                                            verērī, veritus sum (chapter 27) (both +
                                            accusative, despite 'of')

'after'   postquam (conjunction: takes a clause, not an
                                            object) (chapter 47)

'again'   iterum (chapter 54)

'age'   aetās, aetātis (f.) (chapter 61)

'all'   omnis, omne (chapter 21)

'allow': use impersonal verb 'it is   licet, licēre, licuit, – (+ dative and infinitive)
  allowed'   (chapter 45)

'almost'   paene (chapter 7)

'also'   et (chapter 45)

'altar'   āra, ārae (f.) (chapter 61)

'although'   cum (+ subjunctive) (chapter 47)

'always'   semper (chapter 20)

'ancient'	antīquus, antīqua, antīquum (chapter 57)
'and ... not'	neque, nec (chapter 45)
'and'	et (chapter 1); -que (translated before the word to which it is attached: *puerī puellaeque* 'boys and girls') (chapter 33); atque (chapter 45)
'anger'	īra, īrae (f.) (chapter 60)
'animal'	animal, animālis, animālium (n.) (chapter 14)
'announce'	nūntiō, nūntiāre, nūntiāvī, nūntiātum (chapter 58)
'anyone' (with no negative preceding)	aliquis, aliquid (declines like *quis*) (in masculine and feminine) (chapter 57)
'anyone' (when after 'not')	nēmō (m.) (chapter 40); nē quis (m.) (chapter 40)
'anything' (with no negative preceding)	aliquis, aliquid (declines like *quis*) (in neuter) (chapter 57)
'anything' (when after 'not')	nihil (n.) (chapter 40); nē quid (n.) (chapter 40)
'arise'	orior, orīrī, ortus sum (chapter 28)
'army'	exercitus, exercitūs (m.) (chapter 33)
'arrive'	adveniō, advenīre, advēnī, adventum (chapter 47)
'art'	ars, artis, artium (f.) (chapter 54)
'as' (coin worth ¹⁄₁₀ or ¹⁄₁₆ denarius)	as, assis (m.) (chapter 58)
'as ... as possible'	quam (+ superlative) (chapter 38)
'ashamed': use impersonal verb 'be ashamed'	pudet, pudēre, puduit, – (+ accusative of person and genitive of cause) (chapter 45)
'ask'	rogō, rogāre, rogāvī, rogātum (chapter 28); quaerō, quaerere, quaesīvī, quaesītum (chapter 54)
'at once'	statim (chapter 45)
'Athens'	Athēnae, Athēnārum (f. plural) (chapter 35)
'attack'	oppugnō, oppugnāre, oppugnāvī, oppugnātum (chapter 24)
'away from'	ā, ab (+ ablative) (chapter 9)
'bad'	malus, mala, malum (chapter 12)
'badly'	male (chapter 7)
'bake'	coquō, coquere, coxī, coctum (chapter 60)
'be'	sum, esse, fuī, futūrus (chapter 5)
'be!' (imperative singular)	estō (chapter 10)

'be!' (imperative plural)	este (chapter 10)
'be able to'	possum, posse, potuī, – (chapter 7)
'be absent'	absum, abesse, āfuī, āfutūrus (conjugated like *sum*) (chapter 12)
'be afraid of'	timeō, timēre, timuī, – (chapter 12); vereor, verērī, veritus sum (chapter 27) (+ accusative, despite 'of')
'be ashamed'	pudet, pudēre, puduit, – (+ accusative of person and genitive of cause) (chapter 45)
'be born'	nāscor, nāscī, nātus sum (chapter 58)
'be done'	fīō, fierī, factus sum (passive of *faciō*) (chapter 51)
'be healthy'	valeō, valēre, valuī, valitum (chapter 35)
'be ignorant (of)'	nesciō, nescīre, nescīvī/nesciī, nescītum (+ accusative, despite 'of') (chapter 45)
'be made'	fīō, fierī, factus sum (passive of *faciō*) (chapter 51)
'be present'	adsum, adesse, adfuī, adfutūrus (conjugated like *sum*) (chapter 12)
'be well'	valeō, valēre, valuī, valitum (chapter 35)
'beautiful'	pulcher, pulchra, pulchrum (chapter 8)
'because'	quia (chapter 7); quippe quī (chapter 56)
'become'	fīō, fierī, factus sum (chapter 51)
'bed'	lectus, lectī (m.) (chapter 58)
'before'	antequam (conjunction: takes a clause, not an object) (chapter 47)
'beg'	ōrō, ōrāre, ōrāvī, ōrātum (chapter 28)
'believe'	crēdō, crēdere, crēdidī, crēditum (+ dative of person believed) (chapter 54)
'best'	optimus, optima, optimum (chapter 40)
'better' (adjective)	melior, melius (chapter 40)
'better' (adverb)	melius (chapter 43)
'big'	magnus, magna, magnum (chapter 3)
'big' (as part of 'how big?')	quantus, quanta, quantum (chapter 54)
'big' (as part of 'so big')	tantus, tanta, tantum (chapter 33)
'bigger'	maior, maius (chapter 40)
'biggest'	maximus, maxima, maximum (chapter 40)
'black'	niger, nigra, nigrum (chapter 8)
'body'	corpus, corporis (n.) (chapter 14)
'book'	liber, librī (m.) (chapter 8)

'born': use verb 'be born'	nāscor, nāscī, nātus sum (chapter 58)
'both ... and'	et ... et (chapter 45)
'boy'	puer, puerī (m.) (chapter 8)
'brave'	fortis, forte (chapter 21)
'brief'	brevis, breve (chapter 21)
'bright'	clārus, clāra, clārum (chapter 38)
'bring'	afferō, afferre, attulī, allātum (chapter 49)
'brother'	frāter, frātris (m.) (chapter 14)
'bury'	sepeliō, sepelīre, sepelīvī, sepultum (chapter 16)
'but'	sed (chapter 7)
'buy'	emō, emere, ēmī, ēmptum (chapters 1 and 4)
'by'	ā, ab (+ ablative) (chapter 23)
'call'	vocō, vocāre, vocāvī, vocātum (chapter 19)
'camp' (in the military sense)	castra, castrōrum (n. plural) (chapter 7)
'can' (i.e. be able to)	possum, posse, potuī, – (chapter 7)
'capture'	capiō, capere, cēpī, captum (chapter 15)
'careful'	dīligēns, *gen.* dīligentis (chapter 47)
'carry'	ferō, ferre, tulī, lātum (chapter 49)
'carry off'	auferō, auferre, abstulī, ablātum (chapter 49); rapiō, rapere, rapuī, raptum (chapter 35)
'Carthage'	Carthāgō, Carthāginis (f.) (chapter 35)
'case'	causa, causae (f.) (chapter 41)
'cause to flee'	fugō, fugāre, fugāvī, fugātum (chapter 57)
'certain'	certus, certa, certum (chapter 38)
'citizen'	cīvis, cīvis, cīvium (m.) (chapter 14)
'city'	urbs, urbis, urbium (f.) (chapter 14)
'come'	veniō, venīre, vēnī, ventum (chapter 16)
'come back'	redeō, redīre, rediī, reditum (conjugated like *eō*) (chapter 47)
'conduct'	gerō, gerere, gessī, gestum (chapter 57)
'conquer'	vincō, vincere, vīcī, victum (chapters 1 and 4)
'cook'	coquō, coquere, coxī, coctum (chapter 60)
'Corinth'	Corinthus, Corinthī (f.) (chapter 35)
'danger'	perīculum, perīculī (n.) (chapter 61)
'dare'	audeō, audēre, ausus sum (semideponent, i.e. deponent in perfect tenses but not in present, future, or imperfect tenses) (chapter 54)

'daughter'	fīlia, fīliae (f.) (chapter 57)
'day'	diēs, diēī (m.) (chapter 33)
'dear'	cārus, cāra, cārum (chapter 38)
'deep'	altus, alta, altum (chapter 57)
'defend'	dēfendō, dēfendere, dēfendī, dēfēnsum (chapter 24)
'delay'	moror, morārī, morātus sum (chapter 28)
'Delphi'	Delphī, Delphōrum (m. plural) (chapter 35)
'denarius'	dēnārius, dēnāriī (m.) (chapter 58)
'deny'	negō, negāre, negāvī, negātum (chapter 61)
'depart'	discēdō, discēdere, discessī, discessum (chapter 24)
'destroy'	dēleō, dēlēre, dēlēvī, dēlētum (chapter 57)
'die'	morior, morī, mortuus sum (chapter 27)
'difficult'	difficilis, difficile (chapter 21)
'dine'	cēnō, cēnāre, cēnāvī, cēnātum (chapter 57)
'dinner' (when not part of verb 'have dinner')	cēna, cēnae (f.) (chapter 57)
'dinner' (as part of verb 'have dinner')	cēnō, cēnāre, cēnāvī, cēnātum (chapter 57)
'divide'	partior, partīrī, partītus sum (chapter 27)
'do'	agō, agere, ēgī, āctum (chapter 15); faciō, facere, fēcī, factum (chapter 15)
'dog'	canis, canis (m., f.) (chapter 57)
'drink'	bibō, bibere, bibī, – (chapter 60)
'drive together'	cōgō, cōgere, coēgī, coāctum (chapter 58)
'drive'	agō, agere, ēgī, āctum (chapter 15)
'easier'	facilior, facilius (chapter 40)
'easiest'	facillimus, facillima, facillimum (chapter 40)
'easily'	facile (chapter 43)
'easy'	facilis, facile (chapter 21)
'encourage'	hortor, hortārī, hortātus sum (chapter 28)
'end'	fīnis, fīnis, fīnium (f.) (chapter 41)
'endure'	patior, patī, passus sum (chapter 28)
'enemy' (personal enemy)	inimīcus, inimīcī (m.) (chapter 50)
'enemy' (public enemy)	hostēs, hostium (m. plural) (chapter 14)
'enter'	ingredior, ingredī, ingressus sum (chapter 41)
'even' (adverb)	et (chapter 45)
'even' (adjective)	aequus, aequa, aequum (chapter 61)

'every'	omnis, omne (chapter 21)
'excellently'	optimē (chapter 43)
'expensive'	cārus, cāra, cārum (chapter 38)
'extent' (as part of 'to such an extent')	adeō (used only with verbs) (chapter 33)
'fair'	aequus, aequa, aequum (chapter 61)
'faith'	fidēs, fideī (f.) (chapter 33)
'fall'	cadō, cadere, cecidī, cāsum (chapter 57)
'fame'	fāma, fāmae (f.) (chapter 41)
'famous'	clārus, clāra, clārum (chapter 38)
'farmer'	agricola, agricolae (m.) (chapters 2 and 3)
'fast'	celer, celeris, celere (chapter 21)
'father'	pater, patris (m.) (chapter 14)
'fatherland'	patria, patriae (f.) (chapter 45)
'fear' (noun)	metus, metūs (m.) (chapter 33)
'fear' (verb)	timeō, timēre, timuī, – (chapter 12); vereor, verērī, veritus sum (chapter 27)
'feel'	sentiō, sentīre, sēnsī, sēnsum (chapter 16)
'few'	paucī, paucae, pauca (chapter 12)
'field'	ager, agrī (m.) (chapter 8)
'fifth'	quīntus, quīnta, quīntum (chapter 35)
'fight'	pugnō, pugnāre, pugnāvī, pugnātum (chapter 20)
'find'	inveniō, invenīre, invēnī, inventum (chapter 16)
'fire'	ignis, ignis, ignium (m.) (chapter 57)
'first'	prīmus, prīma, prīmum (chapter 35)
'fit': use impersonal verb 'it is fitting'	decet, decēre, decuit, – (+ accusative and infinitive) (chapter 45)
'five'	quīnque (chapter 12)
'flee'	fugiō, fugere, fūgī, fugitūrus (chapter 20)
'fleet'	classis, classis, classium (f.) (chapter 14)
'follow'	sequor, sequī, secūtus sum (chapter 28)
'foolish'	stultus, stulta, stultum (chapter 38)
'foot'	pēs, pedis (m.) (chapter 35)
'for' (conjunction)	nam; enim (chapter 33; *enim* is postpositive, i.e. does not come first in a clause)
'for a long time'	diū (chapter 19)
'force'	cōgō, cōgere, coēgī, coāctum (chapter 58)
'forest'	silva, silvae (f.) (chapter 7)

'forgive'	ignōscō, ignōscere, ignōvī, ignōtum (+ dative) (chapter 45)
'fortunate'	fēlīx, *gen.* fēlīcis (chapter 21)
'four'	quattuor (chapter 12)
'fourth'	quārtus, quārta, quārtum (chapter 35)
'free' (adjective)	līber, lībera, līberum (chapter 8)
'free' (verb)	līberō, līberāre, līberāvī, līberātum (chapter 50)
'friend'	amīcus, amīcī (m.) (chapters 2 and 3)
'from where?'	unde (chapter 54)
'from'	dē (+ ablative) (chapter 9); ā, ab (+ ablative) (chapter 9)
'game'	lūdus, lūdī (m.) (chapter 60)
'gate'	porta, portae (f.) (chapter 60)
'get up'	surgō, surgere, surrēxī, surrēctum (chapter 47)
'gift'	dōnum, dōnī (n.) (chapter 50)
'girl'	puella, puellae (f.) (chapters 2 and 3)
'give'	dō, dare, dedī, datum (chapter 6)
'give back'	reddō, reddere, reddidī, redditum (chapter 47)
'go'	eō, īre, iī/īvī, itum (chapter 9)
'go!' (imperative singular)	ī (chapter 10)
'go!' (imperative plural)	īte (chapter 10)
'go away'	abeō, abīre, abiī/abīvī, abitum (conjugated like *eō*) (chapter 12)
'go back'	redeō, redīre, rediī, reditum (conjugated like *eō*) (chapter 47)
'go down'	dēscendō, dēscendere, dēscendī, dēscēnsum (chapter 41)
'go out'	exeō, exīre, exiī/exīvī, exitum (conjugated like *eō*) (chapter 12)
'go up'	ascendō, ascendere, ascendī, ascēnsum (chapter 41)
'god'	deus, deī (m.) (chapters 2 and 3)
'goddess'	dea, deae (f.) (chapters 2 and 3)
'gold'	aurum, aurī (n.) (chapter 41)
'good'	bonus, bona, bonum (chapter 3)
'grab'	rapiō, rapere, rapuī, raptum (chapter 35)
'grateful'	grātus, grāta, grātum (chapter 38)
'great': use 'so great'	tantus, tanta, tantum (chapter 33)

'greatly'	magnopere (chapter 43)
'Greek'	Graecus, Graeca, Graecum (chapter 8)
'greet'	salūtō, salūtāre, salūtāvī, salūtātum (chapter 41)
'greetings'	salūs, salūtis (f.) (chapter 41)
'guest'	hospes, hospitis (m.) (chapter 60)
'hand'	manus, manūs (f.) (chapter 33)
'happy'	fēlīx, *gen.* fēlīcis (chapter 21)
'hard'	dūrus, dūra, dūrum (chapter 38)
'harsh'	dūrus, dūra, dūrum (chapter 38)
'hatred'	odium, odiī (n.) (chapter 12)
'have'	habeō, habēre, habuī, habitum (chapter 6)
'have dinner'	cēnō, cēnāre, cēnāvī, cēnātum (chapter 57)
'he'	is, ea, id (in masculine) *or omit, if subject of verb* (chapters 1 and 23)
'head'	caput, capitis (n.) (chapter 19)
'health'	salūs, salūtis (f.) (chapter 41)
'healthy': use verb 'be healthy'	valeō, valēre, valuī, valitum (chapter 35)
'hear'	audiō, audīre, audīvī, audītum (chapter 15)
'heavy'	gravis, grave (chapter 21)
'help'	iuvō, iuvāre, iūvī, iūtum (chapter 6)
'her' (pronoun)	eam (feminine accusative of *is*) (chapter 23); sē (reflexive) (chapter 20)
'her' (possessive, e.g. 'her house', when the possessor is not the subject of the sentence)	eius (genitive singular of *is*, so does not agree with the possessed item) (chapter 23)
'her' (possessive, e.g. 'her house', when the possessor *is* the subject of the sentence)	suus, sua, suum (chapter 20)
'her own'	suus, sua, suum (chapter 20)
'here'	hīc (chapter 7)
'herself' (intensive)	ipsa (chapter 52)
'herself' (reflexive)	sē (chapter 20)
'high'	altus, alta, altum (chapter 57)
'him' (pronoun)	eum (masculine accusative of *is*) (chapter 23); sē (reflexive) (chapter 20)
'himself' (intensive)	ipse, ipsa, ipsum (chapter 52)
'himself' (reflexive)	sē (chapter 20)
'hinder'	impediō, impedīre, impedīvī, impedītum (chapter 16)
'his' (when the possessor is not the subject of the sentence)	eius (genitive singular of *is*, so does not agree with the possessed item) (chapter 23)

'his' (when the possessor *is* the subject of the sentence)

suus, sua, suum (chapter 20)

'his own'

suus, sua, suum (chapter 20)

'home'

domus, domūs/domī (f.) (chapter 33)

'homeland'

patria, patriae (f.) (chapter 45)

'hope'

spēs, speī (f.) (chapter 33)

'horn'

cornū, cornūs (n.) (chapter 33)

'horse'

equus, equī (m.) (chapters 2 and 3)

'host'

hospes, hospitis (m.) (chapter 60)

'hour'

hōra, hōrae (f.) (chapter 35)

'house'

domus, domūs/domī (f.) (chapter 33)

'how?'

quōmodo (chapter 54)

'how big?'

quantus, quanta, quantum (chapter 54)

'how many?'

quot (indeclinable) (chapter 54)

'however'

autem (postpositive, i.e. does not come first in a clause) (chapter 33)

'human being'

homō, hominis (m.) (chapter 19)

'hunt'

vēnor, vēnārī, vēnātus sum (chapter 27)

'if' (in an indirect question)

num (chapter 54)

'if' (in a condition)

sī (chapter 33)

'if not' (in a condition, i.e. 'unless')

nisī (chapter 50)

'ignorant': use verb 'be ignorant (of)'

nesciō, nescīre, nescīvī/nesciī, nescītum (+ accusative, despite 'of') (chapter 45)

'immortal'

immortālis, immortāle (chapter 21)

'in'

in (+ ablative) (chapter 9)

'in such a way'

ita (chapter 33)

'in this way'

sīc (chapter 45)

'into'

in (+ accusative) (chapter 9)

'island'

īnsula, īnsulae (f.) (chapter 60)

'it is allowed'

licet, licēre, licuit, – (+ dative and infinitive) (chapter 45)

'it is fitting'

decet, decēre, decuit, – (+ accusative and infinitive) (chapter 45)

'it is raining'

pluit, pluere, pluit, – (chapter 45)

'it is right'

oportet, oportēre, oportuit, – (+ accusative and infinitive) (chapter 45)

'it repents'

paenitet, paenitēre, paenituit, – (+ accusative of person and genitive of cause) (chapter 45)

'it shames'

pudet, pudēre, puduit, – (+ accusative of person and genitive of cause) (chapter 45)

'it'	is, ea, id (in neuter) *or omit, if subject of a verb* (chapters 1 and 23)
'its' (possessive)	eius (genitive singular of *is*, so does not agree with the possessed item) (chapter 23)
'journey'	iter, itineris (n.) (chapter 60)
'joy'	gaudium, gaudiī (n.) (chapter 61)
'joyful'	laetus, laeta, laetum (chapter 57)
'judge'	iūdex, iūdicis (m.) (chapter 41)
'Jupiter'	Iuppiter, Iovis (m.) (chapter 60)
'keen'	ācer, ācris, ācre (chapter 21)
'kill'	interficiō, interficere, interfēcī, interfectum (chapter 16)
'king'	rēx, rēgis (m.) (chapter 14)
'knee'	genū, genūs (n.) (chapter 33)
'know' (when not negative)	sciō, scīre, scīvī/sciī, scītum (chapter 45)
'know' (when negative): use 'not know'	nesciō, nescīre, nescīvī/nesciī, nescītum (chapter 45)
'lack'	egeō, egēre, eguī, – (+ genitive or ablative) (chapter 47)
'language'	lingua, linguae (f.) (chapter 45)
'Latin'	Latīnus, Latīna, Latīnum (chapter 47)
'law'	iūs, iūris (n.) (chapter 54)
'lead'	dūcō, dūcere, dūxī, ductum (chapters 1 and 4)
'lead!' (imperative singular)	dūc (chapter 10)
'leader'	dux, ducis (m.) (chapter 57)
'learn'	discō, discere, didicī, – (chapter 41)
'least' (adverb)	minimē (chapter 43)
'leave behind'	relinquō, relinquere, relīquī, relictum (chapter 24)
'leave' (in the intransitive sense, i.e. 'depart')	discēdō, discēdere, discessī, discessum (chapter 24)
'less' (adverb)	minus (chapter 43)
'letter'	epistula, epistulae (f.) (chapter 5)
'lie' (i.e. be horizontal)	iaceō, iacēre, iacuī, – (chapter 57)
'life'	vīta, vītae (f.) (chapter 12)
'lift'	tollō, tollere, sustulī, sublātum (chapter 47)
'like' (adjective)	similis, simile (+ dative) (chapter 38)
'little' (adverb)	paulum (chapter 43)
'live' (i.e. 'be alive', not 'inhabit')	vīvō, vīvere, vīxī, vīctum (chapter 16)
'London'	Londinium, Londiniī (n.) (chapter 35)

'long' (adjective)	longus, longa, longum (chapter 19)
'long time': use 'for a long time'	diū (chapter 19)
'lose'	āmittō, āmittere, āmīsī, āmissum (chapter 20)
'love' (verb)	amō, amāre, amāvī, amātum (chapter 6)
'love' (noun)	amor, amōris (m.) (chapter 60)
'make'	faciō, facere, fēcī, factum (chapter 15)
'man'	vir, virī (m.) (chapter 8)
'many'	multī, multae, multa (chapter 12)
'many' (as part of 'how many?')	quot (indeclinable) (chapter 54)
'many' (as part of 'so many')	tot (indeclinable) (chapter 33)
'master'	dominus, dominī (m.) (chapter 20)
'matter' (in the sense of 'thing')	rēs, reī (f.) (chapter 33)
'may' (in the sense of 'is allowed to')	licet, licēre, licuit, – (+ dative and infinitive) (chapter 45)
'may' (as a wish)	*use subjunctive verb* (chapter 13)
'messenger'	nūntius, nūntiī (m.) (chapter 58)
'miserable'	miser, misera, miserum (chapter 8)
'mistress'	domina, dominae (f.) (chapter 20)
'money'	pecūnia, pecūniae (f.) (chapter 5)
'more' (adjective)	plūrēs, plūra (chapter 40)
'more' (adverb)	plūs (chapter 43)
'more badly'	peius (chapter 43)
'more difficult'	difficilior, difficilius (chapter 40)
'more easily'	facilius (chapter 43)
'more greatly'	magis (chapter 43)
'more like'	similior, similius (chapter 40)
'more similarly'	similius (chapter 43)
'most' (adjective)	plūrimī, plūrimae, plūrima (chapter 40)
'most' (adverb)	plūrimum (chapter 43)
'most difficult'	difficillimus, difficillima, difficillimum (chapter 40)
'most easily'	facillimē (chapter 43)
'most greatly'	maximē (chapter 43)
'most like'	simillimus, simillima, simillimum (chapter 40)
'most similarly'	simillimē (chapter 43)
'mother'	māter, mātris (f.) (chapter 14)
'mountain'	mōns, montis, montium (m.) (chapter 60)
'much' (adverb)	multum (chapter 43)
'my'	meus, mea, meum (chapter 3)

'name'	nōmen, nōminis (n.) (chapter 14)
'need'	egeō, egēre, eguī, – (+ genitive or ablative) (chapter 47)
'neither'	neque, nec (chapter 45)
'never'	numquam (chapter 20)
'nevertheless'	tamen (chapter 33)
'new'	novus, nova, novum (chapter 3)
'night'	nox, noctis, noctium (f.) (chapter 45)
'no' (adjective)	nūllus, nūlla, nūllum (chapter 40); nē ūllus, nē ūlla, nē ūllum (chapter 40)
'no-one'	nēmō (m.) (chapter 40); nē quis (chapter 40)
'none'	nūllus, nūlla, nūllum (chapter 40); nē ūllus, nē ūlla, nē ūllum (chapter 40)
'nor'	neque, nec (chapter 45)
'not' (in indicative sentences, when not after 'and')	nōn (chapter 1)
'not' (in indicative sentences, when after 'and')	neque, nec (chapter 45)
'not' (with many types of subjunctive)	nē (chapter 13)
'not ... anyone'	nēmō (m.) (chapter 40); nē quis (chapter 40)
'not ... anything'	nihil (n.) (chapter 40); nē quid (chapter 40)
'not know'	nesciō, nescīre, nescīvī/nesciī, nescītum (chapter 45)
'not want'	nōlō, nōlle, nōluī, – (chapter 37)
'nothing'	nihil (n.) (chapter 40); nē quid (chapter 40)
'now'	nunc (chapter 7)
'obey'	pāreō, pārēre, pāruī, – (+ dative) (chapter 61)
'of such a sort'	tālis, tāle (chapter 33)
'often'	saepe (chapter 20)
'old'	vetus, *gen.* veteris (chapter 60)
'old man'	senex, senis (m.) (chapter 58)
'on'	in (+ ablative) (chapter 9)
'on account of'	propter (+ accusative) (chapter 35)
'one'	ūnus, ūna, ūnum (chapter 55)
'onto'	in (+ accusative) (chapter 9)
'or' (except in double questions)	aut (chapter 33); vel (chapter 50)
'or' (in double questions)	utrum ... an (chapter 54)
'order'	imperō, imperāre, imperāvī, imperātum (+ dative) (chapter 28)

'other' (of more than two)	alius, alia, aliud (chapter 55)
'other' (of two)	alter, altera, alterum (chapter 55)
'ought to'	oportet, oportēre, oportuit, – (+ accusative and infinitive) (chapter 45)
'our'	noster, nostra, nostrum (chapter 8)
'out of'	ē, ex (+ ablative) (chapter 9)
'own'	*see* 'his own', 'her own', or 'their own' (chapter 20)
'perceive'	sentiō, sentīre, sēnsī, sēnsum (chapter 16)
'persuade'	persuādeō, persuādēre, persuāsī, persuāsum (+ dative) (chapter 28)
'pick up'	tollō, tollere, sustulī, sublātum (chapter 47)
'place'	locus, locī (m., also n. in plural) (chapter 35)
'plan'	cōnsilium, cōnsiliī (n.) (chapter 5)
'pleasing'	grātus, grāta, grātum (chapter 38)
'poet'	poēta, poētae (m.) (chapters 2 and 3)
'possible': use 'as … as possible'	quam (+ superlative) (chapter 38)
'powerful'	potēns, *gen.* potentis (chapter 38)
'praise' (noun)	laus, laudis (f.) (chapter 19)
'praise' (verb)	laudō, laudāre, laudāvī, laudātum (chapter 6)
'prefer'	mālō, mālle, māluī, – (chapter 37)
'prepare'	parō, parāre, parāvī, parātum (chapter 58)
'present': use verb 'be present'	adsum, adesse, adfuī, adfutūrus (conjugated like *sum*) (chapter 12)
'promise'	polliceor, pollicērī, pollicitus sum (chapter 28)
'provided that'	dummodo (+ subjunctive) (chapter 47)
'put'	pōnō, pōnere, posuī, positum (chapters 1 and 4)
'put to flight'	fugō, fugāre, fugāvī, fugātum (chapter 57)
'queen'	rēgīna, rēgīnae (f.) (chapter 45)
'rain': use impersonal verb 'it is raining'	pluit, pluere, pluit, – (chapter 45)
'rather bad'	peior, peius (chapter 40)
'rather badly'	peius (chapter 43)
'rather big'	maior, maius (chapter 40)
'rather difficult'	difficilior, difficilius (chapter 40)
'rather easily'	facilius (chapter 43)
'rather easy'	facilior, facilius (chapter 40)
'rather good'	melior, melius (chapter 40)

'rather greatly'	magis (chapter 43)
'rather like'	similior, similius (chapter 40)
'rather little' (adverb)	minus (chapter 43)
'rather many'	plūrēs, plūra (chapter 40)
'rather similarly'	similius (chapter 43)
'rather small'	minor, minus (chapter 40)
'rather than'	quam (chapter 37)
'rather well'	melius (chapter 43)
'read'	legō, legere, lēgī, lēctum (chapters 1 and 4)
'reason'	causa, causae (f.) (chapter 41)
'receive'	accipiō, accipere, accēpī, acceptum (chapter 15)
'reliable'	certus, certa, certum (chapter 38)
'remain'	maneō, manēre, mānsī, mānsum (chapter 35)
'repair'	reficiō, reficere, refēcī, refectum (chapter 16)
'repent': use impersonal verb 'it repents'	paenitet, paenitēre, paenituit, – (+ accusative of person and genitive of cause) (chapter 45)
'report'	nūntiō, nūntiāre, nūntiāvī, nūntiātum (chapter 58)
'reputation'	fāma, fāmae (f.) (chapter 41)
'return' (in the sense of 'give back')	reddō, reddere, reddidī, redditum (chapter 47)
'return' (in the sense of 'go back')	redeō, redīre, rediī, reditum (conjugated like *eō*) (chapter 47)
'rich'	dīves, *gen.* dīvitis (chapter 57)
'right' (noun)	iūs, iūris (n.) (chapter 54)
'right' (as part of 'it is right')	oportet, oportēre, oportuit, – (+ accusative and infinitive) (chapter 45)
'river'	flūmen, flūminis (n.) (chapter 14)
'rock'	saxum, saxī (n.) (chapter 7)
'Roman'	Rōmānus, Rōmāna, Rōmānum (chapter 8)
'Rome'	Rōma, Rōmae (f.) (chapter 35)
'roof'	tēctum, tēctī (n.) (chapter 60)
'rough'	asper, aspera, asperum (chapter 8)
'rule'	regō, regere, rēxī, rēctum (chapters 1 and 4)
'rumour'	fāma, fāmae (f.) (chapter 41)
'run'	currō, currere, cucurrī, cursum (chapters 1 and 4)
'sad'	trīstis, trīste (chapter 21)
'sailor'	nauta, nautae (m.) (chapter 61)

'same'	īdem, eadem, idem (chapter 58)
'save'	servō, servāre, servāvī, servātum (chapter 50)
'say'	dīcō, dīcere, dīxī, dictum (chapter 6)
'say!' (imperative singular)	dīc (chapter 10)
'sea'	mare, maris, marium (n.) (chapter 60)
'second'	secundus, secunda, secundum (chapter 45)
'see'	videō, vidēre, vīdī, vīsum (chapter 6)
'seek'	petō, petere, petīvī, petītum (chapters 1 and 4); quaerō, quaerere, quaesīvī, quaesītum (chapter 54)
'seize'	rapiō, rapere, rapuī, raptum (chapter 35)
'-self'	ipse, ipsa, ipsum (chapter 52)
'sell'	vendō, vendere, vendidī, venditum (chapter 16)
'senate'	senātus, senātūs (m.) (chapter 33)
'send'	mittō, mittere, mīsī, missum (chapters 1 and 4)
'serious'	gravis, grave (chapter 21)
'sestertius' (coin worth ¼ denarius)	sēstertius, sēstertiī (m.) (chapter 58)
'seven'	septem (chapter 12)
'seventh'	septimus, septima, septimum (chapter 35)
'shame': use impersonal verb 'it shames'	pudet, pudēre, puduit, – (+ accusative of person and genitive of cause) (chapter 45)
'shameful'	turpis, turpe (chapter 38)
'sharp'	ācer, ācris, ācre (chapter 21)
'she'	is, ea, id (in feminine) *or omit, if subject of a verb* (chapters 1 and 23)
'sheep'	ovis, ovis, ovium (f.) (chapter 14)
'ship'	nāvis, nāvis, nāvium (f.) (chapter 58)
'short'	brevis, breve (chapter 21)
'show'	ostendō, ostendere, ostendī, ostentum (chapter 58)
'silver'	argentum, argentī (n.) (chapter 41)
'similar'	similis, simile (+ dative) (chapter 38)
'similarly'	similiter (chapter 43)
'since'	cum (+ subjunctive verb) (chapter 46); *or use ablative absolute* (chapter 57)
'sister'	soror, sorōris (f.) (chapter 14)
'sit'	sedeō, sedēre, sēdī, sessum (chapter 24)
'six'	sex (chapter 12)
'sixth'	sextus, sexta, sextum (chapter 35)
'skill'	ars, artis, artium (f.) (chapter 54)

'slave'	servus, servī (m.) (chapters 2 and 3)
'sleep'	dormiō, dormīre, dormīvī, dormītum (chapter 57)
'small'	parvus, parva, parvum (chapter 19)
'smaller'	minor, minus (chapter 40)
'smallest'	minimus, minima, minimum (chapter 40)
'so' (i.e. therefore)	ergō; igitur (*igitur* is postpositive, i.e. does not come first in its clause) (chapter 33)
'so' (i.e. to such a degree)	tam (used only with a following adjective or adverb); adeō (used only with a following verb); ita (used with adjectives, adverbs, and verbs) (chapter 33)
'so big'	tantus, tanta, tantum (chapter 33)
'so great'	tantus, tanta, tantum (chapter 33)
'so many'	tot (indeclinable) (chapter 33)
'soldier'	mīles, mīlitis (m.) (chapter 14)
'someone'	aliquis, aliquid (declines like *quis*) (in masculine and feminine) (chapter 57)
'something'	aliquis, aliquid (declines like *quis*) (in neuter) (chapter 57)
'son'	fīlius, fīliī (m.) (chapter 8)
'sorry'	paenitet, paenitēre, paenituit, – (+ accusative of person and genitive of cause) (chapter 45)
'sort' (in 'of such a sort')	tālis, tāle (chapter 33)
'sort' (in 'the sort of person')	*use relative clause with subjunctive* (chapter 56)
'soul'	animus, animī (m.) (chapter 61)
'spare'	parcō, parcere, pepercī, parsūrus (+ dative) (chapter 61)
'speak'	loquor, loquī, locūtus sum (chapter 28)
'speaker'	ōrātor, ōrātōris (m.) (chapter 61)
'stand'	stō, stāre, stetī, statum (chapter 6)
'stay'	maneō, manēre, mānsī, mānsum (chapter 35)
'step'	gradus, gradūs (m.) (chapter 33)
'stone'	saxum, saxī (n.) (chapter 7)
'strong'	fortis, forte (chapter 21)
'such'	tālis, tāle (chapter 33)
'suffer'	patior, patī, passus sum (chapter 28)
'suitable'	idōneus, idōnea, idōneum (chapter 45)
'summer'	aestās, aestātis (f.) (chapter 61)
'supply'	cōpia, cōpiae (f.) (chapter 61)

'sweet'	dulcis, dulce (chapter 38)
'swift'	celer, celeris, celere (chapter 21)
'sword'	gladius, gladiī (m.) (chapter 7)
'Syracuse'	Syrācūsae, Syrācūsārum (f. plural) (chapter 35)
'take'	capiō, capere, cēpī, captum (chapter 15)
'take care (of)'	cūrō, cūrāre, cūrāvī, cūrātum (+ accusative, despite 'of') (chapter 50)
'teach'	doceō, docēre, docuī, doctum (chapter 6)
'teacher'	magister, magistrī (m.) (chapter 8)
'tender'	tener, tenera, tenerum (chapter 8)
'than'	quam (chapter 37)
'that' (conjunction)	*use indirect statement* (chapter 19)
'that' (demonstrative pronoun/ adjective)	ille, illa, illud (chapter 10)
'that' (relative pronoun)	quī, quae, quod (chapter 25)
'that of yours'	iste, ista, istud (chapter 52)
'their' (when the possessor is not the subject of the sentence)	eōrum, eārum (genitive plural of *is*, so does not agree with thing possessed) (chapter 23)
'their' (when the possessor *is* the subject of the sentence)	suus, sua, suum (chapter 20)
'their own'	suus, sua, suum (chapter 20)
'them'	eōs, eās, ea (accusative of *is*) (chapter 23); sē (reflexive) (chapter 20)
'themselves' (intensive)	ipsī, ipsae, ipsa (chapter 52)
'themselves' (reflexive)	sē (chapter 20)
'then'	deinde (chapter 45)
'there'	ibi (chapter 33)
'therefore'	ergō; igitur (*igitur* is postpositive, i.e. does not come first in a clause) (chapter 33)
'these'	hic, haec, hoc (chapter 10)
'they'	is, ea, id (in plural) *or omit, if subject of verb* (chapters 1 and 23)
'thing'	rēs, reī (f.) (chapter 33)
'think'	arbitror, arbitrārī, arbitrātus sum (chapter 28); cōgitō, cōgitāre, cōgitāvī, cōgitātum (chapter 50); putō, putāre, putāvī, putātum (chapter 50)
'third'	tertius, tertia, tertium (chapter 45)
'this'	hic, haec, hoc (chapter 10)
'those'	ille, illa, illud (chapter 10)

'three'	trēs, tria (chapter 55)
'through'	per (+ accusative) (chapter 9)
'throw'	iaciō, iacere, iēcī, iactum (chapter 57)
'thus'	ita (chapter 33); sīc (chapter 45)
'time': use 'for a long time'	diū (chapter 19)
'to'	ad (+ accusative) (chapter 9)
'to such an extent'	adeō (used with verbs) (chapter 33)
'to where?'	quō (chapter 54)
'today'	hodiē (chapter 7)
'together': use verb 'drive together'	cōgō, cōgere, coēgī, coāctum (chapter 58)
'tomorrow'	crās (chapter 7)
'tongue'	lingua, linguae (f.) (chapter 45)
'touch'	tangō, tangere, tetigī, tāctum (chapter 60)
'town'	oppidum, oppidī (n.) (chapter 3)
'tree'	arbor, arboris (f.) (chapter 61)
'troops'	cōpia, cōpiae (f.) (in plural in this meaning) (chapter 61)
'true'	vērus, vēra, vērum (chapter 19)
'trust' (verb)	crēdō, crēdere, crēdidī, crēditum (+ dative of person trusted) (chapter 54)
'trust' (noun)	fidēs, fideī (f.) (chapter 33)
'try'	cōnor, cōnārī, cōnātus sum (chapter 58)
'tuft of wool'	floccus, floccī (m.) (chapter 58)
'two'	duo, duae, duo (chapter 55)
'understand'	intellegō, intellegere, intellēxī, intellēctum (chapter 24)
'uneven'	inīquus, inīqua, inīquum (chapter 61)
'unfair'	inīquus, inīqua, inīquum (chapter 61)
'unless'	nisī (chapter 50)
'until'	dum (chapter 47)
'urge'	hortor, hortārī, hortātus sum (chapter 28)
'use'	ūtor, ūtī, ūsus sum (+ ablative) (chapter 27)
'useful'	ūtilis, ūtile (chapter 47)
'value'	aestimō, aestimāre, aestimāvī, aestimātum (chapter 58)
'verse'	versus, versūs (m.) (chapter 33)
'very bad'	pessimus, pessima, pessimum (chapter 40)
'very badly'	pessimē (chapter 43)
'very big'	maximus, maxima, maximum (chapter 40)

'very difficult'	difficillimus, difficillima, difficillimum (chapter 40)
'very easily'	facillimē (chapter 43)
'very easy'	facillimus, facillima, facillimum (chapter 40)
'very good'	optimus, optima, optimum (chapter 40)
'very great'	summus, summa, summum (chapter 50)
'very greatly'	maximē (chapter 43)
'very like'	simillimus, simillima, simillimum (chapter 40)
'very little' (adverb)	minimē (chapter 43)
'very many'	plūrimī, plūrimae, plūrima (chapter 40)
'very much'	plūrimum (chapter 43)
'very similarly'	simillimē (chapter 43)
'very small'	minimus, minima, minimum (chapter 40)
'very well'	optimē (chapter 43)
'voice'	vōx, vōcis (f.) (chapter 41)
'wage (war)'	gerō, gerere, gessī, gestum (chapter 57)
'wait'	maneō, manēre, mānsī, mānsum (chapter 35)
'walls'	moenia, moenium (n. plural) (chapter 14)
'want' (without a negative)	volō, velle, voluī, – (chapter 24)
'want' (with a negative): use 'not want'	nōlō, nōlle, nōluī, – (chapter 37)
'war'	bellum, bellī (n.) (chapter 3)
'warn'	moneō, monēre, monuī, monitum (chapter 6)
'water'	aqua, aquae (f.) (chapter 7)
'way' (as part of 'in such a way')	ita (chapter 33)
'way' (as part of 'in this way')	sīc (chapter 45)
'wealth'	dīvitiae, dīvitiārum (f. plural) (chapter 50)
'wear'	gerō, gerere, gessī, gestum (chapter 57)
'well' (adverb)	bene (chapter 7)
'well' (as part of verb 'be well')	valeō, valēre, valuī, valitum (chapter 35)
'what?'	quis, quid (in neuter) (chapter 13)
'when' (in a question)	quandō (chapter 54)
'when' (in a subordinate clause)	cum (chapter 47); *or use ablative absolute* (chapter 57)
'where' (with motion towards)	quō (chapter 54)
'where' (with no motion)	ubi (chapter 7)
'where' (as part of 'from where?')	unde (chapter 54)
'whether'	num (chapter 54)

'which?' (interrogative adjective)	quī, quae, quod (chapter 13)
'which' (relative pronoun)	quī, quae, quod (chapter 25)
'while'	dum (chapter 47)
'white'	albus, alba, album (chapter 61)
'who?' (interrogative pronoun)	quis, quid (chapter 13)
'who' (relative pronoun)	quī, quae, quod (chapter 25)
'whole'	omnis, omne (chapter 21); tōtus, tōta, tōtum (chapter 61)
'why?'	cūr (chapter 7)
'wise'	sapiēns, *gen.* sapientis (chapter 38)
'wish'	volō, velle, voluī, – (chapter 24)
'with'	cum (+ ablative) (chapter 9)
'without'	sine (+ ablative) (chapter 9)
'woman'	mulier, mulieris (f.) (chapter 60)
'word'	verbum, verbī (n.) (chapter 3)
'work'	opus, operis (n.) (chapter 14)
'worse'	peior, peius (chapter 40)
'worst' (adjective)	pessimus, pessima, pessimum (chapter 40)
'worst' (adverb)	pessimē (chapter 43)
'worthy (of)'	dignus, digna, dignum (+ ablative) (chapter 45)
'write'	scrībō, scrībere, scrīpsī, scrīptum (chapters 1 and 4)
'year'	annus, annī (m.) (chapter 35)
'yesterday'	herī (chapter 7)
'young man'	adulēscēns, adulēscentis, adulēscentium (m.) (chapter 61)
'your' (plural 'you')	vester, vestra, vestrum (chapter 8)
'your' (singular 'you')	tuus, tua, tuum (chapter 3)

Index of Grammatical Topics Covered

Numbers indicate chapters; references to chapter 65 (the glossary) lead to definitions of the terms concerned.

Index of Latin Passages Included